Policing Los Angeles

Justice, Power, and Politics

The Justice, Power, and Politics series publishes new works in history that explore the myriad struggles for justice, battles for power, and shifts in politics that have shaped the United States over time. Through the lenses of justice, power, and politics, the series seeks to broaden scholarly debates about America's past as well as to inform public discussions about its future.

More information on the series, including a complete list of books published, is available at http://justicepowerandpolitics.com/.

Policing Los Angeles

Race, Resistance, and the Rise of the LAPD

MAX FELKER-KANTOR

The University of North Carolina Press
Chapel Hill

This book was published with the assistance of the Authors Fund
of the University of North Carolina Press.

The University of North Carolina Press has been a member of the
Green Press Initiative since 2003.

Library of Congress Cataloging-in-Publication Data
Names: Felker-Kantor, Max, author.
Title: Policing Los Angeles : race, resistance, and the rise of the LAPD /
    Max Felker-Kantor.
Other titles: Justice, power, and politics.
Description: Chapel Hill : University of North Carolina Press, [2018] |
    Series: Justice, power, and politics | Includes bibliographical
    references and index.
Identifiers: LCCN 2018010264| ISBN 9781469646831 (cloth : alk. paper) |
    ISBN 9781469659183 (pbk. : alk. paper) | ISBN 9781469646848 (ebook)
Subjects: LCSH: Los Angeles (Calif.). Police Department—History—
    20th century. | Police—California—Los Angeles—History—20th century. |
    Police administration—California—Los Angeles—History—20th century. |
    Discrimination in law enforcement—California—Los Angeles—History—
    20th century. | Los Angeles (Calif.)—Politics and government—20th century. |
    Los Angeles (Calif.)—Race relations—History—20th century.
Classification: LCC HV8148.L55 F45 2018 | DDC 363.209794/9409045—dc23
    LC record available at https://lccn.loc.gov/2018010264

Cover illustrations: Top, police officers search a suspect in Watts; bottom,
police officer threatens African American youth with a shotgun. Courtesy of
the *Los Angeles Times* Photographic Archives, Library Special Collections,
Charles E. Young Research Library, University of California, Los Angeles.

Portions of this book were previously published in a different form and are used
here with permission. Throughout is included material from "Liberal Law-and-
Order: The Politics of Police Reform in Los Angeles," *Journal of Urban History*,
OnlineFirst April 28, 2017, http://doi.org/10.1177/0096144217705462. Chapter 4
includes material from "'Kid Thugs are Spreading Terror through the Streets':
Youth, Crime, and the Expansion of the Juvenile Justice System in Los Angeles,
1973–1980," *Journal of Urban History*, 44, no. 3 (May 1, 2018): 476–500,
https://doi.org/10.1177/0096144215623260. Chapter 5 includes material from
"The Coalition against Police Abuse: CAPA's Resistance Struggle in 1970s Los
Angeles," *Journal of Civil and Human Rights* 2, no. 1 (2016): 52–88, https://doi
.org/10.5406/jcivihumarigh.2.1.52.

For Gerald Gill,
And for all the victims of police abuse in Los Angeles

Contents

Graphs, Illustrations, Map, and Table

Introduction

The Police Power

"A strong, visible police force is one of our best crime-fighting tools," said Los Angeles's liberal African American mayor, Tom Bradley, in 1990. In remarks delivered alongside his proposed budget for the year, Bradley committed to providing the department with the resources to effectively combat crime and violence. "Through the use of mobile booking units, horse-mounted police officers and other high-profile deployment strategies, the police are waging an all-out war on crime," he told reporters. "I want to give them the personnel to escalate our attack." Police were the first line of defense against crime and violence, Bradley argued, and they needed all the resources and manpower at the city's disposal to ensure public safety, combat criminals, and maintain social order. Bradley made his administration's position clear: "The city has made our blue-uniformed officers the number-one priority."[1]

Between the 1960s and 1990s, a broad coalition of lawmakers, criminal justice administrators, and police officials advocated expanding the funding and manpower of the Los Angeles Police Department (LAPD) as it fought a war on crime. A force of roughly 5,200 officers in 1960 grew to 8,414 officers in 1990, a per capita increase from 2.1 to 2.4 officers per 1,000 residents. Yet as Bradley's budget remarks suggested, he was still unsatisfied with the state of the police department. In fact, he vowed to do everything within his power to expand the department by 400 additional officers. Even when a recession in the Southern California economy subsequently led to revenue shortfalls and budget cuts, Bradley and other lawmakers pledged to identify additional funding for the police and called on the federal government to provide support for the city's "continuing fight against crime."[2]

But Bradley hoped to accomplish something else as well. Like many mayors across the country confronting the conservative political context of the 1970s and 1980s, Bradley faced pressure to embrace the police to ensure law and order. Though Bradley wanted to contain crime and maintain order, at the same time he intended to rein in abusive police practices by using the regulatory power of the state to assert control over the police department. Yet, contrary to what he and other similarly minded city officials hoped, by the 1990s this approach to reform wound up providing the police with more power and authority. In spite of lawmakers' efforts and Bradley's antagonistic relationship with LAPD chief Daryl Gates, the police expanded their discretionary prerogatives to enforce order in ways that contributed to an "us versus them" attitude toward the residents they were supposed to serve.

Racial targeting was central to the LAPD's expansion of police power and efforts to control the streets at all costs. Residents of color, because the police viewed them as disorderly and lawless, had long been the subjects of the LAPD's police power. As African American and Mexican migrants reshaped Los Angeles's racial geography during the postwar era, they confronted a police force intent on maintaining Los Angeles's reputation as the nation's "white spot." As part of a system of racialized punishment that was rooted in Los Angeles's history of settler colonialism and racism, the growth of police power in the decades after the 1960s was organized around the aim of controlling the city's black and brown populations. Intensified police power and racially targeted policing were not incidental but mutually constitutive.[3]

Just over a year after Bradley's commitment to empower the LAPD to "fight crime on every front," officers revealed the racism embedded in the police power when they were captured on video brutally beating unarmed African American motorist Rodney King. Bradley responded by setting up the Independent Commission on the Los Angeles Police Department to investigate the internal disciplinary procedures and culture of the department. The commission's report called the King beating a "landmark in the recent history of law enforcement, comparable to the Scottsboro case in 1931," and exposed a pattern of discriminatory use of excessive force. Verbal harassment, the "prone-out" tactic requiring a suspect to lie face down with his arms spread out, stop-and-searches, and the use of force were routinely visited on African American and Latino/a residents far more frequently than on whites. After twenty years of the Bradley administration's attempts to regulate the LAPD, reduce police brutality, and root out racist police practices, the department had effectively insulated its power and operated without external oversight or accountability.[4]

The failure to institute systemic reform of the unequal relation of power between the LAPD and the city's black and brown residents produced the conditions for the eruption of the largest urban uprising in American history. Sparked by the acquittal of the officers for beating King, the 1992 rebellion was reminiscent of the six days in August 1965 when Watts erupted in anti-police protest. After the Watts uprising, African American and Latino/a residents and activists placed immense pressure on elected officials and the police department to end racist and abusive police practices, and Bradley was elected in 1973 by a multiracial coalition on a platform of police reform. But the King beating and the reaction to it twenty-seven years after Watts revealed that the police, if anything, had become more powerful, more abusive, more militarized, and more present in areas of social life where they had not been before. Between the 1960s and 1990s, in short, the police power intensified.[5] This book asks how and why this could happen after Watts exposed the racism at the heart of the police power, decades of pressure from an active anti–police abuse movement, and under the twenty-year rule of a liberal administration that sought to control and regulate police behavior.

Within the context of growing electoral pressure for law and order after the urban uprisings of the 1960s, police power in Los Angeles grew as city officials attempted to manage the interaction between the police and residents of color within a political structure that limited mayoral authority over the police department. Liberals in the Bradley administration promoted reforms, such as procedural fairness, better police-community relations, and more training, that sought to soften the power of the police, but because they accepted the legitimacy of the police power and were committed to law and order, they did not fundamentally alter the basic power relations between the police and the city government on the one hand and black and brown communities on the other. As a result, they enabled the police bureaucracy to adapt to—and at some points coopt—ameliorative reforms and assert its authority to maintain social order without disruption until the 1992 rebellion.[6]

But the story told here is more than one of liberal politics and police power. African American and Latino/a residents and activists recognized the threat of an unfettered police power that operated as an occupying force in the city's communities of color, and they routinely mobilized against it. In the decades after Watts, they resisted the LAPD's effort to discipline them by protesting police brutality and demanding greater police accountability. While many residents of color supported liberal reforms based on ensuring procedural fairness, anti–police abuse activists pushed further in their demand that the power of the LAPD be not only reined in but in some cases dismantled entirely. In doing so, activists exposed the racism at the heart of police power, the limits of liberal reforms, and proposed alternatives to get-tough policing.

Tracing the racism at the heart of the police power reveals the historical consequences of expanded police authority. Relying on the police to manage social problems of crime, violence, and drugs that were rooted in Los Angeles's history of segregation, inequality, and poverty led to disciplinary practices of surveillance, harassment, and arrest that criminalized and excluded black and Latino/a residents. In the process, as antipolice activists pointed out and struggled against, the police often deemed residents of color as not only potential threats to the public welfare but also unfit for full benefits of social membership in American society. Police practices thereby produced racialized definitions of criminality and enforced the city's hierarchical racial order.[7]

As a result, the struggle over policing structured and exacerbated deep cleavages in American cities over race, citizenship, politics, and state power.

The Police Power and Urban Politics

After Watts, the city's policymakers responded to fears of rising crime and urban unrest among white voters and a politically influential police department by supporting law enforcement solutions while hoping to rein in the most egregious abuses of officer discretion. But as police authority expanded, the department maintained its prerogative to discipline and control African American and Latino/a residents. In waging a battle for the streets, the LAPD pursued a racist, space-based enforcement of order that rarely lived up to its motto, To Protect and to Serve, for residents of color.[8] The expansion of police power occurred as city officials, with limited authority to oversee the police department, attempted to mediate the interaction between police, people of color, and antipolice protest.

Throughout Los Angeles's twentieth-century history, the police served as the frontline agents in a system that targeted residents of color as outsiders in need of subjugation that Kelly Lytle Hernández has aptly described as "mass elimination."[9] Responding to what they viewed as unfair limits on police practices and discretion imposed by liberal courts during the late 1950s and 1960s, LAPD officials helped create the "wars" it fought on crime, social movements, drugs, gangs, and immigration to legitimate a proactive assertion of their authority to use the coercive power of the state to maintain control and order on the streets. In the process, the police became a powerful partisan force within local, state, and national politics with both material and symbolic authority. In this way, the LAPD interlaced its authority into new areas of urban governance and social life and vastly expanded its prerogatives over Los Angeles citizens.[10]

Police power was not incidental or supplemental, but constitutive of postwar city politics and authority. Yet the story of policing in American cities has not been integrated with histories of urban politics. Most accounts of the growth of the carceral state have also left out the police as the primary point of contact between the state and citizens on the streets of urban America.[11] Many studies have focused narrowly on an institutional history of the police, the internal operation of police departments, the behavior of officers, the role of discretion, and the culture and attitude of officers in isolation from the involvement of policing in its broader social and political context and contribution to a state-building enterprise centered on get-tough policies.[12] Work on the LAPD has tended to focus on police professionalization, the conservative subculture of the department, and the impact of the police on communities of color in mid-twentieth-century Los Angeles but do less to explain the police as actors within the city's social and political power structure, the transformation of discretionary police power, or the expansion of police into new areas of social life and state authority after the 1960s.[13] Police officials strategically positioned the department to become integrated into the city's social institutions and a powerful partisan political entity, in some ways more powerful than the mayors and governors they served.[14]

The LAPD's independent authority was based on the police power of the state. As a broadly defined authority of the state to prevent and dispose threats to the public welfare, the police power insulated the LAPD from political oversight and civilian accountability. Rooted in theories of prevention and security, the police power granted the police discretion to pacify threats to the social order. Wielding broad discretionary authority, officers defined what types of activities constituted disorderly, improper, or criminal behavior. Pacification, in turn, relied on the police use of force, which reflected the centrality of the police to the core component of state power: the monopoly on legitimate violence. The police power made officers, in the words of notorious LAPD chief William Parker, "a thin blue line of defense . . . upon which we must depend to defend the invasion from within." The ordering of the urban environment constituted the police power and released the department to extend its reach into nearly every facet of social life. Because the monopoly over the means of violence was a core element of the police power, it enabled the LAPD to aggressively discipline perceived threats to social order and, in the process, produce and enforce a hierarchical racial order.[15]

The police further constituted their own power in urban politics through the crises they helped manufacture. Raising and mobilizing public fear of radical social movements, the drug trade, gang activity, and undocumented immigrants as threats with the potential to undermine the social order served the department's financial and political interests. By using the department's own crime statistics to justify demands for greater resources and authority, police action produced and legitimized its own existence. The LAPD routinely reported increases in the Part I crime rate in its annual reports and statistical digests, suggesting the need for greater police resources. Crime statistics and arrest rates, however, reflected both spatial concentrations of crime and the LAPD's enforcement priorities. Part I crime was routinely higher in the predominantly African American 77th and Latino/a Rampart than in the white West Los Angeles division. Arrest rates exacerbated the perception of the spatial concentration of violent crime as officers made arrests at rates five and six times higher in black and Latino/a communities than in white ones. Such statistics fueled the LAPD's construction of black and Latino/a communities as places in need of more policing and repressive control.[16]

The media, notably the *Los Angeles Times*, picked up and naturalized police rhetoric and logic by often reporting in terms constructed by the police. Such adoption of police language is one reason why tracking police power is difficult. Because the police helped define the very categories the media and city officials used to interpret urban problems of gangs, the drug trade, and violent crime, they justified police action as the only solution. In doing so, the police and the media also made those groups who fell within those categories, namely black and brown youth, into enemies to be eradicated.[17]

This is by no means to suggest that the drug trade, gang violence, and crime were not real problems facing urban communities. They certainly were.[18] But, in contrast to the suggestion of LAPD officials, they were not problems of law and order that could be resolved by more repressive policing. Rather they were the consequences of spatial segregation, racial discrimination, and economic restructuring that led to unemployment, poverty, and a lack of investment in urban communities. The very real concerns residents of color had about drug dealers, gang activity, and school violence required solutions that addressed those larger structural problems, not policies that strengthened the police. Yet, these solutions lost out to policies that bolstered the LAPD's power and authority to enforce social order.

Constructing a Get-Tough Coalition

A convergence of political interests facilitated the growth of police power. With some exceptions, traditional narratives of post-1970s law and order politics often follow a dichotomy of conservative support for the police versus liberal proponents of reform, especially under black mayoral power. Scholarship has tended to portray support for the police as a conservative project pushed forward by the backlash of suburban white residents and Republican politicians to civil rights and urban uprisings of the 1960s. More recently, scholars have emphasized the proactive role of Republicans in pushing forward law-and-order politics and influencing Democrats to support punitive policies known as "frontlash." Others, however, have suggested that Democrats and liberal policies made key contributions to the burgeoning War on Crime dating back to the interwar and immediate post–World War II years.[19]

Presenting the drive toward mass incarceration and development of punitive policy as a grassroots backlash or elite frontlash, however, ignores how a convergence of multiple interests coalesced to advocate for expanded police power and punitive policies. Scholars of the carceral state have recently demonstrated various converging interests in favor of get-tough policy, including liberal and conservative politicians, prosecutors and judges, and segments of the African American community.[20] But in doing so they miss a central point of the politics of punishment and social control in this period: law enforcement officials, the police in particular, deliberately and strategically expanded their power, authority, and resources. Conservatives, liberals, and, crucially, the police themselves converged to enable the growth of the police power of the carceral state even as they promoted different visions of the police role in the city.[21]

Get-tough policing originated as a right-wing program. Liberals' participation in this get-tough coalition was shaped by a politically influential local police department and a conservative law-and-order environment that fueled the political ascendancy of Richard Nixon and Ronald Reagan. Ronald Reagan's calls for more policing and punishment during his successful campaign for governor of California in 1966 and the expansion of federal funds to police under Nixon after 1968 contributed to the LAPD's legal authority, militarization, and community relations programs that expanded its influence after the 1960s. The passage of determinative sentencing policies in late-1970s California and Reagan's reduced aid to cities and the drug war in the 1980s reverberated at the local level, contributing to political constraints faced by liberal lawmakers and to support for crime control and policing to manage urban spaces of color.[22]

But liberal policymakers in Los Angeles, represented by Bradley and moderate Democrats on the city council, had different goals. They hoped to limit the role of the police even as they contributed to a larger, more repressive policing state. Liberal policymakers' approach to the police in the 1970s sprang from police reforms of the 1960s. Scholars of that earlier period have shown that liberals used the harm principle, which rejected morals policing and justified policing of only those activities that physically or materially harmed others, to decriminalize status crimes, such as loitering, drunkenness, or sexual identity, and pull back police discretion over whites. New laws and legal interpretations meant that criminal law focused only on physical harm. Nowhere was this process more consequential than Los Angeles, where arrests for drunkenness reached nearly 70,000 in 1967, then declined to just over 6,000 in 1982.[23]

Liberal lawmakers intended to bring the police under the rule of law using the harm principle and a commitment to procedural fairness. Yet they often resisted extending the harm principle to people of color and thus faced a problem. They had eliminated and delegitimized law enforcement's traditional discretion. But they also believed that certain populations—especially so-called violent African American and Latino/a youth, drug traffickers in neighborhoods of color, and "alien criminals"—posed a threat to social order and security and thus required discretionary supervision. The spatial concentration of the LAPD's crime and arrest statistics reflected these different priorities. Through the 1970s and 1980s, policymakers and law enforcement officials responded to the limits on the police by engaging in an elaborate state-building project as they attempted to relegitimize police authority and ensure that police only directed these prerogatives toward so-called harmful and disorderly residents, which often meant people of color. The success of police reform in the 1960s motivated the police to carve out new areas of authority and left black and Latino/a activists politically isolated in their challenge to the police power.[24]

The first (and only) African American mayor of Los Angeles, Tom Bradley built a multiracial political coalition and won election five times. Bradley's approach reflected the ways that liberals contributed to the expansion of police power through both a political consensus in support of law and order and liberal policies rooted in ensuring public safety and security. As a twenty-one-year veteran of the LAPD who faced an electorate that was still predominantly white in the late 1960s and early 1970s, Bradley supported law and order to allay white fears of crime, violence, and unrest after Watts. But as the mayor of a city that was becoming more multiracial after 1970, Bradley was also a reformer who wanted to make city government more diverse, inclusive, and fair. Rather than presenting himself as a mayor solely for black residents, he intended to represent "all Los Angeles."[25] Every resident deserved to be safe and secure on the city's streets, which required a strong police department that did not engage in racial discrimination. Ensuring procedural fairness that treated all residents equally, Bradley and Democrats on the city council such as David Cunningham, Robert Farrell, Zev Yaroslavsky, Joel Wachs, and Pat Russell believed, would lead to reductions in police harassment and abuse. Bradley certainly tried more liberal policies, such as juvenile diversion and rehabilitation programs, relative to the punitive policies of conservatives, such as Chief Parker and Mayor Sam Yorty. Those reforms, however, moderated demands for substantive change and enabled the broadening of police authority into social institutions where it had never been before.

Local politics in Los Angeles was a nominally nonpartisan affair because the mayor and city council members were elected on a nonpartisan basis. Prior to Bradley's election, Los Angeles politics had been dominated by pro-business Republicans during the 1950s, and conservative Democrat Sam Yorty continued this close relationship in the 1960s. Pro-business conservatives, backed by the city's civic elite made up of white business owners and lawyers, invested the LAPD with the power to maintain the racial hierarchy, combat dissent, and promote antiunion politics. Bradley's election brought a liberal regime to power, which was made up of moderate Democrats who promoted liberal social policies, notably affirmative action, and pro-business development and growth.[26] While there were conservative Democrats and Republicans on the council, liberals dominated during the Bradley era. Within this context, the LAPD and criminal justice officials filled in as the dominant representative of the city's conservative business interests and white Republican voters in the San Fernando Valley.[27]

Bradley focused on remaking the relationship between both the police and the citizenry and the police and the mayor's office. In Los Angeles, the mayor's authority was constrained by the city charter and a strong city council. Yet, Bradley worked effectively with a council that became more liberal after 1970 and, in contrast to prior mayors, believed he could exert significant power over local government. Bradley pursued reforms aimed at expanding the authority of his office over issues of law and order by appointing liberals to the Board of Police Commissioners and creating the Mayor's Office of Criminal Justice Planning. Liberal law and order was in part a response to electoral pressures to keep white voters in the Bradley coalition and conservative calls for stronger law enforcement institutions and tough-on-crime policies. But it was also a deliberate attempt by Bradley and liberal council members to control law-and-order politics and rein in abusive police practices. This was a technocratic liberalism that allowed Bradley and liberal council members to both pledge strong support for tough law enforcement and propose using the power of government to effectively manage the police. With faith in their own ability to mold public policy in a conservative political era, however, liberals wound up releasing a right-wing police force to enforce its vision of racial hierarchy and social order.[28]

As the city became a hub of global migration and trade between the 1970s and 1990s, liberal law and order gave way to world city liberalism characterized by a bifurcated service economy, the attraction of international capital, and uneven economic development. Bradley hoped to be responsive to a more multicultural constituency and to maintain Los Angeles's attractiveness to international corporations within an increasingly conservative political climate both nationally during the Reagan era and in California with the election of Republican governor George Deukmejian in 1984. During the 1980s, especially after hosting the 1984 Olympics, world city liberalism informed Bradley's and political officials' approach to governing and policing. Making a global Los Angeles rested on embracing diversity and assurances of its safety for investment, trade, and economic development amid growing fears of gang violence and the drug trade. World city liberals, including Bradley and pro-business Democratic city council members, responded by pursuing a two-pronged strategy. On the one hand, they empowered the police to crack down on crime—the drug trade and gangs in particular—to promote the city as a safe space for high-wage workers and investment. On the other, they promoted procedural regulations to bring the police further under the rule of law in response to demands from immigrants, refugees, and residents of color for safety and fair treatment.[29]

Bradley-era reforms aimed at making the police more responsive to residents had the effect of weaving the police ever more tightly into liberal social programs and institutions. Prioritizing police and criminal justice solutions to the urban crisis of the 1970s and 1980s illustrates the tremendous state-building project during an era often characterized by a retreat in state services. It was the epitome of what Ruth Wilson Gilmore calls the "antistate state." Rather than displacing government, the local war on crime produced a punishing state that facilitated a reinterpretation of structural inequalities as the fault of individual behavior and lapsed personal responsibility requiring supervisory discretion of the police. As a result, the police became the primary contact many residents of color had with the state during an era of economic restructuring and government austerity.[30]

Race and Resistance to Police Power

Even as the LAPD's authority became more capacious after the 1960s, many African American and Latino/a residents resisted the coercive power of the police and advocated for alternative visions of policing in their communities.[31] Black and Latino/a activists made the police a central component in the struggle for racial justice and meaning of equality after the 1960s. In the process, they demonstrated how the police power organized around the desire to police African Americans and Latinos/as had significant consequences for racial formation, the meaning of citizenship, and social justice. Many black and Latino/a residents characterized the police as an oppressive force that acted with impunity in their neighborhoods, leading to harassment, arrest, and, ultimately, distrust of state authority. Repression, however, did not destroy resistance but led to movements demanding systemic changes in the relations of power between residents of color and the LAPD, most notably by advocating community control of the police. Focusing on the mobilization around policing counters views of inner-city populations as powerless nonactors in the face of overwhelming punitive policies and aggressive policing.[32] By promoting alternatives to punitive policies, antipolice struggles not only challenged the police power but also exposed how policing was a central arm of state power that operated to exclude people of color from full social membership in American society.

What bridged the experiences of black and brown Angelinos was common treatment by the police as outsiders in need of monitoring and control. A pervasive police presence meant that African Americans and Latinos/as often defined their communities in relation to the police, employing metaphors of their neighborhoods as occupied territory or as communities under siege. Throughout the postwar period, Los Angeles's communities of color understood their position and status in the city through their relationship with and treatment by law enforcement. Policing of Latino/a immigrants enabled the LAPD to extend the police power and prerogatives into immigration enforcement, an overlooked area of policing prior to 9/11. In the process, the department constructed an internal border delineated by racialized conceptions of illegality and criminality.[33]

Police action helped produce the region's racial hierarchy and understandings of criminality. Policing in Los Angeles carried with it a self-serving rationale—the perceived criminal nature of particular racial or ethnic groups—that justified the concentration of police power in communities of color. Policing was, in other words, a social practice that produced intertwined categories of race and criminality which displaced the responsibility for racist policing and state violence from the LAPD onto communities of color themselves. Such police practices resulted in the criminalization of black and brown residents and the near daily interaction between residents of color and the police and justified disciplinary practices of exclusion.[34]

But the LAPD's targeting of black and Latino/a communities also produced resistance to the police. For over thirty years, community activists challenged the liberal assumption that police abuse was a problem of individual "bad apple" officers that could be solved through ameliorative reforms. Instead, local antipolice activists repeatedly drew attention to the ways in which police abuse sprang from the position the police occupied in the city power structure. Activists recognized the constitutive nature of police power to state authority and, in turn, exposed the limits of liberal police reforms, such as ensuring procedural fairness, more training, and diversifying the LAPD, that did not address the underlying power relations between the police and the public. In response, activists pushed for reforms, most notably civilian review boards and community control of the police, as steps toward a fundamental restructuring of the police power.[35] This was why antipolice movements and protests were so significant. They exposed the way the police naturalized categories of criminality and disorder and justified militarized solutions to urban problems to the detriment of social and economic programs. In contesting the police, anti–police abuse activists revealed the problems of disorder and crime were rooted in the police power itself.

Exploring the policing of African American, Latino/a, and immigrant communities brings together experiences in what is all too often thought of as only an African American story. Although existing scholarship on social movements often suggests that African Americans and Latino/as were largely separate in their activism, the experience of repressive policing created potential for solidarity and coalition building.[36] The development of the Coalition against Police Abuse, most notably, demonstrates both efforts at multiracial coalition building and reperiodizing the timeline and alleged decline of Black Power and Chicano/a movements. Together, Coalition against Police Abuse activists drew in a broad group of political officials, middle-class African Americans, Latinos/as, church leaders, and civil rights organizations by concentrating on the issue of police violence. By doing so, they drew attention to the LAPD's get-tough, militarized approach to the production of order and management of social and economic inequality.[37] Anti–police abuse movements did not disintegrate in the face of state-sanctioned violence but extended well into the 1970s and beyond.

Within the African American community, class divisions also shaped the relationship with the police. Rising criminal violence in the 1970s and 1980s led many middle-class African Americans to call for greater police resources and protection. Yet African American residents often did not receive the equitable police service, such as community control, external oversight, and decision-making over urban police strategies, they demanded. By the late 1980s and early 1990s, the police had transformed from the "thin blue line" preventing threats to freedom and order into a militarized force combating and eliminating "terror" in the form of black and brown youth from the streets. Reduced government aid to cities and liberal law-and-order policy had left few options to residents to address social and economic crises other than the police. Instead, they faced a militarized police department intent on waging a war to win the battle for the streets. Police officials entrenched themselves as the first-line defenders of order by appealing to fears of drug crime and gang violence among African American residents and lawmakers intent on ensuring public safety.[38]

Los Angeles as a Model Carceral City

This could easily be a story of policing in nearly any city in postwar America. Yet Los Angeles presents a key site for investigation of politics, policing, and antipolice struggles. The LAPD was at the forefront of many innovations in policing, and political developments in Los Angeles foreshadowed those in cities across the country between the 1970s and 1990s. From concerns around youth violence, the militarized war on gangs and drugs, the surveillance of social movements, and the response to new waves of immigrants, to the antipolice movements, the Los Angeles story informed urban police policies after the 1960s. Los Angeles's long history of jailing and punishment made it, according to historian Kelly Lytle Hernández, "the carceral capital of the world." Policing in Los Angeles was a crucial component of a systemic effort to build a punishing carceral state and contributor to the growth of California's prison landscape since the 1970s, what geographer Ruth Wilson Gilmore calls "the biggest prison-building project in the history of the world."[39]

The machinations and power plays of the LAPD reverberated throughout the country. As Watts and the 1992 rebellion demonstrate, the LAPD symbolized the growth of an expansive police power and the get-tough response to urban uprisings and antipolice protest. Efforts by the police to secure additional funding, to militarize, and to intensify its discretionary authority with the minimal amount of oversight were nationally significant processes led by the LAPD. Such innovations in policing made the LAPD a model department whose structure, hardware, and philosophy were emulated the world over.[40] Due to the prominence of the LAPD in shaping policing nationally and internationally, Los Angeles provides an exemplary site for an investigation of policing, crime policy, and urban politics.

Between the two uprisings that bookend this study, the political conditions shaping the city's policing regime were forerunners of broader trends in cities and urban policy. During the first decades of the postwar period, Los Angeles was a low-density sprawl city marked by the lack of an entrenched political machine characteristic of the Sunbelt. It was ruled by conservative Republicans and business interests who supported police chief Parker. This era unraveled after Watts and was followed by the election of Bradley, part of the election of black mayors across the country in the 1970s. A reformer in a city that was not majority African American, Bradley attempted to ensure fair governance and police service for all Angelinos. As new immigrants further altered the city's demographics and regional economics shifted to a service economy between 1970 and 1990, Los Angeles entered an era as a world city. Reflective of broader patterns in global cities, world city liberalism ushered in a politics of accepting diversity while attracting international capital that guided policing strategies in the 1980s and 1990s.[41]

From the city's inception, Los Angeles power brokers targeted African Americans and Mexican Americans as outside the bounds of social membership requiring disciplinary modes of containment and exclusion. Demographic changes after World War II led to a vibrant African American community alongside an already significant Mexican American population. Between 1940 and 1970, for example, the African American population in Los Angeles County grew from 63,744 to 763,000. African Americans entered a region shaped by a colonial past and a Mexican American population of nearly 1.4 million in 1970. Such racial and ethnic diversity, however, threatened city boosters' vision of the city as a haven for white homeowners. Discriminatory real estate practices confined African Americans and Mexican Americans to South Central and East Los Angeles, respectively. Hovering over 11 percent in 1965, unemployment rates for blacks in South Central were double the average for the city and the poverty rate stood at 27 percent. Conditions for Mexican Americans in East Los Angeles were similar, with an unemployment rate of 7 percent and a poverty rate of nearly 25 percent. Political officials and white residents entrusted the police to ensure safety, to provide domestic tranquility, and to safeguard this racially segregated and hierarchical social order. Black and brown life was thereby structured by pervasive harassment, brutality, and violence from a hostile police department. "Police officers enforce the code of the community," one African American resident explained in 1962, "and here it includes segregation."[42]

Intensified policing and punitive crime policies in Los Angeles emerged from the response to the urban uprisings of the 1960s. Despite the belief among mostly white conservative politicians and police officials that, in the words of conservative Democratic mayor Yorty, "Harlem-type riots could not occur here," chapter 1 foregrounds the racist police practices of the LAPD targeting residents of color as the root of the Watts uprising.[43] As such, the uprising was a demand for an end to police practices that reproduced and upheld white supremacy, segregation, and inequality. Department officials and conservative policymakers, however, used the legitimacy crisis of the police created by the uprising to expand police power.

The LAPD's postwar model of policing routinely served as a standard for departments across the country. Backed by federal funds and support from newly elected governor Ronald Reagan, the LAPD led the way in bolstering its paramilitary function through riot control plans, the use of helicopters, and the invention of Special Weapons and Tactics (SWAT) teams, which was quickly adopted by other departments. At the same time, the department sought to legitimize the iron fist with the velvet glove of community relations and improved officer training. As chapter 2 shows, the LAPD enhanced its martial capacity while expanding its reach through community relations programs.[44]

Get-tough policing was not the only possible response to the urban uprisings of the 1960s. African American and Mexican American residents challenged punitive crime policy, demanded police accountability, and promoted anti–police abuse activism. As chapter 3 reveals, residents and activists reimagined the meaning of safety that rested on community control of the police. Yet the LAPD responded to these movements by framing them as a

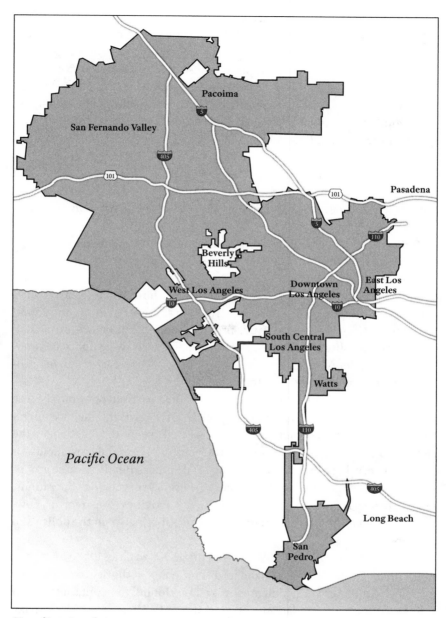

City of Los Angeles, 1970

threat to order to justify increased officer discretion to harass, arrest, and repress. This cut short the possibility for alternative models of policing and ensured that grievances with the police persisted.

The Watts uprising and anti–police abuse activism ushered in a shift in politics and policing marked by Bradley's election and his commitment to liberal law-and-order policies. Focusing on the Mayor's Office of Criminal Justice Planning and efforts to combat youth crime during the 1970s, chapter 4 shows how a combination of liberal and conservative politicians and criminal justice officials focused on reforming a juvenile justice system they believed to be too lenient on youth offenders. By posing rehabilitation and diversion as alternatives to arrest and imprisonment, they provided the police with new discretionary authority to enter social institutions to supervise youth of color.

Reflecting broader trends in cities that had elected black mayors in the 1970s, Bradley's politics rested on a belief that law enforcement could provide equitable police service by committing to pluralist policies that were responsive to all city residents. As chapter 5 argues, however, reforms, such as diversifying the department, enhancing human relations training, and adopting community-oriented policing, provided only a semblance of civilian control of the police. As the police continued to aggressively police communities of color, it produced a new phase of anti–police abuse organizing calling for an end to police crimes and power abuses.

The LAPD's ability to maintain its independent partisan power in the face of procedural reforms and antipolice protest rested on its intelligence operations. Police spying, as chapter 6 shows, targeted groups that challenged the status quo, none more so than anti–police abuse activists and movements for racial justice, using a capacious definition of "disorder." But these same groups exposed the Public Disorder Intelligence Division's surveillance operations, leading to new regulations on the department's activities. The reforms, however, did not change the underlying power relations between the police and residents.

Within the context of global trade and migration to cities in the 1980s, the department remobilized to expand its discretionary authority to combat the growing number of undocumented migrants. Hoping to maintain the trust of new immigrant populations, officials limited police authority to make arrests based on immigration status. Yet, as chapter 7 argues, the LAPD constructed an "alien criminal" category to justify cooperation with the Immigration and Naturalization Service and to arrest undocumented immigrants. In the process, the LAPD employed racialized constructions of illegality that criminalized the city's Latino/a population.

Reductions to social service and urban aid budgets by the Reagan administration, economic crises, and growing conservatism among middle-class white voters reshaped political possibilities during the 1980s. Reductions in urban aid left only punitive solutions available to local policymakers facing drug crime and gang violence. The Bradley administration, as chapter 8 demonstrates, hoped to maintain its multiracial coalition and attract international capital by waging a militarized war on drugs as a war on gangs. The combined drug-gang war rationalized social and economic inequality and constructed black and Latino/a youth as criminal, thereby legitimating disciplinary exclusion and removal from the streets.

Such conditions ultimately contributed to the eruption of the 1992 Los Angeles rebellion. The uprising occurred within the distinctly punitive context of the war on drugs and gangs. Solutions to urban social problems, chapter 9 shows, had become so entangled with the city's and LAPD's various wars on crime that the responses to the uprising depended on partnership with law enforcement and criminal justice programs, leaving police power intact. As *Policing Los Angeles* concludes, the post-1992 reforms expanded the criminal justice system into new areas of municipal governance through the adoption of community and broken windows policing, which focused police enforcement on low-level and quality of life offenses to maintain urban order.[45] Not until the Rampart Scandal (the exposure of widespread corruption in the LAPD's Rampart anti-gang Community Resources against Street Hoodlums unit) in the late 1990s led to a federal consent decree did the LAPD face external oversight. While leading to a new era in the LAPD's history, such oversight also opened possibilities for expanded police authority because decades of get-tough policies embedded police power in local politics.

––––––––

Doing police history is difficult. Access to sources is an obstacle because police archives are often closed. To undertake this study, I mined the archives of city officials, anti–police abuse organizations, and local newspapers for any reference to the police and crime policy. The presence of police materials in a wide-ranging set of archives exposed the extent to which the police power had expanded into every facet of social and political life in Los Angeles and the immense energy of activists to challenge the police. I filed a California Public Records Act request for LAPD materials in 2012 in hopes of including official LAPD records, but the department refused to open its files. A lawsuit by the American Civil Liberties Union (ACLU) based in part on my records request, however, led to the opening of the LAPD's historical records in the fall of 2017.[46] While those files are not reflected here as this book goes to press, the story that this book reveals of how racism and repression was built into the expansion of police power in Los Angeles stands on its own.

Yet there are limits to the scope of any book. *Policing Los Angeles* is a study of policing, politics, and anti-police abuse movements in Los Angeles from Watts to the 1992 rebellion. Its analytical focus centers on the consolidation of the police power in city politics, the impact of policing on African American and Latino/a residents, and black and Latino/a efforts to combat police abuse. As a result, this book does not provide an in-depth discussion of police officers or an institutional history of the LAPD. Nor does it provide a gendered analysis of policing, the efforts of the LAPD to police Los Angeles's homeless or LGBT populations, or Asian American relations with African Americans or the police. The absence of these other areas of police history should not suggest that they are unimportant to understanding the role of police power in Los Angeles or other cities but that they are fruitful avenues for future exploration and research.

Police function to ensure social order varies only in the particulars of geography. As the LAPD produced and enforced racially hierarchical order through its get-tough police practices, however, it led to intense African American and Latino/a discontent that repeatedly erupted in antipolice protest, creating a series of legitimacy crises for the department that linger in the twenty-first century. The police are not neutral. They are mobilized by elites, they are pressured from below, and, especially since 1965, they have organized politically. They define their interests through repressive capacity. This is their story in one of its most vital locales.

Chapter 1

Policing Raceriotland

A Journey into Racist Policing and Urban Uprising

Speaking to the California Commonwealth Club a month after the Watts uprising, Los Angeles civil rights leader H. H. Brookins pinpointed police as the central cause of the unrest. In his aptly titled speech "Watts Close Up—A Lesson for Other Cities," Brookins reminded his audience, "The majesty of the law has for generations of Negroes, really meant the majesty of white authority." For many African Americans, the police were the crux of a racist system of occupation, containment, and control. For African Americans, the law "has had no majesty," Brookins explained; "it has, rather, been the symbol of oppression, and that 'law' has not been viewed by the Negro as an institution of the whole community, but a tool of the white authority to enforce its will on him in almost every aspect of his daily life." Repressive policing had fueled six days of rage in August 1965 and, if left unchanged, would create the potential for future violence.[1] How officials and residents chose to address long-standing patterns of abusive police power would have far-reaching consequences for politics and racial equality in Los Angeles.

The Watts uprising drew strength from a legacy of frustration with racism, employment discrimination, and residential segregation. Yet racist policing was ultimately the uprising's trigger. Under the direction of William Parker, the LAPD had operated as a force unto itself. The police defended the city's dominant white Protestant social and political institutions themselves rooted in a history of colonialism.[2] "Los Angeles is the white spot of the great cities of America today," Parker reminded residents upon his appointment as chief in 1950 of the city's exceptional pattern of low crime but which came to embody a racialized meaning. "It is to the advantage of the community that we keep it that way."[3]

Post–World War II demographic changes threatened Parker's view of Los Angeles. New African American residents migrated from the South, and dissented from white residents' blanket support for the LAPD and the local power structure. African American residents soon lodged demands for police reform and accountability. Parker flatly rejected these calls for change, denouncing them as the work of subversives aimed at undermining the authority of law enforcement. Instead, the LAPD operated as a de facto army of occupation meant to keep the African American community contained.

The arrest of Marquette Frye on August 11, 1965, produced an explosion of antipolice rage that generated an even greater reaction of police violence against the black community, effectively creating a police riot. Residents openly confronted the forces of law and order, expressing their discontent with the police. Law enforcement's aggressive response to the unrest aimed to put an end to any doubts about who owned and controlled the streets.[4]

Many black residents placed the LAPD at the center of their analysis of the rebellion. The potential for violence would remain unless officials dealt with a police force intent on maintaining a race-based hierarchy of social control. Yet any hopes were quickly dashed. Most observers explained the unrest as the work of lawless black criminals, and the Governor's Commission to Investigate the Los Angeles Riots was no exception. Better known as the McCone Commission for its chairman, former Central Intelligence Agency chief John McCone, there was little chance it would indict the police. Testimony revealed widespread discontent with the police and evidence that law enforcement did more to exacerbate the unrest than to prevent it. But the commission accepted the view that complaints of brutality were ruses to undermine the police. Political officials blamed the uprising on a rogue criminal element and absolved the police of responsibility, shoring up the power of the police.[5]

The uprising was ultimately a demand for an end to police practices that maintained white authority, control, and order in black spaces. For law enforcement, it created a crisis in legitimacy that required new strategies to reassert police discretionary authority. Local officials' rhetorical commitment to reform, however, was overshadowed by a reinvestment in law and order and militarization. The Watts uprising and policy responses marked a pivotal moment in the history of policing, politics, and power in Los Angeles after which the city would never be the same. The following pages reveal that the LAPD was a racist, violent institution prior to Watts but the uprising focused attention and critique on the police. The department's response to calls for reform, however, ultimately made things worse by using the crisis of legitimacy created by the unrest to demand more authority, discretion, and resources.

William Parker's "Thin Blue Line"

No one had a greater influence on the LAPD's operations, attitudes, and culture than Chief William Parker. When Parker became an officer in 1927, he found a department mired in graft, political corruption, and scandals. He kept his distance, then returned to the LAPD in 1947 after serving in World War II, building a reputation for discipline, political savvy, and public relations that elevated him to chief of police in 1950, a position he held until his death in 1966. Under Parker the LAPD became the most emulated department in the country, and observers often referred to him as the "second most respected" law enforcement officer in the nation after the FBI's J. Edgar Hoover.[6]

Parker rooted out corruption and improved the department's image through professionalization. His program rested on scientific management, research, efficiency, and a military style of training and discipline. Strict standards for recruitment and training, high salaries for officers, and a well-equipped department would enable the police to maintain authority on the streets. Perhaps most importantly, professionalization ensured the LAPD operated independently from political influence. Despite a Board of Police Commissioners empowered by the city charter to oversee the department and appoint the chief, the board often acted as a rubber stamp following the chief's directives.[7] Parker protected the department's autonomy at all costs, and his power rivaled that of the mayor and city council. This power relied on maintaining the belief that domestic tranquility, social order, and positive community relations all required one thing only: unstinting support for the police.[8]

Insularity led to a profound lack of accountability. The Internal Affairs Division adjudicated all complaints, and city charter Section 202 gave the chief all disciplinary power over officers. While Parker's reforms ensured strict adherence to internal discipline and punished officers for poor moral conduct and behavior, the Internal Affairs Division often returned verdicts of justifiable homicide in police shootings and rarely sustained complaints of abuse that came from citizens. Between January 1, 1964 and July 31, 1965, the police committed sixty-four homicides of which sixty-two were ruled justifiable. In twenty-seven of the cases, the victim was shot in the back; twenty-five of the suspects were unarmed; and four had committed no crime when shot.[9]

Compared with police departments in other major cities such as New York and Chicago, the LAPD had to make do with fewer officers and less financial support. The ratio of police to population in Los Angeles in the mid-1950s, according to department officials, was 1.87 officers per 1,000 residents, compared with 4 per 1,000 residents for cities such as Detroit, New York, and Chicago.[10] Parker developed a strategy of proactive policing to address a chronically understaffed force. Roughly 5,200 LAPD officers were spread across 450 square miles and 2.5 million residents in 1960. Proactive policing put officers into patrol cars, which reduced contact with residents, and required officers to be able to recognize a criminal by appearance, behavior, or demeanor. The proactive philosophy made the police the guardians of a "thin blue line" holding back crime, disorder, and, crucially, civil rights and Communism. Social or economic causes of crime were irrelevant to a proactive police force. "We are not interested in why a certain group tends towards crime," Parker declared. "We are interested in maintaining order."[11]

Because the police power gave the police the discretion to both define and enforce the boundaries of order and model citizenship, any challenge to Parker's vision of an orderly city invited intense reprisals. Nothing challenged Parker's definition of order more than demands for equality by the city's residents of color.[12] Throughout the 1950s Parker linked civil rights activists with Communism, crime, and an erosion of police authority. "The current soft attitude on the part of the public to crime and Civil Rights demonstrations," Parker told the Sherman Oaks Rotary Club, "could lead to a form of anarchy unless halted."[13] When the National Association for the Advancement of Colored People (NAACP) charged that the "police use fear, not respect, to influence conduct" in the ghetto, Parker responded that the claim not only was "false, libelous, and defamatory," but itself undermined social order and police authority.[14] Parker would not tolerate such challenges to police power. "The voice of the criminal, the communist, and the self-appointed defender of civil liberties," Parker warned residents, "constantly cries out for more and more restriction upon police authority."[15]

Command and control tactics inundated black and Mexican American neighborhoods with police, due to the perception that they were high-crime areas. Parker defended his tactics, arguing that though blacks made up only 16 percent of the population, 60.2 percent of all suspects in violent crimes were black. Although Parker acknowledged that racial and ethnic categories were "unscientific breakdowns; they are a fiction," Parker's theory of policing provided a defense for the use of race in proactive police work. "From a police point-of-view," Parker explained, racial categories "are a useful fiction and should be used as long as they remain useful. The demand that the police cease to consider race, color, and creed is an unrealistic demand." Claiming that the police "concentrate on effects, not causes," Parker framed black and Mexican American criminality as a fact, and used it to bolster the police power's discretionary authority to employ race as predictor of criminality and in determining threats to order.[16]

Perceptions of criminality, however, resulted from how the LAPD policed urban space. The department's statistics revealed that arrest rates in neighborhoods of color were much higher when compared with those of white neighborhoods. In 1965, for example, the number of reported Part I incidents—homicide, rape, robbery, aggravated assault, burglary, larceny, and auto theft—in the predominantly African American 77th Division was 92.7 per 1,000 residents with an arrest rate of 29.9. In the white West Los Angeles Division, in contrast, the Part I offense rate was 39.0 but the arrest rate was 3.8 per 1,000 residents. Even as the 77th Division had a higher rate of reported offenses, the proportion of offenses to arrests was much higher—roughly one arrest for every three reported—compared with the West Los Angeles, where there was approximately one arrest for every ten reported incidents.[17] Such disparities led one black resident to complain, "The police is brainwashed that every colored person is a criminal." Policing practices based on racist categorizations thereby confirmed beliefs in black and Mexican American criminality that, as one observer explained, reflected "the views and prejudices held by a majority of the people."[18]

Suggesting criminal behavior was inherent among blacks and Mexican Americans facilitated racist policing. Testifying to the Civil Rights Commission, Parker explained, "You cannot ignore the genes in the behavior pattern of people." Such outright racism was widespread among officers, many of whom came from the South. While on patrol, many called black men "boy" and black women "Negress."[19] Officers in the 77th Street Station, for example, employed the acronym LSMFT for "Let's shoot a motherfucker tonight. Got your nigger knocker all shined up?" In the 1960s, the LAPD referred to the 77th Street Division as "the L.A. Congo" and the Newton Division as "Occupied Newton."[20] Not surprisingly such views produced an "us versus them" attitude within the department that contributed to not only police violence but also hostility toward the police.

Police abuse, unsurprisingly, was common. The University of California, Los Angeles (UCLA) Riot Study found that 71.3 percent of black men felt that the police were not respectful and 65.5 percent believed that they used unnecessary force when making arrests. Nearly 72 percent believed the police used roust-and-frisk tactics, the term then used for what would come to be called stop-and-frisk, on a regular basis, and 65 percent felt that police beat suspects while in custody. While individual experiences with police abuse were lower, with 23 percent of respondents reporting they directly experienced disrespect and 20 percent reporting they experienced roust-and-frisk, twice as many said they witnessed such practices. Mexican Americans held similar views. Sociologist Armando Morales found that 65 percent of Mexican Americans in East Los Angeles believed that police lacked respect, 73 percent believed the police used discriminatory roust-and-frisk tactics, and 68 percent believed that the police used unnecessary force in making arrests.[21]

The number of reported incidents was likely only a fraction of the total, as African American and Mexican American residents saw little value in filing complaints against an unresponsive department. Federal and state law also provided the police with latitude when it came to the use of force, making legal redress difficult for victims of police abuse.[22] During the 1950s, for example, the NAACP filed numerous complaints that either got wrapped up in Internal Affairs Division investigations or were ignored entirely.[23] While

Internal Affairs Division officials claimed that roughly 40 percent of complaints were sustained annually, the statistics did not differentiate between internal complaints and those made by residents. In 1965, for example, the department received 231 complaints of the use of excessive force, sustaining only twelve, or 5.2 percent. That same year, there were 326 complaints of neglect of duty, an internal charge often made by superiors, of which Internal Affairs Division sustained 81.2 percent. Officers were also trained to bring charges of "assaulting a police officer" against suspects who had been subject to the inappropriate use of force or threatened a complaint.[24]

While the police were omnipresent in African American and Mexican American neighborhoods, the service they provided was negligible. Many residents desired better police service, but officers were slow in responding to calls. "It takes a long time for police to respond to calls in Watts," a young resident named David explained, "from forty-five minutes to an hour." Sheriff's deputies in East Los Angeles often failed to respond to calls for emergency service by Mexican American residents. Black youth recognized the need for police service in Watts, but they objected to the constant harassment that came with that service.[25]

The police represented an arm of the state that did little for communities of color but keep them under control. That the department was overwhelmingly white—in 1964 there were no more than 325 black officers, and their proportion of the department ranged between 2 and 5 percent during the 1950s and 1960s, while Mexican Americans fared little better, representing roughly 6 percent of the force in 1966—and the lack of a residency requirement mandating police officers live within the city of Los Angeles heightened perceptions among residents of color that their neighborhoods were occupied territories. Hearings on police-community relations held in 1962 by the U.S. Commission on Civil Rights found widespread distrust of the police among blacks and Mexican Americans.[26] While Parker denied any problems between his department and the black community, the actions and attitudes of the police created a "bad psychological pattern" between minority communities and the police.[27]

As such, police-community contact resulted in a series of escalating "anti-police riot[s]" during the early 1960s. The police often resorted to force when confronted by groups of black residents because, anti–police abuse lawyer Hugh Manes suggested, "the peace officer who sees the crowd gather 'menacingly' does not pause to consider—then or later—whether his arrogant treatment of prisoners is the progenitor of a potentially hostile mob." Between 1961 and 1964, there were eleven episodes of black crowds confronting officers, but LAPD officials brushed them off as isolated incidents rather than a systemic problem within the department. "Regardless of a citizen's own attitude toward the police," Manes concluded, "the latter conduct themselves with an arrogance and contempt for the Negro citizen that seems calculated to invite violence."[28]

One such incident occurred on Memorial Day 1961 when officers arrested a black teenager at Griffith Park for failing to pay for a ride on the merry-go-round. The arrest led to a crowd of 200 onlookers attempting to stop the police. Members of the crowd threw rocks and bottles, yelling, "This is not Alabama." Police swarmed the area with more than seventy-five reinforcements, and the "riot" ended with the arrest of three other black youth. The police charged one youth with assault on an officer and the other two under a 1933 law that made it illegal to remove a prisoner from police custody by "means of a riot." This use of an antilynching law to arrest black youth further enraged many residents. Using such overwhelming force to prevent and contain future incidents, civil rights attorney Loren Miller suggested, was "inept and antagonistic" and likely to lead to violence.[29]

A year later, on April 27, 1962, two members of the Nation of Islam were removing clothing from a car in front of the Muslim temple when two police officers stopped to investigate. Within a few minutes, "the area . . . resembled a modern day street scene in Algiers," as the LAPD flooded the area with seventy-five officers to disperse an antipolice demonstration. The battle ended with the police shooting seven unarmed Nation of Islam members, killing Korean War veteran Ronald Stokes. Following the incident, a meeting of civil rights leaders and civil liberties activists found that the black community "seems to be convinced that the initiator of these problems regarding relations between Negroes and the police is the police chief himself." The Stokes killing emboldened residents who were "no longer afraid to say there is police brutality."[30] While not every episode of police abuse resulted in such violent confrontation, Manes reported that "scarcely a week passes without reports in the Negro press of claims of violence by citizen and police against each other."[31]

Many African American activists, however, urged the police to address perceptions of the LAPD as merely a professionalized version of "white man's law" in the South. The United Civil Rights Committee pled to "Men of Good Will" to alter police practices that left a "long smoldering resentment." But Parker responded with silence, and the lack of change left many black residents pessimistic about the future. "Violence in Los Angeles is inevitable, and that nothing can or will be done about it until after the fact," Loren Miller predicted in 1964. "Then there will be the appointment of a commission which will damn the civil rights leaders and the Chief alike."[32]

The deep roots of racist policing in Los Angeles had created a profound frustration and disillusionment with the possibility of fair treatment by the police. For many black residents, the history of discriminatory police practices and patterns of mistrust left them with few alternatives but to seek remedies to police misconduct in the streets. A routine encounter between blacks and the police on a hot August day a year after Miller's warning would spur an antipolice uprising during which, as the American Civil Liberties Union's Ed Cray reported, "the very sight of blue uniformed officers was enough to provoke new waves of violence."[33] Despite the potential for retaliatory violence and repression by the police, many African Americans understood participation in the unrest as a moment to stand up and assert that black lives mattered. "I been kicked and called 'Nigger' for the last time," one Watts resident stated during the uprising. "There're lots worse things here than dying."[34]

Burn, Baby, Burn!

On August 11, 1965, California Highway Patrol officers pulled over two African American men, Marquette Frye and his brother Ronald, for reckless driving and being under the influence of alcohol on 116th Place and Avalon Boulevard in the Watts neighborhood of Los Angeles. When the California Highway Patrol officers attempted to arrest Marquette Frye, a scuffle ensued and a crowd of 250 to 300 onlookers gathered to observe the situation. The growing crowd and presence of Frye's mother scolding her son produced a volatile situation. When the California Highway Patrol radioed a call of "Officers needs help," the arrival of LAPD and more California Highway Patrol officers added to the tension. As one crowd member described the situation, "They [the police] act like they're fighting in Viet Nam. They have all these cops and everything around."[35]

When officers resorted to the use of force, kicking the Fryes, hitting them with batons, and shoving them into patrol cars, cries erupted. A woman reportedly spit at the officers, causing them to charge into the crowd to apprehend her by the neck. "This," one observer recalled, "is when the crowd became angry." Some cried out, "Goddam! They'd [the police] never treat a white woman like that." Officers on the scene, who formed a line across the street with their batons at the ready, recalled people yelling, "This is just like Selma. . . . We got no rights at all." As they made their retreat, officers hoped the removal of law enforcement would reduce the crowd's hostility. As officers retreated, rumors of police brutality spread quickly, igniting the spark that set South Central aflame in open rebellion against the police.[36]

Law enforcement may have pulled out to reduce tensions, but for the crowd it was a victory. Growing to over 1,500, the crowd hurled rocks, slabs of concrete, and bottles at the police officers as they drove away, then at other passing vehicles. By midnight the area was out of control. As August 11 turned to August 12, crowds gathered throughout South Central, concentrating on 103rd Street, which came to be known as Charcoal Alley. Rumors circulated that young blacks were boasting that "they were going to show the cops that night."[37]

Hoping to stop the violence, leaders from the African American community met with young participants at Athens Park on August 12. Organized by the Human Relations Commission's John Buggs, the meeting of over 200 people was attended by Reverend H. H. Brookins, Congressman Augustus Hawkins, NAACP leader Claude Hudson, and County Board of Supervisors members John Gibson and Kenneth Hahn. Despite constructive proposals, many active in the uprising believed that television outlets fanned the flames of the violence and did not show the positive elements of the meeting. Media coverage undermined peace efforts by focusing on a black youth who exclaimed that they were "not going to fight down here no more. You know where they going? They after the whites."[38]

Buggs worked with youth leaders to address their grievances to stop the unrest. In one meeting the youth felt that the violence would stop if "the Anglo cops" were not in the area. The problem, according to one kid, was that many of them had been arrested on the first day and "had come back to the Watts area with bloody heads" and "believed that the PD [police department] had roughed them up." Confrontation with the police gave many youth a sense of pride and justice for years of harassment and brutality. "Residents in Watts had a feeling that they had given the police a licking and that they were not going to let the police forget it," Buggs recalled. "They were going to impress it on the police more." Recommendations to restore peace aimed at removing white officers and bringing in black officers in plainclothes and employing residents as a community police force. As Brookins summarized, "There ought not to be any concentration of police power in this community tonight."[39]

Buggs relayed the proposals for reduced police power to the LAPD's community relations officer, James Fisk. When asked if the LAPD would accept the recommendations to remove white officers, Fisk sorrowfully replied, "No." Fisk reported that the LAPD would maintain "regular" patrols but did not know if they would include black officers. When Fisk reported to Parker, the chief responded, "Certainly we do not wish to be provocateurs by being in the area," but Parker would not remove police from the area because officers at the meeting "did not believe they could abdicate their responsibility to uphold law and order." The lack of awareness by Parker and LAPD officials of the antipolice sentiment fueling the unrest caused Buggs to exclaim to Fisk, "You've blown it."[40]

Police officials responded with an overwhelming show of force. When six police cars moved into the area near Athens Park with sirens blazing, "it was just like an explosion," Brookins reported; "everything just went haywire." Police cars filled with white officers flooded the streets. As Buggs and Brookins drove through a crew of black youngsters followed by a police car, the youth waited for the pair to pass before pelting police cars with rocks and slabs of concrete. Nearby, "two or three Negroes were backed up against a wall, and all the officers had batons in their hands." The LAPD had responded with overwhelming force, causing Buggs to comment, "Man, it looks like they're [the police] asking for it."[41]

When Buggs and Brookins met with Deputy Chief Roger Murdock at the 77th Street Station later that night, they described the simmering tension. Suggesting that white police officers were the target of the community's anger, they pushed for the use of black officers in plainclothes. Murdock responded that the black leadership's suggestions had failed—"Now let us do it our own way." Upon leaving the station, Brookins told reporters, "The Police Department indicated to us that they were going to run the city their own way, and they would prove who runs the city of Los Angeles. Mr. Roger Murdock's attitude was one I would suspect from a Jim Clark in Alabama. We are not in Alabama, we want to work with the police, we want to work with elected officials, not against them."[42] The department's plan aimed to show the rioters who ruled the streets and primed the city for more violence.

Mired by communication problems, a shortage of vehicles, manpower shortages, inadequate jail facilities, poor field equipment, and a lack of leadership from Parker, the LAPD quickly became overwhelmed by the unrest as the city spiraled out of control. Participants in the unrest attacked cars driven by whites, forced white reporters out of the area, threw objects at firefighters, made Molotov cocktails, and burned buildings. Looting targeted white business owners as crowds, combining to totals of tens of thousands, shouted "Burn, Baby, Burn." Participants did not shy away from confrontations with the symbols of authority, sniping at LAPD officers from rooftops and behind buildings. "The police, sheriffs and highway patrolman," Leonard Carter of the NAACP reported, "were barraged with bricks, bottles, etc. and were overrun during the night."[43]

Although Parker had prepared for unrest after the 1964 Harlem riot, his response was uncoordinated and self-defeating. Parker refused to meet with civil rights leaders to cool tensions, calling participants "agitators" and criminals, while Mayor Sam Yorty would not consult with black leaders because he saw them as "part of the problem." City leaders failed to recognize that the violence was the symptom of a long history of discrimination, abuse, and segregation. Instead of attempting to understand the discontent aimed at his department, Parker dismissed the rioters by suggesting, "One person threw a rock. . . . Then, like monkeys in a zoo, others started throwing rocks."[44]

Sensational helicopter coverage amplified police power by bringing images of urban warfare into people's homes. Jerry Dunphy, a KNXT television news anchor, introduced "The Big News" on August 13, by linking the war in Vietnam to the streets of South Central, claiming, "Newsmen who have been in Vietnam say nothing they have seen elsewhere compares with the unbridled rampaging in Watts." The KTLA television report "Hell in the City of Angels," produced days after the uprising, described the unrest using metaphors of war that pitted the forces of law and order against undifferentiated black masses.[45] The LAPD legitimized views that such spaces were enemy war zones filled with criminals that required aggressive, military-style policing. Law-and-order policies were presented as the only logical response to a situation that Parker described as "very much like fighting the Viet Cong."[46]

After three days, the outmanned and ill-prepared LAPD received reinforcements from the California National Guard. Lieutenant Governor Glenn Anderson called the scene an "extreme emergency," placing a curfew over a 46.5-square-mile area.[47] As one reporter stated, "Sunday saw . . . the balance of power [shift back to the authorities]. . . . Finally we had that overwhelming use of force." As Deputy Chief Daryl Gates described it, "We're taking the gloves off." Anyone outside after 8:00 P.M. was subject to arrest, and white guardsmen and police officers flooded the area and tanks rolled down the streets, creating what resident Robert Oliver recalled as a "little gestapo situation." Mayor Yorty, observing from a helicopter, commented, "It must make those policemen feel pretty good to have those troops behind them. . . . That's the kind of force we've got to have." With the aid of the National Guard, police flushed out snipers, forcing them to lie prone on the street, and yelled at suspected rioters, "One more move and I'll kill ya." An improvised traffic sign on 104th Street and Wilmington warned, "Turn left or get shot."[48]

Years of oppressive policing had created a police state. "If you wanted to stay alive then you pretty much kinda got in line," Oliver explained. "It turned into a police state. . . . They were very serious about what they felt had to be done in order to put these black people back in their places."[49] If black residents viewed the use of force as an instrument of containment, for the state, force was necessary to quell the violence and maintain social control.[50] Believing his officers had turned the tide, Parker reported, "We're on top and they're on the bottom." He praised his officers in responding with high standards and quality performance. Officers, Parker concluded, "demonstrated skill,

Handmade sign in the street, "Turn left or get shot," in front of police barricade, 1965. Reminding residents in South Central who owned the streets, the LAPD doubled down on the threat of force and monopoly of violence in response to the antipolice protest. The LAPD viewed the streets of Los Angeles as a battleground requiring containment and control. Governor's Commission on the Los Angeles Riots Records, BANC MSS 74/115 c; courtesy of the Bancroft Library, University of California, Berkeley.

adaptability, courage, sense of responsibility and professional conduct [that] reflects the quality of our department and our unreserved dedication to the public service."[51]

Mass arrests were a deliberate strategy of incapacitation. As Murdock explained, the way to handle the rioters was "to put as many people as we can in jail. . . . That's certainly no secret."[52] Police arrested 3,952 people, including over 500 youths under the age of eighteen, for any number of offenses including "loitering, looting, and vandalism." When responding to claims that innocent people had been swept up in the mass arrests, city attorney Roger Arnebergh commented, "I doubt that innocent people were swept up. . . . Police did not make arrests indiscriminately." Many of those arrested for burglary or curfew violations, however, stated in interviews afterward that they had not been involved in violence or looting.[53]

In the following weeks, arrest cases overwhelmed local courts. Judges supported the police by setting bail as high as $5,000. The United Civil Rights

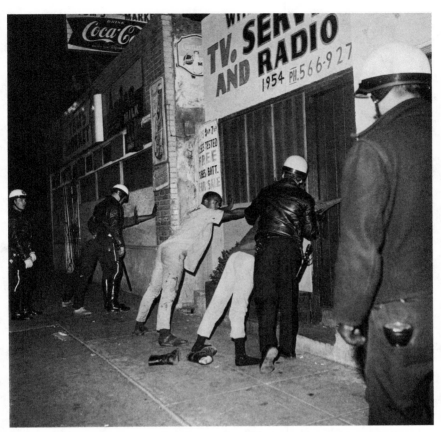

Police officers search suspects in Watts, 1965. Stop, search, and mass arrests targeting young African Americans were at the center of police strategy to address the Watts uprising. Such tactics built on the LAPD's approach to policing after World War II and the targeting and criminalization of the city's African American residents. *Los Angeles Times* Photographic Archives (Collection 1429); courtesy of Library Special Collections, Charles E. Young Research Library, UCLA.

Committee and NAACP offered free legal advice and services, but it was nowhere near enough. The NAACP later filed suit in the California Supreme Court charging twenty-one judges with failure to appoint counsel and to inform arrestees of the charges filed against them. Contrary to claims of prosecutors, many had no prior arrests or convictions. A study of those arrested by the McCone Commission found that 1,232 (35.8 percent) of adults arrested had no prior criminal record and another 930 (27 percent) had one or two convictions resulting in sentences of 90 days or less. Summary justice ensued as cases went forward without juries and judges handed down verdicts of one year to life for looting.[54]

Police officer threatens an African American youth with a shotgun, 1965. The threat of force and militarized response to Watts foreshadowed the police demand for more resources, hardware, and authority in its aftermath. *Los Angeles Times* Photographic Archives (Collection 1429); courtesy of Library Special Collections, Charles E. Young Research Library, UCLA.

By August 17, 103rd Street was barely more than rubble. What most newspapers called "mob rule" had ended and Governor Brown remarked, "We must and will continue to deal forcefully with the terrorists until Los Angeles is safe again."[55] It took 934 LAPD officers, 719 sheriff's deputies, and 13,900 California National Guardsmen to put down the uprising. Property damage amounted to roughly $40 million. The death toll reached at least thirty-four, and 1,032 were wounded. In the following weeks, the coroner's inquest found twenty-six of the deaths to be justifiable homicide. Attempts by Hugh Manes to question officers at the inquest were dismissed, and he was ejected from the courtroom.[56]

Retaliatory actions by LAPD officers confirmed the department's reliance on force and racially targeted policing to reassert police power and en-

U.S. Army troops after the Watts uprising, 1965. Troops of the U.S. Army's
1st Battalion, 160th Infantry leaving after Watts. The use of military troops to reinforce
the LAPD during the Watts uprising blurred the lines between the police power and
military power. *Los Angeles Times* Photographic Archives (Collection 1429); courtesy
of Library Special Collections, Charles E. Young Research Library, UCLA.

force social order. Perhaps the most revealing counteroffensive occurred at
the Nation of Islam Mosque Number 27, where police had attacked three
years earlier. On the morning of August 18, LAPD officers with the support
of sheriffs, highway patrol, and National Guard troops attacked the Nation
of Islam mosque after an anonymous 1:43 A.M. phone call reporting that
"male Negroes were carrying guns into a building at 5606 South Broad-
way." With guardsmen securing the surrounding area, LAPD officers invaded the mosque, firing more than 500 rounds into the building in response
to alleged gunshots. Nineteen men inside and an additional forty outside
the temple were arrested and led away at gunpoint. No guns or bullet casings
were found in the mosque. Most suggestive of the LAPD's retaliatory intent

in assaulting the Mosque occurred after the raid when one officer involved posed for a photograph with a "trophy" pin of Elijah Muhammad's picture, the Nation's leader, pinned to his uniform. While the police commission attempted to downplay the incident to protect the department's image, Councilman Billy Mills pressured the Police, Fire, and Civil Defense Committee to undertake an in-depth investigation of the incident. The committee's report found the law enforcement actions an "unwarranted, unjustified, and irresponsible use of Police power."[57]

Many white residents approved of the use of force to quell the uprising. In the weeks after the uprising, the Chamber of Commerce praised Parker, and he received at least 17,864 letters, of which 99.3 percent were positive.[58] As one constituent wrote to County Board of Supervisors member Kenneth Hahn, "We wish Chief Parker could have more police to cope with his problem—we are for him 100%," while another commented that Parker "has been attacked by undisciplined elements." Others laid blame directly on the black participants, whom they vilified as subversives and criminals. "It's these *hoodlums* standing around waiting," one resident wrote to Lieutenant Governor Glenn Anderson, "*these* are *criminals* out for disregard for '*Authority*.'"[59]

The violence had the potential to raise the veil that hid repressive policing from mainstream society. But, as Hugh Manes explained, the response of city officials and whites served to avoid a reckoning with the culpability of the police and the state in producing the uprising. By ruling all the deaths "JUSTIFIABLE HOMICIDE," the blame rested on lawless rioters, and "the community is relieved; the police are exonerated; and justice is done." Most whites willingly accepted this dominant narrative. Those who chose to consider the source of the unrest, however, could not dismiss the uprising as senseless violence but a response of "a community oppressed by bigoted symbols of white authority whose concept of law enforcement is force."[60] For residents, forcing the attention of the white power structure on a community so often deemed unimportant was the ultimate victory of the uprising. "We won," one resident boasted, "because we made the whole world pay attention to us. The police chief never came here before; the mayor always stayed uptown. We made them come."[61]

The Meaning of Watts

Governor Edmund "Pat" Brown organized the Governor's Commission to Investigate the Los Angeles Riots on August 19, 1965, appointing John McCone to chair the committee. McCone was a conservative with an "impeccable" reputation in the business community who brought a set of ideological blinders to his work that ensured the final report would deemphasize the problems of police brutality that led to the uprising. In his directive to the commission, Brown stated that the violence was a "senseless, formless riot—not a civil rights demonstration." Brown also targeted emergency antipoverty programs for the riot-torn areas, but referred to those involved in the unrest as "hoodlums" and criminals.[62] By framing the rebellion as lawless and criminal at the outset, Brown shaped the commission's approach to solving the police department's legitimacy crisis by absolving it of blame. As one editorial described the commission, "Let's understand one thing. The people now on trial are the rioters, not the police department."[63]

But meetings between state representatives, federal officials, and residents held in the weeks after the uprising revealed bitterness toward the police. One observer reported on a community meeting where most residents "agreed that Police Chief Parker and the police force constituted a provocative force in the general unrest which erupted into a riot."[64] Meetings with black teenagers exposed the dual problem of police brutality and lack of police service that fueled disillusionment and discontent. The teens repeatedly explained that the police motto was To Protect and to Serve and that officers should be respected if they did so but "the police did not protect or serve them or their neighborhood" and routinely failed to "respect people and to respect law and order." As the teens suggested, avoiding violence required eliminating the cause of poor police-community relations: the racist practices of the police. While the community had little faith in the willingness of officials to take on Parker and the LAPD, they were waiting to "see what the Man will do."[65]

The unrest represented a rejection of the way the police operated in the black community. As Watts resident Stan Sanders made clear, the police were targeted because "he comes to the Negro community to impose a legal order so incompatible with its style of life and patterns of conduct as to make it seem that he is imposing an alien civil code." For many the uprising was not senseless violence but a logical demand to be free of state-sanctioned violence and a criminal justice system aimed at keeping blacks in their place. "It's Parker and his police," one twenty-seven-year-old dockworker commented on the cause. "Sure everybody down here's got a record. A Negro can't stay here a year without a record. They want Negroes to have records. Then we can't get those civil-service jobs."[66] The uprising was a calculated political protest against the use of the police to enforce the boundaries of race and social order. "It was a war to break the authority of the police," Wendell Collins of Congress of Racial Equality (CORE) testified, because the police aimed "to accustom him [blacks] to live in an inferior position in society."[67]

The uprising could only be understood in the context of a long history of poor police-community relations. Multiple reports pointed to Parker's refusal to meet with leaders or residents to discuss ways to improve police-community relations as a central cause of the uprising and potential future violence. In a meeting between clergy and Parker facilitated by the McCone Commission, for example, Reverend Joseph Hardwick explained how divides in the community remained and "Parker's words are just adding fuel to the fire. Parker is just as responsible for this riot as anyone."[68] If resentment of the police served as a spark to the uprising, the actions of law enforcement also fueled the violence. "Law enforcement methods played a significant role in the recent disorders," Congressman Augustus Hawkins testified, "serving as the catalyst that set off the rioting and was prevalent as a force that sustained the drive for days." Hawkins implored the commission to consider the role of the police in contributing to the uprising to prevent possible future violence. "Are we safer by ignoring or recognizing the human factor we have described?" he questioned. "That, in the final analysis, is going to be the test of law enforcement unless we intend to have the National Guard on a stand-by basis."[69]

While attention focused on the African American community and involvement in the uprising, Mexican Americans not only played a role during the uprising but also mirrored the concerns with racially targeted police power and demands for law and order. The Mexican American newsletter *Carta Editorial* condemned the police handling of the Frye incident, blaming the police for responding "in the only manner they seem to know how to respond—with more insults and violence." As protests expanded, the "tempo of police violence continued to increase." Rather than a riot, *Carta Editorial* called the unrest a "revolt against all laws, authority, and accepted social norms." It was not limited to African Americans but "combined with many of the Mexican-Americans in the area against the symbols of authority such as the police." Mexican American organizations, such as Community Service Organization and East Los Angeles Community Relations Council, demanded investigation into allegations of brutality.[70]

As with African Americans, testimony from Mexican Americans argued that the need for change rested not with residents but with the police. Even as he acknowledged that police-community relations were better than in the 1950s, Ralph Guzman of UCLA's Mexican American Study Project told the McCone Commission that there was considerable room for improvement. He also suggested that minority groups did not riot for the sake of rioting or due to deficient behavior and criminal tendencies but as a direct reaction to discrimination, segregation, and repression imposed by the police and white society more broadly. Congressman Ed Roybal, who had been a city council member representing East Los Angeles, also suggested the long-standing problem of police brutality in the Mexican American community, which contributed to fear of the police and distrust of law enforcement more generally.[71]

Liberal officials saw the Watts uprising as an opportunity to wrest power away from the police department. Tom Bradley and other African American councilmen, Billy Mills and Gilbert Lindsay, called for increased civilian oversight of the police department. Yet the commission often came to the defense of the department and Chief Parker, who was often on the defensive. During the investigation, Bradley and Parker repeatedly faced off. After questioning from Bradley about the role of the police in provoking the violence, Parker jabbed back, claiming, "Councilman Bradley has been tremendously critical of my department before the riots and he is continuing to be."[72]

Parker denied any and all criticism aimed at his department, quipping that he was "the only police chief that they ever sacked a whole city to get rid of." Speaking to *Meet the Press* on August 29, he suggested his "sacking" remark was "facetious" and "I am sure they didn't burn Los Angeles because of Parker." Citing the widespread support from white residents for his handling of the uprising, Parker claimed the security of the city would be at risk if he left office. When asked if his department was at least partially to blame for the violence due to abusive practices, he gave no ground, saying, "I would have to conclude that we are not responsible for triggering the riot."[73] Compared with the California Highway Patrol, Parker stated in his testimony, his highly disciplined, upstanding officers, in contrast, "have been able to continue to apply law enforcement in the area without retributive violence." When the department issued its own account of the riot in its 1965 annual report, in contrast, it praised officers' "remarkable restraint" while enduring "felonious assault upon their persons."[74]

Law enforcement, political officials, and media outlets routinely rejected claims of police brutality as attacks on the police. Indicative of how marginalized black and Mexican American people were in comparison with the power of the police, Parker repeatedly dismissed charges of police brutality by arguing that they were merely the work of subversives "designed sort of to deaden the police and drive them into a sense of inactivity."[75] Yorty came to Parker's defense, calling the charges of brutality false. Criticism of the police, he argued, undermined faith in the police and public safety. Parker denounced the charges as a "terribly vicious canard which is used to conceal Negro criminality . . . to try to find someone else to blame for their crimes."[76] Deputy Chief Richard Simon explained that cries of police brutality created a hostile attitude that made "the task of law enforcement extremely difficult." And even the testimony from police officers that did acknowledge instances of brutality dismissed them as an individual officer's problem rather than a systemic issue.[77]

The McCone Commission's analysis gave little weight to such testimony.[78] As McCone told the Urban League's Wesley Brazier about the commission's efforts to uncover the role police abuse played in the uprising, "We are having considerable difficulty getting to the bottom of it."[79] McCone believed that the claims of police brutality were overblown and represented a threat to democratic governance. "There's a lot of evidence that it's a two-way street," McCone argued, "that there's a kind of planned aggravation of the police by the Negroes." Brushing aside demands for an in-depth analysis of police brutality, McCone described criticism of the police as a "device that is designed to destroy the law—and after all, law is just the thin thread that holds our society together."[80]

Official accounts portrayed those who participated in the unrest as criminals and hoodlums who did not represent the true feelings of the black community. Yorty believed that Los Angeles's image had been tainted by a small number of radical activists, Communists, and other "subversives" who did not represent the feelings of the black community or reflect what he saw as Los Angeles's upstanding race relations. "We cannot permit a criminal element to destroy the exemplary race relations which must continue to exist in our city," Yorty explained.[81] Backed up by similar testimony from police commissioner John Ferraro, Parker suggested the participants in the unrest had no legitimate grievances, claiming, "We don't have any civil-rights problems here."[82]

Yet the uprising had more support than the McCone Commission suggested. Subsequent studies found that anywhere from 30,000 to 80,000 African American residents participated and that perhaps over 70,000 "close spectators" observed the rebellion, a substantially higher number than the 10,000 active participants outlined by the McCone report. Sympathy for the participants was also more widespread than McCone allowed. As one middle-class black woman and owner of an art gallery testified, "I will not take a Molotov cocktail but I am as mad as they [riot participants] are." Not only did more African American residents participate than Yorty, Parker, McCone, or the average white resident cared to admit, but many of those who were involved could hardly be labeled "hoodlums," violent criminals, or recent migrants. One study found that the average convicted rioter was a black man who had lived in Los Angeles for more than five years, was a high school dropout, was employed as either a domestic or an unskilled laborer, earned between $200 and $400 a month, and had an arrest record.[83]

The reliance on what would come to be known as the riff-raff theory, however, delegitimized black grievances, reinforced beliefs in black criminality, and allowed the commission to absolve city officials and law enforcement of any responsibility for the violence. It also rationalized enhanced policing and punitive crime control policies. The commission's report recommended police reform, but its underlying logic reinforced prevailing views that defended the police and their expansive authority to prevent, contain, and eliminate potential threats to order.[84]

An End or a Beginning?

The McCone Commission released its report, *Violence in the City: An End or a Beginning?*, after one hundred days of testimony and data collection. The ninety-six-page report began with an outline of the chronology of the nearly seven days of unrest. Although police action was a central grievance and source of the discontent, the McCone Report stopped well short of placing responsibility on the LAPD for the uprising. If anyone was to blame for the violence, the commission concluded, it was not the police but the rioters. "However powerful their grievances," the report admonished, "the rioters had no legal or moral justification for the wounds they inflicted. Many crimes, a great many felonies, were committed. Even more dismaying, as we studied the record, was the large number of brutal exhortations to violence which were uttered by some Negroes."[85] The commission sidestepped any serious reckoning with the historical context of repressive policing and harassment highlighted in the testimony it had collected. "The commission was not set up to investigate the police department," one commissioner admitted. "What caused the commission to come into existence? The Riots. Not the police department."[86]

The chronology that began the report betrayed the commission's biases. Rather than viewing the initial spark to the riot—the beating and arrest of the Fryes—as evidence of poor relations between the police and the black community, the report stated "Considering the undisputed facts, the commission finds that the arrest of the Fryes was handled efficiently and expeditiously." Subsequent actions by the police to arrest a bystander who spit at them went unquestioned, and blame centered on "inflated and distorted rumors concerning the arrests." When it described the efforts of the Human Relations Commission, clergy, and youth to stop the violence at the August 12 Athens Park meeting, the report merely said the effort "misfired." Little to no credence was given to the warnings from Buggs, Brookins, or black youth that continued police presence would only add to the rebellion. The McCone Report omitted the vast piles of evidence that the police only added to discontent.[87]

Ignoring testimony demonstrating deep-rooted distrust of the police and Chief Parker personally, the commission defended Parker from criticism. *Violence in the City* concluded that "Chief Parker's statements to us and collateral evidence such as his record of fairness to Negro officers are inconsistent with his having such an attitude" of discrimination against black residents. The report went so far as to conclude that Parker was a "capable Chief who directs an efficient police force that serves well this entire community."[88]

By viewing the unrest as an expression of criminality carried out by a lawless element, the report denied the need for systemic changes in policing. Rather than addressing the deep-seated patterns of harassment and authoritarian policing in neighborhoods of color, the report defended the role of the police in maintaining order. "If police authority is destroyed all of society will suffer because groups would feel free to disobey the law and inevitably their number would increase," the report explained. "Chaos might easily result."[89]

Violence in the City outlined four areas of police reform. These included a stronger Board of Police Commissioners, an inspector general to handle complaints, enhanced cooperation between the community and the police, and new hiring practices to diversify the department. Yet the burden of change rested largely on transforming African American and Mexican American attitudes toward the police rather than changing the police department itself. Rejecting a civilian review board, the report barely acknowledged the existence of dual standards, excessive force, and discriminatory policing practices in black and Mexican American neighborhoods. Systemic problems in the ways the police approached relations with black and Mexican American residents were left largely unaddressed.[90]

The reception of the report was largely negative. Many commentators viewed the report as an opportunity to address grievances but held that it "prescribes aspirin where surgery is required." Even *Newsweek* recognized that the "commission scarcely comes to grips at all with the incendiary issue that finally lit the fire in the streets of Watts: the widespread Negro allegations of police misbehavior ranging from name-calling to outright brutality," and was shocked that the LAPD "got a virtually clean bill from McCone & Co."[91] Groups such as the California Advisory Committee to the U.S. Commission on Civil Rights, the American Civil Liberties Union, and United Civil Rights Committee criticized the report's "modest measures" and pushed for more rigorous solutions to police-community relations. In an exercise of "reverse logic," the McCone Commission called for an end to criticism of Parker while criticizing those who protest injustice rather than "those whose acts give rise to the criticism." The McCone Commission had whitewashed Chief Parker and the department's actions more broadly.[92]

Most importantly, the report failed to consider how routine contact with law enforcement in the black community had created a fear of repression that led communities to seek the expulsion of the police. Bayard Rustin, longtime civil rights activist and advisor to Martin Luther King Jr., suggested that the report fundamentally missed the point of the "Watts Manifesto." By framing the rebellion as the "random work of a 'criminal element,'" Rustin argued, Parker's attitude—and the McCone Commission's inaction—could lead, as Martin Luther King phrased it in a meeting with Rustin and Parker, "into potential holocaust."[93] Black residents and activists hoped that the crisis produced by the Watts uprising would lead to reforms ushering in equitable policing. Their vision, however, was undermined by the McCone Report's deference to police and support for law and order.

Relying on the belief that the riot was caused by a lawless criminal element in the black community, *Violence in the City* ensured that any recommended changes in police complaint procedures would occur slowly. While the LAPD complied with the McCone Commission's basic recommendations focused on developing a community relations program, appointing an inspector to oversee disciplinary practice, and efforts to diversify the officer corps, as the American Civil Liberties Union found a year after Watts, *"No significant reform of the system has resulted."*[94]

The Watts moment focused attention on the long-standing problem of racist police power. The police had been central to sparking the uprising and pushing it forward. "In the riot of 1965, I think it was jus[t] the idea of a policeman, period," resident Paul Williams recalled in a 1969 interview. "I don't think it mattered if it was HP [highway patrol] or Sheriff or what. Anyone with a uniform on."[95] The uprising also provided residents with a sense of power and pride vis-à-vis the police. "Even if the people got nothing else out of it they can always say, 'We beat the L.A.P.D., beat them to the ground," one young resident proclaimed. "They had to call in the National Guard to stop us.'"[96]

Instead of interrogating the depth of police repression that structured relations between law enforcement and the black and Mexican American communities, the McCone Commission doubled down on police-oriented responses. By ignoring the patterns of daily interactions between the police and African American residents that produced such distrust of the police and made law enforcement a symbol of oppression, however, the McCone Commission also enabled the expansion of police power in the aftermath of the Watts uprising. It was part of an emerging national shift toward militarization and get-tough policing.

Law enforcement officials in Los Angeles and across the country capitalized on the dominant framing of the lawless rioter to rebuild and expand the capacity of the police to maintain order in the streets. Police-community relations remained tense. Indeed, the memory of the uprising and the crisis of legitimacy it produced shaped the way LAPD officers policed the areas of "foreign territory" in the following years. "Don't think the LAPD haven't forgotten the 1965 revolt because this is the only thing I hear when I go back to the pen every time—all about the revolt," Watts resident Sedgie Collins reported in 1969. "There always talking that talk up in 77. That's all you hear."[97] Rather than reducing tension between the police and residents of color, the response by police and city officials to the Watts uprising emphasized law and order and intensified militarized policing as a program of revenge that ensured daily contact between the criminal justice system and black and brown residents.

The election of Ronald Reagan as governor of California in 1966 and Richard Nixon to the presidency in 1968 provided a political context conducive to intensifying police power even further. The outburst of urban uprisings in cities across the country in 1967 and 1968 fueled fears of lawlessness. Drawing from this national context as well as the local preoccupation with preventing another Watts, law enforcement and city officials would work to enhance the power of the police through militarization while also attempting to gain buy-in from residents by deploying a more responsive community relations programs. The result would be a new form of policing intent on winning the battle for the streets through a strategy of counterinsurgency.

Chapter 2

The Year of the Cop

Buying and Selling Law and Order

For police department leadership, the challenge created by the Watts uprising could be resolved only by intensified law and order. With the support of
political officials, police department leaders argued that the combination of
urban unrest, violent crime, and civil rights activism would undermine the
social order unless it was met with appropriate force. Tom Reddin, who became chief after Chief William Parker's death in 1966 on promises of improving police-community relations, focused on reasserting the LAPD's
discretionary authority and expanding its martial infrastructure. "The administration is in trouble and that crime is one of the places where they are
in trouble," Reddin told the Kerner Commission. "And I think they want to
do something about it. . . . And if we [police] don't take advantage of what exists in the United States in 1967, we are crazy, because we are never going
to have it so good again." Reddin concluded that 1968 was "the year of the
Cop. Everything you want you get. And I say I want more, and I should be
getting it."[1]

These demands were received warmly, particularly in the wake of Governor Ronald Reagan's and President Richard Nixon's election victories, both
of which had capitalized on fears of urban disorder, campus unrest, and
crime. Operating within the national turn toward law and order under
Nixon, Reagan, as governor, supported the police as the front line holding
back the "jungle" attempting to destroy civilization. His policies catered to
police and prosecutors who viewed Warren Court decisions regulating police
behavior—what law enforcement called granting rights to criminals—as
attacks on police's ability to battle crime, permissiveness, and lawlessness.
Local, state, and federal law enforcement officials claimed that court decisions and liberal policies decriminalizing status offenses like vagrancy laws
were creating the conditions for more unrest.[2] In their view, the perceived
breakdown of law and order required the reassertion—and expansion—of
police power and discretionary authority over "harmful" black and brown
residents to guarantee safety of the "harmless," law-abiding white residents.

Department officials believed that crime, violent conflict, and riots could
be prevented through more-efficient, better trained, and well-equipped police departments. Warning that the streets would be overrun by subversives

and criminals, Reddin demanded more resources from local, state, and federal governments and more authority for the LAPD to wage a counterinsurgent war on crime. As local police budgets expanded, the establishment of the Law Enforcement Assistance Administration (LEAA) in 1968 funneled federal funds into state and municipal crime control programs. The LAPD invested in military equipment, riot control plans, and elite tactical training. Control of the streets would be maintained with an iron fist.[3]

Department officials also attempted to reintroduce community relations programs. These amounted to a "hearts and minds" approach that targeted inner-city youth of color in hopes they would come to respect the officer on the street. These community relations programs aimed to bring black and brown youth into established institutions rather than yielding any power or oversight to residents. Community relations thereby enabled the department to "decentralize police functions without decentralizing police authority."[4] These programs would ultimately enable the monitoring and infiltration of civil rights organizations and youth activity. On the surface, community relations appeared less punitive than militarized policing but left police power intact. Community relations complemented the martial infrastructure built after Watts aimed at reasserting control over those residents that LAPD officials viewed as a threat to order.

The urban uprisings of the 1960s marked a turning point for policing and state authority more broadly. Local politicians and law enforcement officials linked civil unrest, crime, and civil rights activism as causes of lawlessness and permissiveness, further justifying repressive policies.[5] They militarized the police and deployed community relations programs while discrediting marginalized groups' demands for equality. Capitalizing on these developments, the LAPD expanded its purview and legitimacy as an independent political entity after Watts, and became stronger than ever in the process.

The Politics of Law and Order and Personal Responsibility

Aware of the long history of the LAPD's antagonistic approach to dealing with the city's African Americans, the criminalization of Watts participants and absolution of the police worried community leaders. Such depictions threatened to undermine the struggle for equality by blaming the unrest on the criminal behavior and lapsed personal responsibility of African Americans. The NAACP's Leonard Carter explained in a special report on the Los Angeles riots that with "white persons more fearful than before and with bigoted politicians capitalizing upon those fears our struggle may be even more difficult in the days and years to come."[6] Beliefs in a connection between civil rights, urban unrest, and crime not only confirmed Carter's fears but also contributed to the appeal of the politics of law and order and personal responsibility.

Coming on the heels of Barry Goldwater's 1964 Republican presidential campaign, Los Angeles officials borrowed from backlash politics and sympathetic whites to advance their agenda to increase funding for the police and their interest in promoting punitive policies in order to legitimize their production of social order. Mayor Sam Yorty suggested that the unrest was a result not of too much police power but of weakened police authority. "Law enforcement faces a crisis," Yorty claimed. "The recent destructive riots may serve some useful purpose if they awaken the nation to the dangers inherent in the deteriorating ability of law enforcement agencies to function effectively."[7] Instead of undermining faith in the police, proponents of law and order used Watts to mobilize greater support for the police.

Media outlets and criminal justice officials also used Watts to construct and naturalize a connection between civil rights and urban crime. As *U.S. News and World Report* suggested, civil rights protests had turned "away from demonstrations and toward outlawry. For city after city, it's becoming a problem of crime control."[8] Law enforcement officials also recast the unrest as straightforward criminal activity, not a response to decades of racist and exclusionary policing. District Attorney Evelle Younger testified to the McCone Commission, "For whatever this tragedy was—race riot, social revolution, or protest—it was the biggest and wildest crime spree in the history of our country."[9] Framing urban unrest and civil rights activism as a problem of crime control enabled law enforcement and political officials to point to rising crime as a means to justify strengthening police authority.

Equating civil rights with crime and unrest built on growing attention to and concern of rising crime rates in the 1960s. Part I crime rates in Los Angeles, as reported by the LAPD, had increased from 50.7 per 1,000 residents in 1963 to 59.5 per 1,000 residents in 1965. The crime rate continued to increase throughout the late 1960s, reaching 76.8 per 1,000 residents in 1970. Although the LAPD reported a rise in crime during the 1960s, the way police administrators mobilized crime data was of greater consequence than actual crime for the consolidation of police power. Police officials employed crime data, released each year in statistical digests and in the chief's annual report, to either laud their progress in fighting crime if rates decreased or to demand more resources and discretionary authority if crime rose. Crime rates, in other words, were significant not for what they revealed about an actual rise in crime but for the way the police used crime data in a self-interested way to enhance their authority and bolster their resources. By pointing to rising crime rates, and the fabricated connection between civil rights activism, crime, and urban unrest, the police helped create the political

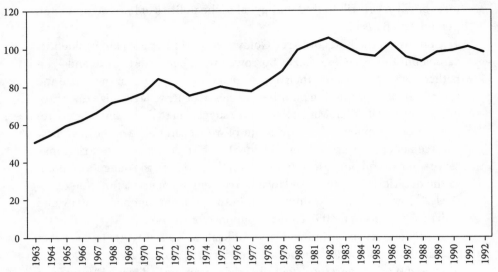

Part I crime rate (per 1,000 residents) in Los Angeles, 1963–1992.
Source: LAPD *Statistical Digests*, 1963–1992.

conditions that allowed officials to empower the police as the primary means to ensure order after Watts.[10]

Police officials employed images of lawless black rioters to urge residents to come to the department's aid. In the week after the uprising, Chief Parker told *Newsweek*, "We had better give the police the support they deserve or next time this happens, they will move in and sack the whole city."[11] Constructing an image of the dangerous black criminal threatening to overrun the city's white, law-abiding residents was central to Parker's efforts to strengthen the police. He warned that by 1970, "45 percent of the metropolitan area of Los Angeles will be Negro, [and] that excludes the San Fernando Valley. Now how are you going to live with that without law enforcement?" The solution required enhancing the power of the police. "If you want any protection for your home and family," Parker counseled the city's white residents, "you're going to have to stop this abuse, but you're going to have to get in and support a strong police department. If you don't do that, come 1970, God help you!"[12]

Parker's rhetoric, and the naturalization of it by the media, steered white citizens toward pro-police policies. Although the UCLA Riot Study—a survey of 2,070 people initiated in the immediate aftermath of Watts—found a high level of sympathy among whites for African American grievances with unemployment, poor housing, and inadequate schools, it also revealed that nearly 78 percent of whites believed that blacks had no respect for law and order. Even more telling of white support for the police, 66 percent of whites believe that the authorities—the police—handled the unrest well compared with 64 percent of blacks who believed the situation was handled poorly. Other pressures pushing whites to embrace the police included findings that half of whites felt either some or a great deal of fear during and after the unrest, over half approved of whites buying guns to protect themselves, and 20 percent felt the best way to prevent further riots was to "take punitive or restrictive action of one form or another." Only 1 percent, however, believed improving the police through hiring more black officers, better training, or community relations would prevent future unrest.[13] As Hugh Manes summarized, "For most Anglo-Saxon Americans justice is simply: crime and punishment."[14]

If the problem at the heart of civil unrest and crime was rooted in the criminal behavior of African Americans, law enforcement solutions and a reassertion of police supervisory discretion over "harmful" residents became more legitimate. To be sure, moderate Republicans and liberal Democrats supported calls for broad social policy to address the underlying causes of urban unrest that repression could never solve. But they also believed in the necessity of the police to maintain order. They believed police power need not be repressive but could be carried out fairly and efficiently through proper oversight in the form of better training, management, and equipment.[15] Faith in better training and management, however, in effect reinforced police power by granting the police discretion to sort out who required supervision— African Americans and Mexican Americans—to ensure law and order.[16]

Republicans saw any government policies and court decisions that regulated police behavior as potential threats to law and order. At the announcement for his candidacy for California governor in 1966, Ronald Reagan placed responsibility for the Watts uprising on the "philosophy that in any situation the public should turn to government for the answer." He campaigned on ideas of individual responsibility and the failure of liberal social policies to adequately deal with growing unrest.[17] Reagan's hard-line approach and his assertion that government services only exacerbated problems of civil disobedience and crime appealed to many voters. Polls conducted prior to the election found that "crime, drugs, and juvenile delinquency" topped the issues of public concern, while "racial problems" came in second. Campaigning on ideas of individual rights, morality, and law and order, Reagan easily defeated incumbent governor Pat Brown in the November 1966 election.[18]

The liberal belief in social and economic inequality as a source of crime and violence, Reagan believed, only absolved individuals for their actions and contributed to conditions that led to further unrest and crime. "We must reject the idea," Reagan argued, "that every time a law is broken, society is guilty rather than the law-breaker. It is essential we restore the American precept that each individual is responsible, and accountable, for his actions. And, it is too simple to trace all crime to poverty. Our time of affluence is also a time of increasing lawlessness." Reagan reinforced the connection between leniency and disorderly inner cities for middle-class television audiences, explaining that every day when the sun goes down, "the jungle gets a little bit closer."[19] Reagan limned a connection between law and order and a free society. Moral bankruptcy, poor behavior, and lapsed personal responsibility surpassed social conditions as the dominant understanding of the source of crime and unrest.[20]

Local law enforcement agencies were elated with Reagan's victory. District Attorney Younger encouraged Reagan to help law enforcement develop new tools to fight the war on crime. "'Business as usual' is not the order of the day," he told Reagan. "We are going to have to be more efficient and more imaginative if we are to be successful in our war on crime."[21] Reagan obliged. His administration produced studies on law and order that outlined the need for a "total and sustained fight against lawlessness . . . if we are to keep our people free and safe." Reagan's approach focused on using "as much force as necessary, as quickly as possible," and reaffirmed his belief that "tougher laws *do* deter crime." By 1969 the Reagan administration had signed twenty laws cracking down on crime and supporting law enforcement agencies.[22] While Reagan occasionally met with black leaders in hopes of developing strategies to reduce tension that led to unrest, he reaffirmed that riots would be crushed with appropriate force through the passage of antiriot bills, civil disturbance control plans, and a statewide network of weapons depots.[23]

The police received high praise from Reagan. Reagan played on growing panics of crime in a speech to the 1969 graduating class at the Los Angeles Sheriff's Department to reinforce support for the officer in blue as the foundation of a free society. "Crime statistics are so continuously shocking," Reagan proclaimed, "that minds are becoming somewhat numbed by the attack." On the front line combating the crime wave was the police officer. "Between us and the jungle holding it back is the man with the badge," Reagan stated. "It is a proud heritage—civilization is in your debt." Yet, Reagan emphasized, "too often the only thanks (the policeman) gets is a charge of 'police brutality.'"[24] Such criticism of the men in blue, Reagan and law enforcement officials believed, limited their authority and undermined their ability to ensure public safety and maintain order on the streets.

Reagan's policies lent support to law enforcement officials who felt under siege from not only rioters and criminals but also liberal politicians and judges. Beginning with the California State Supreme Court's 1955 *Cahan* ruling, which created the exclusionary rule restricting the use of illegally obtained evidence, LAPD officers believed their traditional powers of discretion were under attack from the judiciary. Parker opposed the exclusionary rule as "criminal protecting" and warned that "a dangerous custom has arisen in America wherein the hapless police officer is a defenseless target for ridicule and abuse from every quarter."[25] The Supreme Court's rulings in *Mapp v. Ohio* (1961), *Gideon v. Wainwright* (1963), *Escobedo v. Illinois* (1964), and *Miranda v. Arizona* (1966) provided suspects and defendants with more rights while limiting officer discretion on the street. By the late 1960s and early 1970s the courts had decriminalized status crimes, further reducing officer discretion.[26] Parker believed the decisions "coddled" criminals. "Violence and crime have grown to staggering proportions while the police," Parker proclaimed, "find themselves tragically weakened in their attempts to control the problem." To the police, the decisions were part of an antipolice movement that would result in increased crime, disorder, and violence.[27]

Law enforcement officials criticized the courts for hindering traditional methods of police work and discretion, such as interrogations and searches and seizures. "It's harder today," Younger claimed, "to convict a person who has admittedly committed a major crime than at any time in our history."[28] The combination of liberal court decisions, civil rights activism, and claims of police brutality, Mayor Yorty argued in a report defending the sanctity of law enforcement titled *The Big Lie*, demoralized the police, handicapped their ability to combat crime, and made them vulnerable to attack.[29] Or, as Deputy Chief Ed Davis summarized, "There is no doubt in my mind that there is a conspiracy to eliminate the police."[30]

Law enforcement and police authorities believed that public safety could be guaranteed only if the police had broad discretion to enforce the law and punish offenders. "We feel that to reestablish public order in the streets of our communities," Davis stated in 1967, "the arrest and evidence capabilities of the policeman, which have been denied him by the State and Federal Supreme Court rulings, must, to some degree, be restored."[31]

For the police, American society was at a crossroads. Davis suggested that the decline in personal responsibility represented by increased crime and judicial undermining of law enforcement threatened to unravel society. But Americans, he suggested, had a choice on the direction to take moving forward. Would they choose the road "which glorifies total unrestrained freedom and ridicules individual responsibility—that which sanctifies the rights of the lawless and profanes the rights of society?" he asked. Or would they take the road that "recognizes reverence for law . . . which exalts individual responsibility as one of man's noblest of qualities?" The stakes were high. Would it be, Davis asked, the "law of the jungle, or the law of organized society?"[32] For Davis the choice was clear. Stronger legal, material, and ideological support for the police was necessary to ensure domestic pacification and control of the streets.

Building a Martial Infrastructure

New sources of federal funding bolstered the commitment to law and order. While Lyndon Johnson approved over $29 million for self-help programs in Watts, he also supported legislation to assist law enforcement agencies in waging a War on Crime.[33] Barely a month after Watts, Johnson signed the Law Enforcement Assistance Act into law. The legislation created the Office of Law Enforcement Assistance to disburse funds to states and cities, bringing the federal government into support of local law enforcement in new ways. Federal grants complemented the LAPD's annual operating cost of $88.7 million for 1966–67 and amounted to 26.2 percent of the city budget. By 1972, the department's operating cost, approved by the Yorty regime, had ballooned to $198.5 million, or 34.4 percent of the city budget. The federal War on Crime helped facilitate the LAPD's adoption of riot control plans, military hardware, and computerized systems.[34]

Local officials capitalized on the political support for riot prevention and crime control. Yorty and Parker portrayed segregated inner cities as "armed camps" made up of criminals and potential rioters. They promoted legislation to provide police with the legal means to deal with "agitators" through preemptive measures rather than waiting for the next riot to occur. Before the state legislature, they portrayed South Central on the verge of explosion. Parker testified, "We are sitting on a powder keg. . . . We're talking about putting moats around all our new buildings." Yorty claimed that the city would look like an "armed state" to ward off trouble during the summer of 1966.[35] Despite opposition from African American representatives such as Mervyn Dymally, who called the bills "negative, discriminatory, and punitive," the legislature passed three key pieces of legislation: an act making any person intending to incite a riot subject to prosecution, an act making possession of a Molotov cocktail a felony, and an act making battery of a police officer a felony.[36]

On the surface, Tom Reddin, who served as police chief from 1967 to 1969, represented a more balanced approach to law enforcement. Reddin attempted to downplay the aggressive image of the police by stressing the need for better community relations, communication, and rumor control. Although Reddin's willingness to meet with black representatives after the assassination of Martin Luther King Jr. angered some officers who were members of the John Birch Society, Reddin believed, "We cannot assume that traditional methods are adequate." Because the police had "emerged as the representatives of the establishment," in Watts and other inner-city communities, Reddin hoped to introduce new methods to reduce tensions and ensure order by involving the police as a functioning part of the community and to develop greater support for the police from residents. Under Reddin some officers were put back on the "beat," patrolling areas by foot, and the Community Relations Division expanded its programming and number of officers, making it one of the most extensive in the country.[37]

But community involvement would not succeed without a concomitant emphasis on law and order. For Reddin, the "extreme tides of civil unrest and crime" were evidence of a society on the brink of disintegration. He argued that American society—largely liberal Democrats—coddled criminals and condoned crime under the excuse that a "poor childhood" and "society's failure" caused crime and justified riots. "I do not believe that society causes crime," Reddin explained. "People cause crime." Reddin's sentiments reflected a widely held view among law enforcement officials. They viewed social programs merely as the carrot to the more punitive stick of riot control measures. "Law and order," argued Reddin, "is the main thing that has to be done."[38]

Ready to smash unrest with overwhelming force, the LAPD had internalized the values of a combat unit. "As a matter of fact, we preach what the military calls the overkill—kill a butterfly with a sledge hammer—feeling that we would rather over-police, and control, and run the risk of people saying we are doing that," Reddin explained. "We just do not want to let something get out of control."[39] When a conflict between black and Mexican American youth outside Jordan High School threatened violence in March 1966, the LAPD mobilized a temporary riot control post and deployed massive force to the scene, resulting in at least two killed and fourteen wounded. Yorty praised the actions of the LAPD for deploying "a little faster with bigger force."[40] The police remained ever-vigilant and on high alert for potential violent unrest. During the summer of 1966, for example, the FBI reported that LAPD officers monitored the "situation in the Watts area . . . and continue to remain alert for any signs of heightened racial tension and appropriate steps are thereupon taken to nullify or extinguish the situation."[41] The response of law enforcement to any challenge to its authority on the streets relied on mobilizing more force, more law and order.

Get-tough law enforcement provided the ultimate means of controlling future outbreaks of violence. The McCone Implementation Task Force's second-year report highlighted the success of local law enforcement in preventing unrest.[42] "Los Angeles has not had a riot or major disturbance this summer [1967]," the task force reported. "Tensions are still high and rumors of trouble and violence and impending outbreaks of destruction are daily occurrences, but local law enforcement leaders appear to be prepared with immediate and powerful forces to suppress and quell any eruption of violence."[43] The solution to urban unrest, McCone believed, rested on meeting it with "proper law enforcement tactics."[44]

The department engaged in an arms buildup. For Reddin the reliance on weaponry and the use of force was a psychological and physical tool to be used against city residents and to deter civil insurrection. "We endorse shotguns highly," Reddin stated. "The shotgun is probably the most threatening, forbidding looking hand weapon that exists." The department used shotguns before Watts, but it had increased its supply from one hundred in 1965 to 1,000 in 1967. The LAPD's antiriot arsenal also included a variety of new weapons such as armored personnel carriers, .30 caliber machine guns, .41 Magnums, tear gas launchers, mace, and a smoke screen device.[45] The amassing of weapons, planning, and capacity to deal with urban uprisings reflected the views of law enforcement officials that the police were the protectors of what Ed Davis called "organized society" and needed all tools available to carry out their role effectively and efficiently.[46]

Under Reddin the department established elite tactical units to prepare for potential urban warfare. In one of his first acts as chief in 1967, Reddin created the Tactical Operations Planning Unit and placed it within the Metropolitan Division (Metro Division), an elite group of officers with broad authority to "suppress criminal activity," quickly gaining the nickname "the Shake, Rattle, & Roll Boys." Reddin placed the Tactical Operations unit under the command of Daryl Gates and expanded the Metro Division from fifty-five to 220 officers while reaffirming the directive to "roust anything strange that moves on the streets."[47]

Gates, a disciple of Chief Parker, would play a key role in shaping the LAPD's trajectory over the following three decades. He saw the new tactical units as a way for urban police forces to develop the ability to take on a new type of threat. "We had no idea how to deal with this [the Watts unrest]," Gates recalled in his autobiography. "We did not know how to handle guerrilla warfare." Faced with the responsibility of maintaining order during a time when "the streets of urban America had become foreign territory," Gates intended to regain the offensive.[48] Combining antisniper units with Tactical Operations Planning Units, Gates formed squads based on military models "which were beyond the scope of the conventionally trained and equipped police officer." This was the foundation for Special Weapons and Tactics (SWAT), which represented "the merger of police and military strategies."

Two Los Angeles police officers modeling antiriot gear, 1968. Officers show off a gas mask and fiber shield as part of the LAPD's antiriot arsenal bought in the wake of the Watts uprising. In front of them are tear gas gun and grenades and long- and short-range projectiles. The LAPD used the crisis of legitimacy created by Watts to mobilize for greater authority, funding, and hardware. *Los Angeles Times* Photographic Archives (Collection 1429); courtesy of Library Special Collections, Charles E. Young Research Library, UCLA.

In the words of one SWAT leader, "Those people out there—the radicals, the revolutionaries and the cop haters—are damned good at using shotguns and bombs, and setting up ambushes. We've got to be better."[49]

Worries about Vietnam-style "urban guerrilla warfare" also motivated the development of counterinsurgency units. Under Gates's direction, the Tactical Operations Planning Unit cooperated with military officials and wrote two riot control manuals, one for the department and one for the Kerner Commission. The "Model Civil Disturbance Control Plan" stressed training and readiness to apply quick and overwhelming force to take control of urban space. "Socio-economic causes of riots," the plan outlined, "are not of concern to police." The plan was modeled on a military-style command structure that emphasized the need for swift, aggressive action and harsh penalties for anyone involved in a disturbance.[50] Antiriot legislation, elite paramilitary units, and riot control plans enabled the LAPD to expand its capacity to operate as a military-style counterinsurgency force.

Continued urban unrest and reports of rising violent crime led Johnson to escalate the War on Crime. The Omnibus Crime Control and Safe Streets Act of 1968 provided federal assistance to state and local law enforcement to ensure their efforts were "better coordinated, intensified, and made more effective at all levels of government." Passed with bipartisan support, it created the Law Enforcement Assistance Administration (LEAA), which distributed federal funds for research, planning, coordination, and demonstration projects to state agencies. These agencies, such as the California Council on Criminal Justice (CCCJ), worked with local grantees to disburse funds for criminal justice programs.[51] Compared with other regions in California and cities across the country, Los Angeles received a large—but not disproportionate based on population—amount of the nearly $10 billion disbursed by the LEAA between 1965 and 1981. Between 1969 and 1978, the Los Angeles region received over $100 million in LEAA funds, much of which was allocated for police-related programs. LEAA funding complemented the department's total operating cost, which was nearly $200 million in 1972 alone.[52] Even so, the LEAA enabled the LAPD to look to the state and federal governments to supplement local funds for helicopters, computerized systems, and communications equipment. "As a result of the support provided by the Law Enforcement Assistance Administration," the LAPD reported in 1972, "we can take pride in the fact that Federal funds are turning the *Safe Streets Act* into a reality."[53]

Chief Davis stressed a preference for hardware grants over human relations programs. In fact, he demanded that LEAA funds not be used for a social welfare approach to solving crime "a la the Johnsonian War on Poverty." Rather than approach solving crime through social policy, Davis stressed the need for the LEAA to contribute to a law enforcement program that enhanced the technological capacity of the police. "It is imperative," Davis emphasized, "that the LEAA funds not be used for social approach programs as a means of reducing crime."[54] Although the department was supported by federal funds, Davis stressed that the department should retain discretion to design and control criminal justice planning boards and programs.

Los Angeles's proximity to defense industry contractors enabled this orientation by bringing technology developed for the war in Vietnam to local law enforcement. Obscuring the divide between war and policing, LAPD officials intended to eliminate those whom the department constructed as threats to order. LAPD officials intended to bring law enforcement into the "space age" through cooperation with aerospace corporations. As Reddin explained in 1969, techniques developed for military and space operations "would be of great importance in enhancing the operational ability of the police."[55] State officials believed that scientific experts could help solve the crime problem through data analysis and high-tech approaches, hoping to employ the large number of scientists in Southern California to "turn their efforts earthward" in order to produce better crime-fighting procedures. Hardware, in the form of electronic data processing, communications systems, and research and development projects, however, enhanced the ability of the police to monitor inner-city spaces and residents.[56]

The LAPD developed innovative uses of military hardware. One of the first projects focused on using helicopters as part of the daily patrol operations. Los Angeles's expansive spatial character and a police force assigned to cover nearly 450 square miles made Los Angeles an ideal place for the implementation and experimentation of helicopter patrols "linked by radio with ground units" as a new form of crime control.[57] Following the Los Angeles Sheriff's Department's Project Sky Knight helicopter program, the LAPD developed its own helicopter program called Air Support to Regular Operations (ASTRO). While the department first purchased a helicopter in 1956, it expanded its fleet after Watts with the acquisition of seven helicopters in 1968 equipped with high-intensity searchlights and advanced communications systems. The ASTRO squadron provided "air support for ground units in selected areas of the city" during "special surveillance" and "crowd control" operations. The department's use of helicopters quickly expanded beyond specialized uses and was incorporated into daily police work, intelligence gathering, and coordinating police chases and apprehension of suspects.[58]

ASTRO began full-time operations in the Southwest area and the West Valley by 1970 and quickly expanded to the Wilshire Division. Deputy Chief Gates praised the use of helicopters in discussions with Nixon aide Egil Krogh, boasting that the LAPD had seven Bell helicopters in use with six more on the way. The helicopter, according to Gates, had a significant psychological effect, especially when equipped with loudspeakers and spotlights that made the police a nearly omnipresent force in the city. As the 1970 ASTRO annual report stated, "The chopper acts as their [patrolmen's] backup in the sky which provides the needed psychological edge over the suspect. . . . The suspect cannot escape the view from above." To emphasize the role of helicopters for monitoring and control, the LAPD painted addresses on the tops of buildings to enhance coordination with ground units and antiriot protocols. By 1971, LAPD helicopters logged over 1,500 hours of flight time a month, a rate that "exceeded similar operations of any other law enforcement agency in the United States."[59]

The ASTRO program adhered to and reinforced a racialized geography produced by the LAPD's racially targeted police practices. The program expanded to six of the LAPD's seventeen districts, all but one of which covered neighborhoods that were predominantly African American or Mexican American. In 1972, ASTRO experimented with combined day and night patrols located in five divisions—Southwest, Newton, West Valley, Northeast, and Hollenbeck—all of which, with the exception of West Valley, centered on African American and Mexican American neighborhoods.[60]

Residents in South Central welcomed helicopters when used as part of criminal pursuits. But they also believed that the LAPD overstepped its authority in helicopter operations in ways that contributed to resentment and the escalating use of force. "Many law abiding citizens of minority areas feel they are being subjected to surveillance unnecessarily and without probable cause," Ralph M. Nutter of the Greater Los Angeles Urban Coalition explained. "We are of the opinion that exaggerated and unnecessary use of law enforcement helicopters is causing unnecessary tension in minority areas and stimulating resentment to such an extent that there will be provocation for acts or attitudes which could cause lasting harm to the community."[61]

Law enforcement disregarded these claims. After a study of the program, the Jet Propulsion Laboratory declared that ASTRO was "effective in repressing the crimes of robbery, theft and auto theft to a significant degree in the two test divisions." The LAPD also promoted the qualitative advantage of ASTRO in benefiting response time, coordination, superior aerial surveillance, and increased officer security.[62] This success led to the expansion of the ASTRO program and the adoption of helicopters by other police departments. By 1972 at least 150 departments across the country utilized helicopters in patrol work. The LAPD's ASTRO program covered 75 percent of the city by 1975 and 88 percent by 1977, and continued to purchase helicopters throughout the 1970s and 1980s.[63]

The LEAA also enabled the LAPD to enhance its use of computers, databases, and other technologies to create an efficient police force aimed at preempting crime. The LAPD touted itself as "one of the leaders in the nation in the search for uses of computer-based science and technology in law enforcement." Some of these systems included computers to enhance dispatching based on crime trends, fingerprint and photographic transmittal from police cars to headquarters, record management databases, and an emergency command and control communications center.[64] Chief Davis's "Instant Cop Theory," which centered on the use of computers to help the police quickly respond to crime, guided the use of technology. The theory rested on the idea that data, statistical analysis, and computer programs could help predict and assign officers more efficiently in a city of 450 square miles with a police force of roughly 7,400 officers. By the mid-1970s the LAPD's investment in electronic programs was "truly making the era of LAPD's 'instant cop' a reality."[65]

Once the LAPD came to operate on a military footing, the demand for more weapons and technology became self-fulfilling. Department leadership recognized that the escalating use of force had the potential to increase violence. "In areas where there has been a pattern of using strong physical force to achieve police objectives, a concurrent pattern of resistance develops within the individual or group," Chief Davis explained to his captain school in 1969. "The result is resistance and lack of cooperation on the part of the law violator and the subsequent necessity for resorting to force on the part of the police. The use of force is thus self-perpetuating."[66] To combat such cycles of violence and to justify the expanded coercive capability of the police, the LAPD implemented community relations programs to enhance communication with residents and improve the image of the police officer in the minds of black and Mexican American youth.

Hearts and Minds

Ed Davis, who became chief of police in 1969, believed that the "most explosive" problem faced by police departments was the lack of respect for law and order and image of the police in the black community. As Davis told the League of California Cities, crime would quadruple within ten years unless they "sell the concept of reverence for the law."[67] Community relations programs had the potential to incorporate demands for community control without reducing the discretionary authority of the police.

Throughout the 1950s the LAPD had operated a Deputy Auxiliary Police program to promote mutual understanding between youth and the police, but Parker discontinued it in 1957.[68] Nevertheless, a 1963 order suggested that "the mutual advantages of a friendly relationship between the people of a community and their police force should be widely understood and more fully appreciated." Two months before the Watts uprising, Councilman Tom Bradley described an urgent need for changes in policy to improve police-community relations to stop violence before it erupted. Parker responded to his critics by assigning James Fisk as the department's liaison with the black community in June 1965. While Fisk approached community relations work with all seriousness, Parker hoped that he would gather intelligence about civil rights activists and often referred to Fisk as the "nigger inspector." Community relations continued to be a low priority, with only twenty-nine officers assigned to the section before Watts.[69]

Watts forced Parker's hand. The McCone Commission recommended enhancing police-community relations through "non-punitive" contact with residents. "Little has been done in recent years to encourage the Negro youth's support of the police," the report explained, "or to implant in the youth's mind the true value of the Police Department with respect to the welfare of the youth." To accomplish this goal, the commission recommended intensive human relations training for officers, youth programs, open forums between the police and residents, and frequent contact between officers and junior and senior high school students.[70] While well intentioned, the reforms largely placed the burden for a change in attitude on the residents.

The LAPD soon engaged public relations firms and the LEAA about developing a police-community relations program. The department implemented a crash community relations program headed by four lieutenants who volunteered for the job. Parker appointed Fisk the coordinator for the program, who hoped the Community Relations Program would enhance the efficiency of the police. "With effective community relations," stated Fisk, "the job of the policeman will become an easier one."[71] The initial efforts, the McCone Implementation Task Force found, reflected progress in the reestablishment of community relations programs. "Personal effort of these officers is sincere and commendable," the task force reported in 1966; "they deserve community cooperation and support."[72] Although the LAPD held meetings, workshops, and community councils, the program was initially composed of white officers, many of whom did not live in the neighborhoods in which they patrolled and often viewed residents of color as criminal.[73]

Reddin emphasized community relations. He stressed "effective two-way communication, a mutual development of insights, and a nurture of trust, confidence, and respect" between the police and the people they served. Failure to have such communication could result in violent unrest and increased crime. Upon his appointment, Reddin stated, "Any police department that does not place community relations high (in the scale of importance) is making a bad mistake." The police created tension in the communities they served "because whether we like it or not, the man in the blue suit, the policeman, has suddenly become a symbol of the organization, he is a symbol of the entire White Power structure." Reddin stressed the personalization of police work and reassigned fifty-two officers to community relations. He also authorized Fisk to develop new programs, such as the "Policeman Bill" program, which brought officers into schools to facilitate communication and to encourage young men to consider careers in law enforcement.[74]

The LAPD's Community Relations Program, however, was intended to enhance the department's ability to prevent riots by incorporating the police in the lives of black and brown youth. It built on the department's spring

1968 "Plans of the Los Angeles Police Department for an Enlarged Program to Further Lessen [the] Possibility of Civil Unrest within the City of Los Angeles." The plan aimed to "win the commitment of youth to various causes" and for community organizations to "participate in countering disruptive forces who would create an atmosphere conducive to violence." The program also suggested creating youth councils to enhance communication with the police that would create more "positive non-punitive relationships," increase community relations training and support for uniformed officers, establish neighborhood mentor programs, and cooperate with the academic community to understand urban problems and pacify urban youth who were often viewed as hostile and alienated. Misunderstanding and "mistrust," the report suggested, could be alleviated through increased "person-to-person communication in a non-punitive setting."[75]

Building on the recommendations, the department developed a comprehensive Community Relations Program in November 1968. Operating under a "total community involvement" concept, Reddin stressed that every officer should be a community relations specialist. He instituted enhanced human and community relations training for all new officers. "The achievement of 'social order' by both legal process and by well ordered personal conduct," the program outlined, "can only exist if there is a partnership between citizens of the community and the police." By improving communication between the police and the community, the program hoped to bring residents into the project of crime control, a means of binding the police more closely to the community.[76]

Several black officials and community representatives praised the department's efforts. African American city councilman Tom Bradley stated that if the recommended community relations program passed, "we will have the most advanced police department in the country." Characterizing the proposed plans as a drastic change in the relationship and attitude of the LAPD toward inner-city problems, African American city councilman Bill G. Mills believed that the program was "a great breath of refreshing air over Los Angeles." Mills credited Reddin for the attitudinal change in officers on the beat through the daily filing of "non-punitive contact" reports. The program meant to broaden officers' understanding of the communities in which they worked because the police bore the brunt of "social changes."[77]

Liberal city council members believed enhancing police-community relations would create mutual respect and understanding between residents of color and the police. Such reforms centered on the liberal belief that the problems of policing were ones of discrimination and misunderstanding. Promoting police-community contact and respect would allow officers to better operate in neighborhoods that had little reason to trust the police. As Tom

Bradley suggested in late 1968, the LAPD's participation in the Imperial Courts Public Housing Music Club for young residents reflected the way policing could be "improved and strengthened by developing contacts which go beyond law enforcement." Along with placing officers on the beat to interact with residents, the police would become "cooperative helper[s]" who "would provide greater person-to-person contact in non-criminal situations. It would provide a brief opportunity for socialization, a humanizing activity."[78] Increasing understanding and communication worked hand in hand with efforts to reform the supposed disorderly black and brown youth and, in the process, legitimized the overwhelming presence of police in their neighborhoods.

By the end of 1968, the LAPD's Community Relations Program had become a central component of police operations bolstered by an LEAA special grants project. The program set forth the goal of creating mutual cooperation between the police and the community to maintain social order. The program employed a Special Minority Community Liaison to work with African American and Mexican American residents. The LAPD also worked with the Economic Youth Opportunities Agency to develop a program to enhance the department's Mexican American affairs through language training and cultural understanding. In the African American community, the program focused on the 77th Street Interdenominational Clergy-Police Council, a Ministerial Alliance, and Residents' Councils in public housing projects to develop cooperative crime prevention programs.[79]

Hoping to enhance communication with Mexican Americans, the LAPD held a community relations conference with Mexican American leaders in 1967. The goal was to "encourage our Mexican American communities . . . to accept the outstretched hand of the LAPD in sincerity and friendship. . . . They must be assured that the purpose of this conference is to convince all Mexican-Americans that the Los Angeles Police Department (cares) about you and that it can be trusted."[80] Community relations officers also worked to establish greater grassroots contacts by hiring residents with criminal records as community relations aides from the Mexican American and African American housing projects of Ramona Gardens in East Los Angeles and Imperial Courts in Watts to work with youth.[81]

Community relations programs also focused on winning over youth perceived to be violence prone and oppositional. Community relations officers sought to eliminate the punitive relationship that governed interactions with the police prior to and during the Watts uprising. To change the perception of the department among minority youth, the Los Angeles Police Youth Coordinator developed an Explorer Scout program. By placing officers in inner-city schools, the LAPD's program emphasized the "friendliness" and "humanism" of police officers who came in contact with nearly 8,000 students per week. Police and school officials believed that the program, "presented in an atmosphere of learning, is invaluable in creating a sense of concern for orderly behavior and a sense of responsibility for the maintenance of law and order."[82]

In the African American community, officers worked with local community members to organize a Community-Police Service Corps in hopes of getting black youth to work with—and trust—the police. Of particular concern to law enforcement officials was the growth in "militant Negro youth organizations" associated with the Black Power movement in California, such as the Black Panthers, who emerged in Oakland and Los Angeles after Watts and provided African American youth with a means to express their discontent with the police. While condemning organizations such as the Panthers, US Organization, and Sons of Watts, the LAPD reportedly took the initiative to contact members of these groups. The goal was part of an "effort to channel their interest and activity for constructive purposes in the community, and to discover any valid complaints of the youths concerning police procedures."[83] Other proposals included the creation of youth councils in every high school to facilitate communication and cooperation, psychological understanding and support for uniformed officers who faced intense situations, and placing policemen in public schools to teach courses on police-community contact. Some of the more extravagant events included organized trips to sporting, professional, and entertainment venues for nearly 25,000 "youngsters predominantly from the city's lower socio-economic areas." In 1968, officers took 800 youth from South Central to Camp Radford in the San Bernardino Mountains as part of an "effort to combat the anti-police attitudes learned in the inner city."[84]

Some youth responded positively, but others remained skeptical. One black youth commented, "I don't think that Reddin really made a difference. . . . It's the same thing, but with a different approach."[85] The department could tout its efforts at communication and cooperation, but to black and Mexican American residents, the behavior of the officers on the street had changed little since the 1965 uprising. As South Central resident Paul Williams explained, "Things haven't changed really, in law enforcement. What they've done is eased off and sporadically they harass. . . . Their so-called community relations aren't really relating, not to the community itself. People in the community still feel the police are *harassing*. . . . In fact, the people are more severe toward the poli dept now because they *know* the dept hasn't changed."[86]

Mexican Americans echoed these complaints. They suggested that community relations officers demanded conformity to Anglo norms. The Mexican American Political Association, a moderate political organization, criticized

Reddin's community relations program. "[It] is evasive and, in fact, is deceptive in its approach and intent," association members stated at a 1967 convention. It was "[a] cheap merchandising technique to make palatable an unchanging policy of repressive and discriminatory law enforcement."[87] Leaders of the Mexican American Political Association believed community relations did less to change the attitudes of officers or interactions with people of color and more to mask their punitive discretion and operations in neighborhoods of color. It was, one observer described in the *Los Angeles Riot Study*, a flawed "'con' job."[88]

Community relations officers were not always what they seemed. As programs aimed at pacification, they built on the department's long history of using undercover intelligence, the Red Squad (the moniker for the department's intelligence unit which focused on combating communist and other left-wing organizations), to police morality, temper dissent, and regulate social order.[89] Ron Wilkins of the Student Nonviolent Coordinating Committee recalled how community liaison officers infiltrated groups and participated in raids on the Brown Berets in East Los Angeles. Confirming these fears, Theodore Rankin, the Los Angeles Sheriff's Department's (LASD) former director of community relations, admitted that a central role of the Police Community Relations Officer was intelligence gathering. "We find that most departments are deploying their PCR [Police Community Relations] manpower in the ghetto, barrio, or minority areas," he explained. "Establishing communication with many of the activist groups is improbable if not impossible; yet the police must know what is going on within these groups. The Police Community Relations Officer often infiltrates, first in an undercover capacity followed by open liaison once the objectives of the group have been determined." The LAPD's Community Relations and Liaison Unit outlined the goal of performing "an over all quasi-intelligence function" to keep the department aware of potential racial conflict or tension.[90]

Instead of winning "hearts and minds," community relations ultimately undermined faith in the police. Community relations never outweighed the department's commitment to developing a martial infrastructure. As *The Nation*'s Larry Remer warned in a story on the LAPD, "the militarization of the police, which seems to be the trend of the 1970s, will increase as long as law enforcement persists in 'them-or-us' attitudes toward crime and social unrest."[91]

The police pointed to the absence of major civil unrest in Los Angeles as evidence of the efficacy of the department's policies. Whatever potential there had been for social welfare approaches to solving urban problems of inequality, crime, and violent unrest had been abandoned in favor of an all-out commitment to a War on Crime. As Nathan Cohen, editor of the UCLA Los Angeles Riot Study, described, changing local and national commitments between 1965 and 1970 was part of a "conservative trend" that reflected "a growing belief that an authoritarian approach is necessary to deal with growing urban problems."[92]

The LAPD's response to the crisis produced by Watts set the department on course toward a military model of policing and punitive policy. Aggressive policing predicated on a paramilitary, counterinsurgency model led to an escalation of the use of force and violence with no end in sight. Although paired with community relations and soft forms of police power, the overall project of law enforcement enhanced the mechanisms of social control rather than addressing inequality, disorder, and crime. Both military hardware and community relations rejected limits on police discretionary authority and changes in the relation of power between the police and the community.

During the late 1960s and the early 1970s, the police mobilized their new technological, paramilitary, and legal capacities to reassert discretionary control over African American and Mexican American movements deemed subversive and criminal. Politicians and police officials drew connections among civil rights demonstrations, urban uprisings, and violent crime, which further criminalized communities of color. The discretion of the police to sort "harmless" residents from the "harmful," however, led to conflict with African Americans and Mexican Americans who offered alternative visions of authority, order, and public safety not based on police power. As activists and residents challenged the LAPD's authority, they shaped the meaning and politics of law and order and demonstrated that the turn to repressive policing was not inevitable.

Chapter 3

High Noon in the Ghetto

Occupied Territory and Resistance to Police Brutality

Two years after Watts, Reverend Thomas Kilgore, a prominent Los Angeles civil rights activist and community leader, described how African American youth and community organizations were developing a new "self-image" by "seeking new and creative ways of helping themselves." Perhaps the most symbolic and broad-based example of this development in the African American community was the annual Watts Summer Festival. The festival commemorated the unrest and promoted the rebuilding of South Central. From the ashes, organizers believed, residents could build a community on the basis of racial pride, self-help, equality, and justice. "The fire had not yet died out and the smoke was still in the air when some of the people of Watts talked about the tomorrow they would build," organizers explained. "They talked about a community which served its residents."[1]

Community control of the police was central to the vision of self-determination expressed at the festival. Members of the Community Alert Patrol (CAP), an organization established in 1966 with the goal of monitoring the actions of the LAPD, provided crowd control at the first festival and coordinated its operation with the LAPD to ensure a violence-free festival. Many wondered whether the young men with no formal law enforcement training could maintain peace. Young CAP members put these doubts to rest, and public relations director Chester Wright would boast that "the people of Watts were policing themselves."[2]

If law enforcement and politicians used the crisis of the Watts uprising to intensify police power and authority, African Americans saw an opportunity to promote alternative models of safety and to remove the police from their neighborhoods. Black residents desired protection for long-neglected and underpoliced neighborhoods. They did not, however, want more policing at the expense of equitable treatment. Safe neighborhoods and police accountability were not mutually exclusive in their minds.[3] But patterns of harassment and abuse continued to expose a dual standard of law enforcement—one for whites and another for blacks. Activists and residents turned to alternative, community-based measures, such as the CAP, to ensure safety from both criminals and the police. In response to the patrol, the department worked to contain movements for self-determination and community control of the police.

African American and Mexican American activists' demands for an end to state-sanctioned violence threatened law enforcement. Black and Mexican American activists critiqued the police as an occupying force intent on maintaining the city's racial hierarchy. Groups such as the Black Congress and Black Panthers demanded an end to a dual standard of law enforcement and called for armed self-defense in response to police repression. Similar experiences with the police also led to moments of coalition and collaboration with Mexican American activists. Both groups defined their racial and ethnic identity in relation to their experience with the police and state violence. Yet Mexican Americans organized movements in response to a different historical relationship with the police shaped by colonial occupation and cultural discrimination. Despite their differences, African Americans and Mexican Americans both experienced police repression. They resisted what they saw as a denial of their right to fair treatment by the police as citizens. As racist policing legitimated state violence, these movements challenged the police power and contested the local state's investment in getting tough.[4]

The struggles for alternative models of policing, safety, and security produced another crisis of police authority. The LAPD portrayed these movements as subversive attempts to undermine police authority, responding with a counterinsurgency campaign that treated South Central and East Los Angeles as "armed" camps requiring containment and control. The dual standard of law enforcement exposed how police action criminalized African Americans and Mexican Americans and denied them the full benefits of citizenship. Repression and criminalization of antipolice movements meant to bolster police power, but at the same time, antipolice movements exposed the ways the LAPD's actions attempted to naturalize its broad discretionary authority.[5]

Prosecutor, Judge, and Jury

Civilians responded to Watts in a variety of ways. Some African American residents pressured the department for more police to combat crime, even meeting with the 77th Street Division captain in 1966 to demonstrate their willingness to cooperate with the police and to distinguish themselves from "the small hoodlum element" in South Central. Yet for many black residents, more police did not bring safety or reduce crime; they brought heavy-handed policing. Get-tough policing heightened disillusionment and distrust for the police.[6] "There is indeed a continuous, unbelievably real war game between the police and the young ghettoite," Stan Sanders explained in *The Nation* in 1968.[7] The lack of confidence in the police to fairly enforce the law stemmed from the fact that, according to the American Civil Liberties Union (ACLU), "the police are, for most of the people in the ghetto, their only contact with the white community; and repeated rumors of police brutality, true or not, circulate in the ghetto." Public confidence in the police could be restored if residents felt their complaints of police malpractice would receive a fair hearing. Rather, the ACLU concluded, "the Negro who thinks he has been brutalized or mistreated—often as the result of an arrest sees the police as prosecutor, judge, and jury."[8]

An independent civilian review board would be an important first step in building trust between the police and the community. The National Association for the Advancement of Colored People (NAACP), ACLU, and other community organizations had pushed for a civilian review board during the early 1960s but failed in the face of strong opposition from the Fire and Police Protective League, Chief William Parker, Mayor Sam Yorty, and local businessmen. Picking up on the rhetoric of the police, the *Los Angeles Times* warned a review board would "usurp police authority" and undermine the department's ability to fight crime and keep the city safe.[9] Yet the ACLU pushed city council members to recognize that unaccountable police power was a central grievance that had led to the outbreak of violence the previous August. "The only solution is *an independent reviewing agency*," the ACLU explained; "an independent civilian review board is the only agency which will provide a forum for the grievances deeply felt by minority group members." Such a board would provide confidence that complaints of police malpractice would gain a fair hearing and receive "a full measure of justice." More importantly, a review board would serve as a "safety valve for the hostility to law enforcement officers in a large and growing part of the community."[10]

The proposed board was necessarily narrow in scope. While it would be independent of the department and allow complainants to seek up to $500 in damages, proponents attempted to mitigate arguments that it undermined departmental authority by requiring citizens who used the board to waive the right to sue either the police or the city. More importantly, the board would have no disciplinary power over officers, something that would remain with the chief of police. While proponents acknowledged the limits, they believed establishing a review board was an important first step to improve accountability. "Such a board cannot in and of itself prevent riots such as those which shocked the city in August," the ACLU recognized. "But it can relieve one of the most common and frustrating of the complaints of the Negro community."[11] If activists recognized the limits of the proposed board, any attempt to expand civilian oversight and accountability of the police threatened the agenda of those law enforcement and political officials invested in law and order and get-tough policing.

Local officials ranging from liberal city councilman Tom Bradley to Chief of Police Parker opposed the proposal. The McCone Report similarly argued that a review board "would endanger the effectiveness of law enforcement, which would be intolerable at a time when crime is at an increase throughout the country."[12] Yorty was steadfast, insisting that Los Angeles "will not have a police review board as long as I am mayor."[13] Lacking allies in positions of power and firm resistance from the police department and the Police Protective League, the ACLU's renewed effort to implement a civilian review board made little headway in Los Angeles.[14]

The failure to establish a civilian review board amplified perceptions that the city was neglecting the problem of police accountability. Years of litigation and proposals to work within the structure of the criminal justice system had left the ACLU and other activists despondent at the possibility for change.[15] They sought an independent alternative, initiating police malpractice complaint centers in South Central, East Los Angeles, and Pacoima. The centers presented an independent means of providing residents who believed they had been mistreated by the police with an avenue to file a grievance. The ACLU hoped to achieve two goals: to decrease tension between the police and citizens and to create a permanent and effective complaint procedure. The centers were necessary since the LAPD resisted "any move in that direction [complaint process], would brook no public criticism, and were not about to open up any channel of effective redress."[16]

The malpractice centers offered a way for residents to vent frustrations and provided extensive data on complaints. In a 1969 report, *Law Enforcement: A Matter of Redress*, the ACLU analyzed two years of data gathered at its police malpractice complaint centers. During the first two years, the centers handled 734 cases, of which only 134 were deemed to have no evidence of malpractice. Of the 639 complainants that did show malpractice, 314 were black, 174 Mexican American, 118 Anglo, and 34 other. Approximately one of every ten law enforcement officers in Los Angeles County was engaged in "some form of police malpractice." Many episodes of malpractice often occurred in the presence of witnesses, prompting the ACLU to conclude that officers did not have "any great fear of punishment despite the large number of police and civilian witnesses."[17]

Racially discriminatory law enforcement practices undermined the ability of the police to provide adequate protection for black and Mexican American residents. Based on evidence from the malpractice centers, the ACLU concluded, "there is a dual standard of law enforcement in Los Angeles—one for Negroes and Mexican Americans, one for whites." Faith in the police was routinely challenged by episodes of police abuse, harassment, and shootings. As one seventeen-year-old youth commented on his experience of being beaten by the police after failing to produce a driver's license during a stop, "I don't want to get involved with the police especially after what happened to me."[18] Instead, African Americans created alternative forms, and in some cases the abolition, of policing.

To Protect and Observe

On May 7, 1966, white LAPD officer Jerold M. Bova pulled over twenty-five-year-old Leonard Deadwyler after a high-speed chase in which Deadwyler was taking his pregnant wife to the hospital. When Bova approached the car, he stuck his revolver into the window at Deadwyler. At this moment, Bova claimed the car jolted, causing him to fire and kill Deadwyler. Not only did District Attorney Younger not press charges, but he also ruled the killing "justifiable homicide," enraging civil rights organizations. As the United Civil Rights Committee reported, "Shoot first and ask questions later! Is this the policy of the Los Angeles Police Department? It appears that is what occurred in the Deadwyler incident."[19] It seemed to many that the preventive purpose of police power provided the LAPD overly broad latitude to use deadly force and the legitimacy to devalue black life.

Hundreds of community members, ministers, and activists turned Deadwyler's funeral into a mass protest. Over 300 people took part in a silent "sympathy march" behind Deadwyler's hearse and filled Zion Missionary Baptist Church to capacity with an additional 350 standing outside.[20] Other activists formed the Committee to End Legalized Murder by Cops, and over 200 residents attended a protest at Will Rogers Park that ended with a march to the 77th Street Division police station protesting police brutality. The lack of police accountability, they argued, denied not only justice for Deadwyler but also the rights of all African American citizens.[21]

White officials pushed back by calling for law and order. The *Los Angeles Times* published an editorial comment suggesting the black community should support "our system of justice," and stand up "in support of law and order."[22] Younger openly asked African American ministers to "take the next logical step—address your congregations on the fairness and good of the system and impress upon them the need for law and order."[23] Officials defended the police while criminalizing those who demanded accountability. Yorty and Parker blamed Communists and subversives for whipping the black community into a frenzy and pushed for legislation against individuals who attempted to "incite a riot." When questioned on whether he would take

Crowded Los Angeles County courtroom during coroner's inquest of Leonard Deadwyler. Residents and activists in the African American community mobilized protests in response to the police killing of Deadwyler in 1966 and demanded greater police accountability. In the wake of the killing, activists formed the Community Alert Patrol as a means to observe the police and return the police power to the community itself. *Los Angeles Times* Photographic Archives (Collection 1429); courtesy of Library Special Collections, Charles E. Young Research Library, UCLA.

additional action after a televised coroner's inquest exonerated officer Bova, Parker stated, "I am going to do nothing."[24]

The whitewashing of the Deadwyler killing fueled movements in opposition to the police, state-sanctioned violence, and repression. Black activists and residents formed a new coalition, the Temporary Alliance of Local Organizations (TALO). While concerned with the structural conditions that produced inequality and despair in the black community more broadly, the organization intended to "provide a united voice for the South Los Angeles community in its attempt to prevent a further disintegration of the police-community relations which are threatening the entire city." TALO sought alternatives to law and order through community policing, self-determination, and justice.[25] The "oppressive and brutal police power," TALO chairman Robert Brock explained, "with its roustings, harassments, beatings and killings of black people is the heart and core of the present crisis; and it is because of this that we have come together and are determined to stay together until the pain and suffering in our community is fully redressed."[26]

TALO challenged assumptions of white officials and residents that the black community was in need of aggressive police discretion. Their alternative vision of law and order and public safety saw the police as the true source of disorder in black neighborhoods. "We have found ourselves in a complete outlaw dictatorial police state," Brock explained to the Southern California Council of Churches. "I am not here to ask you to help us violate the law, nor do we wish to violate any, but I am here to ask you to support us in our efforts to establish LAW and ORDER."[27] In effect, TALO reframed the meaning of law and order and crisis from an issue of crime and lawlessness to the lack of legitimacy of white authority and law enforcement in African American neighborhoods. As TALO's public relations director, Chester Wright, pointed out in a sarcastic jab, beliefs that black residents were predisposed to crime, lawlessness, and violence were a construction of the white imagination. "WE disappointed everybody when there was no riot after the Deadwyler inquest," Wright mocked. "WE disappointed them on July 4th. . . . Every white person knew there was going to be a riot. We've yet to find a Negro who knew about it."[28]

Police violence required a community response. The solutions proposed by TALO's Police Alternatives Committee focused on self-defense through community control of the police. "The serious beatings, and killings of black people by police brought on by a get-tough policy in the black and Mexican Communities forces us to protect ourselves as best we can," Brock explained.[29] The primary effort focused on a program whereby civilians would patrol black neighborhoods to observe and monitor the actions of the police known as the CAP. The idea for CAP came out of the work of Ron "Brother Cook" Wilkins and Brother Lennie to observe police practices to prevent incidents aimed at provoking a riot. The goal was to ensure "peace, order, and fair and equitable law in our community." Volunteers drove cars with white cloth tied to their antennas in honor of Deadwyler and monitored the police to document "unequal enforcement and application of the law."[30] CAP put the police on notice that they could not act with impunity and challenged get-tough policing that led to self-fulfilling prophecies of black criminality.

Members met nightly at the office of a local black nationalist organization, which they called the Base, to plan their patrols. Members mapped out routes through areas frequented by black youth, such as the El Rey taco stand on Normandie and Santa Barbara (now Martin Luther King Jr. Boulevard), because the police often selectively enforced the city's antiloitering statute, ambushing black youth with as many as ten to twenty squad cars. The volunteer patrols carried cameras and tape recorders to record information about police arrests, even following arrested youth to police stations to monitor their treatment.[31] CAP instructed members to observe and take pictures but not to talk to officers during routes. Police should know they were being watched, though confrontations should be avoided. CAP played off of the LAPD's own slogan, To Protect and to Serve, by riding in cars marked To Protect and Observe. "When the Man comes on, the reaction of many people is to panic," Tommy Jacquette stated. "We're there to stop the panic, to fight fear."[32]

CAP rejected being labeled vigilantes or antipolice. "We don't think that the Negro community is so angel-like that it doesn't need policing," one member explained. "We're not naive. We are interested in having the Negro community policed in a way that will not cause our children to be conditioned in such a way that they get butterflies in their stomach when they see a policeman."[33] CAP would become so integral to the neighborhood that residents began to see CAP as an alternative form of law enforcement, even calling on patrollers to intervene in street fights and domestic disputes.[34]

The LAPD viewed the organization with suspicion. Officers often pulled over patrol drivers for no reason and given tickets for nonexistent traffic infractions, such as speeding in a parked car or having a torn driver's license. They faced harassment, surveillance, and intimidation. Police officers even planted guns and drugs on members to "give the organization a name—of being hoodlums." The hostile response from officers and department leadership reflected the unwillingness of the police to cede power to black residents even in the name of community relations.[35]

At the suggestion of one of CAP's board members, the patrollers attempted to use the War on Poverty's community action programs to extend the alternative vision of law and order. In its proposal to the Office of Economic Opportunity, CAP described itself as "a grass roots experiment in self-rehabilitation," made up of "ghetto youth, delinquent, out of school, untrained," in its grant application. The program was framed to address juvenile delinquency, and the intent of the program was to serve as a "protective buffer" between the community and the police. The federal funds would help CAP bring about a better relationship between residents and the police department through efforts that would help the community police itself and provide productive outlets for young black men.[36] The grant application demonstrated that CAP was guided by ideas of community action, maintenance of law and order, and juvenile delinquency prevention that fit well with the U.S. Department of Health, Education, and Welfare's (HEW) and OEO's orientation toward "maximum feasible participation." The OEO awarded CAP a grant to assist delinquent youths with records of juvenile arrest "who are performing their first socially useful role in society."[37]

The federal grant produced a mixed response. Some CAP members thought the program was part of a "surrender to the Establishment" that would lead to a co-optation of the organization. State and local officials, including Reagan, Reddin, and Yorty, on the other hand, thought it gave the patrol a quasi-official status, undermining the community's faith in the LAPD.[38] Acting HEW commissioner Joseph H. Meyers believed that had CAP's grant application only dealt with issues of police brutality, CAP would not have received the funds in the first place. Instead HEW officials saw the program as a way to connect individuals to their community, establish a sense of responsibility, and improve communications between the police and the black community. The combination would enhance public safety and reduce the potential of future unrest.[39]

Facing strong opposition from city officials, Meyers wavered. He stated that the grant could be revoked if the LAPD demonstrated or felt that the grant to CAP would impair the operations of the police. Mayor Yorty was skeptical of the grant, believing that the LAPD had done a successful job at repairing police-community relations and that the CAP would get in the way of progress at reform. More important for HEW's decision was Reddin's opposition. He called the CAP a potential "vigilante" committee that would interfere with law enforcement operations, citing occasions when CAP members supposedly encouraged teenagers to challenge officers. "I am opposed to any program," Reddin stated in a condemnation of CAP activities, "that would attempt to usurp responsibilities that rightfully belong to the police."[40]

Convinced by the opposition, federal officials revoked the grant. As Johnson's aide Joseph Califano explained, "This was clearly a goof," and CAP should have known the federal government "cannot support activities that 'monitor or buffer' local police forces." Any future program would have to be approved by the police. For CAP members, on the other hand, any program based on cooperation or endorsement from the police would be "the kiss of death for us in Watts."[41] In effect, the police and white officials countered any attempt by residents to offer alternative modes of policing that threatened to reduce the power and authority of the LAPD. For residents and patrol members, a police force originating from the community would enhance public safety and legitimacy of the police. Such demands for access to protection and safety outside the purview of the LAPD, however, threatened police authority and continued organizing and criticism of the department that would bring more overt—and violent—police repression.

Resisting Containment and Counterinsurgent Warfare

The battle for the streets intensified in 1968 with an increase in shootings, police harassment, frisk rouses, and in-custody deaths. Critiques of the law-and-order paradigm led to a campaign of retribution and terror aimed at disrupting and dismantling black and Mexican American political organizations critical of the LAPD. Black and Mexican American activists viewed repressive policing as a tactic employed by local officials to mobilize the LAPD's riot control arsenal for the containment of civil rights activities. The growth in police repression, according to the Black Congress, an umbrella group consisting of over seventy organizations, signaled that "the Los Angeles Police Dept. has made it crystal clear that they do not want to take the defensive when the revolution comes, they are trying to name the Time, Place and Battlefield."[42]

Due to its efforts to create unity and multiracial alliance in opposition to racially targeted policing, law enforcement officials deemed the Black Congress a threat. Built on a vision of cooperative efforts not only among African American organizations but also between African American and Mexican American activists, the congress used funds provided by the Interreligious Foundation for Community Organizations to develop a collaborative program with the Mexican American umbrella organization Acción de Bronze Collectiva.[43] By developing solidarity across organizational, economic, and racial divisions, the congress hoped to advance "the cause of liberation and human progress" and "to eliminate all forms of oppression and racism in our community."[44]

Combating police abuse was central to the congress's vision. The congress complained about get-tough policing, overenforcement of traffic laws, and the unfair issuance of citations.[45] During the congress's May 4, 1968, meeting at the Second Baptist Church, Margaret Wright, a leader of the United Parents Council, placed changing racially targeted policing and criminal justice at the forefront of the congress's demands. Police roustings and arrests, she argued, were based on unreasonable criteria such as hairstyle, clothing, and mannerisms that were foreign to the policeman, leading to more arrests in the black community. As symbols of the state, the police had created a two-tiered level of citizenship and protection. Describing a "dual personality" of the police, Wright explained how law enforcement protected and served whites, but when confronting blacks they "get out of the car with a gun drawn." Not only did the police fail to investigate crime in black communities, the skewed judicial system meant that inquests into police malpractice were "nothing but a whitewash for trigger-happy cops." Demanding equality before the law, Wright concluded, "Justifiable homicide must stop. Murderers must be punished equally whether they happen to wear a badge or not."[46]

Militant demands for community control of the police by the congress and affiliated groups, such as the Black Panthers, led to reprisals from the police. Chief Reddin warned that the Black Congress was made up of "the most dangerous people in our city today." Labeling social movement organizations as dangerous, subversive, and criminal legitimated the LAPD's efforts to expand the intelligence gathering, surveillance, and policing apparatus.[47] On the streets it amounted to the police carrying out a preemptive strike on organizations struggling against police abuse.

Police harassment and violence escalated in the weeks leading up to the 1968 Watts Summer Festival. On August 5, the situation turned deadly when three young Black Panther members pulled into a service station followed by LAPD officers. When officers ordered the men out of the car, spread-eagled them on the trunk of the squad car, and searched them, an altercation ensued, leaving three Panthers dead and two officers wounded. As with other police shootings, the official reports and media coverage accepted the police accounts of the subversive nature of the Panthers as "aggressive" black men who shot at the police.[48] To residents and activists, the LAPD employed the image of black criminality to justify a crackdown against organizations demanding police reform. "Members of Black organizations in Los Angeles have become targets of the L.A.P.D," the Black Congress concluded. "Their aggressive approach to organized community workers speaks to the conscious premeditation of their activities.[49]

On August 11, thousands of black residents attended the final night of the Watts Summer Festival at Will Rogers Park in the heart of South Central to hear a jazz concert. After the concert, thousands of attendees remained in the park, drinking and enjoying the festivities. On high alert, the LAPD had blanketed the area surrounding the park during the festival.[50] The police presence created a feeling of unease among many participants who knew that a "minor human error" could easily result in violence from police officers. When officials attempting to close down the festival called in the LAPD and Los Angeles Sheriff's Department (LASD) units, members of the crowd threw bottles and rocks at the officers. Following riot control tactics, officers formed squads and moved into the park. According to police reports, unidentified members of the crowd then initiated a gun battle that left three dead and over forty wounded.[51]

The LAPD organized an emergency command center, the "saturation" of a thirty-block area with hundreds of officers, and the use of SWAT teams and helicopters to monitor the area. Sporadic episodes of gunfire and looting ensued but did not erupt into a full-scale uprising, though the police-occupied streets looked eerily similar to the Watts uprising. Over the following two days, the LAPD collected information on 179 separate incidents in South Central including family disputes, standard arrests, broken windows, fires, burglaries, traffic tickets, and false alarms, whether related to the disturbance at the festival or not. "There will be those who said we overreacted," Reddin commented, "but it's better to overreact and control it. In this case we did react massively."[52] One former LASD officer involved in the incident recalled that before going into Will Rogers Park to disperse the festival crowds, officers were instructed to remove their badges, were armed with automatic weapons, and wore "black crepe" outfits similar to those used by the Viet Cong to maintain an element of surprise and that the reported sniper fire was actually friendly fire by officers shooting from across the park.[53] A visiting Marine attending the festival claimed, "The police shot first. I hit the deck the way I was taught in the Marines. . . . Shots were coming from the police. In less than a minute, three policemen were on top of me, clubbing me."[54] The police mobilized riot control and prevention measures for repression and the enforcement of a hierarchical racial order.

Repressive state action fueled organizing. In this case, it linked black and Mexican American activists in common cause. Following the violence, a multiracial cross section of radicals and ministers called the Crisis Coalition mobilized hundreds people to descend on city council hearings held on August 12 and 14. Citing LAPD statistics on the overpolicing of black and Mexican American communities for the protection of white interests, the coalition demanded an end to "oppressive tactics being employed by the police in the ghetto and barrio communities which push tension to the breaking point."[55] The violence at the Summer Festival, therefore, was a product not of community or civil rights actions but of the practices and policies of the police. As Black Congress founder Walter Bremond and Carl Vázquez, a Mexican American activist, stated, "We, Brown and Black, stand here together . . . *hermanos unidos!*" They linked their struggles through a shared history of oppression. They warned that eruptions of violence were likely as long as the "war between the communities and police" continued unabated.[56] If the police did not "de-escalate" from their counterinsurgency policies, the result would be violence. "The man is jamming us," Roy G. Robinson of the Black Congress exclaimed, "and giving us not much choice."[57]

The solution to preventing violence, the coalition argued, required improving the department's accountability to residents and developing alternatives to get-tough policing. The coalition demanded an end to "legal" killings by the police, mass arrests and illegal searches, saturation policing, and the conspiracy to disrupt and destroy civil rights organizing. If the police were not willing to provide adequate service to protect black and brown lives, the coalition was "capable of protecting our own communities." They pleaded for action and explained their lack of confidence in positive change coming from city officials who often listened with open ears but failed to act. As Walter Bremond stated, "When we leave your building of law, you will go back to business as usual."[58]

Council members responded by labeling the coalition participants as subversives. Conservative councilman Louis R. Nowell, who represented the white suburban San Fernando Valley, denounced the critiques of the police as a "shame, travesty, and disservice," called the accusations of brutality "untrue and unfounded," and stormed out of the hearings.[59] Councilman Arthur K. Snyder, a conservative Republican who represented areas of East Los Angeles and Lincoln Heights, as well as the more affluent Eagle Rock, Griffith Park, and Los Feliz neighborhoods, called the Crisis Coalition "phony as a three-dollar bill," and made up of "Marxist- and violence-oriented extremist groups" that did not represent the community.[60] Nevertheless, the coalition was supported by the ACLU, the NAACP, the Neighborhood Adult Participation Program, and the Westminster Neighborhood Association. Through their descriptions, council members criminalized demands for police accountability and implicitly legitimized counterinsurgent police strategies.[61]

Tension between the police and the black community prompted Booker Griffin of the *Los Angeles Sentinel* to advocate for an honest appraisal of the problem of the police in the black community. In contrast to the *Los Angeles Times*' repackaging of police rhetoric, the *Sentinel*, along with Mexican American press outlets such as *Carta Editorial* and select *Times* journalists such as Ruben Salazar, exposed racially targeted police practices. "We must challenge the strategy and policy of the police now or forever live at the mercy of a police-state control," Griffin stated; the "LAPD appears to wish to impose an unannounced South African type curfew on the black community through fear."[62] Police practices, such as officers carrying shotguns on patrol and using the hands-on-the-wall method during stop-and-search operations, contributed to fears of a pervasive police state that united black residents in opposition to the police.[63] Activists would increasingly turn to armed self-defense, just as the police expanded their war on dissent.

The establishment and rapid growth of the Black Panther Party brought immediate attention from the LAPD's Urban Counterinsurgency Task Force as well as the FBI. Part of an attack on the Black Panthers in cities across the country, the local counterinsurgency programs went into high gear, using informants to gather intelligence on the Panthers and prepare plans to disrupt and destroy the organization.[64] The growth of the party led to increased repression, as police often followed members in cars and arrested and charged them under criminal conspiracy statutes that elevated the charges from misdemeanors to felonies. In response to the LAPD's and FBI's targeting of the Panthers for repression, intimidation, and charges of conspiracy, chapter members fortified their offices and homes, led by Vietnam veteran Elmer Geronimo Pratt. The counterinsurgency campaign on the part of law enforcement meant the Panthers "were at war."[65]

Over the course of the summer and the fall of 1969, the LAPD kept watch over Panther locations. A task force surrounded the Central Avenue headquarters on November 28 with over 250 officers in a precursor of what was to come. And then, mere days after the Chicago police raided Panther leader Fred Hampton's apartment and assassinated him, the LAPD carried out an all-out assault on the L.A. chapter. At five-thirty in the morning on December 8, 1969, the LAPD invaded three Panther locations and surrounded the Central Avenue headquarters with over 300 officers and SWAT teams. During the shootout at Forty-first and Central, police armed with M16 rifles, gas masks, a grenade launcher, and armored vehicles fired over 5,000 rounds into the building. The Panthers returned fire with rifles and shotguns. The SWAT team gained approval from the Department of Justice for a grenade launcher and attempted to use dynamite to enter the building from the roof. After the five-hour assault in which three Panthers and three officers were injured, the Panthers surrendered, resulting in twenty-one combined arrests.[66] It was the logical culmination of police policies that had not only viewed but also naturalized inner-city spaces, residents, and anti–police abuse movements as threats in need of monitoring and repression.

The assault on Panther headquarters created a sense of solidarity in opposition to police violence among the city's African American residents. The Panthers called the event an "overt act of massacre" and "genocide against Black People." Indeed, the assault on the Panthers reflected the growing realization that police harassment and abuse did not distinguish among black residents. As a result, in the wake of the assault, the Panthers received support from a number of mainstream civil rights organizations such as the NAACP and the Urban League. John W. Mack, of the Urban League, stated that such police attacks had "the potential for spreading to other blacks," while Earl E. Raines, of the NAACP, commented, "The black community is affected. . . . Next time it may be you." Moderate groups also supported a mass rally of over 4,000 predominantly black youth at Los Angeles City Hall on December 11 and demanded a full investigation into the assault and full public disclosure of the nature and operations of the elite SWAT units.[67]

The shootout with the Panthers, while part of the long-standing assault on organizations believed to be subversive, contributed to a siege mentality among residents who were subjected to a police department bent not on protecting the community but on controlling it. Hopes by Panthers to continue the fight to make South Central "liberated territory" ran headlong into a police project aimed at control and repression. Chief Ed Davis used the incident to praise the SWAT operation and criminalize the Panthers. "I do not intend,"

Black Panther headquarters after police assault. The 1969 police offensive at 41st and Central lasted five hours. The LAPD responded to the organizing of the Black Panthers and their critiques of the police with overwhelming force. Such use of police violence undermined and, ultimately, contributed to the destruction of social movements in the 1960s and 1970s. *Los Angeles Times* Photographic Archives (Collection 1429); courtesy of Library Special Collections, Charles E. Young Research Library, UCLA.

Davis asserted, "to give up one square inch of Los Angeles to any bandit, murderer, law-breaking Minuteman, Ku Klux Klanner, or Black Panther Party member."[68] While the 1969 shootout fueled Black Panther Party growth in the short term, the Panthers dissolved by the early 1970s partly due to the extraordinary level of police harassment and infiltration.[69]

Using its undercover intelligence units, the Urban Counterinsurgency Task Force and Criminal Conspiracy Section, the LAPD waged war on the Panthers and other antipolice groups. Chief Davis suggested that the Black Panthers and the Brown Berets were at the root of growing episodes of disorder. Reflecting on the 1968 Summer Festival, Davis described the explosion of violence as "a very disastrous celebration of the rebirth of Watts after the riots . . . stimulated by Black Panther activity." But they were also categorically different from civil rights activities, requiring the police to prevent the breakdown of the established order. "So this is not just demonstrations now," Davis continued. "You have been in the vital stages of revolution on the installment plan all over the country for a good many years."[70] Criminalizing the activists and organizations critical of get-tough police practices legitimized the LAPD's counterinsurgent war.

Davis took pride in his department's ability to undermine social movement organizations. Calling himself "something like a military general," he recounted the destruction of the Brown Berets, the Black Panthers, and the Black Congress. "See, I ran them out of the city when I became chief," Davis told an interviewer. Indeed, the LAPD, with the help of the FBI and undercover informants, targeted these groups through arrests, infiltration, and surveillance. "The power struggle is all over," Davis stated in 1971; "we knocked them [Black Panthers and Brown Berets] off right and left, and they never did figure, you know, how it was happening."[71]

The police department's counteroffensive cut short attempts to expose the police power and assert alternatives to law and order, in Mexican American neighborhoods just as it had in black neighborhoods. Law enforcement greeted Mexican American antipolice organizing with the same repression it had visited upon the Panthers.

Stranger in One's Land

Though the Watts uprising focused the police department's counterinsurgency campaign in the black community, Mexican Americans in East Los Angeles had long faced police brutality and repression as well. As young Mexican Americans became politicized through police harassment during the 1960s, they placed the police at the center of their grievances. Police and sheriffs often operated on the presumption that "barrios are full of criminals" in need of tough policing. Law enforcement criminalized Mexican Americans due to the perceived language barrier and having to prove "with documents that he is an American citizen." Faced with the deployment of both LAPD and LASD officers in East Los Angeles, Mexican American residents had daily contact with law enforcement.[72] Despite efforts by the LAPD to enhance community relations with the Mexican American community during a series of meetings in 1967, the tension between militant young Chicanos/as and law enforcement quickly reached crisis proportions. Art García, director of the ACLU police malpractice complaint center in East Los Angeles, commented that "the situation in our barrio couldn't get any worse."[73]

The colonial legacy was a crucial determinant in Mexican American relations with law enforcement. As Ruben Salazar explained in his report on U.S. Civil Rights Commission hearings titled *Stranger in One's Land*, antipolice activism was an assertion that "Mexicans are not strangers to this land, especially in the Southwest. They are indigenous to it."[74] While activists pushed law enforcement to recognize that policing Mexican American neighborhoods required a different approach from that used to police South Central, law enforcement relied on the same strategy of criminalizing dissent and waging a counterinsurgent campaign of repression and occupation. The Mexican American Political Association's Manuel Ruíz, for example, challenged Chief Reddin to work more closely with Mexican American leaders because "police understanding of negro community problems will not assist in the understanding of the bi-cultural mores and concerns of the Mexican-American Community, which are not the same." Yet, as Percy Duran of the Mexican American Legal Defense and Educational Fund reported, the police treated East Los Angeles as an "armed camp" requiring the reassertion of control by a militarized police force which was "mainly Anglo, insensitive, fearful, and heavily armed." Not only did Reddin fail to respond, but the department opened an investigation into whether the critics were connected to Communists.[75]

Tense relations between Chicanos/as and the LAPD and LASD exploded during the 1968 school blowouts. Mexican American students walked out of Lincoln High School, Roosevelt High School, and Garfield High School in protest of substandard education. Student organizers recognized the potential for police violence, instructing participants of their right to walk out of school as a "lawful protest" and explaining the need to "Protest! Demonstrate! But we do so peacefully—don't give the police and security guards any excuse to beat up on us or bust us." During the first two weeks of March, nearly 10,000 students walked out of high schools in East Los Angeles holding signs that read "Education not concentration camps" and demanding quality bicultural and bilingual education, community control, and an end to the presence of police on campuses.[76]

The police responded with a tactical alert, deploying riot squads and arresting over one hundred students. Davis criminalized the participants in the blowouts by claiming that they were fomented by "self-avowed Marxist" members of the Brown Berets.[77] District Attorney Younger indicted thirteen of the organizers of the blowouts on sixteen counts of conspiracy to disturb the peace and quiet of a neighborhood, to disturb the operation of a public school, and to remain present during an unlawful assembly, among others. The overt police violence and criminalization of student protests not only enraged the Mexican American community but also reflected how the criminal justice system operated to define dissent as disorderly and criminal, rationalizing the police state response. As David Sánchez, a Brown Beret leader, summed up, "to Anglos justice means 'just us.'"[78]

A lack of political representation on the city council—there were no Mexican American council members—meant there was little political will to address police violence aimed at young Mexican Americans. Indeed, the

Mexican American community faced an "insensitive and sometimes repressive 'government from without.'"[79] Such a history of colonial occupation, Armando Morales explained, contributed to increased "friction between law enforcement and the Mexican American community." Young Mexican Americans, many now identifying as Chicanos/as, experienced repeated arrests, frisk rousts, and beatings on Whittier Boulevard where Chicano/a youth hung out and cruised.[80] Whittier Boulevard was the scene of routine police violence, such as the sheriff's assault on Chicanos/as on July 4, 1970. In response to a rally by Chicanos/as upset over the heavy law enforcement presence, issuance of tickets, and curfew laws, the sheriffs invaded the boulevard with the shock troops of the Special Enforcement Bureau and "busted Chicano heads."[81] Repression and criminalization of Chicanos/as fueled antipolice sentiment. "Police are determined to keep law and order at any cost," Richard Cardoza, director of a probation department youth project in East Los Angeles, observed, "and that's a price the community won't pay any more."[82]

Many residents responded to the harassment and beating of Chicano/a youth by forming defense committees to challenge abusive police practices and reassert a sense of law and order based on a vision of greater police accountability and respect for Chicano/a youth. The Barrio Defense Committee (BDC), formed by Celia Rodríguez and other mothers after the brutality of the 1968 school walkouts, organized for the protection of Chicano/a youth, defended victims of police harassment and abuse, and brought legal action against police killings. They organized self-consciously as mothers and described their work as "the defense of the Barrio."[83]

Part of the BDC's strategy attempted to reframe the police-constructed, but commonly accepted, views of criminality in the community. The real crimes, the BDC suggested, were the ones imposed on students who received poor education and failing schools. But the most galling crime, according to the BDC, was using the police to suppress protest. "And the greatest crime of all," the BDC claimed, was "to turn the cops on the victims."[84] The BDC viewed the police as a source of disorder in the community aimed at discouraging activism. In a letter to its members, the BDC reported, "repression against our Barrio has increased tremendously in an obvious effort to discourage increasing community involvement and protest."[85]

School walkouts and protests in 1970 once again led to police repression, and parents and students mobilized for an end to police violence on school campuses. Administrators at Roosevelt High responded to peaceful protests in March of 1970 by calling the police. Captain Smith of the Hollenbeck Division reported that the police deployed minimal force in restoring order. But community members described the use of the elite Metro Division, which arrived with "riot gear and all." As parents, students, and BDC activists continued to learn, as the forces of law and order, the police operated as agents of repression.[86] Indeed, BDC members often faced harassment, roust-and-frisks, and arrest after leaving their meetings. To such threats they responded with vigilance. "Our Committee again serves notice: We don't scare easily," one newsletter declared. "Having had a taste of Victory, our Barrio will never take it lying down again."[87]

The BDC focused on not only reforming the police but also the oppressive criminal justice system more broadly. Activists worked to inform the community of police malpractice and to mobilize barrio residents to provide legal support for victims of police harassment and abuse. The BDC's expansive view understood the problem of law enforcement as one connected to a discriminatory criminal justice system. They provided legal aid and services to residents facing criminal and felony charges and focused on reforming the processing of prisoners at the county jail. By taking their activity from the streets to the jail, BDC activists recognized how the criminal justice system had made the city a carceral space for Mexican American youth.[88]

Relations between Mexican Americans and law enforcement reached a nadir by 1970. Continued ignorance of the colonial legacy of occupation, negative views of Mexican culture, and lack of language training had, in the eyes of prominent Mexican American journalist Ruben Salazar and other Mexican American activists, made the Mexican American a "Stranger in One's Land." As Brown Beret David Sánchez concluded, "The white policeman and the white judge do not understand our world." Such colonial attitudes created the conditions for violence because law enforcement officials refused to acknowledge the way their policies disregarded Mexican American demands for an end to police treating their neighborhood as occupied territory. As Reverend John P. Luce of the Epiphany Parish in East Los Angeles commented on the state of police-community relations, "We are on a collision course in Los Angeles" that might very well lead to a "police-barrio confrontation."[89]

Police attacked the National Chicano Moratorium demonstration on August 29, 1970, held in East Los Angeles to protest the large number of Mexican American casualties in the Vietnam War. Between 20,000 and 30,000 protestors marched along a three-mile route ending at MacArthur Park. Viewing the demonstration as riotous and violent, the LASD with the aid of LAPD officers charged the protestors with tear gas and nightsticks. Attempts at self-defense resulted in escalating police violence and mass arrest. At the end of the melee, Ruben Salazar lay dead from a tear gas canister that a sheriff's deputy shot at his head while he was sitting in the Silver Dollar Café.[90] The Chicano Moratorium Committee held five subsequent demonstrations during 1970 and 1971, all ending in violence and police or sheriff repression.

Police violence following Chicano Moratorium Committee antiwar protest, 1970. Whereas the police often referred to Chicano/a activists as disorderly and violent, the actions of the police revealed how law enforcement actions led to violence. *Los Angeles Times* Photographic Archives (Collection 1429); courtesy of Library Special Collections, Charles E. Young Research Library, UCLA.

Sheriff Pitchess blamed the violence on the Moratorium Committee and for "a grave disservice to the Mexican American people," while Chief Davis stated that the committee was brainwashed by "swimming pool communists and sophisticated Bolsheviks."[91]

Activists and residents had a different viewpoint. As Rodolfo "Corky" Gonzales, national Chicano leader from the Crusade for Justice in Denver, stated at a press conference, "Los Angeles is the number one police state and city in United States history." Instead of "dissidents" fomenting rebellion, the violence was instigated by "law enforcement agencies throughout the country."[92] The overt repression revealed how the state had abandoned its guarantee of democracy and equal citizenship for Mexican American residents. As one resident commented, "They [the police] certainly must know that when they strip people of their rights and deal the injustices, these people are asked to sever allegiance to their oppressors."[93] Indeed, saturation policing and the use of the elite Metro Division to "shake, rattle, and roll" led to not only disillusionment—and even hostility—with state authority but also the breakdown of law and order itself. One commentator remarked,

"It's ironic that the peace is kept better in East Los Angeles when the police aren't around."[94]

Mexican Americans grew disenchanted with the ability of local governing institutions to adequately respond to demands for fair and equitable policing. Such sentiments pervaded a series of hearings held by the California Assembly's Select Committee on the Administration of Justice on relations between the police and Mexican-Americans during the spring of 1972. Prominent Mexican American organizations, residents, and disaffected law enforcement agents testified to the mounting concern with the violent police behavior in the community, the poor training and knowledge about Mexican culture, and the lack of language skills. Law enforcement agencies rarely acted to protect and serve their communities and criminalized those involved in antipolice demonstrations. "Here in this county, merely because you become an activist and merely because of the fact that you choose not to be on the side of law enforcement when they have inequities, injustice, and so on that prevail," Abe Tapia of Mexican American Political Association summarized, "all of a sudden Chief Davis, with his big mouth that he has, labels everybody Communist, red-baiting."[95]

Repression crushed activism in the Chicano/a community just as it did with the Black Panthers. As Davis proudly explained of his project to destroy the Brown Berets and activists in the Moratorium Committee, "They went into the courts and said we were harassing them and arresting them and we were. . . . They want to move out of the city now. . . . They don't like me. . . . I will make no objection to it."[96] While repression undermined Chicano/a organizing, it also reflected the ways racialized law enforcement practices defined the boundaries of race, criminality, and citizenship and mobilized Mexican Americans to demand an end to police practices based on occupation. As police violence and shootings on the streets of the barrio continued during the 1970s, Mexican American activists mobilized to demand the local state treat them not as "strangers" in their own land but as full members of society by ensuring greater regulation, oversight, and reform of the LAPD.

———

During the late 1960s and early 1970s, police violence was a visible manifestation of the establishment of both the federal and local War on Crime. Demands by African Americans and Mexican Americans for police protection, an end to police violence, and in some cases abolition of the police altogether reflected how policing became a central site of the struggle for racial justice. Many residents and community leaders demanded more and better police services as part of a claim for equal access to state services. Yet the relationship between the police and the black and Mexican American communities continued along a largely antagonistic path. For many inner-city residents, the LAPD was little more than a symbol of a white power structure implicated in a long history of lack of accountability, abusive practices, and aggressive policing. By the early 1970s, African American and Mexican American communities were besieged by law enforcement agencies.[97]

The police responded to protests and organizing with brute force. They labeled activists as subversive and criminal, and destroyed groups like the Black Panthers and Brown Berets. The impact of the LAPD's repression of black and Chicano/a organizing would have repercussions through the 1970s and 1980s, as law enforcement targeted all black and Latino/a youth as potentially delinquent or violent. The response of black and brown residents and activists to police repression, however, reflected an awareness that police practices defined the boundaries of citizenship, sense of belonging, and understanding of place after Watts.

But African American and Mexican American mobilization around police brutality had far more repercussions than simply provoking white backlash. As police violence mobilized African American and Mexican American residents, the election of Tom Bradley brought hope for police reform and a local government that would truly serve all Los Angeles. Bradley's liberal law and order approach envisioned using the power of government to oversee the police and criminal justice system. Yet, though liberals envisioned a different relationship between citizens and the state, the crime control policies that would develop under the Bradley administration created a two-tiered system of justice that treated some residents better than others. During Bradley's mayoral administration, the politics of liberal law and order would ultimately further enable the expansion of police power.

Chapter 4

Kid Thugs Are Spreading Terror through the Streets

Legitimizing Supervision of Black and Latino/a Youth

Speaking to the Los Angeles County Bar after announcing his candidacy for mayor in the 1973 election, Tom Bradley argued that the "ever-present fear" of crime had paralyzed the city. He described schools rife with violent youth, apartment buildings guarded by cameras and armed security, offices patrolled by attack dogs, and downtown streets deserted "not from fear of police spies, but from fear of thugs." He urged those concerned with civil liberties in the audience to take crime seriously. "Are we willing," Bradley asked, "as people committed to the survival of constitutional guarantees—to understand that crime is as clear a threat to the spirit of a free society as the wiretap, the censor, or the billy club? Are we willing to admit that black and white will not live side by side in any degree of trust and friendship, until we have faced the issue of crime and lawlessness head on?"[1] Rather than shying away from law and order, Bradley embraced the war on crime. His vision of a liberal Los Angeles where state institutions could facilitate prosperous and peaceful pluralism for all rested on an empowered police force.

Bradley entered politics in 1963 after twenty-one years as an LAPD officer. As a city councilman, he became one of the department's most ardent critics. Yet when he ran for mayor in 1969, he fought back against the soft-on-crime, antipolice image promoted by incumbent mayor Sam Yorty. Bradley lost to Yorty's race-baiting, red-baiting, tough-on-crime campaign. But in 1973 he won on his second attempt running on a pro-police, law-and-order platform. As the city's first African American mayor, Bradley presented himself as a reformer who would make city government more diverse, inclusive, and fair. Characteristic of a generation of black politicians rising to power in the 1970s, such as Coleman Young in Detroit and Maynard Jackson in Atlanta, not merely responsive to the interests of African American residents, he would represent "all Los Angeles."[2] Liberal law and order expanded police authority within the framework of procedural fairness and government oversight of the criminal justice system. Law and order, in other words, was not merely a response to conservative calls for stronger police and punitive policies but a deliberate attempt by liberals to shape criminal justice policy.[3]

Bradley hoped to use mayoral power to exert more control over the criminal justice system and thereby wrest some authority away from the police.

To do so, he created the Mayor's Office of Criminal Justice Planning (MOCJP). The agency coordinated the city's disparate criminal justice agencies, created its first comprehensive crime control plan, and streamlined grant applications for Law Enforcement Assistance Administration (LEAA) funding. Although LEAA funds were small in comparison to the LAPD's total operating budget, the MOCJP limited some of the department's autonomy by operating as the gatekeeper of federal criminal justice funds in the city. Reflecting liberal law-and-order goals, the MOCJP balanced grants for rehabilitative programs with a commitment to tough-on-crime policies. But it also facilitated new avenues of police discretion by using federal funds to develop intervention programs in partnership with the department. Over time, programs that might have otherwise been independent of the police were incorporated into the widening scope of the department's police power. Framed as reforms, the MOCJP's programs solidified the local criminal justice system and wove the police into the liberal state.

Preventing criminal activity by kids and teenagers in schools and surrounding neighborhoods was the administration's top priority. Working with law enforcement authorities, school administrators, and city council members, MOCJP officials engineered a more punitive juvenile justice system. Liberals, however, made sure that punishment of serious offenders was complemented by diversionary and rehabilitative programs for at-risk kids to prevent lifelong criminal activity. In the hopes of reaching predelinquent youth or first-time offenders before they entered penal institutions, such programs exploited the capacity of social service agencies and schools to monitor children. In effect, criminal justice reform combined social welfare, educational, and penal institutions. Strengthening the juvenile justice system amounted to an elaborate and expensive exercise in state-building as officials attempted to relegitimize police discretion and ensure these prerogatives were directed toward youth of color.[4]

As soon as liberals, such as County Supervisor Kenneth Hahn and MOCJP administrators, implemented these reforms, however, they began expressing fears that state institutions were failing to achieve their pluralist goals. Liberal city and county lawmakers and school administrators claimed that community rehabilitation and diversion were inadequate means of containing hard-core youth offenders who overwhelmed schools with violence. Liberals and conservatives alike blamed the youth crime crisis on the "failure" of community rehabilitation to discipline repeat offenders. They argued that juvenile court was too lenient, amounting to a "revolving door" that allowed repeat offenders to avoid punishment. Liberals joined conservatives in regarding the service-providing state as a threat to society, turning to punitive solutions instead. Detention was necessary, not diversion.

Meanwhile, the new juvenile court legislation created a two-tiered system of rehabilitation and punishment. Black and Latino/a kids were often regarded as hard-core offenders to be targeted for monitoring and supervision. They not only encountered diversionary programs more often than their white counterparts but also were disproportionately represented in the system's penal institutions. Young suburban whites, in contrast, were more likely to be treated as status offenders to be released or referred to counseling programs.[5] The resulting stratified system criminalized, policed, and punished black and Latino/a youth.

Liberal law-and-order reforms, ostensibly aimed at providing alternatives to get-tough policing and incarceration, ended up contributing to the expansion of the city's criminal justice system. The police gained new discretionary powers to monitor and supervise youth of color, as the carceral state expanded into schools and social welfare agencies. All the while, as the criminal justice system responded to fluctuations in crime, it was increasingly used to punish rather than rehabilitate.

The Impossible Dream of Liberal Law and Order

As a twenty-one-year veteran of the LAPD, Bradley was especially aware of the department's problems. As an officer, he had developed a strong commitment to community engagement through work with youth gangs and in the Public Information Division as part of the department's community relations program. These early experiences shaped Bradley's view that police officers could best combat crime through fair and just enforcement of the law that would enhance civilian cooperation. Bradley was well regarded by veteran officers who believed he served the department "well and honorably," but his criticism of the department's approach to policing in the black community made him Chief William Parker's enemy. Leaving the department after rising to the rank of lieutenant, the first African American to do so, Bradley was elected to the city council's predominantly middle-class African American and Jewish Tenth District in 1963. On the council he routinely called for accountability, oversight in complaint procedures, and improved community relations. Prior to the Watts uprising, Bradley earned a reputation as antipolice after raising concerns over the patterns of harassment and officer-involved shootings in neighborhoods of color.[6]

Themes of crime control, policing, and law and order characterized the 1969 mayoral race between Bradley and incumbent Sam Yorty. Capitalizing on the growing divide between liberals and the police after Watts, Yorty's campaign portrayed the LAPD veteran as an antipolice leftist with support from black militants and Communists. Yorty even paid African Americans to drive in the predominantly white San Fernando Valley with fists raised and bumper stickers reading "Bradley for Mayor" and "Black is Beautiful."[7] "[Bradley] is no friend of the Police Department," Yorty proclaimed. "If you don't believe that, ask any policeman. . . . Tell the citizens to stop any policeman they know and ask him how they feel about Tom Bradley."[8] In direct mailings to white voters, Yorty declared, "*We* need a mayor for *our* city!" Yorty also ran racially inflammatory ads in Valley newspapers with Bradley's picture and the caption "Will Your City Be Safe with This Man?"[9]

In response Bradley outlined a liberal law-and-order platform that combined support for strong law enforcement policies with demands for equitable and inclusive policing. The harm principle, which viewed the state as justified in policing only those activities that harmed others, allowed Bradley to call for law and order. "Law and order here and now is essential," a position paper stated; "crime or violence in support of any claim cannot be tolerated." Touting his support for legislative proposals to strengthen the LAPD, such as pay raises, funds for training, and survivor benefits for police wives, Bradley pledged to maintain the more than one-third of the city budget allocated to the department "for more sophisticated detection and greater officer protection."[10]

Support for tough-on-crime policies did not preclude greater civilian oversight of the police department, nor did it demand support for inequitable policing. It did, however, require the government to impose proper oversight of the police. A strengthened police commission would empower it to "use the broad law enforcement review powers which it possesses (a community review board is not the answer)." This vision of oversight directed by mayoral appointees complemented a commitment to a fairer Los Angeles administered by more responsive public servants. "But law enforcement," Bradley continued, "will *not* be the tool of discrimination or the weapon of oppression against any group or person because of his race, economic status, his style of living or his views, whether or not I may agree or disagree with him."[11] Strengthening the police department would be top priority so that all residents could feel safe from urban unrest, crime, and violence.

Yet Bradley made a distinction between civil and criminal violence when framing his position on law and order. Referring to the urban uprisings of the 1960s, he proclaimed that more police would not solve problems rooted in unequal socioeconomic conditions. "The incidence of violence and unrest of the poor, the youth, and the minorities is not the product of what is commonly regarded as a product of the criminal mind," Bradley stated. "It cannot be dealt with as we all know, by the traditional emphasis on techniques of 'catching crooks.'" He warned that attempting to address discontent with the police through force would undermine the department's legitimacy. The city needed a "multi-front program" to improve police-community relations, ensure quality police training and education, diversify the officer corps, strengthen complaint procedures, and guarantee tough-on-crime policies. Emphasizing a framework of equity and fairness would enable get-tough policies to protect all residents.[12]

Yorty defeated Bradley with sizable backing from white residents and police officers, winning 53 percent of the vote to Bradley's 47. Although a group of 117 officers created a "Law Enforcement Committee for Bradley," the vastly more powerful and influential Police and Firemen for Efficient Law Enforcement, a pro-Yorty organization, conducted last-minute polls intended to undercut Bradley's position and shape public perceptions of Bradley as antipolice. Of 895 officers polled, they reported, 98.7 percent supported Yorty. Yorty's hardline law-and-order politics and media campaign to link Bradley with extremists was, in Bradley's words, a "veiled appeal to racism."[13]

The problem for Bradley was not his lack of support for law enforcement or law and order but his campaign's failure to promote his law-and-order vision. As Richard Maullin, a Bradley campaign strategist, recalled, "If Bradley was a policeman and supported true law and order, which he did and which most political liberals do, then he could emphasize that fact clearly." Political conditions meant that support for the police was crucial to win a future mayoral election. "Reforming the police—not destroying them—became a driving purpose for Bradley's supporters and, one may assume, for Bradley himself," Maullin concluded. "That the police were seemingly expressive of a majority's mood, and had therefore become a politically sensitive subject indicative of dominant social trends, was lost in the impulse to reform them to a more liberal image of public service."[14] If Yorty was able to smear Bradley as an antipolice, soft-on-crime candidate in 1969, then in his second campaign Bradley made sure to emphasize his career as a police officer as well as his liberal law-and-order platform.

During the 1973 campaign, Bradley balanced tough-on-crime measures with recognition that unregulated police power threatened the rights of residents. Such themes echoed his law-and-order stance from 1969 but with a more forceful assertion that he would not tolerate crime, violence, or lawlessness. Two major constituencies of Bradley's emerging electoral coalition, African Americans and liberal Westside Jews, influenced his approach to law and order and the police. Black residents had been demanding not only an end to police violence since the 1950s but also more-equitable police service in their neighborhoods. White liberals, on the other hand, supported the LAPD but spoke out against the discriminatory, but not the inherently racist, practices of the department. To win white liberal votes, Bradley distanced himself from black radical movements critical of police power, careful to advocate nothing more revolutionary than fairness and the safety for all law-abiding residents.[15]

Bradley countered his image as a soft-on-crime liberal by running on his police record and the right of all residents to equitable police protection whether in racially diverse areas of the Central City and South Central or the predominantly white conservative San Fernando Valley. "I'm very proud of my service of 21 years on the Police Department, an honorable career," Bradley explained while standing in front of an image of himself as a police lieutenant at the announcement of his campaign. "The people of Los Angeles are entitled to a safe city, safe in the Central City as well as the San Fernando Valley."[16] Bradley portrayed himself as a liberal reformer but not one who would hamstring the police by supporting a civilian review board. "In all my life, I have never proposed a civilian police review board, consistently fought against it since I was a policeman and since I've been a city councilman," he told a journalist. Pledging to work with Chief Ed Davis to wage a more effective war on crime, Bradley demonstrated that if elected, his commitment to fairness would support equitable policing for "all Los Angeles" but also enable the police department to combat crime and violence that threatened the safety of residents across the city.[17]

Promoting Bradley's police record did not mean that the campaign abandoned a liberal law-and-order vision of government oversight of the police and crime control programs. Campaign material routinely criticized Yorty as a do-nothing mayor who hid behind the myth that the mayor's office had no power, especially when it came to regulating the police department or using federal law enforcement funds. An active mayor using the tools of government, Bradley argued, would not only bring more oversight to the department but also ensure safety for all residents through support for new and innovative crime control programs. Campaign flyers, for example, stressed that "if the Mayor says it *can't* be done, it won't be. . . . Tom Bradley says we *can* have safe communities."[18]

From the outset, he promoted a message that liberals were just as concerned with combating crime and ensuring safety as conservatives. "The insane political division which somehow makes it 'conservative' to be against crime and 'liberal' to be for civil liberties," Bradley told the Bar, "has to start coming apart." The tough-on-crime platform continued a commitment to liberal law and order based on fairness and equity through government oversight of the police. When Yorty once again smeared Bradley as antipolice, Bradley's campaign released advertisements of Bradley in his police uniform and made his overwhelmingly positive police file public. The platform also explicitly supported the police department through proposals for a policeman's bill of rights, the use of federal grants to strengthen the juvenile

IF
THE
MAYOR
SAYS
IT <u>CAN'T</u>
BE DONE,
IT WON'T BE

Tom Bradley
says
we <u>can</u>
have
safe
communities

"Crime is an outright attack on our personal liberty and freedom. It is an act of oppression; a threat to the basic rights of an individual citizen, and a danger as well to the very spirit of a free society."

Tom Bradley speaks with a special knowledge about crime because he spent 21 years as a police officer. That experience taught him, more than anything else, that there simply is no justification for redressing a grievance against society by assaulting the property or safety of another citizen.

The Los Angeles Times called Tom Bradley's school violence program "among the more sensible solutions . . . Bradley's reasoning, of course, strikes at the heart of the violence . . . both his plan and his reasoning make it clear that the curbing of school violence remains the responsibility of each of us."

Tom Bradley's other key programs to promote safety in the community include:

A Policeman's Bill of Rights, including provisions for:
Better pay
Expanded insurance in the event of death or injury
Increased educational opportunity (including graduate work)
Improved assignment procedures
Pre-paid liability defense fund

Starting an anti-crime street lighting program to cover all streets. Councilman Bradley was the first Councilman to institute district-wide street lighting program, in his own district.

Seeking additional law enforcement funds for Los Angeles through the Omnibus Crime Control and Safe Streets Act. To date, the County of Los Angeles has received only 19% of the $40 million available to it. Had the leadership of this city taken the initiative Los Angeles could have received the funding it needs to provide better programs for law enforcement. Tom Bradley, as Mayor and as President-elect of the National League of Cities, will provide that leadership.

Severe punishment for hard drug pushers. Reducing the illegal manufacture and distribution of drugs, particularly by organized crime, and suppressing illicit traffickers.

Expanded medical referral program for drug users in junior and senior high schools. To encourage early treatment and more likely success — no criminal punishment for those who apply voluntarily for treatment.

Tom Bradley will be
a working mayor

16B

Tom Bradley campaign flyer. Bradley ran on his special knowledge of combating crime due to his twenty-one years as an LAPD officer. Although he worked for police reform throughout his campaign and subsequent mayoral administration, he also promoted law-and-order politics, especially during his second mayoral campaign in 1973. As campaign flyers outlined, Bradley supported a variety of anticrime measures including a Policeman's Bill of Rights, street lighting programs, increased federal law enforcement funds, and harsher drug sentencing laws. Mayor Tom Bradley Administration papers (Collection 293); UCLA Library Special Collections, Charles E. Young Research Library, UCLA.

Mayor Tom Bradley with LAPD motorcycle drill team during his inauguration. Bradley, a twenty-one-year veteran of the LAPD, was elected by a multiracial coalition in 1973 on a platform of reforming the police. His vision of liberal law and order was an attempt to reform the LAPD but also released the police power into new areas of social life. *Los Angeles Times* Photographic Archives (Collection 1429); courtesy of Library Special Collections, Charles E. Young Research Library, UCLA.

justice system, and legislation requiring strict punishment for "hard drug pushers."[19]

Bradley's promise of making government more responsive to all residents combined with a tough-on-crime platform helped him defeat Yorty with 56 percent of the vote, making Bradley the only black mayor elected in the 1970s in a city with a relatively small—18 percent—black population. Reflective of the prominence of law and order in the campaign, in his victory speech Bradley reiterated his commitment to ensuring law and order and addressing crime and violence in schools. A multiracial coalition of African Americans, Mexican Americans, Japanese Americans, and white liberals fueled Bradley's victory. Among liberal whites, Jews and those of higher income and education levels voted for Bradley. Support from a growing Mexican American base—Bradley won 51 percent of the Mexican American vote—and a less vehement conservative white backlash enabled Bradley to win votes he had lost in 1969.[20] Bradley's time in office would see his approach contribute to an even more robust criminal justice apparatus.

Juvenile Diversion and New Arenas of Control

The Bradley administration and local Democratic lawmakers confronted growing fears of crime, drugs, and youth violence. Just a year before Bradley's election, a "State of the City" report found that crime topped the list of residents' concerns.[21] Such fears were part of a panic surrounding rising juvenile gang crime and violence in schools. "Schools are being described as 'forts,'" County Board of Supervisors member Kenneth Hahn announced after joint city and council hearings on juvenile crime in 1973, "and kid thugs are spreading terror through the streets." Hahn, a liberal Democrat with historically strong support in the African American community, proposed a forty-eight-point crime reduction program aimed at cracking down on some 850 "hard-core" offenders who allegedly committed 25,000 crimes.[22] Within this context, public pressure to strengthen the police force was constant. Throughout the 1970s, constituents routinely made their desires for more police to ensure "security and protection" known. As one resident wrote to Bradley in 1976, "stronger measures must be taken."[23]

Bradley and the city council supported budget appropriations that would increase the number of officers on the beat. At the same time that federal LEAA funding flowed into Los Angeles and cities across the country, the municipal budget process also facilitated the growth in LAPD funding. Under the city charter, the mayor was responsible for submitting a proposed budget to the council. In the process, however, the police department first submitted its annual budget request, routinely asking for significant increases in resources over previous years. In its budget request for fiscal year 1974–75, for example, the LAPD asked for $167 million, a $6 million increase over the previous year. But Bradley used his mayoral authority to propose a reduced police budget of $160 million to the council for approval. Bradley successfully used the budget process to both support appropriations increasing the number of officers on the beat and limit extravagant requests from the LAPD for equipment such as jets and submarines. Yet the council, also concerned with constituent demands for more police, especially in the predominantly white and conservative San Fernando Valley, often restored the department's budget when Bradley attempted to reduce funding in areas such as intelligence gathering. Bradley's ability to rein in the police through the budget process was limited by the combination of public pressure for more officers and the ability of the city council to override his reductions. As a result, the police budget grew through the 1970s.[24]

While he faced city charter rules that limited his direct authority over the police department or the ability to reduce its budget on his own, Bradley believed that the mayor had significant power over city government. "By charter language," Bradley stated in an interview after his election, "it [city government] is what we call a strong-Council-weak-Mayor form of government. I've never accepted that, nor do I believe that it is so. The fact of the matter is that the Mayor has enormous power by law, by charter and by ordinance." Based on this belief, Bradley created the MOCJP in 1974 to exert control over the city's crime control policies and programs. As a city agency, the MOCJP organized grant requests for LEAA funds and sent them to the state coordinating agency, the California Council on Criminal Justice Council. The MOCJP fulfilled Bradley's goal of bringing more federal resources to the city and became the central agency for crime control policy and criminal justice grant administration. It also reflected a fundamental shift in the role of the local state as the mayor's office engaged in organizing, coordinating, and setting crime policy.[25]

The MOCJP was part of Bradley's effort to exert control over LEAA funds as well as crime policy more generally. The police department maintained its autonomy, but the MOCJP allowed Bradley to control the department's access to federal law enforcement funds because it managed all criminal justice planning grants for the city. If the police wanted federal funds for new programs or hardware, the department had to submit a proposal to the MOCJP. While LEAA funding—the Los Angeles region received $12 million in 1971—amounted to a small portion of the LAPD's annual total operating cost of nearly $242 million in 1973, the MOCJP and its effort to systematize the city's federal grant requests represented a shift in authority over criminal justice in the city. By integrating the police department into government institutions that liberals controlled, such as the MOCJP, Bradley hoped to regulate the criminal justice system and the police. But it required him to expand police authority into new areas. Bradley hoped that federal funds previously used by the police to develop new hardware and computer systems would be used by the MOCJP to deal "with criminals and victims on a personalized basis."[26]

As a planning and coordinating agency, the MOCJP brought together seemingly disparate agencies involved with youth services together under a juvenile justice system. "Some of our crime problems and gang problems are serious, and we haven't found the answer there yet," Bradley commented in an interview with *Black Enterprise*. "Part of our strategy is to bring together the different governmental agencies that deal with this problem of criminal justices—the probation department, the police department, the youth authority for schools—and the community to try to help us get a handle on it."[27]

Agencies that fell under the MOCJP's planning umbrella ranged from law enforcement such as the LAPD and the Los Angeles Sheriff's Department (LASD) to those concerned with juvenile delinquency including the California Youth Authority, the Probation Department, and the Los Angeles Unified School District (LAUSD). By bringing a "wide spectrum of community groups and agencies concerned with the criminal justice system" into conversation, the MOCJP facilitated the development of a robust system aimed at crime control, rehabilitation and diversion, and containment and incarceration.[28]

The MOCJP reflected concerns that LEAA funds had not been used for alternatives to punishment. Less than 10 percent of the city's federal criminal justice planning funding, MOCJP officials warned, had gone to "diversionary programs and other programs which seek to deal with offenders outside the formal criminal justice system or through other means."[29] To address the lack of comprehensive programming, the MOCJP developed the city's first criminal justice plan. Prior to Bradley's tenure, the city did not have a crime control plan, which meant that the city's criminal justice system was a result of "ad hoc solutions and political responses to individual situations," that, according to the MOCJP, undermined the city's crime control efforts.[30] The MOCJP's approach reconciled competing criminal justice solutions of punishment and diversion through interagency cooperation and program development.

Increasing citizen participation in the criminal justice system underpinned the MOCJP, its programs, and Bradley's approach to fighting crime more broadly. "It is my conviction that until we can overcome the public's lethargy and feeling of helplessness against the rising tide of crime by actively involving our citizens in the complex systems which deal with that crime," Bradley explained, "lawlessness in our streets will continue to increase."[31] The programs developed by the MOCJP emphasized citizen involvement, and included support for neighborhood watch, domestic violence prosecution, substance abuse and drug treatment, and pretrial intervention programs. Although most of these programs were presented as alternatives to incarceration, Bradley was committed to punishing law-breaking, especially violent crime, even as his administration developed different avenues of redress for less-serious offenders.[32]

Many of the MOCJP's programs reflected growing fears of youth- and school-related violence. As the MOCJP's 1978 crime attitude survey revealed, juvenile crime topped the list of concerns among residents and criminal justice officials.[33] The MOCJP focused on preempting future crime by enhancing the juvenile justice system. "For the first time in our history," Bradley proclaimed in his 1975 State of the City address, "the Mayor's office is taking responsibility for dealing directly with juvenile delinquency . . . that aspect of Criminal Justice Planning that has so often been ignored, but which common sense tells us is the breeding ground for tomorrow's hardened criminals."[34] The juvenile justice system that developed worked in tandem with the adult system to treat hard-core juvenile delinquents as potential criminals.

Initially, the intent of juvenile justice reforms was to reaffirm a distinction between the treatment of child and adult offenders. As the MOCJP suggested, the juvenile court was established not to administer hard justice but to act as a "superparent," following the doctrine of parens patriae, which framed juvenile crime as a delinquent response to social conditions and required the state to act as a surrogate parent to reform wayward children. "Any offenses that a juvenile committed were supposedly done as a result of environmental problems instead of placing individual responsibility on the person," MOCJP officials explained. "Therefore, the intent of the statutes was to allow the court and other social agencies to act in the 'best interests' of the child." By providing education, diversion, and intervention opportunities, MOCJP officials hoped children would avoid criminal stigmatization of the adult courts.[35] The efforts to create a juvenile justice program paired rehabilitative and punitive strategies that, while they seemed to be alternatives, complemented one another. Although rehabilitative programs also allowed for removal of youngsters who committed serious offenses, the preventive goal of many of the MOCJP's early programs targeted a wide range of youth as potential criminals and provided a basis for the extension of crime control measures into areas previously separated from the formal juvenile justice system.[36]

The juvenile prevention projects intended to identify and divert potentially delinquent youth away from the formal juvenile justice system. The primary program, funded with a startup grant from the California Youth Authority in 1974, was Human Efforts at Revitalizing Youth (HEAVY). Initially Project HEAVY created two nonprofit corporations, one in Central City and another in the San Fernando Valley, focused on predominantly African American and Latino/a police divisions where juvenile crime was highest.[37] The project began as a response to requests from the California Youth Authority to develop a "model diversion program" for young offenders. After receiving initial California Youth Authority funding, Project HEAVY incorporated as a nonprofit organization that received funds from LEAA and juvenile delinquency prevention grants in order to "provide alternatives and hope in preventing the cycle of crime and despair."[38]

But the support from the LEAA and the Juvenile Justice and Delinquency Prevention Act of 1974 meant that much of HEAVY's program was funded by money earmarked for criminal justice activities. As HEAVY's organizers reported, 51 percent of the funding had to be oriented toward criminal justice. It could not be a community action agency modeled on the Great Society programs of the 1960s. Even as HEAVY emphasized rehabilitation, it placed such programs under the umbrella of the criminal justice system and augmented the system's growth. Although ostensibly focused on rehabilitation for all youth, HEAVY also contributed to the segmentation of youth offenders into categories of less and more serious, which required and legitimated different treatment. By diverting "carefully screened delinquent and 'predelinquent' youth," HEAVY enabled the use of the more punitive policy of incarceration and detention for the serious offender.[39]

The HEAVY program provided a "total community approach" to the problem of youth crime in Los Angeles. Combining the mayor's office, city council, county supervisors, police, courts, and probation and school officials, HEAVY represented an effort to create a more comprehensive crime control program based on diversion and rehabilitation. The program meant to end the cycle of youth leaving and entering the juvenile justice system by intervening in the lives of at-risk children and teenagers. Intervention workers would steer youth away from gang activity and the criminal justice system and into more productive pursuits, such as job training and recreation programs.[40] "The Project as proposed," the grant application stated, "will establish a system through which carefully screened delinquent and pre-delinquent youth will be diverted from the formal criminal justice system to rehabilitative opportunities and services in the community."[41] While the rehabilitation programs associated with HEAVY were certainly more preferable to punitive policies of incarceration, in effect Project HEAVY extended the reach of the police and juvenile justice system into many more lives.

Project HEAVY focused on keeping kids out of the criminal justice system. Rather than providing direct services, Project HEAVY operated by purchasing services from preexisting community-based treatment, counseling, mental health, job training, and employment agencies for select youth offenders who were yet to be considered hard-core. The project operated on three tiers, which included diversion to community agencies that provided rehabilitation services, a gang consortium to address gang violence, and pretrial intervention to provide alternatives, such as employment, to incarceration in juvenile detention facilities that officials believed contributed to lifelong criminal activity. The Pre-Trial Intervention Project, for example, offered vocational training and job placement for at-risk kids and first-time offenders. Upon completion, the participant would be eligible for dismissal of charges and return to the community. By its second action year, Project HEAVY/Central City reported that over 1,500 children and teenagers had been diverted into HEAVY projects and agencies. The combined projects, MOCJP officials believed, were also "in the process of a rounding out

HEAVY's attempt to place rehabilitation ahead of incarceration as means to combating crime."[42]

By 1978, the city and county had developed a region-wide network of youth diversion services headlined by HEAVY. Many of the programs received grant funds throughout the 1970s from state and federal sources amounting to a region-wide total of nearly $5 million. Such programs were relatively successful. Studies found that the Youth Services Network, the confederation of Youth Services Projects aimed at diversion in the county, treated over 10,000 youth per year. This was roughly 21 percent of the total serious offense pool, although the LAPD and Los Angeles Sheriff's Department referred only 6 percent of the youth they arrested. Project HEAVY in the San Fernando Valley, for example, aimed to provide services for 1,200 kids annually and helped reduce youth arrests by 21 percent between 1975 and 1977.[43] But even as figures showed that diversion rates from all referring agencies in the county, including schools and self-referrals, were nearly 20 percent of the offender pool, those kids arrested by the LAPD or other law enforcement agencies were less likely to be transferred to diversion programs. The LAPD referral rate, for example, rose steadily from the 1.9 percent of youth arrests in 1973 to a high of nearly 10 percent in 1977, but declined to 6 percent in 1980 and 4.5 percent in 1981.[44] Although diversionary programs had a positive impact on some of the kids they reached, and helped reduce arrests in project areas, the programs often had only a marginal impact on the number of youngsters sent to probation. The MOCJP believed that "many more juveniles apprehended by the Los Angeles Police Department could be referred to community social or treatment agencies."[45]

Commitments to prevention, diversion, and rehabilitation did not replace demands for more punishment of young offenders. Diversion programs often had the greatest impact on those offenders who committed the least severe offenses—those who were likely to have been counseled and released by the police—reinforcing a stratified juvenile justice system. Indeed, programs meant to divert at-risk kids from the juvenile court were designed as part of a comprehensive juvenile justice system that combined social services and penal institutions. More significantly, because the diversionary programs actively excluded the so-called serious offender, they complemented a growing imperative of the juvenile justice system to punish through incarceration and removal from the community. Such complementarity between intervention programs and juvenile detention was endemic to liberal law and order. Prevention, diversion, and rehabilitation, in other words, were crucial elements in a juvenile justice system based on a dual strategy of social service and penal approaches that, when combined, drove the development of the city and county's carceral complex. The programs structured a bifurcated juvenile justice system that treated offenders differently by class, race, and geography.

Zero Tolerance

Before liberal politicians adopted law-and-order policies targeting the city's youth, school administrators, such as Superintendent Jack Crowther and his successor William Johnston, sought ways to maintain control over what they believed were increasingly disorderly and unruly schools. School officials were particularly concerned with protests in predominantly African American and Mexican American schools in the late 1960s. Mexican American students involved in the 1968 East Los Angeles blowouts and African American students in the strike at Jefferson School in 1969 demanded better schools, fought for more control over decision-making and curriculum, and opposed discriminatory treatment by teachers and administrators.[46]

Teachers and administrators, mostly white, pushed for more punitive policies and more police on school campuses. The Board of Education passed a motion on March 9, 1968, in the middle of the East Los Angeles blowouts, encouraging the superintendent to seek injunctive relief whenever he felt necessary. The move, which narrowed the role of teachers in disciplinary practices, was a response to principals and teachers who pushed the board to centralize disciplinary policy at the district level, to beef up security on campuses, and to enact punitive measures for disruptions.[47]

What was intended as a limit on the power of teachers to discipline students turned into an expansion of discretionary supervision by the police over potentially violent youth. In 1969, the LAPD, with support from the Los Angeles Unified School District (LAUSD), issued policies giving officers authority to enter schools and put down "unlawful" or disorderly activity. The board also adopted a "get-tough" policy against disruptions. "It [the board] cannot allow acts of violence or intimidation to exist on any of our school campuses," Superintendent Crowther stated. "We are prepared to move to the full extent of the law—against students and nonstudents alike—in those cases where disruptive acts threaten the safety of children and others."[48]

In its response to student protest, the LAUSD administrators facilitated the incorporation of the police into the city's schools. The board coordinated with Chief Davis to develop plans to maintain discipline and order. They also promoted a joint LAPD-LAUSD program, begun in 1969 at David Starr Jordan High School in Watts, which brought officers into schools to teach a course called "Police Role in Government." The program, framed as a way to enhance youth understanding of the police, focused on teaching predominantly black and brown youth proper behavior and "the rules he [the student] is expected to live by." Bringing uniformed officers into schools, the program expanded the authority of the police in new ways. Under pressure from school administrators, the board also increased the presence of police on school campuses during the 1970s because teachers, according to Superintendent William Johnston, "are encountering extreme difficulty maintaining an atmosphere of law and order on campus and report that they are spending virtually all of their school day in this effort."[49]

The Board of Education also expanded the district's police force. Numbering only fifteen officers in 1964, by 1969 the Security Section had 102 full-time agents, and it continued to grow. In 1974 the section operated on a budget of $4.5 million, and it employed 138 full-time agents trained by the Los Angeles Sheriff's Department, six supervising agents, fifty off-duty police officers, and 104 campus safety aides. By 1977 the Security Section's budget had increased to $7 million, and the number of uniformed officers expanded to over 400 in 1977. This growth made the LAUSD security force the fourth largest law enforcement agency in the county.[50] Educators responded to what they believed were growing problems of crime in schools by abandoning their disciplinary responsibilities to security officers who had no role in the education of students.[51]

National newsmagazines routinely described Los Angeles high schools as spaces of crime, violence, and terror. The focus on LAUSD schools highlighted Los Angeles as a national exemplar of the expansion of police power into new areas of social life.[52] Police officials described the violence as a new type of criminal behavior among young African Americans that could be solved only through arrest, punishment, and containment. According to Chief Davis, "the current, new phenomenon of killing someone you have never seen before on the street, by a juvenile, that is a new phenomenon in the black community." Crimes on school premises increased 23 percent in 1973, with assaults on school grounds up nearly 39 and 79 percent for crimes involving firearms on school grounds.[53] Such conditions made education all but impossible. By 1975, Assistant School Superintendent William L. Lucas reported of some 143 gangs in LAUSD schools, leading staff and students to be "intimidated by gang members."[54] The only way to reduce gang activity, Davis asserted, "is through an effective Criminal Justice System."[55] Such views reinforced a growing consensus that the hard-core youth offender was beyond saving.

School administrators blamed the rehabilitation imperative for the explosion of violence on school campuses. The principal of Washington High School, Eugene McAdoo, explained, "The community rehabilitation program is a farce." The tragedy, he added, was "that I, as an educator, should stand here and say some of our young people should be in institutions, but security on our campuses is the problem in our schools today. Not curriculum or new approaches to teaching." Rather than providing programs that some youth demanded to address deteriorating housing, crumbling schools, insufficient recreational facilities, and poor jobs, police, school administrators, and political officials called for an end to a revolving-door system that allowed hard-core youth back onto the streets to "infect" other innocent youth.[56] Such views reinforced a consensus that hard-core offenders could not be saved through rehabilitation and so there was no point in trying.

School administrators responded with enhanced zero-tolerance policies. In the fall of 1972, Superintendent Johnston handed down a rule that made bringing a weapon to campus an automatic suspension and the beginning of expulsion proceedings.[57] Expulsions for the possession of a gun or a knife increased from one in the 1971–72 school year to twenty-five in 1972–73.[58] The impact of these new policies, framed as a district-wide measure, however, targeted a problem that fell disproportionately on black youth, as 80 percent of those expulsions were of black students. Although similar policies aimed at drug sales on school grounds led to the arrest and expulsion of white students in suburban schools through an undercover "school buy program," LAUSD policy reinforced a stratified treatment of offenders. When undercover busts led to forty-three arrests at six predominantly white senior high schools in 1975, for example, students were allowed to complete final examinations and receive grades and diplomas, an option unavailable in black and Latino/a schools.[59]

In 1974 Bradley made good on his campaign promise to increase school security, establishing new security systems in six predominantly black schools in South Central.[60] The beefing up of security did not go unnoticed by school officials or students. Administrators at inner-city high schools described their campuses as being surrounded by mesh fences, padlocked gates, technological alarm systems, armed guards, and helicopter patrols. The predominantly African American Crenshaw High School was nicknamed "Ft. Crenshaw."[61] By 1979 there was a clear pattern of discriminatory "deployment and practices of school security in predominantly Black schools." Whereas inner-city black schools were "prison-like" and employed repressive disciplinary policies, according to the LAUSD's Black Education Commission, predominately white high schools in the Valley had open campuses, fewer security agents, and an absence of regimentation. The increased security measures, however, did not coincide with the severity or number of the offenses, as many Valley schools experienced similar rates of assaults and drug offenses as those in South Central. The two-tiered school security system solidified the converging interests of school administrators and police.[62]

Cooperative police-school programs aimed at monitoring hard-core and at-risk youth, often before they committed a delinquent act. One measure meant for such deterrence was the Disposition Data Coordination Project (DDCP). Initiated in late 1973, the DDCP was a cooperative program between the LAPD and LAUSD to keep track of groups of what the LAPD defined as "hard-core" and "at-risk" kids in South Central. In effect, the DDCP served as a means of monitoring black children and teenagers. The DDCP database, also known as the "Alpha File," was a racist police practice targeting particular neighborhoods and groups for monitoring. Such race- and space-based policing reinforced racialized assumptions of criminality. The project, ostensibly intended to reduce juvenile crime and truancy, not only threatened to treat all black youth as criminals or potential criminals but also made the database public, revealing the names of kids identified as potentially dangerous.[63]

Although city officials believed that the DDCP would provide information necessary to make appropriate decisions about the disposition of juvenile cases, the program's focus on spatial monitoring operated on racialized assumptions of criminality. Rose Ochi, director of the MOCJP, while supporting the DDCP, warned, "Monitoring, which is beyond the scope of legitimate law enforcement agency's activities, is going to be employed nevertheless."[64] The LAUSD's director of Urban Programs, Walter Parker, recognized that the DDCP could easily be viewed as discriminatory because it directly targeted black youth. Residents were unlikely to support the DDCP because, according to Parker, of the "repressive discriminatory matter of the project being concentrated in only certain minority areas in the city."[65]

The American Civil Liberties Union filed a class action suit on behalf of two black students and their parents to prevent compiling, maintaining, and disseminating the Alpha File. The American Civil Liberties Union argued that the project was racist in its targeting of South Central youth and enlisted agencies including Parks and Recreation, the school board, and the Los Angeles Housing Authority with the task of surveillance. More directly, the American Civil Liberties Union asserted that the two black youth were unfairly targeted "based upon the alleged observation of their commission of a 'violent' act not necessarily introduced into the criminal justice system by means of arresting, booking, incarceration and/or diversion prior to arresting, or upon their being identified as a 'gang leader,' 'hard-core gang offender,' 'murderous young person,' or 'hoodlum.'"[66] The city council proposed strict guidelines to avoid potential abuse, and City Attorney Burt Pines approved the program. Due to the publicity surrounding the Alpha File and concerns of violation of privacy, however, the department decided to "let it die a natural death" and stopped adding names to the database in the summer of 1974.[67] Although framed as a preventive measure to stop youth crime, the DDCP reflected the ways the city's two-tiered response to juvenile justice increasingly criminalized black kids through surveillance and monitoring.

Locking up the Kids

If the Alpha File was meant to help the department prevent crime by monitoring potentially delinquent youth, the emergence of specialized anti-gang police units became a more violent and overt example of the use of police power to contain black youth. Chief Davis, for example, committed a one hundred–man task force to combat gang violence in 1972. This task force developed along a Total Resources approach to address the gang and violence problems in the 77th Street Division and on school campuses through integrated criminal justice and social service measures. The development of the Total Resources program built on the LAPD's success in "identification and apprehension of the violent hardcore," but on the belief that "a broader approach was necessary." The initial model was to bring all elements, such as the police, probation, courts, schools, and community, together to address gang violence.[68]

The LAPD initiated the Total Resources Against South Bureau Hoodlums (TRASH) unit in 1973, which consisted of thirty-eight officers who specialized in juvenile crime, and targeted the predominantly African American 77th Street Area and Southwest Area. The TRASH units were renamed Community Resources against Street Hoodlums (CRASH) after community pressure forced them to change the name due to the negative connotations of the acronym. Regardless of the name, CRASH became the LAPD's elite antigang unit and was part of a nationwide investment in elite paramilitary-style police units. CRASH officers functioned as an aggressive assault-type unit meant to break up gangs by arresting and removing gang members from the streets. As the LAPD's Juvenile Division commander Clyde Cronkhite explained to the California State Assembly Select Committee on Juvenile Violence in 1974, "Our emphasis . . . is to remove those hard-cores from the community. . . . And that is a big part of what CRASH is doing in the community."[69]

Support for CRASH revealed the converging demand for police power as council members' district interests encouraged them to build up police programs. The LAPD organized CRASH units in response to demands from residents in other areas of the city, such as a temporary unit in the Oakwood neighborhood of Venice, during the summer of 1978. Residents in the San Fernando Valley also pressured city officials for a unit.[70] Although Bradley threatened to reduce CRASH personnel in 1979 due to budget constraints after the passage of Proposition 13, the council allocated funds for a new Valley unit.[71] By 1981, the South Bureau CRASH unit consisted of fifty-seven officers, and the department established a permanent thirty-man unit in West Los Angeles. The CRASH approach contributed to the police-oriented solution to juvenile crime. The units, as a South Bureau CRASH report explained in 1981, "gained a reputation of aggressive crime suppression."[72]

Monitoring known and potential gang members shaped the CRASH approach. In order to maintain surveillance, CRASH established a file to track known and potential gang members in 1976. The LAPD intended the CRASH file "to enhance the LAPD's ability to protect the public from gang-related crimes." This effort at protection included "prevention and detection of gang-related crimes and the apprehension of suspected gang criminals." Officers kept cards on "suspected gang members," who had not participated in any gang-related crime, leading to the addition of many files on kids with no gang ties but who lived in active gang neighborhoods. A "suspected gang member," for example, meant "a juvenile or adult who is believed to be a gang member, but who has not actively participated in any gang-related crime." CRASH guidelines allowed parents to inquire about their child's inclusion in the file. But the names would not be removed, and "the fact of such protest shall be entered on the file card."[73]

Gang activity was common among all young Angelinos, yet officials focused on African American and Latino/a kids and teenagers. One early CRASH manual on gangs from the late 1970s devoted only minimal attention to white and Asian gangs, while providing thorough details of black and Latino/a gangs. Although most black and Latino/a youth were not gang members, police gang manuals provided descriptions of gang members that could readily apply to all black and Latino/a kids. One early manual, for example, instructed officers to identify Latino/a gang members by clothing such as the wearing of "the Pendleton shirt," "the round or V-neck T-shirt," or shoes that "range from tennis shoes to french-toed shoes." Similar indicators of black gang activity included descriptions such as, "The Black gang member likes to wear the black T-shirt rather than the white T-shirt"; gang members' pants were described as "usually jeans with rolled-up cuffs," and their "shoes range from canvas Crocker Sacks to shiny leather shoes."[74]

Compared with other elite units across the country, CRASH had long staying power. By the 1980s, the CRASH unit's monitoring criminalized all black and brown youth as potential gang members. When the Valley CRASH unit began using intelligence-gathering strategies, such as random street interviews and photographing suspected gang members, to combat gang

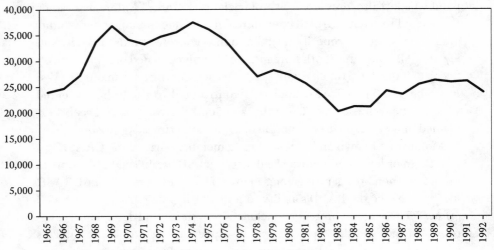

Total juvenile arrests in Los Angeles, 1965–1992. Source: LAPD *Statistical Digests*, 1965–1992.

violence, the unit swept up many innocent Latino/a kids and teenagers. The police were, according to one activist, creating criminals by "stopping people illegally, taking photographs against their will and turning anybody who looked like a gang member into a potential suspect." Although Captain Lawrence Fetters praised the CRASH approach to detention and questioning as the "best tool yet" for rooting out gang violence, residents and activists had a different view. With the help of the American Civil Liberties Union, Latino/a residents from the Valley won a preliminary injunction against the picture-taking of nonconsenting minority youth as an illegal search and seizure. Notwithstanding this initial victory, CRASH procedures pointed to the development of a two-tiered system of juvenile justice system. "Police think they can hassle a bunch of Latino kids hanging around on a Canoga Park street corner, but they wouldn't bother a bunch of white kids with surfboards hanging around Ventura Boulevard," Magdalena Duran, director of El Proyecto del Barrio, stated. "We feel that distinction very keenly."[75]

While arrests of juveniles increased in the early 1970s, they decreased after 1975. The overall reduction in juvenile arrests reflected a general decline in adult arrests during the same period but also the increased attention to monitoring, arresting, and detaining the "hard-core" youth offender. Waging war on youth gangs, for example, rested on the selective enforcement of juvenile laws in predominantly African American and Latino/a neighborhoods. Nancy Boyarsky, a reporter for the *Los Angeles Times*, found that police, the

South Central CRASH unit in particular, used the city's curfew law to "selectively scoop up and arrest tough-looking black youths." In the rest of the city, "curfew-violators are taken to the station and quickly released to their parents. But this is not the practice for children of the ghetto. . . . Inner city curfew violators usually end up for a few days' stay at the county's juvenile hall." Although LAPD leadership denied that officers used curfew laws to target black youth—a violation of the spirit of juvenile laws to treat all children as individuals—one CRASH officer operating in South Central admitted, "We send all our curfews to the hall." As Boyarsky sarcastically concluded, "One way to stop juvenile delinquency is to lock up all the kids."[76]

Closing the Revolving Door and the Stratification of Juvenile Justice

Support for zero-tolerance policies widened the gap between rehabilitative and punitive approaches. Yet, for both liberals and conservatives, these programs failed to address the limits of legal authority to incarcerate violent youth and prevent a revolving-door system. Of particular concern to politicians and law enforcement was the young "hard-core" offender. These kids cycled through the juvenile justice system only to be repeatedly released by juvenile court judges. The LAPD maintained a list of 613 hard-core juvenile offenders whom they believed accounted for 9,287 arrests in 1973, including one individual who had been arrested sixty-two times.[77] The violent, repeat offender, many believed, was responsible for the growth in youth crime.

Violent crime committed by kids and teenagers, local authorities believed, was on the rise in the early 1970s. Clyde Cronkhite, the LAPD's Juvenile Division commander, reported that between 1972 and 1973, Los Angeles experienced a 168 percent increase in youth arrests for felonies and a 220 percent increase in arrests for violent crimes. The inadequacy of the juvenile justice system's carceral capacity was to blame. "At the root of this problem," Cronkhite explained, "is the failure of city and county to place appropriate importance on the handling of juvenile offenders." Solving the juvenile crime crises was crucial to preventing the development of future, lifelong criminals.[78] Legislative proposals for a new juvenile court law allowing for more discretion and punitive approaches to the hard-core offender contributed to the differential treatment of kids by race and geography.

Since its inception in the early twentieth century, the California juvenile justice system operated on the philosophy of community rehabilitation. It was distinct from the adult court and meant to avoid marking children with a stigma of criminality by operating under the doctrine of parens patriae. Under this system, juvenile offenders did not receive due process protections. During the 1960s and 1970s, however, the legal basis of the juvenile justice system shifted after the passage of California's 1961 Arnold-Kennick Juvenile Court Law and the 1967 *In re Gault* Supreme Court decision. Together, Arnold-Kennick and the *Gault* decision cemented a new juvenile justice philosophy based on protecting children in court proceedings through the guarantee of due process rights. These reforms were liberal initiatives meant to safeguard the legal right of children to counsel and due process in juvenile courts.[79]

But liberals and conservatives alike blamed the rise of youth crime during the first half of the 1970s on the permissiveness of the system created by the *Gault* decision. Abandoning the argument that the juvenile justice system was arbitrary and unfair, they charged that it had transformed the system into one akin to the adult criminal court based on adversarial proceedings. The due process protections accorded children, according to liberal County Board of Supervisors member Kenneth Hahn and others, enabled hard-core offenders to escape punishment and thereby created a revolving-door policy that released offenders onto the streets.[80] Chief Davis blamed the juvenile justice system's failures on a "new system of turnstyle justice" which resulted from *Gault* and the state's probation subsidy program that provided $4,000 for every offender sent to the county jail or released straight to probation. He suggested that lenient sentencing and early release for probation, especially for kids who learned to game the system, did little to deter or rehabilitate criminals. Rather, longer sentences were the means to reducing crime. At the same moment when state officials began expanding the California prison system, Los Angeles officials turned to solutions that would fill the new penal capacity with black and brown youth.[81] By reforming the juvenile court law to allow for greater discretion to detain youth offenders, a strategy with bipartisan support, officials hoped to reduce recidivism.

The growth in juvenile crime overburdened the juvenile court, making the revolving door worse. The juvenile justice system was, City Attorney Burt Pines stated, "frankly faced with imminent collapse." Pines explained that an overworked juvenile justice system led to an increase in crime and violence because kids were not sent to the California Youth Authority or other institutions for detention. "I believe there is a direct relationship between the overloading of the Juvenile Justice System and the marked increase in juvenile crime and violence," Pines explained. "Juveniles tend to have a sense, or feeling, about the availability of discipline and how to get around it." The overburdened juvenile system meant that offenders were often released onto the street, where they "infected" innocent children to commit crimes.[82] Law enforcement and political officials proposed that the juvenile system move away from a primary goal of protecting young offenders from the adverse effects of the adult system and toward a greater concern for the safety of the community. This shift meant that punishment, largely through incarceration rather than diversion, would become a cornerstone of the juvenile justice system.

Officials lamented that the juvenile courts did not have proper legislative authority to punish offenders appropriately. "We must handle the juvenile offender," District Attorney Joseph P. Busch suggested, "with the concept that if you break the law you get punished."[83] Proposed solutions focused on separating the "hard-core" offenders, who were predominantly black and Latino/a, from less serious offenders. "The Court must use its influence to effect [sic] a system of segregation," a widely circulated juvenile court "crisis report" developed by local law enforcement and criminal justice officials explained, "to separate detained 'hard core' offenders from minor offenders and non-delinquents detained in Juvenile Hall."[84] The legislative reforms that Busch helped develop were based on this bifurcated approach to juvenile justice and, through the choice of targets, constructed racial and ethnic minorities as criminal while decriminalizing those offenses largely committed by white youth.

The problem, according to local officials, was the emphasis on diversion and rehabilitation rather than incarceration. Serious offenders remained on the street, an LAPD report to the city council suggested, "because of the emphasis on community based rehabilitation." Over time, the report suggested, juveniles learned that the system was a "do nothing" system with few penalties or disciplinary measures. Officials pointed to the juvenile court sending fewer cases to the CYA as evidence for the lack of punishment. Councilman Arthur Snyder reported that the Juvenile Court sent 80 percent fewer cases to the CYA in 1973 than in 1965 despite the increase in juvenile crime. "We need," Snyder suggested, "a new philosophy of how juvenile offenders should be treated by society."[85]

The new philosophy required get-tough policies and a punitive philosophy previously only present in the adult system. The proposed changes would move the juvenile system away from the primary goal of protecting young offenders from the adverse effects of the adult system and toward a greater concern for the safety of the community. "Primary consideration must be given to the protection and welfare of the public," Chief Davis explained. "Only when gang members continually experience swift, certain and positive action will the justice system deter rather than encourage the commission of violent crimes."[86] Following recommendations that punishment was a necessary goal of the juvenile justice system, the council passed motions in support of the passage of strict policies by the state legislature. The council's Police, Fire and Civil Defense Committee issued a statement recommending that the state legislature "change current juvenile court law so that incarceration can be recognized as a means of rehabilitation and that the safety and protection of the community must be considered in handling juvenile delinquents."[87]

Liberals such as Hahn and Bradley lent support to such legislative changes allowing greater discretion in handling hard-core offenders but did not adopt a wholesale punitive war on inner-city youth as they would during the 1980s. Though Bradley supported punishing youth crime with incarceration, he continued to be committed to rehabilitative measures.[88] "Unless the courts understand that we have simply got to remove some of the hard-core offenders from the community where they can infect others or intimidate others we are going to fight a losing battle on this issue," Bradley commented during city council hearings. Although Bradley advocated removal for "rehabilitation and some training," his stance emphasized social services for some offenders because they complemented, rather than replaced, confinement for others. "I would hope we can isolate those few—and they are only a few hundred—remove them to some place where they can receive some rehabilitation and some training."[89] The bipartisan support for get-tough policies, Snyder summarized, "reflected an increased demand for reform by the electorate."[90]

Responding to demands for juvenile justice reform by the city council members and law enforcement officials, Julian Dixon, an African American assemblyman representing South Central, introduced legislation to the California State Legislature to overhaul the juvenile court system. It reflected the converging interests supporting the dual-sided approach to juvenile justice developed in Los Angeles.[91] The legislation, which was titled A.B. 3121, amended California Welfare and Institutions Code 707 to reduce the penalty for status offenses, such as truants or runaways, while adding a section easing the transfer of other sixteen- and seventeen-year-olds to the adult criminal justice system. Those youths who committed violent crimes or felonies, and whom the Probation Department deemed unfit for the services of the juvenile court, could be transferred to adult court. Although A.B. 3121 did not allow an automatic removal of all sixteen- and seventeen-year-old offenders accused of committing violent crimes to adult courts as some legislators had hoped, it represented a move toward treating children as adults and wedded the juvenile system closer to the adult criminal justice system.[92] As one researcher found, "the legislation represents a well known trend away from a rehabilitation focus toward a 'get tough' focus within the juvenile court."[93]

The legislation transformed the treatment of youth in Los Angeles and California more broadly. Within the first five years of implementation, reports found that kids charged with violent crime were incarcerated at higher levels and for longer periods of time. For status offenders, however, the contact with the juvenile justice system resulted in either counseling or diversion.[94] The impact of A.B. 3121's adult court transfer provision fell disproportionately on children of color. In 1978, for example, of the 137 kids sent to adult court from Los Angeles, Mexican Americans represented 30 percent, blacks 66 percent, whites 27 percent, and others 2 percent. In the rest of the state, out of the 809 cases transferred to adult courts, Mexican Americans accounted for 27 percent, blacks 21 percent, whites 46 percent, and others 3 percent.[95] The Los Angeles numbers were not only higher than for the state as a whole but were also disproportionate in comparison to the county's demographics. In 1980, non-Hispanic whites accounted for 67.1 percent of the county population, African Americans 10.8 percent, Latinos/as 18.3, and others 3.1 percent.[96]

Over time, the gap between the two sides of the juvenile justice system widened. By the mid-1980s, black and Latino/a kids were significantly more likely to be arrested and treated harshly than were white kids. The two-tiered system established by A.B. 3121 led to the disparities. Youth of color were more likely to be categorized as hard-core offenders, while the majority of kids arrested for status offenses were white. "Black and Latino youth are generally tracked into the most punitive level of the system, comprised of government administered correctional facilities," the Los Angeles County Human Relations Committee summarized at hearings on the impact of the juvenile justice reforms. In contrast, white kids were "generally placed in treatment and educationally oriented levels of the system comprised of group homes, halfway houses and training schools, or in private psychiatric hospitals."[97]

———

Throughout the 1970s, local officials, operating on the basis of a liberal law-and-order vision of criminal justice, combined social service and punitive solutions to juvenile crime. Even as liberals succeeded in including diversion and rehabilitation as central elements of the juvenile justice system, such approaches complemented more punitive policies because they operated under the purview of the criminal justice system and thereby contributed to the expansion of the carceral state. Over time, however, the critique of community rehabilitation by advocates of more punitive approaches enabled more punishment. While on the decline in the second half of the 1970s, the reemergence of gang violence in the 1980s reinforced the belief that the philosophy of community rehabilitation not only was inadequate but also contributed to criminal activity. The solution to the violence was rooted not in structural understandings of a city undergoing economic and social changes but more punishment. The shift prompted stronger get-tough stances by city and county officials who had maintained a commitment to diversion and rehabilitation programs in the juvenile justice system throughout the 1970s.

The expansion of Los Angeles's juvenile justice institutions had a disproportionate impact on African American and Latino/a kids and teenagers and signaled the striking expansion of the state's prison system. The policy choices at the local and state levels created a two-tiered juvenile justice system that treated certain kids more harshly than others. While many white kids were defined as status offenders, the system focused policing and punishment on black and Latino/a kids. The network of services and institutions that came out of the building of the juvenile justice regime, in other words, was increasingly used to punish rather than to reform. The changes, seemingly benign in their intent, made the juvenile justice system present in the daily lives of black and Latino/a kids.

Alongside the MOCJP's oversight of the criminal justice system and crime control, Bradley's liberal law and order also focused on remaking the relationships between government and the police and between the police and residents. As the police took on new and expanded roles to ensure continued discretionary supervision over so-called hard-core criminals, Bradley intended to ensure an end to discriminatory practices. Through community-based policing, Bradley and the LAPD hoped to restore confidence in the police. While Bradley actively used the power of the mayor's office to assert more control over the police department, limitations on his power to enforce changes in the relationship between the police and residents narrowed the possibilities of reform. As police violence and autonomy remained a fact of life for black and brown residents, it produced new coalitions and possibilities to limit police power during the 1970s.

Chapter 5

Police Crimes and Power Abuses

Police Reform and Anti–Police Abuse Movements

When police officials formed the Operations–South Bureau Community Resources against Street Hoodlums (CRASH) Unit in 1981, they expanded the reach of the department's authority to monitor those residents—especially young African American and Latino/a men—they believed required intensified supervision. The unit included a School Car Program, a Rapid Transit Carrier stop-and-search division, a detective section, and a uniformed gang suppression division. These programs brought officers into routine contact with youth. Over the course of 1981, for example, CRASH school car personnel took 4,588 truants into custody, uniformed gang suppression officers made 2,058 arrests, the Rapid Transit patrol conducted 3,756 bus checks, and the detective section processed 1,011 arrestees—839 of whom were juveniles. All told, South Bureau CRASH made 16,534 contacts with residents in 1981 and added 3,069 names to gang intelligence files.[1] While intensified policing did not necessarily lead directly to arrest, the CRASH Unit enhanced the LAPD's ability and authority to monitor and supervise youth of color. In the process, CRASH officers developed an aggressive, "us versus them" reputation in their interactions with African American and Latino/a youth, sparking increased mistrust and opposition among residents of color.[2]

The integration of police units such as CRASH into service-providing institutions and schools during the 1970s led to renewed questions surrounding the limits of police authority and the need for police reform. Liberal law-and-order politics suggested that transforming the relationship between both the police and the citizenry and the police and the mayor's office would guarantee equitable police service for all the city's residents. While the Police Commission had the power to oversee the police department, the structure of municipal government provided the mayor little direct power over the police and granted the chief of police civil service protection. These limitations enabled Chief Ed Davis, and his successor Daryl Gates, to successfully resist systemic changes aimed at reducing the LAPD's authority. Yet pressure from Mayor Tom Bradley, the Police Commission, and residents led to successful reforms that diversified the officer corps, enhanced human relations training, and established a community-oriented policing philosophy based on increasing officer contact with residents. These approaches provided a semblance of community participation and fair law enforcement practices without limiting officer discretion or leading to greater civilian control of the department. Reform, in other words, largely focused on changing the community's perception of law enforcement, not the daily operation or actions of the police. As a result, these approaches did little to alter the fundamental issue of whom the police served and how the police served them.[3]

Activists responded to the limits of reform and expanded avenues of officer discretion by organizing a movement against police abuse. Formed in 1976, the Coalition against Police Abuse (CAPA) was a grassroots organization made up of African American and Latino/a activists who regarded the LAPD as an occupying force whose mission was to contain poor residents of color. CAPA focused on reducing police violence and the political autonomy of the police. These problems overlapped, but they drew together different political coalitions and produced different reform possibilities. CAPA was started by former members of the Black Panthers and Brown Berets. Its multiracial activism extended the black and brown freedom struggles into the 1980s. It initially represented working-class African Americans and Latinos/as' desires to reduce police political autonomy through community control of the police. Intensified police repression after Watts, the assault on Black Power and Chicano/a social movements, and the expansion of the city's criminal justice system generated distrust of state institutions, especially law enforcement, in both communities. Rejecting the idea that the LAPD could be reformed from within, black and brown activists organized for community control of the police to call attention to the LAPD's militarized operations and to fundamentally alter the relationship between residents and law enforcement.[4]

Between the late 1970s and early 1980s, CAPA drew in a broad-based group of political officials, middle-class African Americans, church leaders, civil rights organizations, and radical activists by concentrating on the more specific issue of confronting police violence. Police killings of African American and Latino/a residents galvanized political officials and middle-class residents in ways that more-radical demands for community control of the police had not. But this coalition was able to make changes only at the margins of the system that did not alter the balance of power between the community and the police. Police abuse mobilized participants across class lines, but its political grounding narrowed over time. Demands for accountability and justice were routed into liberal reforms by city and police officials focused on the most egregious forms of police violence rather than a more far-reaching agenda to alter decision-making or reduce the political autonomy of the LAPD. Although the anti–police abuse coalition challenged law-

and-order politics, its achievements were a far cry from visions of community control.

More Power than the Mayor

On July 13, 1973, less than two weeks after his mayoral inauguration, Tom Bradley looked out on the newest graduates of the LAPD academy. Congratulating the officers, Bradley told them that "after receiving the finest police training available, you are looking forward . . . to a career of public service in one of the most rewarding occupations a man can have." Stressing his own experience as an officer, Bradley also reminded them of their duty to carry out the work of law enforcement in a fair, equitable, and responsible manner. "You now share the tradition of providing the best possible Police [*sic*] service to the people of Los Angeles," Bradley explained. "And it is your responsibility to provide police service with compassion, understanding, common sense, and good judgment." Through greater understanding, communication, and openness with the city's residents, the police "can give equal and fair enforcement of the law everywhere in this city and . . . Police Officers can be responsive to the people they serve." Aligning himself with the officers, Bradley pledged that together they "will do all of this because the people of our great city want, expect, and demand that of us."[5]

Bradley intended to support the police within the framework of procedural fairness and equity. His administration intended to increase civilian authority of the police in hopes of beginning a larger reimagining of the relationships between the police and the citizenry and between the police and the mayor's office. But he faced significant obstacles that limited the impact of procedural reforms. The structure of municipal government limited the mayor's direct power over the police department and granted the police chief civil service protection, while Section 202 of the city charter conferred all power of discipline over officers to the chief. Because the chief wrote a self-evaluation on a yearly basis, there was never evidence of "just cause" for removal.[6] Criticism of the department was also politically risky, given white residents' strong support for the department. Although reforms based on procedural fairness were narrow by definition because they did not address systemic problems of police power, these political constraints limited Bradley's, and the city council's, ability—and willingness—to openly confront the department.[7]

The city charter did give the Board of Police Commissioners the authority to oversee and manage police department policy and to appoint the chief. Yet the board rarely took a stand against the department and often acted as a rubber stamp following the chief's directives. Charter rules that city departments, such as the police, would be run by general managers overseen by part-time mayoral appointees who had to be approved by the city council made police reform a difficult task.[8] As Chief Davis, who rose through the ranks under William Parker, quipped during the 1970s, "I don't want to be mayor of this city. That position has no power. I already have more power than the mayor."[9]

As Bradley had done with the Mayor's Office of Criminal Justice Planning, he hoped to use the power of the city government to exert control over the police department. Yet, Bradley's liberal law-and-order vision narrowed his reform agenda. Bradley's reforms rested on his belief in technocratic governance and faith in the power of the local state to properly regulate law enforcement. Such programs took the form of diversifying the police through affirmative action and appointments to the Board of Police Commissioners. By naming liberal commissioners, Bradley, a strong proponent of the civil service system, believed he could bring accountability to the police department without supporting systemic reforms that would require amending the city charter to limit the LAPD's independence from political oversight.[10]

The professional model of policing, combined with a city charter that granted the chief of police civil service protection, largely insulated the department from accountability to elected officials or external oversight. Discipline of officers was the domain of the chief of police. Officers believed that any external oversight or discipline hampered their ability to keep the city safe and contributed to the coddling of criminals. LAPD officers viewed themselves as professional crime fighters who knew more about the dangers of the streets and how to combat crime than those scrutinizing the department's policies, such as civil liberties groups, civil rights activists, and liberal politicians. As one official close to the department explained, "[The police] don't like to be interfered with by a bunch of people who have never been out in the streets or gone down dark alleys."[11]

Many liberal officials, Bradley in particular, avoided open confrontation and criticism of the LAPD over issues of brutality and harassment in order to not appear antipolice. Many residents feared rising crime rates and youth violence in schools, which shaped Bradley's agenda. After voicing support for law and order on his election night, Bradley recalled his hopes of assuring the department and the public "that we were not going to have any fulfilling of the prophecies or the statements of doom that the opposition had made, that we were going to work together, and we were going to work in the interest of the city." His police commission reinforced the effort to avoid confrontation with the police department to maintain support among residents skeptical of a black liberal's commitment to law and order. "Sam Yorty tried to exploit

[Bradley's race]," William Norris, the president of the police commission, affirmed, "to lead the people to believe that a black mayor would somehow undermine the effectiveness of law enforcement in this community. And we thought it was important to reassure the community—and the department—that Bradley believed in tough law enforcement." Strong law enforcement was not only a campaign commitment in response to electoral pressures but a key component of Bradley's vision for the city.[12]

Fulfilling his campaign promise to maintain a strong police department, Bradley supported the department's requests for, and the city council's allocation of, a high level of city funding to the LAPD. In 1972, for example, the LAPD's total operating cost was $198.5 million, which accounted for 35.5 percent of the city's budget. By 1982, the department's total operating cost increased to $525 million, but the percentage of the city budget declined slightly, to 34.9 percent. Pension reform in the 1980s reduced the overall proportion of funds allocated to the police, but the department continued to receive nearly half of the city's undedicated budget. Bradley and the city council also supported tax measures and budget appropriations that would increase the number of officers on the beat. During Bradley's two runs for governor in 1982 and 1986, aides promoted his tough-on-crime policies and asserted that Bradley had "consistently supported increases in the Police Department's budget."[13]

Although Bradley limited extravagant LAPD proposals to purchase equipment such as planes and submarines and pushed forward pension reform, any attempt to reduce the budget faced stiff opposition from Chief Davis, who was routinely able to get proposed budget reductions overturned. Davis once resorted to fear tactics warning residents to "bar their doors, buy a police dog, call us when we're available, and to pray," in order to convince the city council to maintain a high level of funding. Council members, responding to growing fears of crime in their districts and the political danger of appearing antipolice, often fully funded the department. The LAPD's large share of the city budget enabled the department to develop new elite patrol units, high-tech communication and patrol systems, and experimental crime control programs for inner-city neighborhoods.[14] As the department maintained and expanded its political authority and independence, it also responded to pressure for increased citizen participation and communication to reduce tension between the police and the community.

Civilian Participation without Control

African American residents demanded better policing to deal with fears of crime. A 1972 survey conducted by the LAPD, despite its limits as a source, revealed that black residents not only supported the police but also desired greater police protection and law enforcement resources to deal with the growth in the drug trade, crime, and violence.[15] Some of this sentiment reflected class divisions and a self-help ideology in the African American community as moderate civil rights organizations, such as the National Association for the Advancement of Colored People, cooperated with the LAPD to address crime and safety in the 77th Street Division. Ministerial councils worked with officers to hold meetings with residents and organized neighborhood watch programs.[16] Editorials in the city's African American newspaper, the *Los Angeles Sentinel*, also suggested that neighborhood block associations and neighborhood watch programs modeled on organizing in New York City provided an effective means of crime control and community action.[17]

Yet much as black residents wanted effective crime control, many were reluctant to strongly call for law and order. Anticrime measures too often translated into policies of "shoot first and ask questions later" by the police that eroded "confidence in equal law enforcement." Such a situation led to harassment, a lack of response to complaints of abuse, and targeting entire black communities as criminal. An editorial by *Los Angeles Sentinel* columnist Richard Allen, echoing Bradley, pushed for cooperation between the black community and the police as a more enlightened approach to addressing rising crime rates. He proposed the development of Inner City Crime Control Programs based on the theme of "Law and Order with Justice." The approach would require police officers to live in the neighborhoods they policed and would encourage elected officials to address the socioeconomic causes of crime, including unemployment, poor housing, and inaccessible transportation.[18]

Though crime and violence in black and Latino/a neighborhoods concerned residents, they also supported alternatives to police- and criminal justice–based solutions. Residents participated in programs that aimed to increase civilian involvement, empowerment, and control over criminal justice. The Model Neighborhood grant, for example, provided federal funds that enabled the Legal Aid Foundation to form the Greater Watts Justice Center in 1972 and the Mexican American Lawyers Club to launch the East Los Angeles–based Model Neighborhood Legal Center in 1971. Although the Greater Watts Justice Center and Model Neighborhood Legal Center merged social and penal institutions, in practice they provided resources for underserved residents to challenge punitive criminal justice policies. Both the Greater Watts Justice Center and Model Neighborhood Legal Center provided legal services, information, counseling, and representation to adults and juveniles in black and Latino/a neighborhoods, while also training residents to serve as "law advocates."[19] These organizations intended to give residents decision-making power over the criminal justice system. But liberal officials focused on empowering government to regulate the department's policies and implemented programs that expanded citizen participation without giving up department control or officer discretion.

Bradley understood the need for improved police-community relations and emphasized the necessity of citizen participation in all areas of the criminal justice system. He worked with the Metropolitan Council on Police-Community Relations to enhance cooperation between the police and residents. Addressing the organization in 1974, Bradley praised the LAPD's efforts to bring police out of patrol cars and onto the streets and reinforced his commitment to community involvement in criminal justice. "A city could become a jungle without effective law enforcement and without effective community support," Bradley explained, "for it is by this support that the capability of the police is increased and the respect of the police is increased." Bradley's reforms centered on making the police department the servant of the people rather than the master.[20]

Working with Bradley, Davis developed community-oriented policing programs meant to improve the relationship between the police, the public, and political officials. Davis suggested he would make the department "truly representative and responsive to the needs of the community it serves."[21] To facilitate a more responsive and representative department, Davis developed the Basic Car Plan (BCP). The BCP intended to bring the police out of patrol cars and onto the streets, where they could have more contact with residents. Davis hoped the BCP would improve communication between residents and the police. Officers were required to remain deployed in the same district for two to three years to work with, get to know, and develop trust within the community. Officers also held monthly meetings to gauge community sentiment and receive input from residents.[22]

The effectiveness of the BCP meetings differed based on neighborhood. Middle-class white residents were often more willing to attend BCP meetings than African American and Latino/a residents who distrusted the police. The lack of officers of color also hampered the BCP, as African American and Latino/a residents often viewed the program as an example of the police as an occupying force. If middle-class blacks and Latinos/as desired greater police protection, they also wanted a greater say over how the police operated and interacted with the community, not a mere expansion of the number of police in their neighborhoods or even an increase in black officers if they approached the community with an "us versus them" attitude.[23] Some officers recognized the problem. "We told them what we wanted," stated a former LAPD assistant chief, "rather than finding out what they wanted."[24]

The BCP provided a model for other community-oriented policing programs. As part of the attempt to enhance police-community relationships, Davis introduced the Team Experiment in Area Mobilization (TEAM) concept in the predominantly white beachside Venice neighborhood. Team policing, in Davis's words, was "the combined and integrated delivery of field and investigative services in a police group and geographic area small enough so that the team can act together, on a one-to-one basis, among themselves and can work with the community to perform the crime prevention, deterrent and apprehension functions at an optimum level with full public cooperation."[25] Under the plan, a team of officers worked within a specific area, communicated with residents, and enlisted citizens' help and participation in the fight against crime.

The TEAM approach did not lead to community control of the police. Many officers viewed community-oriented policing skeptically, believing it undermined aggressive police work. Under the LAPD's team policing program, a study of officer discretion by political scientist Michael Brown conducted in the early 1970s found "responsiveness to citizen demands is being sacrificed to the objective of crime control." Although LAPD officials believed that the TEAM experiments were successful, some observers believed that they led to a more aggressive style of policing, and evidence of their impact on crime rates was inconsistent. Brown found that rather than devolving power or control to citizens, the TEAM policing model was "an attempt at formal cooptation—participation without control."[26] In hindsight, even Bradley recognized that the officers involved in the TEAM and BCP programs were "public relations people. . . . They didn't do any police work." The BCP and TEAM projects, in other words, merely enhanced the power of the chief.[27]

Efforts to make the police more responsive to residents through community-oriented policing were hampered by the department's predominantly white composition. Compared with police departments in cities with large black populations, where black officers made up half of the department, such as in Detroit, Atlanta, and Washington, D.C., the LAPD, like the NYPD, had a racial composition that was lacking. In 1978, for instance, the department was over 80 percent white, 6.2 percent black, and 9.7 percent Latino/a. Even after a 1980 consent decree requiring the department to implement affirmative action hiring and promotion programs, officers of the LAPD were still predominantly white. By 1990, the department had become 63.3 percent white, 13.2 percent black, and 20.4 percent Latino/a in a city that was 37 percent white, 13 percent black, 40 percent Latino/a, and 9 percent Asian American. For women the obstacle was higher, as the percentage of female officers increased from a minuscule 2.6 percent in 1980 to a marginal

12.2 percent in 1990. The gradual pace of diversification resulted from slow turnover and an annual goal of minority and female new hires. The department achieved a 23 percent new hire rate for blacks and a 28 percent for Latinos/as during the 1980s. Incremental changes in hiring did increase the number of black and Latino/a officers, achieving "moderate compliance" with hiring goals according to some studies.[28] By 1990 the number of black officers was proportional to the total black population, while Latinos/as and Asian Americans were severely underrepresented within the department. But through the 1980s many residents of color continued to view the police as a predominantly white, masculine department that not only did not represent their interests but operated as an aggressive force on the streets.

The department's commitment to a community-oriented policing philosophy withered over the 1970s. Budget constraints resulting from Proposition 13's limit on property taxes; Bradley's support for police services that directly combated crime; and a new chief of police, Daryl Gates, who opposed any attempt to infringe on police power led to the demise of the BCP and TEAM programs.[29] Community crime control programs did not end with the phasing out of the BCP and TEAM. Indeed, Bradley worked to implement Neighborhood Watch programs during the late 1970s and early 1980s. The Mayor's Office of Criminal Justice Planning, for example, funded a variety of crime prevention programs such as the civilian Rampart Urban Crime Prevention Program and an African American police officer organization's "Bust on Crime" Program.[30] But such community relations programs and community-oriented policing did more to bring residents into the service of the police department's crime-fighting mission and discretionary authority than to produce greater civilian accountability and oversight of the department more broadly.

Community Control of the Police

If Bradley hoped to rely on the Police Commission and community relations programs to change the department's pattern of harassment and abuse in black and Latino/a neighborhoods, he was mistaken. Under Chief Davis the department continued to operate with an "us versus them" attitude and an aggressive approach to crime control. Throughout the 1970s, officer-involved shootings and the use of deadly force continued to affect the lives of black and Latino/a residents. Between 1974 and the first half of 1979, LAPD officers shot 584 suspects: 55 percent were black, 22 percent were Latino/a, 22 percent were white, and 1 percent were "other." Out of 128 suspects killed, 50 percent were black, 16 percent were Latino/a, and 33 percent were white. Much of the escalating police use of force and killings focused on young black men, a response to the fear, elevated to a panic by politicians and media, of youth crime and gang activity stemming from rising unemployment due to the economic recession and the loss of manufacturing jobs in the Los Angeles region during the early 1970s.[31]

As the number of individuals abused, harassed, and killed by the LAPD mounted during the 1970s, residents and activists created defense and justice committees, such as People's United for Barry Evans organized after the killing of Evans, an unarmed seventeen-year-old African American high school student, which was ruled "justifiable homicide" by the district attorney. The energy of defense and justice committees laid the foundation for a broad-based anti–police abuse movement. In response to the fragmented organizing around individual episodes of police violence, a multiracial group of approximately sixty people met at the People's College of Law on March 26, 1976. They established a coalition for mutual support in the struggle against police harassment, killings, and abuses of power in "communities, jails, and prisons."[32] The CAPA, as the organization was called, hoped to address the "isolated and ineffectual" efforts of black and Latino/a residents to respond to what its organizers viewed as a systematic program of "police crimes and power abuses" that "followed a well-established pattern in the poorer minority communities."[33]

CAPA developed out of a tradition of community organizing and Marxist politics passed on by the Black Power and Chicano/a movements. The legacy of the Black Panthers and Black Power ideology was reflected in CAPA's constantly evolving organizing manual. The manual explained the organization's political critique and analysis. It framed the police as an occupying force that did not "'protect and serve' the people" but acted as "armed enforcers of racism, sexism, and other forms of oppression . . . [and] are in our communities for the purpose of intimidation, confinement and control."[34] Yet, CAPA's founders organized around lessons learned from the disintegration of black and ethnic nationalist movements in the early 1970s.

The organization was based on a non-nationalistic and nonsectarian model of coalition building that accepted any group committed to the principle of community control of the police. As CAPA's early literature, printed in both English and Spanish, suggested, organizers framed police abuse as a problem that transcended racial and ethnic lines, and attempted to unite all those who experienced police harassment and abuse. While maintaining the view that the police operated as a colonial force, CAPA eschewed armed confrontation. Instead, members of the coalition channeled their efforts into community organizing, political education, nonviolent protest, political reform, and legal redress.[35]

Coalition against Police Abuse activists protest police killings and the lack of police accountability, ca. 1976. CAPA activists pressured local officials to address the systemic problems and racism at the heart of the LAPD's police power. "Stop Police Killings," undated, box Pulled Materials, CAPA Papers, Southern California Library.

The statement of purpose reflected the importance of community organization and mass mobilization to CAPA's overall strategy. Formed by "community people" concerned that the "reign of terror by the police has remained unchecked for too long," the organizing manual explained, "We have resolved as our main purpose to organize and mobilize the masses in the black and brown communities as well as other poor communities, through block clubs, church organizations, senior citizen clubs and concerned individuals and families, to organize against police terrorism in our communities." The manual explained the process for developing community support based on a three-part program. It required the documenting of abuse cases through interviews with witnesses and public officials as well as by gathering any information in the public record. After documenting cases of abuse, CAPA sought to "reach the people" to keep them informed through flyers, fact sheets, newsletters, educational meetings, and media exposure. The final step was to mobilize the people. This included filing complaints with the police, organizing defense and justice committees, holding protests and marches, attending city council meetings, and pursuing legal action.[36]

Politicizing the community, CAPA recognized, was a time-consuming, step-by-step process that required continuous reinforcement. Members attended seminars to discuss American history, analyze Marxist theory, and read texts on African American history.[37] Early meeting minutes demonstrated how a diverse group of left-wing activists worked to provide "political education" for the community while also responding to the desires, demands, and hopes of local residents. "Develop the base!," organizers exclaimed in a motion blending reformist and revolutionary tactics through educational programming.[38] Using rhetorical questions and statements such as, "HAVE YOU BEEN HARASSED BY THE POLICE?" and "They'd Like Us To Think We Can't Do Anything about It . . ." in its flyers and literature, CAPA worked to politicize residents to take a stand. Community members were not always responsive to CAPA's radical left agenda. Throughout its existence, CAPA grappled with the tension between its political and ideological positions to push residents to action and the effort to respond to the needs and desires that grew out of the community itself.[39] CAPA's development as an organization, as a result, evolved through on-the-ground efforts aimed at politicizing residents through mass education, marches, rallies, and protests.

Perhaps the most basic but also one of CAPA's most important activities was the collection of complaints against law enforcement agencies. Using police malpractice complaint forms, CAPA recorded complaints of police misconduct in person and by phone to create an archive revealing patterns of police abuse. The complaint files provided evidence of police abuse and combined with similar lists compiled by the American Civil Liberties Union police malpractice complaint centers to provide a foundation for tracking over time the relationship between the police and the community.[40] By 1982, CAPA received an average of 1,500 complaints annually, which CAPA used to reinforce arguments that law enforcement agencies in Los Angeles were unaccountable and operated with impunity, especially in communities of color. The number of complaints and their geographic diversity suggest that even though CAPA relied on a core group of fifteen to twenty activists, it was recognized in the community as a site to file complaints, get advice, and mobilize around police abuse.[41]

Filing and maintaining a record of complaints of police abuse was no mundane activity. Rather, it was central to the political project of holding the police accountable to the residents they were supposed to serve. On May 5 and 7, 1976, for example, LAPD officers, acting on legal instruction from the city attorney, shredded thousands of internal affairs files pertaining to unsustained citizen complaints against officers.[42] CAPA held a picket line in front of City Hall to protest the "gross unprofessional, unethical misconduct of both Chief Davis and City Attorney Burt Pines for the destruction of the Internal

Affairs Division Files which they told the city council were merely miscellaneous records." While the destruction of the complaint records did not lead to a criminal investigation, it ultimately led to a lawsuit overturning twenty-three cases where the LAPD charged defendants with assault or battering a police officer or resisting arrest—charges often used to cover up cases of police abuse—because the LAPD destroyed the records and therefore could not produce sufficient evidence to pursue such cases.[43]

By collecting its own complaints, CAPA circumvented not only the LAPD's destruction of documents but also the lack of transparency and accountability in Internal Affairs adjudications of cases of police abuse. Working with legal services organizations, such as the American Civil Liberties Union police malpractice complaint centers, the Police Misconduct Lawyer Referral Service, and the Greater Watts Justice Center and Model Neighborhood Legal Center, allowed CAPA to pursue legal redress for some complainants. CAPA pushed individuals to become aware of their right to bring criminal charges against the police and file claims for damages against the city of Los Angeles, something that lawyers from the American Civil Liberties Union such as Hugh Manes had been supporting—winning many monetary claims against the police—since the early 1960s. With the help of lawyers like Manes, CAPA informed people how to act during an arrest or confrontation with the police in order to provide a strong legal basis for a defense if they filed a lawsuit.[44]

Suits could be successful, such as when Michael Zinzun sued the Pasadena Police Department in 1985 after permanently losing sight in one eye from a severe beating by officers after attempting to observe the arrest of one his neighbors. This resulted in a settlement of $1.2 million but did little to alter the operations of the police or change policy. CAPA recognized that suits were not a "substitute for an organized community to end police crimes," but understood that filing charges against the police could have a monetary impact on the city.[45]

One of CAPA's central strategies focused on pressuring public officials, Mayor Bradley and the Board of Police Commissioners in particular, to rigorously oversee the LAPD's use of force. The killing in 1977 of Ron Burkholder, a thirty-five-year-old white man with mental illness who was gunned down by police while nude in the street, provided CAPA the opportunity to demand oversight of the department's use-of-force policy. Bradley responded by pushing the commission to review the use-of-force guidelines, resulting in the first overhaul of the LAPD's use-of-force regulations since the 1960s. Although limiting the use of firearms in fleeing felon incidents, the new guidelines were vague, stating that all officers should take into consideration "the reverence for human life" in deciding to use force. Such a change, while criticized by Davis as "likely to imperil the safety of police officers and to eliminate sixth sense police work," did not alter the use of deadly force. The routine abusive practices, shootings, and killings by the LAPD officers continued with little comment from the mayor or other officials.[46]

While believing that progress had been made in establishing government regulation of the LAPD, liberals recognized they—and the police department most importantly—needed to address lingering discontent in the African American community with the police. The primary grievances continued to revolve around the department's lax oversight and discipline of the use of deadly force. "I think the general level of hostility and tension between the general black community and the Police Department in 1965 was considerably greater than it is today," Bradley told the Urban League in 1978. "That is not to suggest that there isn't a problem, because there is a serious problem. The number of incidents involving law enforcement officers and the use of their guns, and the number of incidents in which people have been killed as a result of police restraint holds, have created serious problems." There had been improvements in human relations training and increased sensitivity to community concerns, but "much more," Bradley admitted, "is going to have to be done."[47]

For all the work of CAPA activists to raise community control of the police as the solution to police violence, interactions with a hostile police force gave African American and Latino/a residents little reason to believe that much had improved. As the relationship between the police and residents of color continued on a largely antagonistic path, events would soon prove Bradley right and mobilize a broad movement calling for systemic police reform.

Resisting Police Violence

On January 3, 1979, Eula Mae Love, a thirty-nine-year-old African American widow raising three daughters in South Central, attempted to pay a $22 overdue gas bill. After resisting the effort of a Southern California Edison Company representative to turn off her gas by hitting him with a shovel, Love went to a local market to purchase a money order for the unpaid bill. In the meantime, the gas company representative reported the incident to his supervisor, who called the police for backup. Two LAPD officers, Lloyd O'Callaghan and Edward Hopson, one white and one black, responded to the case, which was labeled a "business dispute." When the officers arrived at the house, they found Love in her front yard holding a kitchen knife. The officers approached Love with guns drawn. O'Callaghan knocked Love down and hit the knife out of her hand with a baton. When Love reportedly reached for the knife, the officers opened fire and emptied their guns, killing her on the scene.[48]

Despite widespread outcry from residents and activists, the police department and criminal justice system's response revealed an unwillingness to hold officers accountable. The district attorney refused to prosecute the officers, and the LAPD's Shooting Review Board found that they acted within the department's use of deadly force guidelines. While eventually acknowledging that they could have handled the situation differently, Chief Gates vigorously defended his officers' actions as "legitimate self-defense." Gates's response reflected his perspective that the police were an aggressive force tasked with maintaining law and order. The dismissive attitude toward the killing of Love and other such abuses on the part of the police department and criminal justice system, however, led to an escalating battle that mobilized a wide variety of interests and undermined support for the police in black and Latino/a communities.[49]

In the weeks that followed, the African American community and Latino/a allies reacted, the Board of Police Commissioners noted, with an "outpouring of criticism, anger, fear and distrust" directed at the police, city council, Mayor Bradley, and the Board of Police Commissioners. For many, the Love killing was indicative of the long history of repressive police practices. As Carey McWilliams of *The Nation* criticized, "by any rational standard their [the officers'] response was excessive to a degree that indicates panic, faulty training and wretched judgment. For years there have been far too many police killings in South-Central Los Angeles. It is the kind of district in which police officers tend to fire first and ask questions later." The Love incident became a "lightning rod" for the expression of deeply felt hostility toward the police and fueled CAPA's anti–police abuse campaign. The Love killing was critical in connecting the police's use of excessive force with residents' daily experience of harassment and discrimination.[50]

Frustration with the police was directed not only at the department but also at political officials. Some observers condemned Bradley's failure to reform the police department. Perhaps the most strident criticism came from the *Los Angeles Sentinel* when it called on the mayor to take more direct measures, claiming, "For the past 5½ years, Mayor Bradley has walked rather softly whenever matters of the police came about." The *Sentinel* also printed an editorial cartoon portraying Bradley walking past signs of "police brutality" with the caption: "I Don't See Anything."[51]

The editorial brought strong criticism from Reverend Thomas Kilgore, who championed Bradley's efforts to bring more accountability to the police department. While middle-class blacks had been concerned with police abuse prior to the Love killing, they had placed their faith in Bradley and black city council members to bring the LAPD under control. Kilgore cited how Bradley

I Don't See Anything

"I Don't See Anything," *Los Angeles Sentinel* editorial cartoon. The *Sentinel*'s editorial cartoon criticized Mayor Tom Bradley's inaction on police killings and harassment in the African American community after the police killing of Eula Love. While many African Americans had hoped that Bradley's election would lead to more police accountability, Bradley had not lived up to the demands from residents and activists to take on the LAPD. *Los Angeles Sentinel*, March 1, 1979.

had worked to expand the power of the mayor's office over the department. As Kilgore pointed out, Bradley pushed the police commission to alter the police use-of-force policies in 1977. He had also pressured the police commission to investigate the LAPD's intelligence-gathering operations and the department's use of the controversial choke hold. These technocratic reforms, however, did little to reduce the number of fatal shootings or police use of force.[52]

The Love killing came on the heels of several highly publicized episodes of police harassment of black clergymen. Love was also a middle-aged black woman, which provided new ground for cross-class activism. The killing mobilized residents across class lines and broadened the movement against police abuse. New organizations and moderate residents, especially those who did not align with CAPA's politics, joined the demand for reforming the LAPD. Combined with a pattern of arrests and harassment of activist ministers such as Reverends Thomas Kilgore and M. M. Merriweather, the Love killing prompted a group of 169 ministers representing nearly 250,000 black churchgoers to form a group called The Gathering, charging the LAPD with brutality and racism.[53] The Gathering hoped to develop a "cooperative movement for the redemption and renewal of our town" by focusing on holding the police accountable for shootings and systematic abuse. The Gathering addressed police-community relations through a "Working Committee on Community and Police Issues" and developed a ten-point program for addressing discriminatory police treatment. The program laid out an agenda that demanded meetings with public officials, a new shooting policy, affirmative action in hiring and recruitment, and a civilian review board.[54]

When Gates criticized The Gathering as conducting a "public lynching" of his department, Mayor Bradley took his stand. He defended The Gathering and acknowledged the widespread concern surrounding police violence. He also criticized the officers involved in the Love shooting and suggested that police violence could lead to another Watts uprising. Such comments left Chief Gates "dumbfounded," and he vehemently disagreed with Bradley's criticism of the officers, even downplaying the significance of the Love killing, saying he would be "amazed—clearly amazed," if police use of force led to another Watts riot.[55] Bradley's stand brought praise from local organizations and reflected how systematic police violence broadened the anti-abuse movement.

The district attorney added to the discontent with a thirty-seven-page report ruling the killing a justifiable homicide because the officers acted in self-defense. The finding reflected the lack of change in the daily operations of officers even as the police commission had instituted new use-of-force guidelines. Responding to the pressure from community organizations, civil rights groups, and ministerial alliances, Bradley proposed enhanced human relations training, greater limits on officer discretion, and an investigation by the Board of Police Commissioners.[56] The shift in Bradley's public stance on police violence was a relief to many in the black community. The *Sentinel* commented in an editorial titled "Plaudits for Tom" that Bradley should be commended for taking a strong stance criticizing the LAPD. Activists and community leaders wanted Bradley to push for more substantive accountability to the department. While continuing to praise Bradley, Reverend Kilgore also insisted upon the need to "weed out racism" that plagued the department to its core. Paul Hudson of the National Association for the Advancement of Colored People concluded that Bradley's emphasis on training and procedural reforms enabled the department to avoid criticism by blaming the problem on individual officers, not on the department as a whole, and was therefore no different from other responses to police shootings. "Every time there's a shooting," Hudson proclaimed, "somebody asks for better training." Focusing on issues of procedural fairness without systemic changes in the department's racist practices and policies, saturation policing, and "us versus them" culture, they believed, would do little to stop shootings and abuse.[57]

The Love killing helped shift attitudes and public perceptions of the LAPD. Whereas polls conducted by the LAPD in 1972 had revealed broad support for the police, a 1979 *Los Angeles Times* poll revealed that 62 percent of blacks,

37 percent of Latino/as, and nearly 25 percent of Anglos disapproved of how the LAPD did its job. Some of the discrepancy between blacks and Latinos/as reflected different levels of politicization around police abuse; the fact that Latinos/as lived in areas on the border between the city and county, making them more susceptible to abuse from the sheriff's department; and concerns related to Immigration and Naturalization Service raids. The poll, however, found that the department "suffered a serious decline in public support during the last year and a half, especially among blacks." Survey participants believed that the Love killing was an example of police brutality—rather than the proper use of force—and, moreover, that it reflected a perception, among African Americans especially, that the LAPD was "tougher on blacks." Indeed, 62 percent of blacks, 42 percent of Latinos/as, and 41 percent of Anglos responded that officers treated African Americans more harshly. Many whites supported the police when it came to their overall view of the department. But with Bradley's commitment to reform and a shift in the *Los Angeles Times* reporting, which had become more critical of the LAPD and exposed episodes of police abuse, many whites began to acknowledge the unequal nature of policing in the city. In contrast to the 1972 LAPD poll suggesting support for the police among black residents, by 1979 the repeated experiences with harassment and abuse had turned public opinion against the department and its aggressive practices.[58]

The police commission investigation led to a multipart report finding that the officers involved made "serious errors" in approaching Love with guns drawn. The report recommended changes in the LAPD's policies regarding the use of force, investigatory and disciplinary procedures, and human relations training.[59] Gates criticized the board's findings but eventually accepted limited changes to human relations training, the use-of-force policies, and disciplinary guidelines. On September 26, 1979, Gates issued Special Order 32, which revised complaint procedures, stressing the thorough review of all complaints in "an atmosphere free of real or imagined intimidation, without fear of reprisal." The commission also made another revision to the LAPD's shooting policy that stressed "reverence for human life" and the gradual escalation of force, and permitted the use of firearms only in self-defense or physically threatening situations. Subsequent agreements also led to use-of-force training for officers, the programs to facilitate communication between the police and residents, and the creation of black and Hispanic advisory councils to improve the image of the police in minority communities.[60] For all the changes, however, none of the reforms altered disciplinary authority over officers, a power that remained with the chief.

Police violence also mobilized the Latino/a community. The LAPD's Hispanic Advisory Council's Subcommittee on Police and Use of Deadly Force found that the Love killing "also tended to accentuate old police/minority-community wounds in the psyche of the Hispanic community." The police killing of nineteen-year-old Kenneth Ramírez on October 15, 1980, confirmed these sentiments and revealed the inability of changes in use-of-force policies to limit officer discretion. LAPD officers in pursuit of a robbery traced the suspect to a car registered to Ramírez's father. When they arrived at the Ramírez home in Mission Hills, Kenneth Ramírez approached the patrol car. Officer Wendell Rhinehart, who had not left his vehicle, pulled his gun and fired a shot, killing Ramírez instantly. The LAPD's investigators found the shooting of Ramírez an accident and that the officer's gun misfired when it was taken out of the holster.[61] The Officer-Involved Shooting investigator also asserted that Officer Rhinehart acted "well within department policy" by drawing his weapon.[62]

The Hispanic Advisory Committee reported that many in the community found it difficult to accept the department's conclusions as officers continued to resort to the use of firearms in nonlethal situations. The Hispanic Advisory Committee indicted both the Board of Police Commissioners and the LAPD for doing nothing to alter police use of deadly force and called for a more responsive, "humanistic soldier" as the model for LAPD officers while representatives from the Mexican American Bar Association reiterated long-standing demands for more Spanish-language training for officers. Although the LAPD implemented Spanish-language programs, they were limited, such as showing officers a three-and-a-half-minute video on Spanish translations of verbal commands, and did not address police power or use of deadly force.[63]

While police shootings decreased in the two years after the Love killing, the publicity from police violence in the black and Latino/a communities mobilized residents and activists to continue to demand substantive reform. The publicity and public outcry led to a series of local hearings on police abuse and the convening of congressional hearings in 1980 on police and the use of deadly force. The House subcommittee on crime did not plan to focus on Los Angeles, but the "almost daily attention" to police brutality in Los Angeles demanded investigation.[64] Although the hearings exposed the broad-based discontent with police violence, police officials successfully resisted any further limits on the department's autonomy and political power.

Hopes that the LAPD would work to train more humane officers and implement changes in policies relating to the escalation of the use of force ran headlong into controversy surrounding a series of deaths by police choke holds. Rhetoric from police officials and officers describing black suspects who displayed "maniacal behavior" and "superhuman" strength while on PCP were picked up by the media, leading to beliefs that black residents disproportionately used PCP and influencing the LAPD's use of force in inner-city communities. Suspects were referred to as "crazed" users, and such descriptions ensured that officers approached black residents with heightened suspicion and fear. The result was the widespread use of two types of holds, the "bar-arm," whereby officers placed an arm across a suspect's throat, and the "modified carotid," in which pressure applied to arteries in the neck cut off oxygen to the brain. Most of the use of choke holds occurred in situations that did not warrant such an escalation of force. These holds were used to make black victims, in the words of officers, "do the chicken," flopping around until they lost consciousness due to lack of oxygen.[65] Between 1975 and 1985, the use of the choke hold resulted in sixteen deaths. Twelve of the victims were black.[66] When compared with incidence of choke hold use in cities that had been the subject of allegations of racism and abuse, such as New York, where only one choke hold death had occurred in a decade, the LAPD's use of the choke hold looked particularly problematic.[67]

City Councilman Robert Farrell, who had served as Bradley's African American community coordinator, pushed the council to act on the LAPD's use of the choke hold beginning in 1978. After initial efforts went nowhere, Farrell gained more traction after the Love killing and the growing evidence of discriminatory use of the choke hold. He presented a motion on June 18, 1980, demanding that the city council investigate the choke hold policies. "If the reports are accurate," Farrell stated, "then the issue of appropriate use of force by police officers in the field must be reviewed. . . . A baton applied across the throat is *NOT* an acceptable technique."[68] Public opposition to the use of the choke hold resulted in the filing of a lawsuit to enjoin Los Angeles law enforcement from using the technique. In *Lyons vs. Los Angeles*, the court issued a preliminary injunction against the use of the choke hold in 1981. The Board of Police Commissioners also ordered Gates to conduct a thorough investigation of the LAPD's control hold policy. But Gates vehemently defended the department's use of the choke hold as an appropriate technique necessary to keep residents safe.[69] Officers continued to use the choke hold despite the federal injunction.

To many in the black community, the clearly discriminatory use of the choke hold undermined the LAPD's credibility. Gates attempted damage control, proposing revised policies for the use of the choke hold and banning the bar-arm control hold.[70] Gates further angered the black community, however, when he suggested that blacks were biologically more susceptible to injury from the choke hold because "we may be finding that in some blacks when it (the hold) is applied, the veins or arteries do not open up as fast as they do in normal people."[71] Councilman David Cunningham responded by comparing Gates to the segregationist governor of Georgia, Lester Maddox, and argued that he should have no role in public leadership.[72] Although Gates retracted his statement, it did little to alleviate distrust of the LAPD among residents and local African American politicians. Outrage, political pressure, and rulings by the Police Commission pushed Gates to restrict the use of the choke hold "in any situation other than one in which the use of deadly force is authorized."[73]

The moratorium on the choke hold was a victory for black and Latino/a Angelinos. It also led to the filing and settlement of several multimillion dollar lawsuits against the department's inappropriate use of the choke hold throughout the 1980s.[74] In response, however, the LAPD resorted to aluminum batons, chemical irritants, and TASERs, and injuries to suspects during arrests increased.[75] The reforms brought by the Board of Police Commissioners regarding the use of force, while a clear departure from the past, left the department the authority to discipline officers and investigate claims of misconduct.

The Campaign for a Civilian Review Board

The more rigorous oversight of officer-involved shootings by the Board of Police Commissioners and the ban of the use of the chokehold reflected popular support for the anti–police abuse movement. But these were still moderate changes that left open significant questions about accountability. The more fundamental proposal, put forward by CAPA activists since 1976 and supported by many after the Love shooting, was for the establishment of a civilian review board. Such a board would provide more substantive change to the relationship between the police and community because it would have the authority to enforce discipline of officers involved in cases of the improper use of force. The proposed board, if passed, would also go a long way toward achieving CAPA's goal of community control of the police.[76]

A civilian review board was an uphill proposition. Previous efforts to get a review board had gone nowhere in the face of stiff resistance from the LAPD. Disciplinary power over officers, moreover, was reserved for the chief of police in the city charter, meaning that a review board would require an amendment to the charter. Such a change could be initiated by either the city council or a general election ballot initiative. City council support was negligible, so activists pursued a ballot initiative instead. The initiative process required 15 percent of registered voters in the city to sign a supporting petition 150 days prior to the election. In 1980 this meant soliciting 116,588 signatures. CAPA joined with groups including the National Association for the Advancement of Colored People, the California Democratic Club–Black Caucus, and the Coalition for Economic Democracy among others to create the Coalition for a Civilian Review Board in the summer of 1979. The organization took formal shape in 1980 under the name Campaign for a Civilian Review Board (CCRB).[77]

CAPA provided the outline of an effective review board rooted in community input and decision-making that CCRB used as a model for its initiative campaign. The proposed board, CAPA explained, "attempts to create a system of procedures which would result in just arbitration of police crimes against civilians." Board members would be chosen by the community, rather than by appointment. The board should have broad access to vital records and information from the police department in deciding cases of alleged misconduct. An independent prosecutor, not associated with the LAPD or the city council, would oversee the board. The board would also hire a corps of lawyers to replace the district attorney, who had a dismal record of indicting officers. To ensure community involvement, CAPA's proposal suggested setting up eighteen documentation centers in each of the LAPD's divisions with a central review board at City Hall made up of community representatives. Since the community could not rely on the police to discipline officers, CAPA argued, "the People must take their fate in their own hands and establish a more responsive mechanism for filing criminal charges against police officers." The overwhelming statistical evidence of systematic patterns of discriminatory harassment and the excessive use of force, CAPA suggested, made Los Angeles stand "out as a battleground for who will control accountability and police discipline."[78]

Although the CCRB had its own organization and statement of purpose, it modeled its structure and proposal for a review board on CAPA's. The influence of CAPA was also evident in the CCRB's motto, "For accountable police practices, end police crimes."[79] The CCRB linked its call for a review board to the failure of the LAPD and Board of Police Commissioners to adequately address demands for greater disciplinary oversight of officers. "The community has made numerous appeals," the CCRB explained in its reason for demanding a review board, "but the pleas of the community (particularly Black and Brown, where the problem is most prevalent) have gone unheard, or received token responses."[80]

The petition developed by the CCRB to place an initiative on the November ballot also reflected CAPA's vision. The CCRB proposal gave the board powers of oversight that, while not entirely redistributing police power and disciplinary authority, would have at least acknowledged police abuse as a systemic and structural problem.[81] It called for fifteen members elected by district, provided for the appointment of a special prosecutor, and assigned broad powers to oversee disciplinary cases, including the suspension and removal of officers.[82] On January 3, 1980, the anniversary of the killing of Eula Love, the CCRB launched its petition drive, with a June deadline, to put an initiative for a review board before the voters. To account for invalid signatures, the CCRB intended to collect 150,000 names.[83]

The LAPD, Board of Police Commissioners, and supporters of law enforcement strongly opposed a civilian review board, regarding it as an unnecessary limitation on the department's discretion. The Police Protective League felt that review of LAPD disciplinary procedures was unnecessary because "we have more than adequate remedies and avenues for redress should violations of law or policy occur involving a police officer."[84] Believing that his department was "under siege," Chief Gates vehemently defended his department's autonomy and called the proposed review board a "kangaroo court." He attacked proponents of a review board as part of a conspiracy to handcuff the police, a sign of federal officials hoping to meddle in his department, and "hard core" civil rights activists who portrayed the police in the worst light and wanted "to change the complexion of the department." Ceding no ground, Gates portrayed the police as victims of unfair limitations on their discretion to keep the city safe in order to shore up the department's autonomy. If the board was approved, Gates warned, "the aggressive work that this department does, the efficiency with which this department works, will end."[85]

Although Gates attacked liberal lawmakers as plotters against the police, opposition to the review board reflected the converging interests that had supported various forms of law and order. A number of city officials, including Bradley, conservative Republican councilman Art Snyder, and Democratic councilwoman Joy Picus, rejected any form of review board. Few lawmakers, such as African American councilman Robert Farrell and Assemblywoman Maxine Waters, expressed strong support. Bradley had never supported a civilian review board. But he also recognized that creating such a board in 1980 was a political impossibility, since there was little support in the city council and the police department, and the Police Protective League strongly opposed it. As Bradley told reporters after the Love killing, "You and I both know it [a civilian review board] is not going to happen."[86]

Bradley's position revealed the breaking point of liberal law and order that was willing to fix procedure and enhance civilian accountability but not the underlying authority of the police power. While public officials and the police commission had been willing to hear complaints about the most blatant forms of police use of excessive force, they adamantly opposed to shifting power and decision-making to an external review board. Activists exposed the way the media and politicians accepted the framing created by the LAPD that a review board would hurt the morale of the department, weakening officers' ability to protect public safety. "Reporters only talk about morale of the police because they accept the notion that the police are to be treated as

Needed: A Civilian Police Review Board

"The Time Is Now!," *Los Angeles Sentinel* editorial cartoon. Building on the work of activists, the *Sentinel* promoted the passage of a civilian review board. African American activists had pushed for a civilian review board since the early 1960s but now suggested that the continued police killings and lack of indictments or disciplinary action required more systemic changes to the nature of police power itself. *Los Angeles Sentinel*, February 28, 1980.

a military outfit, just as Chief Gates refers to officers as 'his troops,'" Jerry Cohen, a research associate for the CCRB, explained. "If we looked at police as public servants instead of combatants in a war, maybe their conduct would be different."[87]

Prior to the June deadline, African American and Latino/a activists collected over 80,000 signatures and received support from a number of local institutions including the *Los Angeles Sentinel*. The *Sentinel* ran an editorial cartoon in favor of the CCRB plan that represented the rise of police shootings by showing a smoking gun as a symbol of the need for a civilian review board to provide oversight of the LAPD.[88] The campaign also received support from The Gathering in April after the ministerial coalition concluded that despite the changes made by the Board of Police Commissioners to improve community relations, citizen input was necessary.[89]

Yet the CCRB was unsuccessful at gaining the required signatures to place a referendum on the November ballot. The campaign faced a hostile conservative political climate marked by the passage of Proposition 13 in 1978 and Ronald Reagan's election in 1980, which anticipated the election of Republican George Deukmejian as California governor in 1983. The campaign lost momentum, lacked political support from city officials, and faced hostility from Chief Gates and law enforcement authorities. For CAPA and CCRB activists, however, the failure was not due to a lack of community support but rather due to evidence of their opponents' efforts to sabotage the campaign. According to CAPA's co-chairman Charles Chapple, the petitioners had been advised that they did not need to collect precinct numbers of those who signed the petition, but were later told that precinct numbers were required. The change, occurring four weeks before the deadline, meant the CCRB had to purchase twenty precinct books at $16 each and review every signature. Chapple also believed that many residents had been reluctant to sign petitions out of fear of police harassment or violent repercussions if they signed. The struggle would continue, however. As Chapple explained, "We are not going to drop it. . . . There hasn't been a change in anything. . . . Police abuse is still there."[90]

———

The failure to collect enough signatures for a referendum on a civilian review board reflected the difficulty of transforming broad-based mobilization around police abuse into fundamental political change. The response to the Love killing and the choke hold deaths suggested that many residents, civil rights organizations, and local politicians were concerned with police violence and willing to demand reforms to make the LAPD more account-able. The anti–police abuse movement pushed mayor Bradley and the Board of Police Commissioners to demand changes from the LAPD. They succeeded in pushing the LAPD to hire more black and Latino/a officers, enhancing the complaint process of the Internal Affairs Division, and alter-ing the investigatory procedures in officer-involved shootings. The move-ment also led to a citywide moratorium on the use of the choke hold, which had been connected with discriminatory treatment of black men. These re-forms were meant to ensure that the police served and protected all resi-dents equally.

Support for these reforms, however, did not translate to CAPA's more radical agenda of reorienting the relationship between residents and the police through community control. Such a goal required fundamental changes in the balance of power between the LAPD and the community it served, something Gates refused to consider. It also challenged the political system and struc-ture of authority in the city. Even as Bradley and select city council members supported greater oversight of the LAPD by the Board of Police Commis-sioners, they opposed changes that would have resulted in the devolution of power away from city officials, placing that power directly in the hands of residents. As a result, the more substantive demands for civilian review failed, disciplinary control stayed with the chief of police, and the underlying relation of power between the community and the police remained unchanged.

CAPA's organizing was generative. By constantly challenging city officials, LAPD leadership, and the Board of Police Commissioners, CAPA politicized the issue of police abuse and the criminal justice system more broadly. It provided an opening for residents, activists, and community organizations to challenge white institutions and to articulate alternative visions of police authority and relations. As episodes of police abuse, use of excessive force, and lethal violence persisted, resistance and protest expanded to a wide variety of groups in the black and Latino/a communities. As the focus of organizing shifted from police autonomy to police violence, moderate civil rights organizations, ministers, and local officials took up the issue of police violence. Opposition from the LAPD notwithstanding, CAPA's efforts ensured that holding the police accountable to the community it served continued to be at the center of the meaning of justice.

Police violence motivated a broad coalition in favor of giving civilians greater oversight and decision-making in how they were policed. Yet for all the criticism brought by activists, the LAPD's position as an unchecked partisan entity in the city remained largely intact. To maintain its power as an autonomous political entity and to expand discretionary authority to ensure order and manage so-called disorderly residents, the department relied on intensive monitoring, surveillance, and intelligence gathering. Whereas the forces opposed to police autonomy and violence made only marginal inroads in guaranteeing transparency and accountability of the department, they would win a significant victory in challenging the LAPD's overreach of authority in surveillance operations.

Chapter 6

The Rap Sheet

The Nimble Surveillance State

The LAPD would often use surveillance to combat potential crime, establish control of the streets, and enforce public order. Intelligence-led policing operated by instilling fears of an omniscient police force in the hopes of maintaining social order by preempting crime before it occurred. At a hearing titled "The Erosion of Law Enforcement Intelligence Gathering Capabilities" in 1976, Chief Davis proclaimed, "The existence of a potential threat of detection or the knowledge of close surveillance on unlawful activities can . . . prevent future misconduct." To enable such a pervasive police presence, officers required broad authority to surveil residents and infiltrate organizations regardless of their actual criminal activity. While attentive to far-right groups, the LAPD focused on monitoring, tracking, and disciplining progressive organizations whose demands for equality and social justice challenged the department's enforcement of a hierarchical racial order but also police legitimacy. Nothing threatened Chief Davis more than "sinister forces" with the goal of "the partial and complete paralysis of municipal police agencies."[1] By containing, repressing, and eliminating threats to its legitimacy through surveillance and infiltration, the LAPD consolidated power and enhanced its ability to define, fabricate, and enforce the boundary between criminality and order.

The LAPD had a long history of information-gathering, maintaining intelligence files as early as the 1920s. The Red Squad combated so-called subversives and protected the city's dominant political and economic interests. Challenges to the department's legitimacy after Watts, however, led the LAPD to reinvest in intelligence-gathering capacity and restructure the division, establishing the Public Disorder Intelligence Division (PDID) in 1970. While the FBI's better-known counterintelligence program (COINTELPRO) monitored activists and infiltrated civil rights organizations across the country during the 1960s, the PDID established a more extensive local covert action network aimed at disciplining and neutralizing radical activists and progressive movements. National attention to Watergate and counterintelligence programs, however, focused criticism on intelligence operations and led to the dismantling of federal surveillance programs during the 1970s. Yet, even within such a critical context, LAPD officials capitalized on the evolving fears of violent unrest, street crime, and terrorism to justify and expand the PDID's operations, funding, and choice of targets. A key component of police power generally, and the LAPD's law-and-order power play in particular, surveillance was key to shifts in policing strategies between the 1970s and 1980s and insulated the police department's independent authority.[2]

Conservative and liberal political interests overlapped in support of LAPD intelligence operations. Even so, liberal lawmakers, poised between conservative national context supportive of get-tough policies and increased wariness of rights violations by law enforcement intelligence units, pushed for regulation and oversight of the PDID. Meanwhile, the PDID broadened the definition of "terror" and "terrorist activity" to justify the repression and monitoring of social justice movements and anti–police abuse activists. The LAPD, in other words, defined domestic radicalism as a form of terrorism and thereby yoked policing to antiterrorism prerogatives in ways that criminalized the same people of color they had long targeted as a threat to order. In light of these powers, attempts to limit surveillance activities through state oversight only wound up legitimizing the unit.[3]

But the PDID's efforts to monitor, infiltrate, and discipline social movements did not go unnoticed or unchallenged. Activists and radical movements, most notably the Coalition against Police Abuse (CAPA) and the Citizens' Commission against Police Repression (CCPR), exposed the LAPD's far-reaching surveillance network. They revealed a police department more intent on neutralizing threats to its legitimacy and undermining demands for accountability than on upholding the law or democratic principles. By confronting the PDID and uncovering its operations, antipolice activists created a new legitimacy crisis for the police.

From Red Squad to Public Disorder Intelligence

The LAPD began intelligence operations in the 1920s at the height of the first "red scare." Though its targets included groups such as the Ku Klux Klan, the Red Squad's core mission was to guard the city from the scourge of Communist infiltration. Its right-wing zealotry protected the city's business interests from unions and radical organizing. After becoming chief, Parker reorganized and expanded the department's intelligence operation, establishing the Intelligence Division in 1960 ostensibly to monitor organized crime. But Parker's intelligence files were a crucial part of his and the department's political power. There were rumors, for example, that he had "the goods on everybody," even maintaining tabs on members of the Board of Police Commissioners. More than a narrow focus on organized crime, by the 1960s the files contained information ranging from labor activists to alleged Communist subversives of the 1950s, antiwar demonstrators, and civil rights organizers. The Organized Crime Intelligence Division, known as the Red Squad, functioned as a countersubversive arm aimed at molding Los Angeles in Parker's vision of morality and order. It was a John Birch Society dream of right-wing, pro-business, white-supremacist politics backed by an all-out attack on progressive social movements and civil rights activists.[4]

For all of Parker's efforts to make the LAPD a counterinsurgent force able to identify perceived troublemakers, the intelligence unit utterly failed to predict the Watts uprising. Rather than reassess the utility of counterintelligence programs, under Chief Reddin and his successor, Ed Davis, the LAPD expanded its intelligence apparatus in response to Watts. "Intensive intelligence gathering by LAPD/PDID sprang from 1965 riots," one intelligence officer observed. "[The] LAPD reacted by wanting to snoop around to know, beforehand, who the 'troublemakers' were."[5] By deliberately working to enhance its preemptive capacity, the LAPD became a key player in developing surveillance practices and national law enforcement intelligence sharing. Department officials participated in the creation of the Law Enforcement Intelligence Unit (LEIU), which incorporated military intelligence practices into domestic policing and created a network for information sharing.[6] The LAPD also led workshops for law enforcement agencies and police departments across the country on management, control, and utilization of informants. As the *Los Angeles Times* observed, the "police place great emphasis on their intelligence system, and the LAPD has a reputation for unusually good undercover work."[7]

Preemptive intelligence operations focused on maintaining a social order based on racial hierarchy. No group raised as serious concerns for law enforcement as Black Power organizations. "We feel that the present Negro movement is just as subversive as the past Communist movement or just as dangerous as the organized crime movement," Reddin claimed. "And we have even re-tooled our intelligence efforts . . . in the Negro community because we found that we were really woefully unacquainted with what was going on."[8] The department responded by placing people "underground," often as paid informants, with the Criminal Conspiracy Section. Using an "aggressive surveillance style," in police surveillance scholar Frank Donner's words, the Criminal Conspiracy Section explicitly worked to neutralize and eliminate the department's most vocal critics and threats to its legitimacy.[9]

Infiltration of progressive organizations often began as part of the LAPD's community relations programs. Community relations officers were not only tasked with keeping tabs on activity in neighborhoods of color but also recruited by the Intelligence Division. Perhaps the most prominent example was Sergeant Robert Thoms, who had spent time as a community relations officer before being transferred to counterintelligence operations. In congressional hearings held in 1970 on the Internal Security Act, Thoms revealed a wide-ranging effort to infiltrate, investigate, monitor, and undermine a wide range of nonviolent, left-leaning groups in Los Angeles. Surveillance efforts portrayed civil rights organizers as subversive and violent, leading to arrests on charges including conspiracy to disturb the peace, unlawful assembly, assault with a deadly weapon, and inciting a riot.[10]

Conservative lawmakers attempted to capitalize on reports of left-wing subversives to undermine civil rights and liberal social programs. Councilmen John Gibson and Art Snyder, for example, introduced a summary of the Thoms Report to the Chamber of Commerce in Washington, D.C., in hopes of persuading legislators and other officials of the danger of continuing to fund projects that they found objectionable. "There is no doubt whatsoever in my mind that the Federal Government is subsidizing agencies in Los Angeles," Gibson claimed, that "are harassing citizens and government officials to the extent that it is very difficult for local agencies and local government to function properly." Most of the organizations included in the report, however, merely provided social services for impoverished residents using War on Poverty funds.[11] When community organizers and activists countered that such surveillance was employed as an ideological tool of repression, the councilmen and Chief Ed Davis portrayed liberal social programs and civil rights organizations as subversive threats fomenting violent unrest to rationalize enhanced counterintelligence activities.[12]

Expanding surveillance capacity, police officials argued, was not only needed to prevent urban uprisings and social protest but also used to attack the limits placed on police discretion during the 1960s. Fears that liberal restrictions on police power would allow criminals to run rampant on the streets and force law-abiding residents to become prisoners in their homes, as police authorities and conservative officials from Nixon to Reagan had lamented after Watts, had apparently come home to roost. By politicizing Nixon's and Reagan's portrayal of law-abiding urban and suburban whites "locked in" their homes by fear of street crime, Davis framed the threat to society as not just crime but "revolutionaries" and radicals. Warning the Senate Internal Security Committee in 1970 that "we have revolution on the installment plan," Chief Davis justified the need for greater surveillance capacity, resources, and discretion in choosing targets. "Public officials are absolutely at the mercy of conspirators who have decided to overthrow this form of government," Davis explained, "and it's going to get worse." If legal and political support for surveillance programs was not forthcoming, Davis suggested, law-abiding citizens would continue to live in fear. "It is a tragic irony," Davis concluded, "that revolutionaries are running free on the streets and that the people are locked in their homes and even in their public buildings."[13] Counterintelligence operations, in effect, were part of an attempt to use the harm principle to reassert the department's discretion to define, prevent, and police threats to the public welfare in the name of protecting law-abiding residents. Attacks on the left, in other words, opened the way for generalized repression by granting the LAPD expansive police power to decide what behaviors and types of people constituted a threat to the social order.[14]

The LAPD worked diligently to expand its discretion to define what constituted a subversive or violent threat by transforming the focus of its counterintelligence apparatus. Under Chief Davis, the department slowly shifted its program from one concerned largely with organized crime to a deliberately vague, and thereby expansive, targeting of "public disorder." "Since I have been in I have virtually doubled my intelligence capacity, because intelligence 20 years ago, when we started it, was essentially a matter of keeping organized crime out of the city," Davis bragged at congressional hearings. "We found we have been gradually borrowing organized crime–type intelligence people into disordered-type [public disorder] intelligence."[15] The shift away from concerns for organized crime to "disordered" types rested on the belief that social movements were intent on limiting the power of law enforcement. Although Davis suggested that rigorous planning based on "the gathering of intelligence information" enabled the police to better protect the public, surveillance activities often exceeded such limits as officers became the arbiters of which activities were disorderly or criminal.[16]

Davis formally shifted the Intelligence Division's focus from organized crime to public disorder by establishing the PDID as an independent unit in 1970. In creating the PDID, Davis expanded the department's surveillance capacity and reoriented the target from the criminal to the subversive. The PDID operated as an updated Red Squad gathering "practically all" information on "potential threats" and storing as much information as possible. It was, in other words, a comprehensive surveillance program that significantly expanded the department's intelligence operations. Carving out broad discretionary authority, the PDID monitored and sorted activities deemed potentially harmful to Los Angeles's law-abiding residents.[17] Doing so intensified police surveillance of African American and Latino/a social movements under the pretense of preempting criminal activity.

Ensuring discretionary authority, however, required a demonstration of the PDID's success at keeping violence at bay. When the Board of Police Commissioners pushed Davis to study the possibility of redeploying personnel from the PDID to other divisions because of a reported decline in civil unrest and a budget crunch during the early 1970s, the chief vehemently defended the PDID's record. The roughly $1.7 million allocated to the division, the commission felt, would be better spent for patrol officers to combat rising crime rates. Davis opposed any reduction in the department's intelligence budget. The PDID operations, he argued, had been crucial to "quashing potential disorders in East Los Angeles and other areas," not mentioning that these "disorders" were often peaceful protests that became violent only upon police intervention. Davis defended the PDID, claiming that "in our case, it's preventing disorder on the streets of Los Angeles. . . . We were doing a good job keeping ahead of terror on the streets." Arguing that Los Angeles experienced less violent disorder than any other big city in the country, Davis capitalized on growing fears of gang violence and conflict with Black Power organizations to bolster the department's mission and convince the city council to maintain full funding to the PDID.[18]

Despite Davis's ability to maintain funding for the PDID, the Board of Police Commissioners recognized that counterintelligence operations threatened civilians' constitutional rights. As the Watergate scandal and the Church Committee investigation of U.S. intelligence agencies' covert action programs and spying on foreign leaders and American citizens exposed widespread federal surveillance and violation of constitutional rights, the commission became concerned with the growing backlog of old or irrelevant files. To address the problem, the commissioners ordered the purging of obsolete PDID files, resulting in the destruction of nearly two million intelligence records between 1975 and 1976. Mayor Bradley called the destruction of the files an "unprecedented move" that put Los Angeles in the lead of cities seeking "positive social change." The destruction of records, while on the surface painted as a move toward greater accountability and transparency, ultimately covered up past activities, destroying evidence of the PDID's politically motivated surveillance program.[19]

Alongside file destruction, the Police Commission proposed revisions to the guidelines regulating PDID operations in April 1975, which intended to balance the need for proper law enforcement functions and to prevent the erosion of residents' constitutional rights and liberties. To be sure, Bradley's liberal-leaning commissioners recognized that police surveillance damaged community relations, led to unrest, and undermined faith in government institutions. Commissioners such as Mariana Pfaelzer and Allan Bersin hoped that the review and revision of the PDID guidelines and procedures would place limits on the intelligence-gathering operation while maintaining the functions of a proactive and aggressive police force. "Intelligence information," the guidelines outlined, "will be gathered only in connection with those individuals or organizations found in accordance with the guidelines, to have threatened, attempted or performed illegal acts disruptive of the public order or disruptive of the legally protected civil rights of citizens." The proposed regulations also coincided with another audit of intelligence files, which resulted in the destruction of 850,000 additional old file cards.[20]

Revisions focused on file maintenance, retention, and destruction did little to limit the PDID's methods of intelligence gathering. The guidelines even allowed the PDID to operate anywhere in the country to monitor potentially disruptive activities "reasonably expected to affect the city of Los Angeles."[21] Board members, apparently convinced by Davis's claims of success, supported intelligence gathering because it "has been critical to police efforts to protect the public from those who would break the peace by creating riotous situations as well as from those who attempt to terrorize society by mass killings, wanton bombings or individual murders."[22] Continuing to believe in the power of government to rationally manage the coercive power of the state, Mayor Bradley praised the guidelines as evidence of the successful limits on police power in a democratic society. "The city must maintain the law enforcement balances of collecting information on violent people who are either ready to or have committed violence," he asserted, "but we must not at anytime collect information by the Police Department on people who break with the status quo and express political opinions that some, even if a majority, do not believe in." Concern for politically motivated spying did not preclude the prerogative of the police power to engage in intelligence operations.[23]

While Bradley and the Police Commission praised the guidelines, critics worried that PDID officers still possessed too much room to abuse their authority. Councilman David Cunningham opposed the PDID's ability to define who and what groups were subversive and criminal, while Mae Churchill of the Urban Policy Research Institute (UPRI), a local nonprofit group concerned with the abuse of police power and the violation of civil liberties, skewered the standards and procedures as a threat to constitutional rights. UPRI and the American Civil Liberties Union (ACLU) representatives were particularly concerned with the preventative monitoring of "potentially disruptive" groups, which they viewed as an illegitimate expansion of police authority. During hearings on the revised guidelines held in the spring of 1975, UPRI spokespeople made repeated demands that the commission needed to consider "a fundamental change in the definition of police power and police activity." At a second public hearing on the revised guidelines held in December 1975, seventeen witnesses representing organizations such as the Los Angeles County Bar Association, the NAACP, the ACLU, and UPRI testified to the PDID's politically motivated spying and threat created by providing the police with discretionary authority to determine who was harmful and who was law abiding. The revised guidelines, the UPRI's George Abdo claimed, did nothing to stop the PDID from being the "sole definer of public order and the sole judge of what threatens it."[24]

In response, Davis capitalized on the fears of international terrorism as a smokescreen for the PDID's repression of left-wing movements. Los Angeles, according to Davis, "has been among those suffering least from urban guerillas during the 70's." He suggested that the city's safety from bombings, kidnappings, hostage extortions, and killings was the result of the vigilance of the department's intelligence officers. "The relative freedom from serious harm to individual citizens in this City from terrorist activities," Davis told the Los Angeles Times in 1975, "is largely attributable to the creation of a highly sophisticated, totally lawful, and extremely effective public disorder intelligence function within the department." Calling the PDID and other intelligence functions "worth their weight in gold," Davis suggested that surveillance operations were central to preventing future violence.[25]

Yet the claim that the PDID's constant vigilance successfully thwarted terrorist plots was overblown. While left-wing "terrorism" was nearly nonexistent in the city, Davis failed to acknowledge that Los Angeles continued to lead the nation in right-wing bombings. In 1974 the city experienced 152 bombings by groups such as the American National Socialist Party, the Nazi Liberation Front, and the Ku Klux Klan. Local news media reported on some of these incidents, such as a 1975 bombing of the Socialist Workers Party office, but nowhere near the extent of attention placed on the 1974 SWAT shootout with the left-wing Symbionese Liberation Army in Compton. A lack of attention to growing right-wing terrorism nationwide reified police-constructed threats made up of those solely on the left.[26] Although Davis provided little evidence of success in stopping left-wing plots, he capitalized on fears of urban unrest to bolster the PDID's mission and discretionary authority. When Bradley attempted to reduce the PDID's ninety-one officers by half in 1976 due to his belief that the division duplicated state and federal intelligence units, Davis defended PDID operations as necessary to ward off an increase in "terrorist activity." Davis's fear-mongering convinced the city council to restore thirty of the proposed forty-six reductions made by Bradley in his initial budget.[27]

Nevertheless, the Police Commission believed that regulating file maintenance and retention would rein in the department's unwarranted surveillance practices. Responding to persistent criticism that the guidelines were vague and provided too much discretion to the PDID, in the final hearing on December 16, 1976, the Board of Police Commissioners stated that the revised guidelines had been approved by the city attorney as constitutional. Few public officials, including Mayor Bradley, were willing to openly challenge the chief or the PDID's autonomy to define what sorts of activities constitute potential disorder or criminal activity.[28] The commission passed the new guidelines, lauding them as "an important and valuable police innovation for which Chief of Police Edward M. Davis and his staff are to be highly recommended . . . a contribution . . . in the best leadership traditions of the Los Angeles Police Department."[29]

Despite the requirement of annual audits, the first of which was conducted nearly eighteen months later than required, the commissioners allowed the PDID operational freedom. The Police Commission routinely defended the PDID when questioned about the division's secrecy surrounding intelligence gathering.[30] "So far as attempting to have a Department that operates within the guidelines," Commissioner Pfaelzer reported, "I think that they have tried to do that . . . and that they were genuinely grateful that there was a long, long discussion about the organizations and the individuals." While recognizing that the "anticipatory intelligence function" made it difficult to determine exactly what types of activities would fit the definition of actions that could lead to, threaten, or "reasonably be expected to lead to or threaten" property damage or physical injury, the board did not question the clear potential for slippage into partisan surveillance based on the discretion of both police officials and officers. Pfaelzer's report concluded with the affirmation, "I am satisfied that they have made a genuine effort to confine their efforts to the kinds of organizations which are a threat."[31] The latitude provided to the PDID allowed it to maintain undercover officers, photographs, and files on nonviolent and law-abiding groups because the division defined what constituted disorder.

Policing Radicals, Fabricating Order

While Davis nominally accepted the new limits to the PDID's mandate, he vehemently defended intelligence gathering as a fundamental police function because it was central to the department's ability to contain both threats to liberty and the department's legitimacy. Davis routinely portrayed counterintelligence operations as part of defending the bedrock of a free society, claiming that "if the price of liberty is eternal vigilance, then abandonment of the intelligence function must be regarded as a first sign of impending death for American freedom." Surveillance activities, however, more often functioned to safeguard the freedom of the police and their legitimacy than the civilians the police were tasked to protect. They were crucial to the department's ability to combat and preempt its critics.[32] Indeed, as PDID lieutenant Charles Kilgo admitted, "One PDID function was to know anything about everybody that might come into conflict with the City of L.A., whether it be from a philosophical, political, or national standpoint."[33] Covert action was a tool of repression wielded by a department bent on enhancing its discretionary authority to define threats to the public and enforce social order.

Few groups were targeted as heavily as those who challenged the department's authority or attempted to bring accountability to the police. Concerned about CAPA's mission to root out the "police reign of terror," officers Connie Milazzo and Georgia Odom infiltrated the organization from its inception. As one briefing warned, "This organization is rapidly becoming one of the most militant we have encountered."[34] Within three months of CAPA's founding, PDID investigators were astonished at the organization's growth and the number of organizations brought together around the common complaint of police harassment, abuse, and killings. "The growth of CAPA has been phenomenal," a PDID briefing stated. "The May 21 meeting was attended by representatives of the following 21 organizations, all of which are involved in varying degrees in disruptive activities." The activities were certainly critical of the LAPD's prerogatives, but they could hardly be classified as potentially criminal. They included the collection of complaints against police malpractice, door-to-door organizing, steering committee meetings, development of a research and speaker bureau, and nonviolent protest.[35]

PDID officers routinely commented on the internal conflicts created by the paranoia over police spying and infiltration, a sign to the officers of the efficacy of their operation. "At one of our rallies we were trying to keep things calm and not give off bad vibes," a CAPA member and onetime friend of Odom stated. "But Georgia insisted on initiating chants like, 'Today's pig is tomorrow's bacon.' It disrupted our entire demonstration."[36] Undercover officers attempted to push CAPA to become a paramilitary organization that was a threat to the public order, justifying police infiltration and repression. The infiltration created divisiveness within CAPA, which hindered organizing and contributed to a loss of credibility with the community, and paranoia, distrust, and anxiety within the organization. The very presence of police infiltrators and surveillance, CAPA leader Anthony Thigpenn reaffirmed, "was a disruption" and "impeded and impaired our ability to organize."[37] The intelligence operation successfully created tension and hostility within target organizations in hopes of destabilizing and criminalizing them.

The surveillance of CAPA was part of the department's larger effort to discredit the groups' work to mobilize the community around police abuse, harassment, and killings. Chief Gates recalled discussions during briefings and roll call meetings to determine the validity of complaints against the department brought by CAPA's Police Misconduct Complaint Bureau. Assessing validity of complaints, however, was less about making the department more accountable to residents than it was a means of monitoring CAPA's activities and devising ways to turn the community against the anti–police abuse movement and undermine the legitimacy of complaints. "We are always concerned with that kind of complaint," Gates stated in reference to CAPA, "that is, basically interested in what they are doing in the community to convince others that their complaints are valid and what we might do to disabuse people in the community who believe that they are valid complaints."[38]

Black Power organizations also came under intense surveillance. As one former PDID officer admitted, "they were trying to destroy the black movement in L.A."[39] The PDID had a section devoted to infiltrating and providing information on African American community groups called the Black Power section, which grew to over twenty officers at its height in the late 1970s. Edward Brimmer, who became the supervisor of the Black Power Section, for example, oversaw the activity of the Black Panthers for at least seven years and recalled, "We basically kept records on all Panther activity in Southern California as a primary objective." Brimmer's concern for the Panthers was based on a belief that they represented a violent threat to the police. The Black Panthers had "had some violent situations involving the police. And specifically L.A. Police Department," Brimmer recalled. "And so any of the chapters that opened in Los Angeles, the City of Los Angeles, were—to my mind, would have to be investigated. And that's exactly what we set out to do."[40]

One such officer was David Bryant, who infiltrated a number of organizations including CAPA and the Black Panthers. An African American officer, Bryant started his career on the Narcotics Buy Team, where he worked undercover to arrest drug dealers, making busts largely in East and South Central Los Angeles. In November 1974, he began work in the PDID as one of the officers assigned to the Black Power section, where commanding officers asked if he had friends or relatives who were political and gave him books on socialism, Communism, and Marxism for training purposes. As a PDID informant, Bryant was told to take on the role of the observer, to be the eyes and ears of the department. Throughout his work as an undercover agent, Bryant recalled that he always worked to "further my status in the group," suggesting that PDID officers intended to become central to the organizations they infiltrated.[41]

Far from witnessing potentially criminal behavior, he witnessed multiple episodes of members of the groups under his purview actively opposing actions that could be conceived as disorderly or criminal. In fact, Bryant never observed any criminal activity as an organizer in the Black Panther Party's survival programs. When Panthers attempted to bring guns to a CAPA meeting, for example, Bryant recalled that Michael Zinzun would not let them enter. CAPA had a no weapons policy. Bryant's and other PDID officers' work in the Black Power section, overseeing a range of groups from the National Association for the Advancement of Colored People to the Black Panthers, reflected the attempt to monitor, preempt, and ultimately contain organizations and communities of color in the wake of the civil rights movement, practices that labeled them as de facto criminals.[42] The concern for the Black Panthers also led to the sharing of information between the PDID and the Oakland police about Panther activity. The widespread attention to the Panthers facilitated a statewide, if not interstate, network of surveillance. Yet, agents were pulled from investigations of the Panthers in 1978 due to a combination of a loss of funding and a lack of evidence of criminal activity and violence.[43]

Oftentimes, PDID officers infiltrated groups that were not even authorized as targets for surveillance. Bryant testified that he was "assigned to undercover non-file [unapproved surveillance] leftist groups to determine if criminal activity was planned." Bryant revealed in his deposition that most of his work did not result in an arrest, nor did it neutralize or prevent criminal activity. After infiltrating the Black Panthers, for example, he concluded that they improved the community through services, education, and job training and that the intense surveillance was a waste of resources. When he reported on the lack of criminal activity to his superiors, however, he was ordered to continue monitoring the group and was never told he was acting improperly, recalling that he was instructed to include all political groups at events and that they should be the focus of the reports. In fact, Edward Brimmer, a supervisor of the Black Power section, testified that the purpose of constant monitoring and file maintenance of political groups was to have information to be used when "necessary."[44]

The PDID also targeted Chicanos/as and American Indians for monitoring, infiltration, and disruption. During the early 1970s, for example, the PDID reported on United Farm Worker pickets, boycotts of liquor stores selling Gallo wines, and meetings with Mayor Tom Bradley.[45] The American Indian Movement was also under constant surveillance, and the FBI and PDID monitored the American Indian Movement's organizing on the Pine Ridge Reservation in South Dakota and sympathy protests and rallies held in Los Angeles in support of American Indian sovereignty and treaty rights.[46] One of the most dangerous Chicano/a groups in the eyes of PDID agents was El Centro de Acción Social Autónomo/the Center for Autonomous Social Action (CASA), an organization established by Bert Corona and other activists concerned with issues of labor and immigration. Working with the FBI, the PDID agents paid particular attention to CASA's work supporting local unionization efforts, protests of the arrest of undocumented workers by the LAPD and Immigration and Naturalization Service, and demonstrations against immigration bills requiring employers to investigate and remove undocumented aliens from their jobs.[47]

Instead of enforcing the law, the PDID's intelligence operations aimed at monitoring, containing, and disrupting the work of a variety of movements that challenged the police or attempted to expose police intelligence operations. The exposure of widespread spying in the late 1970s led to public admissions from officers about the extent of the department's political motivations. Two former PDID officers, for example, revealed in anonymous interviews with the *Herald Examiner* that the PDID spied on and infiltrated any group that challenged the status quo. "We were accountable for peaceful organizations as much as the ones that were a definite threat," one officer stated. They would identify themselves as Community Relations Section officers to get peaceful groups to complain about the police. "When I started to realize what the department was doing, I was humiliated," one officer explained. "They wanted us to report anything to show these people had ulterior motives."[48] The indiscriminate practices of PDID officers led to widespread violations of departmental policy regulating intelligence gathering. But the overreach of officer discretion also led to the demise of the PDID.

The PDID's Downfall

For all the effort to keep the inner workings of the PDID shrouded in secrecy, covert police action did not go unnoticed. Spurred by the disclosure of the LAPD's shredding of intelligence files and a police video crew and photographer collecting information and taking pictures of city council hearings, a coalition of thirty-six organizations formed the Southern California Network against Government Spying in August 1977—renamed the Citizens' Commission on Police Repression (CCPR) in 1978—to expose and publicize police spying, infiltration, and intelligence networks targeting organizations and individuals based on politics and ideology.[49] In the spring of 1978, the CCPR circulated a leaked official list of over 200 organizations that had been subject to PDID infiltration and spying. The groups included a few violence-prone organizations based in California prisons such as the Mexican Mafia, the Black Guerilla Family, and the American Nazi Party. The majority of groups, however, were nonviolent and on the liberal-left side of the political spectrum. The exposure not only increased public opposition to intelligence gathering but also revealed the inability of the Police Commission and city officials to effectively regulate the LAPD.[50]

If the circulation of the list of organizations under observation or infiltration raised concerns among organizations and liberal city council members, such as Zev Yaroslavsky, it did not faze Chief Gates. Although never denying the authenticity of the list, Gates criticized Yaroslavsky's proposal of a municipal Freedom of Information Ordinance, prohibiting photography in city council sessions, and an investigation into the police intelligence review process and operating guidelines. Gates feigned ignorance, claiming, "I don't know what police spying is," and a department spokesman denied wrongdoing, insisting, "We don't engage in political spying so what is there to talk about?"[51] Even after information regarding the breadth of PDID spying came to light, police commissioner Mariana Pfaelzer defended the commission's audit record and flatly denied the CCPR's charges of illegal activities, claiming, "No organization is being spied on now because it is a political activist group."[52]

Activists from CAPA, CCPR, and the ACLU filed a lawsuit in 1978, *CAPA, et al. vs. Gates, et al.*, which came to be made up of six cases on behalf of twenty-three groups and 108 individuals charging that the LAPD engaged in illegal surveillance operations based on political or ideological motivations.[53] The lawsuit stopped the destruction of file cards to preserve evidence of spying. Discovery motions unearthed thousands of pages of intelligence records and led to evidence that connected the LAPD to national and international intelligence operations and conservative political organizations.[54] The lack of restriction on PDID activity created serious doubts about the scope of state authority, constitutional rights, and civil liberties. Police surveillance, the CCPR's Linda Valentino, who had also been under investigation, told the city council, was at the center of the "moral and legal crisis in this country today."[55]

Discovery documents undermined claims that the PDID operated within the limits set by the 1976 guidelines. Releases of documents between 1980 and 1982 disclosed that PDID officers had infiltrated city council meetings, spied on elected officials, including Mayor Bradley, and routinely spied on nonviolent community organizations protesting police abuse. On a number of occasions, such as hearings held after the police killing of Eula Love, PDID officers attended council meetings with cameras and video equipment to photograph participants and record testimony related to police abuse. Evidence of undercover officers monitoring noncriminal activity critical of the police reaffirmed the PDID's role in monitoring, containing, and neutralizing threats to its legitimacy.[56] The revelations of police spying on elected officials, however, drew outrage from Bradley and city council members.

In the face of mounting criticism, Gates defended PDID operations. Gates refused to disclose the PDID's budget to the city council's Finance and Revenue Committee, citing the need for secrecy. If he released the budget, Gates opined, "the whole operation (PDID) itself would be in jeopardy. The potential terrorists assessing the potential of their being under surveillance would place the welfare of this community in jeopardy."[57] Any excesses or past errors were, according to Gates, merely "honest mistakes" in the course of doing what was necessary to thwart terrorist plots. Gates allowed for some criticism but was unwilling to cede any ground on the validity of intelligence functions.[58] Commissioner Stephen Reinhardt backed up Gates using circular logic by claiming that if infiltration had occurred there was likely a "legitimate reason" for the operation.[59] When Gates refused to comment on PDID activities to the city council, Yaroslavsky commented that "the statements made today reflect the department's traditional policy of tight lips and delays and lack of candor," to which Gates replied that that was "pure, unadulterated baloney."[60]

Mayor Bradley also put pressure on the police. After Gates's dissembling at city council hearings, Bradley admonished the department and its chief. "I will not tolerate the gathering of intelligence information on individuals or organizations that are not involved in either criminal or terrorist activities," Bradley stated. "Since recently released information indicates an apparent past infringement on those constitutional rights, steps must be taken now so that this never again occurs in the future."[61] Bradley asked Gates for a written report on intelligence operations targeting civil rights activists such as H. H. Brookins in light of what Bradley called "illuminating disclosures" and that "such conduct destroys the credibility of the department."[62]

Far from undermining the credibility of the department, Gates did not believe PDID activities represented an overreaching of state authority or an illegitimate discretionary police power. Nor did the PDID, according to Gates, infiltrate organizations based on political ideology but solely out of the need to enforce order. "Contrary to the allegations of the Citizens' Commission and their supporters your police department does not engage in mass infiltrations of peaceful organizations nor do we conduct indiscriminate 'spying' on the private or public lives of individuals," Gates told the Rotary Club. "The Public Disorder Intelligence Division is responsible for investigating specific and critical areas of concern that have a serious impact on the public order in our city." Gates not only defended the PDID but also called for the expansion of intelligence gathering in 1981 and early 1982 because he claimed that terrorism threatened to disrupt the city's hosting of the 1984 Summer Olympics.[63]

Instead of following Gates in lockstep, the Board of Police Commissioners followed Bradley's demand for greater transparency of police surveillance operations and passed a series of revisions to its PDID guidelines. The first came in 1980 but made only nominal changes to intelligence-gathering regulations.[64] Investigations by the police commissioners into allegations of improper PDID operations focused on the surveillance of city council meetings and lawful organizations but did not result in strong reprisals of the intelligence function per se. Audits of the PDID conducted by the Police Commission were hardly critical and commented only on the files removed from the PDID's active investigation list.[65] The LAPD also conducted its own annual reviews of PDID files, which produced mere two-page reports on the number of individuals and organizations removed from the files. The reports made no mention of how many or which organizations were added, failing to properly regulate the type of information gathered and target selection.[66]

There was little effort, in other words, to limit or manage the gathering of intelligence beyond restricting politically motivated spying on elected officials. In another revision to the Standards and Procedures passed in 1982, the commission promoted intelligence gathering as a legitimate police function that could be properly regulated by the local state. Passed unanimously, the revised guidelines asserted the principle that "public disorder intelligence information, properly gathered, maintained, and used, is essential to the performance of the Los Angeles Police Department's mandated duty of preventing significant disruption of the public order." The board admitted that in the past intelligence gathering was "directed towards organizations or individuals with 'subversive' ideologies," and limited the collection of intelligence files to groups who advocated criminal conduct or had planned or threatened disruptions of the public order. While the board lauded its efforts to revise the guidelines, claiming "that no other metropolitan police department in this country has imposed such far-reaching restrictions on its own behavior," the commissioners continued to justify the purpose of the PDID based on the need for "anticipation and prevention of crimes." If political ideology was an illegitimate reason for target selection, the 1982 guidelines continued a pattern of vague and ambiguous limits on intelligence collection and transparency.[67]

When the ACLU released a forty-page report documenting infiltration and surveillance of organizations critical of the department and the city council later in 1982, the credibility of Gates and the police commission eroded. Councilman Cunningham called the operation "damnable." Continued document releases revealed not only intelligence briefings on city council members but also deliberate efforts of Chief Gates to deceive the Board of Police Commissioners about the scope of the PDID's choice of targets. Spying on the council, Police Commission, and Mayor Bradley seemed to be one scandal too many for the city to swallow. As Zev Yaroslavsky wrote to Commissioner Reva Tooley in 1982, it was time to address the widespread political spying because the police have "steadfastly maintained" that they did not conduct investigations on peaceful, law-abiding groups. What was more, the Police Commission had not fully implemented the new regulations and denied that the PDID had acted well outside its operational guidelines.[68]

Released documents also unearthed the *Connection Report*, which was an effort by the PDID to link various left-wing organizations together in a criminal conspiracy for use in the trial defense. In the *Connection Report*, the PDID investigators listed the organizations involved with the CCPR, the eighty-eight organizations tied to CAPA, and every individual involved in the case against the department as potentially subversive. "CAPA, CCPR, and CES [Coalition for Economic Survival, a multiracial grassroots organization for economic justice] are similar in their ideology demographic makeup, and areas of interest," the report explained. "The common theme among the organizations is the control of the police department by progressive civilians." The PDID went on to outline the "massive interlocking ties" that connected the organizations in a common fight and even labeled government-funded groups, such as the Greater Watts Justice Center, as a "staging ground" to attack the police. These groups certainly had similar agendas and common grievances, but the attempt to frame them as part of a left-wing criminal conspiracy was evidence of the department's paranoia and fear of losing its power to enforce order and limits on discretionary authority.[69]

The investigation into the PDID also revealed a spy network that extended well beyond Los Angeles. Revelations that intelligence documents had been in the possession of an officer by the name of Jay Paul, who had distributed some of the PDID files to an ultra-right-wing organization called Western Goals, led to an investigation revealing an extensive network of government spying and sharing of information with public and private agencies across the country.[70] The Paul inquiry, undertaken by the city council and Board of Police Commissioners, revealed that the PDID had avoided compliance with civilian oversight and regulations of the Board of Police Commissioners. As Officer Jesus Mejia stated, "the guidelines had no effect on investigations and only had a procedural effect on in-file documentation." Most detectives and supervisors determined that information was appropriate if the "chief needed to know."[71]

The confidential report on the Paul investigation exposed not only the PDID's virtually unrestrained intelligence operations but also the gross negligence on the part of the Police Commission, city officials, and police brass to keep its intelligence officers in check. "The evidence we have reviewed indicates that recordkeeping and record security at PDID was negligent," the report found. "Insufficient controls and lack of management concern made it possible for Paul to have unchecked, unrecorded access to most materials." Investigators concluded that the PDID was mostly concerned with groups attempting to reform the department rather than complying with surveillance guidelines. "Of greater magnitude," the Paul Report stated, "was the amount of PDID energy and time spent studying, infiltrating and reporting on peaceful organizations which were critical of police such [as] CAPA, CCPR, ACLU, NLG [National Lawyers Guild] & AFS [American Friends Service Committee]."[72] Investigations into the Paul documents suggested that the PDID had conducted widespread illegal spying and infiltration operations that overstepped its authority.

Public attention from the lawsuit led to harsh scrutiny of the department and calls to dismantle the division. City Attorney Ira Reiner, for example, called for the cutoff of all funds to the department's intelligence unit. The 1982 guidelines, Reiner charged, had created a façade of accountability. The exposure of Jay Paul's intelligence network and open sharing with right-wing countersubversive organizations had destroyed the credibility of any PDID activities. Gates, however, denied any wrongdoing. He reverted to the argument that limits on the ability of the police to operate at will, would hamstring the department's ability to keep the city safe, commenting, "I'll bet there are several terrorists clapping their hands in glee over the panic that has set in . . . [who] are not going away by having the City Council withhold funds from PDID."[73]

If Gates hoped to use terrorism to manipulate the council into supporting the PDID, he now faced certain defeat. Mounting pressure from activists and city council members, such as Zev Yaroslavsky, led the Board of Police Commissioners to request Chief Gates submit a full report on the PDID in the fall of 1982 after evidence confirmed that Gates had lied about surveillance activities relating to the CCPR, CAPA, and other nonviolent groups. Discovery documents revealing that Gates had directed intelligence officers to infiltrate anti–police abuse organizations and report all activities did not square with his statements to the commission that the PDID had "absolutely no interest in peaceful groups."[74] Despite Gates's stonewalling, Police Commission chair Reva B. Tooley concluded after a months-long investigation in January 1983, "Recent events have led me to conclude that PDID has not been operating in the manner contemplated by Commission guidelines."[75]

Pressure from the city council, Mayor Bradley, and City Attorney Ira Reiner ultimately led to the demise of the PDID. On January 17, 1983, Reiner submitted a proposal to the city's Police, Fire and Public Safety Committee that the PDID be disbanded. The following day, the Police Commission, in conjunction with the city council, formally disbanded the PDID. Deciding to dismantle the PDID was an attempt to renew faith in law enforcement's ability to protect constitutional rights by removing all political and ideological considerations from intelligence gathering.[76]

The PDID scandal not only revealed the surveillance of community groups but also pointed toward a broader threat posed by the coercive power of the state to limit dissent and infringe on basic rights of citizens. As Yaroslavsky reported to the Police, Fire and Public Safety Committee on February 14, 1983, the history of the LAPD's surveillance was shameful and frightening. "Shameful, because we have behaved in an unabashedly irresponsible manner, violating constitutional precepts," he explained. "Frightening because it has unveiled an arrogance of power in the department which, if not curtailed, will continue to plague the citizens of this City indefinitely." Police surveillance and intelligence activities that began with the intention of curtailing and even destroying movements for racial and social justice ended up threatening the constitutional rights and civil liberties of all of Los Angeles's residents. But the enhanced guidelines and freedom of information ordinance stopped short of questioning what Yaroslavsky described as the benefits of "bona fide police intelligence gathering."[77]

For all the outrage at police spying by city council members and Bradley, most of the opposition generated in response to revelations of spying was based on their political point of view, not the question of the validity of the police intelligence function. Instead of questioning the underlying police power of surveillance itself, liberals attempted to reorganize intelligence regulations so that the police focused their spying on "harm" based on expansive definitions of "terrorism." Only a decade earlier, the LAPD justified its need for secrecy and wide latitude in surveillance to root out dangerous "revolutionaries," a category that led to vast police discretion to target and repress. The department would now focus on the need to neutralize "terrorists."

From Disorder to Terrorism

Rather than interrogate the legitimacy of intelligence gathering, the Board of Police Commissioners reorganized the PDID into the Anti-Terrorist Division (ATD) with new standards and procedures on July 1, 1983. The guidelines attempted to construct narrow definitions of what types of activities qualified for surveillance while leaving the police enough discretion to protect public safety. Only organizations that advocate "criminal conduct *and* its members have planned, threatened, attempted or performed such criminal conduct which could reasonably be expected to result in significant disruption of the public order" could come under ATD surveillance. The regulations specifically defined nonviolent civil disobedience and public protest as legitimate forms of expression, behavior, and political activity.[78] The transition team overseeing the move from the PDID to the ATD made recommendations intended to strictly monitor and limit any politically motivated spying.[79]

At the federal level, terrorism gained new political saliency in the years after the Iran Hostage crisis and as the Reagan administration ramped up proxy wars and support for anti-Communist paramilitary operations in Central America.[80] The ATD reinforced the growing concern with international terrorism and, according to one source, ensured "the last vestige of the old Red Squad days has come to an end in Los Angeles."[81] The turn to "terror," however, was productive of a new era in police power. The LAPD both followed and helped set new national priorities related to police power and the prevention of "terrorist" threats, with long-lasting consequences.

The *CAPA v. Gates* lawsuit ended in a settlement of $1.8 million to the plaintiffs in 1984.[82] The associated consent decree, according to the *Los Angeles Times*, "establishes the toughest controls on police intelligence activities in the nation." The agreement gave civilian authorities the power to approve or reject undercover operations by the ATD. The settlement in Los Angeles was part of similar efforts in cities across the nation to curb police abuses, including Chicago, Memphis, Washington, D.C., Michigan, New York, and Seattle.[83] The settlement agreement ended a long fight against the PDID, and CAPA felt that it had succeeded in forcing the city and the LAPD to make concessions toward greater accountability. "These guidelines are the toughest in the Country," CAPA reported; "the LAPD Anti Terrorist Division has already began to squawk about not being able to spy on whoever they choose."[84]

The consent decree was a victory. But the investigation ultimately blamed LAPD management for lack of adequate oversight to contain rogue agents rather than a systemic problem in the department or of police power writ large. As Jack B. White, commander and Police Commission investigator, reported to the commission, officer discretion had led to serious overreaching. "The Commission concluded that the intelligence function was limited to protecting the city from those persons who would attempt serious disruptions of the public order through violent or unlawful means," White explained. "Some departmental personnel, however, viewed the intelligence function as much more global, and apparently saw as its mandate the amassing and collection of information from every conceivable source."[85] By framing the problem as one of individual discretionary overreach instead of a systemic, department-wide culture, the solution left the fundamental legitimacy of surveillance as a discretionary police power intact.

In the wake of the lawsuit that led to the dissolution of the PDID, Gates criticized the groups who demanded changes in the PDID as having no interest in making the city safe from terrorists and that they did not care about the stability of the city. Gates felt that the new guidelines unduly limited the LAPD. "For anyone to say that we are going to be able to operate effectively with these guidelines I think they would be foolish," Gates reported. "I think it's senseless to have this kind of detailed, demanding guidelines for any detective work."[86] Indeed, Gates continued to defend the broad collection of information even after the PDID had been disbanded and more stringent regulations had been established for the ATD. "There is absolutely no way that we cannot, on occasion," Gates explained, "trample on some people's privacy and freedom."[87]

Aided by CAPA and the CCPR, Councilman Zev Yaroslavsky also proposed a local freedom of information act through the city council in order to safeguard the community from future secrecy of public records.[88] In the face of Gates's opposition and wild claims that the ordinance would undermine the ability of the police to maintain safety during the 1984 Olympics, the council passed a version of Yaroslavsky's ordinance. The local ordinance, though a watered-down version of the original bill, provided residents with access to intelligence records and was a step toward increasing transparency in the department and local governance.[89]

Although the ATD consent decree placed limitations on the LAPD's ability to initiate preliminary investigations without a "reasonable and articulated suspicion" that a person or group was planning to disrupt the public order and required yearly audits, the police routinely balked at such limits on their power. Indeed, it was no secret that Gates had nothing but contempt for the 1983 regulations instituted by the consent decree. Initial audits of the ATD suggested that the department complied with the strict guidelines governing intelligence gathering. Even when more outspoken members of the police commission suggested in 1988 that the ATD should be dismantled or, at the least, officers should be rotated out of undercover operations every five years to prevent corruption, Gates stonewalled, once again calling the suggestion "foolish."[90]

But by the late 1980s and early 1990s, charges of politically motivated spying and secret intelligence files arose in spite of Gates's denunciations of any unlawful surveillance carried out by his department. Yet in 1991 the Police Commission was two and a half years behind in conducting required annual audits. Questions about the department's intelligence program also erupted after the police commission's controversial decision to not place Gates on leave after the Rodney King beating in 1991. Indeed, the liberal members of the Police Commission appointed under Bradley had done little to rein in or criticize the department in the decade after the consent decree. While no concrete evidence surfaced and Gates called the allegations "outrageous," there were many who believed that Gates had continued to use information gathered on political officials to ensure support for the department.[91]

If the ACLU and CAPA continued to warn of the possibility of politically repressive police counterintelligence operations, city officials had a short historical memory. In 1996, just over a decade after the consent decree, the department once again organized to roll back the limitations on intelligence gathering to combat new terrorist threats. Even before the 1995 Oklahoma City bombing, renewed fears of domestic terrorism provided support for the LAPD's push for more expansive discretion in surveillance operations. Despite opposition from the ACLU, CAPA activists, and editorials in the *Los Angeles Times* warning of the dangers of loosening police surveillance guidelines, the board, working with LAPD officials, went ahead with revisions that significantly broadened the LAPD's authority to initiate investigations based on "reasonable suspicion" of criminal activity and to utilize electronic surveillance tools.[92]

Surveillance, infiltration, and the maintenance of intelligence files were central components of an expanding criminal justice system used to manage the material consequences of urban decline and social protest within the context of civil rights victories. The LAPD's efforts at monitoring, social control, and preemptive measures aimed at inner cities framed organizations and individuals struggling against repressive policing as disorderly, subversive, and criminal. As the number of organizations and individuals under PDID surveillance suggested, most of the intelligence gathering was aimed at nonviolent and law-abiding activities. The PDID's intelligence officers, however, repeatedly made decisions that the types of activities and politics of these groups constituted disorderly, improper, or criminal behavior; in effect, surveillance produced, rather than reflected, criminality. Such thinking reinforced ideas within the department, at the leadership level in particular, that movements for social justice and civil liberties threatened the American social order and required monitoring and surveillance.

Yet, the story of the relationship between surveillance and social movements also reveals the ways that police intelligence operations were shaped by the actions of local community organizations. Although the publicity from media attention and city council furor over PDID abuses were crucial to ending police spying, CAPA and the CCPR presented key challenges to the PDID and what they saw as the development of a surveillance state, ultimately dismantling the PDID.

Liberal officials and anti–police abuse activists hoped that strict regulation of police intelligence gathering would limit police power, enhance procedural fairness, and protect the rights of citizens. But as the LAPD's capacity to target elected officials narrowed in the wake of the PDID scandal, its ability to define what constituted "terrorism" and potential harm to the public welfare left intact the power to monitor people of color and social movements under the guise of enforcing order. Changing definitions of the threat to public safety, from the radicals and revolutionaries of the 1960s and 1970s to the terrorists of the 1980s and 1990s, provided the LAPD with continued latitude in surveillance operations. As the department pivoted to the 1980s, it remobilized to expand its discretionary authority to attack urban social problems, such as rising immigration, drugs, and gangs. In the process, the police circumvented procedural reforms meant to limit officer discretion and contributed to new methods of racially targeted governance and control.

Chapter 7

Policing an Internal Border

Constructing Criminal Aliens and Exclusive Citizenship

On May 13, 1977, Roque Placentia Arenas was sipping a beer in the Las Vegas Bar when two LAPD officers entered on a routine patrol. After surveying the patrons, the officers approached Arenas because "[he] was very small in stature and had a very youthful appearance." They apprehended Arenas and tried to leave the bar to verify his age when Juan López Ibarra stepped in front of the officers. Ibarra asked them what they were doing with Arenas, claiming, "You don't have any right to take him. He isn't drunk." Brushing Ibarra aside, the officers arrested Arenas, who had no identification and "spoke Spanish only," for "illegal entry." But the officers were not finished. They returned to Ibarra, whom they described as speaking "broken English." When Ibarra could not provide identification, the officers detained him for illegal entry as well and reported the arrests to the Immigration and Naturalization Service (INS).[1]

During the 1970s, LAPD officers often arrested undocumented Mexican immigrants and transferred them to the INS. While some police officials viewed Mexican immigrants as a source of rising crime, they recognized that enforcement of immigration status violations not only made immigrants wary of reporting crime out of fear of deportation but also strained local police budgets. In response, police officials and lawmakers attempted to incorporate immigrants into the war on crime. Revisions to department policy in 1970 and 1972 made arrests based on immigration status "less important" than fighting crime. They also established programs to encourage immigrants to report crime. Hopes that immigrants and Latino/a residents would support the police required limiting arrests based solely on immigration status and ending cooperation with INS agents. As such, police officials framed the undocumented immigrant-as-potential-crime-victim in need of police protection but not a legitimate target for arrest or detention.

Although the LAPD nominally accepted limits to policing immigration status violations, the department did not abandon assumptions that undocumented immigrants contributed to rising crime.[2] Rather, the police circumvented policies limiting their discretion by employing a new category of criminality, the "alien criminal," a precursor to the more widespread use of "criminal aliens" after the INS's 1986 Criminal Alien Program. Using the harm principle to frame "alien criminals" as a potential threat to law-abiding citizens, the police legitimated continued cooperation with the INS and targeting of immigrants for arrest, detention, and deportation. The police often portrayed this alien criminal as an undocumented Mexican immigrant. The racialized construction of categories of illegality and exclusion led to the violation of the rights of immigrants and discriminatory treatment of Mexican migrants and Mexican American citizens as potentially "illegal" and criminal. Aggressive immigration enforcement thereby treated all Mexican American residents as perpetual foreigners.[3] By constructing a racialized category of the "alien criminal" as any ethnic Mexican in need of supervision, the LAPD simultaneously avoided violating its own policy of nonenforcement of immigration status and expanded its authority to enforce order and define exclusionary boundaries of citizenship.

Lawsuits filed by the Mexican American Legal Defense and Educational Fund exposed police cooperation with the INS. It led LAPD authorities to implement orders further narrowing officer discretion to make arrests based on immigration status. The policy put the LAPD in the forefront of national standards when it came to regulating local enforcement of immigration law. During the 1980s, however, the police circumvented these policy limitations within the context of the city's war on drugs and gangs. Flipping the standard narrative of federal enforcement of immigration law reveals how the LAPD expanded the police power into immigration enforcement during an era when the INS had limited resources and manpower. Police and city officials pointed to undocumented immigrants as a source of rising gang crime and violence in Latino/a and immigrant neighborhoods. Addressing the problem required empowering officers to arrest immigrants and cooperate with the INS. Within the context of the war on drugs and gangs, law enforcement officials labeled immigrants as violent criminals and thereby subject to arrest by local police and transfer to the INS for detention and deportation.[4]

Even as Mayor Bradley promoted Los Angeles as a "world city" welcoming visitors—and capital—from around the globe, new waves of immigrants and refugees from Central America during the 1980s and 1990s threatened the LAPD's vision of social order, raising questions about which residents it was required to protect and to serve.[5] In doing so, the LAPD repackaged old tactics, such as status arrests and dragnet tactics that were staples of 1950s policing, as new and novel strategies. Using a theory known as public order policing (broken windows), the LAPD targeted activities immigrants and refugees used to earn a living, such as street vending and day labor, for aggressive policing. They framed this informal economy as a nuisance to public order and a sign of neighborhood decay leading to more serious crime. In the process, the police produced another category of criminality and illegality that led to the discriminatory policing of Latino/a immigrants and refugees. By the early 1990s, the LAPD's war on crime was enmeshed in a program of immigration control.[6]

A Multiracial Metropolis, World City Liberalism, and the Crisis of Immigration

Following the 1965 Hart-Cellar Immigration Act, Los Angeles experienced profound demographic changes. Mexican immigrants came to Los Angeles in large numbers between the 1970s and 1990s due to demands for cheap labor in the city's burgeoning service economy and economic pressures in Mexico. While Mexican immigrants represented the largest migrant stream, the 1965 act's removal of discriminatory national origins quotas opened new sources of immigrants who contributed to an increasingly diverse metropolitan region. Los Angeles experienced rapid growth during the 1980s in immigrants from Central and South America and Asia, particularly China and Korea. In 1980, whites accounted for 68 percent of the county population, African Americans represented 12.6 percent, Latinos/as 27.6 percent, and Asian and Pacific Islanders 5.8 percent. By 1990, whites represented 56.8 percent of the population in the county, while blacks represented 11.2, Asian and Pacific Islanders 10.8, and Latinos/as 37.8 percent. Los Angeles had become a world city. In 1988, for example, 13.7 percent of all new immigrants to the United States moved to Los Angeles, and the foreign-born population of the city in 1990 was 32.7 percent. By the end of the twentieth century, the Los Angeles International Airport had become a new Ellis Island.[7]

As the city became more diverse, Mayor Bradley hoped to be responsive to a more multicultural constituency. Between the 1970s and 1990s, world city liberalism characterized Bradley's and political officials' approach to governing and policing a global Los Angeles. Bradley advanced multicultural programs and promoted diversity as central to effective governance for Los Angeles. Positioning Los Angeles as a "world city" required making it a safe place for global investment, trade, and commerce. While attracting capital from Asia—Japan in particular—was a central goal of world city liberalism, it also relied on a burgeoning low-wage service sector filled by immigrant and refugee labor. But maintaining the city's diversity and attracting international corporations also required assurances of public safety and a crackdown on crime. World city liberals responded by pursuing a dual strategy. On the one hand, it required empowering the police to crack down on crime to promote the city as a safe space for high-wage workers and investment. On the other hand, it required responding to demands from the city's immigrant populations for fair treatment by the police.[8]

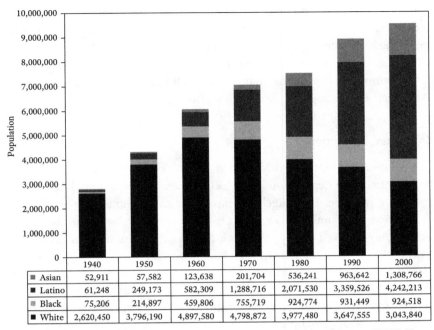

	1940	1950	1960	1970	1980	1990	2000
▪ Asian	52,911	57,582	123,638	201,704	536,241	963,642	1,308,766
▪ Latino	61,248	249,173	582,309	1,288,716	2,071,530	3,359,526	4,242,213
▪ Black	75,206	214,897	459,806	755,719	924,774	931,449	924,518
▪ White	2,620,450	3,796,190	4,897,580	4,798,872	3,977,480	3,647,555	3,043,840

Los Angeles County demographics, 1940–2000. Source: Phil J. Ethington, W. H. Frey, and D. Myers, "The Racial Resegregation of Los Angeles County, 1940–2000," *Race Contours*, 2000.

The rise of world city liberalism and the growth in immigration to Los Angeles coincided with a series of economic crises during the 1970s. Recession and unemployment followed the oil crisis of 1973, and the region's manufacturing base experienced a significant decline, losing tens of thousands of jobs over the decade. Despite global economic forces and U.S.-backed counterinsurgency wars in Latin America that forced Mexicans and Central Americans to flee to American cities where they faced low-wage and exploitive labor conditions, local and national media blamed immigrants for the economic crisis. The *Los Angeles Times* fanned such fears and attributed local budget woes on immigrants, publishing negative stories, such as one with the headline "Aliens Reportedly Get $100 Million in Welfare." Local officials and law enforcement doubled down on fears of immigrant invasion, often describing undocumented Mexican immigrants as a drain on the region's social services, to expand the ability of the police to target migrants.[9]

By the early 1990s, Los Angeles's law enforcement and political officials framed the city's multiracial demographic transformation as a problem of violence and criminality. The City Human Relations Commission reported, "Rather than having this city's diversity understood as a rich resource as an economic crossroad, it has been cast as tribal conflict, fraught with crime, violence and tension."[10] Rather than a reflection of the immigrants or refugees who had come to Los Angeles, police and city policy established between the 1970s and 1990s produced exclusive categories of citizenship that not only linked immigrants with criminality but also framed both the city's Mexican American and immigrant populations as foreign outsiders.

Perpetual Foreigners

In the late-night hours on July 16, 1970, two officers from the northern California city of San Leandro and six LAPD officers arrived at a Skid Row apartment in downtown Los Angeles in pursuit of an individual suspected of an "execution-type" murder. The officers kicked in the door of the apartment where they believed the suspect was hiding. Without announcing their presence, officers proceeded down a dark hallway, then fired shots from service pistols and shotguns at a door that had been pushed closed. In the barrage, the officers killed two Mexican nationals, cousins Guillermo and Guillardo Sánchez, one with a .38 caliber bullet and the other by buckshot that left forty holes in his body. The officers notified LAPD headquarters of the shooting, reporting, "No officers injured."[11]

Upon hearing about the killings, LAPD inspector Kenneth McCauley called U.S. attorney Robert L. Meyer to report the shooting of two Mexican "illegals." The two men were unarmed, they had nothing to do with the murder investigation, and police entered their apartment without a warrant. But the LAPD portrayed the killings as a mere mistake of routine police work and argued that the officers should not be disciplined. Deputy Police Chief Daryl Gates called the shootings "a tragic series of mistakes, and a tragedy all around." The killings, however, led to national publicity surrounding the problem of police abuse and the limits of police authority in dealing with the city's immigrant community. The U.S. attorney general intervened to determine if civil rights violations had been committed, and the Department of Justice requested the impaneling of a grand jury, leading Mexican American journalist Ruben Salazar to praise the "System's" ability to achieve justice.[12]

Despite indictments of the officers by the grand jury, the federal case was dismissed in August 1971. A crucial element in the case was the fact that the Sánchez cousins were undocumented residents. During the trial and in public statements, defense attorneys made references to the Sánchez cousins and witnesses to the shooting as aliens, wetbacks, and illegals.[13] The defense questioned whether undocumented—"illegal"—residents were entitled to civil rights protections, arguing in a brief that "it is inconceivable that an illegal alien could be an inhabitant. . . . At best he is a fugitive subject to criminal sanctions when discovered."[14] Rather than viewing the Sánchez cousins as victims, the defense criminalized them as illegal and therefore devoid of rights. "Of importance," a Mexican American Legal Defense and Educational Fund lawyer lamented, "is the fact that the judge instructed the jury that if the victims were not 'inhabitants' of Los Angeles, they were not protected by the Civil Rights acts and officers could not be found guilty."[15]

The Sánchez killings revealed how the targeting of "illegal aliens" also criminalized Mexican American citizens based on racialized constructions of illegality. The Mexican American community criticized law enforcement's racist assumptions of criminality and illegality. The Barrio Defense Committee used its newsletter, *La Voz Del Barrio*, to warn all Mexican Americans, Latinos, Hispanos, and Chicanos that "you must prove daily, you're a U.S. citizen" due to the actions of the police and the INS. "If the officers are acquitted a precedent will be established giving a blank check to policemen not only to shoot and kill Mexican Nationals, but to rationalize the shooting of Chicanos," the Barrio Defense Committee warned. "After all, cops can 'mistake' a Chicano for a National."[16] As police enforced immigration law, in short, they contributed to the exclusion of Mexican immigrants and Mexican Americans as perpetual foreigners based on the stereotype of Mexicans as the prototypical "illegal aliens." "Police see Chicanos as foreigners, intruders, illegals anyway," one resident told researchers investigating police use of deadly force, "and therefore not having any rights."[17]

Immigration enforcement constructed and operated on racist views of undocumented immigrants that treated all Mexicans as potential "illegal aliens" and subject to detention. In the spring of 1973, for example, the INS conducted "Operation Cleansweep," during which agents arrested and detained more than 2,000 immigrants. Reports from religious groups and activists suggested that many Mexican Americans were targeted "based solely on skin color or language."[18] The Centro de Acción Social Autónomo/the Center for Autonomous Social Action (CASA) held demonstrations in front of the Mexican Consulate to protest the blanket targeting of Latinos/as. "The raids, purportedly undertaken to apprehend 'illegal aliens,'" a CASA press release explained, "have occurred on a door-to-door basis, and have led to the harassment of all persons with brown skin."[19] Many constituents also wrote to Congressman Ed Roybal, complaining about the racist nature of the raids. "The raids have primarily focused on the roundup and deportation of thousands of persons of Mexican descent," Roybal concluded. "This concentration of effort has led to the serious charge that the Service has detained and arrested persons on the basis of race or color."[20]

Over the 1970s, arrests of immigrants for "illegal entry" and cooperation with INS agents in raids and routine arrests reflected how the LAPD policed the boundaries of race and citizenship by targeting Latinos/as as "illegal." Department officials recognized that the Mexican American community opposed police enforcement of immigration law because it often led to interrogation, harassment, and arrest of Mexican American citizens, "not because they are suspected of being illegal aliens, but because of their ethnicity." As one LAPD community relations study found, "indiscriminate stopping and questioning of the illegal alien element will not be accepted." Such policing alienated the community and increased distrust of law enforcement.[21] Police officials responded by implementing new policies and programs aimed at incorporating immigrants and Mexican Americans into the war on crime.

Immigrants as Potential Crime Victims

Immigration control and policy had long been established as a prerogative of the federal government. But state and local law enforcement routinely worked with federal officials in enforcing immigration law during the mid-twentieth century. Although the Immigration Act of 1929 classified unauthorized entry as a misdemeanor, Border Patrol agents largely treated it as a civil rather than criminal offense. The Immigration and Nationality Act of 1952 further bifurcated the immigration and criminal justice systems by making civil violations the jurisdiction of the INS, while local police departments could arrest immigrants for criminal violations. Within this legal structure, the LAPD was an important partner to federal immigration enforcement, especially in the 1940s and 1950s. Accompanied by INS agents, Daryl Gates recalled of his early tenure on the force, "we used to go down to the railroad stations and pick 'em up by the dozens." While this federal-local arrangement remained in place through the 1960s, the rise of unauthorized immigration in the 1970s, pressure on local police budgets, and growing pressure from Mexican Americans fearful of being targeted as "illegal" challenged the LAPD's cooperative relationship with federal immigration enforcement.[22]

As the LAPD's relationship with Mexican American residents and immigrants grew tense due to police harassment and abuse during the early 1970s, police and city officials feared that it would lead both Mexican American citizens and undocumented immigrants to lose trust in the police and a reluctance to report crime. Undocumented immigrants were particularly subject to exploitation by "bunco" artists and immigration consultants. Unauthorized experts and "errant attorneys" often promised aid to immigrants in obtaining visas, for representation during deportation proceedings, and in establishing residency but did not provide the promised service. Undocumented immigrants were often victims of such crimes but were reluctant to approach the police department for aid out of fear of being reported to the INS.[23]

If officer discretion to enforce immigration law was limited, officials reasoned, immigrants would be more willing to approach officers when they were victims of crime. Recognizing the problem, Chief Davis issued Memorandum Number 9 in 1970, which stated, "Arrests for illegal entry [to the United States] shall be considered subordinate to police activities directly related to the interests of the people of Los Angeles." Such language, however, left officers with significant discretion when it came to making arrests based on status. Two years later, Davis strengthened the limits on officers with Special Order 68, stating that "officers shall not initiate police action where the primary objective is directed toward discovering the alien status of a person." But the policy allowed officers to contact the INS to determine the status of a person involved in criminal investigations. Nor did it prevent officers from making arrests based on status. It merely emphasized that "arrests for illegal entry should be considered less important than other police activities." While narrowing discretion, the reforms aimed to soften the image of the police in immigrant neighborhoods and incorporate residents into the fight against crime.[24]

The department also hoped to facilitate trust by establishing a storefront station in East Los Angeles where residents could report crimes and scam artists without being asked about their immigration status. With the backing of the city council and Mayor Bradley, the LAPD established Operación Estafadores in 1972.[25] The city council described the program "both as a device to enhance community relations and as a badly needed crime repressant."[26] The program operated on a "no questions asked" basis and intended to "extend police assistance to that segment of the Latin community that is reticent to seek contact with official agencies due to language difficulties, immigrational status, or the foreboding image that a police agency represents to some people."[27]

City council members and community residents praised Estafadores as a step toward improving relations with both Mexican American citizens and Mexican immigrants. Detectives manning the storefront believed it helped create a liaison between the community and the police, as an estimated 75 percent of those who used the service were undocumented.[28] "It has probably been one of the most successful efforts to develop trust and cooperation," stated Captain Richard J. Stevens, who oversaw the project from Hollenbeck Division. "I can see very few programs that have had an impact like Operación Estafadores."[29]

Working with residents enabled prosecutors to make cases against "Immigration Consultants." The district attorney, Joseph Busch, for example, told

LAPD officials that Estafadores strengthened the district attorney's Consumer Protection Division because "members of the Mexican-American Community who previously would not or could not complain to a government agency such as ours, are now providing, through Operación Estafadores, the information necessary for us to prepare cases for court."[30] Within the first two years of operation, the department claimed over 8,000 contacts with residents and indictments against major players, such as All Nations, Inc., in the immigrant consulting business.[31] One woman, for example, was given notice to move from her apartment despite on-time rent payments but had not reported the eviction because she "did not want to have attention focused on herself due to her illegal status." After she moved to a new apartment, her manager padlocked her door, prompting her to approach Operación Estafadores "because she had heard that she would not be asked what her status was." An investigator helped negotiate with the manager, who was surprised that "just a wetback" had reported the incident to the police. Although the case was under investigation, the LAPD reported it as a successful demonstration of the ability to bring redress in cases "where fear of deportation would have prevented corrective action."[32]

The project was a departure from the usually antagonistic relationship with the Mexican American and immigrant communities. Yet, Chief Ed Davis's claim that "persons heretofore reluctant to seek police assistance due to a language barrier or immigrational status now openly seek the aid of this Department in solving their problems" was an overstatement. After the passage of Proposition 13 in 1978 placed pressure on city budgets and newly appointed Chief Daryl Gates's reduction in funding and commitment to community relations programs, the department cut Estafadores personnel to three officers. Estafadores continued to operate through the 1980s on a limited budget. There were still only three detectives assigned to the program in 1991 despite the growth of the immigrant population and immigrants' susceptibility to becoming victims of crime and fraud. Even with programs such as Estafadores in operation, however, many immigrants were still wary of approaching the police to report crimes. For all the efforts to incorporate immigrant crime victims into the department's war on crime, the police continued to link another category of undocumented immigrants with criminality and as a law-and-order threat requiring aggressive enforcement of immigration laws, coordination with INS agents, and expansive discretionary supervision.[33]

Alien Criminals and Constructing a New Threat to Order

By the mid-1970s, the LAPD and other city officials worried that an element within the undocumented population was responsible for rising crime.

According to a survey conducted by the Hollenbeck Area commanding officer, which used police data to examine the connection between "illegal" immigrants and "crime," "a high percentage of crimes in Hollenbeck Area are being committed by members of the illegal entry faction."[34] While recognizing that undocumented immigrants were hard working and industrious, motivated to make a better life for themselves and their families, the report also framed the "illegal alien" as a threat to the social order. The LAPD and city officials pointed to a study of three immigrant neighborhoods, Hollenbeck, Harbor, and Rampart, after INS sweeps to support claims that undocumented immigrants represented a criminal threat.[35] "During the sweep repressible crimes fell 32 percent in Hollenbeck, 17.4 percent in Harbor, and 18 percent in Rampart," Deputy Mayor Grace Davis reported. "Although there were a number of variables involved in these statistics, they do tend to indicate a correlation between the sweep of undocumented aliens and the decrease in crime."[36]

Many law enforcement personnel and city officials advocated for greater cooperation with the INS to contain undocumented immigrants. "In view of the severity of the social and economic problems generated by the illegal alien element in our society," an LAPD report explained, "the recommendation was made that the Department actively cooperate with the Immigration and Naturalization Service by arresting illegal aliens solely for their unlawful status and releasing them to the Immigration Service for immediate deportation if these individuals were not involved in criminal activity." Despite pressure to broaden officer discretion, the report concluded that Special Order 68 should remain as policy because police cooperation with the INS threatened the department's crime-fighting mission, as it reduced support and trust in the Mexican community.[37]

Even as the department officials who penned the report advised against mass arrests of undocumented immigrants by the LAPD because of the risk of alienating residents from the department, other recommendations supported targeting of undocumented immigrants. Officials supported increased resources to the INS for apprehension and promoted legislation that would allow for prosecution before deportation of undocumented immigrants. The LAPD argued that "swift and vigorous prosecution *before deportation*" would create a "convicted alien" status, which, the department hoped, would make attempts at reentering less appealing.[38]

By the late 1970s, however, the department warned that immigrants were a growing criminal element in the city. Chief Davis reported to Attorney General Edward H. Levi in 1976 that illegal aliens brought a surge of crime and "added to the dope problem" in Southern California.[39] When taking into consideration the potential growth of the immigrant population, the police

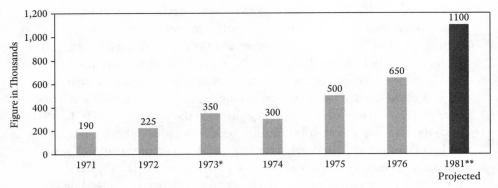

Growth of the illegal alien population in Los Angeles, 1971–1981. Sources: 1971/76 population based on INS estimates. The Illegal Alien Committee, "The Illegal Alien Problem and Its Impact on Los Angeles Police Department Resources: Briefing Paper Prepared for Staff Officers' Mini-Retreat."

estimated—from a speculative survey of officer opinions—that undocumented residents would account for 18.7 percent of crimes committed in the city. "Whether this crime level extrapolation is higher or lower than the actual is not as significant as the fact that any crime committed by an illegal alien should not be occurring in the City of Los Angeles," the department's Illegal Alien Committee argued. Undocumented immigrants, in other words, represented a new criminal threat. As the committee summarized, "there are increasing reports of illegal alien involvement in crime, including street gang activities, narcotics trafficking and usage and organized criminal activities."[40]

The LAPD employed statistics to mobilize fears that undocumented immigrants would have a detrimental impact on the department's resources and ability to fight crime. A 1977 LAPD Illegal Alien Committee report warned of a wave of undocumented immigrants predicted to reach over one million by 1981. The LAPD used the number of "illegal aliens" to reinforce the claim that the department was underfunded and understaffed, especially in relation to other departments across the country. Based on per capita expenditures, the LAPD reported that the cost of providing police services to illegal aliens was $37 million annually. The ratio of officers to residents—"'thin blue line' of police coverage"—the department lamented, was 18.6 percent less than "commonly accepted" when accounting for the undocumented aliens in the population. If fully counted, the number of undocumented immigrants in the city would reduce the officers per 1,000 people from 2.63 to 2.14. To

Population and sworn strength comparisons of five largest U.S. cities, 1975

City	Census Population	Estimated* Illegal Aliens	Adjusted Population	Police Strength**	Stated Police Ratio	Actual Police Ratio	Reduction in OFCR per 1,000	% Change in Police Ratio
Los Angeles	2,824,828	650,000	3,474,828	7,440	2.63	2.14	-0.49	-18.60%
New York	7,896,000	850,000	8,746,000	26,891	3.41	3.07	-0.34	-10.00%
Chicago	3,335,000	250,000	3,585,000	14,059	4.22	3.92	-0.30	-7.10%
Philadelphia	1,916,000	42,000	1,958,000	8,564	4.47	4.37	-0.10	-2.20%
Detroit	1,500,000	26,000	1,526,000	5,509	3.67	3.67	-0.06	-1.60%

*Estimates of illegal aliens obtained from INS District Directors for each city.

** Authorized sworn strength per 1975 budgets.

Source: The Illegal Alien Committee, "The Illegal Alien Problem and Its Impact on Los Angeles Police Department Resources: Briefing Paper Prepared for Staff Officers' Mini-Retreat."

make up for the difference in ratio, the city would have to hire 1,703 officers at an annual cost of nearly $60 million. The committee warned that an already woefully undermanned police force was even more understaffed and under-resourced than previously thought. As Deputy Mayor Grace Davis concluded in testifying to Congress, "the undocumented aliens do cause a substantial drain on police resources."[41]

The burden of immigration enforcement on police resources led the LAPD to push for a federal crackdown on undocumented immigration. Chief Davis called for a shift in national policy away from "benign neglect," in which federal law enforcement did not interfere in state or local immigration enforcement, to more rigorous federal enforcement of border laws and efforts to reduce the incentive for immigrants to come to the United States. The Illegal Alien Committee also recommended intensified enforcement of immigration laws when undocumented immigrants were suspected of criminal activity. "In special problem areas of the City where illegal aliens are inordinately contributing to the crime rate, vice or gang activities," the committee explained, "intensified enforcement by Immigration and Naturalization personnel should be requested for the purpose of removing deportable alien criminals."[42]

The Illegal Alien Committee capitalized on reports of the criminal alien problem not only to demand more resources but also to expand officer discretion. Alongside requests for the hiring of more officers to contain the illegal alien crime surge, the committee proposed a surveillance project to monitor undocumented immigrants involved in criminal activity. Maintaining a database of file cards on known criminal aliens, they believed, would allow easy identification of deported aliens who "upon their reentry, [can] be arrested for a felony violation of the U.S. immigration laws." The creation of an "alien criminal" category fueled public fears of undocumented immigrants as the source of rising crime and enhanced the department's discretionary authority of exclusion to control and contain undocumented immigrants within the framework of nonenforcement of immigration law.[43]

Police Discretion and the Limits of Immigration Enforcement

For all the efforts to limit local enforcement of immigration laws, the LAPD continued to carve out discretionary authority to target "alien criminals" for arrest as part of its crime control prerogative and to collaborate with INS agents on its deportation agenda. As Chief Davis reported to Mayor Bradley in 1976, INS officials "agreed to assist the Police Department in deporting career criminal illegal aliens who are identified by this Department." In return, the LAPD could "assist his Department [the INS] by publicly calling attention to the illegal alien problem."[44] Department officials routinely met with INS agents to discuss and plan potential joint actions. Over the course of three days in September 1974, for example, the LAPD and the INS conducted a Joint Crime Suppression Task Force in Rampart Division. Officers justified their participation, which resulted in 428 arrests, based on evidence that "arrest after arrest has repetitively demonstrated that many illegal aliens are members of the criminal element within the City of Los Angeles." The LAPD claimed that officers targeted only vice and narcotics violations while the INS agents enforced immigration laws. The department also received legal sanction from State Attorney General Evelle Younger, who concluded, "Local law enforcement officers have not only the right, but the duty to enforce all laws, both State and Federal, including those concerning the apprehension and detention of illegal aliens."[45] As interpreted by LAPD officials, this meant that they could not make arrests based solely on immigration status, but it did allow officers to contact the INS when they learned of an individual's "illegal" status in the course of making arrests for criminal activity.[46] Such collaboration with the INS based on the threat posed by the "alien criminal," in effect, represented police enforcement of immigration status by another means.

Close ties between the LAPD and the INS led to claims that the department violated Special Order 68. The Immigration Coalition, an immigrant rights organization, challenged Davis's claim that the LAPD did not collaborate with the INS or target undocumented status for arrest. "It is interesting to note that although the LAPD has a 'policy' of not arresting persons for immigration violations alone," the coalition argued, "60% of the aliens arrested in the 1974/75 fiscal year were for this reason, according to the department's own statistics." In fact, the LAPD reported that 1,376 "illegal aliens" were taken into custody in 1975, many for "alien related" charges, such as forged green cards. Such data, the Immigration Coalition concluded, revealed that "the inappropriate use of law enforcement officials in Los Angeles County for the apprehension of undocumented aliens, a responsibility of the INS, is common."[47]

Chief Davis responded that the LAPD not only did not target undocumented immigrants for arrest but also did not share files with the INS except in cases where immigrants were involved in criminal cases. Davis asserted that when he became chief in 1969, nearly 25 percent of felony arrests were for illegal entry but, "I said, 'Let John Mitchell (then U.S. attorney general) enforce these laws.' We have no obligation to enforce federal laws." Although

Davis acknowledged that he sent officers to observe a series of 1975 INS raids to ensure public safety, the officers, according to Davis, did not assist INS officers in making arrests. Davis apparently convinced Police Commissioner Sal Montenegro of the need for police discretion to not only observe INS raids but also make arrests. "We can't treat these people as citizens," Montenegro concluded, "but we have to treat them as human beings."[48]

Police enforcement of immigration status violations and collaboration with the INS were more common than law enforcement officials admitted, however. Testimony at hearings held by the Los Angeles County Bar Association in 1974 on the deportation and removal of aliens highlighted police collaboration with the INS and enforcement of immigration status violations. One individual, for example, recounted a 1974 raid in which uniformed police officers accompanied plainclothes INS agents to raid a bar on 7th and Wilshire. The predominantly Latino/a clientele was made to exit the bar one by one and show legitimate proof of legal status to INS agents as LAPD officers stood by. "The black and whites are going out and assisting the immigration officers in the course of conduct," one CASA activist summarized. "Not only is there not probable cause for the immigration agents to go out and bust into people's apartment houses and to pick people up off the bus stops, and go to the places of amusement and recreation, but the LAPD is assisting them in this." City Councilman David Cunningham gave the police the benefit of the doubt, stating they made a determination of status only when it was "forced upon them" by immigrants involved in criminal activity. Yet the bar concluded that cooperation with the INS was widespread, was intentional, and created a climate of fear in the Spanish-speaking community.[49]

Despite a lack of jurisdiction to enforce federal immigration law, local police used their discretion to enforce public order to arrest individuals for immigration status violations.[50] On April 13, 1978, for example, Miguel García, an undocumented Mexican immigrant, called a police officer in hopes of helping him receive a warranty replacement for a defective car stereo he bought at Lee Imports in downtown Los Angeles. The officer spoke with García, asked him for his driver's license, and then asked for his immigration papers. When García was unable to produce documentation, the officer arrested García for illegal status and transported him to a detention center, where he was held for two hours. Released on bail after a week in detention, the INS initiated deportation proceedings.[51]

Initial proceedings found García deportable. With the aid of the Southeast Legal Aid Center, García appealed the deportation proceedings based on claims that extreme hardship would result from deportation. The Southeast Legal Aid Center based the argument for the appeal on the longtime residence of García, arguing that he and his wife left temporarily between December 1974 and April 1975 to have their child in Mexico, but maintained their jobs and apartment in Los Angeles while away. They also claimed that "extreme hardship" would result to his family, especially his daughter, who was an American citizen, if he was deported.[52]

When García's lawyer approached Mexican American Legal Defense and Educational Fund attorneys to aid in the case, they added an element to the case. They viewed the problem of "harassment of undocumenteds by local police" as a significant piece of the case and exposed "illegal practice by local police in cooperation with the INS." As Mexican American Legal Defense and Educational Fund attorneys suggested to the attorney general the year prior to García's case, "California police officers are alleged to have blatantly violated the rights of Mexican American citizens and aliens while engaged in unauthorized activities. . . . They have one unifying theme: the blatant, and often brutal, violation of constitutional rights."[53] Such arguments had little impact on García's deportation proceedings, however. On appeal, the court dismissed García's request to stay his deportation and required García to voluntarily leave within thirty days or be forcibly deported.[54] Although García lost his case, continued blanket sweeps and police circumvention of Special Order 68 led local political and law enforcement officials to scrutinize LAPD practices due to fears that the city's immigrant population would become more distrustful of the police.

When the INS ramped up residential raids in 1979, city officials criticized the arrests and demanded the clarification of the limits of local enforcement of immigration law. Mayor Bradley pressured the INS to stop blanket sweeps in residential neighborhoods, calling them "unpopular and counterproductive."[55] The controversy led the Board of Police Commissioners to adopt a formal policy instructing officers that immigration status alone was not a basis for arrest. The move, lauded by city council members, aimed to bring undocumented immigrants into a partnership with the police. "Now these people [undocumented immigrants]," Commissioner Montenegro stated, "will be able to report crimes without fearing that the police will turn them over to immigration officials." Newly appointed chief Daryl Gates claimed the policy was a significant change from an era "when our officers engaged in wholesale arrests of illegals, merely for their immigration status." Though couched as a "dramatic step in restoring confidence" in the police, the policy operated to protect the immigrant crime victim while leaving the ability to arrest the "alien criminal" intact.[56]

Gates also established a nationally significant policy in 1979 limiting officer discretion in the realm of policing immigration status. "It is," Special Order 40 affirmed, "the policy of the Los Angeles Police Department that undocumented alien status in itself is not a matter for police action." Under Special Order 40, officers were directed to enforce the law in an equal manner regardless of "alien status" because of the need for immigrants to report crime and cooperate with the police. Because enforcement of federal immigration law threatened to alienate residents and treat all Latino/a residents as illegal, in other words, the policy made arrests based on immigration status explicitly out of an officer's jurisdiction.[57]

The new policy developed in response to a lawsuit arising from arrests of Mexican residents to determine their immigration status. In the spring of 1979, two legal residents, Juan Villalvazo Grajeda and Raúl Oswaldo Rivera, filed a suit in which they sought "to enjoin the LAPD from engaging in a pattern and practice of discrimination and denial of rights to persons of Latin American descent." Both Grajeda and Rivera had been picked up for jaywalking and sitting in a parked car but questioned about their immigration status by LAPD officers and sent to INS. While they were released by INS, the case raised the question of the LAPD's use of racialized categories of illegality and overstepping of authority to enforce immigration law.[58]

The trial court found the LAPD's actions unconstitutional. Both Special Order 68 and Special Order 40 violated the federal Immigration and Naturalization Act "because they permitted questioning persons about their immigration status." On appeal, however, the Court of Appeals overturned the decision in 1987. The pre-1979 policy (Special Order 68) still violated state law because a policy allowing officers to arrest individuals based on civil violations related to immigration "impermissibly intruded upon the federal preserve." Yet, Special Order 40 was valid because it did not permit arrest or detention of undocumented immigrants based solely on their immigration status. "Where an LAPD officer legitimately comes across information in the course of investigating a crime which reasonably leads to the belief the person arrested is illegally present in this country," the court found, "nothing in either the state or the federal constitution prevents the officer from advising INS of this data."[59] The finding left Special Order 40 intact and provided officers discretionary authority over immigration referrals.

By the early 1980s, city officials believed Special Order 40 limited police power to ensure cooperation from the city's growing immigrant communities. A briefing memo to Mayor Bradley, for example, praised LAPD policy in relation to undocumented immigrants. "The L.A.P.D. is progressive with respect to our policy regarding the local enforcement of U.S. immigration laws," the memo stated. "This policy is sensitive to the principle that effective law enforcement depends on a high degree of cooperation between the department and the public it serves."[60] Yet Special Order 40 continued to categorize immigrants into the law-abiding and the criminal. The rise of drug crime and gang violence in the 1980s provided the LAPD the ability to expand its discretion to police criminal aliens. The construction and use of these categories reinforced racist assumptions of illegality and criminality.

Policing a City of Immigrants amid the War on Gangs and Drugs

By the 1980s, law enforcement emphasized the problem of the criminal alien as a law-and-order threat to expand police authority to enforce immigration law. New immigrants from Central and South America faced growing poverty, low-wage work, and residential segregation. Multiple forms of marginalization that led many Latino/a immigrants toward what the police defined as "gang" behavior. The collapse of industrial work in the region and the rise of the "world city's" dependence on a highly unequal high-wage financial sector and low-wage service industry led many immigrants toward informal economic activity. If the region's shifting political economy created the conditions for immigrants' involvement in illicit activities, the police responded by doubling down on repression and racially defined categories of citizenship and exclusion through the 1980s.[61]

LAPD officers portrayed undocumented immigrants as the source of rising crime, especially narcotics and gang activity in Latino/a neighborhoods. Without supporting evidence, an assistant chief believed that "illegal aliens" were potentially responsible for 30 percent of the city's crime in 1986.[62] As such, the police required greater discretion to arrest and remove the criminal alien element. The Rampart Division Narcotics Task Force, for example, found that out of more than 2,000 drug-related arrests in 1986, 78 percent were undocumented immigrants and "much of the crime involving undocumented aliens is gang related." Of those arrested, 756 were reported to the INS. Collaboration with the INS on activities, such as drug raids, even when the department was aware of illegal activity by undocumented immigrants made local political officials wary of alienating Latino/a residents. As members of a city task force on immigration expressed, "the involvement of the INS at such a stage may have a negative effect on the department's efforts to gain the community's trust and confidence (especially the undocumented community)."[63]

Despite reassurances that the department adhered to its policy in Special Order 40, when it came to drug and gang activity, the LAPD worked closely with the INS. By the mid-1980s, a study of INS enforcement activities related to criminal aliens reported that the Los Angeles INS district office "has undertaken a number of special projects with local agencies," to identify and remove undocumented immigrants involved in drug and gang activity. Gang activities section commander Robert Ruchoft, for example, launched a program in conjunction with the INS in 1986 to deport undocumented immigrants involved in gangs to their country of origin. Accompanied by a four-man INS team, Community Resources against Street Hoodlums (CRASH) patrols in immigrant neighborhoods circumvented the limits of Special Order 40 by focusing on gang violence. "We don't arrest people for being illegal aliens," a department spokesperson stated, "but it is a pilot program in our campaign to obliterate violence by gangs." The INS agents made arrests while on patrol with LAPD officers because, according to Ruchoft, "we know who they are, and where they are, and the criminal activities in which they are taking part."[64]

Joint LAPD-INS efforts to deport criminal aliens often operated as a form of immigration control rather than crime control. A similar LAPD, Los Angeles Sheriff's Department (LASD), and INS task force targeted undocumented gang members in 1988. Deportation often occurred even if LAPD officers were unable to charge the individual with a crime. "If a gang member is out on the street and the police can't make a charge," assistant district director for the INS John Brechtel explained, "we will go out and deport them for being here illegally if they fit that criteria." Deputy Chief Bernard Parks praised the task force because using deportations allowed "our officers to concentrate on gang members in another fashion." Police, according to Parks, could remove undocumented gang members from the streets without having to bring criminal charges against them.[65] In effect, the LAPD used the war on gangs and drugs to reassert the department's authority to create racialized categories of exclusion and police immigrants.

Attention to the role of foreign-born and deportable immigrants in drug crimes and gang violence threatened to overwhelm the criminal justice system. A study of deportable immigrants in the Los Angeles county jail conducted in May 1990 found that out of 17,774 inmates, 3,327, or 19 percent, were foreign-born. Over half (1,933) were classified by INS as deportable, and nearly 25 percent of the 1,602 who had been convicted were charged for drug possession and drug trafficking.[66] To deal with the high level of criminal activity, mostly drug related, by immigrants, the committee suggested greater integration of justice agencies. "The INS is charged with the task of apprehending and removing criminal aliens, but it cannot be expected to carry this burden alone and to perform it effectively without the full cooperation of both local and federal justice agencies," the County Subcommittee on Criminal Aliens concluded. "Therefore, strong working partnerships between local and federal justice agencies must be developed to effectively reduce the impact and expense of this criminal population on the justice system."[67] Using the connection between "criminal alien" drug violators and an overburdened

Police and eighteen undocumented aliens with hands tied outside raided house, 1981. Although the LAPD had committed to the nonenforcement of immigration law in order to ensure trust in the police, they found means of extending the police power and authority into new areas of social life. Such policing of immigrants contributed to exclusion from full social membership and citizenship. *Los Angeles Times* Photographic Archives (Collection 1429); courtesy of Library Special Collections, Charles E. Young Research Library, UCLA.

criminal justice system, in other words, enabled the expansive use of police power to police immigrant communities.

Sweeps aimed at finding and deporting undocumented drug dealers and gang members, however, relied on dragnet policing that reaffirmed racist views of illegality. During a three-month operation in the summer of 1985 called Retake the Streets, for example, the LAPD arrested more than 1,700 people in an antidrug sweep. Deputy Chief Clyde Cronkhite reported that 63 percent of those arrested were "illegal aliens," mostly from Mexico and El Salvador. Cronkhite suggested that such widespread policing of undocumented immigrants who, he believed, were at the center of a growing drug trade "will continue until they get the message, 'You come to Los Angeles to sell drugs, and you'll be in big trouble.'" The antidrug sweep relied on close cooperation between LAPD officials and the INS agents who met with residents in the target area to address fears of blanket arrests based on race or ethnicity.[68]

Cooperation between the LAPD and INS in the name of the war on drugs rested on racially defined categories of illegality. Condemning a "daylight 'drug' raid" conducted in the heart of the Salvadoran community on June 30, 1989, the Latino Community Justice Center claimed that the joint action "is sowing Latino community anger and distrust against the department and city government." The joint operations blurred the line between legitimate police raids based on evidence and investigation and immigration raids. "But when the INS and Police Department conduct joint raids, the operations necessarily become immigration raids," the Latino Community Justice Center's Antonio Rodríguez stated. "They may apprehend some criminals, but they target and capture in their net many innocent persons who are taken prisoner by INS agents if they are undocumented."[69] Mexican American residents faced harassment as the police used their discretionary authority to police the boundaries of citizenship. On November 4, 1988, for example, eight LAPD officers harassed and arrested Félix Narváez and a group of friends who "were called 'Mexican pendejos.' We were called wetbacks and told we would be kicked out to Mexico." The officers also questioned the group's legal status and "threatened to cut up his [one member's] visa card with a knife."[70]

While police practices framed "illegal alien criminals" as one source of gang violence and drug trafficking, it simultaneously reaffirmed a connection between racial identity and illegality. With the growth of immigrants and refugees from Central America during the 1980s, the LAPD's police practices contributed to exclusive categories of citizenship. In doing so, the department created new avenues of supervisory discretion and criminal categories based on public order policing to circumvent policy restricting enforcement of immigration status.

Vendors, Not Criminals

The influx of refugees and asylum seekers from Latin America, El Salvador and Guatemala in particular, created new challenges for law enforcement. Prior to 1980, the Central American population in Los Angeles was relatively small, especially in comparison to the Mexican population. By 1990, however, 301,600 Salvadorans and 159,200 Guatemalans resided in Los Angeles, representing a fivefold increase for both groups since 1980. Although the Reagan administration's foreign policy funded civil war and dislocation in Central America, it did not grant refugees from El Salvador and Guatemala status as asylum seekers, leaving them without protection prior to the extension of Temporary Protected Status in 1990.[71] Yet the city council responded to the refugee crisis with a policy of sanctuary. Spearheaded by Councilman Michael Woo, the city council passed a resolution in 1985 granting asylum status to refugees, and declaring Los Angeles a "city of sanctuary" for "law abiding" Salvadoran and Guatemalan refugees. While largely a symbolic step, the resolution reaffirmed policy restricting the LAPD's arrest or detention of residents based on immigration status.[72]

The resolution irked INS western regional director Harold Ezell and conservative city council members. "I think it's unfortunate," Ezell commented. "It's an absolute mistake for the city of Los Angeles. I think we have tantamount to a City-Council trying to be their own immigration and naturalization service." During council hearings, Ezell claimed that such a resolution would be an "open invitation" to the world to see Los Angeles as a "safe haven" from the INS and would "lead to a massive influx of immigrants into Los Angeles, depletion of resources and increased crime." Pressure from Ezell and conservative councilman Ernani Bernardi led to a revision in 1986 removing the reference to Los Angeles as a city of "sanctuary." The change reaffirmed Special Order 40 but removed protection for refugees seeking asylum. Instead, policing strategies targeting public nuisances constructed refugees as criminals requiring supervision.[73]

While liberal council members and Mayor Bradley hoped to present Los Angeles as a welcoming city for the world, INS sweeps and local law enforcement profiling threatened to undermine their effort. Beginning in the early 1980s, the LAPD targeted unlicensed produce vendors in the Pico-Union neighborhood. Ostensibly organized to target Los Mercados for selling and packaging produce illegally, such raids effectively targeted Latino/a refugees and immigrants. "The thing is most of these people are Latinos—from Mexico, (San) Salvador, Nicaragua, Honduras—and who knows how many of them are undocumented?" Commander Rick Barton stated. "So even though the INS has no part in this task force, it could be that a lot of them are afraid we might have the INS with us."[74] Focusing on street vending provided police and city officials a means of expanding police authority by claiming to enforce standards of public health, safety, and order.[75]

The focus of the LAPD's attention centered on the Rampart Division, where many newly arrived immigrants lived and sold goods. During the fall of 1989, officers from Rampart arrested street vendors and bystanders around 7th and Alvarado Street.[76] One such incident occurred to Jorge Cruz Cortés. Originally from Oaxaca, Mexico, Cortés made a living selling items in the area surrounding MacArthur Park because he had "no other way to make money." On October 27, 1989, Cortés was standing on 7th Street "not selling anything . . . not very close to the vendors who had set out their wares on the sidewalk" when over ten LAPD officers ran toward him, grabbed him, pushed him into the wall of a nearby store, and handcuffed him. One officer then kicked his leg out from under him, causing him to fall to the ground, where the officer hit him with his nightstick three times and stood on his left leg. The officers took Cortés to the patrol car, where they told him, "You're going back to Mexico." When he was released from jail, he was threatened with retaliation if he made a complaint about his treatment.[77]

The targeting of street vendors and day laborers mobilized immigrant rights activists to challenge the LAPD's use of the "criminal alien" category to justify their broad discretionary authority. Protesting excessive use of force by LAPD officers, nearly seventy demonstrators carried signs reading "We are vendors, not criminals," and shouted in Spanish, "Work, yes. Repression, no" in front of the Rampart Police Division Headquarters on November 16, 1989.[78] "In a city with a large immigrant and refugee population, it is essential that people understand that the LAPD and the INS are not one and the same," said Father Luís Olivares, chairman of the Coalition for Humane Immigration Rights of Los Angeles (CHIRLA). "If people fear that contact with the police [will] result in their deportation, victims and witnesses of crimes will not go to the police, a situation which hurts all residents." Activists demanded an end to LAPD cooperation with the INS and asked the city council to prohibit any joint actions between the agencies. LAPD commander William Booth dismissed the demands, stating, "I'm not going to bar the door to any other law enforcement agency." INS officials agreed, calling the relationship with the LAPD "positive."[79]

Due to the transformation of the economy, many vendors had no other choice but to continue to sell goods on the streets. In response to mistreatment from local businesses and police, a group of forty-seven vendors formed the Street Vendors Association (SVA) in 1986 to protect their rights. As SVA president Dora Alicia, who was born in San Salvador and migrated to Los Angeles in 1980 to escape the brutal civil war in El Salvador, commented, "Selling is my life and I found that my trade was my only means of survival when I came to this country." The SVA fundamentally challenged dominant constructions of illegality, and led vendors to be "treated more like human beings" instead of "objects to the police."[80]

By 1991 the SVA forced the city council to consider an ordinance legalizing vending. Despite opposition from the LAPD, the city council eventually passed an initial ordinance in January 1992 allowing vendors to sell in designated zones in the city, and later passed a Sidewalk Vending Ordinance on January 4, 1994.[81] The ordinance placed restrictions on where vendors could legally sell, but the SVA attempted to limit punitive enforcement of vending outside of designated areas by proposing education and workshops for vendors caught selling in undesignated areas.[82] Selective enforcement of street vending laws continued in the following years, however. On the eve of the passage of Proposition 187 in 1994, which made undocumented immigrants ineligible for public benefits, one observer reported the way the police began to "implement proposition 187 in their old fashioned way," by cracking down on street vendors.[83]

City ordinances regulating street vending granted the LAPD power to enforce public order. Expanding the categories of criminality and illegality to include street vending and day labor ensured that the police would be involved in policing immigrants and refugees.[84] As the LAPD's enforcement activities in immigrant neighborhoods ramped up in the early 1990s, however, they came under increased scrutiny from liberal politicians and activists. While claiming they aided those undocumented immigrants who were victims of crime, such as immigration smugglers, the LAPD employed crime control imperatives to resist attempts to limit their discretion to enforce immigration law and cooperate with the INS.

Crime Control as Immigration Control

When the families of some twenty-six undocumented immigrants who were held hostage for $1,000 each by smugglers in a South Central "drop house" contacted the Central American Refugee Center in June 1990, they reignited debates about the proper limits to the LAPD's cooperation with the INS. The Central American Refugee Center reported the hostage situation to the LAPD, and within hours, eight LAPD officers rescued the hostages. While the smugglers escaped, the immigrants' ordeal continued. The Newton Division officers, in violation of policy, reported the undocumented immigrants to the INS for detention. Commander James Chambers argued that the officers acted correctly, and "if this circumstance comes up again as it did [Wednesday] night, I believe we will handle it the same way."[85]

Officers involved in the rescue contacted the INS to bring the smugglers to justice. "The reason we call the INS is because that's their jurisdiction," Commander Findley explained. "They're the ones who know how to interrogate. They know how to get these smugglers." Brushing aside the claims of immigrant rights attorneys that the immigrants were victims, INS officials felt the LAPD acted appropriately in notifying the INS. "If they find people who are illegally in the country and encounter individuals who are suspected of having smuggled illegal immigrants into the U.S., that is [a] federal felony," INS Los Angeles District director Robert Moschorak stated. "I think the officers used suberb judgment if they notified the INS and I fully support their decision."[86]

The following month, the LAPD received another report of smugglers holding immigrants hostage. When officers located the hostages, they seized evidence of illegal smuggling operations and contacted the INS. After the police raid, Chief Gates claimed that "the entire matter is now in the hands of I.N.S." and "the manner in which this case is being handled is in keeping with the policy of the L.A.P.D." In effect, the LAPD used charges of smuggling not only to expose illegal operations but to criminalize immigrants who were for all intents and purposes victims. "This department makes absolutely no effort to seek out undocumenteds in responding to calls for service and otherwise protecting people in Los Angeles," Gates argued. "But, when we are confronted by serious criminal actions involving feloniously conspiring to violate the laws of the United States, kidnapping, hostage taking, threats of great bodily harm, extortion and bondage, we can not look the other way."[87] In the name of helping those victimized by smugglers, the LAPD turned them over to the INS for removal.

If the LAPD hoped cooperating with the INS would help stop smuggling operations, their actions further undermined the immigrant community's faith in the police. The Board of Police Commissioners' Hispanic Advisory Council criticized the department, calling the actions a "flagrant violation of policies" for handling undocumented immigrants that could lead to a potential deterioration of the "positive relationship" with the Latino/a community. One *Los Angeles Times* editorial titled "How to Make Allies into Enemies," suggested that in order to maintain the trust of the immigrant community, police officers had to ensure that immigrants recognize the difference between the LAPD and the INS. But the LAPD's actions did little to allay the fears of the Latino/a community.[88] "The feeling in the immigrant community," stated Madeline Janis, executive director of CARECEN, "is that the police and the INS are the same thing and that they [immigrants] have no recourse if they're victims of a crime."[89]

Cooperation between the LAPD and the INS circumvented both the spirit and the letter of Special Order 40. Protest from immigrant rights groups, such as the Central American Refugee Center, the Coalition for Humane Immigration Rights of Los Angeles, and La Resistencia, demanded an end to police cooperation with the INS. Protestors held banners criticizing the LAPD's cooperation with "La Migra" and the INS, including a graphic of a police officer gladly handing over an immigrant and child to a gleeful INS agent. Handing over victims of smuggling was only the latest episode of police-INS cooperation protested by these groups. On May Day, for example, protestors from La Resistencia demonstrated outside an INS detention facility in Pico-Union and were arrested by the LAPD. The protests and publicity forced the city council to hold hearings to reassess police cooperation with the INS, and a review of departmental policy.[90]

The publicity led to city council hearings on the department's immigration policy. Councilman Michael Woo, who had spearheaded the Sanctuary resolution in 1985, responded with a proposal that the LAPD should not "assist or cooperate with any Immigration and Naturalization Service investigation, detention, or arrest procedures." Woo was concerned that the actions of officers in the June raid threatened the status of Los Angeles as a "city of refuge." "The policy that we fought to enact back in 1985 is becoming unraveled," he stated. "Ultimately, it's going to be the Police Department that is going to suffer if victims or witnesses are afraid to contact the Police Department. We can't leave the current policy as it is."[91] Councilman Richard Alatorre and Woo, with the support of Mayor Bradley, proposed new guidelines to help stop crimes from going unreported. "Those crimes [against immigrants] go unreported for one simple reason," Alatorre summarized: "people are afraid of being turned over to the INS."[92]

Gates opposed restrictions on LAPD cooperation with immigration officials. He claimed that regulations "would seriously endanger our ability to ensure public safety in the city." While the chief expressed understanding of the concerns raised in the council motion, which would have barred police cooperation with an INS investigation except in service of a search warrant or arrest, he defended the expansive discretionary authority of the LAPD. "I believe all residents of Los Angeles are best served," Gates explained, "when its Police Department is able to work cooperatively with all segments of government to provide for the public's safety."[93]

Framing immigration control as crime control enabled extensive cooperation between police and the INS. As the council's Public Safety Committee learned, the LAPD's cooperation with INS agents was widespread and included handing children, victims of crime, and people arrested for minor misdemeanors over to the INS.[94] The council approved a motion recommending the department clarify the limits of Special Order 40 and the police department's relationship with the INS. The recommendations centered on ensuring narrow discretion by leaving "little room for interpretation by individual officers." Yet the changes were not meant to "prevent the LAPD from upholding its responsibilities to enforce the law." The proposals reiterated that arrests should not be made based solely on alien status and the police should not turn arrestees over to the INS "EXCEPT for felony, drug or gang (Street Terrorism Enforcement and Prevention Act) Misdemeanors."[95] The recommended clarifications to LAPD policy, in other words, continued to recognize categories of "alien criminals" where authority to police immigration status and cooperate with the INS was necessary.

Concern for the ability of the police to ensure safety by arresting and detaining undocumented immigrants outweighed demands aimed at limiting police power and discretion. Although the motion meant to clarify and update departmental policy to limit officer discretion surrounding arrests based on "alien status," it did not remove the police from questions related to immigration. Even after the efforts of the Central American Refugee Center and liberal city council members to limit the actions of the police in the realm of immigration law, suspected undocumented immigrants were routinely arrested and turned over to the INS.[96]

Tension surrounding the LAPD's cooperation with the INS continued in 1991 after the fatal shooting of an LAPD officer by an El Salvadoran immigrant whom the officer intended to cite for public intoxication. The episode once again revealed how discretionary authority surrounding activities labeled a public nuisance intersected with the police department's immigration enforcement and assumptions of racialized categories of illegality. Chief Gates criticized the lack of aggressive deportation enforcement by the INS and called the man "an El Salvadoran drunk—a drunk who doesn't belong here." Activists and a police commissioner criticized the chief's comments as racist, and demanded an apology. Under pressure, Gates agreed to better educate officers on immigration issues and acknowledged the need for cooperation with the Salvadoran community to maintain public safety.[97]

Yet programs aimed at enhancing collaborative efforts between the LAPD and undocumented immigrants, such as Operación Estafadores, worked at cross purposes with the department's reliance on racialized categories of illegality and criminality. Community relations programs and initiatives to provide equitable police services to Latino/a communities, in other words, required narrowing the range of officer discretion on the street in order to enhance the LAPD's ability to work with communities to combat crime. But the department's construction of the "alien criminal" category developed an alternative means for the police to enforce immigration status violations during an era of rapidly changing demographics. By the 1980s and 1990s, the department's attention to policing day laborers, street vendors, and victims of immigration smugglers contributed to distrust between immigrant communities and the police. In the process, the police contributed to the construction—and enforcement—of exclusionary conceptions of illegality, criminality, and citizenship.

Even as the LAPD gave up discretion to police immigration status and collaborate with the INS under Special Order 40, it turned to other areas where it retained authority, such as enforcing public order, to contain the perceived threat the rapidly growing immigrant population posed to the city's racial hierarchy. In effect, the police attempted to square their ability to work with immigrant crime victims to combat crime with the department's efforts to expand authority through targeting the criminal alien. Nowhere did discretionary authority and criminalization of residents of color expand as greatly during the 1980s and early 1990s than with the LAPD's waging of an aggressive war on gangs and drugs in South Central.

Chapter 8

The Enemy Within

Drug Gangs and Police Militarization

On the evening of August 1, 1988, after months of surveillance and consultation with SWAT and narcotics experts, approximately eighty officers from the LAPD's Southwest Area Gang Task Force raided four apartments at 3900 South Dalton Avenue. Searching for drugs and Rolling 30's Crips gang members, their operation resembled a search-and-destroy mission. Officers broke windows, ripped open walls, smashed toilets, and destroyed furniture. Exchanging high-fives and shouting antigang slogans, officers spray-painted "LAPD Rules—Death to Crips" on walls, and sang a song with the refrain "Wild Wild Southwest" to the tune of a popular hip-hop song. They also detained fifty residents and bystanders who were cuffed, hit with flashlights, kicked, and humiliated for nearly two hours. Yet the raid produced little evidence of drug or gang activity. Officers confiscated one rifle, less than an ounce of crack cocaine, and less than five ounces of marijuana. Of the thirty-three residents detained at the Southwest Division station, six were booked for drug possession, and only one was ever prosecuted.[1]

Despite leaving the apartments uninhabitable and residents battered, officers blamed the victims for their injuries and told reporters that gang members damaged the apartments after the raid. Their after-action reports claimed that the operation had been well planned, flawlessly executed, and carried out with restraint. But media attention and resident complaints led to an Internal Affairs Division investigation revealing that officers obtained the search warrant with false data, employed an inappropriate use of force, and allegedly fabricated after-action reports to cover up wrongdoing. Internal affairs recommended disciplinary action for thirty-eight officers. None were fired. Chief Gates acknowledged that things had "got out of control," but believed adequate disciplinary measures had been taken. Following the Internal Affairs Division report, however, the department continued to hide evidence, keeping records of the investigation secret and even promoting thirty-seven of the officers in subsequent years.[2]

For many residents, the raid symbolized how a combined drug and gang war empowered an unaccountable and militarized police force to wage a scorched-earth campaign in black neighborhoods of South Central. Aided by the Police Misconduct Lawyer Referral Service, who described the raid as "an orgy of violence," residents sued the LAPD, the city, and Mayor Bradley. The raid, they claimed, was part of a "policy, custom and practice of the City of Los Angeles to harass, intimidate and violate the rights of minority residents, particularly blacks." It was the "inevitable result of unconstitutional policies, customs and practices . . . which incite the police to disregard basic democratic rights in the course of purported 'gang sweeps.'" They demanded equitable police protection for residents of color and for an end to racist police tactics associated with the war on gangs and drugs. Though they failed to shift the city's tactics, the suit culminated in over $3 million in settlements.[3]

The Dalton raid exposed how the LAPD used its broad discretion to wage a racialized war against drugs and gangs during the 1980s. Drugs, gangs, and crime were real problems facing urban communities of color, which police capitalized on to expand their authority, discretion, and martial capacity. But the LAPD also leveraged fears of gang violence and the drug trade to do political work for their law-and-order agenda. Los Angeles police "experts" framed gangs and drugs as a problem of violent African American youth which were promoted by journalists and shaped perceptions of these intertwined crises as enemies that could be eradicated only by the police. Indeed, the response from city and law enforcement officials overwhelmingly focused on empowering the police to wage a war of suppression. Yet, this approach was hardly the way to deal with the real issues of gangs and drugs, since they were social problems rooted in poverty, inequality, disinvestment and unequal development, and the economic transformation of the world city. As police-produced categories, the war on "gangs" and "drugs" did little but justify police action to eradicate its enemies while diverting attention from deeper social and economic causes and protecting vested interests of the world city vision.[4]

By framing violent drug gangs as the dominant players in the crack cocaine trade, criminal justice officials rationalized a militarized war to protect law-abiding residents. Using federal law enforcement resources and from hosting the 1984 Olympics, the LAPD's battle for the streets became an all-out war on entire communities. The department's "Battle Plans" focused on monitoring and removing gang members from the streets through mass arrests, gang sweeps, drug raids, asset forfeiture, and civil injunctions.[5] Deploying a martial infrastructure to this end was part of a buildup of police power during an era of decreased tax revenues, reduced federal aid to cities, and retrenchment in social programs that exacerbated the exclusion of working-class black and Latino/a Angelinos from full social membership.

While fights over police abuse and civilian oversight of the LAPD were often divisive, in the fight against drugs and gangs, liberals, conservatives, and law enforcement officials were often closely aligned. Within the context of fears of the omnipresent danger that drugs and gangs posed to social order, rescuing the dream of making Los Angeles a world-class city attractive for international investment and economic development required a political commitment to eliminating drug crime and gang violence. To do so, Mayor Bradley and liberal lawmakers, however at odds they were with Chief Gates over his hostile attitude toward political oversight of the department by the early 1990s, aligned with Gates and conservatives in support of suppression. Cracking down on the enemies within was a central component driving world city liberalism in a punitive direction. By redeploying the harm principle within the wars on drugs and gangs, liberals reconciled their decades-long effort to bring accountability to the LAPD with broadened police discretion, police militarization, and punitive policies. To contain so-called hoodlums and urban terrorists, local officials' interests converged on empowering the police.[6]

Law enforcement relied on and produced new definitions of what constituted a gang and gang membership. Targeting daily life and behaviors they associated with African American and Latino/a youth as evidence of gang membership, police and lawmakers employed racialized assumptions in constructing the term "gang" as one that marked all youth of color as potential criminals.[7] Although the LAPD targeted Latino/a youth, media attention and public debate focused on black gangs because the police, notably Chief Gates, defined the problem in relation to crack cocaine sales concentrated in South Central. African American gang members and drug users, in the eyes of politicians, the police, and many residents, did not deserve inclusion in society as full citizens. Such attitudes legitimized repressive policing and punitive legislation to remove black and brown youth from the streets using counter-insurgency tactics developed after Watts, albeit with fancier weapons. Once again, the LAPD looked to the past and repackaged its strategies for a new era. In the process, police officials and lawmakers criminalized residents for social problems related to drugs and gangs while downplaying their roots in in economic restructuring, concentrated poverty, and urban divestment.[8]

Middle- and working-class residents and religious organizations turned to the police to help "save" their communities from the drug and gang crisis. But residents demanded an end to assumptions that all black and Latino/a youth were gang members. Yet these challenges did little to alter the city's get-tough policies. Policing strategies based on waging war on entire neighborhoods and nuisance abatement—targeting behaviors deemed disorderly, a parallel to the more well-known adoption of broken windows policing in New York City, which postulated that strong repression of minor violations of law or nuisances would result in greater adherence to social order, norms, and reverence for the law and ultimately would stop urban decay, became the means of addressing the fallout of social and economic crises of the 1980s and 1990s.[9] As funding and support for social services disappeared, the police not only retained but expanded authority on the streets.

Economic Restructuring, Urban Divestment, and the Unequal World City

Los Angeles had been home to a vibrant manufacturing sector after World War II. During the early 1980s, employers left the region as the economy restructured. Part of a national pattern, deindustrialization hit Los Angeles particularly hard, and the city lost some 70,000 manufacturing jobs between 1978 and 1982 alone. The manufacturing jobs that remained relocated to manufacturing parks in newly industrialized suburban areas, such as the South Bay and the Inland Empire, where few African Americans lived. But compared with cities in the so-called Midwestern and northeastern rustbelt, Los Angeles attracted corporations for a new service-based economy and oversaw massive internationalized growth. Low-wage service industries and high-paying financial institutions replaced good-paying jobs in auto plants and other manufacturing industries, creating a polarized local economy that exacerbated inequality and social ills of drugs and gangs.[10]

Instead of investing in local communities using municipal resources, however, the Bradley administration hoped to rely on federal social service and urban development grants to help impoverished neighborhoods. Yet, when Reagan cut aid to cities, these funds did not get replaced, and Bradley focused on a real estate growth strategy that would reinvigorate downtown Los Angeles through economic development projects aimed at attracting global capital. Bradley's approach led to vastly uneven development that brought high-rise office buildings and cultural centers to the downtown district while providing few benefits to poor neighborhoods. "High-rise towers soon sprouted on Bunker Hill," the *Los Angeles Times* observed. "But South Los Angeles stayed in its slump."[11]

As the region's economy restructured from one based on manufacturing to one centered on services, economic inequality, unemployment, and poverty grew. While Latinos/as faced low-wage and exploitative labor in the region's service economy, those African Americans who were left out of Bradley's use of affirmative action to expand access to public service jobs experienced high rates of unemployment and poverty. Unemployment rates among black youth in the early 1990s remained at a staggering 45 percent, while poverty rates in parts of South Central hovered at 40 percent.[12] As government policies and structural processes exacerbated social and economic inequality, joblessness and poverty left many black and Latino/a youth with few alternatives to the informal drug economy. For many African American and Latino/a Angelinos, the world city brought continued social and economic marginalization that officials attempted to contain with policing, incarceration, and exclusion.

Waging the War on Drugs as a War on Gangs

Poor economic conditions and changing federal drug policies made inner-city neighborhoods fertile ground for increased drug use and trafficking. Much as the LAPD referred to South Central as the "PCP capital of the world" in the late 1970s, by the 1980s cocaine flooded into the city as drug interdiction in Florida rerouted international supply lines, and Reagan's Cold War foreign policy in Latin America backed anti-Communist forces reliant on drug trafficking to fund counterinsurgency wars. The cheap price of "rock" cocaine combined with high rates of unemployment in impoverished African American neighborhoods to create a devastating social problem. The year 1984 saw a 70 percent increase in admittances to Martin Luther King Jr. Hospital for addiction. At the same time, the ability to make large sums of cash facilitated the growth of the crack economy. One eighteen-year-old South Central high school student, known as "Dap," claimed he could make upwards of $70,000 a week selling cocaine.[13]

By 1986 the LAPD's war on drugs reached new heights. The LAPD confiscated six and a half tons of cocaine in 1986, a 7,000 percent increase from 1980, and made 47,000 drug-related arrests, a 90 percent increase. Building on such police reports and law enforcement rhetoric, media reports helped elevate the panic of a "drug crisis" into a full-blown "drug war."[14] Local officials used these statistics and rhetorical escalation to make the fight against drugs a militarized campaign and a central component of the city's crime control program. "We are engaged in a war against the criminals of this city," Bradley told residents at an anticrime rally in 1985. "We are engaged in a war to save our youth." Employing military analogies, Bradley organized a "Mayor's D-Day in the War on Drugs," and held conferences to address the drug crisis. Nothing was off the table. While liberal officials recognized the need for prevention and intervention programs, adherence to the harm principle requiring them to ensure the safety of law-abiding residents made punishment a priority. Such policy choices were a function of a drug crisis that officials understood as a gang problem.[15]

Los Angeles's long history of youth gang activity in African American and Latino/a neighborhoods reached new heights in the 1980s. Young, unemployed black and Latino/a men, faced with an economy that provided few jobs and poor educational opportunities, turned to alternative forms of employment and socialization. As one self-described gang member mocked officials who asked youth how to solve gang violence, "You all going to get us jobs?"[16] Pointing to a rise in gang-related homicides from 168 in 1977 to 351 in 1980, prosecutors and the police mobilized the discourse of crisis to construct a need for greater police power in the years that followed.[17] "We are threatened by gang violence to a greater degree than ever before," the mayor's Gang Program coordinator stated in 1985. "Activities by members of youth gangs represent a crime problem of the first magnitude which shows little prospect of early abatement." By 1987, criminal justice officials routinely referred to Los Angeles as the nation's gang capital, as District Attorney Ira Reiner proclaimed: "With no sense of pride, we're No. 1."[18]

Although Latino/a gangs remained prominent in East Los Angeles, political officials and law enforcement agencies focused on the notorious African American Bloods and Crips gangs because they framed the rise of gang violence as a product of crack cocaine trafficking within African American neighborhoods of South Central. Doing so also justified expanding the police department's authority to wage a militarized war on drugs in African American neighborhoods. In 1986, the LAPD reported a 20 percent surge in gang violence related to narcotics street sales. Federal law enforcement agencies and initiatives bolstered the LAPD's framing of the war on drugs rooted in gang activity. "Drugs are these gangs' lifeblood," one Drug Enforcement Administration agent commented in reference to the city's African American gangs. "To stop gang violence, it is imperative that we stop drug trafficking."[19] Testimony by law enforcement officials, politicians, and community organizations at federal hearings held by the Select Committee on Narcotics Abuse and Control in 1986 and 1988 connected gang violence and crack cocaine trafficking. As Reiner testified at the "Organized Criminal Activity by Youth Gangs" hearings, "the gang wars are truly drug wars, the result of cheap cocaine that is flooding the streets."[20]

The connection between drugs and gangs was not so straightforward, however. Though gang members were certainly involved in the crack trade, studies conducted using police data found that only 25 percent of cocaine-related arrests in 1985 were gang related. Even if some gang violence resulted from competition over drug markets, experts concluded, the drug trade "was in no way dominated by gang involvement." While gang violence was on the rise more generally in the 1980s, media framings of violent drug gangs did more to shape perceptions that gang-related drug trade was tied to rising criminal violence than an actual connection between gang drug sales and violence. "Gang homicides," experts found, "were no more likely to involve drug sales than nongang homicides." Yet such findings did little to alter public perceptions or policies promoted by police and the media that defined the war on drugs as part of the violence associated with the war on gangs, rationalizing force, containment, and repression.[21]

Drive-by shootings, retaliatory killings, and crack cocaine pushers holed up in fortified "rock houses" with Uzis and Mac-10s certainly differed from mid-twentieth-century gang violence. But it occurred alongside new capacities for state violence led by the police. Law enforcement officials envisioned themselves engaged in low-intensity warfare. As the head of the district attorney's Hardcore Drug Unit stated in 1988, "This is Vietnam here." Solutions resembled counterinsurgency campaigns. "It's like having the Marine Corps invade an area that is still having little pockets of resistance," Gates said in describing the war on gangs. "We can't have it. . . . We've got to wipe them out."[22] Media portrayals reinforced views of urban neighborhoods as war zones. In an exposé on South Central titled "The Drug Gangs," *Newsweek* explained that crack had transformed "some of the country's toughest street gangs into ghetto-based drug-trafficking organizations" that facilitated a "form of urban-guerilla warfare," creating "a nightmare landscape inhabited by marauding thugs and hard-nosed cops."[23]

Fighting the drug war as part of the gang crisis led to broadened police authority and capacity. Bradley deployed a joint task force of antigang units and narcotics specialists to South Central, explaining, "We will not give up another inch of this city to this kind of violence and urban terrorism." While stressing the need to cooperate with residents, the task force focused on saturation policing, mass arrest, and strict prosecution. "The Task Force shall give its highest priority to increased surveillance, arrests, support for successful prosecutions, and probation and parole revocations in order to break the back of gang violence and urban terrorism," Bradley stated. "Special emphasis shall be placed on persons involved in drug trafficking in any matter whatsoever."[24]

New police counterinsurgency programs emerged. In January 1988, the LAPD, working with Mayor Bradley, established the Gang-Related Active Trafficker Suppression (GRATS) system under an antigang, antidrug czar. The GRATS program combined a computer-based system for tracking gang-related narcotics activity with task forces geared toward arresting dealers and seizing property. While the GRATS program curbed some gang-related drug activities, it led to the arrest of a wide range of non-gang-affiliated individuals. The definitions of what qualified as a GRATS arrest were broad and targeted entire neighborhoods for punitive enforcement campaigns. In September 1988 alone, for example, the monthly report stated that there had been 955 arrests, yet only 345 of those arrests were gang members or associates.[25] The approach centered on "significant enforcement activity." Mass arrest tactics did not concern LAPD officials or Bradley, who praised the program for making numerous arrests and drug seizures. By 1992, the program's fourth anniversary, GRATS arrests totaled 45,991, only 13,523 of which were gang members or associates. Although focused on supposed "hot spot" locations of narcotic and gang activity, GRATS operations rested on an "us versus them" attitude, spatially selective policing, and mass arrests.[26]

Local get-tough policing foreshadowed national trends. Chief Gates's quip to the Senate Judiciary Committee in 1990 that the "casual [drug] user ought to be taken out and shot" may have been hyperbole, but it suggested that the punitive approach had become common sense.[27] As early as 1981, Gates called for greater state capacity to solve social problems through warehousing. "I am for separation, long and short-term," Gates argued. He stated that the roughly 26,000 inmates in California's prisons—0.1 percent of the population—was a measly fraction of the 2 or 3 percent of the population that needed to be incarcerated. Gates's ideas would help launch an unprecedented prison-building boom in California over the coming years. Linking the drug crisis with gang violence combined with strict enforcement of the law enabled the police power to carry out what District Attorney Reiner described as the need to put "every one of these little murderous hoodlums in jail" for as long as possible.[28] The LAPD's ramped-up drug and gang war to protect "all Los Angeles" both drove and legitimated the massive investment in the city's martial infrastructure.

Building a Martial State

Relying on punitive institutions to fight the drug and gang war required a massive state-building enterprise to prevent the criminal justice system from being overwhelmed by mass arrests. As Gates told the County Board of Supervisors in 1989, "There's going to be in this county a need for courts, prosecutors, and jail space because the city is going to continue to supply you with lots of [arrests]."[29] Gates was a key player within a broader political bloc pursuing incapacitation, but it required an expansion of the city's martial infrastructure. "It is additionally recommended," Gates wrote in a position paper titled "Needs to Eradicate Violent Street Gangs," "that the City Council support the building of new prisons and jails rather than alleviate the current jail overcrowding condition by releasing prisoners, especially those who are repeat offenders." Strengthening and expanding the criminal justice system would combat gang violence and drug crime by keeping "the criminals 'off the street.'"[30]

Binding the drug war to gang violence justified the use of military-style weaponry and technology. Under Reagan, the Military Cooperation with Civilian Law Enforcement Agencies Act enabled local police agencies to obtain military hardware, intelligence, and research to fight the War on Drugs, which brought military-grade weapons onto the streets of America's cities. The 1988 Anti–Drug Abuse Act also established new federal grants for law enforcement, funneling billions to local law enforcement and enabling the city to expand Special Weapons and Tactics (SWAT) teams and Community Resources against Street Hoodlums (CRASH) units, create specialized narcotics units, and offer overtime pay to officers involved in drug-related investigations.[31] Reagan-era legislation fundamentally transformed domestic policing as local law enforcement agencies relied on the new military hardware, weaponry, and training to combat drugs and gangs.[32]

Deeming law enforcement the primary solution to drug and gang crime, Mayor Bradley exempted the LAPD from across-the-board budget cuts in 1983. While continuing to promote fair and equitable policing, Bradley hoped to expand the size and scope of the department in the post–Proposition 13 era. This stance reflected his liberal law-and-order vision of pairing procedural fairness and government regulation with expanded police power. Hoping to win the governor's seat in 1986 within the context of the panic over drugs and gangs, Bradley was, in part, responding to surveys conducted by his administration and the *Los Angeles Times* revealing rising fear of crime, growing federal support and resources for the war on drugs, and ire from the Los Angeles Police Protective League over his successful reform of the police pension system.[33] Budget constraints and the antitax mood initially limited Bradley's efforts to fund the LAPD to his preferred level. Nevertheless, Bradley's efforts to "fight crime on every front" grew the LAPD from a force of 6,900 in 1984 to 8,414 in 1990.[34]

Elite antigang police units became the primary beneficiary of the militarized drug war. The LAPD expanded its CRASH units to a citywide presence of 127 officers by 1988 and 235 by 1992. The Los Angeles Sheriff's Department and district attorney's office followed with their own elite antigang units, Operation Safe Streets and the Hardcore Program. Such units represented a new type of crime-fighting force that was more intensive in their operations and took up the bulk of the city's antigang resources. The city allocated 80 percent of its 1980 antigang budget for CRASH. Working in partnership with the district attorney and city prosecutors who promoted an aggressive approach to criminal prosecution in the 1980s, CRASH units aimed to intimidate, remove, and incarcerate as many gang members as possible, conducting geographically targeted gang and drug sweeps in predominantly African American and Latino/a neighborhoods.[35]

By the mid-1980s, CRASH units conducted routine sweeps to round up known and suspected gang members and drug dealers. They focused on combating the Bloods and Crips in South Central. Targeting African American

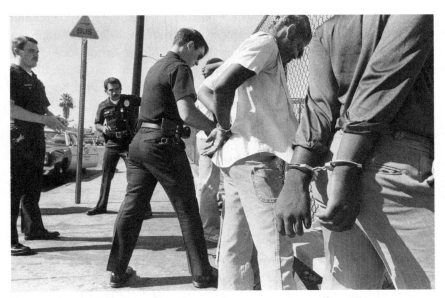

Los Angeles Southeast Division police officers arresting four young African American men, 1980. The LAPD's targeting of young African American men in its war on drugs and gangs constructed them as criminal and a threat to order that required disciplinary modes of exclusion from full social membership. *Los Angeles Times* Photographic Archives (Collection 1429); courtesy of Library Special Collections, Charles E. Young Research Library, UCLA.

gangs in South Central reflected the city's long history of residential discrimination that produced a segregated racial geography. But it also revealed how the racialized category of the "gang" resulted from choices made by the police to wage the war on drugs and gangs in a spatially selective manner. Operations reached upwards of 280 officers making 780 arrests in coordinated actions. Mobilizing bipartisan support for punitive policies to protect innocent civilians, Gates stated that such sweeps would continue until "we have recaptured our streets for good people."[36] Despite the military-style sweeps and overwhelming force, the gang war was a battle, according to one officer, "we seem to be losing."[37] After defining success through militarization for two decades, accelerating militarization and suppression was part of the police department's common sense and the obvious—and only—answer to problems rooted in economic and social crises of the 1980s.

The hosting of the 1984 Summer Olympics enabled the LAPD to buy military hardware and to rehearse spatially targeted policing operations that they would transfer to the drug and gang war in the late 1980s. The LAPD fast-tracked a new wave of recruits through training to conduct what

Commander William Rathburn, the department's Olympic coordinator and future director of the drug and gang sweep program, called an "unprecedented" crime-fighting project. The Olympics Major Crime Task Force, made up of LAPD, Los Angeles Sheriff's Department, and FBI officers, conducted mass sweeps to rid the Coliseum area of gang members, drug dealers, and homeless residents during the games. The LAPD also used its Olympic budget to buy an arsenal of machine guns, infrared-enhanced viewing devices, and a radio system for SWAT. Police partnered with the Department of Defense to coordinate security and flooded venues, especially the Coliseum and Exposition Park on the edge of South Central, with additional officers at a total cost of more than $20 million for the duration of the games. At the cost of "trying to sanitize the area," the overwhelming show of force kept crime and violence to a minimum during the games. But the militarized capacity of the police enabled a dramatic expansion of the department's war on drugs and gangs.[38]

Military equipment bought for Olympic security was remobilized to wage the war on drugs and gangs. On February 6, 1985, an LAPD SWAT team used a military-grade V-100 tank-like vehicle received after the Olympics, emblazoned with "LAPD Rescue Vehicle" on the side and equipped with a fourteen-foot battering ram, to smash down a wall of a suspected "rock house" in Pacoima. The officers found two women and three children eating ice cream, a small amount of marijuana, no guns, and no cocaine. Chief Gates, along with some residents and Councilman David Cunningham, praised the tactics, believing that such a show of force would cause "rock houses" to shut down.[39]

Meanwhile, many community members and civil rights and civil liberties organizations argued that police protection need not entail "storm trooper" tactics. The chairman of the San Fernando chapter of the National Association for the Advancement of Colored People (NAACP) explained, "We don't need new weapons to be tried out on us." Representing residents who were neither drug dealers nor gang members but who had been subjected to improper use of a ram, the American Civil Liberties Union (ACLU) filed a suit against the LAPD. After the suit had been in the legal system for two years, the California Supreme Court ruled that the LAPD had to receive judicial approval showing immediate danger to officers before each use of the ram. Community pressure and legal restraints successfully limited the LAPD's use of the ram but did little to deter the department's commitment to a campaign of eradication.[40]

Law enforcement and local political officials leaned on asset forfeiture to fund the drug war. Developed at the national level during the 1940s but greatly expanded under the Reagan administration, asset forfeiture allowed state and local law enforcement agencies who aided in federal drug raids to receive a portion of the spoils. The Comprehensive Crime Control Act of 1984 and the

Scene of damaged house and Los Angeles police battering ram in Pacoima, 1985. The use of the battering ram revealed the consequences of the LAPD fighting the war on drugs as a war on gangs. Instead of finding drugs, however, the officers found only a family eating ice cream. *Los Angeles Times* Photographic Archives (Collection 1429); courtesy of Library Special Collections, Charles E. Young Research Library, UCLA.

Anti–Drug Abuse Act of 1986 made cities eligible for massive infusions of state and federal funds received from narcotics seizures and allowed the LAPD to confiscate not only drugs but up to 90 percent of the property and cash related to drug cases, filling the department's coffers. When the city council approved the expanded asset forfeiture guidelines, it created the potential for huge financial windfalls for the city's Forfeited Assets Trust Fund and encouraged local politicians and police departments to see drug cases as a source of income during an era of economic stagnation and fiscal constraints.[41]

Asset forfeiture produced significant revenue for the department to reinvest. Between 1984 and 1990, the LAPD reported an expected return of $20,746,935 from drug raids, arrests, and confiscation of property.[42] Alongside funneling drug case money back into larger narcotics-related enforcement and stings, Bradley proposed using the funds to finance an increase in police officers in non-narcotics work and to pay overtime while Gates devised a city-approved Forfeited Assets Trust Fund budget to purchase military-grade hardware.[43] In 1988 the LAPD requested Forfeited Assets Trust Fund funds for twelve new positions in the Asset Forfeiture Detail of the Narcotics Division because it estimated that "funding these positions could result in an annual increase of $15 million in asset seizures." Bradley, in turn, justified a $1.5 million Forfeited Assets Trust Fund transfer to the Narcotics Abatement Account out of a belief that "the proposed expenditures will increase the effectiveness of the Department's war on drugs."[44] The use of forfeited assets funds and the Narcotics Abatement Account enabled the department to purchase information, narcotics, equipment, and logistical support for its war on drugs.

City officials also extended the militarized approach to the built environment through property destruction. Operation Knockdown epitomized a Vietnam-era philosophy of destroying neighborhoods in order to save them. Announcing the program on January 5, 1989, Bradley stated, "Under 'Operation Knockdown,' we will rid neighborhoods of abandoned, unsafe buildings . . . which often serve as drug centers or gang hideouts. . . . Unsafe buildings will be erased." Police officers identified derelict buildings, filling out a "Community Enhancement Form" to target the property for destruction. The city then bulldozed known "rock houses," leaving lots vacant, and giving streets the look of war zones in the name of "keeping neighborhoods safe."[45]

Spatial control and containment was a key component of the city's martial state. On October 20, 1989, the LAPD launched a "Neighborhood Rescue Operation" in the Pico-Union neighborhood. As the *Los Angeles Times* reported, "The 'Neighborhood Rescue Operation' is an attempt by police to eliminate drug dealing in the one-square-mile area by cordoning off intersections and dispatching an additional 60 patrol officers daily."[46] The program, formally named Operation Cul-de-Sac, meant to "design out" gang crime by designating certain streets as Narcotics Enforcement Zones. "In conceptualizing a strategy for Operation Cul-de-Sac I wanted to give the socially disadvantaged neighborhoods what the middle-class neighborhoods already had—that is, a physical characteristic something like cul-de-sacs that naturally deters gangs and drive-by shootings," the program's designer, Assistant Chief Vernon, explained.[47] Using the built environment to reduce gang violence was a stopgap measure that did not address social or economic conditions at the root of drug and gang activity, leading only to an increased police presence and a barricading of inner-city neighborhoods.[48]

The LAPD introduced Operation Cul-de-Sac to one of South Central's most segregated and marginalized neighborhoods in February 1990, closing off fourteen streets of the Newton Area. Within the neighborhood, which residents called a "war zone," the department set up a twenty-four-hour field command center, increased patrols, and established checkpoints to stop and search suspicious-looking persons attempting to enter the targeted area. Feigning to protect residents, Gates claimed that the police were "not here to occupy the territory. This isn't Panama. It's the city of Los Angeles and we're going to be here in a lawful manner. . . . People's constitutional rights will be protected in every way."[49] Gates attempted to allay fears by reaffirming that Los Angeles was not a police state akin to Central American dictatorships, which was exactly the point made by long-standing critics of the department when challenging the LAPD's repressive practices. Yet the carceral environment created by the barricades, checkpoints, and command center undermined his claims.

The barricades drew mixed comments from area residents. While many clergymen and school officials supported the program, residents feared that increased police patrols would lead to harassment. "This just allows the police to do whatever they want here," one black youth living in the neighborhood commented. "We have to answer their questions and submit to the harassment whether or not we are in a gang. It is all legal." While LAPD officials claimed that an overwhelming majority of residents supported the barricades, the *Los Angeles Sentinel* critiqued the plan, observing that the measure "automatically associates all teen-age youth in the barricaded zone with [criminal] activity."[50] Yet Operation Cul-de-Sac, according to the LAPD, succeeded in reducing crime in the target area by 20 and 14 percent in its first and second years, respectively.[51] But the positive outcomes came at the cost of policing measures that contained communities, perpetuated their identity as criminal spaces, and reinforced an "us versus them" approach of the police.

By the late 1980s and early 1990s, the emphasis on arrest and incarceration led to overcrowding in the city's jails. In 1988, for example, the Board of Police Commissioners asked the city for $246,000 to open a jail in the Rampart police station and to expand the existing Valley jail. City jails, the board explained, needed to expand by 14 percent in order to cope with a 22 percent increase in annual bookings from arrests for felonies and drug crimes. Between 1977 and 1986, for example, arrests for narcotics violations rose 75 percent, which increased the proportion of narcotics arrests from 10 percent to 20 percent of total arrests. "The Department attributes this jail capacity problem to the increasing proportion of felony arrest, especially those for narcotics related violations," the city administrative officer reported, "which require a longer period of detention than less serious crimes."[52] Many of those arrested and incarcerated were black and Latino/a youth. As the police carved out a dominant role in the drug and gang wars, the selective and spatially targeted policing based on assumptions of the drug-gang connection created racialized categories of criminal behavior.

Criminalizing Behavior and Counterinsurgency Campaigns

As with the city's approach to juvenile justice in the 1970s, African American and Latino/a youth remained the central targets of the war on drugs and gangs. CRASH unit operations focused on preempting gang crime through identification, monitoring, and intelligence gathering through the compilation of a file card database of suspected gang members. As one Board of Police commissioner wrote, "The Department believes that CRASH intelligence information has been effective in charting crimes and thereby detecting patterns and identifying suspects."[53] Yet the result of the CRASH file indiscriminately targeted most black and brown youth as either gang members or potential members.[54]

The ACLU filed a suit against the use of arbitrary questioning and photographing of Latino/a youth in 1980. The ACLU charged that officers often stopped youth on the street without any evidence of criminal activity. Officers would use the opportunity to fill out a "field information card" and enter it into the department's database. The ACLU charged that the photographing of youth was "invidious discrimination based on race and poverty." In an early victory, the judge issued a civil injunction against the department, stating that the LAPD's operations constituted an illegal search and seizure while discounting the claims of racial discrimination.[55]

The limits on the CRASH file card system did not last long. In 1985 a Superior Court judge dismissed the injunction on maintenance of gang files. The department issued new guidelines calling for the amassing of information about youth believed to be gang members or affiliated with gang members into a database. Officers who encountered individuals they suspected of being gang members were instructed to fill out a field information card, which contained names, aliases, addresses, and other identifying information in addition to dates of police encounters.[56] Due to the routine contact between the police and communities of color, many black and Latino/a youth who were not gang members were included in the database.[57]

When computerized gang databases replaced the CRASH file card system, it reinforced the ability of the police to criminalize black and brown youth through surveillance technology. The LAPD developed a Gang Reporting, Evaluation, and Tracking (GREAT) project in conjunction with the Los Angeles Sheriff's Department intended to monitor gang crime through a powerful computerized database. The development of Gang Reporting, Evaluation, and Tracking and the LAPD's internal Gang Tracking System placed Los Angeles at the forefront of computerized gang programs. Using the twenty-four-hour file to monitor gang members, officers subjected a growing number of inner-city residents to constant criminal justice system oversight and made recidivism more likely because of the LAPD's policy of enforcing minor violations of probation and parole.[58]

The statistics of the Gang Reporting, Evaluation, and Tracking database reflected the disparate nature of gang enforcement. According to Reiner, 47 percent of black youths and 9 to 10 percent of Latinos/as compared with 0.5 percent of white youth were involved in gangs. Antigang CRASH officers reinforced such beliefs through racially targeted policing. As one Latino activist remarked, "When you see [CRASH officers] out there . . . they look at every kid as problematic."[59] Profile-based stops and searches also rounded up some youth who happened to look like gang members or drug users, a profile that in the eyes of the police fit most black and Latino/a youth. Yet, even Reiner understood that the disproportionate number of black youth perceived to be gang members resulted from the fact that "black youth are more likely to be arrested than other youths" due to heavy policing and, therefore, added to the database.[60] Despite awareness that "youth gang membership is but a small percentage of the overall Latino and Black youth population of Los Angeles County," law enforcement produced racialized definitions of "gangs" and gang membership.[61]

The war on drugs and gangs criminalized the everyday activity and behavior of black and brown youth, leading to disciplinary policies that excluded them from public life. A 1989 Drug Enforcement Administration report on crack cocaine, for example, outlined a series of behaviors and signs that pointed to a "Crips and Bloods Gang Member Profile." These included "Black Males 12 to 24 years of age" who did not carry identification, used nicknames, had closely cropped hairstyles, wore red or blue clothes, used nonverbal communication, or wore gold chains and rings. The "Gang Member Profile," however, could easily describe many non–gang members. The California Attorney General's Office, led by former Los Angeles district attorney John Van de Kamp, also warned in a confidential "Crips & Bloods Street Gangs" report that gang members had started to avoid wearing gang attire in order to "throw off law enforcement authorities." As a result, the report suggested, any black man could legitimately be stopped and questioned as a potential gang member.[62]

Similar characterizations of gangs informed city and local law enforcement policy. "It is no surprise that 'gangs,' a term created by the criminal justice system, is used to describe violent youths or the more visible violent offenders, usually of minority status in Los Angeles," Miguel Duran, a youth gang worker, recognized. As city policy and policing strategies relied on racialized gang categories, they divorced drug and gang activity from the social and economic conditions that produced such behaviors and reinforced beliefs in the inherent criminality of black and brown youth.[63]

The logic behind this understanding of gangs dovetailed with new law enforcement philosophies aimed at combating gang crime by policing behaviors regarded as public nuisances. The LAPD's proposal marked a commitment to the broken windows theory of policing developed by James Q. Wilson and George Kelling in 1982. When combined with the aggressive policing of the war on drugs and gangs, the theory worked in Los Angeles as it did in other cities like New York under the NYPD's quality of life policing campaigns to stigmatize and justify those wars as wholesale attacks on poor communities of color who did not fulfill mainstream standards of respectability and personal responsibility.[64]

The adoption of "broken windows" inspired strategies that criminalized behaviors associated with black and brown youth, such as graffiti. Using the same rhetoric as the campaign against drugs and gangs, City Councilman Gilbert Lindsay organized a month-long "War on Graffiti" in 1987. Bringing together community leaders, church groups, block clubs, school officials, the Department of Recreation and Parks, and the LAPD in his South Central district, Lindsay envisioned the campaign as a means of neighborhood renewal.[65] The antigraffiti program, Operation Clean Sweep, culminated with city ordinances making graffiti illegal. The city distributed "NO GRAFFITI" signs and antigraffiti pamphlets to property owners. In effect, the campaign criminalized all street art associated with blacks and Latinos/as under the pretense of it being gang related.[66]

The California legislature also targeted low-income minority youth through antigang legislation. Following federal antidrug legislation passed in 1986 and 1988, the legislature passed the Street Terrorism Enforcement and Prevention (STEP) Act, which reinforced racialized categories of criminal behavior under the pretense of fighting gangs. The passage of the STEP Act, which was first drafted by Los Angeles city attorney James Hahn's Gang Unit under the name the California Street Terrorism and Anti-Gang (STAG) Act in 1987, committed local officials to producing and warehousing more criminals. Hahn's efforts to pass antigang legislation at the state level extended his fight against the Playboy Gangster Crips, in which he deployed a Civil Gang Abatement program, which made legal activities, such as owning a pager, making hand signals, wearing specific attire and colors, and congregating in known drug sale locations, illegal for gang members or suspected gang members. Although an ACLU challenge limited the reach of such injunctions, subsequent court decisions broadened gang abatement and injunction laws to provide no mandatory legal assistance or right to counsel to defendants by treating street gangs as a form of organized crime.[67]

The STEP Act created new criminal classifications for gang members, affiliates, and anyone who had knowledge of the criminal actions conducted by gangs. The STEP Act operated on the belief that gang violence created a "clear and present danger" to the public order.[68] As Hahn stated, "This comprehensive package of laws will give us a vital new arsenal of legal weapons to use against street gang crime."[69] Because the law was aimed at anyone "who willfully promotes or assists any felonious conduct" of gang members, STEP Act notices could be served to both the juvenile offender and their parents, thereby criminalizing many non–gang members. As such, the STEP Act criminalized otherwise legal behaviors associated with poor families dealing with the fallout of deindustrialization, failing schools, and residential segregation.[70]

Following the passage of the STEP Act, the LAPD's South Bureau CRASH Unit created "criminal profiles" of sixteen different gangs between 1989 and 1991 and served 993 STEP warnings to gang members in the area, adding the Rollin 30's Crips to the STEP Profile database, and increasing the prosecution of gang members and affiliates. The act enabled the police and the district attorney to trigger sentencing enhancements for gang-related crimes. After the LAPD served STEP notices, the department reported, gang members responded by making gang affiliation less overt or readily identifiable, and STEP arrests began to result in increased convictions.[71] The STEP Act's attention to behaviors perceived to be gang related not only targeted known gang members but also marked many black and Latino/a youth as potentially criminal.[72]

The legal dragnet worked hand-in-hand with mass arrest tactics to sweep up as many gang members as possible. When a stray bullet from a gang shooting in Westwood killed suburban teenager Karen Toshima on January 30, 1988, the LAPD's repressive apparatus swung into action. The LAPD assigned more than thirty officers and detectives to the case and increased foot patrols in the area, and the city council announced a $25,000 reward for Toshima's killer. Residents of South Central Los Angeles, where 114 people were killed by gang violence in 1987, argued that city officials and the police did not react with the same level of resources or concern when black residents were killed by gang violence.[73] As Councilman Farrell commented, "Unfortunately there is a perception that a life lost in South L.A. or East L.A. does not measure up to a life lost somewhere else."[74] African American residents speaking at community meetings expressed hopes that officials would respond to the sources of gang violence in social, political, and economic inequality rather than solely ratcheting up policing and criminal justice solutions.[75]

The LAPD responded to the Toshima killing with an antigang summit that resulted in the development of "Battle Plans" for an all-out war on gangs in 1988, the "Year of Gang Enforcement." Gang crime would no longer be the concern of only gang and narcotics specialists; it would now become the concern of the entire department. "Every member of the Office of Operations is responsible for the suppression of gang activity," the LAPD reported. "Each officer is required to take every available opportunity to bring the full weight of the Department to bear on those who have chosen to be involved in gang crime." In their daily work, officers were provided with "great discretion" when it came to gang suppression. Because department officials believed individuals chose a career of gang crime, rather than responding to social and economic conditions, officers should use every legal tool available when dealing with gang members. Ratcheting up its militaristic rhetoric, the LAPD proclaimed, "We are in the midst of a war over who is going to control the streets of this City and we shall prevail."[76]

Although Gates proposed a five-pronged "Needs to Eradicate Violent Street Gangs" strategy consisting of preventative measures and legislation to support courts and corrections, the focus was on an escalation of tactics resembling search-and-destroy missions in foreign territory. "The most effective means of suppressing street gang criminal activity is to remove gang members from City [sic] streets through lawful arrests," Gates proclaimed. "In this effort, the Los Angeles Police Department has launched continual Gang Task Forces in specific Areas and City-wide which focus on gang members."[77] The city council approved $2.45 million in overtime pay for the sweeps in April 1988, which Gates praised as a necessary tool to address violence that he claimed was worse than Beirut, Lebanon.[78] Department officials in charge of the task forces believed that a "posture of aggressive enforcement will increase the community's confidence in the Police Department."[79] As they played out, however, the task forces led to abuses of police power that criminalized and alienated residents while doing little to reduce crime or violence.

The Gang Abatement Task Forces, known as Operation Hammer, resulted in wholesale surveillance, arrest, and criminalization of a generation of black and Latino/a youth. As one LAPD spokesman bluntly stated, "Tonight we pick 'em up for anything and everything."[80] The spatial concentration of the task forces targeted the predominantly African American South Central neighborhood. In one deployment formula, for example, out of the 1,000 officers on the task force, 500 would be deployed in the Operations South Bureau, 200 in Operations Central, 150 in West, and 150 in Valley. After the sweeps, the LAPD removed the task forces from most areas of the city but left a 160-officer antigang unit in South Central to conduct nightly sweeps.[81]

Focusing on street corners known as gang hangouts, Operation Hammer led to indiscriminate stops, searches, and arrests of many black residents who fit the "drug gang" profile. During sweeps, officers made 24,684 arrests, of which 13,746 were reportedly gang members, and held suspects in a special holding facility at the Los Angeles Coliseum. Yet, few of the arrests were for felonies, and many of those picked up were never charged with a crime, though their names were entered in gang databases and they were released after twenty-four hours in holding. Such practices left many black

77th Street Division police officers arresting and searching suspect, 1989. Black youth, men in particular, bore the brunt of the LAPD's combined drug and gang war. As the police criminalized black youth in the department's attempt to win its self-proclaimed war to control the streets of Los Angeles, black youth faced routine stops and searches. *Los Angeles Times* Photographic Archives (Collection 1429); courtesy of Library Special Collections, Charles E. Young Research Library, UCLA.

and Latino/a youth with criminal records and increased vulnerability to incarceration.[82]

The sweeps drew a variety of responses, ranging from hopes that the "benign neglect" of the problem had been lifted to concerns that the "jacking up" of all black youth of a certain age and dress was a form of racist policing. For many middle-class residents, such as local clergy, the sweeps did not solve the problem but were a welcome effort to rid their streets of violent youth. In contrast, the NAACP charged that officers harassed black residents and made petty arrests that would likely never be prosecuted.[83] The abuses of power even prompted a critic for the *Los Angeles Times* to call out Bradley's one-sided approach to the gang problem, arguing that it was "up to Bradley to make the city's commitment to the social aspects of the gang crisis match the strengthened law-enforcement response."[84]

Mass criminalization of black and brown youth based on the assumption they were gang members, activists claimed, was the inevitable result of such law enforcement practices. The LAPD's response to demands for help in reducing gang and drug violence, the Coalition against Police Abuse explained, "has been the implementation of a 'scorched earth policy' in which the defendants have not attempted to distinguish between the innocent and those for whom they have legitimate reason to believe are engaged in illegal activity." The Police Misconduct Lawyer Referral Service received numerous complaints of harassment as a result of gang sweeps where police operated as if they had a "blank check."[85] Sweeps and mass arrests ensured that many black and Latino/a youth in target areas would have direct experience with the criminal justice system. Indeed, police questioning of youth became so routine that the *Los Angeles Sentinel* published a feature titled "What to Do When Approached by Cops." The single-minded approach not only resulted in mass criminalization but also contributed to the gang problem. "Those youngsters know you can't put them all in jail," one gang intervention worker remarked of the sweeps. "And when they go in the jail, they come back a little meaner and a lot tougher, and the problem just gets worse."[86]

Yet Gates, who referred to gang members as "rotten little cowards," defended the practice. Law enforcement personnel had no qualms about identifying the primary objective of the sweeps as a reassertion of police authority. "We're going to arrest them to death," Deputy Chief Glenn Levant, the city's antigang and antidrug czar, explained. Gates also rationalized harassment and profiling as a legitimate police strategy. "I think people believe that the only strategy we have is to put a lot of police officers on the street and harass people and make arrest for inconsequential kinds of things," Gates stated. "That's part of the strategy, no question about it."[87]

While the effectiveness of mass sweeps, militarized policing, and legal dragnets on reducing gang crime was unclear, it certainly led to an increase in the number of black youth believed to be gang members in the hands of the criminal justice system. The LAPD's 1989 report *State of the Los Angeles Gang Crisis* found that gang crime remained relatively stable at an average of 4,600 violent crimes a year between 1980 and 1988, yet gang membership recorded in databases soared from roughly 15,000 to 30,000 over the same period.[88] In the two years after Operation Hammer, gang homicides in the city climbed to 329 in 1990 and 375 in 1991 (county statistics reached 650 and 771 in the same two years), higher than in any year over the previous decade, and by 1992, District Attorney Reiner estimated that there were 1,000 gangs in the county with an estimated membership of 150,000.[89] Estimates by some scholars suggested that by 1990 at least 25 percent of young black men in Los Angeles were under control of the criminal justice system, while a 1991 study by the County Adult Detention Center found that nearly one-third of black men aged twenty to twenty-nine in the county had been arrested at least once in that same year.[90] By the early 1990s, the policing regime constructed to fight the drug and gang war had not reduced drug crime or gang violence but had criminalized a generation of black youth by its omnipresence in South Central's African American neighborhoods.

A War to Save the Neighborhood

The emphasis on spatial containment, mass arrests, and incarceration, while dominant, was not the only approach to dealing with gangs and drugs. Some city officials recognized that more policing would not solve the problem. Councilman Lindsay pushed for solutions that would address the economic and social crisis in the city. "But we also need to give our young people some better alternatives," Lindsay proclaimed. "We have to treat the root cause of these problems rather than just trying to arrest more people and seize more drugs."[91] Some in police leadership recognized that "law enforcement activities alone will not effectively handle the situation," and the department's top antigang officer recognized that there was no magic answer to stopping gang violence. "For every gang member you put in jail, there are two or three replacements waiting in line to take their place," Commander Larry Kramer explained. "We have to deal with the social dynamics."[92]

Perhaps the most significant alternative to get-tough policing and punishment in the 1980s was the Community Youth Gang Services Project (CYGS). While complementing the city's ongoing youth diversion programs, such as Project HEAVY (Human Efforts at Revitalizing Youth), CYGS employed ex–gang members and youth specialist staff to curb street gang violence and prevent gangs from recruiting new members. The CYGS teams used an intervention model to help mediate gang-on-gang conflicts, and they provided violence prevention services and surveillance in target areas to reduce violence. This intervention model represented an effort to facilitate cooperative work between law enforcement, social agencies, and the community.[93] Intervention measures were crucial to reducing violence but were never designed to prevent gang and drug activity in the first place. As Miguel Duran, a CYGS administrator, admitted, their prevention programs aimed at addressing social and economic roots of gang activity received less funding compared with "after the fact" suppression programs.[94]

What prevention programs did exist focused on changing the behavior of youth of color, not racial hierarchies or unequal socioeconomic structures. The LAPD pioneered drug and gang resistance education programs, such as the well-known Drug Abuse Resistance Education (DARE) program established by the department in 1983. In line with the soft side of Reagan's War on Drugs, LAPD instructors taught elementary and junior high school children to develop self-esteem and to resist peer pressure in order to "just say no" to drugs and gangs.[95] The program was so successful, according to Gates, that it resulted in a 53 percent decrease in substance abuse by high school students. After the first year of operation, the LAPD operated DARE programs in sixty-four elementary and junior high schools across the city. By 1988, DARE operated in all local elementary and junior high schools, and it was a national model adopted by school districts across the country, reaching nearly 1.5 million students. Programs such as DARE, however, reinforced the dominant belief that changing behavior—rather than social or economic conditions—would solve drug use and gang violence. These programs also complemented and justified the punitive side of the drug war. For if youth who were exposed to antidrug and antigang programs continued to demonstrate lapses of personal responsibility they knew the consequences: policing and punishment.[96]

Yet the primary emphasis of the city's gang and drug policies continued to center on law enforcement programs and suppression. The funding disparity between police programs and community-based intervention and rehabilitative models was stark. The LAPD operated its elite antigang CRASH units at roughly $10 million a year. The CYGS, in contrast, operated on an annual budget of roughly $2 million. The primary strategy continued to consist of locking up gang members as often and for as long as possible.[97]

As residents and religious organizations in South Central and East Los Angeles became concerned with gang violence and the drug trade during the 1980s, there were few options open to them but to call for more police. Support for intensified policing and punitive measures from religiously affiliated organizations such as the South Central Organizing Committee (SCOC) and the United Neighborhoods Organization (UNO) framed aggressive measures that linked the war on drugs and gangs as part of a war to save the ghetto and barrio. The work of SCOC and UNO, however, demonstrated the ways the overarching framework of solving urban social problems through policing, pro-market economic development, and personal responsibility dominated the thinking of city officials and residents alike. The demands for more police revealed class-based fissures in African American and Latino/a communities. With few resources available for prevention programs, the police remained, but instead of the police creating safer neighborhoods, residents faced abuse and discriminatory treatment.

The SCOC and UNO organized around the belief that through development of local leaders and bold initiatives they could "rebuild the Los Angeles inner city from the bottom up." UNO had been concerned with the widespread public and private divestment in East Los Angeles, which resulted in the lack of a retail sector, unemployment, inadequate health services, poor schools, family instability, gang violence, and crime.[98] Although many resi-

California governor George Deukmejian presenting Daryl Gates and Sherman Block with check for gang suppression projects, 1986. Funding for the war on gangs routinely flowed into programs aimed at suppression rather than prevention. Social or employment programs that gang members had asked for in the 1970s were no longer available in the 1980s. *Los Angeles Times* Photographic Archives (Collection 1429); courtesy of Library Special Collections, Charles E. Young Research Library, UCLA.

dents were initially wary of the SCOC's white leadership, the group's commitment to law and order, connections with political officials, politics of self-help, and confrontational style when addressing drug dealers led to increased support. Community support enabled them, along with UNO, to reap a number of concessions from local officials that helped fuel the city's war on crime in the name of saving the inner city from itself.[99]

The LAPD's saturation tactics during the Olympics prompted demands for more police by the SCOC and UNO. "Los Angeles cared enough about its international image to deploy hundreds of extra officers in the South Central area for four short weeks," Grace Trejo of the SCOC remarked, and she asked, "Does the fact that these police officers were removed along with the Olympic banners mean that the city does not care that in any given month roughly 26 residents of the South-Central area are murdered, 65 raped and 729 assaulted?"[100] The SCOC, along with politicians such as Maxine Waters, expressed concern for violent crime in the black community and called for a greater police presence to combat drugs and provide equitable services across the city.[101] Councilwoman Joan Milke Flores responded by filing a motion to review the LAPD's deployment policy, which privileged property value of committed crimes.[102] Although Gates defended the deployment formula, protests by SCOC and UNO, along with a lawsuit filed by the NAACP, succeeded in changing the deployment formula to reduce the importance of protection of property and shifted officers from the more affluent San Fernando Valley and West Side to underserved areas in South and East Los Angeles.[103]

An explosion of gang violence that left seven dead and five wounded in early October 1984 led SCOC to demand stricter punishment for gang members. Edith Nealy of the SCOC described the community as "virtually at the mercy of the gangs. We're people who are afraid to walk the streets." With political support from Bradley, Gates, and Ira Reiner, residents held anticrime rallies and proposed the Jericho Plan to send more police to South Central. The SCOC and UNO supported programs to rebuild their neighborhoods through rehabilitation but also believed that illegal drug and gang activity had to be dealt with swiftly and to the fullest extent of the law.[104]

Anticrime organizations worked with the Bradley administration to rid the streets of drug peddlers and criminals. UNO and SCOC joined with lawmakers to hold a war-on-crime rally in 1985 to mobilize residents to take back the streets. UNO and SCOC also cooperated with Bradley and Reiner to "free the city from the grip of violence," by forming Special Combat Zone Teams to "retake our city's streets by putting rock houses and corner dope peddlers out of business." The rhetoric of war and military-style tactics adopted by anticrime community organizations provided political space for Bradley and Gates to expand law enforcement programs and suppressive crime control policies.[105]

By the late 1980s and early 1990s, groups dissatisfied with the punitive approach began organizing to develop alternatives. The NAACP organized a 1988 concert titled "Save Our Community, Save Our People," promoting gang intervention and prevention as an alternative "to the continual support of resources being funneled into gang suppression (police overtime) which has yet to be proven effective in deterring gang violence."[106] Survey results from NAACP gang seminars held in 1987 revealed that residents saw drugs and alcohol as a significant contributor to gangs, but residents also understood that unemployment and poverty were key elements of the gang problem. While residents saw law enforcement as necessary, they also thought prevention programs, employment, and police community involvement were important measures. In calling out a welfare culture and need for parents to gain "control of their families," however, the NAACP linked drug and gang problems to declining family values, the nihilistic culture of black youth, and lack of parental responsibility—falling back on individual failings rather than structural explanations.[107]

South Central residents demonstrate against crime. These are some of the protestors who gathered near Mt. Pleasant Hill Baptist Church, July 10, 1983. Many African Americans were concerned with the problems of drugs and gangs in their community. But their calls for more police and punitive policies existed alongside a range of other proposals, including jobs programs, social services, and an end to police abuse and brutality associated with the war on drugs and gangs. *Los Angeles Times* Photographic Archives (Collection 1429); courtesy of Library Special Collections, Charles E. Young Research Library, UCLA.

Alternative views that regarded crack as a public health crisis also challenged the focus on punishment. Future California representative Karen Bass and City Councilman Mark Ridley-Thomas organized a Community Coalition for Substance Abuse Prevention and Treatment. Their inaugural conference, "Crack: Crisis in the African-American Community," offered solutions that "represent an alternative to the present response which is dominated by law-enforcement activities." Organizers worked to dispel myths produced by the police and disseminated by the media that gangs controlled the crack trade, and attendees discussed the LAPD's indiscriminate targeting of black men. While participants split on recommendations, the conference suggested that growing numbers regarded law enforcement's response to the combined crack and gang problem insufficient.[108] Community members interested in proposing alternatives to police-oriented solution to drugs and gangs, however, were unable to influence the broad convergence of interests that supported a punitive war on drugs, and the harassment, profiling, and aggressive policing persisted as the city's drug and gang crises lingered on.

———————

State-sanctioned violence and intensified militarization of the police were part and parcel of rising gang and drug conflict during the 1970s and 1980s. In combining the drug and gang wars, local officials vastly broadened the powers of the police, investing in a punitive state-building project to contain the fallout of social and economic crises facing impoverished black and Latino/a communities. Police maintained a belief, exhibited in mass arrests as in the Dalton Street Raid or Operation Hammer, that removal and warehousing were the only solution. These punitive policies criminalized and excluded a broad class of largely poor black and Latino/a youth from full participation in American society within the shifting context of the 1980s and 1990s marked by economic crises, reduced federal aid to cities and social services, global migrations and attention on the multicultural transformation of American cities, and the emphasis on broken windows and community-based policing. The desire of world city liberals to build a city safe for a diverse population and secure for economic development ultimately extended the power of the police.

By the 1990s, the get-tough approach and expanded police authority had produced a vastly more punitive milieu than the conditions that led to the uprisings of the 1960s. While many middle-class residents of color continued to support punitive policies, many impoverished residents of color regarded the police as little more than the frontline agents of control, containment, and exclusion. Punitive actions and the excessive force created a culture of disrespect and a lack of faith in law enforcement. This volatile combination of punitive policy, police militarization, and long-standing antipolice sentiment would come to a head in the largest episode of civil unrest in American history.

Chapter 9

The Chickens Have Come Home to Roost

Police Violence and Urban Rebellion Redux

The Webster Commission was established to investigate the uprising that rocked Los Angeles for five days in April 1992 after the acquittal of four LAPD officers on trial for beating Rodney King. In testimony and community meetings before the commission, South Central residents described a long history of discriminatory criminal justice policies, police brutality, and lack of accountability. "We saw Don Jackson's head smashed through a plate glass window by cops out in Long Beach. The cops were acquitted," activist Tut Hayes proclaimed. "We saw on television Latasha Harlins shot in the back of the head and the Korean grocer that got no time, straight probation, and we saw what happened to Rodney King. We were informed, we were alert, we viewed all that, and nothing happened. But we responded." Media outlets and lawmakers portrayed so-called rioters as criminals lacking legitimate grievances just as they did after Watts. But many participants had a clear political message for lawmakers and police officials. They explicitly rejected the intensified police authority, racist police practices, and punitive policies that had worked to keep them contained for the previous two and a half decades.[1]

Video evidence of the King beating, the officers' acquittal, and ensuing rebellion vindicated the claims of activists and residents of color who had struggled against a repressive police department and criminal justice system since the 1965 Watts uprising. In the wake of the 1992 rebellion, community organizations, activists, and residents once warned that a get-tough response would only perpetuate the crisis in impoverished neighborhoods and reinforce the city's racial hierarchy. "Right now in L.A., making the right choice between the welfare state or the police state is critical; no amount of police can protect people from the spiraling social cost of poverty," argued activists from the Labor/Community Strategy Center (LCSC), a progressive, multiracial organization that emerged from labor and economic justice struggles of the 1980s. "Hiring 1,000 police will overcrowd more schools and close a few health centers, but for the millions of poor Angelenos who live in fear, it will not buy safety. . . . The further transformation of the LAPD into an occupying force is the wrong solution."[2] Nevertheless, police authorities and lawmakers responded with initiatives that reasserted state authority and police-oriented solutions to urban problems.

In contrast to the 1960s uprisings, the 1992 rebellion was multiracial, its context more punitive. Often referred to as a poverty or bread riot in response to the dire economic conditions and inequality faced by people of color in the city, the rebellion was also rooted in a rejection of the excessive police power and the LAPD's broad discretionary authority to criminalize, contain, and incarcerate those residents the police deemed a threat to the social order.[3] As such, human relations programs or halfhearted community-based policing initiatives to incrementally reform the LAPD would not be enough. Substantive changes would be necessary.

Many residents had high hopes after the rebellion. Economic development and social programs developed by lawmakers, however, relied on a partnership with the criminal justice system. Operation Weed and Seed, in particular, paired federal funding for social services in impoverished and high-crime neighborhoods with increased resources for law enforcement to weed out criminals. But the police were not equipped to solve social problems that manifested through crime, drug use, and gang violence. As LCSC activists predicted during their campaign against Weed and Seed, programs aimed at solving socioeconomic inequality were linked with law enforcement, and the welfare state was absorbed by the carceral state.[4]

In the years after 1992, Los Angeles's first African American chief of police, Willie Williams, promoted community policing. An outsider who had come to Los Angeles after serving as chief of the Philadelphia police department, Williams faced stiff opposition from veteran LAPD officers and commanders. Yet hopes for reform and external oversight by the police commission were hampered by the election of law-and-order conservative Richard Riorden as mayor in 1993. The department capitalized on the city's continued need for law enforcement to address social problems to continue to consolidate its power and authority.

Policing and Excessive Force in the Multiracial Metropolis

By the 1990s, the city was no longer one the police knew. Police officers assigned to inner-city districts were rarely from the area and brought with them a hostile mentality toward the residents they served. A study by the American Civil Liberties Union (ACLU) found that 83.1 percent of LAPD officers lived outside the city limits. Segregation exacerbated this geographic divide. Not only did officers live outside the city boundaries, they lived in areas much less ethnically and racially diverse than the neighborhoods they patrolled. "The most pronounced, consistent difference is that police enclave communities have extraordinarily small African-American populations," the ACLU explained, "making it more likely that officers and their families have few social interactions with African-Americans outside the context of police work."[5]

The combination of demographic changes between the 1970s and the 1990s, racial segregation, and officer residency patterns worsened the department's "us versus them" attitude. Officers tasked with patrolling high-crime, violent neighborhoods felt vulnerable. Rarely viewing their role as ensuring public safety, they enforced order. "In response to the enormous influx of Mexicans and Central Americans, the police have come to feel like mercenaries fighting a war in a foreign land," one observer suggested. "The result is what one officer calls 'the John Wayne Syndrome—you and me, pardner, against the world. Who do we stop? The dummies. It's us against the dummies.'"[6] But for residents, the police were a force of outsiders. "There is a widespread belief," the ACLU concluded, "that the Los Angeles Police Department . . . is a dominantly white force of suburban outsiders who function as a de facto army of occupation in the urban communities of Los Angeles."[7]

Suppression and containment strategies associated with the wars on crime, drugs, and, gangs of the 1980s and early 1990s amplified the divide between police and residents of color. The martial imperative increased the potential for police abuse and removed limitations on the excessive use of force. "The political rhetoric about a 'war' on drugs and a 'war' on crime has helped turn the police into soldiers," the ACLU concluded in the wake of the King beating, "not civil servants or guardians of community order—making them sometimes more aggressive and forceful than they have a right to be in the pursuit of criminals and suspects."[8] Seeing themselves at war, the police used whatever means necessary to control the streets.

Such attitudes had dire consequences for many black and Latino/a residents. In June of 1986, six officers from Community Resources against Street Hoodlums raided the home of Jessie Lárez in East Los Angeles in search of a murder weapon supposedly in the possession of one of Lárez's sons. During the raid, the officers turned the home upside down and broke Jessie Lárez's nose. As the U.S. Court of Appeals summarized, officers "hurled Jessie across the room, grabbed him by the hair, forced him to lie face down on the floor where one of the officers held Jessie down with his knee on Jessie's neck and handcuffed him. . . . The officers laughed and sneered; they told him they had him where they wanted him. At one point Officer Holcomb pointed his service revolver at Jessie's head and said to him, 'I could blow your fucking head off right here and nobody can prove you did not try to do something.' Officer Keller told Jessie, 'we finally got you motherfucker.'"[9] Officers failed to find any weapons and did not bring any charges against members of the Lárez family for gun possession. As was common when officers used improper force, they arrested Jessie Lárez for battery of a police officer.[10]

Lárez lodged a complaint and the Internal Affairs Division (IAD) assigned a Community Resources against Street Hoodlums officer to investigate. Unsurprisingly, none of the allegations of brutality, excessive use of force, or property destruction were sustained. In response, Lárez brought a lawsuit against Gates and the LAPD in federal court. Gates defended his officers, asking, "How much is a broken nose worth? . . . I don't think it's worth anything. [Lárez] is probably lucky that's all he had broken."[11] Although a federal judge found in favor of Lárez and ordered Gates to pay a $170,000 fine, the city council and Bradley appropriated funds to pay the settlement, infuriating Latino/a residents and activists who viewed the action as a failure to hold the department accountable to civilian authority.[12] As the Latino Community Justice Center, an organization that worked on behalf of police abuse victims in the Latino/a community, explained, "Gang violence has been repeatedly used by Chief Gates to justify police harassment of Blacks and Latinos."[13]

Routine police abuse had a significant impact on city resources. But skyrocketing expenditures from lawsuits and settlements had done little to change disciplinary practices within the LAPD. Between 1972 and 1990, individuals filed 15,054 complaints and 5,598 lawsuits against the LAPD, which resulted in the city paying out over $43 million in claims to residents for the actions of LAPD officers.[14] By the early 1990s, an observer of the Board of Police Commissioners explained that "multi-million dollar verdicts, if not exactly commonplace, were no longer extraordinary events." In 1989 and 1990, for example, the city paid out over $6 million and $8 million in settlements, respectively. While using taxpayer resources to protect the police, the same observer found, the commission also recognized that the "specter of future litigation" and fiscal repercussions made them wary of aggressive investigations into the accusations of abuse or the department's disciplinary permissiveness.[15] As the board was caught between protecting the department and avoiding the financial strain of future judgments, the board's oversight withered.

In the late 1980s and 1990s, Robert Talcott led the police commission in an effort to restore peace and harmony with the department. Talcott's approach heralded back to an era when the mayor's office attempted to create an amicable relationship with the police department in which the commission took a backseat to the prerogatives of the chief of police. After LAPD officers assaulted protestors involved in the Century City Justice for Janitors march in June 1990, for example, the Police Commission did not undertake an investigation until ordered to by Mayor Bradley. As former commissioner Reva Tooley told investigators tasked with probing the King beating, the LAPD was "so out of control in terms of oversight that they only investigate what they want to." The department was "getting away with murder."[16]

Department officials routinely absolved officers charged with the use of excessive force. Deputy Chief Glenn Levant, who directed the war on gangs, believed that under Assistant Chief Robert Vernon, the department rarely sustained complaints of excessive force or abuse. Between 1986 and 1990, for example, IAD sustained only 19 percent of all citizen-generated complaints and officer discipline was lax. Out of 1,988 complaints of officer use of excessive force or improper tactics, only 7.9 percent were sustained. The IAD did not even review every complaint. The IAD investigated only sixty-six complaints of excessive force or improper tactics during the study period, leaving the remaining 1,922 complaints to be investigated by area commanders who were less likely to sustain complaints of excessive force. Indeed, Levant believed the complaint and discipline system had "gone to hell."[17]

The accountability problem rested with department leadership. Supervisors often knew who the most problematic officers were and recommended disciplinary action. But when those recommendations for discipline reached Gates, who held ultimate disciplinary authority over officers, he routinely overturned punishments, especially for excessive use of force. In 1986, F. E. Piersol, commander of the Operations–South Bureau, wrote to the director of the Office of Operations, Assistant Chief Vernon, complaining that Gates overturned sustained complaints of officer misconduct for three officers who "had conducted themselves in a manner inconsistent with established Department standards." In each case, the chief disregarded the recommended disciplinary action, which undermined the commander's credibility with officers and weakened the ability of the oversight system to prevent misconduct. "The unfortunate by-product of these reversals was that the involved officers were led to believe that their conduct in these matters was acceptable although the Bureau deemed it inappropriate," Piersol concluded. "Each of the three involved officers have subsequently become involved in similar, and in one case, almost identical, acts of misconduct." What was needed was a loud and clear message that the department would not tolerate acts of misconduct. Such suggestions went unheeded.[18]

For Gates the department remained exemplary. In his annual self-evaluations and end-of-year messages to officers, Gates praised his department as respectful, communicative with residents, and innovative. The end-of-year message in 1989, for example, suggested that the LAPD had concluded another successful year and through "expansion and innovation" was a department "on the move."[19] Gates rarely, if ever, admitted the problems of excessive force and violations of civil liberties that accompanied the gang and drug war. In 1986, the same year officers beat Lárez without facing any repercussion or disciplinary action, Gates rated the department "Outstanding" in every category, including Community Relations and Unit Management.[20] But Gates's rosy vision was about to come crashing down.

On March 3, 1991, California Highway Patrol officers pulled over Rodney King after a high-speed chase. Called in for support, LAPD officers confronted King, who was drunk and failed to respond to verbal commands. While some seventeen other officers stood by, three LAPD officers, under the direction of a sergeant, viciously beat King using aluminum batons and TASERs. Unbeknownst to the officers, a bystander filmed the beating and gave the tape to a local news station. The clip became an international news story, providing startling evidence of the LAPD's excessive use of force.[21]

When residents and political leaders saw the video of the King beating, they reacted with disbelief. Mayor Bradley was "shocked and outraged." Even Chief Gates appeared astonished, demonstrating his inability to accept that officers in his self-proclaimed model department would treat suspects with such force. "It was very, very extreme use of force—extreme for any police department in America," Gates stated. "But for the LAPD, considered by many to be the finest, most professional police department in the world, it was more than extreme. It was impossible." While Gates denied the beating reflected systemic problems in his department, calling it an aberration, residents and media outlets mocked Gates's claims of a police department in tune with racial equality and civil rights through protests and political cartoons. For his part, Bradley pledged action. "This is something we cannot tolerate," Bradley stated. "I assure you . . . appropriate action will be taken by the department and the Police Commission."[22]

The footage of the King beating exposed the failure of the department's disciplinary system to keep officers in check. Officers ordinarily able to hide behind the code of silence, which informally forbade an officer from testifying against a fellow officer, were exposed on videotape. Gates attempted to head off criticism by announcing internal investigations by the IAD and Major Crimes Investigation section, calling his department a "model department" emulated by law enforcement agencies across the nation, and eventually issuing a half-hearted apology in which he emphasized King's criminal past. "He's on parole," Gates stated. "He's a convicted robber, I'd be glad to apologize." Yet, Gates denied that the beating reflected a systemic problem in the department, concluding, "This [incident] is an aberration."[23]

But for many black and Latino/a residents, such episodes of abuse were hardly aberrations. A Los Angeles Times poll found that 92 percent of residents believed the police used excessive force against King and two-thirds thought police brutality was common. Another poll conducted for the mayor's office found that 78.1 percent of people believed blacks and Latinos/as were more likely to be victims of police brutality.[24] "There are so many incidents of police brutality in our community," the ACLU's Paul Hoffman stated, "that it has become part of the fabric of our daily lives, especially the lives of the African-Americans and Latinos in Los Angeles."[25]

Pressure for Reform

The King beating mobilized many residents to demand change. Over 10,000 people wrote to the ACLU demanding that Gates resign.[26] Hundreds of protestors, led by the National Association for the Advancement of Colored People and the Urban League, converged on the Parker Center to demand Gates's resignation. Protestors chanted "Gates must go! Gates must go!" for over three hours. With support from Gates and Bradley, the district attorney indicted four officers. The FBI also investigated to determine if King's civil rights were violated, and the Department of Justice closely monitored the outcome of the city's handling of the situation.[27]

Removing Gates was not an easy task. Gates flexed the LAPD's political muscle after the Board of Police Commissioners decided to put him on inactive duty pending an investigation into the department. Infuriated, Gates refused to accept the order, appealing to the city council and suing the Board of Police Commissioners for illegally convening and overstepping their power to remove the chief. The city council reinstated Gates the following day. After a month, Bradley publicly demanded Gates's resignation, something he had not previously done when episodes of abuse surfaced. To be sure, in the decades prior to 1991, Bradley had operated within the context of structural constraints of the city charter that gave the mayor only so much authority over the police department. But video evidence provided Bradley with the leverage he did not have before. Yet Gates remained steadfast in dismissing any call for his removal. "I will never leave when there is controversy," Gates stated. "I will leave when I choose to leave."[28]

But Bradley took action. He appointed deputy secretary of state and former FBI director Warren Christopher, who had served on the McCone Commission, to lead an independent investigation of the policies, practices, and culture within the LAPD. The ten-member Independent Commission on the Los Angeles Police Department, known as the Christopher Commission, was intended to be "a comprehensive effort to deal with the entire problem of police brutality in Los Angeles." With the cooperation of Gates, commissioners interviewed more than fifty experts, 150 community representatives, and 500 police officers in its review of LAPD policies, culture and attitudes, and supervision and management procedures.[29]

The Christopher Commission's investigation exposed a systemic lack of accountability and failure of leadership that would ultimately force Gates out. Beyond general use-of-force disparities, the report exposed the LAPD's racist use of the K-9 Unit, including a wide disparity in dog bites and attacks in black and Latino/a neighborhoods. Despite a lawsuit filed by the ACLU and a nationally televised CBS news airing of an LAPD-sanctioned video showing a dog attack on an unarmed suspect, Gates denied that the department trained dogs to bite people, that they only bite if attacked, and that the dogs were "the most gentle things you'll ever find in your life."[30]

The release of the LAPD's Mobile Digital Terminal transcripts and interviews with officers compounded the damning evidence of a racist subculture in the department. One officer, for example, commented that he was "back over here in the projects, pissing off the natives," and that he "would love to drive down Slauson with a flamethrower. . . . We could have a barbecue." Although the most blatant racist selections represented a small percentage of the total number of transmissions, a survey of 650 officers found that nearly 25 percent of officers believed "racial bias (prejudice) on the part of officers toward minority citizens currently exists and contributes to a negative interaction between police and the community." A lack of management supervision contributed to the excessive use of force and an insular culture that operated to bury complaints of excessive force or punish officers who spoke out or criticized the department. More surprising, however, was that 4.9 percent of respondents believed that an officer was justified in administering physical punishment to a suspect who has committed a heinous crime, while 4.6 percent believed an officer was justified in using physical punishment with a suspect who had a bad or uncooperative attitude.[31]

Testimony also uncovered a failure of leadership and management to ensure accountability. While some officers, such as Assistant Chief Vernon, defended the department against criticism, others expressed concern with the way Gates had managed the department. Assistant Chief David Dotson was blunt. "Essentially," he explained, "we have not had, in my opinion, at the top, very effective leadership." To be sure, the department's policy manual had "high-sounding statements of purpose" about how officers should treat residents, but very little was translated into day-to-day operations. Rather, the department was stuck in a 1950s-era mentality that rewarded officers for "doing this hardnosed, aggressive, proactive police job." The perceived failures of the criminal justice system, Assistant Chief Brewer added, led officers to adopt tactics of street justice, the attitude that "perhaps maybe we should teach you that you shouldn't do these kinds of things [crime and violence]."[32]

The philosophy of managing rather than preventing crime isolated the police from the people they were supposed to serve and made the use of force much more likely. "This police department is aggressive," Gates admitted. "We're going to use all the means at our disposal that we can to bring down the crime and violence."[33] Officers and representatives of the Los Angeles Police Protective League, however, testified that the department's emphasis on statistics as the sign of good police work—arrests as an indicator of productivity and means of promotion—and response time to emergency calls reduced incentives for officers to cooperate with residents or adopt community-oriented policing practices. The result, the commission concluded, was a "siege mentality" that "alienates the officer from the community."[34]

The commission's report identified and criticized the LAPD's policies and practices in a way that only anti–police abuse activists had done in the past. It condemned the department's discriminatory practices, such as the "pretty routine" use of the prone-out tactic and stops of black and Latino/a youth without "probable cause" or "reasonable suspicion" in neighborhoods of color, and revealed a racist culture that influenced the use of excessive force in black and Latino/a communities. "The problem of excessive force," the commission concluded, "is aggravated by racism and bias within the LAPD." The central recommendations reflected the liberal law-and-order emphasis on procedural oversight and responsiveness to all residents, including Gates's retirement, the adoption of community policing, new training and supervisory procedures, and policies to make the department more accountable to the mayor and Board of Police Commissioners.[35]

The Christopher Report proposed 130 specific changes to departmental operations and made thirty-six major recommendations in need of immediate redress. The most far reaching aimed to overhaul departmental culture starting with top leadership, the elimination of discriminatory practices, a return to the philosophy of community-based policing, transparency in disciplinary and complaint proceedings, a greater oversight role for the police commission, and limits on the tenure of the chief.[36] Praising the report, Bradley called for implementation of the most pressing recommendations. "I say to those who would block the road to change: stand aside or we will leave you behind," Bradley said. "We cannot, we will not, rest until the Christopher Commission has changed the way we police our city."[37]

Gates "strongly opposed" all recommendations limiting the power or autonomy of the department. He rejected proposals that would remove the chief's civil service protection, change the selection process of the chief curbing preferences for internal candidates, increase mayoral power to appoint the chief, provide greater authority for the Police Commission to remove the chief, and limit the chief's tenure to two five-year terms. He also hesitated when it came to changes limiting officer discretion, such as the recommendation to end use of the prone-out tactic. Gates ordered further study of the practice and defended the gradual approach by claiming, "This research is necessary because a delicate balance must be reached. Crime prevention, officer safety, community perceptions, employee relations concerns and 'Service Excellence' all must be taken into account."[38]

Gates did eventually announce a plan to retire in April 1992, and begrudgingly accepted the recommendation that the department expand community-based policing strategies. Beginning in January 1992, the department implemented pilot community-based policing initiatives in divisions around the city. Gates promoted community-based policing as "an attitude, not a program," and as a philosophy of cooperation with residents to solve long-term community problems. The department's adoption of community-based policing as a "value-laden philosophy of policing that consists of an open-ended dynamic process emphasizing partnerships and problem solving to provide service excellence" reflected the potential for a transformation of policing in the city. But it required a reorientation in departmental culture that was rigidly hierarchical and committed to aggressive tactics based on the "us versus them" attitude.[39]

Progress was slow, and convincing officers to buy in required work. Supervisors from the Southeast and Southwest areas, responding to widespread criticism of the department after the King beating and pressure from the department brass to implement new initiatives, supported community-based policing and recognized that they "must listen and respond to community desires." Supervisors emphasized the desire to "instill the service mentality into the troops; citizens want to be treated well." Within Operations–South Bureau, Chief Hunt promoted implementation of community-based policing philosophies and challenged officers to act in ways that would "prove the greatness" and restore the faith, credibility, and image of the LAPD as a model department. But supervisors also noted a "need to get officers on board; present in positive manner," which in practice often meant subordinating community desires for control to police objectives and interests.[40]

A more fundamental change came when residents overwhelmingly passed Charter Amendment F in June of 1992. Coming on the heels of the 1992 Los Angeles rebellion, discussed below, Charter Amendment F gained support from blacks, Latinos/as, and white liberals, Jews in particular. Opposition was centered in the San Fernando Valley, but even there, voters approved the measure with just over 50 percent of the vote.[41] Charter reform altered the process of hiring the chief of police, limited the chief's tenure to two five-year terms, provided the mayor and police commission greater power to fire the chief, and appointed a civilian member to departmental disciplinary panels to promote greater accountability in complaint and disciplinary proceedings. Such reforms would provide the foundation for a transformation in the relationship between the police and civilian oversight that LAPD officials had opposed for half a century.[42] Unsurprisingly, Gates and the Police Protective League opposed the measure. Gates argued the amendment was a "power play—it will politicize the Police Department right down to the man on the street," while Police Protective League president Bill Violante called it "a sham, a bunch of garbage." Public support for charter reform, however, was a clear rejection of Gates and his style of policing. Groups such as the Urban League believed that it represented a "new climate" and "sends out the message to officers on the street that says, 'Hey, this is a new day, you can't brutalize people anymore.'"[43]

Yet activists would point out that the reforms were limited in scope. As LCSC activists argued, the charter amendment narrowly focused on the power of the chief, failed to address systemic problems of racism and excessive violence in the LAPD, and aimed at pacifying community outrage through the appearance of significant change. Instead, the Coalition against Police Abuse, as it had done for nearly two decades, suggested a fundamental reordering of police power through proposals for social and economic investment in communities, an independent review board, and community control of the police. In demanding investment in the welfare state instead of the police state, LCSC activists warned that surface-level reforms to the LAPD would enable the further transformation of the department into an occupying force.[44]

But the police department did not change overnight. Cosmetic changes, such as setting up a toll-free hotline to receive complaints and creating more easily accessible and bilingual complaint forms, as activists suggested, did not overturn the prevailing power structure of the department.[45] Early audits, in fact, found significant noncompliance with the changes in complaint procedures and limited implementation of community policing. In 1992 an ACLU study concluded, "More than a year after the beating of motorist Rodney King focused attention on the LAPD's handling of incidents of severe police misconduct, meaningful reform of citizen complaint operations remains woefully incomplete."[46] As public outcry and pressure led to the indictment of four LAPD officers involved in the King beating, the outcome of the trial would test the city's commitment to justice and equality.

No Justice, No Peace

The trial of the LAPD officers for beating King became a judgment on the police, racism, and justice in the city. Four months later, the California Court of Appeals changed the venue of trial from downtown Los Angeles to the re-mote, nearly all-white suburban enclave of Simi Valley thirty-five miles to the northwest. The jury, composed of ten whites, one Latina, and one Filipino-American, included no African Americans. To the shock of many Angelinos, on April 29, 1992, the jury acquitted the officers. In the hours and days that followed, thousands of residents took to the streets, many yelling, "No justice, no peace," in what quickly became the largest urban uprising in American history.[47]

The trial followed a series of new injustices and abuses of police power. The most recent affront for many African Americans occurred after Judge Joyce Karlin handed down a light sentence of probation and community ser-vice for Korean merchant Sun Ja Du after the murder of Latasha Harlins, an African American teenager. Karlin's leniency combined with the acquittal of the four officers in the King trial and the longer history of police abuse in the city symbolized a racist and unequal criminal justice system. As one Ingle-wood Blood told Mike Davis: "Rodney King? Shit, my homies be beat like dogs by the police every day. This riot is all about the homeboys murdered by the police, about the little sister killed by the Koreans, about twenty-seven years of oppression. Rodney King just the trigger." When the jury handed down its acquittal, hip-hop artist Chuck D of Public Enemy summarized the reaction: it "was like throwing a match in a pool of gasoline."[48]

Peaceful protestors gathered in front of Parker Center, while other marched in the streets holding signs condemning chief Gates, racism in the LAPD, and police practices that gave officers a "license to kill." As protest grew, it evolved into sporadic episodes of violence city-wide. City officials and LAPD commanders were unprepared, even though Gates had written the Model Riot Control Plan after Watts, telling interviewers, "No one knows how to handle a riot better than I do." Even after the sporadic violence broke out, Gates attended a fundraiser with opponents of Charter Amendment F in the posh West Side neighborhood of Brentwood rather than organize his department's response.[49]

Looting and burning spread to vast swaths of the city, reaching Koreatown, Hollywood, and parts of the San Fernando Valley. An unorganized and uncoordinated LAPD command responded slowly, without any clear direc-tive. Outnumbered and ill-equipped, officers retreated from the scene at the corner of Florence and Normandie in South Central while the city watched on television as white truck driver Reginald Denny was brutally attacked. The department's command structure broke down during the initial hours of the rebellion, and the nation's top police department—unwilling to ask for help unless forced to do so—looked on helplessly as the violence quickly spun out of control.[50]

Protesting the LAPD during the 1992 Los Angeles rebellion. Protestors march in the streets and hold up signs condemning the racism at the core of the LAPD and demanding the firing of Chief of Police Daryl Gates. The acquittal of the four officers on trial for the beating of Rodney King sparked and fueled the rebellion, which quickly became the largest episode of civil unrest in American history. Photographer: Gary Leonard; Gary Leonard Collection, Los Angeles Public Library.

Law enforcement officials believed that gangs were organizing the violence and that counterinsurgency tactics of mass arrest, occupation, and containment would be necessary to restore law and order. Mayor Bradley declared a state of emergency, called on the State of California to send troops, and instituted a citywide sunset-to-sunrise curfew.[51] After assuring the nation that he would "use whatever force is necessary to restore order," President George H. W. Bush provided federal law enforcement officers with the authority to act as peace officers and to enforce state laws.[52] Over 7,000 National Guardsmen and more than 3,500 federal troops from a variety of agencies such as the FBI; SWAT Teams; special riot control units from the U.S. Marshals Service; Immigration and Naturalization Service (INS); Alcohol, Tobacco, and Firearms; and the Bureau of Prisons mobilized to aid local law enforcement. It took over 20,000 law enforcement and military forces to stop the unrest, which ended after five days, 16,291 arrests, 2,383 injuries, at least fifty-two deaths, 700 businesses burned, and nearly $1 billion in damage. Cooperation between local and federal law enforcement agencies resulted in mass arrests and criminalization of the city's black and brown residents.[53]

Local officials and the Bush administration blamed the violence on gang members and criminals. In a public address to the nation, President Bush declared the violence was "not about civil rights" or a "message of protest," but "the brutality of a mob, pure and simple."[54] Deputy City Attorney John Wilson claimed that background checks on the arrestees revealed that 40 percent had criminal records. "This was not an instantaneous 'good guy rage' kind of thing," Wilson suggested. "This was a 'bad guy' taking advantage of a situation out of control." City officials brushed off charges of civil liberties violations by portraying much of involvement in the violence as the work of hardened criminals. "The public defenders have made a point of saying we've caught up people who were homeless. (And) yes, we have seen some of those," said Deputy City Attorney Dennis Jensen. "But there was a criminal element out there."[55]

Mass arrests targeted areas that had been punitively policed since the 1970s. Emphasizing the high proportion of criminal records among those arrested ignored how the war on drugs and gangs had produced higher rates of arrest among blacks and Latinos/as. Indeed, between 1987 and 1992, California expanded criminal justice spending by 70 percent, and at least 25 percent of black youth in South Central had some sort of criminal record. By framing the uprising as an episode of lawlessness, criminality, and illegality, officials justified punitive responses of aggressive policing, mass arrest, and incarceration.[56]

Yet unlike the uprisings of the 1960s, this was a multiracial and multiethnic rebellion. Studies found that 50.6 percent of those arrested were Latino/a and 36.2 percent were African American. Many of the targets of violence were Latino/a immigrants—or perceived immigrants—and Korean shopkeepers. Predominantly immigrant neighborhoods of Pico-Union and Koreatown became focal points of the unrest. As immigrants transformed American cities between 1965 and the 1990s, many blamed urban problems on immigrants themselves. In this case, many observers placed responsibility for the violence on the city's immigrant populations, especially the undocumented. The cooperation of the INS and police in response to the unrest reflected both a broader anti-immigrant nativism and the expansion of police authority to criminalize and contain immigrants.[57]

Federal law enforcement agencies helped restore order, but the cooperation between INS agents and the police led to mass criminalization and violations of civil liberties of the city's immigrant population. Nearly 400 Border Patrol and INS agents aided local law enforcement during the rebellion, which provided cover for operations targeting immigrants. When the police responded to calls for service in the predominantly immigrant areas of Pico-

Union and the Alvarado corridor, they often arrived with INS officers who conducted dragnet sweeps to arrest undocumented immigrants. INS officials denied they conducted mass sweeps but went where they were directed by commanders. INS officers also went to the county jail to interview arrestees to identify undocumented immigrants and to initiate the deportation process. "We should be seeking to restore peace and calm in this city," City Councilman Mike Hernandez stated. "It is intolerable to have INS engaging in border patrol type immigration sweeps."[58]

The arrest and deportation of many undocumented immigrants revealed the extension of police power and violations of the LAPD's Special Order 40. Of the 16,291 arrests, some estimated that 1,240 of them were undocumented immigrants, many of whom were handed over to the INS for immediate deportation. Statistics revealed that of the 1,240 alien arrests, 1,105 were deportable and 1,064 were removed from the country.[59] The Central American Refugee Center documented widespread violations of the civil and human rights of Latino/a residents living in the central Pico-Union district in the weeks following the riots. The Central American Refugee Center found at least 452 persons were stopped for no reason by the LAPD, interrogated as to their immigration status, and summarily handed over to the INS, with no criminal charges ever brought against them. Such practices were in direct violation of city law and policy regarding intervention into immigration matters. The official investigation into the rebellion, however, exonerated the LAPD and INS from any wrongdoing.[60] "We are becoming the guinea pigs, the Jews," the Central American Refugee Center's Roberto Lovato stated, "in the militarized laboratory where George Bush is inventing his new urban order."[61]

When the violence ended, Mayor Bradley appointed former CIA and FBI director William Webster to lead yet another commission on civil unrest. Although this commission acknowledged increased levels of poverty, demographic changes, and tense relations between residents and the police, the bulk of the investigation focused on the LAPD's lack of preparation, poor intelligence gathering prior to the verdict, and inability to control the unrest. It avoided an in-depth investigation of community grievances or police brutality. Finding new ways to mobilize overwhelming police power and new tactics for "rapid containment" took precedence over identifying the roots of the rebellion in police-community conflict.[62]

The failure of the criminal justice system to treat African Americans or Latinos/as fairly had come home to roost. At community meetings, commissioners stressed their desire to hear opinions about "the LAPD's response to the civil unrest, what worked and what didn't work, and how the LAPD should prepare for the future to respond to any future emergencies that might come up." Residents responded by reciting a long history of racist law enforcement practices and criminal justice policies that were at the root of the violence. "Our policemen have been trained from infancy to see people of color as people who are substandard, less than equal," one testified. As another resident commented, "I see police and they're like strangers in a foreign land. You know, you drive through—they can drive through south central and it's like, you know—but all they know is they're going in there to deter crime. That's fine, but you got to know—there's a community in there also. It's not Vietnam. It's not just a war going on."[63]

After 160 days of investigation, neighborhood meetings, and interviews with police officers, the commission released its report, *The City in Crisis*, on October 21, 1992. The report revealed the utter lack of preparation by the city and the police for the King verdict and the failure of the LAPD leadership to respond to the warnings of division officials and officers of the growing tension between the police and residents. A failure in political leadership was also cited as a fundamental problem. In fact, Bradley and Gates had barely spoken to one another for nearly thirteen months. The report contributed to the framing of the rebellion as acts carried out by "criminals" and thugs" by emphasizing the impact of rising drug and gang activity. Yet the report did not interrogate the impact of the aggressive and punitive policies of the LAPD's war on drugs and gangs. The war on drugs had not only failed to stem the flow of drugs to American cities but, as one observer wrote, "helped ignite the recent riots."[64]

The Webster Report, *The City in Crisis*, provided the opportunity to produce a new approach to the city's problems. In its recommendations, the Webster Commission reemphasized calls for community-oriented policing and a shift in the LAPD's orientation from crime fighting to prevention and problem solving through community control of the police. Instead of interrogating the systemic practices of policing and criminal justice in the city that led to criminalization, containment, and incarceration, *The City in Crisis* focused on the ways law enforcement could control future disorder and civil unrest.[65]

The narrow scope led to criticism from activists from the LCSC and the Coalition against Police Abuse. They issued their own reports and recommendations, such as the LCSC's *Reconstructing Los Angeles from the Bottom Up*, that assailed the LAPD's practices as racist. A more systemic investigation of policing practices, activists argued, would require rethinking the reliance on the police power to solve problems rooted in social and economic crises and implementation of community control of the police. As activists pointed out, the singular focus of the Webster Commission on better preparing the police to handle unrest opened the door to new avenues of police power, which led to greater police integration into the social life of residents of color.[66]

Integrating the Police into Social-Welfare Institutions

Bradley recognized that poverty, unemployment, and economic inequality fueled the unrest. Yet instead of promoting public investment and funding jobs programs as LCSC activists suggested, Bradley sought to empower the private sector to rebuild Los Angeles. Bradley organized not a government agency but a nonprofit corporation called Rebuild L.A., which would facilitate private investment and development. Led by Peter Ueberroth—who had organized the 1984 Olympics—Rebuild L.A. intended to attract investment to the "neglected areas" of the city, but ultimately delivered very little. Promises of corporations willing to build new stores and reinvest in South Central quickly faded. Vons opened a supermarket in 1994 which closed a mere six years later.[67]

Meanwhile, city and police officials vied for federal grants linking social spending with law enforcement measures to rebuild Los Angeles. President George H. W. Bush responded by fast-tracking funds from a national crime prevention program called Operation Weed and Seed.[68] Weed and Seed first provided funding for law enforcement to "weed" out criminals through community-based policing, then "seeded" the target area with social service funding to prevent future crime.[69] "The philosophy that underlies the program," Attorney General William Barr admitted, "is that social programs must be closely coordinated and integrated with law enforcement efforts."[70] Out of $19 million in federal Weed and Seed funds for Los Angeles, according to Bradley aide Wendy Greuel, $1 million would go toward law enforcement programs, and the other $18 million would be used for education, job training, housing and urban development, and health and human services. Of the funds directed toward law enforcement, city officials claimed they would not be used for "aggressive law enforcement tactics" but for community-based policing.[71] Weed and Seed revealed how liberal law and order empowered police discretion to sort the criminals from the law-abiding residents by integrating the police into service-providing institutions.

Officials targeted areas within South Central and Pico-Union for Weed and Seed funding. Although many residents welcomed efforts at community policing, they feared that the Weed portion of the program would undermine efforts to achieve greater police accountability and community control by funneling more resources to the police under the direction of the Department of Justice. Residents and activists wanted to address problems of crime and violence but not at the expense of continued police abuse, repression, and discrimination. "No one in these communities is denying that widescale crime exists, or that the LAPD has not been helpful in policing them," City Councilman Mark Ridley-Thomas suggested. "But that does not wipe away sentiments of unfair and abusive treatment by the LAPD."[72]

The image produced by the term "Weed" to characterize their neighborhoods and youth who were often targets of law enforcement proved especially frustrating to residents and activists. After a series of hearings with residents and LCSC activists, for example, Ridley-Thomas and Councilwoman Rita Walters submitted a motion asking for the rejection of the program because the "Weed portion of this program has been imposed on communities of color with the purpose of incarceration and not rehabilitation. The people of South Central and Pico Union are not 'weeds' to be pulled out of their communities and put into jail."[73] Representatives of community organizations echoed the warning by arguing that treating social and economic problems as an issue of crime control contributed to violent conflict. "Coding serious urban social problems as crime issues serves to perpetuate alienation, hopelessness and police abuse in the inner city," the executive director of the Southern Christian Leadership Conference explained. "These are the very conditions that generated the rebellion in the first place."[74]

LCSC activists led the opposition to Weed and Seed. They saw the program as a means of using community-based policing to criminalize black and Latino/a youth and not a substantive solution to inner-city problems or police reform.[75] It reflected the smoke-and-mirrors operation of community-based policing that promised a lot but delivered very little in the way of empowering residents to make decisions. "The way the Weed & Seed Proposal was developed is indicative of how community and community-based policing is viewed," the LCSC explained. "LAPD's orientation is to develop the program without community participation, assign the community a role, then get [the] community to sign off on [a] program under the guise of Community-Based Policing."[76] Coming within the context of a militarized war on drugs, LCSC activists were wary of federal law enforcement programs that integrated criminal justice, social services, and enterprise zones. Operation Weed and Seed, the LCSC summarized, "imposes a federal police presence in inner city." Social service programs, they argued, would be placed under the authority of the Department of Justice, the FBI, and the INS, which was "a move towards the imposition of a police state on the public life of low-income, communities of color."[77] By linking social-service programs to law enforcement, Weed and Seed was a "'warfare' approach to urban problems."[78]

The struggle over Weed and Seed produced a compromise between community organizations, city officials, and the police department. Chief of Police Williams and council members Mike Hernandez and Mark Ridley-Thomas agreed to seek community input to "determine how best to use the federal funds to implement community-based policing programs." The Department of Justice also agreed to change the name of the Los Angeles portion of the federal Weed and Seed program to "Community Projects for Restoration." Further compromise allowed the social-service component to move forward while requiring the law enforcement section to include community input and approval. Officials hoped that the new name would reflect an emphasis on community building and cooperation rather than on policing.[79]

Although unsuccessful at stopping Weed and Seed funds, the work of activists from the LCSC highlighted the concern that social problems should not be treated as crime problems and that an authentic commitment to community control of the police, civilian oversight, and a renewed progressive approach to poverty would be necessary. "The system has no intention of dealing with poverty and racism but it *will* hire a few more cops," the LCSC's Eric Mann observed. "The crime is real *now*, a policeman can answer my phone call *now*, and any new war on poverty is pie in the sky." But hiring a handful of new officers did little to ensure the city could address the need for public safety for the entire city. Despite a proposal from the LCSC to reconstruct Los Angeles from the bottom up, most funding went to public safety to support strategies of arrest and incarceration. This commitment to incapacitation meant that as the California prison population grew to over 135,000 prisoners in 1995, 40 percent came from Los Angeles County.[80] Weed and Seed ultimately enhanced police power by integrating the police into service-providing institutions.

The More Things Change, the More They Stay the Same

Although the changes brought about in response to the King beating and the 1992 rebellion represented victories for reformers, the LAPD maintained its autonomy and resisted fundamental changes. The unwillingness, and inability, of department commanders to crack down on problem officers or to rein in a gunslinger style of policing aimed at winning the battle for the streets continued to characterize the department's approach. Bradley's announcement that he would not run for a sixth term in 1993 set the city up for one of its most important mayoral elections in two decades. Conservative Richard Riorden, whose campaign slogan was "Tough enough to turn Los Angeles around," triumphed over the progressive, pro–police reform city councilman Michael Woo in 1993, stalling the reform effort. Woo attempted to maintain Bradley's multiracial coalition, but his broad support in immigrant neighborhoods did not translate to votes. Despite broad support for Charter Amendment F just a year earlier, most residents rejected the blatant racism of the

LAPD but not the need for more police, enabling Riorden to capitalize on white fears of rising crime and violence. Chief Williams's hopes for community policing faced immediate resistance from Riorden. As the economy emerged from a recession and budgets recovered, Riorden made good on campaign promises of expanding the police force, which grew to 9,192 active-duty officers by 2000, and supporting tough-on-crime measures. During Riorden's two terms, the Christopher Commission recommendations were not high priorities.[81]

When Willie Williams was appointed the first African American chief of the LAPD, he told residents, "You should expect change today; you should expect change tomorrow. . . . But change unfortunately comes very slow."[82] Critical observers continued to be skeptical. "As far as Los Angeles' business and political elites are concerned, police reform is now finished business," Mike Davis observed. "Focusing on the 'managerial crisis' in Parker Center (the police headquarters), the commissioners have substituted a superficial administrative overhaul, symbolized by the appointment of Williams, for substantive institutional change."[83]

Williams was an outsider from the start. He did little to win over sergeants and patrol officers, nor did he address their questions and concerns about the direction of the department. In his second-year review, the Board of Police Commissioners opened the door to criticism. "Consistently," the commission wrote, "you seem to lack focus and discernible purpose in managing the Department. It is often unclear throughout the ranks exactly who is in charge and who is making decisions affecting the operations and direction of the LAPD. Often, you seem unable to move the Department, to have your decisions understood and followed in a timely matter, if at all." Appointing a chief from outside the department had done little to alter or influence the insular culture of career officers.[84]

Progress on Christopher Commission reforms remained halting. Williams was successful in implementing elements of community policing and voters agreed in 1995 to create a new Office of Inspector General to review IAD findings on behalf of the police commission. Katherine Mader, the first inspector general, however, quickly criticized Williams's lack of leadership in disciplining officers and the limited effort to fundamentally reshape the culture of the department. "The department has not undergone reform to the extent that was possible or required," the special counsel to the Police Commission reported in 1996. "We have seen no evidence of a meaningful, institutionalized effort by the Department to do work history reviews for officers generating an unusually high number of uses of force or force-related complaints." Problem officers continued to plague the department, and Williams had not sent a strong signal to supervisors that they would be held account-able for actions of subordinates.[85]

Opposition from rank-and-file officers and a lack of progress on reforms ultimately proved Williams's undoing. A series of personal scandals involving comped rooms at Las Vegas casinos added fuel to the fire, and on March 10, 1997, the Police Commission refused to reappoint Williams for a second term. His successor, Bernard Parks, was a career LAPD officer who began as a traffic officer, rose to the rank of commander by 1980, and was second-in-command of the department under Williams. As chief, Parks vehemently opposed external control of the department. While supported by the African American community—he would be elected to the city council representing the predominantly African American District 8 in 2003—Parks disregarded recommendations from the Police Commission for a new disciplinary policy, instituting his own guidelines. Parks sent a message that his department would not be controlled by the Police Commission, nor by the inspector general established on the Christopher Commission's recommendation. Parks worked to limit the ability of the inspector general to initiate investigations, and eventually forced inspector general Mader, to resign, which left the LAPD to once again police itself.[86]

The 1992 uprising was a referendum on the coalition of lawmakers and law enforcement officials' nearly thirty-year-long faith in police power and an expanded criminal justice system to protect the city's law-abiding residents from the harmful ones. But an empowered LAPD had operated less to protect and to serve all residents than as a police force bent on holding up the city's hierarchical racial order. The rebellion was an explicit rejection of repressive police power and administrative reforms that failed to control police abuse. For participants, the explosion of anger and discontent was the logical outcome of three decades of policies privileging get-tough policing at the expense of addressing unequal social and economic conditions. In contrast to the views of local and national political officials and law enforcement agents, the rebellion was not an apolitical expression of criminality or evidence of failed social welfare programs. Rather, it exposed how the reliance on punitive policies criminalized the poor, resulted in hostility between the police and residents of color, and fueled mass incarceration.

In the rebellion's aftermath, however, the use of the police to manage unequal socioeconomic conditions and enforce a hierarchical racial order remained a cornerstone of city and federal policy. Reforms such as Weed and Seed and community-based policing may have been well intentioned, but they appeared more focused on changing the image of the police as equitable enforcers of the law than on transforming the actions or attitudes of officers on the streets. The police continued to operate with impunity, especially in neighborhoods of color. By responding to fear of crime and urban uprisings with calls for more efficient policing, Bradley and city officials had created a program of police reform that enabled aggressive enforcement of the law. Charter Amendment F represented a significant change in the city's political structure, but neither charter reform nor the removal of Gates led to greater accountability. Politicians still relied on law enforcement to address social problems, and the structure of the department and its position within city politics enabled it to resist changes aimed at reducing its authority.

The 1992 uprising had presented a moment of possibility for alternative visions of the city's future. Residents and activists proposed solutions based on achieving justice through community control of the police and nonpunitive approaches to addressing urban social problems and inequality. These movements built on and extended the anti–police brutality organizing of 1970s and 1980s. Activists continued to challenge the politics of law and order and get-tough solutions to urban problems in the wake of the rebellion. Even if they were unsuccessful in altering city or law enforcement policy, they continued to engage the struggle to move urban policy away from a punitive, get-tough framework. Nevertheless, the intensified, military-style policing continued to define Los Angeles as a carceral city.

Epilogue

The Rampart Way: A Gang Truce,
Gangster Cops, and a Consent Decree

The police were the front-line agents in a battle for the streets, key to build-ing the carceral state during the final decades of the twentieth century. Spurred by a crisis of legitimacy created by the 1965 Watts uprising and the challenge of activists, a broad coalition of local authorities—liberal and conservative—advocated get-tough policies, enshrining the police as enforcers of order and unleashing their discretionary authority over communities of color. In the process, they integrated the police into other areas of governance. Faced with rising immigration, a drug crisis, and gang violence in the 1980s, local author-ities responded to each challenge by shoring up the state's capacity to protect the "harmless" law-abiding residents from "harmful" violent ones. The police and punitive crime control policy became the solution to demographic change, social discontent, and economic inequality alike, with devastating consequences for African American, Latino/a, and immigrant communities.[1]

In the decades after Watts, local authorities invested in the police power and the capacity of the police to monitor, supervise, and eliminate potential threats to the social order. People of color bore the brunt of this reliance on the police, and, as a result, experienced virtual exclusion from full social membership as citizens. Police surveillance, harassment, arrest, and incar-ceration structured their daily lives and the very meaning of citizenship, race, and identity. Policing served as an index of inequality in postwar Los Angeles and urban America more broadly.[2]

Residents and activists resisted, challenging police authority and demand-ing an end to state-sanctioned violence, criminalization, and incarceration. The LAPD's repressive policing fueled the disillusionment and discontent that culminated in the 1992 Los Angeles rebellion and exposed the depart-ment's enforcement of racial hierarchy through order-maintenance policing.

Although the changes ushered in after 1992 represented a significant victory for reformers, LAPD authorities did not give up their hard-won discretionary authority easily. Through the 1990s, the police department continued to operate with impunity in neighborhoods of color and claimed the need to keep potentially harmful groups, especially African American and Latino/a gangs, under discretionary supervision. In the process, LAPD leadership both enabled and reinforced a systemic culture within the department characterized by a lack of accountability, warrior policing, and racism.[3] As the police continued to be tasked with maintaining the boundary between "civilization and chaos," the lack of restraint produced another legitimacy crisis for the police that brought the department to its knees.

———

A month prior to the King verdict, Los Angeles's two prominent street gangs, the Crips and the Bloods, formed a truce. Modeled after the 1949 cease-fire between Israel and Egypt, the aim of the truce was to reduce killings and help create jobs. The change came because gang members "woke up and realized what we were doing to ourselves and our families," in the words of former gang member Charles Rachal. Attempting to set aside grievances, they hoped to redirect energy toward positive community change. "We are putting the war on hold to see if we can make this work," participants explained. "This means instead of killing each other we are going to defend each other and defend our communities." For a brief time, the truce held, greatly reducing gang-related violence in South Central neighborhoods. Compared with 1991, gang-related homicides declined by 88 percent, attempted murders dropped by 45 percent, and robberies declined by 13.2 percent. "As far as I know," said LAPD lieutenant John Dinkin a year after the truce in August 1992, "there have been no drive-by shootings between gangs in south and central Los Angeles since the riots."[4]

Gang members endeavored to rebuild Los Angeles after the rebellion. They understood the unrest as an expression of discontent with unemployment, racism, and criminalization. "The riot has been our voice," one truce member explained in a statement reminiscent of those made after Watts, "the only voice that you will listen to."[5] Mobilizing around claims for social justice, gang members offered a political analysis of unemployment, the drug trade, and the role of the police.[6] They proposed a program for Los Angeles's "Face Lift" that included $2 billion for education, community-based law enforcement, public beautification, economic development, and welfare and health programs. In return, the proposal stated, the Bloods and Crips would push drug traffickers out of the community, promote the use of drug profits for rebuilding the community, and work to attract private investment and development. "Give us the hammer and the nails," they stated memorably, and "we will rebuild this city."[7] Although the proposal incorporated dominant elements of free-market ideology, it sought to pair it with community control of the police and nonpunitive solutions to urban inequality.

Yet for the millions of dollars fueling the city's carceral state–building, none of the money was redirected in support of the truce or of efforts to rebuild the city on an equitable basis. Law enforcement officials responded skeptically, claiming the truce "was an excuse for young gang members to unify against the police." As Mike Davis observed, "The ecumenical movement of the Crips and Bloods is their worst imagining: gang violence no longer random but politicized into a black *intifada*."[8] Officers openly harassed truce leaders. Rampart Division Community Resources against Street Hoodlums (CRASH) officers even arrested one prominent truce leader, Alex Sanchez, handing him over to the Immigration and Naturalization Service on immigration charges in violation of Special Order 40.[9] As the truce tenuously held on, evidence of a different type of gang—one centered on police corruption and abuse—rocked the city.[10]

It was no coincidence that Rampart CRASH officers arrested Sanchez and harassed other truce leaders. Rampart CRASH officers openly flaunted attempts to limit officer discretion, taking full advantage of the department's lack of accountability. In 1994, Rafael Pérez had joined Rampart CRASH, referred to by other officers as "Rampage Division." There, he enjoyed wide latitude to wage war on the area's thirty to sixty local gangs. As Pérez would later describe to investigators, Rampart CRASH officers acted as if they were above the law and played by their own rules. Planting evidence, such as guns and drugs, was a common practice to ensure sentencing enhancements from a misdemeanor to a felony. Abuse of suspects and arrestees went uninvestigated and unpunished. Anyone could be arrested for any reason. Rampart CRASH was an unaccountable force following its own rules—what its members called "the Rampart Way."[11]

In 1998 evidence of corruption by Pérez and other Rampart CRASH officers surfaced when agents found that six pounds of cocaine, evidence from drug raids, was missing from the LAPD property room. Pérez and his partner had stolen the seized cocaine from police evidence, engaged in drug sales, and engineered cover-ups of dirty shootings. Along the way, they routinely beat suspects and arrestees, intimidating witnesses into testifying against individuals who were not involved in crimes or acts of violence. Most galling, Pérez had shot an unarmed man, covered it up, and framed him, sending him to prison for a crime he didn't commit.[12]

Chief Parks immediately suspended twelve officers and dismantled all the department's CRASH units. Yet these revelations threatened to undermine the city's criminal justice system. In nearly 4,000 pages of testimony, Pérez implicated approximately seventy officers who had also engaged in illegal conduct. Five were fired, and eight others resigned. Multiple investigations overturned nearly one hundred convictions for false arrest or imprisonment. Victims of police misconduct filed suit, winning over $75 million in damages. Daily coverage by the *Los Angeles Times* pushed Parks to initiate a Board of

Inquiry review and external investigations by the FBI and the U.S. attorney. It was called "the worst scandal in the history of Los Angeles," and "one of the worst police scandals in American history."[13]

The Rampart scandal produced a new impetus for fundamental reform and oversight. Parks had initially attempted to bottle up the corruption within a single division, sidestepping evidence that it might reflect systemic problems within the department. The LAPD's Board of Inquiry released a 362-page report with 108 recommended reforms, likewise denying systemic corruption. Once again, the problem was one of "bad apples" in the middle and lower ranks.[14]

Constitutional scholar Erwin Chemerinsky, who had been asked by the Police Protective League to analyze the report, argued that the Board of Inquiry recommendations would do nothing to address systemic problems in the department's management, culture of control, or adherence to a code of silence. Downplaying the scope of the problems within the department had become a routine response to abuse, shootings, and corruption. "The Board of Inquiry report," Chemerinsky wrote, "fails to convey the unconscionability of what occurred."[15]

A similar sentiment arose from the Board of Police Commissioners' Rampart Independent Review Panel. The panel found that the Rampart misconduct grew into a scandal because of a "systematic failure of supervision." As one officer who was later convicted and fired told interviewers, "If I'd known that a 'by the book' sergeant could have turned up on my street action at any given time, I wouldn't have tried to get away with a third of what I did." A culture of warrior policing and defending the department's image at all costs had been drilled into officers. Department leadership had also failed to learn from past crises, which undermined the faith of residents in the department's ability to operate fairly and equitably.[16]

The LAPD's attempts to head off criticism did not quiet the department's critics, which included veterans of anti–police abuse movements dating back to the 1970s such as the Coalition against Police Abuse and the American Civil Liberties Union. More than forty organizations joined to form the Coalition for Police Accountability, demanding civilian control of the department and federal oversight. Independent reviews by the Police Commission and the Los Angeles Bar Association further exposed a cowboy-gunslinger mentality predisposed to the use of force and lacking discipline and accountability. Policies of containment and suppression had produced a department-wide culture that viewed residents as the enemy rather than participants in a problem-solving approach to policing. This was particularly the case in neighborhoods of color. "They really don't want to know everything that occurs down here," one Southeast gang officer remarked. "And they don't put us in a position to win. We're not here to win anything. We're here to maintain control between civilization and utter chaos." A group initiated by Parks's replacement, Chief William Bratton, summed it up: "In short, the CRASH crisis did not happen because a few LAPD rogues stole drugs. It happened because the Los Angeles criminal justice system's anemic checks on police abuse and LAPD's feeble constraints on its 'warrior policing' failed across the board."[17]

Coming on the heels of the King beating and the 1992 rebellion, the LAPD could no longer escape the movement for external oversight and regulation that activists had been building for so many years. The Department of Justice, using legislation passed in the wake of the King beating which permitted the Civil Rights Division to sue cities with a history of discriminatory policing, initiated an inquiry into the department in 1996 in response to continued complaints of the excessive use of force. The investigation led the Department of Justice to file a civil rights suit against Los Angeles and the LAPD. The press release announcing the suit implicated the department in a wide range of unconstitutional practices, including excessive use of force, improper search and seizures, and making arrests without probable cause. The LAPD could either go to trial, risking further exposure of the department's corruption, insularity, and unaccountability, or agree to a consent decree with the Department of Justice.[18]

The city council overwhelmingly voted to accept a consent decree requiring federal oversight and departmental compliance with strict regulations on operations on September 19, 2000. Riorden and Parks initially opposed the consent decree, but they had little choice other than to accept it due to support in the city council. The consent decree gave the federal district court jurisdiction to monitor the department's progress in implementing reforms. The agreement required annual Integrity Audits of the department to ensure compliance. It was, as some experts believed, "one of the most ambitious experiments in police reform ever attempted in an American city."[19]

Though flawed, the consent decree led to changes and oversight of a department that had systematically opposed any semblance of external control or regulation since the end of World War II. The Department of Justice started the long process of reining in the LAPD. Yet it required a change in leadership willing to accept the conditions of the consent decree to ensure full compliance. When James K. Hahn was elected mayor in 2001, he worked to remove Chief Parks from office and to bring in William Bratton from New York City as the new chief. Bratton, a pioneer of computer statistics (CompStat) policing and a devotee of the broken windows philosophy, worked to implement the reforms required by the consent decree. To gauge the scope of change required, he initiated a Rampart after-action report headed by civil rights lawyer and anti–police abuse activist Connie Rice. In a departure from his predecessors, Bratton seemed willing to accept external scrutiny and to work with groups traditionally at odds with the police.[20]

Bratton hoped to reestablish trust between the LAPD and the community through what he called "public trust policing." He worked not only to repair the relationship between the department and the city's elected officials but also to transform how officers viewed their job. Instead of racking up arrests, Bratton's public trust policing promoted community engagement and service, a model of policing that challenged the LAPD's ingrained "us versus them" culture. Within Rampart, this job fell to career officer and assistant chief Charlie Beck, who had been "as hard-charging a CRASH officer as you could have found" during the 1980s. But he realized "search and destroy wasn't working," and began the long process of rooting out the Rampart Division's gunslinger mentality and "us versus them" attitude. Beck pioneered a new style of policing aimed at reducing crime with the support of the community, and transforming how officers thought about and performed their jobs. As the Rampart Review Committee found and noted in its after-action report in 2006, "it resulted in a turnaround of the division, the transformation of a local park and a 180-degree difference in officer mindset."[21]

By other measures, the department had not lived up to the consent decree's requirements. Significant questions remained as to whether the changes produced in Rampart Division under Beck, especially the transformation in outlook and mentality of officers to see the community as a resource rather than an opponent, could be replicated throughout the department. Supervision and accountability problems continued to plague other divisions, and the "thin blue line" model of policing had long staying power. And it revealed the interest of the police and city power structure to maintain a social order based on inequality. "We have only enough police officers here to make certain that the wealthier neighborhoods stay safe," one expert admitted. "The question . . . Los Angeles has to confront is . . . do we want to make the whole city safe?" The lack of police service in neighborhoods of color had not only led to disillusionment with the police but also meant the only view of the police that residents had was of aggressive, proactive crime control.[22]

Even as Bratton attempted to make the department more responsive to residents' needs, his policies produced a new type of techno-police based on computer algorithms and quality of life arrests that reconstituted racially targeted police power. Calls for public trust and positive impact policing were undermined by the continued emphasis on the use of CompStat by-the-numbers policing as the measure of productivity and promotion potential. Focusing on statistics created incentives for officers to either fabricate or make illegitimate arrests to meet their goals. What some observers viewed as a positive trend—increased traffic stops and arrests—created new avenues of police power. Increased efficiency and accountability, in other words, came with a vast expansion of the use of gang injunctions and stop-and-frisk policing.[23]

Expansion of police authority under the framework of community- and broken windows policing reinforced racially targeted police practices. A study conducted for the American Civil Liberties Union found evidence that "African Americans and Hispanics are over-stopped, over-frisked, over-searched, and over-arrested." Blacks were 127 percent more likely and Latinos/as 43 percent more likely to be frisked than whites. In contrast to claims of high levels of black or Latino/a crime, frisked African Americans were 42.3 percent and Latinos/as 31.8 percent less likely to be found with a weapon than frisked whites. Searches of blacks and Latinos/as were also less likely to uncover drugs than searches of whites. Although Bratton and the president of the Police Protective League disputed charges of discrimination and unwarranted stop-and-frisks, not one of the 320 profiling complaints filed in 2007 was sustained. Neither were any of the profiling-based complaints filed in the previous five years.[24] In focusing on the failure of the study to decipher an officer's intent in making a stop, the department's defenders ignored the structural and institutional practices of the LAPD that had long criminalized the city's black and Latino/a residents. The approach to public safety in the city's communities of color had not fundamentally changed, as it continued to rest on police power and the criminal justice system.

Federal oversight eventually led to nominal compliance. By the end of the decade, there was a growing consensus among observers and law enforcement officials that the department had improved policing in the city and fulfilled the requirements of the consent decree. One 2009 study found that civilian satisfaction with the department was up by 83 percent, crime was down, the frequency of the use of excessive force had declined every year since 2004, and the management and governance of the department had improved. Yet, the number of arrests, most notably for drug crimes and public order charges, increased under the consent decree. Police killings also reached a high of thirty in 2011 for the period between 2000 and 2017.[25] Gary Feess, the district court judge overseeing the LAPD's compliance, removed the consent decree in 2009 with a transition period requiring routine check-ins with the Board of Police Commissioners and federal judges. In 2013, Feess released the LAPD from monitoring under the transition agreement, stating, "The LAPD has fully complied with the requirements and has institutionalized constitutional and community policing."[26] But the LAPD continued to use order maintenance and CompStat policing alongside new methods of big data policing to maneuver within the constraints of the consent decree to relegitimize its authority and power on the streets.[27]

––––––––

Over more than thirty years, the LAPD worked to create, exploit, or otherwise leverage urban crises in ways that bolstered its own authority. The result was an intensified police power that was most evident in the lives and deaths of the city's black and Latino/a communities. But the lasting result of this history has been the almost impenetrable dominance of policing in American society. Police power not only survived the late-1960s crisis of legitimacy but expanded through the rest of the century. Although liberals, such as Bradley, advocated reform, their solutions often focused on administrative changes meant to enhance procedural fairness and government oversight of the police but did not question the fundamental role or power of the police. Policing, as a result, did not narrow its focus but instead intensified between the 1960s and 1990s. In the process of reclaiming their legitimacy and expanding their reach after the 1960s, urban police used the very standards of liberal reform—police professionalization, procedural fairness, and the "harm" principle—to transform themselves into frontline agents in the production of a social order rooted in a system of racist mass incarceration.

Police violence has once again sparked rebellions and anti–police abuse movements across the country. The story of policing and politics in Los Angeles, bookended by two major urban uprisings, suggests that relying on the police power and punitive crime policies exacerbates the very problems they are intended to solve. Despite attention to the militarization of the police in the wake of Ferguson and Baltimore, the story is not a particularly new one. But the story told in this book reveals that the militarization of the police is only one facet of the much deeper, insidious, and all-encompassing police power in American cities and society.[28]

In a moment when federal officials have escalated rhetoric and support for the police, there are important lessons to be learned about the threat of an expansive police power to democratic citizenship and social justice.[29] The police themselves played a crucial role in expanding their own authority, constructing a get-tough political coalition, and instantiating themselves as a virtually unassailable political and military institution in Los Angeles and cities across the country. Police officers were not simply pawns of government officials, federal law enforcement grant funders, or business elites. Rather, the police opportunistically involved themselves in the functions of other government agencies, and department officials were active in public debates and electoral politics. As a result, this book offers a cautionary note to anyone who thinks that more racially inclusive and politically progressive city governments will naturally produce more just law enforcement.

Police reform has been at the center of public debate with the rise of #BlackLivesMatter, antipolice uprisings, and President Obama's Task Force on Twenty-First Century Policing. The story of policing, antipolice movements, and politics in Los Angeles demonstrates the problems associated with reforms aimed at attempting to bring the police under the rule of law. The persistence of illiberal police violence reveals the limitations of liberal approaches to law and order and police reform. In particular, it demonstrates that liberal beliefs in narrowing the discretion of officers and bringing the police under the rule of law will not solve the underlying problems of harassment, abuse, and violence related to an expansive police power.[30]

Such is the case in Los Angeles, where the Board of Police Commissioners implemented new regulations on the LAPD's use-of-force policy to emphasize de-escalation in 2016. But the police killed sixteen people in 2017, down from eighteen the year before. Given the history of underreporting of officer-involved shootings, however, such changes may not represent significant progress. For all the attention to the LAPD's recognition of its racist history and continued problems of distrust in communities of color, the suggested solutions continue the long line of reasoning surrounding liberal reform.[31] Yet, police power is not merely one focused on the enforcement of law, but is a central part of the state's broader power to regulate and preserve order backed by a monopoly on the use of violence. As such, discretion is an administrative power of the state given to the police, which leaves the police significant latitude to enforce order even when brought under the rule of law. Within this context, reforms based on narrowing discretion, enhancing accountability, and increasing government oversight of the police did not and will not result in far-reaching change.[32]

Given the history presented in this book, it should come as no surprise that a quarter century after the 1992 rebellion, relations between the LAPD and communities of color remain tense.[33] This historical study forces a reconsideration of the role of community activists in police reform. Most late-twentieth-century histories of urban law enforcement have portrayed community protest movements against police abuse as largely ineffectual. More recently, there has been pressure for the use of federally directed consent decrees as the most effective approach to police reform. Consent decrees, unlike earlier piecemeal efforts, understood police abuse as a structural problem. Yet, the experience with consent decrees has shown that progress is often costly and slow; departments' resist the Department of Justice as a meddlesome outsider; and making the reforms last, especially ending racial profiling, has been a challenge.[34]

Anti–police abuse activists have been essential in creating the political conditions and possibility for Los Angeles's own 2001 federal consent decree.

The decree sprang from decades of antipolice community activism. For over thirty years, Los Angeles community activists had been challenging the liberal assumption that police abuse was a problem of individual "bad apple" officers or the need to bring the police even more fully under the rule of law. Instead, local activists repeatedly drew attention to the ways in which police abuse sprang from structural arrangements inherent to the police power itself. And they proposed alternatives ranging from community control to the abolition of the police. Community activists were behind the lawsuit leading to Los Angeles's consent decree, and their arguments ultimately influenced the terms of that decree. They were responsible for the federal recognition that police abuse was a structural issue. The current anti–police abuse movement's structural perspective is built on decades of rigorous community analysis, messaging, and protest in the streets.

If not for the tireless struggle of anti–police abuse activists, the LAPD would likely have continued on its trajectory—an unaccountable force committed to suppression and containment with impunity. For decades, the LAPD had navigated challenges to its authority from activists and lawmakers, becoming a powerful partisan entity with a broad reach. Its punitive state-building project was not easily unwound. Federal oversight would finally yield some systemic reforms to the department's insularity and "us versus them" style. But for all its progress, the new era of community-based and order-maintenance policing once again expanded police discretionary authority in innovative ways. Although crime rates declined, stop-and-frisk and quality of life policing strategies persisted, and beliefs about African American, Latino/a, and immigrant criminality continued to drive up the number of arrests and reliance on incarceration. Through the first decades of the twenty-first century, the police have continued to be the primary contact between people of color and the state, fueling distrust with law enforcement as well as movements resisting state violence and demanding justice.[35]

Rather than relying on the police as the solution to urban problems and thereby expanding the ability to track, arrest, criminalize, and, ultimately, discipline residents of color, activists routinely called for alternative strategies to solve problems rooted in structural social and economic inequality. Much of this work has already begun, and it is necessary to achieve a more just, equal, and antiracist vision of citizenship and inclusive social membership in American society.[36] As long as the police power is viewed narrowly around a role of preventing crime and harm rather than as a powerful independent entity in urban politics and a productive force in the maintenance of a racially unjust social order, the police will continue to receive the legitimacy to wage and win the battle for the streets.

Acknowledgments

As with any work of scholarship, there are far too many people to thank for their support, comments, and critiques. Robin D. G. Kelley has been a source of advice and guidance throughout the process of researching and writing this book. He pushed me to think more deeply, ask harder questions, and recognize the significance of my scholarship. His feedback and encouragement always left me more energized to take on the long process of completing this book. At the University of Southern California, a number of scholars provided critical readings and insight. I thank Bill Deverell, Phil Ethington, and George Sanchez. At the University of Oregon, I thank Laura Pulido.

While finishing the writing of this book, I had the fortune to teach at Marian University and DePauw University. Both institutions provided supportive environments for teaching and research. My colleagues at Marian made for an energetic teaching environment. DePauw University has provided the time necessary to complete the project and crucial financial support. My colleagues at DePauw, including Ayden Adler, Ryan Bean, Julia Bruggemann, Yung-Chen Chiang, Theresa Dazey, Bob Dewey, Mac Dixon-Fyle, Nayhan Fancy, David Gellman, and Sarah Rowley created a welcoming and supportive place to teach and write. The DePauw Wednesday Writing group, organized by Salil Benegal and Nicole Lobdell, offered important space to focus on writing in the midst of a teaching-heavy semester.

This book could not have been possible without the help of numerous archivists and librarians. Raquel Chavez, Yusef Omowale, and Michele Welsing at the Southern California Library deserve enormous thanks. Michele offered invaluable aid and guidance into some of the key collections that served as the foundation for the entire project. The archivists and staff at UCLA Special Collections, including Susan Anderson, Kelly Besser, Megan Fraser, Robert Montoya, and Cesar Reyes, offered key insight into large and unprocessed collections. Michael Stone at the Chicano Studies Research Center helped me access partially unprocessed collections. Dace Taube at USC Special Collections helped me navigate collections and provided access to important material from the 1992 Los Angeles rebellion. Todd Gaydowski and Michael Holland at the Los Angeles City Records and Archives provided insight into the nature of city records that was invaluable. I also thank Renee James at Cal State Los Angeles Special Collections, David Sigler at the Urban Archives Center at Cal State Northridge, Polly Armstrong at Stanford's Green Library Special Collections, and the staff and reading room supervisors at the Huntington Library.

Sections of this book have been previously published in scholarly journals and benefited from editorial and reader comments. Michael Ezra at the *Journal of Civil and Human Rights* provided important feedback and editorial advice for a piece exploring the Coalition against Police Abuse. An article on juvenile justice for the *Journal of Urban History* benefited from reader comments and suggestions. Chris Agee and Themis Chronopolous generously asked me to submit an article for a special section of the *Journal of Urban History* on current scholarship on the history of policing. Finally, my thinking about the legacies of police militarization and its connection to the present benefited from Nicole Hemmer, Katie Brownell, and Brian Rosenwald at Made by History at the *Washington Post*.

This book has benefited from comments provided by colleagues at a number of conferences and workshops. I received important feedback on various parts of the manuscript at annual meetings and conferences including the American Historical Association, American Studies Association, Urban History Association, the Interdisciplinary Conference on Race at Monmouth University, and Social Science History Association. Clay Howard generously invited me to present a chapter at the Ohio State History Workshop, and Xóchitl Bada and Adam Goodman gave me the opportunity to present a chapter alongside Delia Fernández at the Newberry Library Latino Borderlands History Seminar. Both workshops provided crucial space, conversations, and feedback that pushed me to think more deeply and clearly about chapters 6 and 7. The conference on the 1990s at Purdue University organized by Katie Brownell, Lily Geismer, and Niki Hemmer allowed me to think through the 1992 Los Angeles rebellion in new ways.

Much of my thinking about the power of the Los Angeles Police Department and the importance of activists stemmed from my work with the City of Inmates Working Group organized by Kelly Lytle Hernández and Gaye Theresa Johnson in the spring of 2015. Kelly and Gaye graciously invited me to share my ideas and research about the LAPD and anti–police abuse movements and were enthusiastic supporters of the project. Engaging with activists, such as Pete White from LACAN, Kim McGill of the Youth Justice Coalition, and Manuel Criollo of the Labor Community Strategy Center revealed the long legacies of the stories of activism I have attempted to uncover in the previous pages.

The editors of the Justice, Power, and Politics series at UNC Press, Heather Thompson and Rhonda Williams, supported this project from the start. Heather has offered especially important guidance, insight, and enthusiasm throughout the research and writing of this book. My editor, Brandon Proia, has offered indispensable insight, guidance, and editing that made this book possible. It is a far better book because of his involvement. Thanks to Michael Tuber for preparing the index. I would also like to extend a special thank you to Dan Berger and Chris Agee. They have been incredibly generous and engaged with the manuscript in ways that any author would be privileged to receive and offering in-depth, insightful comments that have shaped this book in innumerable ways.

Kelly Lytle Hernández and Donna Murch have been key supporters of this project and provided important guidance and feedback throughout the process. A number of other friends and colleagues have offered comments and support in the writing of this book. At Tufts University, Steve Cohen and Jeanne Penvenne have gone above and beyond in their support over many years. I thank Lauren Acker, Matt Amato, Eric Avila, Andy Baer, Betty Bruther, Jordan Camp, Sarah Coleman, Will Cooley, Michael Durfee, Alex Elkins, Garrett Felber, Anne Gray Fischer, Michael Fortner, Holly Gastineau-Grimes, Lily Geismer, Leah Gordon, Allison Gorsuch, Sarah Haley, Karen Halttunen, Deb Harkness, Hillary Jenks, Annie Johnson, Shannon King, Joanne Klein,

Nora Krinitsky, Christine Lamberson, Marisol LeBrón, Mary Ellen Lennon, Tim Lombardo, Toussaint Losier, Gordon Mantler, Amber Nelson, Becky Nicolaides, Caitlin Parker, Peter Pihos, Keith Pluymers, Dan Royles, Eric Schneider, Stuart Schrader, David Stein, Carl Suddler, Caitlin Verboon, and Pat Wyman. A few people deserve special thanks. Julilly Kohler-Hausmann, Elizabeth Hinton, Melanie Newport, and Alyssa Ribeiro have been key sources of support, enthusiasm, and friendship. They have been especially important sounding boards, and my discussions with them have enriched my scholarship. Adam Goodman offered critical readings and advice on new areas of research, and I appreciate our intellectual camaraderie, engagement, and friendship. My longtime friends and comrades Heather Ashby, Christian Paiz, and Monica Pelayo have offered support, companionship, and humor throughout the research and writing process. I would not have made it this far without them. Ray Haberski has been an important mentor and friend who gave me the time and space to present sections of this book to his American Studies courses. Simon Balto has been a crucial companion and sounding board who made the writing and revision process much more bearable.

Most importantly, my family has been a constant source of support and encouragement. Mostly they have been patient. Without them this book would not have been possible. I cannot express how grateful I am for the love and support of my parents, Janet Felker and Harvey Kantor. They have never ceased in their encouragement and have been models of how to live with compassion and an open mind. My dad has been a model of scholarly rigor, and he has been involved in every aspect of this book. He often acted as an additional reader and provided invaluable feedback on the manuscript that made my writing and arguments stronger, clearer, and more concise. My sister, Erica, has been overwhelmingly supportive and championed my work, especially in the most challenging times. She has been with me through ups and downs and deserves enormous love and thanks. And, of course, Dudley has been a loyal companion throughout the writing process. Finally, I could not have finished this book without the love and support of Mary Appel. She deserves enormous thanks and I love her dearly. She has never ceased in her encouragement during a process that too often became all-encompassing. She has been a voice of reason keeping me grounded, reminded me to take breaks, and made every aspect of life more enjoyable.

Notes

CCF	City Council Files, Los Angeles City Archives, Los Angeles, California
CCM	City Council Minutes, 1850–1978, Los Angeles City Archives, Los Angeles, California
CCR	Commonwealth Club Records, Hoover Institution Archives, Stanford, California
CEC	California Ephemera Collection, University of California, Los Angeles Library Special Collections, Charles E. Young Research Library, UCLA, Los Angeles, California
CEPCCRA	The Church of the Epiphany Chicano Civil Rights Archive 1960–94, UCLA Chicano Studies Research Center, University of California, Los Angeles
CHP	Chester Earl Holifield Papers, University of Southern California, Regional History Collection, Special Collections, Information Services Division, University of Southern California, Los Angeles, California
CRCR	Community Relations Committee Records, California State University, Northridge, Urban Archives Collections, Northridge, California
CSM	*Christian Science Monitor*
DLC	Debbie Louis Collection on Civil Rights, University of California, Los Angeles Library Special Collections, Charles E. Young Research Library, UCLA, Los Angeles, California
EDE	Papers of Edmund D. Edelman, The Huntington Library, San Marino, California
EGP	Ernesto Galarza Papers, Stanford Green Library, Special Collections, Stanford, California
EPP	Elwin H. Powell Papers, State University of New York at Buffalo, University Archives, Buffalo, New York
EQP	Eduardo Quevedo Papers, Stanford Green Library, Special Collections, Stanford, California
ERP	Edward R. Roybal Papers 1919–2003, UCLA Chicano Studies Research Center, University of California, Los Angeles
FDOC	Frank Del Olmo Collection, California State University, Northridge, Urban Archives Collections, Northridge, California
GAP	Glenn M. Anderson Papers, California State University, Dominguez Hills, Special Collections, Carson, California
GCLARM	Governor's Commission on the Los Angeles Riots Records, Microfilm Edition
GCLARR	Governor's Commission on the Los Angeles Riots Records, Bancroft Library, University of California, Berkeley, Berkeley, California
GLP	Gilbert Lindsey Papers, Los Angeles City Archives, Los Angeles, California

GMDP	Grace Montañez Davis Papers, 39, UCLA Chicano Studies Research Center, University of California, Los Angeles
HBC	Herman Baca Collection, MSS 649. http://libraries.ucsd.edu/speccoll/testing/html/mss0649a.html, University of California, San Diego, The Library, San Diego, California
HMP	Hugh R. Manes Papers, University of California, Los Angeles Library Special Collections, Charles E. Young Research Library, UCLA, Los Angeles, California
HRCR	Human Relations Commission Records, Los Angeles City Archives, Los Angeles, California
ICR	Independent Commission on the Los Angeles Police Department Records, University of Southern California, Regional History Collection, Special Collections, Information Services Division, University of Southern California, Los Angeles, California
IFCOR	Interreligious Foundation of Community Organizations Records, Schomburg Center for Research in Black Culture, Special Collections, New York, New York
JABP	John Allen Buggs Papers, 1939–64, Amistad Research Center, Tulane University, New Orleans, Louisiana
JHP	John Holland Papers, California State University, Los Angeles, Special Collections, Los Angeles, California
JNC	Julian Nava Collection, California State University, Northridge, Urban Archives Collections, Northridge, California
JNP	Julian Nava Papers, California State University, Los Angeles, Special Collections, Los Angeles, California
JPR	Johnson Presidential Recordings, Miller Center Presidential Recordings Program, University of Virginia, Charlottesville, Virginia
JWHCF	Civil Rights during the Johnson Administration, 1963–69, Part 1: The White House Central Files, ProQuest History Vault (Online Database Access)
JWP	Joel Wachs Papers, Los Angeles City Archives, Los Angeles, California
KCR	Civil Rights during the Johnson Administration, 1963–69, Part 5: Records of the National Advisory Commission on Civil Disorders Records, Proquest History Vault (Online Database Access)
KHC	Collection of Kenneth Hahn, The Huntington Library, San Marino, California
LACU	Los Angeles Civil Unrest, 1992 Collection, Southern California Library, Los Angeles, California
LAHE	*Los Angeles Herald-Examiner*
LAPL	Los Angeles Public Library, Los Angeles, California
LAS	*Los Angeles Sentinel*

LAT	*Los Angeles Times*
LATR	Los Angeles Times Company Records, The Huntington Library, San Marino, California
LAUSDR	Los Angeles Unified School District Records, University of California, Los Angeles Library Special Collections, Charles E. Young Research Library, UCLA, Los Angeles, California
LAWCR	Los Angeles Webster Commission Records, University of Southern California, Regional History Collection, Special Collections, Information Services Division, University of Southern California, Los Angeles, California
LCRKP	Lou Cannon—Rodney King Papers, University of California, Santa Barbara, Department of Special Collections, Davidson Library, University of California, Santa Barbara
LHFC	Liberty Hill Foundation Collection, Southern California Library, Los Angeles, California
LMP	Loren Miller Papers, The Huntington Library, San Marino, California
MALDEFR	Mexican American Legal Defense and Educational Fund Records, Stanford Green Library, Special Collections, Stanford, California
MDP	Mervyn Dymally Papers, California State University, Los Angeles, Special Collections, Los Angeles, California
MR	Meyerson vs. City of Los Angeles Records (MSS 081), Southern California Library, Los Angeles, California
MRP	Manuel Ruíz Papers, Stanford Green Library, Special Collections, Stanford, California
MRTP	Mark Ridley-Thomas Papers, Los Angeles City Archives, Los Angeles, California
MTBAP	Mayor Tom Bradley Administration Papers, University of California, Los Angeles Library Special Collections, Charles E. Young Research Library, UCLA, Los Angeles, California
NAACPRLC	National Association for the Advancement of Colored People Records, Library of Congress, Manuscripts Division, Washington, D.C.
NAACPRR	National Association for the Advancement of Colored People, Region 1, Records, Bancroft Library, University of California, Berkeley, Berkeley, California
NARA	U.S. National Archives and Records Administration, Archives II, College Park, Maryland
NCLRP	National Council of La Raza Records, Stanford Green Library, Special Collections, Stanford, California
NYT	*The New York Times*
OEOR	State Office of Economic Opportunity Office Records, California State Archives, Sacramento, California

OZAP	Oscar Zeta Acosta Papers, University of California, Santa Barbara, CEMA 1, Department of Special Collections, University Library, University of California, Santa Barbara, Santa Barbara, California
PBP	Paul Bullock Papers, University of California, Los Angeles Library Special Collections, Charles E. Young Research Library, UCLA, Los Angeles, California
PDX	Police Department Records, Los Angeles City Archives, Los Angeles, California
PDX/82	Police Department Records/82, Los Angeles City Archives, Los Angeles, California
PDX/95A	Police Department Records, Correspondence and Subject Files, Los Angeles City Archives, Los Angeles, California
PDX/BSI	LAPD Bureau of Special Investigations, Los Angeles City Archives, Los Angeles, California
PRP	Pat Russell Papers, Los Angeles City Archives, Los Angeles, California
PRWA	FBI Case File 157-LA-2712 (Possible Riot in Watts Area) received through FOIA, U.S. National Archives and Records Administration, College Park, Maryland
RBOHC	Ralph J. Bunche Oral History Collection, Moorland-Spingarn Research Library at Howard University, Washington, D.C.
RDC	Robert Docter Papers, California State University, Northridge, Urban Archives Collections, Northridge, California
RFP	Robert Farrell Papers, Los Angeles City Archives, Los Angeles, California
RG 60	Department of Justice Records, U.S. National Archives and Records Administration, College Park, Maryland
RG 423	Law Enforcement Assistance Association Records, U.S. National Archives and Records Administration, College Park, Maryland
RG 453	U.S. Civil Rights Commission Records, U.S. National Archives and Records Administration, College Park, Maryland
RGPGOF	Governor's Papers Governor's Office Files, Ronald Reagan Presidential Library, Simi Valley, California
RGPRU	Governor's Papers Research Unit, Ronald Reagan Presidential Library, Simi Valley, California
RLAC	Rebuild L.A. Collection, Loyola Marymount University, Department of Archives and Special Collections, William H. Hannon Library, Los Angeles, California
RLGF	WHORM Local Government Files, Ronald Reagan Presidential Library, Simi Valley, California
RMC	Rosalio Muñoz Collection, UCLA Chicano Studies Research Center, University of California, Los Angeles

RMP	Rosalio Muñoz Papers, University of California, Los Angeles Library Special Collections, Charles E. Young Research Library, UCLA, Los Angeles, California
SHP	Saul Halpert Papers, Southern California Library, Los Angeles, California
SLAC	South Los Angeles 20th Century Documentation Collection, Southern California Library, Los Angeles, California
SSC	Stanley K. Sheinbaum Collection, University of California, Santa Barbara, Department of Special Collections, Davidson Library, University of California, Santa Barbara, Santa Barbara, California
SVAR	Street Vendors Association Records, Southern California Library, Los Angeles, California
SWP	Samuel L. Williams Papers, University of California, Santa Barbara, CEMA 1, Department of Special Collections, University Library, University of California, Santa Barbara, Santa Barbara, California
SWPR	Socialist Workers Party Records, Hoover Institution Archives, Stanford, California
TCOF	20th Century Organization Files, Southern California Library, Los Angeles, California
TWP	*The Washington Post*
UAEC	Collection of Underground, Alternative and Extremist Literature, University of California, Los Angeles Library Special Collections, Charles E. Young Research Library, UCLA, Los Angeles, California
UCCR	Records of the U.S. Commission on Civil Rights, Special Projects, 1960–70, ProQuest History Vault (Online Database Access)
UCIS	Vertical Files, U.S. Citizenship & Immigration Services History Library, Washington, D.C.
UPRI	Urban Policy Research Institute Records, Southern California Library, Los Angeles, California
WCSCL	Watts 1965 Collection, Southern California Library, Los Angeles, California
WHCFCF	White House Central Files Confidential Files, Richard Milhous Nixon Presidential Library, Yorba Linda, California
WHCFHU	White House Central Files—HU 3-1, Richard Milhous Nixon Presidential Library, Yorba Linda, California
WHCFJL	White House Central Files JL—6, Richard Milhous Nixon Presidential Library, Yorba Linda, California
WHCFLA	White House Central Files LG/Los Angeles, Richard Milhous Nixon Presidential Library, Yorba Linda, California
WOHC	Watts 1965 Oral History Collection, Southern California Library, Los Angeles, California

Introduction

1. "Bradley, for Sixth Consecutive Year, Enlarges Police Force," January 23, 1990, folder 19, box 951, MTBAP.

2. "Bradley, for Sixth Consecutive Year"; City of Los Angeles, Office of the Mayor and City Administrative Officer, *Budget, City of Los Angeles* (Los Angeles, 1990–1992); Rose Ochi to Tom Bradley, "Mayor Bradley's Testimony Before House Committee on Government Operations," July 2, 1990, folder 16, box 98, MTBAP.

3. Parker and Wilson, *Parker on Police*, 8. On settler colonialism see Hernández, *City of Inmates*; Deverell, *Whitewashed Adobe*. On the history of racialized punishment rooted in slavery, see Wagner, *Disturbing the Peace*; Childs, *Slaves of the State*.

4. Independent Commission on the Los Angeles Police Department, *Report of the Independent Commission on the Los Angeles Police Department* (Los Angeles, 1991), i, 31.

5. For a discussion of crime control as a governing process, see Simon, *Governing through Crime*.

6. On the police power and security, see Neocleous, *Fabrication*; Neocelous, *War Power, Police Power*, 117–18. On the police and the maintenance of a particular class-based political order see Harring, *Policing a Class Society*.

7. Neocleous, *Fabrication of Order*, 65, 99–118; Harcourt, *Illusion of Order*, 1–22; Robinson, *Terms of Order*, 7. On criminalization see Muhmmad, *Condemnation of Blackness*. On limits of citizenship and exclusion from social membership see Lerman and Weaver, *Aresting Citizenship*; Soss, Fording, and Schram, *Disciplining the Poor*; Tonry, *Punishing Race*; Beckett and Herbert, *Banished*; Stuart, *Down, Out, and Under*; Muñiz, *Police, Power, and the Production*.

8. See Domanick, *To Protect and to Serve*; M. Davis, *City of Quartz*; Escobar, *Race, Police*. On early twentieth-century police repression in multiracial neighborhoods and labor organizing see Wild, *Street Meeting*.

9. Hernández, *City of Inmates*, 1, 8–9.

10. This is what some scholars refer to as a "net widening" effect. Beckett and Herbert, *Banished*, 11; Kohler-Hausmann, *Misdemeanorland*, 244; Cohen, *Visions of Social Control*, 50–69; Frampton, Haney-López, and Simon, *After the War*; Simon, *Governing through Crime*. For a more recent exploration of this in Los Angeles, see Stuart, *Down, Out*. For the LAPD's connection of court decisions with rising crime see Los Angeles Police Department, *Annual Report*, 1976.

11. Thompson and Murch, "Rethinking Urban America"; Katz, *Why Don't American*. For a recent study of policing and politics in the nineteenth century see Malka, *Men of Mobtown*. Other works on policing coming out in the near future include Balto, *Occupied Territory*; LeBrón, *Policing Life and Death*; Lombardo, *Blue-Collar Conservatism*; Schrader, *Policing Revolution*; Suddler, *Presumed Criminal*. Some recent dissertations on policing include Elkins, "Battle of the Corner"; Fischer, "Arrestable Behavior"; Krinitsky, "Politics of Crime Control"; Pihos, "Policing, Race."

12. Brown, *Working the Street*; Chevigny, *Edge of the Knife*; Chevigny, *Police Power*; Cray, *Enemy in the Streets*; Fogelson, *Big-City Police*; Reiss Jr., *Police and the Public*; Skolnick, and Fyfe, *Above the Law*; Skolnick and McCoy, *Justice without Trial*; Wilson, *Varieties of Police Behavior*; Zimring, *When Police Kill*. For work on black police officers see Dulaney, *Black Police in America*.

13. Woods, *Police in Los Angeles*; Appier, *Policing Women*; Escobar, *Race, Police, and the Making*; Escobar, "Dialectics"; Escobar, "Bloody Christmas"; Escobar, "Unintended Consequences"; Kramer, "William H. Parker"; Woods, "Be Vigorous but Not Brutal"; McClellan, "Policing the Red Scare." Some studies have explored the LAPD since the 1960s: Davis, *City of Quartz*; Cannon, *Official Negligence*; Phillips, *Operation Fly Trap*; Herbert, *Policing Space*; Domanick, *To Protect and to Serve*; Domanick, *Blue*; Leovy, *Ghettoside*. There have been a number of memoirs from LAPD officers both critical and celebratory: Rothmiller and Goldman, *L.A. Secret Police*; Owens and Browning, *Lying Eyes*; Gates, *Chief*; Vernon, *L.A. Justice*.

14. For a discussion of the broadening of police authority nationally and the implications for constitutional rights in the late twentieth century see Friedman, *Unwarranted*.

15. Parker and Wilson, *Parker on Police*, 60. On the police power, see Dubber, *Police Power*; Wagner, *Disturbing the Peace*; Singh, *Race and America's Long War*; Neocleous, *Fabrication*. On the connection of police, power, and violence see Seigel, "Violence Work"; Bittner, *Functions of the Police in Modern Society*; Weber, "Politics as a Vocation," 77–79. On ordering the urban environment and disciplining, see Neocleous, *War Power*, 119, 134. On enforcing order, see Fassin, *Enforcing Order*, xv; Harcourt, *Illusion of Order*, 1–22; Harcourt, *Illusion of Free Markets*, ch. 9–10; Robinson, *Terms of Order*, 7. For a more popular take on these themes, see Hayes, *Colony*.

16. LAPD, *Statistical Digests*, 1965–1982. Part I offenses included homicide, rape, aggravated assault, robbery, theft-larceny, burglary, and auto theft.

17. Hall et al., *Policing the Crisis*; Johnson, Sears, McConahay, "Black Invisibility"; Reeves and Campbell, *Cracked Coverage*; Hagan, *Who Are*; Davis, *City of Quartz*; Butler, *Chokehold*, 17–46.

18. Leovy, *Ghettoside*; Phillips, *Operation Fly Trap*. In general see Forman Jr., *Locking Up*; Fortner, *Black Silent Majority*.

19. Edsall and Edsall, *Chain Reaction*; Flamm, *Law and Order*; Flamm, *In the Heat of the Summer*; Weaver, "Frontlash." One longtime exception to this dichotomy is Thompson, *Whose Detroit*. For scholarship that pushes the origins of mass incarceration back in time see Gottschalk, *Prison and the Gallows*; Frydl, *Drug Wars*. For the growing scholarship on liberals see Agee, "Crisis and Redemption"; Thompson, "Why Mass Incarceration"; Kohler-Hausmann, *Getting Tough*; Hinton, *From the War*; Murakawa, *First Civil Right*; Camp, *Incarcerating the Crisis*. For alternative views of the origins of mass incarceration see Enns, *Incarceration Nation*; Pfaff, *Locked In*; Miller, *Myth*; Schoenfeld, *Building the Prison State*.

20. Enns, *Incarceration Nation*; Hinton, *From the War*; Kohler-Hausmann, *Getting Tough*; Murakawa, *First Civil Right*; Gottschalk, *Prison and the Gallows*; Miller, *Perils of Federalism*; Pfaff, *Locked In*; Schept, *Progressive Punishment*. On the role of African Americans see Forman Jr., *Locking Up*; Fortner, *Black Silent Majority*. Heather Schoenfeld has recently added to this debate with an argument about the role of partisan competition to building the carceral state, Schoenfeld, *Building the Prison State*.

21. Here I am making a distinction between law and order rooted in liberalism as a political ideology and policies and politicians that can be defined as liberal in

contrast to conservative ones. For a more in-depth discussion of the law and order roots in liberalism, see Murakawa, *First Civil Right*; Hinton, *From the War*; Camp, *Incarcerating the Crisis*; Schept, *Progressive Punishment*. For the role of suburban residents in this coalition, see Lassiter, "Pushers"; Lassiter, "Impossible Criminals."

22. Alexander, *New Jim Crow*; Hinton, *From the War*; Kohler-Hausmann, *Getting Tough*; Stuart, *Down, Out*; Herbert, *Policing Space*.

23. Hobson, "Policing Gay LA"; Goluboff, *Vagrant Nation*; Agee, *Streets of San Francisco*, 11–15; Hurewitz, *Bohemian Los Angeles*; LAPD, *Statistical Digest* (1967); LAPD, *Statistical Digest* (1982). For a discussion of the use of low-level offenses by the police and criminal courts as a racialized form of social control see Kohler-Hausmann, *Misdemeanorland*.

24. Neocleous, *Fabrication*, 22–44; 98–99, 110–11; Agee, "Crisis and Redemption"; Agee, *Streets of San Francisco*, 11–15, 251; Beckett and Herbert, *Banished*, 12–14; Self, "Sex in the City"; Stewart-Winter, *Queer Clout*. Others have addressed the way the carceral state has been integrated with the welfare state, see Garland, *Culture of Control*; Foucault, *Discipline & Punish*; Kohler-Hausmann, "Guns or Butter"; Soss, Fording, and Schram, *Disciplining the Poor*; Wacquant, *Punishing the Poor*.

25. I explore these themes in Felker-Kantor, "Liberal Law-and-Order." See also Sonenshein, *Politics in Black and White*; Keil, *Los Angeles*. For a similar analysis of black mayors and their efforts to represent more than African American interests, such as Carl Stokes in Cleveland, see Taylor, *From #BlackLivesMatter*, 85–87.

26. When using the term "liberal" in this book, I am referring to Mayor Bradley and the group of Democratic city council members who promoted liberal social policies, most notably affirmative action and police reform, and who promoted pro-business economic development.

27. Gottlieb et al., *Next Los Angeles*, 136–42; Sonenshein, *Politics in Black and White*, 155–56, 266; Fulton, *Reluctant*, 46–51.

28. On the constraints of Los Angeles politics, see Sonenshein, *Politics in Black and White*; Sonenshein, *City at Stake*. On liberals and use of government regulation, see Agee, *Streets of San Francisco*, 5–8, 11–13. For strains of liberal ideology, see Murakawa, *First*; Self, *American Babylon*. For discussions of black political power, see Yamahtta Taylor, *From #BlackLivesMatter*. For an exploration of police impunity and black political power in Chicago see Losier, "Public Does not Believe." My argument stems from a broader critique of liberal approaches to discretion and beliefs that bringing the police under the rule of law will result in narrowing police power. However, the police power is rooted not merely in the enforcement of law but in the regulation and preservation of order. As such, discretion is an administrative power of the state given to the police, which leaves the police significant latitude to enforce order even when brought under the rule of law. See Neocleous, *Fabrication*, 99–106.

29. Kurashige, *Shifting Grounds*, 279–81; Keil, *Los Angeles*, xxviii–xxix, 80–88, 137–50; Fulton, *Reluctant*, 52–54; Erie, *Globalizing L.A.*; Gottlieb et al., *Next Los Angeles*, 139–58; Gottlieb, *Reinventing Los Angeles*, 6–7.

30. Gilmore, "In the Shadow"; Camp and Heatherton, *Policing the Planet*; Hinton, *From the War on Poverty*; Kohler-Hausmann, *Getting Tough*; Camp, *Incarcerating the Crisis*; Agee, "Crisis and Redemption."

31. A note on terms: I use Mexican American prior to the 1970s due to the predominance of Mexican Americans in the makeup of the city's Latino/a population. In the period after the 1970s, I use the broader term Latino/a due to widespread immigration from Central and South America and the resulting changes in the makeup of the city's Latino/a population.

32. For discussions of resistance to police abuse and imprisonment, see Berger, *Captive Nation*; Berger and Losier, *Rethinking the American*; Chase, "We Are Not Slaves"; Camp, *Incarcerating the Crisis*; Márquez, *Black-Brown Solidarity*; Murch, *Living for the City*; Taylor, *From #BlackLivesMatter*.

33. Beckett and Murakawa, "Mapping"; Hernández, "Amnesty or Abolition?"; Hester, "Deportability"; Gottschalk, *Caught*. Some recent exceptions that focus more on the INS not local police include Macías-Rojas, *From Deportation to Prison*; Goodman, *Deportation Machine*; Hernández, *Migra!*. On the disproportionate policing of black communities see Butler, *Chokehold*; Davis, *Policing the Black Man*; Hayes, *A Colony*.

34. For my thinking on this and the use of the term racist policing throughout the manuscript, see Fields and Fields, *Racecraft*, 16–18. For the ways the LAPD produced race through racist practices, see Haney-López, *Racism on Trial*. On exclusion, see Reeves and Campbell, *Cracked*, 40–41; Beckett and Herbert, *Banished*, 3–15.

35. On the limits of police reform, see Davis, *Policing*; Vitale, *End of Policing*; Butler, *Chokehold*.

36. Mantler, *Power to the Poor*; Lee, *Building a Latino Civil Rights Movement*; Brilliant, *Color of America Has Changed*; Bernstein, *Bridges of Reform*; Pulido, *Black, Brown, Yellow, and Left*; Kun and Pulido, *Black and Brown*; Márquez, *Black-Brown Solidarity*; Behnken, *Struggle in Black and Brown*; Johnson, *Spaces of Conflict*.

37. Felker-Kantor, "Coalition"; for work on anti–police abuse activism, Camp and Heatherton, *Policing the Planet*; Moore, *Black Rage in New Orleans*; Johnson, *Street Justice*; Watson, *Race*.

38. Murch, "Crack"; Agee, "Crisis and Redemption"; Forman Jr., *Locking Up Our Own*.

39. Hernández, *City of Inmates*, 1; Gilmore, *Golden Gulag*, 7–8, 26; Berger, *Captive Nation*.

40. Balko, *Rise of the Warrior*, 96; Seigel, "Objects of Police History"; Schrader, *Policing Revolution*; Hernández, *City of Inmates*.

41. My use of these eras and political frameworks is based on Kurashige, "Between 'White Spot' and 'World City'"; Ethington, "Regional Regimes"; Erie, *Globalizing L.A.*; Gottlieb et al., *Next Los Angeles*, 136–72. On business and real estate interests, see Fulton, *Reluctant Metropolis*. On Sunbelt cities, see Nickerson and Dochuk, *Sunbelt Rising*. On global cities, see Abu-Lughod, *New York, Chicago, Los Angeles*; Sassen, *Global City*.

42. Gene Sherman, "Housing Is Key to Aspirations: NEGRO'S ROLE," *LAT*; July 4, 1962; Carey McWilliams, "Watts: The Forgotten Slum," *Nation*, August 30, 1965, 89–90; County of Los Angeles Commission on Human Relations, *Urban Reality* (1965); California Department of Industrial Relations, *Negroes and Mexican Americans in*

South and East Los Angeles (1966); Bullock, "Negro and Mexican American Experiences"; Pulido, *Black, Brown, Yellow, and Left*, 45–48; Kurashige, *Shifting Grounds*, 269–70; Katz, *Why Don't American*, 84; Schmidt Jr., *This Is the City*, 69–99.

43. Charles Abrams, "Rats among the Palm Trees," *Nation* 170, no. 8 (February 25, 1950): 177–78; Platt et al., *Iron Fist and the Velvet Glove*, 143.

44. G. N. Beck, "SWAT—The Los Angeles Police Special Weapons and Tactics Teams," *FBI Law Enforcement Bulletin*, April 1972; Daryl F. Gates, "Control of Civil Disorders," *Police Chief*, May 1968, 32–34; Paul M. Whisenand, "Use of Helicopters by Police," *Police Chief*, February 1969, 32–39; Edward M. Davis, "Key to the Future of Policing," *Police Chief* 43, no. 11 (1976): 18–21; Edward M. Davis, "Policing, 1960s and 1970s," *Police Chief*, 1982, 42–43.

45. For a discussion of broken windows and low-level enforcement see Kohler-Hausmann, *Misdemeanorland*.

46. Along with the ACLU, Ali Winston, Kelly Lytle Hernández, and Shawn Nee helped bring the suit. Kate Mather, "ACLU sues LAPD over 'systemic violation' of public records law," *LAT*, April 25, 2017.

Chapter 1

1. H. H. Brookins, "Watts Close Up—A Lesson for Other Cities," September 17, 1965, folder Watts (Correspondence) 1965, box 146, Part 6, CRCR; Thomas Pynchon, "A Journey Into The Mind of Watts," *New York Times Magazine*, June 12, 1966.

2. Hernández, *City of Inmates*.

3. Parker and Wilson, *Parker on Police*, ix, 8.

4. In general, see Horne, *Fire This Time*. On police and riots, see Elkins, "Stand Our Ground."

5. Fogelson, *Los Angeles Riots*, 116–19; Murakawa, *First Civil Right*, 77–78.

6. Woods, *Police in Los Angeles*, 223–42; Crump, *Black Riot in Los Angeles*, 27–32; Domanick, *To Protect and to Serve*, 103, 108; Kramer, "William H. Parker," 45–49.

7. David Johnston, "Police Commission: Bradley-Appointed Panel Reshapes LAPD," *LAT*, September 22, 1980, sec. Part 2; Woods, *Police in Los Angeles*; Woods, "Be Vigorous but Not Brutal."

8. Domanick, *To Protect and to Serve*, 108; Kramer, "William H. Parker," 45–49; William Parker, "The Police Role in Community Relations," October 3, 1955, folder 14 (Mold box 4), box 24, LMP.

9. Manes, *Report*; City of Los Angeles, "Rules Governing Personnel Complaint Procedures," May 12, 1964, folder 9, box 67, ACLUSCR; Hugh R. Manes, "Policemen with Guns," 1966, folder 2, box 39, HMP.

10. Kramer, "William H. Parker," 96–97, 97n231.

11. Bollens and Geyer, *Yorty*, 151; Parker, "Invasion from Within," in Parker and Wilson, *Parker on Police*, 49–65; Kramer, "William H. Parker," 49; Domanick, *To Protect and to Serve*, 111; "The Police: An Interview by Donald McDonald with William H. Parker," 1962, folder Police Community Relations, box 200, ACLUSCR.

12. For a discussion of the intersection of race and gender in the LAPD's approach to policing between the 1930s and 1960s see Fischer, "Arrestable Behavior."

13. Community Relations Conference of Southern California, "Police Chief William H. Parker Speaks," folder Watts (Correspondence) 1965, box 146, Part 4, CRCR; Ed Cray, "The Governor and the Police," *Frontier*, May 1961, folder 29, box 77, CAPA.

14. Ed Cray, "The Police and Civil Rights," *Frontier*, May 1962, folder 29, box 77, CAPA; Willietta Schley Kendrick, *Summer Task Force—Watts: A Confidential Report to the NAACP*, May 13, 1966, folder Riots Watts, Cal, 1966–1967, box 66, Part 4, NAACPRLC.

15. Parker, *Parker on Police*, 64, 65; Kramer, "William H. Parker," 68.

16. Parker, *Parker on Police*, 162; Singh, *Race and America's*, 58–59.

17. Los Angeles Police Department, *Statistical Digest*, 1965; Gilbert Geis and the California Advisory Committee to the U.S. Commission on Civil Rights, "Statistics Concerning Race and Crime," September 13, 1962, folder 1, box 6, JABP; Haney-López, *Racism on Trial*, 135–38.

18. Jacobs, *Prelude to Riot*, 62; Paul Jacobs, "The Los Angeles Police: A Critique by Paul Jacobs," *Atlantic*, December 1966, folder 21, box 35, UPRI.

19. Community Relations Conference of Southern California, "Police Chief William H. Parker Speaks," 1965, folder Watts (Correspondence) 1965, box 146, Part 4, CRCR; Governor's Commission on the Los Angeles Riot letter to Chief Counsel, "Report of Interview with Sgt. Vivian Strange, LAPD," November 15, 1965, folder 31 I, box 13, GCLARR.

20. Conot, *Rivers of Blood*, 38, 40–41; Tullis, "A Vietnam at Home," 208.

21. Cohen, *Los Angeles Riots*, 386; Armando Morales, "A Study of Mexican American Perceptions of Law Enforcement Practices in East Los Angeles," n.d., folder 10, box 22, FDOC; On the origins of stop-and-frisk and the role of the LAPD in pioneering the tactic see Elkins, "The Origins of Stop-and-Frisk."

22. Reiss, *Police and the Public*; Chevigny, *Police Power*; Cray, *Enemy in the Streets*; Skolnick and McCoy, *Justice without Trial*; Vitale, *End of Policing*, 19–20.

23. Jacobs, *Prelude to a Riot*, 40; Hugh R. Manes, "In the Name of Liberty," April 8, 1963, folder 2, box 39, HMP; Loren Miller, "Miller on Police," 1960, folder 14 (Mold box 4), box 24, LMP; Los Angeles Branch NAACP, *Police Brutality Report*, March 1962, folder 1, box 37, LMP.

24. ACLU Southern California Branch, *Law Enforcement: The Matter of Redress* (1969); Lloyd M. Smith letter to Alfred Wolf, "THREE BITS OF HISTORY Concerning the Processing of Complaints against the Los Angeles Police Department," October 30, 1963, folder 14 (Mold box 4), box 24, LMP; American Civil Liberties Union Southern California Branch, *Police Malpractice and the Watts Riot: A Report*, 1966; Chevigny, *Police Power*.

25. Bullock, *Watts*, 134, 136–37, 139; California Legislature, Select Committee on the Administration of Justice, *Relations between the Police and Mexican-Americans* (Sacramento, April 28, 1972).

26. Kramer, "William H. Parker," 226; Domanick, *To Protect and to Serve*, 140; Homer F. Broome Jr., "LAPD's Black History, 1886–1976," 1977, folder loose, box 10, SWP. The larger proportion of Mexican American representation in the LAPD is likely a result of the statistic year from 1966, after programs implemented to pro-

mote minority hiring as a result of Watts; see Woods, *Police in Los Angeles*, 235; California State Advisory Committee to the United States Commission on Civil Rights, *Report on California: Police-Minority Group Relations* (Washington, 1963). The city council passed a residency ordinance in 1972, but it was overturned in 1974 by California voters. See Edward Davis to Honorable Board of Police Commissioners, "Impact of the Residency Ordinance on Hiring and Retention of Department Employees," March 19, 1974, folder General 1974, box 664052, AKS; Eisinger, "Municipal Residency Requirements and the Local Economy"; ACLU, "From the Outside In."

27. Manes, *Report*.

28. Manes, *Report*; Hugh R. Manes, "In the Name of Liberty," April 8, 1963, folder 2, box 39, HMP; Ed Cray, "Peoples' Rights," September 4, 1965, folder 5, box 7, CAPA.

29. Hugh R. Manes, "In the Name of Liberty," April 8, 1963, folder 2, box 39, HMP; "2 More Suspects Jailed in Riot at Griffith Park," *LAT*, June 1, 1961; "Two Cited under Lynch Law After Park Riot: Suspects Accused of Assault by Force; Preliminary Hearing Set for June 14," *LAT*, June 2, 1961; "These Are Notes Taken from an Informal Conference at the Office . . . ," July 27, 1962, folder Los Angeles, box 3, RG 453; John A. Buggs letter to County Board of Supervisors, "Confidential Preliminary Report on The Memorial Day Disturbance at Griffith Park," July 1, 1961, folder 27, box 5, JABP; Committee to Fight Police Brutality, "Stop the Griffith Park Frame-Up!," 1961, folder 7, box 1, DLC.

30. "The Racial Disturbance in Los Angeles," *Frontier*, June 1962, folder Watts—Source Material, Watts '65 Project; Los Angeles County Commission on Human Relations, "Human Relations Commission Calls for Positive Program on Police-Community Relations (Muslim Incident)," May 14, 1962, folder 4, box 6, JABP; Knight, "Justifiable Homicide." For an in-depth discussion of the Stokes killing see Felber, *Those Who Know Don't Say.*

31. Manes, "In the Name of Liberty."

32. Christopher Taylor, Wendell Green, Marnesba Tackett, Thomas G. Neusom, Norman B. Houston, and H. H. Brookins, "To Men of Good Will," June 6, 1963, folder 7, box 67, ACLUSCR; Loren Miller, "The Fire This Time," November 16, 1965, folder 9, box 29, LMP. On warnings of violence, see also Howard H. Jewel letter to Stanley Mosk, May 25, 1964, folder 9, box 29, LMP; Los Angeles County Commission on Human Relations, *Report and Recommendations Concerning Recent Incidents Involving Police and Minority Groups*, 1964, folder 11, box 6, JABP; County of Los Angeles Commission on Human Relations, *Special Citizen's Law Enforcement Committee: Report and Recommendations*, January 6, 1964, folder 31 g, box 13, GCLARR.

33. Ed Cray, "Peoples' Rights," September 4, 1965, folder 5, box 7, CAPA. On the deep history of racist policing see Hernández, *City of Inmates.*

34. Willietta Schley Kendrick, "Summer Task Force—Watts: A Confidential Report to the NAACP," May 13, 1966, folder Riots Watts, Cal, 1966–1967, box 66, Part 4, NAACPRLC.

35. Evelle Younger, *Report Concerning Riot in Los Angeles (Vol. 2)*, May 17, 1966, 220, box 109, entry: A1-ENC 144 (144-12-1102), RG 60 (Courtesy of Alex Elkins); "SNCC

Filed Secretary's Report: The Negro Revolt in L.A.—From The Inside," *Movement*, August 1965; California Highway Patrol, *California Highway Patrol Report to the Governor's Commission on the Los Angeles Riots*, 1965, folder 3-d, box 4, GCLARR; "1,000 Riot and Battle Police in Watts Area," *LAT*, August 12, 1965, sec. Part 1.

36. Evelle Younger, *Report Concerning Riot in Los Angeles* (Vol. 2), May 17, 1966, 184; Evelle Younger, *Report Concerning Riot in Los Angeles* (Vol. 4), May 17, 1966, 120, 217–24; Evelle Younger, *Report Concerning Riot in Los Angeles* (Vol. 1), May 17, 1966, all in box 109, entry: A1-ENC 144 (144-12-1102), RG 60.

37. Leonard H. Carter letter to Roy Wilkins and Gloster B. Current, "Special Report on the Los Angeles Riots," September 10, 1965, folder 3, box A 333, Part 3, NAACPRLC; H. W. Sullivan letter to Honorable Board of Police Commissioners, "Communication from Police, Fire and Civil Defense Committee Requesting Information Re: The Disturbance which Occurred in South Central Los Angeles in August, 1965," May 18, 1966, folder 6, box 60, JHP.

38. Columbia Broadcasting System, "CBS Reports: Watts: Riot or Revolt?."

39. Governor's Commission on the Los Angeles Riot, "Interview of Mr. John A. Buggs," October 2, 1965, folder 5-b, box 5, GCLARR; Interview of James Fisk, "Volume XVI Documents," October 11, 1965, vol. 16, reel 5, GCLARM; Interview of Rev. Casper Glenn, "Volume XV Documents," November 5, 1965, vol. 15, reel 4, GCLARM; Wendell Collins Interview, 1990, WOHC.

40. Governor's Commission on the Los Angeles Riot, "Interview of Mr. John A. Buggs," October 2, 1965, folder 5-b, box 5, GCLARR; Interview of James Fisk, "Volume XVI Documents," October 11, 1965, vol. 16, reel 5, GCLARM.

41. Governor's Commission on the Los Angeles Riot, "Interview of Mr. John A. Buggs," October 2, 1965, folder 5-b, box 5, GCLARR.

42. CBS, "Watts: Riot or Revolt?"; Governor's Commission on the Los Angeles Riot, "Interview of Mr. John A. Buggs."

43. Robert E. Conot, "The Superchief," *LAT West Magazine*, June 9, 1968, folder 18, box 8, MRP; Conot, *Rivers of Blood*; Cohen and Murphy, *Burn, Baby, Burn!*; Leonard H. Carter letter to Roy Wilkins and Gloster B. Current, "Special Report on the Los Angeles Riots," September 10, 1965, folder 3, box A 333, Part 3, NAACPRLC.

44. National Guard, "The California National Guard and the Los Angeles Riot, August 1965," 1965, folder 7-a, box 5, GCLARR; Leonard H. Carter letter to Roy Wilkins and Gloster B. Current, "Special Report on the Los Angeles Riots," September 10, 1965, folder 3, box A 333, Part 3, NAACPRLC; "Los Angeles: Why," *Newsweek*, August 30, 1965, folder 12, box 49, UPRI.

45. KTLA, "KTLA Film: 'Hell in the City of Angels,'" November 29, 1965, folder 3-a, box 4, GCLARR; Connor, "Creating Cities and Citizens," 429–30.

46. Kohler-Hausmann, "Militarizing the Police," 48, 64.

47. "100 Hours—City in Crisis," 1965, 6.6.1.5 (folder 9, box 317), KHC; "Timetable of Phone Calls to and from Police Chief," 1965, folder 5, box 288, *LAT*; Raymond G. Parker to Ed Ainsworth, November 9, 1965, folder 5, box 288, *LAT*.

48. "Los Angeles: Why," *Newsweek*, August 30, 1965, folder 12, box 49, UPRI; KTLA, "KTLA Film: 'Hell in the City of Angels.'"

49. Robert Oliver interview, 1990, WOHC; Wendell Collins interview, 1990, WOHC; "Watts Is Burning . . . A Movement Supplement," *Movement*, August 1965.

50. H. W. Sullivan letter to Honorable Board of Police Commissioners, "Communication from Police, Fire and Civil Defense Committee Requesting Information Re. The Disturbance Which Occurred in South Central Los Angeles in August, 1965," May 18, 1966, folder 6, box 60, JHP.

51. "LA Police 'On Top'—Parker," *Outlook*, August 16, 1965, folder 7, box 33, JHP; Gladwin Hill, "Relief Job Begun: 20 Agencies Give Aid to Riot-Torn Area—Patrols Continue Calm Returning to Los Angeles," *New York Times*, August 17, 1965.

52. KTLA, "KTLA Film: 'Hell in the City of Angels'"; Horne, *Fire This Time*, 64. The goal of incapacitation anticipated the post-1970s era when the purpose of the prison was one of warehousing and incapacitation; see Simon, *Mass Incarceration on Trial*.

53. Gene Blake, "Criminal Justice Meets Challenge Successfully in Wake of L.A. Riots," *LAT*, August 22, 1965, sec. C; *Preliminary Report of Persons Arrested in the Watts' Riots*, November 17, 1965, folder 12 a (27), box 7, GCLARR; Governor's Commission on the Los Angeles Riot, "Outline of Interview of Persons Arrested in Riot: D.R. Bowie," 1965, folder 16, box 6, GCLARR. For other interviews of arrestees see box 6 in the GCLARR.

54. Thomas Bradley, "Bradley Release," 1965, folder 2, box 1687, MTBAP; "Courts Twist Laws In Effort To Keep Watts Defendants From Receiving Counsel," *Movement*, October 1965; NAACP, "Legal Defense Fund Intervenes in Behalf of 4,000 Watts Rioters," October 3, 1965, folder 31, box 82, NAACPRR; Stanley R. Malone Jr. letter to Leonard Carter, "Special Committee for NAACP Legal Defense of Indigent Persons Involved in Watts Incident," September 23, 1965, folder 7, box 2584, Group 5, NAACPRLC; Governor's Commission on the Los Angeles Riot letter to Chief Counsel, "Arrests of Persons in the Riot," November 22, 1965, folder 12 c, box 7, GCLARR; *Preliminary Report of Persons Arrested in the Watts' Riots*, November 17, 1965, folder 12 a (27), box 7, GCLARR.

55. Art Berman, "Some Coast Violence Goes On as Governor Says 'Worst Is Over,'" *TWP*, August 17, 1965.

56. Governor's Commission on the Los Angeles Riots, *Violence in the City—An End or a Beginning?* (December 2, 1965); James N. Adler, "Coroners Inquest and the Los Angeles Riots," November 12, 1965, folder 2, box 189, APP; "Coroner Ejects Lawyer,'" *LAHE*, September 14, 1965.

57. Billy G. Mills, *Special Report*, November 22, 1965, 352.209794 M657, LAPL; Ed Cray, "The Curious Incident of the Raided Mosque," *Frontier*, 1965 (Courtesy of Alex Elkins); Horne, *Fire This Time*, 126–29; For a more in-depth discussion of the LAPD raid on the Nation of Islam mosque see Felber, *Those Who Know Don't Say*.

58. "Watts Riot, 1965, Including Report of the President's Task Force on the Los Angeles Riots, from the Files of Joseph A. Califano Jr., 1965," 1965, JWHCF; Los Angeles Chamber of Commerce, "L.A. Chamber Reaffirms Support for Law Enforcement Agencies," August 16, 1965, 6.6.1.6, KHC.

59. See Angela Riggs letter to Kenneth Hahn, August 15, 1965 and W. D. Letter to Kenneth Hahn, August 16, 1965, 6.6.1.6, KHC; Marie letter to Edmund Brown, Sam Yorty, Glenn Anderson, and William Parker, August 14, 1965, folder 5, box 189, GAP.

60. Manes, "The Meaning of Watts," *Lincoln Law Review* 1, no. 1 (December 1965): 17–27, folder 2, box 39, HMP.

61. Bayard Rustin, "The Watts 'Manifesto' & The McCone Report," *Commentary* 41, no. 3 (March 1966): 29–35; see also Thomas Wolf, "ABC Scope: Face of Watts," January 22, 1966, folder 2, box 190, APP. Another version of this quote came from a group of black youth who told Martin Luther King Jr., Bayard Rustin, and Andrew Young while they were touring Watts in the aftermath of the unrest, "We won." King Jr., *Where Do We Go*, 120.

62. Edmund G. Brown, "Remarks by Governor Edmund G. Brown," August 19, 1965, folder Watts (Correspondence) 1965, box 146, CRCR; Wallace Turner, "McCone Heads Panel of 8 to Study Riots on Coast: Leaders in Region Named by Brown to Seek Causes and Avert Recurrence McCone Heads Coast Panel of 8 to Study Causes of the Rioting," *NYT*, August 20, 1965, p. 1; Paul O'Rourke letter to Brown, "An Emergency Anti-Poverty Program in Los Angeles," August 19, 1965, folder 4, box 60, JHP; Art Berman, "City Moves on Many Fronts to Aid Riot Area," *LAT*, August 24, 1965, sec. Part 1; On residents' views of the commission, see Hugh Taylor letter to Becker, "Watts," September 1, 1965, folder 4, box 60, JHP; Jacobs, *Prelude to Riot*, 238.

63. KPOL Radio, "Fixing the Blame," August 23, 1965, folder 2, box 1687, MTBAP; "Who's to Blame," *Time*, August 27, 1965, folder 13, box 4727, MTBAP; "A Dispute over Blame for the Los Angeles Riots," *U.S. News & World Report*, August 30, 1965, folder 13, box 4727, MTBAP; KMPC Radio and KTLA Television, "The Second Civil War," 1965, folder 2, box 61, JHP.

64. "Civil Rights: Watts, Los Angeles, Selected Office Files Related to Civil Rights—Lee C. White 1965," 1965, Part 1, JWHCF; Norman Houston letter to Edmund Brown, August 1965, folder 31, box 82, NAACPRR.

65. Governor's Commission on the Los Angeles Riot letter to William Becker, "Meeting of August 26," September 1, 1965, folder 21-f, box 11, GCLARR; William Becker letter to Brown, "A Summary of Statements Made about 15 Meetings of People Who Live in the Riot Area," August 20, 1965, folder 8, box 60, JHP; Virna M. Canson letter to Brown, "Report from Meeting with Watts Area Citizens Held at Westminister Neighborhood Center, August 20, 1965," August 23, 1965, folder 4, box 60, JHP; Louise Meriwether, "What the People of Watts Say," *Frontier*, October 1965.

66. Stanley Sanders, "The Language of Watts," *The Nation*, December 20, 1965; "Los Angeles: Why," *Newsweek*, August 30, 1965, folder 12, box 49, UPRI; Bullock, *Aspiration vs. Opportunity*, 151–55.

67. Wendell Collins, "Testimony of Wendell Collins," November 4, 1965, Volume 5, reel 2, GCLARM.

68. Governor's Commission on the Los Angeles Riot letter to Chief Counsel, "Allegations of Police Brutality," October 12, 1965, folder 31 m, box 14, GCLARR; "Meeting of the Council of Churches Officers and Elected Negro Clergymen with Chief Parker at the Council's Offices on September 7, 1965," September 21, 1965, Volume 15, reel 4, GCLARM; Governor's Commission on the Los Angeles Riot, "Rev. Joseph Hardwick," October 27, 1965, folder 16, box 8, GCLARR.

69. Augustus F. Hawkins, "Remarks of Augustus F. Hawkins to the McCone Commission," September 20, 1965, folder Anti-Poverty Programs—Misc., box 91, AHP; "Minority Group Relations in the San Francisco Bay Area and Aftermath of 1965 Watts Riot, 1962–1963, 1965–1966," UCCR.

70. *Carta Editorial*, August 30, 1965.

71. Ralph Guzman, "Testimony of Ralph Guzman," October 27, 1965, Volume 7, reel 3, GCLARM; Edward R. Roybal, "Testimony Edward R. Roybal," October 28, 1965, Volume 12, reel 4, GCLARM; MAPA, "Statement of the Mexican American Political Assoc. on the Watts Situation," 1966, folder 2, box 4, EQP.

72. "Riot Hearings Boil, Parker, Bradley in Row over 'Mystery Man,'" *LAHE*, September 14, 1965; Sonenshein, *Politics in Black and White*, 81–82.

73. NBC, "Meet the Press," August 29, 1965. F869.68.9.N4N3, Bancroft Library; "Who's to Blame?," *Time*, August 27, 1965.

74. William H. Parker, "Testimony of William H. Parker before the California Governor's Commission on the Los Angeles Riots," September 16, 1965, Volume 11, reel 3, GCLARM, 82; Los Angeles Police Department, *LAPD Annual Report*, 1965, folder 23, box 35, UPRI.

75. NBC, *Meet the Press*, August 29, 1965, F 869.68.9 n4n3, Bancroft Library; Will Herberg, "Who Are the Guilty Ones?," *National Review*, September 7, 1965, 769–70; Committee on Un-American Activities, "Guerilla Warfare Advocates in the United States," 1968, folder Civil Disorder 72, box RS13a, Series I: Subject File, RGPRU.

76. NBC, *Meet the Press*, August 29, 1965, F869.68.9 n4n3, Bancroft Library; "Race Friction—Now a Crime Problem?," *U.S. News & World Report*, August 30, 1965.

77. Kevin O'Conell, "Conference with Richard Simon, Deputy Chief, LAPD," October 15, 1965, folder 31I, box 13, GCLARR.

78. Governor's Commission on the Los Angeles Riots letter to Chief Counsel, "Police Brutality—Jack Halliburton, Source," November 8, 1965, folder 7, box 13, GCLARR; Governor's Commission on the Los Angeles Riots letter to Chief Counsel, "Police Brutality—Mrs. Billie Dymally, Source," November 8, 1965, folder 7, box 13, GCLARR; Yvonne Brathwaite, "Letter from the Rev. John H. Brown," September 22, 1965, folder 31e, box 13, GCLARR.

79. Wesley Brazier, "Wesley Brazier," October 14, 1965, Volume 4, reel 1, GCLARM.

80. Jacobs, *Prelude to Riot*, 271–72; George Slaff, "Testimony George Slaff," October 12, 1965, Volume 13, reel 4, GCLARM.

81. Sam Yorty, "Testimony of Sam Yorty," September 21, 1965, Volume 14, reel 4, GCLARM.

82. Parker quoted in "Race Friction-Now a Crime Problem?," *U.S. News & World Report*, August 30, 1965; John Ferraro, "Testimony of John Ferraro," October 13, 1965, Volume 6, reel 3, GCLARM.

83. "'Average' Rioter In Watts Had Job: State Study Upsets Belief Most Were Newcomers," *New York Times*, September 4, 1966; see also Thomas Wolf, "ABC Scope: Face of Watts," January 22, 1966, folder 2, box 190, APP; Aljean Hacker, "What the McCone Commission Didn't See," *Frontier*, March 1966, folder 1, box 191, APP; Interview with Middle-aged Negro Housewife Living in the Center of the Curfew Area, "Volume XVI Documents," September 29, 1965, Volume 16, reel 5, GCLARM; Fogelson, *Violence as Protest*, 50.

84. Warren Christopher letter to Fellow Commissioners, October 21, 1965, folder 31 j, box 13, GCLARR.

85. Governor's Commission, *Violence in the City*, 6–9.

86. Jacobs, *Prelude to a Riot*, 270–71.

87. Governor's Commission, *Violence in the City*, 11; Jacobs, *Prelude to a Riot*, 273–76.

88. Governor's Commission, *Violence in the City*, 28.

89. Governor's Commission, *Violence in the City*, 28–29.

90. Governor's Commission, *Violence in the City*, 29; Willietta Schley Kendrick, *Summer Task Force—Watts: A Confidential Report to the NAACP*, May 13, 1966, folder Riots Watts, Cal, 1966–1967, box 66, Part 4, NAACPRLC.

91. "Report on Watts," *Newsweek*, December 13, 1965; Horne, *Fire This Time*, 345.

92. U.S. Commission on Civil Rights, California Advisory Committee, *Analysis of McCone Commission Report* (Washington, D.C., 1966); Phil Kerby, "The Report on the McCone Commission Report on Watts," *Frontier*, February 1966, folder 1, box 191, APP; ACLU, "McCone's Modest Measures," *Open Forum*, January 1966; Aljean Hacker, "What the McCone Commission Didn't See," *Frontier*, March 1966, folder 1, box 191, APP; Augustus F. Hawkins, "Hawkins Chides McCone Report on Watts," January 31, 1966, folder 13, box 22, MDP; Robert Blauner, "Whitewash over Watts: The Failure of the McCone Commission Report," *Trans-Action*, April 1966, Vertical Files, LAPL; Kendall O. Price, Kent Lloyd, Ellsworth E. Johnson, D. Richard McFerson, and William J. Williams, *A Critique of the Governor's Commission on the Los Angeles Riot* (Public Executive Development and Research, 1967); United Civil Rights Committee, "United Civil Rights Committee's Response and Counter Proposals to A Report by the Governor's Commission on the Los Angeles Riots," December 13, 1965, folder 4, box 189, APP.

93. Rustin, "Watts 'Manifesto.'"

94. ACLU of Southern California, "A Project to Reduce Police-Citizen Tension," 1966, folder Police Malpractice Complaint Centers, box 159, ACLUSCR; Governor's Commission on the Los Angeles Riot, *Staff Report of Actions Taken to Implement the Recommendations in the Commission's Report*, August 17, 1966, folder 28, box 23, NAACPRR.

95. Paul Williams interview by Paul Bullock, 1969, folder 7, box 2, PBP; Pynchon, "Journey"; Stanley Sanders, "New Breed in the Ghetto," *LAT*, May 19, 1968, sec. West magazine.

96. John Gregory Dunne, "The Ugly Mood of Watts," *Saturday Evening Post*, July 16, 1966, folder Watts '68, box 230, ACLUSCR.

97. Sedgie Collins interview by Paul Bullock, March 1969, folder 8, box 2, PBP.

Chapter 2

1. National Advisory Commission on Civil Disorders, "Proceedings of the National Advisory Commission on Civil Disorders," November 2, 1967, 311, folder 15, box 38, UPRI.

2. Agee, *Streets of San Francisco*; Goluboff, *Vagrant Nation*.

3. Hinton, *From the War on Poverty*; Murakawa, *First Civil Right*; Platt et al., *Iron Fist and the Velvet Glove*; Los Angeles Police Department, *Annual Report*, 1966. On counterinsurgent war and the police see Harcourt, *Counterrevolution*; Seigel, "Objects of Police History"; Schrader, *Policing Revolution*.

4. Platt et al., *Iron Fist and the Velvet Glove*, 16, 130; Goldstein, *Poverty in Common*, 117; Harcourt, *Counterrevolution*, 89–100.

5. Murakawa, "Origins of the Carceral Crisis."

6. Leonard H. Carter letter to Wilkins, "Special Report on the Los Angeles Riots," September 10, 1965, folder 3, box A 333, Part 3, NAACPRLC.

7. Yorty letter in Evelle Younger, "Report Concerning Riot in Los Angeles (Vol. 1)"; Evelle J. Younger, *Report by Evelle J. Younger to the Governor's Commission on the Los Angeles Riots*, October 28, 1965, 6.6.1.5, folder 9, box 317, KHC.

8. "Race Friction-Now a Crime Problem?," *U.S. News & World Report*, August 30, 1965.

9. Evelle J. Younger, *Report by Evelle J. Younger to the Governor's Commission on the Los Angeles Riots*, October 28, 1965, 6.6.1.5, folder 9, box 317, KHC; Taylor, *From #BlackLivesMatter*, 117–18; Murakawa, "Origins of the Carceral Crisis."

10. Los Angeles Police Department, *Statistical Digest*, 1964; Los Angeles Police Department, *Statistical Digest*, 1965; Los Angeles Police Department, *Statistical Digest*, 1970; see also Los Angeles Police Department, *Annual Report*, 1965–1970. The reliance on crime data and the use of rising crime rates during the 1960s to explain the origins of mass incarceration has been subject of debate among scholars. While I am not intervening in the debate over whether crime actually rose during the 1960s, I am suggesting that the police used their own data to advance their position and power in city politics. For a succinct discussion of the way crime rates reflected crime reporting see Hinton, *From the War*, 6–7.

11. "Los Angeles: Why," *Newsweek*, August 30, 1965, folder 12, box 49, UPRI.

12. Schmidt Jr., *This Is the City*, 85.

13. Cohen, *Los Angeles Riots*, 484–92; Seventy-nine percent of whites believed that Police Chief Parker handled the unrest well. White respondents also split nearly equally between Republican and Democrat in their responses, 499.

14. Hugh R. Manes, "The Meaning of Watts," *Lincoln Law Review* 1, no. 1 (December 1965): 17–27.

15. On conservatives, see Alphonzo Bell, "Excerpt from a Speech on Police and the Courts in Los Angeles," February 28, 1969, folder 41, box 110, ABP. John Ferraro was a conservative Democrat; see John Ferraro, "Testimony of John Ferraro," October 13, 1965, vol. 6, reel 3, McCone Transcripts—Microfilm; on liberals, see Thomas Bradley, *Report to the People—XIX*, 1965, folder 2, box 1687, MTBAP; Erwin Baker, "$100 Million Urged to Aid Negro Plight: Lindsay Makes Plea for Federal, State Assistance Funds," *LAT*, August 17, 1965, sec. Part O; Chet Holifield, "Riots, Crime and Civil Responsibilities," 1968, folder Riots, Crime and Civil Responsibilities—Whittier 4_16_68 and Montebello Rotary 4_17_68, box 82, CHP; Hinton, *From the War on Poverty*; Murakawa, *First Civil Right*.

16. Dubber, *Police Power*; Neocleous, *War Power, Police Power*.

17. Flamm, *Law and Order*, 71; Healey and Isserman, *California Red*, 197–200.

18. Bell, *California Crucible*, 237; Rarick, *California Rising*; Perlstein, *Invisible Bridge*, 408–14; Matthew Dallek, "Up from Liberalism," 201.

19. Kohler-Hausmann, "Militarizing the Police," 51.

20. Ronald Reagan, "Law and Order in California," n.d., folder Legal Affairs—Law + Order, box GO 190, RGPGOF; Office of the Governor, "Creative Paper on Law

and Order," May 14, 1968, folder Legal Affairs—Law + Order—R. Reagan Statements (1 of 3), box GO 190, RGPGOF.

21. Evelle J. Younger letter to Ronald Reagan, November 14, 1966, folder Legal Affairs—Law Enforcement (1 of 3), box GO 190, RGPGOF.

22. California Bureau of Criminal Statistics, "Do Tougher Laws Deter Crime?," 1970, folder Legal Affairs—Law + Order, box GO 190, RGPGOF; Ronald Reagan, "Law and Order in California," n.d., folder Legal Affairs—Law + Order, box GO 190, RGPGOF; Office of the Governor, "Creative Paper on Law and Order," May 14, 1968, folder Legal Affairs—Law + Order—R. Reagan Statements (1 of 3), box GO 190, RGPGOF.

23. Norman Kempster, "Urgent," July 19, 1966, folder Riots 67 (1 of 3), box RS 25, Series I: Subject File, RGPRU; Lee Fremstad, "State Has Top Quality Riot Control Gear in Readiness," *Sacramento Bee*, November 12, 1973, folder Legal Affairs—Law Enforcement (3 of 3), box GO 190, RGPGOF.

24. Office of the Governor, "Excerpts of Speech by Governor Ronald Reagan at the Sheriffs Training Academy," September 12, 1969, folder Legal Affairs—Law + Order—R. Reagan Statements (2 of 3), box GO 190, RGPGOF.

25. Ed Cray, "The Police and Civil Rights," *Frontier*, May 1962, folder 29, box 77, CAPA; Ed Cray, "The Governor and the Police," *Frontier*, May 1961, folder 29, box 77, CAPA; William Parker, "The Cahan Decision Made Life Easier for the Criminal," in Parker, *Parker on Police*, 113–23.

26. Goluboff, *Vagrant Nation*, 320–21.

27. Los Angeles Police Department, *Annual Report*, 1964; Ed Cray, "Crime as a New Political Problem," *Frontier*, November 1965, folder 15, box 1083, ACLU Records, Princeton Special Collections (Courtesy of Alex Elkins).

28. "Escalation in Crime War," *LAT*, December 16, 1965, sec. Part 2; Yale Kamisar, "When the Cops Were Not 'Handcuffed,'" *NYT*, November 7, 1965, sec. Magazine.

29. U.S. Congress, House, Committee on Un-American Activities, *Subversive Influence in Riots, Looting, and Burning*, 1967, 837–43.

30. U.S. Congress, Senate, Committee on the Judiciary, Subcommittee to Investigate the Administration of the Internal Security Act and Other Internal Security Laws, *Assaults on Law Enforcement Officers*, 1970, 331.

31. Edward M. Davis, "An Address by Deputy Chief E.M. Davis at the Mayors and City Councilmen Session of the League of California Cities Conference in San Francisco," October 16, 1967, Notebook 1-A Speeches Articles, PDX/82; LEAA, "LEAA Newsletter," June 1972, folder F8369: 73, box 2275, CCCJR.

32. Edward M. Davis, "America at the Crossroads," October 3, 1967, Notebook 1-A Speeches/Articles, box 2275, PDX/82.

33. "Watts Riot, 1965, Including Report of the President's Task Force on the Los Angeles Riots, from the Files of Joseph A. Califano Jr., 1965," 1965, JWHCF.

34. Hinton, *From the War on Poverty*, 79–81, 87–88; Daniel Skoler letter to Clark, "California Grants," September 21, 1966, folder California, box 8, RG 423; "Los Angeles Police Department Budget 1963–1972 in Millions of Dollars," 1972, folder 4, box 2803, MTBAP. The overall operating budget included police pensions. While pension funding did not translate directly to the LAPD's martial infrastructure, it did reflect the ability of the department to carve out authority and resources in city politics.

35. Ray Zeman, "Yorty and Parker Urge Riot Laws: Tell Legislators L.A. May Face 'Sacking' in Guerrilla Warfare," *LAT*, June 29, 1966, sec. Part 1.

36. Governor's Commission on the Los Angeles Riot, *Staff Report of Actions Taken to Implement the Recommendations in the Commission's Report*, August 17, 1966, folder 28, box 23, NAACPRR; "McCone Commission Implementation: Problems and Recommendations Check List for Suggested State Response," 1966, folder 6, box 187, APP; Mervyn Dymally, "Reply to Robert F. Sutton's Remarks," March 24, 1966, folder 18, box 27, MDP; "Proposed Riot Laws Labeled as 'Negative,'" *LAS*, March 17, 1966; "State Senate Unit OKs Stricter Arson Laws," *LAT*, March 23, 1966, sec. Part 2.

37. Conot, "The Superchief," *LAT West Magazine*, June 9, 1968, folder 18, box 8, MRP; Saul Halpert, "Los Angeles Police Are De-emphasizing a Reported Buildup . . . ," February 22, 1968, folder 1, box 3, SHP.

38. Thomas Reddin, "Law Enforcement Faces Grave Challenges," *FBI Law Enforcement Bulletin* (January 1968): 12–16; National Advisory Commission on Civil Disorders, "Proceedings of the National Advisory Commission on Civil Disorders," November 2, 1967, 307–8, folder 15, box 38, UPRI.

39. National Advisory Commission on Civil Disorders, "Proceedings of the National Advisory Commission on Civil Disorders," November 2, 1967, folder 15, box 38, UPRI, 54, 259. On the LAPD's combat image, see Kendall O. Price, Kent Lloyd, Ellsworth E. Johnson, D. Richard McFerson, and William J. Williams, *A Critique of the Governor's Commission on the Los Angeles Riot* (Public Executive Development and Research, 1967).

40. Loring Emile letter to Gloster B. Current, March 16, 1966, Part 4: folder Riots Watts, Cal, 1966–1967, box 66, NAACPRLC; Art Berman, "Police Close Watts Riot Control Post," *LAT*, March 18, 1966, folder Riots Watts, Cal, 1966–1967, box 66, Part 4, NAACPRLC; Eric Malnic, "'Code 77' Radio Call Set Police Plan Into Action," *LAT*, March 17, 1966, sec. Part 1; "Warning from Watts," *NYT*, March 17, 1966; Richard Bergholz, "Governor, Mayor Laud Riot Police: Officers Didn't Fire Shot, Yorty Notes; Brown Hits Lawlessness," *LAT*, March 17, 1966, sec. Part 1; "This Time It Was Contained," *LAT*, March 17, 1966, sec. Part 2.

41. U.S. Department of Justice, Federal Bureau of Investigation, "LA 157-943," 1966, folder 27, box 3, CAPA; U.S. Department of Justice, Federal Bureau of Investigation, "Possible Racial Violence Major Urban Area, July 4, 1966," June 21, 1966, folder 27, box 3, CAPA; "Chief Reddin's Talk Hurts Area's Image," *LAS*, March 2, 1967, A6.

42. Governor's Commission on the Los Angeles Riot, *Staff Report of Actions Taken to Implement the Recommendations in the Commission's Report*, August 17, 1966, folder 28, box 23, NAACPRR.

43. "Los Angeles Riots Update Report Submission to National Advisory Commission on Civil Disorders," August 7, 1967, KCR.

44. "Statement of McCone, August 7, 1967 Meeting of National Advisory Commission on Civil Disorders," August 7, 1967, KCR.

45. Paul Houston, "Reddin Stresses Firm, Fast Control of Riots," *LAT*, August 20, 1967, sec. A; Bill Lane, "Police Test Anti-Riot Arsenal," *LAS*, November 30, 1967; National Advisory Commission on Civil Disorders, "Proceedings of the National Advisory Commission on Civil Disorders," November 2, 1967, folder 15, box 38, UPRI, 269.

46. Edward M. Davis, "Preparation for Civil Disturbance," September 13, 1967, Notebook 1-A Speeches/Articles, box 2275, PDX/82.

47. Balko, *Rise of the Warrior*, 60; Gates, *Chief*, 112.

48. Gates, *Chief*, 110, 114; Kohler-Hausmann, "Militarizing the Police," 48.

49. Gates, *Chief*, 114; Burt Miller, "The Los Angeles Police Dept. Special Weapons and Tactics (SWAT) Team," *Guns & Ammo*, July 1975, folder 1, box 40, UPRI; Larry Remer, "SWAT: The Police Berets," *Nation* 220, no. 20 (May 24, 1975): 627–28; Saul Halpert, "SWAT Squad," December 10, 1969, folder 1, box 3, SHP; Bill Hazlett, "Police Specialists—Grim Training Aimed at Saving Lives," *LAT*, October 29, 1972, sec. C; LAPD, *Symbionese Liberation Army in Los Angeles*, 1974, BC.

50. Los Angeles Police Department, *Model Civil Disturbance Control Plan*, 1968; "Police Mobilization during Riots, October 27, 1967–October 30, 1967," October 27, 1967, 001346-010-0736, KCR; Daryl F. Gates, "Control of Civil Disorders," *Police Chief* (May 1968): 32–34; Paul Houston, "Reddin Stresses Firm, Fast Control of Riots," *LAT*, August 20, 1967, sec. A; Gates, *Chief*, 107; Edward M. Davis, "Preparation for Civil Disturbance," September 13, 1967, Notebook 1-A Speeches/Articles, box 2275, PDX/82; Edward M. Davis, "Linear Riot Strategy," August 1, 1967, Notebook 1, box 2276, PDX/82.

51. Hinton, *From the War on Poverty*, 134–38; Lyndon B. Johnson, "The Challenge of Crime to Our Society," February 7, 1968, folder 3_4_68, box 82, CHP; James Kilpatrick, "A New Federalism Project That's Working," *LAT*, September 18, 1969, sec. Part 2; California Council on Criminal Justice, "Evaluation of Crime Control Programs in California," April 1973, folder 23, box 20, UPRI.

52. Comptroller General of the United States, "Federal Funding Provided To 10 Police Departments for Intelligence Activities," November 6, 1975, folder 9, box 42, UPRI; Robert Lawson, "Distribution of LEAA Funds in California," 1971, folder 25, box 19, UPRI; Law Enforcement Assistance Administration, "Funding Summary—1969," 1970, folder Law Enforcement Assistance Administration—1969/70, box 25, BKF; U.S. Department of Justice, Law Enforcement Assistance Administration, "Program Announcement: Special Grant for Crime Control Projects in Largest Cities," May 10, 1969, folder Cities, box 1, RG 423; U.S. Department of Justice, Law Enforcement Assistance Administration, *Crime Control in Los Angeles County, 1973–1978* (1978); U.S. Department of Justice, Law Enforcement Assistance Administration, *Safe Streets . . . the LEAA Program at Work*, Washington, 1971; U.S. Advisory Commission on Intergovernmental Relations, *Safe Streets Reconsidered*, 245–84; Hinton, *From the War on Poverty*, 2, 93–94.

53. LEAA, "LEAA Newsletter," June 1972, folder F8369: 73, CCCJR; Edward M. Davis, "Financing Local Police Departments," n.d., Notebook 1, box 2276, PDX/82; Thomas Reddin, "Proposed Federal and State Financial Assistance to Local Law Enforcement," December 8, 1969, Notebook 1, box 2276, PDX/82; California Council on Criminal Justice, "Evaluation of Crime Control Programs in California," April 1973, folder 23, box 20, UPRI; Law Enforcement Assistance Administration, "Application for Action Grant by State of California," 1969, folder California, box 8, RG 423; Chet Holifield, "Holifield Announces Law Enforcement Grants," December 30, 1968, folder Riots, Crime and Civil Responsibilities—Whittier 4_16_68 and Montebello Rotary 4_17_68, box 82, Chester CHP; "Crime Memo," 1972, folder Law Enforcement/Crime Control, box 25, BKF.

54. Edward M. Davis, "The Gordian Knot," *Police Chief*, April 1976, Notebook 1, box 2276, PDX/82.

55. Thomas Reddin, "Proposed Federal and State Financial Assistance to Local Law Enforcement," December 8, 1969, Notebook 1, box 2276, PDX/82; Thomas Reddin, "Non-Lethal Weapons—Curse or Cure?," *The Police Chief*, December 1967, 60–63; Robert Barkan, "Big Brother Bringing His Toys Home From Vietnam Battlefield," *LAT*, July 2, 1972, sec. E. On blurring war and policing, see Singh, *Race and America's*, 26; Seigel, "Violence Work."

56. "Aerospace—Down to Earth," March 15, 1966; "Crime Control A Space-Age Approach," n.d., both in folder—, box 70, RG 423; California Council on Criminal Justice, "Science and Technology Program Document," July 21, 1971, folder F8369: 68, CCCJR; Edward M. Davis, "Police Communications and Riot Control," November 16, 1966, Notebook 1-A Speeches/Articles, box 2275, PDX/82; Los Angeles Police Department, *Annual Report*, 1968.

57. Ronald Reagan, "Law and Order in California," n.d., folder Legal Affairs—Law + Order, box GO 190, RGPGOF.

58. City of Los Angeles Police Department, *Annual Report*, 1968; C. Robert Guthrie, *Project Sky Knight* (Office of Law Enforcement Assistance, U.S. Dept. of Justice, 1968); Robert Dyment, "Sky Knight," *American County Government*, November 1968; Ann Frank, "7 Cities Ponder Using Copters to Cut Crime," *LAT*, June 2, 1968, sec. San Gabriel Valley; Paul M. Whisenand, "The Use of Helicopters by Police," *The Police Chief*, February 1969, 32–39; Tullis, "A Vietnam at Home," 146; Gilmore and Gilmore, "Beyond Bratton," 177.

59. Los Angeles Police Department, Helicopter Section, *Helicopter Section Annual Report*, 1970, folder 24, box 35, UPRI; Egil Krogh, "LAPD Notes," 1970, folder [L.A.P.D. (Los Angeles Police Dept.)], box 26, BKF; "Rooftop Number Painting Program Offered by Police," *LAT*, August 3, 1975, sec. West Side; Los Angeles Police Department, *Annual Report*, 1972.

60. Los Angeles Police Department, Helicopter Section, *Helicopter Section Annual Report*, 1971, folder 24, box 35, UPRI; Los Angeles Police Department, Helicopter Section, *Helicopter Section Annual Report*, 1972, folder 24, box 35, UPRI.

61. Ralph H. Nutter letter to Murdock, June 13, 1969, folder 15, box 36, UPRI.

62. LAPD, "Effectiveness of LAPD Helicopter Program," 1973, folder Police Helicopters, 1970–1974 (Part 1 of 2), box 664052, ASP.

63. Los Angeles Police Department, Helicopter Section, *Helicopter Section Annual Report*, 1975; Los Angeles Police Department, Helicopter Section, *Helicopter Section Annual Report*, 1976, both in folder 24, box 35, UPRI; Bill Hazlett, "Squads Growing: Police Copters," *LAT*, November 16, 1972, sec. Part 1; City Administrative Officer letter to Tom Bradley, "Purchase of Three Surplus Military Helicopters," June 13, 1977, folder 2, box 1295, MTBAP; Los Angeles Police Department, *Annual Report*, 1977.

64. LAPD, "Emergency Command Control Communications System Information Sheet," 1980, folder 9, box 36, UPRI; Aerospace Corporation, "Evaluation of the Proposed Tactical Information Correlation and Retrieval System (PATRIC)," May 12, 1970, folder 11, box 35, UPRI; Los Angeles Police Department, *Annual Report*, 1970.

65. Edward M. Davis, *LAPD and Computers, 1972–1973* (1972); Edward M. Davis, "The Instant Cop Theory," September 16, 1966, box 2275, Notebook 1-A Speeches Articles, PDX/82.

66. Edward M. Davis, "Professional Police Principles," July 1969, Notebook 1-A Speeches Articles, box 2275, PDX/82.

67. Edward M. Davis, "Chief of Police," n.d., Notebook 1, box 2276, PDX/82; Edward M. Davis, "An Address by Deputy Chief E. M. Davis at the Mayors and City Councilmen Session of the League of California Cities Conference in San Francisco," October 16, 1967, Notebook 1-A Speeches/Articles, box 2275, PDX/82.

68. Community relations had never been high on Chief Parker's list of priorities except as a means of creating "habitual patterns of conduct" among residents. His vision for improving community relations rested on professional and efficient policing, which would lead to buy-in from the public. Community relations, for Parker, would improve if the police had the tools to guarantee social order. Parker, *Parker on Police*, 148; Singh, *Race and America's*, 58–60.

69. Governor's Commission on the Los Angeles Riot letter to Thomas Sheridan, "Police-Community Relationships," November 5, 1965, folder 31, box 13, GCLARR; Los Angeles Newsletter, "Los Angeles Newsletter," September 18, 1965, folder 4, box 40, JHP; Kramer, "William H. Parker," 267–68; Kevin O'Conell, "Interview with Inspector James Fisk," October 11, 1965, folder 4-a, box 4, GCLARR; Tom Bradley letter to Honorable Board of Police Commissioners, June 10, 1965, folder 11, box 11, MDP.

70. Governor's Commission on the Los Angeles Riots, *Violence in the City*, 35.

71. "Better Police-Minority Relations," *LAT*, January 20, 1966, sec. Part 2; Pat Murphy, Daniel Skoler, and John Jemilo letter to Paul E. Kataver, "Los Angeles Police Community-Relations Development," January 14, 1966; Thomas Reddin letter to Gene S. Muehleisen, "Los Angeles Police Community-Relations Development," July 25, 1966, both in folder Police Community Relations, box 69, RG 423; Edmund Brown letter to Thomas C. Lynch, "Law-Enforcement—Community Relations Program," January 21, 1966, folder 2, box 189, APP.

72. Governor's Commission on the Los Angeles Riot, *Staff Report of Actions Taken to Implement the Recommendations in the Commission's Report*, August 17, 1966, folder 28, box 23, NAACPRR.

73. Bill Lane, "Citizens, Police Review Problems," *LAS*, February 17, 1966.

74. "The Police and the Ghetto," *LAT*, March 8, 1968, folder Civil Disorder 72, box RS 13a, Series I: Subject File, RGPRU; "Prerequisite for a Police Chief," *LAT*, October 12, 1966, sec. Part 2; "LAPD and Community Relations," *LAT*, March 24, 1967, sec. Part 2. For other youth programs and initiatives see Los Angeles Police Department, *Annual Report*, 1966; Los Angeles Police Department, *Annual Report*, 1967.

75. Los Angeles Police Department, "Plans of the Los Angeles Police Department for an Enlarged Program to Further Lessen Possibility of Civil Unrest within the City of Los Angeles," April 1968, folder 1, box 3, SHP.

76. LAPD, "Community Relations Program," November 1968, folder [L.A.P.D. (Los Angeles Police Dept.)], box 26, BKF; UCLA and LAPD, "The Role of the Police in Los Angeles: A Proposal to Design a Training Program in Community-Police Relations," 1968, folder 4, box 19, UPRI.

77. Saul Halpert, "The Los Angeles Police Department Today Outline a Far-Reaching Program . . . ," April 24, 1968, folder 1, box 3, SHP; "Unrest," April 24, 1968, folder 1, box 3, SHP.

78. Thomas Bradley, *Report to the People #186*, November 15, 1968, folder 2, box 4728, MTBAP.

79. LAPD, "Community Relations Program," November 1968, folder [L.A.P.D. (Los Angeles Police Dept.)], box 26, BKF; "Wanted: A Police-to-People Program," *LAT*, July 19, 1968, sec. Part 1; California Council on Criminal Justice, "Grant Programs for Police Services Task Force," 1970, folder 33, box 19, UPRI.

80. Los Angeles Police Department, *LAPD Mexican-American Community Conference Proceedings and Recommendations*, Los Angeles, 1967.

81. Saul Halpert, "Halpert Notes," March 29, 1968, folder 13, box 2, SHP.

82. LAPD, "Youth and the Police," July 1972, folder Los Angeles, Calif—Police Department, box 56, CEC; Los Angeles Police Department, "Plans of the Los Angeles Police Department for an Enlarged Program to Further Lessen Possibility of Civil Unrest within the City of Los Angeles," April 1968, folder 1, box 3, SHP; Los Angeles Police Department, *Annual Report*, 1969; Los Angeles Police Department, *Annual Report*, 1971.

83. *Los Angeles Riots Update Report Submission to National Advisory Commission on Civil Disorders*, August 7, 1967, KCR; Murch, *Living for the City*.

84. LAPD, "Organized Youth Activities in the Los Angeles Area," April 1969, folder [L.A.P.D. (Los Angeles Police Dept.)], box 26, BKF; Los Angeles Police Department, "Community Relations Programs of the Los Angeles Police Department," 1971, LAPL.

85. Bullock, *Watts*, 54, 136–37.

86. Paul Williams interview by Paul Bullock, 1969, folder 7, box 2, PBP.

87. "MAPA Assails Chief Reddin and Police Brutality," *People's World*, July 22, 1967, folder 8, box 10, MRP.

88. Cohen, *Los Angeles Riots*, 406.

89. Donner, *Protectors of Privilege*, 245–54.

90. Tullis, "A Vietnam at Home," 199; Theodore Rankin, "Fact or Farce?," *Police Chief* 38, no. 3 (March 1971): 62–64; L.A.P.D. "Organization & Function of Community Relations Program & Liaison Unit," March 10, 1971, folder 6, box 1564, MTBAP.

91. Larry Remer, "SWAT: The Police Berets," *Nation* 220, no. 20 (May 24, 1975): 627–28; Keith Comrie letter to Tom Bradley, June 6, 1980, folder 4, box 2802, MTBAP.

92. Cohen, *Los Angeles Riots*, 718; see also John W. Mack, "Testimony to Be Presented before the National Urban Coalition Commission on the Cities," April 13, 1971, folder 7, box 4, SHP.

Chapter 3

1. Thomas Kilgore Jr., "What's Been Done in Watts," *Commonwealth Club Radio Program*, August 25, 1967, CCR; "Watts Summer Festival," Watts Summer Festival Committee, (1967), ScSer.M.W257, Schomburg Center; Mervyn Dymally, "Assembly Interim Resolution No. 4 Relative to the Watts Summer Festival," July 28, 1966, folder 4, box 34, MDP.

2. Ray Rogers, "Watts Patrol Proved It Could 'Cool Things' at Festival," *LAT*, August 23, 1966, sec. Part 2; "A Meeting with Brother Lennie," *The Movement*, September

1966; Betty Pleasant, "Watts Summer Festival Surpasses Expectations," *LAS*, August 18, 1966; Tommy Jacquette interview by Stevenson (2006), UCLA Oral History Collection.

3. Forman Jr., *Locking Up Our Own*.

4. Escobar, "Unintended Consequences"; Hernández, *City of Inmates*; Márquez, *Black-Brown Solidarity*; Lerman and Weaver, *Arresting Citizenship*; Kohler-Hausmann, *Getting Tough*.

5. Berger, "Social Movements."

6. Jack Jones, "Groups in Watts Act to Change Negative Image,'" *LAT*, August 3, 1966, sec. Part 2; "Survey Bares Ghetto Tragedies," *Chicago Daily Defender*, September 6, 1966.

7. Stanley Sanders, "New Breed in the Ghetto," *LAT*, May 19, 1968, sec. Magazine.

8. ACLU of Southern California, "Re Watts: ACLU Again Proposes a Police Review Board," 1965, folder 2, box 2, DLC; ACLU, "ACLU Action Memorandum—Urgent!!," 1966, folder Police Community Relations, box 200, ACLUSCR.

9. "Undermining the Police Force," *LAT*, July 19, 1960, folder 3, box 24, ACLUSCR; Leanne Golden letter to Affiliates, "Police Advisory Boards," April 18, 1963, folder 3, box 24, ACLUSCR; ACLU, "Police Review Board Summaries," 1960, folder 3, box 24, ACLUSCR; Edward M. Davis, "Move Over, Chief," October 23, 1962, Notebook 1-A Speeches/Articles, box 2275, PDX/82.

10. ACLU Southern California Branch, *Police Malpractice and the Watts Riot* (Los Angeles, 1966); Willietta Schley Kendrick, *Summer Task Force—Watts: A Confidential Report to the NAACP*, May 13, 1966, folder Riots Watts, Cal, 1966–1967, box 66, Part 4, NAACPRLC.

11. ACLU of Southern California, "Re Watts: ACLU Again Proposes a Police Review Board," 1965, folder 2, box 2, DLC.

12. "Reforms Urged to Ease Race Tension," *LAT*, December 7, 1965, sec. Part 4.

13. "'No Review Board For L. A., Yorty,'" *LAS*, December 22, 1966.

14. Flamm, "'Law and Order' at Large"; Hudson, "Civilian Review Board."

15. ACLU of Southern California, "A Project to Reduce Police-Citizen Tension," 1966, folder Police Malpractice Complaint Centers, box 159, ACLUSCR.

16. Interview of Eason Monroe by Gardner, 1974, UCLA Oral History Project; ACLU of Southern California, "Release on Police Malpractice Centers," July 11, 1966, folder Police Community Relations, box 200, ACLUSCR; ACLU of Southern California, "A Project to Reduce Police-Citizen Tension," 1966, folder Police Malpractice Complaint Centers, box 159, ACLUSCR.

17. American Civil Liberties Union Southern California Branch, *Law Enforcement: The Matter of Redress*; ACLU of Southern California, *East Los Angeles Police Malpractice Complaint Center: A Report*, August 28, 1968, folder PMCC—Report Data, box 200, ACLUSCR; ACLU of Southern California, *The Watts Police Malpractice Complaint Center: A Report*, August 30, 1968, folder PMCC—Report Data, box 200, ACLUSCR.

18. American Civil Liberties Union Southern California Branch, *Law Enforcement: The Matter of Redress*; ACLU, "ACLU New Release," 1968, folder Urban Unrest—Crisis Coalition: 1968, box 664092, ASP.

19. Arthur S. Black and Norman Houston, *The Legal Redress Committee Special Report*, May 1966, folder 5, box 2560, Group 5, NAACPRLC; United Civil Rights Council, "Deadwyler Incident," May 31, 1966, folder 10, box 1, DLC; Don Wheeldin, "The Situation In Watts Today," *Freedomways* (Winter 1967); Philip Fradkin, "Bitter Negroes Mourn Man Killed by Policeman's Bullet: Bitter Negroes Mourn Man Shot by Officer," *LAT*, May 17, 1966, sec. Part 1; "Public Deserves Facts In Deadwyler Slaying," *LAS*, May 12, 1966; Tom Bradley, *Report to the People—LVI*, May 20, 1966, folder 11, box 11, MDP.

20. Philip Fradkin, "Bitter Negroes Mourn Man Killed by Policeman's Bullet," *LAT*, May 17, 1966, sec. Part 1; Bob Lucas, "Hundreds In Killing Protest," *LAS*, May 19, 1966.

21. Bob Lucas and Betty Pleasant, "Quiet Meet Erupts into Disturbance," *LAS*, May 19, 1966; Art Berman, "New Watts Violence Provides Backdrop for Inquest Today," *LAT*, May 19, 1966, sec. Part 1.

22. "Stand Up for Law and Order!," *LAT*, May 24, 1966, sec. Part 2.

23. "Political Issue Injected in Deadwyler Proceedings," *LAS*, May 26, 1966.

24. "Yorty Asks for Law Against Inciting Riot," *LAT*, May 28, 1966, sec. Part 1; "Parker Says 'Outsiders' Stir Racial Unrest," *LAS*, June 16, 1966.

25. TALO, "The (Temporary) Alliance of Local Organizations Press Release," May 31, 1966, folder 8, box 32, MDP; Carl Westmann, "Temporary Alliance of Local Organizations," 1966, folder 7, box 42, TCOF.

26. Robert L. Brock, "Speech of the Presentation of TALO," July 31, 1966, folder 7, box 42, TCOF.

27. Robert L. Brock, "Speech of Robert L. Brock, Chairman of the Temporary Alliance of Local Organizations, before the Southern California Council of Churches," June 20, 1966, folder 7, box 42, TCOF.

28. Carl Westmann, "Temporary Alliance of Local Organizations," 1966, folder 7, box 42, TCOF; Clifford McClain interview by Stevenson, n.d., UCLA Oral History Collection.

29. Robert L. Brock, "Speech of the Presentation of TALO," July 31, 1966, folder 7, box 42, TCOF.

30. The initial patrol started as an "Observer Corps" by a coalition of civil rights groups, black nationalists, and private citizens. See "Observer Corps," July 31, 1966, folder 7, box 42, TCOF; Chester Wright, "Will L.A. Cops Trigger the Next Riot?," *Movement*, November 1966; "A Meeting with Brother Lennie," *Movement*, September 1966; "We Have to Get the Police Off Our Backs," *Movement*, September 1966; S. W. Collins, *Temporary Alliance of Local Organizations Police Alternatives Committee Report*, June 6, 1966, folder 8, box 32, MDP; Tullis, "A Vietnam at Home," 222–23; SA Roy Andrew Peters to SAC, Los Angeles, "Temporary Alliance of Local Organizations (TALO) Racial Matters," July 15, 1966, RD 38314 URTS 15950, DOCID-70100730, FOIA—FBI Files, RG 60, NARA.

31. Tullis, "A Vietnam at Home," 223; Terence Cannon, "A Night with the Watts Community Alert Patrol," *Movement*, August 1966, folder The Movement, WCSCL; "Community Alert Patrol," May 1967, RD 38314 URTS 15950, DOCID-70100730, FOIA—FBI Files, RG 60, NARA.

32. Betty Pleasant, "Cop Watching Serious Business with Community Alert Patrol," *LAS*, June 16, 1966; Student Nonviolent Coordinating Committee of California, "The

Movement," August 1966, folder The Movement, WCSCL; Tullis, "A Vietnam at Home," 224.

33. Student Nonviolent Coordinating Committee, "We Have to Get the Police off Our Backs," *Movement*, September 1966.

34. Tullis, "A Vietnam at Home," 225–27; SA Leslie F. Warren to SAC, Los Angeles, "Community Alert Patrol (CAP) Racial Matters," August 12, 1966, RD 38314 URTS 15950, DOCID-70100730, FOIA—FBI Files, RG 60, NARA.

35. Terence Cannon, "A Night with the Watts Community Alert Patrol," *Movement*, August 1966, folder The Movement, WCSCL; Tullis, "A Vietnam at Home," 227–28; "Transcript of Tape Recorded Confidential Report from XXXX: NAACP & Community Alert Patrol Meeting," June 27, 1966, RD 38314 URTS 15950, DOCID-70100730, FOIA—FBI Files, RG 60, NARA.

36. U.S. Department of Health, Education, and Welfare, "Release," May 18, 1967, F3751: 181, OEOR; Herbert T. Brown letter to Theron Bell, "Community Alert Patrol," May 23, 1967, F3751: 181, OEOR; Community Alert Patrol, "Release," May 24, 1967, F3751: 181, OEOR.

37. "Role of the 'Community Patrol,'" *LAT*, May 26, 1967, sec. Part 2; U.S. Department of Health, Education, and Welfare, "Release," May 18, 1967, F3751: 181, OEOR; Vincent J. Burke, "U.S. Might Cancel Alert Patrol Fund at Police Request," *LAT*, May 30, 1967, sec. Part 1; Tullis, "A Vietnam at Home," 229–31.

38. Ronald Reagan letter to Sargent Shriver, June 12, 1967, F3751: 181, OEOR; Jackie Beam letter to Jim Barber, June 20, 1967, F3751: 181, OEOR; George Murphy, "Release," June 5, 1967, F3751: 181, OEOR; "Dangerous Policy," *LAHE*, May 28, 1967, RD 38314 URTS 15950, DOCID-70100730, FOIA—FBI Files, RG 60, NARA.

39. "Whites Grab Cash Marked For CAP Use," *LAS*, May 25, 1967; Vincent J. Burke, "U.S. Might Cancel Alert Patrol Fund at Police Request," *LAT*, May 30, 1967, sec. Part I.

40. Vincent J. Burke, "U.S. Might Cancel Alert Patrol Fund at Police Request," *LAT*, May 30, 1967, sec. Part 1; Erwin Baker, "Alert Patrol Grant 'Political'—Yorty," *LAT*, May 25, 1967, sec. Part 2; "Yorty Complains to President on Fund for Patrol," *LAT*, June 2, 1967, sec. Part 2; "Federal Officials Assigned To Clarify CAP Operation," *LAS*, June 22, 1967; James B. Utt, "Poverty Funds to Destroy Police Departments?" *Congressional Record Appendix*, June 12, 1967; KNXT editorial, "Community Alert Patrol," May 26, 1967, folder 3, box RS 13a, Series I: Subject File, RGPRU.

41. Byron E. Calame, "Community Patrol: Los Angeles' Planned Police-Slumdweller 'Buffer' in Dispute," *Wall Street Journal*, August 2, 1967; "Politics, Civil Rights," *LAS*, June 8, 1967; Wesley R. Brazier, "Your Urban League: Advantages of the CAP Program," *LAS*, June 22, 1967; Tullis, "A Vietnam at Home," 233.

42. Los Angeles Black Congress, "Black Voice," August 1968, 2012 Folio S3, BV (thanks to Allison Gorsuch for this source).

43. Walt Bremond letter to Mervyn Dymally, July 18, 1967, folder 5, box 106, MDP; Walter Bremond Interview by Robert Wright, November 18, 1968, RBOHC; Los Angeles Black Congress, "IFCO Proposal #203," 1968, folder 24, box 30, IFCOR; Los Angeles Black Congress, "Afro-Mex Proposal," 1968, folder 24, box 30, IFCOR.

44. The Black Congress, "Charter of the Black Congress," 1968, folder 26, box 83, NAACPRR.

45. "Black Congress Beefs to Chief," *LAS*, April 18, 1968; IFCO, "IFCO Evaluation: The Los Angeles Black Congress—Structure, Program and Projection, 1969–70," November 20, 1968, folder 25, box 30, IFCOR.

46. KPFK, "Black Congress Aircheck," May 4, 1968, BB4523a, Pacifica Radio Archives; on Wright, see O'Toole, *Watts and Woodstock*, 134.

47. National Advisory Commission on Civil Disorders, "Proceedings of the National Advisory Commission on Civil Disorders," November 2, 1967, folder 15, box 38, UPRI; "Extent of Subversion in the 'New Left' (testimony of Robert J. Thoms)," January 20, 1970, folder 15, box 36, UPRI.

48. Los Angeles Black Congress, "Black Voice," August 1968, 2012, folio S3, BV; Phil Fradkin and Dial Torgerson, "Negro Leaders Urge Suspect in Police Shootout to Give Up: Man Who Fled Gunfight Urged to Give Self Up," *LAT*, August 7, 1968, sec. Part 1; Crisis Communications Task Force, Crisis Mobilization Task Force, *Crisis Report: LAPD*, August 23, 1968, folder 26, box 39, UPRI.

49. L.A. Black Congress Legal Council, "Statement," 1968, folder Watts '68, box 240, ACLUSCR; For a discussion of the way the FBI and LAPD relied on informants to provide information about the Black Congress and Black Panthers during the summer of 1968, see SA Robert H. Claudius to SAC, Los Angeles, "Black Panther Party, Racial Matters," September 18, 1968, RD 38314 URTS 15950, DOCID-70100738, FOIA—FBI Files, RG 60, NARA.

50. Watts Summer Festival Committee, "Watts Summer Festival," 1968, CC.

51. "FBI Case File 157-LA-2712 (Possible Riot in Watts Area)," 1968, PRWA; Frankie Kay, "'The Observer' and Mingler," August 16, 1968, folder 7, box 48, UPRI.

52. "FBI Case File 157-LA-2712 (Possible Riot in Watts Area)," 1968, PRWA.

53. California Legislature, Assembly Select Committee on the Administration of Justice, *Relations between the Police and Mexican-Americans* (Sacramento, April 28, 1972).

54. Hubert E. Wesson, "On Sunday, August 11, 1968, I Was in Los Angeles on a Pass from . . . ," 1968, folder Watts '68, box 240, ACLUSCR.

55. Arthur K. Snyder, "City Council Hearings with Crisis Coalition Notes," August 1968, folder Urban Unrest—Crisis Coalition: 1968, box 664092, ASP; Crisis Communications Task Force, *Crisis Report: LAPD*, August 23, 1968, folder 26, box 39, UPRI; Community Reporter, "Coalition Statement Presented to the Los Angeles City Council Police, Fire & Civil Defense Committee," August 1968, folder 2, box 36, UPRI; Linda Mathews, "Minorities, Councilmen Stage Stormy Session," *LAT*, August 15, 1968.

56. Crisis Coalition, "Crisis Coalition Release," August 12, 1968, folder Urban Unrest—Crisis Coalition: 1968, box 664092, ASP; Phil Kirby, "Riding Shotgun in Watts," *Nation* 207, no. 7 (September 2, 1968): 166–67.

57. Crisis Communications Task Force, *Crisis Report: LAPD*, August 23, 1968, folder 26, box 39, UPRI. On counterinsurgency see Harcourt, *Counterrevolution*.

58. Crisis Coalition, "Crisis Coalition Statement," August 14, 1968, folder Urban Unrest—Crisis Coalition: 1968, box 664092, ASP; Arthur K. Snyder, "City Council Hearings with Crisis Coalition Notes: Day 2," August 1968, folder Urban Unrest—Crisis

Coalition: 1968, box 664092, ASP; Linda Mathews, "Minorities, Councilmen Stage Stormy Session," *LAT*, August 15, 1968.

59. "Brutality Charges Burled; Hearings Termed 'Shameful,'" *Los Angeles Herald*, August 1968, folder Urban Unrest—Crisis Coalition: 1968, box 664092, ASP; "Brutality Charges Hurled; Hearings Termed 'Shameful,'" *Los Angeles Herald*, 1968, folder Urban Unrest—Crisis Coalition: 1968, box 664092, ASP; Jack Jones, "Police Action Hearings Harden Opposite Views," *LAT*, August 25, 1968, sec. A.

60. Arthur K. Snyder, "City Council Hearings with Crisis Coalition Notes," August 1968, Arthur K. Snyder letter to Rae R. Wilkin, September 18, 1968, both in folder Urban Unrest—Crisis Coalition: 1968, box 664092, ASP. On Snyder, see Southern California Public Radio, "PHOTOS: LA Councilman Art Snyder Remembered as a 'Rascal,'" Southern California Public Radio, https://www.scpr.org/news/2012/11/08/34868 /former-la-city-councilman-art-snyder-remembered-ra/, accessed December 19, 2017.

61. Arthur K. Snyder, "Statement of Councilman Arthur K. Snyder," August 25, 1968, folder 2, box 36, UPRI; Arthur K. Snyder, "List of Speakers and Misc. for Council Hearings Re. Crisis Coalition," 1968, folder Urban Unrest—Crisis Coalition: 1968, box 664092, ASP.

62. Booker Griffin, "It's High Noon in The Ghetto," *LAS*, August 22, 1968; Jack Jones, "Police Plan Oct. 21 Response on Accusations of Harassment," *LAT*, September 29, 1968, sec. B; Thomas Reddin letter to Friend of Law Enforcement, August 16, 1968, folder Urban Unrest—Crisis Coalition: 1968, box 664092, ASP.

63. Informant report in SA Leslie F. Warren to SAC, Los Angeles, "Black Congress," April 14, 1969, RD 38314 URTS 15950, DOCID-70100738, FOIA—FBI Files, RG 60, NARA.

64. Black Panthers, "Police Repression Hits All People!," 1969, folder Black Panthers, box 38, UAEC; Black Panther Party, "Black Panther Party Bulletin No. 2 Southern California Edition," January 22, 1969, folder 3, box 1, BPC; Roy Haynes, "Panthers vs. Police: Where They Stand Today: Panthers Follow Mao Teachings in Training," *LAT*, June 21, 1970, sec. B; Tackwood, *Glass House Tapes*.

65. Cleaver and Katsiaficas, *Liberation*, 98; Black Panther Party, Black Students Alliance, Black Youth Alliance, Students for a Democratic Society, and Student Non-Violent Coordinating Committee, "Joint Press Statement—Preventive Detention, FBI Intimidation, 'Conspiracy,'" April 3, 1969, folder 4, box 1, SHP; "Chronology of Panther Incidents," December 9, 1969, folder 4, box 1, SHP.

66. Saul Halpert, "SWAT Squad," December 10, 1969, folder 1, box 3, SHP; "The Central Avenue Blitz," *LAS*, December 11, 1969; Bloom and Martin, *Black against Empire*, 238–40; Black Panther Party, Southern California Chapter, "The Black Panther Community News Service," 1969, folder 4, box 1, BPC.

67. The Black Panther Party Southern California Chapter, "The Black Panther Community News Service," 1969, folder 11, box 10, DLC; San Fernando Valley Community—Police Relations Council, "The Community and the L.A.P.D.—December, 1969," December 1969, folder 1, box 2, BPC; Black Panthers, "Police Repression Hits All People!," December 1969, folder Black Panthers, box 38, UEAC; Bloom and Martin, *Black against Empire*, 240.

68. "Subversive Influences in Riots, Looting, and Burning, Part 3, Los Angeles–Watts, Hearings before the Committee on Un-American Activities House of Repre-

sentatives," November 28, 1967, folder HUAC, WCSCL; Edward M. Davis, "Chief Davis Sees Closer Police-Community Relationship," *Town Hall Journal*, December 16, 1969, Notebook 1, box 2276, PDX/82.

69. Davis, *City of Quartz*; Alex Alonso, "Out of the Void: Street Gangs in Los Angeles," 147–50. Internal divisions within the Panthers also contributed to its decline, see Bloom and Martin, *Black against Empire*.

70. U.S. Congress, Senate, Committee on the Judiciary, Subcommittee to Investigate the Administration of the Internal Security Act and Other Internal Security Laws, "Assaults on Law Enforcement Officers," 335.

71. Robert Kaiser, "Partial Transcript of Tape Recording of Interview with Chief Edward Davis," January 20, 1971, folder 21, box 38, UPRI. For FBI and LAPD surveillance and infiltration of TALO, CAP, NAACP, Black Panthers, Black Congress, and Brown Berets, see documents in RD 38314 URTS 15950, FOIA—FBI Files, RG 60, NARA.

72. California State Advisory Committee to the U.S. Commission on Civil Rights, "Issues of Major Concern to the Mexican-American in Southern California," 1967, folder SAC Meeting re—MA Problems in Los Angeles, Calif, box 26, RG 453; Gómez, *Somos Chicanos*, 144–45; Morales, *Ando Sangrando*.

73. Los Angeles Police Department, *LAPD Mexican-American Community Conference Proceedings and Recommendations* (Los Angeles, 1967); "Ve Ri Tas?," *La Raza*, September 16, 1967, see also advertisements for the Police Malpractice Complaint Center in *La Raza*, March 31, 1968.

74. U.S. Commission on Civil Rights, *Stranger in One's Land*, 49.

75. Manuel Ruíz letter to Leopoldo G. Sánchez, "L.A. Police Department," May 6, 1968, folder 12, box 7; Bert N. Corona letter to Thomas Reddin, September 9, 1967, folder 12, box 7, both in MRP; Armando Campero, "Comentario Grafico," *La Opinion*, September 1967, folder 18, box 8, MRP; U.S. Commission on Civil Rights, California Advisory Committee, *Police-Community Relations in East Los Angeles, California*, 1970; California Legislature, Assembly Select Committee on the Administration of Justice, *Relations between the Police and Mexican-Americans*, April 28, 1972, 67; see also Joe C. Ortega letter to Peter R. Chacon, "Police Hearings," September 29, 1971, folder 8, box 18, RG 9, MALDEFR.

76. "Cops Invade Schools," *La Raza*, March 31, 1968; "Chicano Power," *The Movement*, May 1968; "White Reform?," *La Causa*, May 23, 1969; Garfield High School Strike Committee, "Garfield High School Striker," March 7, 1968, folder 11, box 4, OZAP; Carta Editorial, "Carta Editorial," March 27, 1968; Los Angeles Board of Education, "Minutes," March 7, 1968, folder Minutes March 7, 1968, box 415, LAUSDR; Jack P. Crowther letter to Board of Education Members, "Staff Response to Demands and Requests Presented in Connection with Student Walkouts," March 26, 1968, folder 3, box 1898, LAUSDR.

77. Robert Kaiser, "Partial Transcript of Tape Recording of Interview with Chief Edward Davis," January 20, 1971, folder 21, box 38, UPRI.

78. "Summary of Grand Jury Transcript and Argument in Opposition to Motion Under Penal Code Section 995," 1968, folder 16, box 4, OZAP; "Indictment," 1968, folder 25, box 4, OZAP; "Indictment (2)," 1968, folder 26, box 4, OZAP; "Indictment (3)," 1968, folder 27, box 4, OZAP.

79. Subcommittee on Review of Los Angeles City Redistricting Practices, *Report on the Reapportionment of Los Angeles' 15 City Councilmanic Districts to the United States Commission on Civil Rights*, September 7, 1972, folder 22, box 40, FDOC; "Los Angeles City Council Redistricting," 1972, folder 15, box 27, Part 1, JNC.

80. U.S. Commission on Civil Rights, *Stranger in One's Land*, 39; "Cruising Whittier Bloulevard," *La Causa*, May 23, 1969; "Police Genocide," 1970, folder 24 box 14, BCP; National Council of La Raza, "Los Angeles: Introduction," 1980, folder 2, box 478, NCLRP.

81. "La Raza," *La Raza*, 1970, folder Urban Unrest La Raza Chicano Moratorium, box 664092, ASP; "Rally on Whittier Blvd.," July 1970, folder Urban Unrest General: 1968–1971, box 664092, ASP.

82. California State Advisory Committee to the U.S. Commission on Civil Rights, *Police-Community Relations in East Los Angeles, California*, 1970.

83. Barrio Defense Committee letter to Friends, July 13, 1970, folder 10, box 38, BCP; Barrio Defense Committee, "La Voz Del Barrio," November 1971, folder 19, box 5, UPRI; Barrio Defense Committee, "Arturo Varela, 17, of Lincoln Heights, Shot by Police, Dies in Chains," January 22, 1971, folder 19, box 5, UPRI; Mothers Who Care, "Program of the Mothers Concerned with Police Brutality," 1971, Los Angeles Police Department Bureau of Special Investigations, folder City Council January thru June, 1971, box B-2272, PDX/BSI; "Victoria," *Carta Editorial*, December 1969; on other Mexican American efforts to form defense committees see "This Must Not Happen Again" *Carta Editorial*, December 1969.

84. Barrio Defense Committee, "Police Strike Again at Roosevelt," March 10, 1970, folder 3, box 49, JNP.

85. Celia L. de Rodríguez, Julia Luna Mount, and Susan V. Torres letter to Friends, "Barrio Defense Committee," July 13, 1970, folder 1, box 22, FDOC; Celia L. de Rodríguez letter to Joe C. Ortega, July 20, 1971, folder 16, box 19, RG 9, MALDEFR; Escobar, "Dialectics," 1506.

86. Barrio Defense Committee, "Police Strike Again at Roosevelt," March 10, 1970, folder 3, box 49, JNP; Captain Smith, "Statement of Captain Smith of the Hollenbeck Division concerning Roosevelt at Second Street School Community Meeting Held on Tuesday, March 17, 1970," March 17, 1970, folder 3, box 49, JNP.

87. Barrio Defense Committee, "Window Smashed Again at the Home of the Barrio Defense Committee President," December 22, 1970, folder 3, box 22, FDOC.

88. Barrio Defense Committee, "Legal Panel and Community," 1971 1970, folder 16, box 19, RG 9 MALDEFR; Barrio Defense Committee, "Inefficiency by Sheriff Personnel in Processing Prisoners," July 9, 1970, folder 10, box 38, BCP; Susan Torres letter to Peter J. Pitchess, July 9, 1970, folder 10, box 38, BCP; Barrio Defense Committee, "Inquest Hearing," February 16, 1970, folder 10, box 38, BCP.

89. U.S. Commission on Civil Rights, *Stranger in One's Land*; Sydney Reibscheld, "The Plight of a People-Strangers in One's Own Land," *LA Daily Journal*, August 1971, folder 14, box 20, FDOC.

90. Oropeza, *Raza Sí!*, 145–82; "Provoca protestas la muerte de Ruben Salazar," *La Opinion*, 1970, folder 10, box 18, MRP; "Se Exige Que El F.B.I. Investigue La Muerte de Salazar," *La Opinion*, September 10, 1970, folder 10, box 18, MRP; Herman Baca,

"Day the Police Rioted! Remembering 32 Years Ago!," August 15, 2002, folder 17, box 1, HBC.

91. Peter J. Pitchess, "Statement by Sheriff Peter J. Pitchess Regarding East Los Angeles Disturbances," 1971, folder 10, box 15, FDOC; National Chicano Moratorium Committee, "Ya Basta!," 1970, folder 10, box 38, BCP; Donner, *Protectors of Privilege*, 255; National Chicano Moratorium Committee, "Marcha Por La Justicia," 1971, folder 8, box 1, SHP; National Chicano Moratorium Committee, "Release," January 20, 1971, folder 8, box 1, SHP.

92. "Riots Called 'Planned Conspiracy' at Board of Supervisors Meeting," *Los Angeles Daily Journal*, September 2, 1970, folder 10, box 18, MRP.

93. "Reflections on Law and Order in East Los Angeles," n.d., folder 11, box 38, BCP.

94. California State Advisory Committee to the U.S. Commission on Civil Rights, *Police-Community Relations in East Los Angeles, California*, 1970.

95. California Legislature, Select Committee on the Administration of Justice, *Relations between the Police and Mexican-Americans*, 1972, 124; California Legislature, Select Committee on the Administration of Justice, *Relations between the Police and Mexican-Americans*, April 21, 1972.

96. Robert Kaiser, "Partial Transcript of Tape Recording of Interview with Chief Edward Davis," January 20, 1971, folder 21, box 38, UPRI.

97. John Fleischman, "Police Blast Citizens 33-1 The Score on the Killing Ground," 1971, folder 20, box 30, CAPA.

Chapter 4

1. Thomas Bradley, "Remarks of City Councilman Thomas Bradley before the Los Angeles County Barristers," December 14, 1972, folder Scan, box 5, Part 2, RDC.

2. Keil, *Los Angeles*, 77–91; Thompson, *Whose Detroit*; Taylor, *From #BlackLives-Matter*, 75–106.

3. Agee, *Streets of San Francisco*; Goluboff, *Vagrant Nation*; Murakawa, *First Civil Right*; Self, "Sex in the City."

4. Hinton, *From the War on Poverty*, 218–49.

5. Lassiter, "Impossible Criminals." For longer histories of juvenile justice and criminalization of children of color see Chávez-García, *States of Delinquency*; Agyepong, *Criminalization of Black Children*.

6. Police, Fire, and Civil Defense Committee, "Undersigned Member of Your Police, Fire and Civil Defense Committee Submits the Following Minority Report," 1965, folder 5, box 40, JHP; Police Commission letter to Thomas Bradley, May 5, 1965, folder 4, box 40, JHP; Thomas Bradley letter to Board of Police Commissioners, June 10, 1965, folder 4, box 40, JHP. On Bradley's time in the LAPD, see Domanick, *To Protect and to Serve*, 135–42; 164–65. Quote of officers: "Police Officers Form Group to Back Bradley's Election," *Beverly Hills Reporter*, May 14, 1969, folder 17, box 181, ABP.

7. "Mayor Yorty's Big Upset," *Newsweek*, June 9, 1969; James Q. Wilson, "The Urban Mood," *Commentary Magazine*, October 1, 1969; "Tom Bradley Lambasts Yorty's Scare Tactics," *LAS*, August 21, 1969; Gregory Rodríguez, "Race Is His Magical Shield," *LAT*, May 15, 2005.

8. Kenneth Reich, "People Should Ask Police for Opinions on Bradley—Yorty," *LAT*, April 9, 1969, sec. Part 2; "Anti-Bradley Group Seeks Donations," *LAT*, April 30, 1969, sec. Part 1; Sam Yorty, "Yorty Statement," 1969, folder 4, box 4709, MTBAP.

9. Kurashige, *Shifting Grounds*, 279; Sonenshein, *Politics in Black and White*, 85–100; "Sam Yorty Takes Low Road," *LAT*, May 18, 1969, sec. F.

10. Thomas Bradley, "Law and Order Position Text," 1969, folder 1, box 4728, MTBAP; Tom Bradley, "The Position of Councilman Tom Bradley: Law Enforcement and Community Relations," February 4, 1969, folder 14, box 1687, MTBAP; Bradley for Mayor Committee, "Bradley's Work for the Police," 1969, folder 16, box 17, ABP.

11. Thomas Bradley, "Law and Order Position Text," 1969, folder 1, box 4728, MTBAP; Tom Bradley, "Bradley Release to Junior Barristers," May 1, 1969, folder 3, box 1685, MTBAP; Tom Bradley, "Bradley Release," May 20, 1969, folder 3, box 1685, MT-BAP; Tom Bradley, "Draft: Law and Order Speech," 1969, folder 16, box 17, ABP; Tom Bradley, "Speech by Councilman Thomas Bradley, THE RULE OF LAW IN LOS ANGELES," April 28, 1969, folder 16, box 17, ABP.

12. Tom Bradley, "The Position of Councilman Tom Bradley: Law Enforcement and Community Relations," February 4, 1969, folder 14, box 1687, MTBAP; Tom Bradley, "On Police Community Relations," February 1969, folder 29, box 4727, MTBAP.

13. Sonenshein, *Politics in Black and White*, 93; Richard Bergholz, "White Voter Made The Difference," *LAT*, June 3, 1969, sec. Part 1; "Police Officers Form Group to Back Bradley's Election," *Beverly Hills Reporter*, May 14, 1969, folder 17, box 181, ABP; "Yorty Backed by Officers, Poll Claims," *LAT*, May 23, 1969, sec. Part 1; "Poll 5/22/1969," May 22, 1969, folder 6, box 1685, MTBAP; Richard Bergholz, "Stress on Law and Order Credited for Yorty Victory," *LAT*, May 29, 1969, sec. Part 1; "The LAPD: How Good Is It?" *LAT*, December 18, 1977, folder 3, box 36, UPRI; Bradley quoted in "Mayor Yorty's Big Upset," *Newsweek*, June 9, 1969.

14. Richard Maullin, "Los Angeles Liberalism," *Trans-Action* 8 (May 1971): 40–48.

15. Sonenshein, *Politics in Black and White*, 91–92, 103–13; Gottlieb et al., *Next Los Angeles*, 34–35, 139–41; Hahn et al., "Cleavages, Coalitions"; Halley et al., "Ethnicity and Social Class."

16. Tom Bradley, "Remarks of City Councilman Thomas Bradley before the Los Angeles County Barristers," December 14, 1972, folder Scan, box 5, Part 2, RDC; Kenneth Reich, "Bradley in Second Mayoral Bid; Stresses Law and Order," *LAT*, December 6, 1972, sec. Part 1.

17. Tom Bradley, "Police Days," 1973, folder 3, box 4704, MTBAP; Boyarsky, "Bradley, Reddin Again Move In on Yorty's Law-and-Order Issue," *LAT*, February 2, 1973, sec. Part 2.

18. Citizens for Bradley, "If the Mayor Says It CAN'T Be Done, It Won't Be," 1973, folder 2, box 3160, MTBAP.

19. Bradley, "Remarks of City Councilman Thomas Bradley before the Los Angeles County Barristers," December 14, 1972, folder Scan, box 5, RDC; Yorty for Mayor, "Your City? What Will Happen . . . ," 1973, folder 1, box 3160, MTBAP; Bill Boyarsky, "Bradley Releases His Police Personnel Records to Public," *LAT*, January 27, 1973, sec. Part 2.

20. Sonenshein, *Politics in Black and White*, 107–9, 164; Carl Greenberg, "Bradley and Yorty: Words Grow Hotter as Days Grow Shorter," *LAT*, May 10, 1973, sec. Part 1;

Bill Boyarsky, "Bradley Defeats Yorty In Landslide: L.A. Becomes Largest U.S. City to Elect a Black Mayor," *LAT*, May 30, 1973, sec. Part 1; Booker Griffin, "Yorty Years End As Most Areas Go Bradley," *LAS*, May 31, 1973; "Bradley Gained Over '69 Vote in 6 Key Precincts," *LAT*, May 31, 1973, sec. Part 1.

21. City of Los Angeles, Community Analysis Bureau, *The State of the City: Volume 1*, vol. 1 (Los Angeles: The Bureau, 1972); City of Los Angeles, Community Analysis Bureau, *The State of the City: Volume 2*, vol. 2 (Los Angeles: The Bureau, 1972).

22. Kenneth Hahn, "Release," January 4, 1973, folder 29, box 32, UPRI; Kenneth Hahn, "Motion by Supervisor Kenneth Hahn," January 9, 1973, folder 29, box 32, UPRI; Hahn 48 Point Program, 1972, 6.4.2.1; Juvenile Crime Control Update, 1973, 6.4.2.3, KHC.

23. Mark J. Sachey letter to Tom Bradley, October 10, 1976, folder 2, box 1211, MTBAP. Other examples on need for police: Susie Littlejohn letter to Tom Bradley, January 5, 1976, folder 3, box 1211, MTBAP; Irene Denoyer letter to Tom Bradley, March 14, 1980, folder 2, box 1211, MTBAP.

24. City Budget of Los Angeles, 1974–1975; City Budget of Los Angeles, 1975–1976; Los Angeles City Budget during the Bradley Administration, Fiscal Years 1974–75 through 1993–94, ACP. For a broad overview, see Sonenshein, *Politics in Black and White*, 158. On the charter and budget process, see Ingram, "Rules of Ruling," 340, 392.

25. "The Example of Los Angeles Will Encourage Others: An Interview with Mayor Bradley," *Black Enterprise*, January 1974, 34–37.

26. Tom Bradley, "Law Day Speech," May 2, 1974, folder 33, box 2129, MTBAP; "Police Department Budget Data," 1979, folder 2, box 1644, MTBAP; Robert Lawson, "Distribution of LEAA Funds in California," 1971, folder 25, box 19, UPRI; California Council on Criminal Justice, "Current Project Listings," 1972, folder 4, box 21, UPRI; Hinton, *From the War on Poverty*, 285.

27. "The Example of Los Angeles Will Encourage Others: An Interview with Mayor Bradley," *Black Enterprise*, January 1974, 34–37.

28. Mayor's Office of Criminal Justice Planning, "Project Narrative Submitted to the Office of Criminal Justice Planning State of California," 1974–1975, folder 7, box 1314, MTBAP; "The MOCJP Planning Effort," 1976, folder 1, box 115, MTBAP.

29. Mayor's Office of Criminal Justice Planning, "Project Narrative Submitted to the Office of Criminal Justice Planning State of California," 1975–1974, folder 7, box 1314, MTBAP.

30. MOCJP, *Two Year Report of the Mayor's Office of Criminal Justice Planning*, March 16, 1976, folder 1, box 115, MTBAP; Criminal Justice Planning Office, Los Angeles, "Crime Control Plan (Mini Block Plan)," 1979, folder 2, box 1358, MTBAP; Terry J. Hatter Jr., "Prospectus for a Comprehensive Criminal Justice Plan for the City of Los Angeles," June 1975, folder 1, box 118, MTBAP.

31. Tom Bradley, "A Court System in Which All the People Have a Part," *Judicature* 58 (1974): 270; Tom Bradley, "Law Day Speech," May 2, 1974, folder 33, box 2129, MTBAP.

32. Mayor's Office of Criminal Justice Planning, "Summary of Major Programs/Projects," June 13, 1975, folder 7, box 1314, MTBAP.

33. Criminal Justice Planning Committee, "Priority Problems," April 13, 1978, folder 2, box 118, MTBAP.

34. Mayor's Office of Criminal Justice Planning, *Quarterly Report to the Department of the Youth Authority*, March 1, 1975, folder 4, box 90, MTBAP; Mayor's Office of Criminal Justice Planning, *Quarterly Report to the Department of the Youth Authority*, June 1, 1974, folder 4, box 90, MTBAP.

35. Criminal Justice Planning Office, "The Juvenile Justice Offender Flow in Los Angeles," August 9, 1976, folder 1, box 118, MTBAP.

36. Cohen, *Visions of Social Control*, 40–86.

37. Mayor's Office of Criminal Justice Planning, "HEAVY Central City Component Grant (Full)," 1975, folder 4, box 1552, MTBAP; Mayor's Office of Criminal Justice Planning, "HEAVY San Fernando Valley Component (Full)," 1975, folder 4, box 1552, MTBAP; Project HEAVY-WEST, *Quarterly Report of Project HEAVY-WEST*, December 31, 1977, folder 3, box 1211, MTBAP.

38. Mayor's Office of Criminal Justice Planning, "Project Narrative for Project HEAVY Central City Component," 1975, folder 7, box 19, UPRI; CAO to Bradley, [1975], folder 7, box 19, UPRI; see also Rose Matsui Ochi letter to Tom Bradley, "Project HEAVY Central City 'Humanitarian of the Decade' Recognition," June 2, 1987, folder 4, box 125, MTBAP.

39. William J. Carey, Henry C. Marin, and William Wilson, "Juvenile Justice: Project Heavy," *Town Hall Reporter*, June 1976, folder 1, box 115, MTBAP.

40. Mayor's Office of Criminal Justice Planning, *Final Report to the Department of the Youth Authority*, June 1, 1974, folder 4, box 90, MTBAP; MOCJP, *Two Year Report of the Mayor's Office of Criminal Justice Planning*, March 16, 1976, folder 1, box 115, MTBAP; Project HEAVY Abstract (and Clippings), folder 7, box 19, UPRI.

41. Criminal Justice Planning Committee, *Quarterly Report of the City of Los Angeles Criminal Justice Planning Office to the California Office of Criminal Justice Planning*, May 1, 1974, folder 7, box 1314, MTBAP.

42. MOCJP, *Two Year Report of the Mayor's Office of Criminal Justice Planning*, March 16, 1976, folder 1, box 115, MTBAP; Project HEAVY, "Project HEAVY/Central City," 1987, folder 4, box 125, MTBAP; Summary of Major Programs/Projects, June 13, 1975, folder 20, box 1339, MTBAP; John Flores letter to Pat Russell, August 10, 1977, folder Mayor's Office of Criminal Justice, box C-0560, PRP.

43. Criminal Justice Planning Office, "The Juvenile Justice Plan," 1979, folder 2, box 1358, MTBAP; Los Angeles Regional Criminal Justice Planning Board, *Crime Control in Los Angeles County, 1973–1978* (Department of Justice, 1978); Mark W. Lipsey and Judith E. Johnston, "Impact of Juvenile Diversion in Los Angeles County," Claremont Graduate School Center for Applied Social Research (1979); Roderick, Kevin, "Project HEAVY Cuts Arrests of Youngsters 21%," *LAT*, March 17, 1977, sec. San Fernando Valley.

44. Los Angeles Police Department, *Statistical Digest*, 1980; Los Angeles Police Department, *Statistical Digest*, 1981.

45. Criminal Justice Planning Office, "The Juvenile Justice Plan," 1979, folder 2, box 1358, MTBAP.

46. Kafka, *History of "Zero Tolerance,"* 75–78, 89–91; Sojoyner, *First Strike*, 126–27.

47. Los Angeles Board of Education, "Minutes," March 7, 1968, folder Minutes March 7, 1968, box 415, LAUSDR; Kafka, *History of "Zero Tolerance,"* 75–78, 89–91.

48. Los Angeles City Schools, "City Schools Adopt 'Get Tough' Policy against Disruptions," March 14, 1969, folder 4, box 1900, LAUSDR; Los Angeles Police Department, "Policy of the Los Angeles Police Department Regarding Regulation of Conduct at School Campuses," February 1969, folder 4, box 1901, LAUSDR; Otto E. Buss letter to Principals of Secondary Schools, "Suggestions for Maintaining Control During Major Disturbances," June 4, 1969, folder Student Rights: Board Covers & Memos, 1969, box 8, Part 1, RDC.

49. Los Angeles Board of Education, "Meeting Minutes," November 20, 1969, folder 3, box 1831, LAUSDR; Los Angeles Police Department, "The Police Role in Government School Programs," 1972, folder 7, box 32, UPRI; Superintendent of Schools letter to Board of Education, "Proposed Transfer of Funds to Security Section from Undistributed Reserve," October 15, 1973, folder 2, box 1,459, LAUSDR; Sojoyner, *First Strike*.

50. Jack P. Crowther letter to Members of the Board of Education, "Questions by Dr. Docter Regarding Security Agents," October 16, 1969, folder Scan, Part 2, RDC; Superintendent of Schools letter to Board of Education, "Additions to Security Capabilities," November 20, 1972, folder 2, box 1,459, LAUSDR; Superintendent of Schools letter to Los Angeles City Board of Education, "Reorganization of the Security Section," October 31, 1977, folder 3, box 1,460, LAUSDR; Superintendent of Schools letter to Los Angeles City Board of Education, "Security Assistance for Schools," April 2, 1979, folder 3, box 1,460, LAUSDR; Security Section, LAUSD, "Security Section Statistical Digest, 1975–1976," 1976, folder Scan, box 5, Part 2, RDC; Joan C. Baratz, "Police Presence in the Schools: Cops and Kids," February 11, 1977, folder 31, box 32, UPRI.

51. Kafka, *History of "Zero Tolerance,"* 109, 117.

52. William J. Johnston letter to Members of the Board of Education, "Informative Report on Gang Activities," October 6, 1972, folder 3, box 78, JNP; William J. Johnston letter to Members of the Board of Education, "Testimony from the Special Board Meeting on Juvenile Justice," March 25, 1974, folder 11, box 52, JNP; "In Public Schools, A Crime Invasion," *U.S. News & World Report*, January 26, 1970; "Terror in Schools," *U.S. News & World Report*, January 26, 1976.

53. U.S. Congress, House, Committee on Education and Labor, Subcommittee on Equal Opportunities of the Committee on Education and Labor, *Juvenile Justice and Delinquency Prevention and Runaway Youth* (Washington, 1974), 21, 25.

54. "Street Gangs Turn from 'Rumbles' to Wanton Crime," *U.S. News and World Report*, July 7, 1975; "Violence in L.A. Schools Comes Under Fire From 3 Directions: Bradley, Head of Teachers' Group and Black Students Offer Proposals Aimed at Combating Growing Problem," *LAT*, December 15, 1972, sec. Part 1.

55. Edward M. Davis, "Juvenile Violence in the City of Los Angeles," April 26, 1974, Notebook 1, box 2276, PDX/82.

56. David Rosenzweig, "Black Principal Describes School as 'Ft. Crenshaw': Terror Makes Learning Impossible, Supervisors Told; Crackdown Urged Principals Call for Help on Violence in Schools," *LAT*, December 19, 1972, sec. Part 1; Jack V. Fox, "'Atmosphere of Fear Was So Thick You Could Cut It,'" *LAS*, January 25, 1973; Subcommittee to Investigate Juvenile Delinquency, *School Violence and Vandalism*, 134.

57. William J. Johnston letter to Elementary and Secondary School Administrators, "Possession of Deadly Weapons on School Premises," October 13, 1972, folder 6, box 69, JNP.

58. Los Angeles Unified School District, "Pupil Expulsions," March 19, 1974, folder Violence, box 5, Part 2, RDC.

59. "'Get Tough' Policy Hits 9 Students," *LAS*, February 22, 1973; "Student Violence Draws Expulsions," *LAS*, March 15, 1973; Pat Sterne letter to Bill Smith, "Description of Drug Survey," February 12, 1975, folder 7, box 34, UPRI; William J. Johnston letter to Members of the Board of Education, "Drug Arrests on School Campuses," May 28, 1975, folder 7, box 53, JNP; Kafka, *History of "Zero Tolerance,"* 208.

60. Chris Carr letter to The Files, "Locke High School," June 4, 1974, folder 13, box 33, UPRI; Los Angeles Unified School District, "Bid Form: Manual Arts High School," March 15, 1974, folder Scan, box 5, Part 2, RDC; William J. Johnston letter to Members of the Board, "Deployment of Security Personnel," March 26, 1974, folder Violence, box 5, Part 2, RDC.

61. David Rosenzweig, "Black Principal Describes School as 'Ft. Crenshaw': Terror Makes Learning Impossible, Supervisors Told; Crackdown Urged Principals Call for Help on Violence in Schools," *LAT*, December 19, 1972, sec. Part 1.

62. Black Education Commission, "Racism, Repression and Inefficiency in the Deployment and Practices of School Security," July 30, 1979, folder 93, box 110, CAPA; Black Education Commission, "Black Education Commission's Statement to Los Angeles City Board of Education on School Security Program," April 16, 1979, folder 6, box 4, Part 1, JNC.

63. Louis L. Sporrer, "Disposition Data Coordination," 1974, folder 7, box 37, UPRI; Burt Pines letter to the Board of Police Commissioners of the City of Los Angeles, "Guidelines for Utilization of Disposition Data Coordination Index," n.d., folder 8, box 37, UPRI; Chief Legislative Analyst letter to Board of Grants Administration and Mayor Tom Bradley, April 16, 1974, folder 7, box 37, UPRI; Louis L. Sporrer, "Disposition Data Coordination," 1974, folder 7, box 37, UPRI; Chief Legislative Analyst letter to Board of Grants Administration and Tom Bradley, "Disposition Data Coordination Project," 1974, folder 5, box 1320, MTBAP.

64. Rose Matsui Ochi letter to Terry J. Hatter Jr., "City Attorney Proposed Guidelines for the Disposition Data Coordination Index Project," February 13, 1975, folder 5, box 1320, MTBAP.

65. Walt Parker letter to William Johnston, "Disposition Data Coordination Project," December 13, 1974, folder 7, box 37, UPRI.

66. Complaint for Injunctive and Declaratory Relief to Redress Deprivation of Civil Rights, December 11, 1974, folder 5, box 1320, MTBAP; Greater Watts Justice Center, "Police Surveillance Tactics," 1974, folder 6, box 16, CAPA.

67. Burt Pines letter to Honorable Police, Fire and Civil Defense Committee of the City of Los Angeles, "Re: Council File No. 75-4750," February 19, 1975, folder 8, box 37, UPRI; "City Orders Alpha File Outline," *LAS*, January 23, 1975; Robert Rawitch, "LAPD Halts Listing of Violent Juveniles," *LAT*, July 14, 1975, sec. Part 1.

68. LAPD, "South Bureau Total Resources Approach to Group Violence," 1974, folder Police-Juvenile: 1973–1975 (Part 1 of 2), box 664063, ASP; Los Angeles Police Department, *Annual Report*, 1973.

69. "Special Report on Total Resources Attack on South Bureau Hoodlums," in Edward M. Davis, "Pertinent Matters of Interest in Police Affairs," December 6, 1973, folder 3, box 1746, MTBAP; Chico Norwood, "CRASH Unit, Curtails Violence," *LAS*, October 16, 1980; California State Assembly Select Committee on Juvenile Violence, *California State Assembly Report on the Los Angeles Hearing on Juvenile Violence Held April 26, 1974* (Sacramento: California Legislature, 1974), 95. Aside from the LAPD's own SWAT model, one of the most notorious examples of elite tactical patrols developed in Detroit: "Stop the Robberies, Enjoy Safe Streets" (STRESS). Operating in plainclothes, STRESS patrols focused on low-income, mostly black neighborhoods, making more than 6,000 arrests and killing eighteen people—all but one were black—over two years. Developing a reputation for the use of force, STRESS and CRASH were part of an interlinked, deadly expansion of the police power's battle for the streets. Compared with many of its peers, such as STRESS, which disbanded in 1974, however, CRASH had long staying power. Hinton, *From the War*, 191–202.

70. Nancy Baltad, "Police CRASH Unit Hits Oakwood—It Doesn't Hurt," *LAT*, August 3, 1978, sec. The West Side; Bob Baker, "Special Patrol Urged to Curb Youth Gangs: 28-Man L. A. Police Unit Would Attempt to Break Them Up," *LAT*, November 12, 1978, sec. Glendale-Burbank.

71. Josh Getlin, "Bradley Keeps Anti-Gang Program Funds in Budget," *LAT*, June 7, 1979, sec. San Fernando Valley.

72. LAPD, *Operations South Bureau CRASH Annual Report*, 1981, folder Loose, box 758964, RFP; City of Los Angeles, *Budget, City of Los Angeles*, 1977–1978; City of Los Angeles, *Budget, City of Los Angeles*, 1978–1979; Nancy Graham, "Police Concentrate Manpower: CRASH Unit Deployed Against Gangs," *LAT*, August 21, 1980, sec. West Side.

73. Joel Edelman to Commander Lou Ritter, "CRASH File Standards & Procedures," June 29, 1976, folder 7, box 1338, MTBAP; "Questionnaire: Community Resources against Street Hoodlums," 1976, folder 7, box 1338, MTBAP.

74. Excerpts of gang manual quoted in Armando Morales, Yvonne Ferguson, and Paul Munford, "The Juvenile Justice System and Minorities," UCLA Center for the Health Sciences (January 1981), folder 1, box 1644, MTBAP. On LAUSD attention to African American and Latino gangs, see William J. Johnston letter to Members of the Board of Education, "Informative Report on Gang Activities," October 6, 1972, folder 3, box 78, JNP.

75. Josh Getlin, "Police, Minorities: Uneasy Communication," *LAT*, June 22, 1980, sec. Valley; Myrna Oliver, "Police Photographing of Hispanics Hit: ACLU Sues to Block Arbitrary Questioning of Youths on Streets," *LAT*, March 7, 1980, sec. Part 2; Myrna Oliver, "Judge Bars LAPD Photos Without OK," *LAT*, March 29, 1980; Jeff Simmons letter to Rose Matsui Ochi, "Assembly, Criminal Justice Committee Gang Hearing: East Los Angeles," November 8, 1976, folder 9, box 1338, MTBAP.

76. Nancy Boyarsky, "Justice and the 10 O'Clock Curfew," *LAT*, January 26, 1975, sec. Part 4.

77. Hahn 48 Point Program, 1972, 6.4.2.1; Juvenile Crime Control Update, 1973, 6.4.2.3, KHC; Kenneth Hahn, letter to Alfred J. McCourtney, "LAPD Report on Juvenile Offenders," January 3, 1973, 3.4.1.7, KHC; Ad Hoc Committee on Juvenile Justice, *Juvenile Court Crisis Report*, June 14, 1974, folder 5, box 1746, MTBAP; LAPD, "Illustrative

Cases of Juvenile Court 'Revolving Door' and Administrative Problems," June 14, 1974, folder 5, box 1746, MTBAP; Los Angeles Police Department, *Annual Report*, 1973.

78. Clyde Cronkhite, "Juvenile Crime Crisis—Cause and Remedy," *The Police Chief* 41, no. 12 (1974): 40–42.

79. Nunn et al., "From the Mexican"; Boches, "Juvenile Justice."

80. U.S. Congress, House, Committee on Education and Labor, Subcommittee on Equal Opportunities of the Committee on Education and Labor, *Juvenile Justice and Delinquency Prevention and Runaway Youth* (Washington, 1974), 85; Kenneth Hahn, *Hahn Report*, January 16, 1973, 6.4.2.3, KHC; Kenneth Hahn, *Hahn Report*, May 3, 1973, 6.4.2.2, KHC.

81. Edward M. Davis, "Juvenile Justice Since Gault Decision," *The Police Chief* 77 (1977): 8; "CHIEF CALLS IT 'BLOOD MONEY': Davis Says Probation Subsidies Fuel Crime," *LAT*, December 31, 1972, sec. A; Ed Davis, "Address by Los Angeles Police Chief Edward M. Davis to the Los Angeles County Bar Association," October 25, 1973, folder 4, box 1746, MTBAP; Gilmore, *Golden Gulag*, 88–92.

82. City Attorney, *Supplemental Report RE: Juvenile Crime*, June 20, 1974, folder 5, box 1746, MTBAP; Ad Hoc Committee on Juvenile Justice, *Juvenile Court Crisis Report*, May 21, 1974, folder 5, box 1746, MTBAP.

83. Peyton Canary, "Busch Says Juvenile Justice System Is Not Doing the Job," *LAT*, September 26, 1974, sec. Southeast.

84. Ed Davis letter to Board of Police Commissioners, "Juvenile Court Crisis Report," May 31, 1974, folder Police-Juvenile: 1973–1975 (Part 2 of 2), box 664063, ASP.

85. Arthur K. Snyder, "The Case for More Stringent Justice for Juvenile Offenders," 1975, folder Police-Juvenile: 1973–1975 (Part 2 of 2), box 664063, ASP; "The Problem: Youth Violence," January 7, 1975, folder Police-Juvenile: 1973–1975 (Part 2 of 2), box 664063, ASP; LAPD quote in State, County and Federal Affairs Committee, *State, County and Federal Affairs Committee Report*, January 22, 1975, folder Police-Juvenile: 1973–1975 (Part 1 of 2), box 664063, ASP.

86. Edward M. Davis, "Punishment Will Halt 'Contagion,'" *LAT*, December 15, 1974, sec. Part 6.

87. Police, Fire and Civil Defense Committee, *Police, Fire and Civil Defense Committee Report*, December 1974, folder Police-Juvenile: 1973–1975 (Part 1 of 2), box 664063, ASP; Los Angeles City Council, "Minutes," December 12, 1974, CCM.

88. Rose Matsui Ochi letter to Terry J. Hatter Jr., "Response—Los Angeles Police Department's Position on Council Motion to Amend State Law Regarding Detention, Incarceration and Trial of Juveniles," January 20, 1975, folder 1, box 1338; Los Angeles City Youth Advisory Council, "Statement Regarding Juvenile Justice System," January 7, 1975, folder 1, box 1338, all in MTBAP; Erwin Baker, "Council Urges Toughness on Serious Youth Crime: Recommends Juveniles 16 or Older Involved in Major Cases Be Considered for Trial as Adults," *LAT*, January 29, 1975, sec. Part 2.

89. Irv Burleigh, "Sparked By School Drug Arrests: L. A. Studies Stance on Juvenile Law," *LAT*, January 2, 1975, sec. Centinela-South Bay.

90. Arthur K. Snyder, "The Case for More Stringent Justice for Juvenile Offenders," 1975, folder Police-Juvenile: 1973–1975 (Part 2 of 2), box 664063, ASP.

91. Tom Bradley, "Statement of Mayor Tom Bradley in Support of AB 3121," 1976, folder 8, box 1338, MTBAP.

92. Erwin Baker, "Tougher Attitude Sought: Major Changes Urged in Juvenile Justice System," *LAT*, January 24, 1975, sec. Part 2; Julian C. Dixon, "Juvenile Justice in Transition," *Pepperdine Law Review* 4 (1977 1976): 469; Richard A. Gadbois Jr. and Kenneth A. Black, "1976 Amendments to the Juvenile Court Law: Adult Treatment of 16–17 Year-Old Offenders," *U. West LAL Rev.* 9 (1977): 13.

93. Anonymous, *Implications of California's 1977, Volume 8*.

94. California Youth Authority, *AB 3121 Impact Evaluation Final Report*; Teilmann Van Dusen, *Implications of California's 1977, Volume 6*.

95. Donna M. Hamparian, "Youth in Adult Courts: Between Two Worlds, West Region, Major Issues in Juvenile Justice and Delinquency Prevention," (Washington, D.C.: National Institute for Juvenile Justice and Delinquency Prevention, January 1982).

96. Abu-Lughod, *New York, Chicago, Los Angeles*, 376.

97. Zara Taylor and Los Angeles County Commission on Human Relations, *Kids, Crime and Jail: The Color of Juvenile Justice: Report on a Public Hearing Held by the Los Angeles County Commission on Human Relations* (Los Angeles, CA: Los Angeles County Commission on Human Relations, 1988).

Chapter 5

1. Based on the evidence, it is unclear how many contacts were unique individuals or contact with the same people many times.

2. LAPD, *CRASH Annual Report*, April 1982, box 758964, RFP; LAPD, *Operations South Bureau CRASH Annual Report*, 1981, box 758964, RFP.

3. John Hagan, John D. Hewitt, and Duane F. Alwin, "Ceremonial Justice: Crime and Punishment in a Loosely Coupled System," *Social Forces* 58, no. 2 (1979): 506–27; Brown, *Working the Street*, 283–84.

4. I explore these themes in more depth in Felker-Kantor, "Coalition against Police Abuse."

5. Tom Bradley, "Police Graduation," July 13, 1973, folder 33, box 2129, MTBAP.

6. Edward M. Davis letter to Thomas Bradley, January 16, 1975, Notebook 1, box 2276, PDX/82.

7. Woods, *Police in Los Angeles*, 164–65.

8. Raphael Sonenshein and League of Women Voters, *Los Angeles: Structure of a City Government* (League of Women Voters, 2006).

9. Joe Domanick, "The Mind-Set Is 'Us Against Them': Police: Chief Gates Gets Away with Outrageous Expressions of Intolerance Because LAPD Operates in a World of Its Own," *LAT*, September 11, 1990.

10. "The Example of Los Angeles Will Encourage Others: An Interview with Mayor Bradley," *Black Enterprise*, January 1974, 34–37; Thomas Bradley, *The Impossible Dream: Thomas Bradley*, Interview by Bernard Galm, 1984, UCLA Oral History Project; Sonenshein, *Politics in Black and White*, 155–58, 164; "Biography, Chances of Winning, Comparison with Other Candidates," 1969, folder 2, box 1434, MTBAP.

11. "The LAPD: How Good Is It?," *LAT*, December 18, 1977, folder 3, box 36, UPRI.

12. "The LAPD: How Good Is It?," *LAT*, December 18, 1977, folder 3, box 36, UPRI.

13. "Los Angeles Police Department Budget 1963–1972 in Millions of Dollars," 1972, folder 4, box 2803, MTBAP; "Los Angeles Police Department Budget 1973–1983 in Millions of Dollars," 1983, folder 4, box 2803, MTBAP, UPRI; Mark Fabiani, letter to Tom Houston and Craig Lawson, "The Mayor's Record: Crime and Criminal Justice," December 21, 1984, folder 17, box 194, MTBAP; Talbot T. Smith, letter to The Honorable City Council of Los Angeles, "Blue Ribbon Pension Committee," December 23, 1981, folder 6, box 3118, MTBAP; Superior Court of the State of California for the County of Los Angeles, "Deposition of Tom Bradley," June 18, 1986, folder 8, box 3118, MTBAP.

14. Quote in Brown, *Working the Street*, 62–63; Anton Calleia, "Los Angeles City Budget during the Bradley Administration," 1994, ACP (Courtesy of Caitlin Parker).

15. Erwin Baker, "Secret L.A. Study: Blacks' Favorable View of Police Told," *LAT*, March 24, 1972, sec. Part 2; L. Knowles and J. Brewer, "The Black Community: Attitudes toward Community Problems, Crime and the Police," *The Police Chief* 40, no. 8 (1973): 48–51; *A Special Report: Citizens in South Los Angeles Don't Want a Riot*, 1970, folder Chief's Office 1970, box B-2272, PDX/BSI. The LAPD survey was limited because police officers conducted the survey with residents and given the history of distrust between the police and the African American community, many residents may not have been willing to criticize the department in front of officers. For debates on African American support for the police and punitive policies, see Forman Jr., *Locking Up Our Own*; Fortner, *Black Silent Majority*.

16. Daryl F. Gates letter to Tom Bradley, "Pertinent Matters of Interest in Police Affairs, Police Department Biweekly Report No. 329," April 8, 1976, folder 7, box 1942, MTBAP; Bill Boyarsky, "Law and Order Major Issue in Mayor's Race: Gang Warfare Causes Blacks to Worry More About Violence than Whites, Survey Reveals," *LAT*, January 8, 1973, sec. Part 2.

17. "A Crime Answer," *LAS*, October 18, 1973.

18. Richard Allen, "'We Must Separate the Issue of Race from the Issue Of Crime,'" *LAS*, May 24, 1973; Richard Allen, "'Let's Put an End to Murder, Rape, and Robbery,'" *LAS*, May 17, 1973.

19. Los Angeles Model Cities Program, "Los Angeles Model Cities Program: Greater Watts Justice Center," 1971, folder 10, box 1407; Los Angeles Model Cities Program, "Model Neighborhood Legal Center," March 12, 1971, folder 5, box 1407; Greater Watts Justice Center, "Proposed Agreement with the Legal Aid Foundation of Los Angeles," September 1970, folder 10, box 1407, all in MTBAP.

20. Los Angeles Area Metropolitan Council on Police-Community Relations, *Police Community Report*, February 1974, folder Police-Community Relations, box 268, Part 4, CRCR. The Los Angeles County Human Relations Commission had a similar committee; see Los Angeles County Commission on Human Relations, "Minutes of Special Law Enforcement Committee," October 8, 1971, folder 3, box 18, MRP.

21. E. M. Davis letter to Thomas Bradley, "LAPD Goals," November 1, 1973, folder Police General July–December 1973, box 664052, ASP; Doug Shuit, "Bradley, Davis Call Meeting Productive," *LAT*, June 6, 1973, sec. Part 1; Los Angeles Police Department, *Annual Report*, 1974.

22. Edward M. Davis, "Community Policing," August 6, 1976, Notebook 1, box 2276, PDX/82; Kenneth Hansen, "Police Plan for Public Contacts Implemented," *LAT*, January 13, 1970, sec. San Fernando Valley.

23. Booker Griffin, "'L.A.'s Finest' Must Make up Its Mind about Race," *LAS*, December 3, 1970; Robert Rawitch, "Police Basic Car Plan—Review a Year Later," *LAT*, February 21, 1971, sec. C; "Lost Appeal: Basic Car Plan Failed to Help," *LAT*, May 22, 1975, sec. The West Side.

24. Domanick, *To Protect and to Serve*, 224.

25. Edward M. Davis, "The Basic Car Plan and the TEAM Program," September 23, 1974, Notebook 1, box 2276, PDX/82; Los Angeles Police Department, "Final Evaluation of Team-28," November 1, 1973, box 2275, PDX/82; Los Angeles Police Department, *Annual Report*, 1975.

26. Brown, *Working the Street*, 299–302; "The LAPD: How Good Is It?" *LAT*, December 18, 1977, folder 3, box 36, UPRI.

27. Interview of Tom Bradley by Lou Cannon, January 19, 1994, folder Bradley, Tom, box 10, LCRKP.

28. Sonenshein, *Politics in Black and White*, 154–55; LEAA, "The City of Los Angeles California and the Los Angeles Police Department and Law Enforcement Assistance Administration Voluntary Compliance Agreement," February 3, 1976, folder LAPD/LEAA 2, box 36, RG 60; Leonard Carter letter to Robert Lawson, "Statewide Conference of Police Chiefs Re: Discrimination against Minorities and Women," April 12, 1973, folder 91, CCCJR; Randall Sullivan, "Disparities in Officers' Pay and Duties Persist," *LAHE*, August 14, 1979, folder 97, box 110, CAPA; George Felkenes, T. Lasley, Lawrence C. Trostle, and James Lasley, "The Impact of Fanchon Blake v. City of Los Angeles on the Selection, Recruitment, Training, Appointment and Performance of Women and Minorities for the Los Angeles Police Department and the City of Los Angeles" (Claremont, Calif.: Center for Politics and Policy, Claremont Graduate School, 1990), 6; Samuel Walker, "Employment of Black and Hispanic Police Officers, 1983–1988: A Follow-up Study," *Review of Applied Urban Research* 89–1 (February 1989): 1–8.

29. Brown, *Working the Street*, 61–73, 75; "Lost Appeal"; Daryl F. Gates letter to Tom Bradley, December 29, 1980, folder 1, box 1644, MTBAP.

30. Mark Fabiani letter to Tom Houston and Craig Lawson, "The Mayor's Record: Crime and Criminal Justice," December 21, 1984, folder 17, box 194, MTBAP; "Rampart Community Crime Program Info," n.d., folder 3, box 107, MTBAP; Oscar Joel Bryant Association, "OJB Bust on Crime," 1983, folder 5, box 107, MTBAP.

31. Board of Police Commissioners, *The Report of the Board of Police Commissioners Concerning the Shooting of Eula Love and the Use of Deadly Force: Part II Investigation and Adjudication of Use of Force Incidents*, 1979, folder 7, box 102, CAPA; Ruben Smith, Karen Posnick, Davis Ortiz, and Joel R. Daniel, "Systems Analysis of Officer Involved Shootings, 1978 The Los Angeles Police Department," January 22, 1979, folder 30, box 12, CAPA; Pulido, *Black, Brown*, 45–48.

32. CAPA, "C.A.P.A. Proposal to Liberty Hill, Exhibits," 1976, folder 6, box 3, LHFC; "People United Newsletter," June 1977, folder 53, box 116, CAPA; C.A.P.A. "Steering Committee Meeting Minutes—CAPA (2)," October 1, 1976, folder 39, box 86, CAPA; Betty Liddick, "To Be Young, Gifted, Black . . . and Dead: Tragedy of a Pacoima

Youth," *LAT*, March 5, 1976, sec. Part 4. I explore CAPA in more depth in Felker-Kantor, "Coalition against Police Abuse."

33. C.A.P.A., "C.A.P.A. Proposal to Liberty Hill," 1977, folder 5, box 3, LHFC; Duren, Bob D., and Michael Zinzun, "C.a.p.a.," n.d., folder Federal Agencies, box 10, CAPA.

34. C.A.P.A. "C.A.P.A. Organizing Manual," 1977, folder 5, box 3, LHFC; Vargas, *Catching Hell*, 111–12.

35. C.A.P.A. "By-Laws Committee," July 20, 1976, folder 49, box 18, CAPA; Roche, "Unfinished Business," 137–39; Vargas, *Catching Hell*, 109–40.

36. C.A.P.A. "C.A.P.A. Organizing Manual," 1977, folder 5, box 3, LHFC; see also Roche, "Unfinished Business"; Vargas, *Catching Hell*.

37. Vargas, *Catching Hell*, 113.

38. C.A.P.A., "Steering Committee Meeting—CAPA," August 7, 1976, folder 49, box 18, CAPA.

39. C.A.P.A., "Steering Committee Workshop Minutes—CAPA," September 4, 1976, folder 40, box 86, CAPA.

40. Joe Williams, "C.A.P.A. Research Committee," May 24, 1977, folder 13, box 110, CAPA.

41. Roche, "Unfinished Business," 189; For examples of complaint forms, see ACLU, "ACLU Complaint Forms," 1979, folder ACLU Complaint 1979, box 8, CAPA.

42. John Van de Kamp, "Statement of District Attorney John K. Van De Kamo RE Final District Attorney/Attorney General Report on Destruction of 'Other-Than-Sustained' Complaint Files by the Los Angeles Police Department," February 6, 1978, folder 1, box 34, HMP; *Final Report on the Investigation of the Destruction of Internal Affairs Division of the Los Angeles Police Department Documents*, February 3, 1978, folder 1, box 34, HMP.

43. C.A.P.A., "Radio Statement," March 11, 1977, folder Correspondence—In, box 10, CAPA; Gene Blake, "Police, Attorney Hit for Destroying Files: Judge Says Deceit Was Used to Get OK to Shred Records Criticizing Officers," *LAT*, January 24, 1977, sec. Part 1; Gene Blake, "Police Shredding of Files Leads to Case Dismissals," *LAT*, April 8, 1977, sec. Part 1.

44. Hugh R. Manes, "What to Do When Police Stop You," n.d., folder 23, box 46, CAPA.

45. Michael Zinzun Defense Committee, "Michael Zinzun vs Penal Code 69," 1982, folder 1, box 39, RMP; Coalition Against Police Abuse, *C.A.P.A. Report 1983–84*; Michael Zinzun Defense Committee, "For Release: Demand Justice for Steve Rivers/A. Frank Taylor/Michael Zinzun," July 21, 1986, folder Choke Holds LAPD, box 10, CAPA.

46. Cohen, *Deadly Force*; "Police Station Demonstration: 70 Protest Shooting Death of Nude Man," *LAT*, August 15, 1977, sec. Orange County; Commanding Officer, Public Disorder Intelligence Division, "Divisional Intelligence Summary," September 7, 197, folder 9, box 82, CAPA; "What Took So Long?," *LAS*, September 8, 1977; Dale Fetherling and Michael A. Levett, "Police Gun Rules Tightened: Value of Human Life Must Be Guide, Commission Says," *LAT*, September 9, 1977, sec. Part 1; Board of Police Commissioners, "Police Commission Meeting Transcript," September 8, 1977, folder 11, box 40, UPRI; Craig D. Uchida, Lawrence W. Sherman, James F. Fyfe, and Police

Foundation (U.S.), *Police Shootings and the Prosecutor in Los Angeles County: An Evaluation of Operation Rollout*, Police Foundation, 1981.

47. Julian Bond, ed., "Forum: 'Ten Years after the Kerner Report: The Mayors Look at Their Cities,'" August 8, 1978, folder 9, box 2728, MTBAP.

48. Board of Police Commissioners, *The Report of the Board of Police Commissioners Concerning the Shooting of Eula Love and the Use of Deadly Force: Part I The Shooting of Eula Love*, 1979, folder 7, box 102, CAPA; [Michael Zinzun], "Mrs. Eula Mae Love—WHAT REALLY HAPPENED?," 1979, folder 25, box 55, CAPA. There was some debate over the amount of the gas bill and the $22 figure referred to the amount needed to keep Love's gas on, see L.C. Fortenberry, "GAS BILL RESULTS IN DEATH: Cops Slay Widow," LAS, January 11, 1979, p. A1.

49. Domanick, *To Protect and to Serve*, 259.

50. Board of Police Commissioners, *The Report of the Board of Police Commissioners Concerning the Shooting of Eula Love and the Use of Deadly Force: Part III Training and Community Relations*, 1979, folder 7, box 102, CAPA; Carey McWilliams, "Second Thoughts," *Nation*, May 19, 1979, 558.

51. "The Time Is Now," *LAS*, March 1, 1979.

52. Thomas Kilgore, "Rev. Tom Kilgore Censures *The Sentinel*," *LAS*, March 22, 1979; Jim Cleaver, "You Can't Be Everything to Everybody," *LAS*, March 22, 1979.

53. Citizen's Commission on Police Repression, "The Rap Sheet," April 1979, folder 10, box 4, RG 9, MALDEFR; Doug Shuit, "Black Leaders Voice Anger with LAPD: Claim Excessive Force and Harassment Are Prevalent in South-Central L.A. Black Leaders Angry with Police Policies," *LAT*, August 10, 1978.

54. Charles Blake et al., letter to Fellow Clergymen, January 17, 1979, folder 3, box 2736, Group V, NAACPRLC; The Gathering, "Working Committee on Community and Police Issues," March 22, 1979, folder 3, box 2736, Group V, NAACPRLC.

55. "The Chronology of the Eula Love Case," 1979, folder 15, box 40, UPRI; Penelope McMillan, "Mayor Calls Meeting on Police 'Tension,'" *LAT*, October 13, 1979, sec. Part 2; "Gates 'Dumbfounded' by Mayor's Remarks," *LAS*, May 10, 1979.

56. District Attorney, *District Attorney Report on Fatal Shooting of Mrs. Eula Mae Love*, April 16, 1979, folder 13, box 40, UPRI.

57. Ed Davis, "Bradley: Review Love Shooting!: 'Weed Out Racism'—Kilgore," *LAS*, April 26, 1979; "Plaudits for Tom," *LAS*, May 10, 1979.

58. George Skelton, "Public Taking Dimmer View of L.A. Police," *LAT*, May 15, 1979, sec. Part 1; Racial disparities in approval developed prior to the Love killing; see "The LAPD: How Good Is It?," *LAT*, December 18, 1977, 5, folder 3, box 36, UPRI.

59. Board of Police Commissioners, *The Report of the Board of Police Commissioners Concerning the Shooting of Eula Love and the Use of Deadly Force: Part I The Shooting of Eula Love*, 1979, folder 7, box 102, CAPA; Board of Police Commissioners, *The Report of the Board of Police Commissioners Concerning the Shooting of Eula Love and the Use of Deadly Force: Part III Training and Community Relations*, 1979, folder 7, box 102, CAPA.

60. Daryl F. Gates, "Special Order No. 32," September 26, 1979, folder 4, box 7, MR; City Administrative Officer letter to Finance and Revenue Committee and Police, Fire and Civil Defense Committee, "Police Procedures for Reviewing Officer Actions,"

October 29, 1981, folder 7, box 2802, MTBAP; Claire Spiegel, "Gates, Reinhardt Agree to End Love Shooting Dispute," *LAT*, October 16, 1979, b1; Doug Shuit, "Board Seeks to Mend LAPD Ties to City's Blacks: Black Panel on Police Formed," *LAT*, January 9, 1980, sec. Orange County; Doug Shuit and Penelope McMillan, "Commissioners Oppose Police Review Board," *LAT*, October 17, 1979, a7.

61. Hispanic Advisory Council, "Statement of Purpose," n.d., folder 4, box 7, MR; J. Michael Kennedy, "Youth Slain in Policeman Error," *LAT*, October 16, 1980, sec. Part 1.

62. Eric Malnic and J. Michael Kennedy, "L.A. Officer Shoots, Kills Unarmed Man," *LAT*, October 17, 1980, sec. Part 2.

63. Hispanic Advisory Council, "Evaluation and Critical Analysis of the Report on LAPD Officer-Involved Shootings, 1974–1978/9," 1980, folder 4, box 7, MR; Hispanic Advisory Council, "Hispanic Council Urges More Spanish Language and Culture Training for Police," June 9, 1981, folder 4, box 7, MR; Fred David, "L.A. Police to Get More Training in Latin Culture: LAPD: Cultural Training," *LAT*, August 3, 1985, sec. Valley.

64. U.S. Congress, House, Committee on the Judiciary, Subcommittee on Crime, Committee on the Judiciary, *Police and the Use of Deadly Force*, 3.

65. Police, Fire and Public Civil Defense, *Police, Fire and Civil Defense Report*, June 13, 1978, folder PDID, box 758964, RFP; Robert Farrell letter to Mariana R. Pfaelzer, July 25, 1978, box 758964, RFP.

66. David Johnston, "Bradley Orders Probe of Statements by Gates: 'Disparaging' Remarks about Blacks, Jews, Latinos to Be Investigated by Police Commission," *LAT*, May 11, 1982. On deaths between 1975 and 1981, see "Appendix on Choke Hold Case," 1982, box 758964, RFP.

67. Cannon, *Official Negligence*, 97.

68. Robert Farrell, "Motion," June 18, 1980, folder 20, box 23, CAPA.

69. "Lyons vs. City of Los Angeles: Court Docs," 1980, folder City of Los Angeles v. Lyons, box 76, Group 5, NAACPRLC; Robert Farrell, "Statement of Robert C. Farrell Re: James Mincey, Jr.," April 14, 1982, box 758964, RFP; Howard Finn, "Councilman Howard Finn's Statement before the Police, Fire and Public Safety Committee," April 14, 1982, box 758964, RFP; City Council letter to Tom Bradley, "City Council: Choke Holds," August 21, 1981; Daryl F. Gates letter to Honorable Board of Police Commissioners, "Update on Use of Force 'Choke Hold,'" March 30, 1981; Daryl F. Gates, "Restatement of Department Position on the Limitations to the Use of the Upper Body Control Holds," 1982; Daryl F. Gates, "Statement of Department Position on Proposed Moratorium on the Use of Upper Body Control Holds by the Los Angeles Police Department," 1982, all in box 758964, RFP.

70. Cannon, *Official Negligence*, 100; Gates, *Chief*, 214–16.

71. David Johnston, "Bradley Orders Probe of Statements by Gates," *LAT*, May 11, 1982, folder 35, box 74, NAACPRR; "L.A. Furor on Chief's Words about Blacks," *San Francisco Chronicle*, May 11, 1982, folder 34, box 74, NAACPRR; John W. Mack, "Statement by John W. Mack, President Los Angeles Urban League," May 11, 1982, folder 3, box 3178, MTBAP.

72. Dave Cunningham, "Statement by Councilman Dave Cunningham," May 10, 1982, folder 3, box 3178, MTBAP.

73. Daryl F. Gates, "Memorandum No. 6 Moratorium on the Use of Upper Body Control Holds," June 18, 1982, folder Choke Holds LAPD, box 10, CAPA.

74. Myrna Oliver, "Chokehold Victim Wins $1.3 Million," *LAT*, December 18, 1982, sec. Part 1; "Richard Simon, "L.A. Will Pay $585,000 in Chokehold Death," *LAT*, April 3, 1986, sec. Valley; James Rainey, "Final Suit over LAPD's Use of Chokehold Settled," *LAT*, September 29, 1993, sec. Metro.

75. Daryl F. Gates, "Training Bulletin: Use of Force, Chemical Irritant Control Devices," August 1983, folder 9, box 102, CAPA; Los Angeles Police Department, *Annual Report*, 1980.

76. Campaign for a Citizens Police Review Board, "For an END to POLICE CRIMES," 1980, folder 2, box 39, RMP; Campaign for a Citizens Police Review Board, "Statement of Campaign for a Citizens' Police Review Board," January 3, 1980, folder 3, box 39, RMP.

77. Campaign for a Citizens' Police Review Board, "Campaign for a Citizens Police Review Board Flier," 1980, folder 2, box 40, UPRI; Interim Steering Committee of the Coalition for a Civilian Review Board letter to All L.A. Residents and Organizations Concerned about Police Abuse, "Initiative Campaign Meeting," July 2, 1979, folder 2, box 16, CAPA; Campaign for a Citizens Police Review Board, "Release," April 10, 1980, folder 1, box 39, RMP.

78. Coalition against Police Abuse, "Proposal: Civilian Police Review Board and Documentation Centers," 1980, folder 8, box 14, EPP.

79. Campaign for a Citizens' Police Review Board, "Vote for Citizens Review Board," 1980, folder 11, box 7, CAPA.

80. Citizens for a Civilian Review Board, "Citizens Review Board Recommendation Statement of Purpose," 1980, folder 101, box 110, CAPA.

81. For a general discussion of civilian review and oversight, see Walker, *Police Accountability*; Walker and Archbold, *New World*. For a critique of police reform, see Vitale, *End of Policing*.

82. Quentin Banks, Anne F. Davis, Jeff Cohen, Mark Ridley-Thomas, and R. Samuel Paz. "Proposed Amendments to the City Charter Establishing an Elected Citizens' Police Review Board and a Special City Prosecutor," 1980, folder 6, box 7, CAPA; Campaign for a Citizens' Police Review Board, "Campaign for a Citizens Police Review Board Flier," 1980, folder 2, box 40, UPRI.

83. Penelope McMillan, "Coalition Begins Drive to Place Civilian Police Review Board on November Ballot," *LAT*, January 4, 1980, sec. Part 2; Campaign for a Citizens' Police Review Board, "Campaign for a Citizens Police Review Board Flier," 1980, folder 2, box 40, UPRI.

84. Doug Shuit and Penelope McMillan, "Commissioners Oppose Police Review Board," *LAT*, October 17, 1979, a7; Fred W. Kline, "The Effort Is On in Los Angeles to Emasculate Police Department," April 11, 1980, folder 11, box 22, CAPA.

85. Ron Burns, "Gates: Review Board a Potential 'Kangaroo Court,'" *LAHE*, March 24, 1980, folder 3, box 39, RMP.

86. "Critics Seeking Review Board Say They're Trying to Help Police: Critics Seeking Review Board Claim to Aid Police," *LAT*, January 13, 1980, sec. West Side; Doug Shuit, "Calls for Police Review Board Renewed: Mrs. Love's Neighbors Voice Shock, Anger over DA's Decision," *LAT*, April 18, 1979, sec. Part 1; Michael Marten, "Policing the LAPD," *LAHE*, May 12, 1979, folder 6, box 16, CAPA.

87. Jeff Cohen, "Campaign Begins for Police Review Board in L.A.," *Open Forum*, February 1980, folder 12, box 9, TCOF.

88. "The Time Is Now!" *LAS*, February 28, 1980.

89. Nick Brown, "Review Board Support Grows," *LAS*, April 17, 1980.

90. Nick Brown, "Police Review Board Push Still On," *LAS*, August 28, 1980; "Review Board Push Nears End," *LAS*, May 22, 1980; Campaign for a Citizens' Police Review Board, "Rally against Police Abuse," September 13, 1980, folder 8, box 19, SLAC.

Chapter 6

1. U.S. Congress, Senate, Committee on the Judiciary, Subcommittee to Investigate the Administration of the Internal Security Act and Other Internal Security Laws, *Erosion of Law Enforcement Intelligence Gathering Capabilities*, 3–5, 7.

2. Donner, *Protectors of Privilege*, 1–6, 272; Churchill and Wall, *Agents of Repression*; Rothmiller and Goldman, *L.A. Secret Police*; in general, see Marx, *Undercover*; Parenti, *Soft Cage*; Rosenfeld, *Subversives*; Perlstein, *Nixonland*; Perlstein, *Invisible Bridge*; Kohler-Hausmann, *Getting Tough*. For a timeline, see Stop LAPD Spying Coalition, "Timeline of LAPD Spying and Surveillance," www.stopladpspying.org. On surveillance and domestic counterinsurgency see Harcourt, *Counterrevolution*. On repression of radical movements, surveillance, and the carceral state, see Berger, "Social Movements"; Browne, *Dark Matters*.

3. Dave Lindorff, "Police Spies in the City of Angels," *Nation*, May 5, 1984, 537–40. For the broadening of the definition of terrorism, see Davis, *Freedom*, 78–79; Singh, *Race and America's*.

4. Donner, *Protectors of Privilege*, 245–46, 249–54; Board of Police Commissioners, "Statement of the Los Angeles Board of Police Commissioners on the Public Disorder Intelligence Function of the Los Angeles Police Department," April 10, 1975, folder 24, box 41, UPRI; McClellan, "Policing the Red Scare."

5. *Confidential Report on Paul Documents*, n.d., unfiled, box B-1834, PDX/BSI; Donner, *Protectors of Privilege*, 252–53. On LAPD intelligence units monitoring "racial matters" and "potential violence," see SAC, Los Angeles to Director, FBI, "Racial Riots, Los Angeles Division, Racial Matters," September 7, 1964, RD 38233 URTS 15945, DOCID-70100614, FOIA—FBI Files, RG 60, NARA.

6. "Proceedings of the National Advisory Commission on Civil Disorders," November 2, 1967, folder 15, box 38, UPRI; Vigil, *Crusade for Justice*, 154.

7. John Dreyfuss, "Secret Program to Put Down Riots Drafted by L.A. Police," *LAT*, February 15, 1968, sec. Part 2; Joe Gunn, "Management Control and Utilization of Informants," April 10, 1974, folder 22, box 77, CAPA.

8. National Advisory Commission on Civil Disorders, "Proceedings of the National Advisory Commission on Civil Disorders," November 2, 1967, folder 15, box 38, UPRI. See also FBI and LAPD surveillance and use of informants in RD 38314 URTS 15950, FOIA—FBI Files, RG 60, NARA.

9. Donner, *Protectors of Privilege*, 260–66; Tackwood, *Glass House Tapes*, 30; J. W. Thompson, "Divisional Intelligence Summary," September 17, 1971, folder 2, box 88, CAPA; Patty Lee Parmalee, "Los Angeles Police Agent Reveals Frameup of Left," *Guardian*, November 10, 1971, folder 28, box 33, CAPA; Roy Haynes, "Former Panther

Was Police Agent, Shootout Trial Told: PANTHER TRIAL," *LAT*, November 24, 1971, sec. Part 1.

10. U.S. Congress, Senate, Committee on the Judiciary, Subcommittee to Investigate the Administration of the Internal Security Act and Other Internal Security Laws, *Extent of Subversion in the 'New Left' Testimony of Robert J. Thoms*, 1970; Julian J. Keiser, "An Analysis of Sergeant Thoms' Testimony: A Presentation before the Law and Justice Task Force of the Los Angeles Urban Coalition," April 13, 1970, folder Appropriations—Controversial Documents, box 91, AHP.

11. "This Material Is Supplied by the President of the Los Angeles City Council to the Members of the Los Angeles Area Chamber of Commerce Leadership Trip to Washington, D.C. and to Members of the Los Angeles Five County Delegation in Congress for Information and Use as Deemed Appropriate by the Recipients," April 1970, folder Appropriations—Controversial Documents, box 91, AHP.

12. Jack Jones, "Report That Militants Get Poverty Funds Hit," *LAT*, May 26, 1970, sec. Part 2; David Martin letter to Brownlee Haydon, "Information Regarding Thoms Testimony," May 26, 1970, folder 1, box 45, UPRI.

13. U.S. Congress, Senate, Committee on the Judiciary, Subcommittee to Investigate the Administration of the Internal Security Act and Other Internal Security Laws, *Assaults on Law Enforcement Officers*, 329.

14. Dave Lindorff, "Police Spies in the City of Angels," *Nation*, May 5, 1984, 537–40. On the intersection of surveillance and social control see Cohen, *Visions of Social Control*.

15. U.S. Congress, Senate, Committee on the Judiciary, Subcommittee to Investigate the Administration of the Internal Security Act and Other Internal Security Laws, *Assaults on Law Enforcement Officers*, 331.

16. U.S. Congress, Senate, Committee on the Judiciary, Subcommittee to Investigate the Administration of the Internal Security Act and Other Internal Security Laws, *Erosion of Law Enforcement*, 2.

17. Donner, *Protectors of Privilege*, 253–56; Edward M. Davis, "Statement by Chief Davis for the L.A. Times," December 10, 1975, folder 1, box 42, UPRI; Chief of Police letter to Honorable Board of Police Commissioners, "Management Accountability for PDID—Chief of Police's Perspective," December 21, 1984, folder Police Deployment and Increase (2), box B-665, JWP.

18. Doug Shuit, "Davis Requested to Study Cut in Police Intelligence Squad," *LAT*, November 8, 1973, sec. Part 2; Anton Calleia, "Los Angeles City Budget during the Bradley Administration," 1994, ACP.

19. Jeffrey Kaye, "Better Shred than Read," *New West*, June 5, 1978, folder 12, box 9, TCOF. This was a different file shredding scandal than the one mentioned in chapter 5 related to complaints of police abuse. On Watergate and the Church Committee see Perlstein, *Invisible Bridge*.

20. Board of Police Commissioners, "Statement of the Los Angeles Board of Police Commissioners on the Public Disorder Intelligence Function of the Los Angeles Police Department," April 10, 1975, folder 24, box 41, UPRI; Board of Police Commissioners, *Audit Report: Public Disorder Intelligence Division*, October 31, 1978, folder 2, box 103, SWP.

21. Donner, *Protectors of Privilege*, 267.

22. Board of Police Commissioners, "Statement of the Los Angeles Board of Police Commissioners on the Public Disorder Intelligence Function of the Los Angeles Police Department," April 10, 1975, folder 24, box 41, UPRI.

23. Tom Bradley, "Statement by Mayor Bradley on Public Disorder Related Intelligence Gatherings," April 10, 1975, folder 24, box 41, UPRI; L.A.P.D., "The Los Angeles Police Department Public Disorder Intelligence Division Standards and Procedures," April 10, 1975, folder 28, box 33, CAPA; Los Angeles County Bar Association, *Los Angeles County Bar Association's Report on the Public Disorder Intelligence Division Standards*, October 30, 1975, folder 1, box 42, UPRI.

24. Mae Churchill, "Statement by Mae Churchill to the Los Angeles Police Commission on the Subject of Public Disorder Intelligence Files," April 26, 1975, folder 24, box 41, UPRI; Mae Churchill, "A Modest Proposal," December 4, 1975, folder 24, box 41, UPRI; George Abdo, "Statement to the Los Angeles Police Commission," December 4, 1975, folder 1, box 42, UPRI.

25. Donner, *Protectors of Privilege*, 269; Edward M. Davis, "Statement by Chief Davis for the L.A. Times," December 10, 1975, folder 1, box 42, UPRI; U.S. Congress, Senate, Committee on the Judiciary, Subcommittee to Investigate the Administration of the Internal Security Act and Other Internal Security Laws, *Erosion of Law Enforcement Intelligence Gathering Capabilities*, 3.

26. On Los Angeles press coverage of right-wing bombings, see Donner, *Protectors of Privilege*, 422n55. For the LAPD's portrayal of the SLA shootout, see LAPD, *The Symbionese Liberation Army in Los Angeles* (Los Angeles: Los Angeles Police Department, 1974), BC. On national right-wing movements, see Cunningham, *There's Something Happening Here*; Cunningham, *Klansville, U.S.A.*; Belew, *Bring the War Home*.

27. Donner, *Protectors of Privilege*; 269; Erwin Baker, "Bradley Disputes Davis Claim of Opposition to Police Unit," *LAT*, December 4, 1976, sec. Part 2.

28. Board of Police Commissioners, "Police Commission Meeting," December 16, 1976, folder 2, box 103, SWP; LAPD, "Standards and Procedures for the Los Angeles Police Department Public Disorder Intelligence Division Files," December 16, 1976, B-2209, Police Department, PDX.

29. Donner, *Protectors of Privilege*, 267.

30. John K. Van de Kamp and William R. Weisman, *Report Concerning the Investigation of the Public Disorder Intelligence Division of the Los Angeles Police Department*, October 15, 1985, folder 26, box 42, UPRI.

31. Board of Police Commissioners, "In the Matter of the Report on Status of Public Disorder Intelligence Division," October 24, 1978, folder 2, box 103, SWP.

32. U.S. Congress, Senate, Committee on the Judiciary, Subcommittee to Investigate the Administration of the Internal Security Act and Other Internal Security Laws, *Erosion of Law Enforcement Intelligence*, 3; Escobar, "Dialectics of Repression," 1493.

33. *Confidential Report on Paul Documents*, n.d., unfiled, box B-1834, PDX/BSI; "Intelligence Briefing (July 18)," July 18, 1978, folder 13, box 82, CAPA.

34. "Intelligence Briefing: 009556," May 4, 1976, folder 16, box 92, CAPA; "Divisional Intelligence Summary," June 14, 1976, folder 13, box 82, CAPA.

35. "Intelligence Briefing," June 1, 1976, folder 14, box 82, CAPA; L.A.P.D., and PDID, *Confidential Report on NLG*, n.d., folder 7, box 92, CAPA; "Intelligence Briefing: 009087 (Sam Paz Letter)," 1979 1978, folder 16, box 92, CAPA.

36. Dick Roberts, "Pdid," n.d., folder 5, box 103, SWP; C.A.P.A., "C.A.P.A. Steering Committee Meeting and Special Program," June 5, 1979, folder Correspondence—Outgoing, box 10, CAPA; "Intelligence Briefing: CAPA Update," March 17, 1978, folder 14, box 82, CAPA.

37. L.R. Linn & Associates, "Anthony J. Thigpenn Deposition," 1983, folder 5, box 76, CAPA; Dick Roberts, "Pdid," n.d., folder 5, box 103, SWP.

38. Superior Court of the State of California for the County of Los Angeles, "Deposition of Daryl F. Gates, Vol. III," May 20, 1983, folder 7, box 43, UPRI.

39. Citizens' Commission on Police Repression, "The Rap Sheet," July 1980, folder Coalition to Free Geronimo Pratt, box 8, CAPA. Two examples of such intelligence briefings are J. W. Thompson letter to Jack G. Collins, "Intelligence Summary," September 10, 1973, folder CAPA v. PDID, box 16, CAPA; W. J. Thompson, "Divisional Intelligence Summary," May 21, 1973, folder 3, box 82, CAPA.

40. "Deposition of Edward Brimmer," August 31, 1983, folder 32, box 42, UPRI.

41. Superior Court of the State of California for the County of Los Angeles, "Deposition of David Bryant, Vol. I," July 25, 1983, folder 1, box 43, UPRI.

42. "Deposition of David Bryant, Vol. I"; Superior Court of the State of California for the County of Los Angeles, "Deposition of David Bryant, Vol. III," July 27, 1983, folder 3, box 43, UPRI.

43. Superior Court of the State of California for the County of Los Angeles, "Deposition of Edward Brimmer," August 31, 1983, folder 32, box 42, UPRI.

44. "Superior Court of the State of California for the County of Los Angeles, "Deposition of David Bryant, Vol. III," July 27, 1983, folder 3, box 43, UPRI; Superior Court of the State of California for the County of Los Angeles, "Deposition of David Bryant, Vol. II," July 26, 1983, folder 2, box 43, UPRI; Superior Court of the State of California for the County of Los Angeles, "Deposition of Edward Brimmer," August 31, 1983, folder 32, box 42, UPRI.

45. Citizens' Commission on Police Repression, "Release of Discovery Documents—Bradley/UFW Reports," 1981, folder Public Disorder Intelligence Division [PDID]/Freedom of Information, box C-0562, PRP; Melonson, "Intelligence Briefing: CAPA Holds Meeting on Police Infiltrators," June 7, 1979, folder 2, box 82, CAPA.

46. "Divisional Intelligence Summary," October 20, 1975, folder 3, box 82, CAPA; "Intelligence Briefing," n.d., folder 32, box 16, CAPA.

47. Thompson, J. W. Letter to R. F. Rock, "Intelligence Briefing," April 23, 1974, folder 32, box 16, CAPA; Thompson, J. W. Letter to R. F. Rock, "Intelligence Briefing," April 30, 1974, folder 32, box 16, CAPA; "Intelligence Briefing," February 4, 1975, folder 3, box 82, CAPA; Thompson, J. W. Letter to Jack G. Collins, "Divisional Intelligence Summary," July 15, 1974, folder 32, box 16, CAPA; "CASA FOIA Documents," n.d., FBI FOIA Request, 1199189-000-105-LA-31729—Section 1-4; Haney-López, *Racism on Trial*, 37–40. For more on Bert Corona see García, *Memories of Chicano History*. For CASA see Pulido, *Black, Brown, Yellow, and Left*.

48. Joel Sappell, "Two LAPD Spies Tell Their Story," *LAHE*, June 16, 1980, folder 7, box 16, CAPA.

49. Southern California Network against Government Spying letter to Friend, n.d., folder 2, box 16, CAPA; Unknown, "Intelligence Briefing: New Anti-Surveillance Group Formed," 1978, folder 13, box 82, CAPA; Citizens' Commission on Police Repression, "The Rap Sheet," May 1979, folder 11, box 22, CAPA.

50. "Snooping by the LAPD," *LAHE*, March 20, 1978, folder 4, box 16, CAPA; Elizabeth Thompson, "'Police Spying' on L.A. Activist Groups Scored: 200 Organizations Purported to Be Surveillance Targets Reforms in L.A. Police Intelligence Urged," *LAT*, July 19, 1978, sec. Part 2; Elizabeth Thompson, "L.A. Councilman Criticizes 'Police Spying' on Activists," *LAT*, July 19, 1978, sec. Part 2.

51. Jeff Gottleib, "Police Spying in Los Angeles," *Inquiry*, January 8, 1979, folder 2, box 16, CAPA; "Police Spying: Wrong—and Right," *LAT*, July 21, 1978, sec. Part 2; Zev Yaroslavsky, "Statement by Councilman Zev Yaroslavsky to the Police, Fire, and Public Safety Committee," August 31, 1978, folder 4, box 16, CAPA; Citizens' Commission on Police Repression, "The Rap Sheet," September 1979, folder 10, box 42, UPRI.

52. "Untitled Summary of PDID Investigation," after 1984, folder 20, box 44, UPRI; Board of Police Commissioners, *Audit Report: Public Disorder Intelligence Division*, October 31, 1978, folder 2, box 103, SWP; Jeff Gottleib, "Police Spying in Los Angeles," *Inquiry*, January 8, 1979, folder 2, box 16, CAPA.

53. Nick Brown, "LAPD to Answer Spying Charges," *LAS*, July 6, 1978; Joel Sappel, "LAPD Accused of Spying on Anti-Spying Citizen's Group," *LAHE*, March 25, 1980, folder 1, box 39, RMP; Nick Brown, Citizens' Commission on Police Repression, "Statement by the Citizens' Commission on Police Repression on the Lawsuit against Los Angeles Police Department Spying," July 15, 1981, folder 2, box 16, CAPA; Citizens' Commission on Police Repression, "The Rap Sheet," August 1981, folder 12, box 6, MR; David Johnston, "5 L.A. Police Spy Suits May Be Settled: Out-of-Court Negotiations Under Way in Actions by Rights Groups," *LAT*, February 24, 1982, sec. Orange County.

54. Citizens' Commission on Police Repression, "The Rap Sheet," December 1979, folder 4, box 16, CAPA; John K. Van de Kamp and William R. Weisman, *Report Concerning the Investigation of the Public Disorder Intelligence Division of the Los Angeles Police Department*, October 15, 1985, folder 26, box 42, UPRI.

55. Linda Valentino, "Remarks before the Los Angeles City Council," July 18, 1978, folder 3, box 89, CAPA; Citizens' Commission on Police Repression, "Citizens Commission on Police Repression Minutes," November 3, 1978, folder 12, box 9, TCOF.

56. Citizens' Commission on Police Repression, "The Rap Sheet," April 1980, folder Coalition to Free Geronimo Pratt, box 8, CAPA; Citizens' Commission on Police Repression, "The Rap Sheet," May 1980, folder Coalition to Free Geronimo Pratt, box 8, CAPA; Linda Valentino letter to Pat Russell, July 5, 1983, folder Public Disorder Intelligence Division [PDID]/Freedom of Information, box C-0562, RFP; Patricia Klein, "Commission to Probe Claim of LAPD Spy in Eulia Love Group," *LAHE*, February 9, 1982, folder 16, box 16, CAPA.

57. David Johnston, "Panel Sides With LAPD on Spending: Controversy over Spy Unit Funding Expected to Continue," *LAT*, May 16, 1980, sec. Orange County.

58. Susan Schmidt, "Gates: Davis Target of 'Persecution,'" *LAHE*, June 4, 1980, folder 7, box 16, CAPA; City Council, "City Council File 82-1915," 1982, City Council

Files, folder File 82-1915, box C-521, Los Angeles City Archives; [PDID], "Intelligence Is Rarely the Mysterious Operation Decried by Its . . . ," 1980, folder 6, box 82, CAPA.

59. Citizens' Commission on Police Repression, "The Rap Sheet," April 1980, folder Coalition to Free Geronimo Pratt, box 8, CAPA; "LAPD Spy Charge: 'Was Political,'" *LAHE*, June 2, 1980, folder 7, box 16, CAPA.

60. Joel Sappell, "The Mayor 'Will Not Tolerate' LAPD Spying," *LAHE*, June 5, 1980, folder 7, box 16, CAPA.

61. Donner, *Protectors of Privilege*, 278; Joel Sappell, "The Mayor 'Will Not Tolerate' LAPD Spying," *LAHE*, June 5, 1980, folder 7, box 16, CAPA.

62. Joel Sappell, "Bradley Will Ask Gates to Report on Spying Charges," *LAHE*, June 18, 1980, folder 7, box 16, CAPA.

63. Daryl F. Gates, "Speech on the Activities of the Los Angeles Police Department's Public Disorder Intelligence Division," July 11, 1980, folder 31, box 3, CAPA; "Gates to Push for More Police Spying," *LAHE*, October 16, 1980, folder 7, box 16, CAPA; L.A.P.D., "L.A.P.D. White Paper to Media," January 21, 1982, folder 7, box 92, CAPA.

64. Jack B. White letter to Honorable Board of Police Commissioners, "Summary of the Public Disorder Intelligence Division Investigation," December 20, 1984, folder 17, box 16, CAPA.

65. Reva Berger Tooley, "Report by Commissioner Tooley to the Board of Police Commissioners on PDID Guideline Development," April 22, 1980, folder 2, box 103, SWP; LAPD, "Los Angeles Police Department Public Disorder Intelligence Division Operational Guidelines," April 22, 1980, folder 2, box 103, SWP; Board of Police Commissioners, *Audit Report: Public Disorder Intelligence Division*, November 17, 1981, folder 2, box 103, SWP.

66. Chief of Police letter to Honorable Board of Police Commissioners, "Annual Review of Public Disorder Intelligence Division Files," March 1, 1977, folder 2, box 103, SWP; see annual reviews from 1978–1982 in folder 2, box 103, SWP.

67. Donner, *Protectors of Privilege*, 281; LAPD, "Standards and Procedures for the Collection of Intelligence Information by the Los Angeles Police Department Public Disorder Intelligence Division," February 24, 1982, folder 28, box 33, CAPA.

68. [PDID], "PDID Information Regarding Organizations," 1982, folder 2, box 67, CAPA; Superior Court of the State of California for the County of Los Angeles, "Exhibit 7: Zaroslavsky to Tooley Letter October 12, 1982," 1983, folder 4, box 44, UPRI; Joel Sappell, "LAPD 'Spying' on the Council," *LAHE*, May 7, 1980, folder 6, box 103, SWP.

69. [PDID], "PDID Information Regarding Organizations," 1982, folder 2, box 67, CAPA.

70. Jack B. White letter to Honorable Board of Police Commissioners, "Summary of the Public Disorder Intelligence Division Investigation," December 20, 1984, folder 17, box 16, CAPA.

71. *Confidential Report on Paul Documents*, n.d., Los Angeles Police Commission, box B-1834, unfiled, Los Angeles City Archives; Superior Court of the State of California for the County of Los Angeles, "Deposition of Robert R. Loomis," October 14, 1983, folder 10, box 43, UPRI.

72. *Confidential Report on Paul Documents*, 1984, box B-1834, PDX/BSI; Superior Court of the State of California for the County of Los Angeles, "First Amended Complaint

for Injunctive and Declaratory Relief; Alliance for Survival Et al. vs. Western Goals Foundation, Et al.," December 16, 1982, folder 22, box 42, UPRI.

73. Donner, *Protectors of Privilege*, 284–85. During his tenure, Gates continued the longstanding argument of LAPD chiefs of police decrying the limits placed on police discretion, gathering of evidence, and intelligence operations by liberal politicians, court decisions, and anti–police abuse activists, see Los Angeles Police Department, *Annual Report*, 1978 for Gates' view and a photograph of an LAPD officer with his hands tied behind his back in front of a courthouse.

74. Reva Berger Tooley, "Statement Regarding PDID by Reva B. Tooley, President of the Los Angeles Police Commission," October 12, 1982, folder 3, box 3178, MTBAP; Board of Police Commissioners, "Hearing before the Board of Police Commissioners of the City of Los Angeles," 1983, folder Public Disorder Intelligence Division, box 758965, RFP; Joel Sappell and David Johnston, "Spying Probe Expanded by Police Board," *LAT*, October 13, 1982, sec. Part 2; Andy Furillo, "Study Blames Gates, Top Aides for Spying Violations: PDID: Report Says Gates Misled City on Spying PDID," *LAT*, November 18, 1984, sec. Part 2.

75. Superior Court of the State of California for the County of Los Angeles, "Deposition of Reva Berger Tooley, Vol. I," September 23, 1983, folder 1, box 44, UPRI; Board of Police Commissioners, "Hearing before the Board of Police Commissioners of the City of Los Angeles," 1983, folder Public Disorder Intelligence Division, box 758965, RFP; Board of Police Commissioners, "In a Matter of Consideration of a Statement Relative to the Public Disorder Intelligence Division," January 18, 1983, folder 2, box 103, SWP.

76. City Council, "City Council File 83-1216," 1980–1985, folder File 82-1915, box C-521, CCF; City Council, "City Council File 82-1915," 1982, folder File 82-1915, box C-521, CCF; Board of Police Commissioners, "In a Matter of Consideration of a Statement Relative to the Public Disorder Intelligence Division," January 18, 1983, folder 2, box 103, SWP.

77. Zev Yaroslavsky, "Statement from Zev Yaroslavsky to Los Angeles City Council's Police, Fire and Public Safety Committee," February 14, 1983, folder 2, box 1547, MTBAP; Superior Court of the State of California for the County of Los Angeles, "Exhibit 7: Zaroslavsky to Tooley Letter October 12, 1982," 1983, folder 4, box 44, UPRI.

78. Los Angeles Police Department, "Standards and Procedures for the Collection, Maintenance and Dissemination of Intelligence Information by the Anti-Terrorist Division," July 1, 1983, folder 16, box 37, CAPA.

79. J. Brewer, M. Kroeker, and L. Kramer, *Report of the Public Disorder Intelligence Division Transition Team*, February 24, 1983, folder 2, box 1547, MTBAP.

80. Farber, *Taken Hostage*; Westad, *Global Cold War*, 331–64.

81. Dick Roberts, "Pdid," n.d., folder 5, box 103, SWP.

82. "LAPD Spy Settlement," *LAT*, February 21, 1984, sec. Part 1—Late Final; Dave Lindorff, "Police Spies in the City of Angels," *Nation*, May 5, 1984, 537–40.

83. Roxane Arnold and Joel Sappell, "Consent Decree Leaves L.A. with Toughest Police-Spy Rules in Country," *LAT*, February 23, 1984, sec. San Diego County.

84. "Settlement Agreement," 1984, folder 17, box 16, CAPA; CAPA., *C.A.P.A. Report 1983–84*, 1984, folder 5, box 55, CAPA.

85. Jack B. White letter to Honorable Board of Police Commissioners, "Summary of the Public Disorder Intelligence Division Investigation," December 20, 1984, folder 17, box 16, CAPA.

86. Daryl F. Gates, "Open Letter to Citizens of Los Angeles," July 1, 1983, folder Public Disorder Intelligence Division [PDID]/Freedom of Information, box C-0562, RFP; Daryl F. Gates, "Speech on the Activities of the Los Angeles Police Department's Public Disorder Intelligence Division," July 11, 1980, folder 31, box 3, CAPA; Joel Sappell, "Gates Admits Failure to Guide Intelligence Unit," *LAT*, January 24, 1983, sec. Part 2.

87. Richard Hansen, "L.A. Unit Being 'Deactivated': Activists Harass Police 'Red Squad,'" *Guardian Bureau*, n.d., folder 5, box 103, SWP; Superior Court of the State of California for the County of Los Angeles, "Exhibit 8: Before the Board of Police Commissioners January 18, 1983," folder 4, box 44, UPRI.

88. CCPR, "The Rap Sheet," September 1979, folder 10, box 42, UPRI.

89. Daryl F. Gates, "Proposed City of Los Angeles Freedom of Information Ordinance: Position of the Chief of Police," March 11, 1983, folder Public Disorder Intelligence Division, box 758965, RFP; Zev Yaroslavsky, "Summary of 1983 Freedom of Information Ordinance," 1983, folder 25, box 41, UPRI. On the LAPD's response to the freedom of information ordinance and the role of the ATD see Los Angeles Police Department, *Annual Report*, 1983.

90. William Overend, "Schlei Bids a Tearful Farewell to LAPD," *LAT*, September 21, 1988, sec. Part 2.

91. Rich Connell, "Police Commission Neglected Required File Audits: Surveillance: Turnover on the Panel Has Prevented Review of Data Mandated in Settlement of Spying Lawsuit, Officials Say," *LAT*, June 14, 1991, sec. Ventura County; Rich Connell and Glenn F. Bunting, "King Aftermath Rekindles Police Spying Controversy: Politics: No Proof of Secret Dossiers Exists, but Some Say Fear Alone Is Enough for Public Figures to Back Gates," *LAT*, June 18, 1991.

92. Jim Newton, "LAPD Pushing to Relax Limits on Undercover Probes; Enforcement: Officials Say Electronic Surveillance and Other Techniques Are Needed to Counter Terrorist Threats. Critics Recall Spying Scandal That Prompted Restrictions," *LAT*, October 11, 1996, sec. Part A; Metro Desk; "Balancing Anti-Terrorism with Prudence Police Commission Needs to Be Careful Not to Grant LAPD Too Much Discretion," *LAT*, July 9, 1995, sec. Opinion; Jim Newton, "Police Panel Votes to Loosen Curbs on Intelligence Work; Law Enforcement: Officials Cite Threat of Terrorism in Seeking Changes. Commissioners Vow Strong Oversight to Prevent Recurrence of Past Spying Scandals," *LAT*, October 16, 1996, sec. Part A; Metro Desk. On the expansion of police surveillance more broadly see Friedman, *Unwarranted*.

Chapter 7

1. Chief of Police, "Undocumented Aliens," August 15, 1977, folder Chief of Police, box 126, GMDP. See also the arrest of Rosa Gallegos for illegal entry in the same document.

2. For the LAPD's view of undocumented immigrants and crime see Joint Crime Suppression Task Force, "Los Angeles Police Study of Impact of Illegal Aliens on Crime in L. A.—Ramparts Division Case Study," September 3, 1974, HV 7595.L71j, UCIS;

The Illegal Alien Committee, "The Illegal Alien Problem and Its Impact on Los Angeles Police Department Resources: Briefing Paper Prepared for Staff Officers' Mini-Retreat," January 1977, folder 1, box 36, UPRI.

3. Molina, *How Race Is Made*; Provine and Doty, "Criminalization of Immigrants"; Carbado, "Racial Naturalization."

4. Hernández, "Amnesty or Abolition?"

5. Keil, *Los Angeles*, 113–50; Gottleib, *Reinventing Los Angeles*.

6. Stumpf, "Crimmigration Crisis"; Beckett and Murakawa, "Mapping the Shadow Carceral State."

7. U.S. Department of Commerce, *General Social and Economic*, 1980; U.S. Department of Commerce, *General Social and Economic*, 1990; Phil J. Ethington, W. H. Frey, and D. Myers, "The Racial Resegregation of Los Angeles County, 1940–2000," *Race Contours*, 2000; Keil, *Los Angeles*, 56, 116–20; Sawhney, *Unmasking L.A.*; Ngai, *Impossible Subjects*, 227–39.

8. Kurashige, *Shifting*, 279–81; Keil, *Los Angeles*, xxviii–xxix, 80–88, 137–50.

9. On economic crisis, see Camp, *Incarcerating the Crisis*, 104–5; Steinberg, Lyon, and Vaiana, *Urban America*, 31; Jacobs, *Panic at the Pump*. On counterinsurgency wars see Westad, *Global Cold War*. On immigrants as a burden, see Goodman, *Deportation Machine*; James C. Hankla, Letter to Each Supervisor, "Impact of Undocumented Aliens on Los Angeles County," December 23, 1985, folder 4, box 980, EDE; Ruben Castaneda, "Studies Paint Confusing Picture of Illegal Aliens," *LAHE*, January 12, 1986, folder 4, box 980, EDE; CJM letter to Ed Edelman, "Comments about Illegal Alien Costs to County and Revenues Generated," January 23, 1986, folder 4, box 331, EDE; "Aliens Reportedly Get $100 Million in Welfare," *LAT*, January 27, 1973, sec. Part 1; Waldinger, "Not the Promised City."

10. Los Angeles City Human Relations Commission, "Proposal for Activities to Respond to Growing Intercultural Tensions," May 1, 1992, folder Intercultural Tensions, box C-2667, HRCR.

11. Julia Kessler, "Peace Keeping in the City of Angels," April 1972, folder 24, box 5, UPRI; Julia Kessler, "Julia Kessler Transcript of Grand Jury Hearings on 17th Street Killings," 1971, folder 23, box 5, UPRI.

12. Kessler, "Julia Kessler Transcript"; Kessler, "Peace Keeping"; National Council of La Raza, "Los Angeles: Introduction," 1980, folder 2, box 478, NCLRP; Ruben Salazar, "A Beautiful Sight: The System Working the Way It Should," *LAT*, July 24, 1970, sec. Part 2; Ronald J. Ostrow and Howard Hertel, "Concern Over L.A. Police Policy Led to U.S. Probe of 2 Killings: U.S. Concern Over L.A. Police Policy Reported," *LAT*, July 25, 1970, sec. Part 1; "Roybal Acusa a La Policia de L.A.: Condena la muerte aquí de 2 mexicanos," *La Opinion*, July 21, 1970, folder 4, box 18, MRP.

13. "Sánchez Police Killings," 1971, folder 5, box 1022, RG 5, MALDEFR; California Legislature, Assembly Select Committee on the Administration of Justice, *Relations between the Police and Mexican-Americans* (Sacramento, April 28, 1972), 65–66, 166–67.

14. Kessler, "Peace Keeping."

15. Joe C. Ortega, letter to Peter R. Chacon, "Police Hearings," September 29, 1971, folder 8, box 18, RG 9, MALDEFR; Gene Blake and Howard Hertel, "4 Counts Dismissed in 'Mistake' Slaying Trial: But All Policemen Face Other Charges as Defense Opens 'MISTAKE' KILLING," *LAT*, August 4, 1971, sec. Part 1.

16. Barrio Defense Committee, "La Voz Del Barrio," August 1971, folder 13, box 18, MRP; Barrio Defense Committee, "La Voz Del Barrio," November 1971, folder 13, box 18, MRP; Barrio Defense Committee, "Sánchez Memorial March," July 16, 1971, folder 1, box 26, CASA. The family of Guillermo Sánchez brought a wrongful death suit against the LAPD for $500,000, Magana & Cathcart, "Claim for Wrongful Death: Alcazar V. City of Los Angeles," August 26, 1970, folder 6, box 1022, RG 5, MALDEFR.

17. National Council of La Raza, "Perceptions of 'Why' Police Are Excessively Violent," 1980, folder 4, box 478, NCLRP.

18. Joshua Eilberg letter to James Greene, June 29, 1973, folder 10, box 413, ERP; U.S. Dept. of Labor, Immigration and Naturalization Service, *Annual Report of the Immigration and Naturalization Service*, 1973; Frank Del Olmo, "600 Arrested in Roundup of Illegal Aliens," *LAT*, May 24, 1973, sec. Part 2; "Clergy Meeting with Mr. Joseph Sureck, District Director of Immigration," June 22, 1973, folder 10, box 413, ERP; "The Law, Morality and the Immigration and Naturalization Service: Human Crisis in Los Angeles, June 1973," June 1973, folder 10, box 413, ERP.

19. CASA, "CASA Release on INS Raids," May 29, 1973, folder 8, box 24, Part 1, JNC; Letter to Acting Director, "CASA," May 30, 1973, folder 10, box 24, CASA; Nestor Carrion, "Acusan a inmigración en el caso de los ilegales," *La Opinion*, June 23, 1973, folder 3, box 1024, RG 5, MALDEFR.

20. Edward Roybal letter to Joshua Eilberg, July 20, 1973, folder 10, box 413, ERP. On constituent letters, see Edward Roybal letter to Mark Olvera, July 11, 1973, folder 15, box 405, ERP; Mark Olvera letter to Edward Roybal, June 29, 1973, folder 15, box 405, ERP; ACLU of Southern California, MALDEF, and John F. Sheffield, "Plaintiffs-Appellants' Opening Brief in Loya v. INS," n.d., folder 15, box 1023, RG 5, MALDEFR; Vilma S. Martínez letter to Joaquin G. Avila, "Yoland Yola V. INS," November 5, 1974, folder 17, box 1023, RG 5, MALDEFR; Loya v. Immigration and Naturalization Service (U.S. Court of Appeals, Ninth Circuit 1978).

21. Community Relations Section Office of the Chief of Police, "Illegal Aliens: Composite Profile," January 1975, folder 19, box 29, FDOC; Bill Steiner letter to Vilma Martínez, Jane Couch, and Joel Contreras, "Coalition of Mexicanos/Latinos Against Defamation," November 10, 1977, folder 3, box 42, RG 9, MALDEFR.

22. Ngai, *Impossible Subjects*, 60–63; Macías-Rojas, *From Deportation*, 17; Sarah Coleman, "Iowa, Local Immigration Enforcement and Immigrants' Rights," unpublished paper presented at the Newberry Latino and Borderlands History Seminar, in author's possession. On the border patrol see Hernández, *Migra*. The history of Immigration federalism had a long history in the twentieth century; see Goodman, *Deportation Machine*.

23. Frank del Olmo, "Bunco Artists Capitalize on Aliens' Fears: Some Firms Advising on Immigration Laws Are Unfit, Do Little," *LAT*, April 21, 1975, sec. Part 1.

24. Edward Davis, "Special Order No. 68: Illegal Entry Arrests," November 24, 1972, folder 18, box 29, FDOC; "Laws Violated," *LAHE*, January 11, 1975, folder 19, box 29, FDOC.

25. Tom Bradley, "Estafadores," May 24, 1974, folder 5, box 1746, MTBAP; Los Angeles City Council, "Minutes," November 14, 1972, CCM; Los Angeles City Council, "Minutes," December 11, 1972, CCM.

26. Los Angeles City Council, "Minutes," November 14, 1972, CCM.

27. Joseph P. Busch letter to Dan Sánchez, "Letter to Captain Sánchez," September 6, 1972, folder 6, box 22, FDOC; E. M. Davis letter to Honorable Board of Police Commissioners, "Operación Estafadores," January 4, 1973, folder 6, box 22, FDOC.

28. Michael A. Castillo letter to H. D. Sánchez, "Letter to Captain Sánchez," August 24, 1972, folder 6, box 22, FDOC; Fernando Del Río letter to Tony Porrate, August 21, 1972, folder 6, box 22, FDOC; Joseph P. Busch letter to Dan Sánchez, "Letter to Captain Sánchez," September 6, 1972, folder 6, box 22, FDOC; Ed Davis letter to Thomas Bradley, "Pertinent Matters of Interest in Police Affairs, Police Department Biweekly Report No. 321," December 18, 1975, MTBAP; Los Angeles City Council, "Minutes," November 14, 1972, CCM; Frank Del Olmo, "Latin Consumers Swamp Police as Storefront Station Opens," LAT, August 22, 1972, folder 6, box 22, FDOC.

29. John Kendall, "Bilking of Thousands of Aliens in L.A. Told: Victims Report on Sham Marriages, Consumer Traps," LAT, September 30, 1976, sec. Part 2.

30. Joseph P. Busch letter to Dan Sánchez, "Letter to Captain Sánchez," September 6, 1972, folder 6, box 22, Frank FDOC.

31. Edward M. Davis, "Pertinent Matters of Interest in Police Affairs, Attachment 1, Part 1," July 25, 1976, Notebook 1, box 2276, PDX/82.

32. Nelson, S. A. Intra-Departmental Correspondence to J. A. McAllister, "Status Report—Operación Estafadores," Intra-Departmental Correspondence, November 20, 1972, folder 6, box 22, FDOC.

33. Ronald L. Soble, "Swindle Squad Helps Latin Community: Police 'Operación Estafadores' Offers Haven of Last Resort to Fraud Victims Operación Estafadores Aids the Swindled," LAT, August 12, 1979, sec. Part 2; Sebastian Rotella, "Crime, Abuses Hound Latino Immigrants," LAT, December 30, 1991, p. A1.

34. E. M. Davis, "Pertinent Matters of Interest in Police Affairs," March 3, 1974, folder Mayor's Report 272 through 279, box B-2272, PDX/BSI; Joint Crime Suppression Task Force, "Los Angeles Police Study of Impact of Illegal Aliens on Crime in L. A.—Ramparts Division Case Study," September 3, 1974, HV 7595.L71j, UCIS.

35. Community Relations Section Office of the Chief of Police, "Illegal Aliens: Composite Profile," January 1975, folder 19, box 29, FDOC.

36. "Testimony of the City of Los Angeles before the House Subcommittee on State, Justice, Commerce and the Judiciary of the Appropriations Committee," February 24, 1978, folder 10, box 115, GMDP.

37. Community Relations Section Office of the Chief of Police, "Illegal Aliens: Composite Profile."

38. Community Relations Section Office of the Chief of Police, "Illegal Aliens: Composite Profile."

39. "Crime Surging Over Mexican Border into U.S., Chief Davis Says," LAT, October 24, 1976, sec. Part 1.

40. The Illegal Alien Committee, "The Illegal Alien Problem and Its Impact on Los Angeles Police Department Resources: Briefing Paper Prepared for Staff Officers' Mini-Retreat," January 1977, folder 1, box 36, UPRI.

41. The Illegal Alien Committee, "The Illegal Alien Problem and Its Impact on Los Angeles Police Department Resources"; John Kendall, "L.A. to Have Million 'Illegals' by '81 at Present Rate: Police Study Calls Peaceful Image False L.A. May Have 1 Million Illegal Aliens by 1981," LAT, January 30, 1977, sec. Part 2; House Subcommittee

on Appropriations, *Undocumented Aliens: Hearings before a Subcommittee of the Committee on Appropriations,* 1978, 276; Los Angeles Police Department, *Annual Report,* 1976; Peter J. Pitchess, "The Impact of Illegal Aliens on Los Angeles County: A Compendium Compiled by the Los Angeles County Sheriff's Department," April 1977, Vertical Files: California Illegal Aliens California, UCIS; Grace Davis, "Testimony of the City of Los Angeles before the House Subcommittee on State, Justice, Commerce and the Judiciary of the Appropriations Committee," February 24, 1978, folder 10, box 115, GMDP.

42. The Illegal Alien Committee, "The Illegal Alien Problem and Its Impact on Los Angeles Police Department Resources."

43. "The Illegal Alien Problem and Its Impact on Los Angeles Police Department Resources"; Patt Morrison, "Illegal Aliens Blamed for Increasing Crimes: Officers Compile Data on Gangs of Transient Burglars RISE IN ILLEGAL ALIEN CRIME," *LAT,* January 30, 1977, sec. Part 2.

44. Edward M. Davis, "Pertinent Matters of Interest in Police Affairs, Attachment 1, Part 1," July 25, 1976, Notebook 1, box 2276, PDX/82.

45. Joint Crime Suppression Task Force, "Los Angeles Police Study of Impact of Illegal Aliens on Crime in L. A.—Ramparts Division Case Study," September 3, 1974, HV 7595.L71j, UCIS. On cooperation, see "CASA FOIA Documents," 1972–1975, Report 4, p. 144, FBI FOIA Request; "More Than 400 Aliens Seized in Factory Raid," *LAT,* May 17, 1975, B1; Edward M. Davis, "Pertinent Matters of Interest in Police Affairs, Attachment 1, Part 1," July 25, 1976, Notebook 1, box 2276, PDX/82.

46. California State Advisory Committee to the U.S. Commission on Civil Rights, *Open Meeting* (Courtesy of Adam Goodman).

47. Immigration Coalition, "Plight of Undocumented Immigrants in America," February 7, 1977, folder 8, box 23, HBC; Edward M. Davis, letter to Arlene Falk Meyers, "With Attachments on LAPD Immigration Policy," August 20, 1975, folder 12, box 15, BCP; Richard Hybels letter to Vilma Martínez, Al Pérez, Mike Baller, Esther Estrada, and Jane Couch, "Summary of the Illegal Alien Problem and Its Impact on Los Angeles Police," June 29, 1978, folder 5, carton 856, RG 9, MALDEFR.

48. "La Policia No Arresta Indocumentadoes Por El Hecho de Estar Llegales: Davis," *La Opinion,* November 17, 1975, folder 18, box 29, FDOC; Kenneth Reich, "LAPD Doesn't Go after Illegal Aliens, Davis Says," *LAT,* November 27, 1975, folder 18, box 29, FDOC; "More Than 400 Aliens Seized in Factory Raid," *LAT,* May 17, 1975, B1.

49. Ad Hoc Committee of the Los Angeles County Bar Association, "Public Hearings on the Deportation and Removal of Aliens," December 18, 1974, folder 12, box 123, GMDP; Los Angeles Bar Association, *Report on the Deportation and Removal of Aliens,* 1976, folder 19, box 115, GMDP.

50. Ed Davis, "Undocumented Aliens," August 15, 1977, folder Chief of Police, box 126, GMDP; Mexican American Legal Defense and Education Fund letter to Griffin B. Bell, "State and Local Police Officer Enforcement of Federal Immigration Laws," January 11, 1978, folder 14, box 129, RG 4, MALDEFR; "Authority of State and Local Police Officers to Enforce Federal Immigration Laws," April 17, 1978, folder 7, box 115, GMDP; Evan Maxwell, "Police Restricted in Arrests of Aliens: Ruling Says Illegals May Not Be Seized Merely for Unlawful Entry," *LAT,* August 26, 1977, sec. Part 2;

Immigration Coalition, "Statement of Concern," 1977, folder 4, box 4, Series 4, RMC; Richter, "Uneasy Border State," 204–5.

51. Bill Steiner letter to Mike Baller, "Miguel García v. LAPD," May 24, 1979, folder 22, box 1096, RG 5, MALDEFR; Miguel García, "Miguel García Interview," February 7, 1979, folder 22, box 1096, RG 5, MALDEFR.

52. INS, "Respondent's Written Argument Regarding the Issue of Suspension of Deportation and Hardship, in Re Matter of Miguel García," 1979, folder 22, box 1096, RG 5, MALDEFR.

53. Bill Steiner letter to Mike Baller, "Miguel García v. LAPD," May 24, 1979, folder 22, box 1096, RG 5, MALDEFR.

54. U.S. Department of Justice, Board of Immigration Appeals, "Application: Suspension of Deportation," February 28, 1980, folder 22, box 1096, RG 5, MALDEFR.

55. "The Raids Are Wrong," *LAT*, October 30, 1979, folder 10, box 2175, MTBAP; Tom Bradley, "Mayor Bradley Tries to Get INS Raids Stopped," November 2, 1979, folder 9, box 122, GMDP; Goodman, *Deportation Machine*, ch. 4.

56. "Aliens, Fearful of Deportation, Shun Police, Even When They're the Victims," *LAT*, July 9, 1978, sec. San Gabriel Valley; Evan Maxwell, "LAPD Eases Policy Toward Illegal Aliens: Officers Won't Question Status Except in Serious Crimes," *LAT*, March 21, 1979, sec. Part 2; California Advisory Committee, "Open Meeting."

57. Daryl F. Gates, "Special Order No. 40: Undocumented Aliens," November 27, 1979, folder 17, box 29, FDOC; Daryl F. Gates letter to Richard Alatorre, "Suggested Amendments to LAPD Special Order No. 40," July 20, 1990, folder 17, box 29, FDOC.

58. U.S. District Court for the Central District of California, "Complaint for Injunctive, Declaratory and Other Relief in Grajeda v. Gates," July 20, 1979, folder 22, box 1096, RG 5, MALDEFR; Myrna Oliver, "Court Asked to Halt LAPD Immigration-Status Action," *LAT*, December 11, 1979, sec. Part 1; City Clerk letter to Southeast Legal Aid Center, "Your File No. 205521," July 28, 1978, folder 22, box 1096, RG 5, MALDEFR; U.S. Department of Justice, Board of Immigration Appeals, "In Deportation Proceedings," 1979, folder 22, box 1096, RG 5, MALDEFR; Southwest Legal Aid Center, "Brief in Opposition to Decision of Immigration Judge," 1979, folder 22, box 1096, RG 5, MALDEFR.

59. Gates v. Superior Court, 193 Cal.App.3d 205 (Cal. Ct. App. 1987).

60. Rose Ochi letter to Tom Bradley, "Attached Briefing Memo. Also Attached for Background—Immigration," April 16, 1981, folder 10, box 2175, MTBAP.

61. Davis, *City of Quartz*, 315–16; Vigil, "Cholo!"

62. U.S. General Accounting Office, *Criminal Aliens: INS' Enforcement Activities - Report to the Chairman, Subcommittee on Immigration, Refugees, and International Law, Committee on the Judiciary, House of Representatives*, GAO, November 1987.

63. Los Angeles City Task Force on Immigration, *Interim Report of the Los Angeles City Task Force on Immigration*, April 1987, folder 13, box 1172, MTBAP.

64. Jerry Belcher, "Police Launch Program against Illegal Aliens: L.A. Seeking to Deport Gang Members," *LAT*, September 5, 1986, sec. Part 2; Richard B. Dixon letter to Each Supervisor, "Projects to Identify Alien Drug Offenders," May 15, 1987, folder 13, box 331, EDE; U.S. General Accounting Office, *Criminal Aliens*.

65. Stephen Braun, "U.S.-L.A. Task Force Deports 175 with Ties to Drug, Gang Activity," *LAT*, April 12, 1989, A3.

66. County of Los Angeles, *Criminal Aliens*; Michael D. Antonovich letter to Each Supervisor, "Criminal Aliens," March 29, 1991, folder 6, box 238, EDE.

67. Ad Hoc Subcommittee on Criminal Aliens, *Criminal Aliens in the Los Angeles County Jail Population: Final Report.*

68. Leonard Greenwood, "1,700 Arrested in LAPD Anti-Drug Sweep," *LAT*, August 14, 1985, sec. Part 2; U.S. General Accounting Office, *Criminal Aliens.*

69. Antonio H. Rodriguez, "L.A. Police and La Migra—an Overbearing Partnership," *LAT*, July 18, 1989; Jesús C. Hernández, "Protestan contra supuestos abusos de la Policía," *La Opinion*, April 20, 1989, folder 23, box 61, CAPA.

70. Cynthia Anderson and Latino Community Justice Center, "Police Abuse in Los Angeles," April 1989, folder 1, box 7, CAPA.

71. López, Popkin, and Telles, "Central Americans," 279–81; Macías-Rojas, *From Deportation*, 34.

72. Victor Merina, "Council Votes 8-6 for L.A. Sanctuary: Symbolic Step for Central American Refugees Seen as Slap at U.S. Policy SANCTUARY: City Approves Symbolic Step," *LAT*, November 28, 1985, sec. Orange County; City Council, "City Council File 85-1948," 1986, folder 85-1948, box C1159, CCF; CARCEREN, "CARCEREN Launches Mass Media Campaign to Urge Salvadorans to Apply for Temporary Protected Status before the October 31st Deadline," 1990, folder 6, box 1170, MTBAP.

73. Michael D. Antonovich, "Antonovich Denounces Council's Sanctuary Action," November 27, 1985, folder 13, box 331, EDE; Victor Merina, "Young L.A. Councilman Gets Badly Bruised in Sanctuary Battle," *LAT*, February 18, 1986, sec. San Diego County; "Council Drops L.A. Designation as 'Sanctuary,'" *LAT*, February 7, 1986; Richter, "Uneasy Border," 218.

74. Dave Smith, "Bad Produce Is Target of Quiet L.A. Raids on Unlicensed Vendors: RAIDS: Crackdown on Produce Vendors," *LAT*, November 24, 1983, sec. Orange County.

75. City of Los Angeles, "Important Notice: Selling on Streets, Sidewalks, Private Property, Etc.," 1987, folder 3, box 4, TCOF.

76. Latham & Watkins letter to Gloria Molina, "Misconduct of Certain Police Officers on 7th and Alvarado Streets," December 6, 1989, folder 9, box 1170, MTBAP; Various authors, "Street Vendor Declarations," December 1989, folder 9, box 1170, MTBAP; "Fact Sheet—Background on the Los Angeles Police Department's Relationship and Collaboration with the Immigration & Naturalization Service," 1990, folder INS-Police Cooperation Declarations & Testimony, carton 1681, RG 5, MALDEFR.

77. Jorge Cruz Cortes, "Declaration of Jorge Cruz Cortes," December 1, 1989, folder 9, box 1170, MTBAP; Latham & Watkins, letter to Gloria Molina, "Misconduct of Certain Police Officers on 7th and Alvarado Streets," December 6, 1989, folder 9, box 1170, MTBAP.

78. "Street Vendors Protest Police Arrest Methods," *LAT*, November 17, 1989, folder 16, box 4, SVAR.

79. George Ramos, "Activists Claim Police Help INS to Expel Aliens," *LAT*, January 19, 1990, sec. Metro News.

80. CRECEN, "CRECEN Eighth Annual Dinner Dedicated to the Central American Refugees and Street Vendors in Los Angeles," 1990, folder 4, box 1164, MTBAP.

81. CARECEN, *Report from CARECEN*, Fall 1991, folder 3, box 1164, MTBAP; Louis Sahagun, "Council OKs Districts for Street Vendors," *LAT*, January 15, 1992, sec. Ventura County; "Anniversary for LA's Street Vending Ordinance Comes but Vendors Don't Celebrate," January 5, 1995, folder 1, box 1, SVAR; "Sidewalk Vending Fact Sheet," 1994, folder 9, box 4, SVAR; "Sidewalk Vending Program," 1994, folder 9, box 4, SVAR; City Council, "City Council File 90-2591," 1991, folder 90-2591, box C2462, CCF.

82. "Enforcement Outside Special Districts," November 8, 1993, folder 9, box 4, SVAR; City Council, "City Council File 90-2591 S2," 1991, folder 90-2591 S2, box C2462, CCF.

83. Javier H. Rodríguez, "Pattern of Selective Enforcement Is Alive and Well . . . ," 1994, folder 5, box 2, SVAR.

84. Rosa Maria Villalpando, "INS Claims Round-Ups Have Not Reduced Number of Day-Laborers," *La Opinion*, June 28, 1989, folder Press Coverage INS/Police, carton 1681, RG 5, MALDEFR; Rosa Maria Villalpando, "Policía Ayuda Al INS En Redada," *La Opinion*, July 1, 1989, folder Press Coverage INS/Police, carton 1681, RG 5, MALDEFR; Rosa Maria Villalpando, "Policía Ayuda Al INS En Redada," *La Opinion*, July 1, 1989, folder Press Coverage INS/Police, carton 1681, RG 5, MALDEFR.

85. Hector Tobar, "27 Hostages Turned Over to INS After Police Rescue," *LAT*, June 16, 1990, sec. Metro; CARECEN, "What Is CARECEN?," 1990, folder 2, box 1164, MTBAP.

86. Tobar, "27 Hostages."

87. Daryl F. Gates, "Statement by Chief Daryl F. Gates Re: Undocumented Being Held Hostage," July 19, 1990, folder 8, box 1170, MTBAP.

88. Hispanic Advisory Council, "Newsletter," December 1990, folder 7, box 1169, MTBAP; "How to Make Allies into Enemies," *LAT*, August 15, 1990, folder 9, box 1170, MTBAP.

89. Tobar, "27 Hostages."

90. CHIRLA, "Stop the Cooperation between the Police and the INS," October 16, 1990, folder 9, box 1170, MTBAP; Edward J. Boyer, "Police, Protesters Clash at INS Detention Center," *LAT*, June 11, 1990; José Luis Sierra, "Cabildo Limita Las Instancias de Cooperación Entre Policía e INS," *La Opinion*, November 14, 1990, folder Press Coverage INS/Police, carton 1681, RG 5, MALDEFR; La Resistencia, "Coast to Coast: Step Up the Struggle to Shut Down America's Concentration Camps!," 1990, folder 15, box 21, CAPA.

91. Hector Tobar, "Woo Seeks Curbs on INS Cooperation: Law Enforcement: His Proposal Follows Incident in Which L.A. Police Rescued 27 Illegal-Alien Hostages and Turned Them over to Federal Agents," *LAT*, June 21, 1990, sec. Metro News; CARECEN, *Report from CARECEN*, Summer 1990, folder 3, box 1164, MTBAP.

92. Hector Tobar, "Proposed Curbs on LAPD Fought," *LAT*, July 31, 1990, p. B1, folder 18, box 29, FDOC; Richard Alatorre and Michael Woo, "Motion," June 20, 1990, folder 8, box 1170, MTBAP; Anton Calleia letter to Yolanda Chávez, "Suggested Amendments to LAPD Special Order No. 40 Woo-Alatorre Motion," August 22, 1990, folder 8, box 1170, MTBAP.

93. Tobar, "Proposed Curbs"; Hector Tobar, "Gates Opposes Bar to Police, INS Cooperation," *LAT*, June 22, 1990, sec. Metro News.

94. Public Safety Committee letter to Los Angeles City Council, "INS-LAPD Memo," November 13, 1990, folder 8, box 1170, MTBAP.

95. Los Angeles City Council, "Motion Adopted Relative to Modification of Los Angeles Police Department's Cooperation Policy with Immigration and Naturalization Service (INS) in Its Treatment of Undocumented Persons," November 15, 1990, folder 8, box 1170, MTBAP; Public Safety Committee letter to Los Angeles City Council, "INS-LAPD Memo," November 13, 1990, folder 8, box 1170, MTBAP; "Fact Sheet—Background on the Los Angeles Police Department's Relationship and Collaboration with the Immigration & Naturalization Service," 1990, folder INS-Police Cooperation Declarations & Testimony, Carton 1681, RG 5, MALDEFR. The STEP Act will be discussed in more depth in chapter 8.

96. Permanent Subcommittee on Investigations of the Committee on Governmental Affairs, *Criminal Aliens in the United States*, 22–23; Edward J. Boyer, "Immigrants Sent to INS by Police, Suit Alleges," *LAT*, May 8, 1991, sec. Valley.

97. Richter, "Uneasy Border," 233; Michael Connelly, "Insults Add to the Tragedy," *LAT*, February 13, 1991, sec. San Diego County; Louis Sahagun, "Group Seeks Gates' Apology for Remarks," *LAT*, February 15, 1991, sec. Metro.

Chapter 8

1. Martin Martínez and Connie Castruita letter to Carlo Cudio, "Department Complaint against Alleging Neglect of Duty and Excessive Force against the Following Southwest Patrol Division Officers," 1989, folder 4, box 129, CAPA; Pamela Klein, "By All Means Necessary: The Dalton Street Raid Showed Just How Far the Police Were Willing to Go. It Is Also Showing Just How Many Residents Aren't Willing to Take It Anymore," *L.A. Weekly*, January 30, 1988, folder 26, box 61, CAPA.

2. "Department Complaint against Alleging Neglect of Duty and Excessive Force against the Following Southwest Patrol Division Officers"; Dan Saunders letter to David Huebner, "Promotions of 39th & Dalton Officers," June 20, 1991, folder 12, box 27, ICR; David Huebner, "39th & Dalton Incident (August 1, 1988)," 1991, folder 11, box 27, ICR; Andrea Ford, "Officer Used False Data for Warrant in Raid, LAPD Alleges," *LAT*, August 8, 1989, sec. Metro.

3. Charissa Jones, "Probe Ordered in Drug Raid Called 'Orgy of Violence,'" *LAHE*, August 5, 1988, folder 26, box 61, CAPA; Dalton Avenue Legal Team, "Complaint for Damages for Violations of Civil Rights under Color of State Law," 1988, folder 26, box 61, CAPA; Dalton Avenue Legal Team, "Joint Venture Agreement," October 1, 1988, folder 26, box 61, CAPA; Henry Weinstein, "Award in Final Dalton Case OKd by Court Police," *LAT*, January 23, 1992, sec. Metro.

4. On moral panics, see Hall et al., *Policing the Crisis*; Davis, *City of Quartz*; Reeves and Campbell, *Cracked Coverage*; Umemoto, *Truce*.

5. Office of Operations, "Battle Plans," February 1989, folder 6, box 30, LAWCR. On Reagan administration support see Terence Dunworth and Aaron Saiger, *National Assessment of the Byrne Formula Grant Program*, December 1996; Balko, *Rise of the Warrior Cop*, ch. 6.

6. Widener, *Black Arts West*, 276. For the mutual hostility between Bradley and Gates, see Sonenshein, *Politics in Black*, ch. 13.

7. Department of Justice, "Crack Cocaine: Overview 1989," Department of Justice, 1989, folder 4, box 12, CAPA; Division of Law Enforcement and John K. Van de Kamp, "Crips & Bloods Street Gangs: A Confidential Publication for Law Enforcement," n.d.; "Background Information Regarding Street Gangs," 1987, folder 2, box 131, MTBAP; Mike Duran, "Gangs," n.d., folder 4, box 3873, MTBAP.

8. Gilmore, *Golden Gulag*; Davis, *City of Quartz*; Hayden, *Street Wars*; Vigil, *Rainbow*; Umemoto, *Truce*; Hagedorn, *People and Folks*.

9. Murch, "Crack in Los Angeles"; Stuart, *Down, Out, and Under*; Forman Jr., *Locking Up Our Own*; Vitale, *City of Disorder*; Wacquant, *Punishing the Poor*.

10. Davis, *City of Quartz*, 300–309; Keil, *Los Angeles*, 53–56; Camp, *Incarcerating the Crisis*, 104–5.

11. Ruth A. Ross, *The Impact of Federal Grants on the City of Los Angeles* (Long Beach: Center for Public Policy and Administration, California State University, Long Beach, 1980); Waldinger and Bozorgmehr, *Ethnic Los Angeles*, 7; Los Angeles Times Staff, *Understanding the Riots*; Johnson et al., "Los Angeles Rebellion"; Keil, *Los Angeles*, 79–87; Fulton, *Reluctant*, 43–61; 291–92.

12. Davis, *City of Quartz*, 300–309; Keil, *Los Angeles*, 53; Gottleib et al., *Next Los Angeles*, 84–85.

13. "L.A. Becomes PCP Capital of World," *LAS*, October 25, 1979; "South-Central Cocaine Sales Explode Into $25 'Rocks,'" *LAT*, November 25, 1984; Los Angeles Police Department, *Annual Report*, 1980; Mike Davis, "Los Angeles: Civil Liberties between the Hammer and the Rock," *New Left Review* 170 (August 1989), WCSCL; Webb, *Dark Alliance*.

14. Tom Bradley and Daryl F. Gates, "LA's War on Drugs," May 1987, folder 4, box 1961, MTBAP; Ralph Brauer, "The Drug War of Words," *Nation* 250, no. 20 (May 21, 1990): 705–6. In general, see Reeves and Campbell, *Cracked Coverage*, 127–50; Hagan, *Who Are*, 100–109; Louis Sahagun, and Carol McGraw, "Former First Lady Says Yes to Drug Raid as She Sees Police Move on Rock House," *LAT*, April 8, 1989. For the LAPD's concern for drugs see Los Angeles Police Department, *Annual Report*, 1980–1992.

15. Tom Bradley, "UNO/SCOC Crime Rally," July 14, 1985, folder 4, box 2206, MTBAP; Tom Bradley, "Drug Abuse: The Scourge of the Generation," September 1, 1986, folder 22, box 2208, MTBAP; Tom Bradley, "Bradley Joins Mayors Nationwide in Anti-Drug Effort by Proclaiming Tuesday, November 18 'Mayor's D-Day in War on Drugs,'" November 18, 1986, folder 1, box 329, MTBAP; Deane Dana letter to the White House, "Writes Regarding Requests by the City of Los Angeles for Increased Staffing for the FBI, Coast Guard, DEA, Immigration, and the U.S. Attorney's Office in Order to Combat Drugs," April 12, 1988, folder 554191–566999, box 10, RLGF.

16. Paul Feldman, "Police Use a Wide Broom LAPD's War on Gangs and Drugs Has Shifted Emphasis, Concentrating on South-Central L.A., with Mixed Reactions from Residents," *LAT*, May 8, 1988, sec. Metro.

17. For the LAPD's attention to gang activity see Los Angeles Police Department, *Annual Report*, 1979–1992. On police and prosecutors using discourses of crises and police power, see Forman, *Locking Up Our Own*; Pfaff, *Locked In*.

18. California Council on Criminal Justice/State Task Force on Youth Gang Violence, "Testimony of the Mayor's Office of Criminal Justice Planning, City of Los Angeles—

Jamesetta Hawthorne, Gang Program Coordinator," September 4, 1985, folder 2, box 131, MTBAP; "Gang Violence Informational Packet," n.d., folder 4, box 5084, MTBAP; Paul Feldman, "L.A. County's Gang Wars Engulf Peace Efforts: Millions Spent to End Violence, Curb Membership and Protect Bystanders," *LAT*, November 12, 1987, sec. SD36; On gangs, see Vigil, *Rainbow*; Moore, *Going*.

19. Kenneth Reich, "Surge in Gang Crime Caused by Narcotics, Police Assert," *LAT*, July 17, 1986, sec. Part 2.

20. U.S. Congress, House, Select Committee on Narcotics Abuse and Control, *Narcotics Trafficking and Abuse in the Los Angeles Area*, 1986; U.S. Congress, House, Select Committee on Narcotics Abuse and Control, *Federal Law Enforcement Role in Narcotics Control in Southern California*, 1988; U.S. Congress, House, Committee on the Judiciary, Subcommittee on Criminal Justice, *Organized Criminal Activity by Youth Gangs*, 1988, 18.

21. Quotes from Klein et al., "'Crack,' Street Gangs, and Violence," 623–27, 628, 645; Ira Reiner, "Gangs, Crime and Violence in Los Angeles: Findings and Proposals," 1992, folder Gangs, box 212, SSC; Murch, "Crack."

22. Scott Harris, "Anti-Gang Funds for Police Backed by Council Panel," *LAT*, April 6, 1988, sec. Part 2; David Freed, "Gates Blames Drugs, Gangs for 4% Rise in L.A. Crime," *LAT*, December 25, 1986, sec. Metro.

23. "The Drug Gangs," *Newsweek*, March 28, 1988, 20–27.

24. Bill Chandler et al., *Tom Bradley Commemorative Booklet* (Los Angeles, 1989); "Task Force on Gang Violence and Urban Terrorism: Priority Assignments," n.d., folder 4, box 5084, MTBAP; Tom Bradley, "Mayor's Statement for Press Conference on Gang Violence," 1984, folder 3, box 132, MTBAP; Marvin D. Iannone letter to Gordon K. Pederson, "Long Range Recommendations," December 18, 1984, folder 3, box 132, MTBAP.

25. Tom Bradley, "Mayor, Police Chief Tout Plan to Stamp-Out L.A. Street Drug Sales and Gang Drug Dealers," January 13, 1988, folder 2, box 329, MTBAP; Chief of Police letter to Honorable Board of Police Commissioners, *GRATS Chronic Location Statistical Report*, September 13, 1988, folder 2, box 2807, MTBAP; *GRATS Overview and Statistical Reports*, December 18, 1990, folder Los Angeles Police Department, box 659104, RFP; Gang-Related Active Trafficker Suppression, *GRATS Monthly Report*, September 1988, folder 4, box 4408, MTBAP; Los Angeles Police Department, *Annual Report*, 1988.

26. "Bradley Praises LAPD's GRATS Program on the Occasion of Its Second Anniversary," folder 7, box 275, MTBAP; Board of Police Commissioners letter to Tom Bradley, "Gang-Related Active Traffickers Suppression (GRATS) Semi-Annual Overview, 1992," August 19, 1992, folder 3, box 5021, MTBAP.

27. "Gates on Drugs: 'Casual Users Should Be Shot,'" *LAS*, September 13, 1990; see also statements in U.S. Congress, Senate, Committee on the Judiciary, *One-Year Drug Strategy Review: Hearing before the Committee on the Judiciary*, 101st Cong., 2nd Sess., 1990, 77.

28. Attorney General of the United States, *Task Force on Violent Crime*, 1981, 181; Reiner quoted in Feldman, "L.A. County's Gang Wars." On the city's punitive approach to gangs and drugs, see Daryl F. Gates and Robert K. Jackson, "The Situation in Los Angeles," *Police Chief* (November 1990): 20–23; Gilmore, *Golden Gulag*.

29. Deane Dana letter to the White House, "Writes Regarding Requests by the City of Los Angeles for Increased Staffing for the FBI, Coast Guard, DEA, Immigration, and the U.S. Attorney's Office in Order to Combat Drugs," April 12, 1988, folder 554191–566999, box 10, RLGF.

30. Chief of Police letter to Honorable Board of Police Commissioners, "Needs to Eradicate Violent Street Gangs," October 11, 1988, folder Los Angeles Police Commission, Gangs, box 11, SWP.

31. Balko, *Rise of the Warrior Cop*, 166–67, 243–45; Terence Dunworth and Aaron Saiger, *National Assessment of the Byrne Formula Grant Program*, December 1996.

32. Wesley D. McBride and Robert B. Jackson, "In L.A. County, a High-Tech Assist in the War on Gangs," *Police Chief* (June 1989): 28–29.

33. Pettigrew and Alston, *Tom Bradley's Campaigns for Governor*, 22; Tom Bradley, "Position on Crime," 1982, folder 1, box 3017, MTBAP; Thomas Bradley, "Bradley Lays Out Detailed Program to Stem 'Flood of Criminal Activity,'" April 30, 1982, folder 3, box 3009, MTBAP; Tom Houston and Craig Lawson letter to Mark Fabiani, "The Mayor's Record: Crime and Criminal Justice," December 21, 1984, folder 17, box 194, MTBAP; Joan Milke Flores, "Results of Survey Regarding Increase in Police Protection," 1984, folder 5, box 2803, MTBAP; Kevin Roderick, "The Times Poll: Most in L.A. Are Satisfied Despite the Fear of Crime," *LAT*, March 25, 1985, p. 1. Bradley did successfully reform the police and fire pension system, which had grown to 15 percent of the city budget, by placing limits on the cost of living increases through a ballot proposition in 1982; see Sonenshein, *Politics in Black and White*, 159.

34. Tom Bradley, "Bradley, for Sixth Consecutive Year, Enlarges Police Force," January 23, 1990, folder 19, box 951, MTBAP.

35. Keith Comrie letter to Bradley, "Police Anti-Gang Resources," November 14, 1980, folder 4, box 5084, MTBAP; Los Angeles County Interagency Gang Task Force, *Task Force Report 1982*, June 1983, folder 3, box 131, MTBAP; Malcolm W. Klein, Cheryl L. Maxson, and Margaret A. Gordon, "Evaluation in an Imported Gang Violence Deterrence Program: Final Report," Social Science Research Institute, 1984. On prosecutors, see Pfaff, *Locked In*; Parrish, *For the People*.

36. Michael Seiler, "780 Seized Citywide in Massive Weekend Police Drug Sweep," *LAT*, June 4, 1985, sec. Part 2; Daryl F. Gates, "Attachment: War against Gang Activities," 1985, folder 4, box 3178, MTBAP; David Freed, "Gates Defends His Officers' Search Methods in Court," *LAT*, November 30, 1988, p. D3; Daryl Gates, "Gates Reply," *LAT*, December 22, 1988, sec. Part 2.

37. Von Jones, "Police Struggle against Street Gangs Continues," *LAS*, June 20, 1985.

38. Bill Farr and Ronald J. Ostrow, "FBI, L.A. Police End Olympic 'Turf War': Agencies Sign Agreement Defining Their Tasks, but Some Situations Are Left Vague," *LAT*, February 29, 1984, p. A3; Boris Yaro, "Street Crime Crackdown Begins Near Coliseum," *LAT*, June 16, 1984, p. C4; LAPD, "Equipment Purchases," 1983–1984, folder SID, 1983–1984, box C-654, PDX/95A; LAPD, "Military Assistance Request," 1984, folder Intrusion Detection System, box C-653, PDX/95A; "Deployment—Exposition Park," 1982, folder Exposition Park Field Task Force Deployment and Cost Analysis, box C-653, PDX/95A; *CAPA Report*, 1983–84, folder 20, box 30, CAPA; Los Angeles Police Department, *Annual Report*, 1983, 1984. Parker, "The Capitalist Games," in author's possession.

39. Patricia Klein, "L.A. Police Say 'The Ram' Has Drug Dealers on Run," *LAT*, March 14, 1985; "LAPD's Battering Ram Draws Suit," *LAS*, February 28, 1985; Patricia Klein, "Battering Ram Nets 2 Women, 3 Children, Criticism," *LAT*, February 8, 1985, sec. Valley.

40. Patricia Klein and Stephanie Chávez, "Pacoima Leaders Protest Police Use of Motorized Ram," *LAT*, February 9, 1985, sec. Part 2; Dolores Langford et al. v. The Superior Court of Los Angeles County, Respondent; Daryl Gates, as Chief of Police et al., Supreme Court of California, 43 Cal. ed. 21.

41. Brad Cates letter to Tom Bradley, June 17, 1987, folder 6, box 2804, MTBAP; Sam Enríquez, "Seized in Raids: Police Seek Bigger Share of Drug Cash," *LAT*, April 20, 1986, sec. Valley; Blumenson and Nilsen, "Policing for Profit."

42. "LAPD Gets $1.4 Million in Seized Drug Money," *LAS*, November 28, 1985; *Narcotics Group—Financial Unit, Report of Money Seized and Returned to LAPD*, April 16, 1990, folder 13, box 4400, MTBAP.

43. Kerman Maddox letter to Tom Bradley, "Police Commission Meeting November 5, 1985," November 7, 1985, folder 1, box 2803, MTBAP; Chief of Police letter to Honorable Board of Police Commissioners, "Narcotics Abatement Account Expenditure Plan," June 29, 1987, folder 2, box 2806, MTBAP.

44. City Administrative Officer letter to Thomas Bradley, "Police Department Request for Positions and Resources for the Asset Forfeiture Detail," August 4, 1988, folder 1, box 2807, MTBAP; Tom Bradley letter to Council of the City of Los Angeles, August 17, 1988, folder 1, box 2807, MTBAP; Tom Bradley letter to Zev Yaroslavsky, "Narcotics Abatement Account (NAA) Expenditure Plan VII and Confidential Equipment List," July 24, 1992, folder 6, box 5021, MTBAP.

45. Thomas Bradley, "Bradley, Gates Unveil 'Operation Knockdown' to Demolish Unsafe, Dilapidated Buildings Serving as Havens for Drug Dealers," January 5, 1989, folder 2, box 329, MTBAP; Frank V. Kroeger letter to Tom Bradley, "Property Demolition," November 10, 1988, folder 2, box 4436, MTBAP. For the link to Vietnam, see Tullis, "A Vietnam at Home"; and Schrader, *Policing Revolution*.

46. Bob Sipchen and Darrell Dawsey, "Neighborhood Has Learned Coexistence Secret," *LAT*, October 20, 1989, sec. Part A.

47. James R. Lasley, "Using Traffic Barriers to 'Design Out' Crime: A Program Evaluation of LAPD's Operation Cul-De-Sac," National Institute of Justice, November 1996; Los Angeles Police Department, *Annual Report*, 1990.

48. John M. Glionna and Jesse Katz, "LAPD Cuts Back on Pico-Union Narcotics Patrol Drugs," *LAT*, October 22, 1989, sec. Metro, Part B.

49. Steve Valdivia, "Fax Information on LAPD Press Conference Statement Regarding 'Special Enforcement' Area," February 2, 1990, folder 2, box 149, EDE; Jane Fritsch, "Police Barricades Go Up In South Central War Zone," *LAT*, February 2, 1990.

50. Maurice Miller, "Drug Enforcement Barricades Not Accepted By All Residents," *LAS*, March 1, 1990, A1; Anthony Maceo Givhan, "Residents' Reaction Mixed On South-Central Barricaded Area," *LAS*, January 25, 1990.

51. James R. Lasley, "Using Traffic Barriers to 'Design Out' Crime: A Program Evaluation of LAPD's Operation Cul-De-Sac," November 1996.

52. City Administrative Officer letter to Tom Bradley, "Request for Interim Financing to Expand Jail Facilities," April 27, 1988, folder 5, box 2806, MTBAP; Tom Bradley and Daryl F. Gates, "LA's War on Drugs," May 1987, folder 4, box 1961, MTBAP.

53. Joel Edelman letter to Commander Lou Ritter, "CRASH File Standards & Procedures," June 29, 1976, folder 7, box 1338, MTBAP; Samuel L. Williams letter to Thomas Bradley, June 9, 1981, folder 4, box 1643, MTBAP.

54. See Ira Reiner, "Gangs, Crime and Violence in Los Angeles: Findings and Proposals," 1992, folder Gangs, box 212, SSC.

55. Myrna Oliver, "Police Photographing of Hispanics Hit: ACLU Sues to Block Arbitrary Questioning of Youths on Streets," *LAT*, March 7, 1980, sec. Part 2. Myrna Oliver, "Judge Bars LAPD Photos Without OK," *LAT*, March 29, 1980.

56. "The Region: Police Lawsuit Dropped," *LAT*, May 2, 1985, sec. San Diego County; Marvin D. Iannone letter to All Concerned Personnel, Office of Operations, "Gang File Guidelines," June 13, 1985, folder CAPA/ACLU, box 12, CAPA.

57. James Queally, "Los Angeles barred from enforcing nearly all gang injunctions, federal judge rules," *LAT*, March 15, 2018.

58. Operations-Headquarters Bureau, "State of the Los Angeles Gang Problem," March 1, 1989, folder Los Angeles Police Commission, Gangs, box 11, SWP; Director, Office of Operations letter to All Personnel, Office of Operations, "1988: Year of Gang Enforcement," February 25, 1988, folder Los Angeles Police Commission, Gangs, box 11, SWP.

59. David Freed, "Policing Gangs: Case of Contrasting Styles," *LAT*, January 19, 1986, sec. Part 2; Ira Reiner, "Gangs, Crime and Violence in Los Angeles: Findings and Proposals," 1992, folder Gangs, box 212, SSC.

60. Ira Reiner, "Gangs, Crime and Violence in Los Angeles: Findings and Proposals," 1992, folder Gangs, box 212, SSC.

61. Los Angeles County Commission on Human Relations, *Today's Conflicts, Tomorrow's Challenges: A Report on Five State of the County Hearings*, January 1984, folder 2, box 704, EDE.

62. Department of Justice, "Crack Cocaine: Overview 1989," Department of Justice, 1989, folder 4, box 12, CAPA; Division of Law Enforcement and John K. Van de Kamp, "Crips & Bloods Street Gangs: A Confidential Publication for Law Enforcement," n.d.

63. "Background Information Regarding Street Gangs," 1987, folder 2, box 131, MTBAP; Mike Duran, "Gangs," n.d., folder 4, box 3873, MTBAP.

64. LAPD, "Fact Sheet Community-Oriented Policing Program," May 16, 1988, folder Los Angeles Police Commission, Gangs, box 11, SWP; "Los Angeles Pride Week: Community Oriented Policing (Preliminary Draft)," 1984, folder Los Angeles Police Commission, Gangs, box 11, SWP; George L. Kelling, and James Q. Wilson, "Broken Windows," *Atlantic*, March 1982; David M. Kennedy, "Neighborhood Policing in Los Angeles," 1987, folder 44, box 17, ICR; Vitale, *City of Disorder*; Harcourt, *Illusion of Order*.

65. Gilbert Lindsay, "War on Graffiti," 1987, folder 10, box 104, MTBAP.

66. Tom Bradley, "Proclamation: Anti-Graffiti Awareness Day," October 27, 1988, folder 2, box 104, MTBAP; "Operation Clean Sweep Fact Sheet," 1989, folder 1, box 102, MTBAP; Joel Wachs, "Motion—Graffiti," May 11, 1990, folder 1, box 102, MTBAP; City of Los Angeles, "No Graffiti Pamphlet," n.d., folder 2, box 102, MTBAP.

67. James K. Hahn, *Civil Gang Abatement: A Community Based Policing Tool of the Los Angeles City Attorney* (Los Angeles, 1989); "Hahn's STAG Act To Take Gang Profits," *LAS*, April 2, 1987; *Iraheta v. Superior Court*, 70 Cal. App. 4th 1500, 1514 (Ct. App. 1999); Grogger, "Effects"; Stewart, "Black Codes and Broken."

68. Cal. Penal Code S 186.21.

69. "'Step' Act Clears Hurdle in Assembly," *LAS*, August 18, 1988; "Attorneys Support STEP to Halt Gang Violence," *LAS*, June 18, 1987.

70. Gene Johnson, "LAPD Serves Law To Hardcore Gangs," *LAS*, June 22, 1989; Beckett and Herbert, *Banished*, 9–10; Muñiz, *Police, Power.*

71. Commanding Officer, Operations–South Bureau CRASH letter to Commanding Officer, Operations–South Bureau, "Activities Report for Deployment Period February 24, 1991–March 23, 1991," March 26, 1991, folder 27, box 37, LAWCR; Commanding Officer, Operations–South Bureau CRASH letter to Commanding Officer, Operations–South Bureau, "Activities Report for Deployment Period April 21, 1991–May 18, 1991," May 17, 1991, folder 27, box 37, LAWCR.

72. Davis, *City of Quartz*, 282–84.

73. Robert Reinhold, "In the Middle Of L.A.'s Gang Wars," *New York Times Magazine*, May 22, 1988.

74. Stephen Braun, "The Politics of Murder," *LAT*, February 4, 1988, sec. Part 2.

75. "The Gangs," *LAT*, June 11, 1988, sec. Part 2.

76. Director, Office of Operations letter to All Personnel, Office of Operations, "1988: Year of Gang Enforcement," February 25, 1988, folder Los Angeles Police Commission, Gangs, box 11, SWP; James K. Stewart, "Remarks by the Honorable James K. Stewart, Director of the National Institute of Justice at the LAPD Battle Plans Seminar," Rancho Mirage, California, September 28, 1988.

77. Chief of Police letter to Honorable Board of Police Commissioners, "Needs to Eradicate Violent Street Gangs," October 11, 1988, folder Los Angeles Police Commission, box 11, Gangs, SWP.

78. Scott Harris, "Anti-Gang Funds for Police Backed by Council Panel," *LAT*, April 6, 1988, sec. Part 2.

79. Office of Operations, "Gang Abatement Task Force Operations Guidelines," May 5, 1988, folder 21, box 33, LAWCR.

80. Eric Malnic and Mark Arax, "1,000 Officers Stage Assault Against Violent Youth Gangs," *LAT*, April 9, 1988, Part 2.

81. Office of Operations, "Gang Abatement Task Force Operations Guidelines," May 5, 1988, folder 21, box 33, LAWCR; Operations–Headquarters Bureau, "State of the Los Angeles Gang Problem," March 1, 1989, folder Los Angeles Police Commission, Gangs, box 11, SWP; Davis, *City of Quartz*, 267–315; Davis, "Los Angeles"; Los Angeles Police Department, *Annual Report*, 1988.

82. Operations–Headquarters Bureau, "State of the Los Angeles Gang Problem," March 1, 1989, folder Los Angeles Police Commission, Gangs, box 11, SWP.

83. Paul Feldman, "Police Use a Wide Broom LAPD's War on Gangs and Drugs Has Shifted Emphasis, Concentrating on South-Central L.A.," *LAT*, May 8, 1988, sec. Metro; Bob Baker, "'The Hammer:' Is Nailing Gangs, LAPD Reports," *LAT*, March 13, 1988, sec. Metro; David Ferrell, "NAACP Raps Police Over Gang Sweeps," *LAT*, April 15, 1988, sec. Part 2.

84. "The Gangs," *LAT*, June 11, 1988, sec. Part 2.

85. "Draft Complaint on Gang Sweeps," May 20, 1988, folder CAPA/ACLU, box 12, CAPA; David Lynn letter to John Conyers, March 17, 1989, folder 12, box 51, CAPA; Police Misconduct Lawyer Referral Service, "Police Misconduct Lawyer Referral Service Proposal to the Sunflower Foundation," 1989, folder 7, box 36, CAPA.

86. Paula Brown, "For Kids: Tips On Dealing With 'Sweep' Cops: What To Do When Approached By Cops," *LAS*, April 21, 1988, A1; Nielson Himmel, "L.A. Gang Killings Put at 236—Up 15% from '87," *LAT*, December 16, 1988, sec. Part 2; David Lynn, "Caught between Gang and Police Violence with No Where to Run," April 6, 1988, folder 12, box 51, CAPA.

87. Karol Heppe, "Examples of Police Abuse (Notes)," 1991, folder 12, box 51, CAPA; Paul Feldman and David Freed, "Police 'Czar' Assigned to Spearhead Assault on Gang-Drug Tie-In," *LAT*, January 14, 1988, sec. Metro.

88. Operations–Headquarters Bureau, "State of the Los Angeles Gang Problem," March 1, 1989, folder Los Angeles Police Commission, Gangs, box 11, SWP.

89. Ira Reiner, "Gangs, Crime and Violence in Los Angeles: Findings and Proposals," 1992, folder Gangs, box 212, SSC.

90. Waldinger and Bozorgmehr, *Ethnic Los Angeles*, 402; Miller, *Search and Destroy*, 5.

91. U.S. Congress, House, Select Committee on Narcotics Abuse and Control, *Federal Law Enforcement Role in Narcotics Control in Southern California*, 30.

92. Jesse Brewer letter to Sam Williams, April 21, 1987, folder Los Angeles Police Commission, Gangs, box 11, SWP; "L.A. County's Gang Wars Engulf Peace Efforts," *LAT*, November 12, 1987.

93. Community Youth Gang Services Project, CCJCC, April 21, 1982, 1.36.2.1.1, KHC; Claire Spiegel, "City Council Awards $560,000 to County Anti-Gang Program," *LAT*, August 19, 1981, folder 4, box 7, CEPCCRA.

94. Mike Duran, "Youth Gangs Presentation," February 4, 1982, folder 4, box 3873, MTBAP.

95. Daryl Gates, "Testimony on Progress in the War on Drugs during the First Year of the National Drug Strategy Presented to the United States Senate Judiciary Committee," folder 10, box 4400, MTBAP.

96. U.S. Congress, House, Select Committee on Narcotics Abuse and Control, *Federal Law Enforcement Role in Narcotics Control in Southern California*, 85; Evaluation and Training Institute, "DARE Evaluation for 1985–1989," January 1990, folder 6, box 5021, MTBAP; Daryl F. Gates, "Los Angeles Is in 'Jeopardy,'" 1989, folder Los Angeles Police Commission, Gangs, box 11, SWP. On the LAPD's promotion of DARE, see Los Angeles Police Department, *Annual Report*, 1987, 1990.

97. "L.A. County's Gang Wars Engulf Peace Efforts"; City Council, "Council File: 80-2133 S-3A," September 4, 1980, folder Project HEAVY, box 758965, RFP; Mike Duran, "Gangs," n.d., folder 4, box 3873, MTBAP; "The Situation in Los Angeles."

98. United Neighborhoods Organization Program Outline, folder 4, box 7, CEPCCRA; "La hora politica," *La Opinion*, October, 5, 1982, folder 4, box 7, CEPCCRA.

99. UNO, SCOC, and EVO, "We the People," July 12, 1987, folder 1, box 2511, MTBAP; South Central Organizing Committee, 1983, folder 12, box 320, MTBAP; S.C.O.C., *The S.C.O.C. Report*, July 23, 1984, folder 10, box 19, TCOF.

100. Grace Trejo, "South-Central L.A. Fights Crime Itself," *LAT*, November 23, 1984, sec. Part 2.

101. John T. McDonald letter to Marvin Braude, March 26, 1984, folder NAACP Los Angeles, box 758929, RFP.

102. Joan Milke Flores, "Motion," August 22, 1984, folder Police Department, 1981–85 (1 of 2), box C-1661, GLP.

103. Frank Clifford, "Gates Speaks Out on Deployment: Police Chief Chides 2 Complaining Community Groups," *LAT*, January 17, 1985, sec. Part 2; Public Administration Service, *Patrol Deployment Progress Report for the Los Angeles Police Department*, October 1988, folder Police Patrol Deployment, box 211, SSC.

104. Marita Hernández and Sandy Banks, "Deaths Spur Call for L.A. Gang Control," *LAT*, October 17, 1984, sec. Orange County; Chico Norwood, "SCOC Unveils Jericho Plan to Fight Crime," *LAS*, May 31, 1984; U.S. Congress, House, Select Committee on Narcotics Abuse and Control, *Narcotics Trafficking and Abuse in the Los Angeles Area*, 6–7.

105. Tom Bradley, "UNO/SCOC Crime Rally," July 14, 1985, folder 4, box 2206, MTBAP; UNO, SCOC, and EVO, "We the People," July 12, 1987, folder 1, box 2511, MTBAP.

106. "Save Our Community, Save Our People," 1988, folder NAACP Los Angeles, box 758929, RFP.

107. James K. Hahn letter to Tom Bradley, "NAACP Gang Awareness Survey Results," September 17, 1987, folder 2, box 131, MTBAP; Melanie Lomax to Community Relations Commission, November 26, 1984, folder 12, box 3880, MTBAP; Steven R. Churm, "Pushers' Rule of Streets Challenged in South L.A.: South-Central Residents Fight Back against Pushers, Gangs," *LAT*, November 17, 1986.

108. Community Coalition for Substance Abuse Prevention and Treatment, "Community Coalition," 1991, folder 18, box 19, LAWCR; SCLC and Los Angeles Martin Luther King Legacy Association, "Crack Cocaine Crisis Conference (and Supporting Documentation)," Fall 1989, folder 6, box 35, LHFC.

Chapter 9

1. Office of the Special Advisor of the Los Angeles Police Commission, "Community Meeting No. 1," September 8, 1992, folder 38, box 1, LAWCR; Melvin L. Oliver, James H. Johnson Jr., and Walter C. Farrell Jr., "Anatomy of a Rebellion: A Political-Economic Analysis," in Gooding-Williams, *Reading Rodney King*, 11.

2. Labor/Community Strategy Center, *Reconstructing Los Angeles from the Bottom Up* (Los Angeles, CA: The Center, 1993); On the LCSC, see Mann, *Taking on General Motors*.

3. Katz and Smith, "L.A. Intifada."

4. Labor/Community Strategy Center, *A Call to Reject the Federal Weed and Seed Program in Los Angeles*, 1992; in general, see Hinton, *From the War on Poverty*; Kohler-Hausmann, *Getting Tough*; Harcourt, *Counterrevolution*, 142–43. For an in-depth study of Weed and Seed, see Miller, *Politics of Community*.

5. ACLU, *From the Outside In: Residency Patterns within the Los Angeles Police Department* (ACLU: 1994).

6. Fredric Dannen, "Gates's Hell," *Vanity Fair*, August 1991, folder 4, box 4400, MTBAP.

7. ACLU, *From the Outside In*, 25; Blue Ribbon Rampart Review Panel, "Rampart Reconsidered," 2006, 19–21.

8. ACLU, "On the Line: Police Brutality and Its Remedies" (1991); Paul L. Hoffman, "Testimony of Paul L. Hoffman before the House Sub-Committee on Civil and Constitutional Rights of the House Committee on the Judiciary," March 20, 1991, folder ACLU PCID, box 206, SSC.

9. Lárez v. City of Los Angeles (1991).

10. Skolnick and Fyfe, *Above the Law*, 5–7.

11. David Freed, "Gates Defends His Officers' Search Methods in Court," *LAT*, November 30, 1988, D3; Daryl Gates, "Gates Reply," *LAT*, December 22, 1988, sec. Part 2; Kim Murphy and David Freed, "FBI Probes Alleged Brutality by LAPD's Anti-Gang Division," *LAT*, February 15, 1989.

12. Antonio H. Rodríguez, "Can't Anyone in L.A. Hold Chief Gates Accountable?," *LAT*, January 10, 1989.

13. Cynthia Anderson, Latino Community Justice Center, "Police Abuse in Los Angeles," April 1989, folder 1, box 7, CAPA.

14. "Police Litigation," 1991, folder 3, box 29, MTBAP. The turn to lawsuits reflects what Charles Epp calls "legalized accountability"; see Epp, *Making Rights Real*.

15. "The Final Bradley Five," May 31, 1994, folder The Final Bradley Five, box 212, SSC; Chevigny, *Edge of the Knife*.

16. Lindsee P. Granfield letter to Raymond C. Fisher, "Independent Commission on the Los Angeles Police Department—Second Session with Robert Talcott," May 6, 1991, folder 55, box 18, ICR; Gia Cincone letter to Distribution, "Interview with Reva Tooley," April 30, 1991, folder 59, box 18, ICR; *Subcommittee Report Justice for Janitors Demonstration*, November 20, 1990, folder 1, box 181, MTBAP; Bob Baker, "Inquiry into Strike Violence Ordered: Labor: Mayor Bradley Directs Police Commission to Investigate Clash between Officers and Demonstrating Janitors so It 'Doesn't Happen Again,'" *LAT* June 19, 1990, sec. Metro.

17. Los Angeles Police Department, Office of Administrative Services, "OIS Statistics and Legend," May 31, 1991, folder 2, box 16, ICR; Independent Commission on the Los Angeles Police Department, "Complaint Statistics and Analysis," June 30, 1991, folder 1, box 16, ICR; Yolanda Orozco letter to Independent Commission on the Los Angeles Police Department, "Interview of Captain Jan Charlson, Commanding Officer, Internal Affairs Division," May 3, 1991, folder 32, box 17, ICR; Thomas E. Holliday letter to Richard Drooyan and Gary Feess, "Independent Commission," June 27, 1992, folder 11, box 10, ICR.

18. Commanding Officer, Operations-South Bureau letter to Director, Office of Operations, "Disciplinary Audit," August 26, 1986, folder 25, box 17, ICR; Commanding Officer, Operations-South Bureau letter to Director, Office of Operations, "Disciplinary Audit (with attachments)," August 26, 1986, folder Brewer, box 208, SSC.

19. Chief of Police, "Chief of Police Year End Message—1989," 1989, folder 14, box 32, ICR.

20. Daryl F. Gates letter to Honorable Board of Police Commissioners, "Merit Pay Self-Evaluation for Fiscal Year 1986–7," October 30, 1987, folder 4, box 15, ICR; see other self-evaluations ibid.

21. William H. Webster and Hubert Williams, "The City in Crisis: A Report by the Special Advisor to the Board of Police Commissioners on the Civil Disorder in Los Angeles," Los Angeles, October 21, 1992.

22. Hector Tobar and Leslie Berger, "Tape of L.A. Police Beating Suspect Stirs Public Furor Law Enforcement: Mayor Says He's 'outraged.' The Department, FBI and District Attorney Are Investigating," *LAT*, March 6, 1991, sec. Part A; Gates quote in Stevenson, *Contested Murder*, 284.

23. Daryl F. Gates, "News Conference," 1991, folder 6, box 946, MTBAP; David Ferrell, "Grim Gates Faces Heated Questions," *LAT*, March 8, 1991, sec. Valley; "Gates Offers an Apology," *LAT*, March 9, 1991, sec. Metro.

24. Ted Rohrlich, "Majority Says Police Brutality Is Common," *LAT*, March 10, 1991; "Los Angeles Residents Police Brutality Survey," March 16, 1991, folder 3, box 3182, MTBAP.

25. Paul L. Hoffman, "Testimony of Paul L. Hoffman before the House Sub-Committee on Civil and Constitutional Rights of the House Committee on the Judiciary," March 20, 1991, folder ACLU PCID, box 206, SSC.

26. ACLU of Southern California, "ACLU Presents Police Commission with over 10,000 Letters Asking for Resignation of Los Angeles Police Chief Daryl Gates," March 20, 1991, folder LAPD—Gates/King, box 4, LCRKP; Committee for Justice and a Civilian Police Review Board, "The Effort to Get a Civilian Police Review Board Has Begun: Kick-Off Rally," August 9, 1991, folder 8, box 7, CAPA.

27. Ira Reiner, "Statement by Ira Reiner Announcing the Indictments in the Rodney King Case," March 15, 1991, folder 6, box 946, MTBAP; Sheryl Stolberg, "Hundreds of Protesters Demand That Gates Resign," *LAT*, March 10, 1991, sec. Metro.

28. Honorable Board of Police Commissioners, "Executive Session of Board of Police Commissioners," April 4, 1991, folder Correspondence—Brown Act Invest, box 10, SWP; "Summary of Documents (Chief Gates Lawsuit v. Police Commission)," 1991, folder 10, box 15, ICR; Gates, *Chief*, 385–90; Tom Bradley, "I Called upon Chief Gates to Retire," May 7, 1991, folder 3, box 946, MTBAP; Tom Bradley, "Gates Resignation," April 2, 1991, folder 9, box 1172, MTBAP; Sheryl Stolberg, "Hundreds of Protesters Demand That Gates Resign," *LAT*, March 10, 1991, sec. Metro.

29. Tom Bradley, "Bradley Appoints a High-Level Independent Citizens Commission to Restore Public Confidence in the Police Department," April 1, 1991, folder 35, box 21, ICR; Daryl F. Gates, "Memorandum No. 4: Cooperation with the Independent Commission on the Los Angeles Police Department," May 7, 1991, folder 8, box 29, MTBAP.

30. Robert Mann letter to Los Angeles Police Commissioners, "Los Angeles Police Department Police Dog Deployment," May 7, 1991, folder 7, box 10, ICR; "LAPD K-9 Unit Binder," 1991, folder 2, box 4410, MTBAP; Thomas Mann and Donald W. Cook letter to Thomas Bradley, "Use of LAPD Dogs and Chief Daryl F. Gates," December 16, 1991, folder 9, box 4400, MTBAP; Independent Commission on the Los Angeles Police Department, *Report of the Independent Commission*, 75–79.

31. Independent Commission, "MDT Selections," March 1, 1989; "Los Angeles Police Department Opinion Survey Summary of Results," 1991, folder 23, box 19, ICR; David Huebner, "Issues of Racism and Bias Affecting the Use of Excessive Force (Draft)," June 24, 1991, folder 10, box 27, ICR; Thomas E. Holliday letter to John W. Spiegel, "Summary of LAPD Interviews," June 24, 1991, folder 69, box 33, ICR; see also Amnesty International, *United States of America: Torture, Ill-Treatment and Excessive Force by Police in Los Angeles, California* (New York: Amnesty International Publications, 1992).

32. David D. Dotson, "Independent Commission on the Los Angeles Police Department Executive Session, Testimony of Assistant Chief David D. Dotson," June 14, 1991, folder 2, box 28, MTBAP; Jesse Brewer, "Transcript of Testimony before the Independent Commission of Former Assistant Chief Jesse Brewer," June 19, 1991, folder 2, box 28, MTBAP.

33. Los Angeles Times, *Understanding the Riots*, 39.

34. Independent Commission, *Report of the Independent Commission*, xiv; Brad Seiling letter to Witness File, "March 26, 1991, Interview with Commander Michael Bostic, Captain Robert Riley, Lieutenant George Ybarra, Lieutenant, Him Vogue, and Sergeant Earl Paysinger," May 1, 1991, folder 4, box 19, ICR; Thomas Holliday letter to File, "Interview of Captain Noel Cunningham," May 2, 1991, folder 10, box 19, ICR; Lt. George V. Aliano, "Initial Comments of the Los Angeles Police Protective League to the Special Independent Commission of the Los Angeles Police Department," May 1, 1991, folder 23, box 24, ICR; John B. Sherrell letter to Independent Commission File, "Interview of LAPD Officers," June 20, 1991, folder 6, box 19, ICR.

35. Independent Commission, *Report of the Independent Commission*, xii, 76–77.

36. Ann Reiss Lane and Stanley Sheinbaum letter to Board of Police Commissioners, "Implementation Subcommittee Review of Department Status Report on Independent Commission Recommendations," June 20, 1992, folder LA BD of Police Commissioners—Analysis, box 208, SSC.

37. Tom Bradley, "Bradley Directs Police Commission to Begin Implementing 36 Components of the Christopher Commission Report Immediately," July 16, 1991, folder 1, box 28, MTBAP; Tracy Ford, Wilkinson Andrea, and Tracy Wood, "Panel Urges Gates to Retire Report on Police Cites Racism, Excess Force Investigation," *LAT*, July 10, 1991, sec. Part A.

38. Chief of Police letter to Honorable Board of Police Commissioners, "Recommendations of the Independent Commission on the Los Angeles Police Department," July 23, 1991, folder Christopher Commission, box 1, LCRKP; Daryl F. Gates, *Implementation Status Report—December, 1991*, December 31, 1991, folder LA BD of Police Commissioners Implementation Status Report, box 208, SSC.

39. Los Angeles Police Department, "A Working Definition of Community-Based Policing for the City of Los Angeles," January 1, 1992, folder Area Stations—Community Policing, box 206, SSC; Chief of Police letter to President, Board of Police Commissioners, "Community-Based Policing Pilot Program," January 13, 1992, folder Area Stations—Community Policing, box 206, SSC; Office of the Chief of Police, "Administrative Order No. 1: Community-Based Policing—Phase I," January 26, 1992, folder 13, box 30, LAWCR. On planning for implementing community-based policing, see Community Based Policing Model Executive Committee, "Community-Based Polic-

ing Model (CBPM) Executive Council Meeting," February 12, 1992, folder Comm Based Pol Comt, box 210, SSC.

40. Southeast Area Supervisor, "Southeast Area Supervisors Meeting," May 1, 1991, folder 32, box 37, LAWCR; Chief Hunt, "Supervisors Meeting Notes," May 22, 1991, folder 2, box 38, LAWCR; "LT's Meeting," June 7, 1991, folder 2, box 38, LAWCR; "OSB Meeting," April 2, 1991, folder 2, box 38, LAWCR; "Supervisors Meeting Southwest Area," August 7, 1991, folder 2, box 38, LAWCR; Operations South Bureau, "Notes from OSB Staff Meeting," 1991, folder 27, box 37, LAWCR; "OSB Meeting," April 2, 1991, folder 2, box 38, LAWCR.

41. The conservative Twelfth District opposed the measure 54 to 46 percent. Sonenshein, *Politics in Black and White*, 224–26.

42. "Charter Amendment F," 1991, folder 1, box 946, MTBAP; Meir J. Westreich letter to Members, Public Safety Committee, "Implementation of Charter Amendment F—Selection of Civilian Member of Boards of Rights," June 22, 1992, folder Bd. of Rights, box 208, SSC.

43. Louis Sahagun and John Schwada, "Measure to Reform LAPD Wins Decisively," *LAT*, June 3, 1992, sec. Part A.

44. LCSC, *Reconstructing Los Angeles from the Bottom Up*, 1993.

45. Gloria J. Romero letter to Stanley Sheinbaum, "Complaint Procedures," March 20, 1992, folder ACLU Complaints, box 206, SSC; Director, Office of Operations letter to All Personnel, Office of Operations, "1-800 Citizen Complaint Line," April 3, 1992, folder ACLU PCID, box 206, SSC.

46. Ann Reiss Lane and Stanley Sheinbaum letter to Board of Police Commissioners, "Implementation Subcommittee Review of Department Status Report on Independent Commission Recommendations," June 20, 1992, folder LA BD of Police Commissioners—Analysis, box 208, SSC; ACLU of Southern California, "The Call for Change Goes Unanswered," March 1992, folder ACLU Complaints, box 206, SSC; ACLU of Southern California, "ACLU Finds Major Flaws in LAPD Handling of Citizen Complaints," March 30, 1992, folder ACLU PCID, box 206, SSC.

47. Richard A. Serrano and Carlos V. Lozano, "Jury Picked for King Trial; No Blacks Chosen," *LAT*, March 3, 1992; Gooding-Williams, *Reading Rodney King*; Webster and Williams, *City in Crisis*.

48. On black-Korean relations and the need to understand underlying structural relations, see Camp, *Incarcerating the Crisis*, 99, 104–5; Stevenson, *Contested Murder*; Mike Davis, "In L.A., Burning All Illusions," *Nation* 254, no. 21 (June 1992): 743–46. Media attention focused on black-Korean tension, a reflection of the changing nature of American cities during an era of immigration and white flight. But the concern surrounding Korean-American vigilantism among African Americans was as much about the underlying structure of a racially discriminatory criminal justice system as it was about interracial tension. On the demographic transformation of cities in the late twentieth century, see Katz, *Why Don't American*.

49. Abu-Lughod, *Race, Space, and Riots*, 231; Terry W. Bird, Richard J. Stone, and Elizabeth D. Lear letter to William H. Webster and Hubert Williams, "Interview of Los Angeles Police Chief Daryl F. Gates—June 25, 1992," July 1, 1992, folder 84, box 19, LAWCR.

50. G. J. Church and S. Monroe, "The Fire This Time," *Time*, May 11, 1992; "Analysis of the Los Angeles Police Department's Planning, Preparedness and Response to the 1992 Riot (The First Six Hours)," 1992, folder LAPD—Riot Report, box 5, LCRKP; John D. Vandevelde and Terry W. Bird letter to Richard J. Stone, "Interview of Lt. Michael Moulin—Part 2," June 8, 1992, folder 24, box 23, LAWCR.

51. D. H. Hackworth, "This Was No Riot, It Was a Revolt," *Newsweek* 119, no. 21 (May 25, 1992): 33; "Administrative Messages—Re: Gangs Targeting Police," May 1, 1992, folder 18, box 4404, MTBAP; Tom Bradley, "Declaration of Local Emergency," April 30, 1992, folder 16, box 4406, MTBAP; Tom Bradley, "Regulation and Directive Ordering Curfew and Other Specific Restrictions during Existence of a Local Emergency," April 30, 1992, folder 16, box 4406, MTBAP; Tom Bradley, "Regulation and Directive Ordering Curfew and Other Specific Restrictions during Existence of a Local Emergency Amendment No. 1," April 30, 1992, folder 16, box 4406, MTBAP; see amendments to the Emergency Amendments ibid.

52. George Bush, "Address to the Nation on Civil Disturbances in Los Angeles, California," May 1, 1992, the American Presidency Project, University of California, Santa Barbara; Daniel E. Lungren letter to All Sheriffs and Chiefs of Police in Areas Encompassed by the Governor's Declaration of a State of Emergency, "Utilization of Federal Law Enforcement as Peace Officers," May 1, 1992, folder 18, box 4404, MTBAP; Roger E. Venturi Letter to Larry Buffalow, "Federal Officers, Authority to Enforce State Law," May 1, 1992, folder 18, box 4404, MTBAP; Inter-Agency Team, *Inter-Agency Team Final Report*, "Appendix: Federal Law Enforcement Agencies," 1992, folder 1, box 23, LAWCR.

53. Webster and Williams, *City in Crisis*, 26, 11–27; Abu-Lughod, *Race, Space, and Riots*, 237–39; Horne, *Fire This Time*, 355–56; Paul Lieberman, "40% of Riot Suspects Have Criminal Records," *LAT*, May 19, 1992, sec. Metro.

54. George Bush, "Address to the Nation on Civil Disturbances in Los Angeles, California," May 1, 1992, the American Presidency Project, University of California, Santa Barbara.

55. A. T. Callinicos, "Meaning of Los Angeles Riots," *Economic and Political Weekly* 27, no. 30 (July 25, 1992): 1603–6; Jack Nelson, "After the Riots: The Search for Answers; Bush Reaction to Riots Splits Republicans Unrest," *LAT*, May 8, 1992, sec. Part A; Paul Lieberman, "40% of Riot Suspects Have Criminal Records," *LAT*, May 19, 1992, sec. Metro.

56. Miller, *Search and Destroy*, 5; Johnson et al., "Los Angeles Rebellion," 364; James H. Johnson and Walter C. Farrell, "The Fire This Time: The Genesis of the Los Angeles Rebellion of 1992," *North Carolina Law Review* 71 (1992–1993): 1416.

57. Manuel Pastor, Barbara Cox, and Tomás Rivera Center, *Latinos and the Los Angeles Uprising*, 9; Katherine A. Schmidt, "RAND Study: Blacks Represented Just 36% of Riot Suspects," *Outlook*, June 24, 1992, folder 39, box 4, LAWCR; Sánchez, "Face the Nation." On immigration and urban transformation, see Katz, *Why Don't American*; Barber, *Latino City*.

58. Mike Hernandez, "Hernandez Denounces INS Sweeps; Urges Council Solidarity in Asking Federal Government to Halt Sweeps as City Recovers," May 6, 1992, folder 13 box 1201, LAWCR; Inter-Agency Report, *Inter-Agency Team Final Report*, September 2, 1992, folder 20, box 22, LAWCR; ACLU, "Civil Liberties in Crisis."

59. Roel Campos and Laurie Levenson letter to Richard J. Stone, Vincent J. Marella, and Jan Hanzlik, "Interview with INS (with Attachments)," August 5, 1992, folder 30, box 20, LAWCR; Office of the Commissioner, Immigration and Naturalization Service letter to George J. Terwilliger, III, "Plans for Processing Aliens Arrested during the Los Angeles Disturbance," May 20, 1992, folder 58, box 21, LAWCR.

60. Ronald J. Nessim letter to File, "Webster Study—CARECEN Documents," September 1, 1992, folder 3, box 21, LAWCR; Webster and Williams, *City in Crisis*, 160.

61. Mike Davis, "In L.A., Burning All Illusions," *Nation* 254, no. 21 (June 1992): 743–46.

62. Davis, "Who Killed Los Angeles? Part Two"; Special Advisor's Study Report, *Special Advisor's Study Report re Information Obtained from Public Officials and the Community*, September 14, 1992, folder 8, box 22, LAWCR; LAPD Team, *LAPD Team Final Report*, September 2, 1992, folder 9, box 22, LAWCR.

63. Office of the Special Advisor of the Los Angeles Police Commission, "Community Meeting No. 1," September 8, 1992, folder 38, box 1, LAWCR; Oliver et al., "Anatomy of a Rebellion," 119.

64. Hazen, *Inside the L.A. Riots*; Webster and Williams, *City in Crisis*; "Agreement between the City of Los Angeles and the Special Advisor to the Police Commission Concerning the Events Following the Rodney King Verdict," 1992, folder 23, box 23, LAWCR.

65. Webster and Williams, *City in Crisis*, 165–81; Ashley Dunn, "Commission Reveals Little to Riots' Victims Reaction: While They Applaud the Call for Better Planning, Most Feel the Recommendations Don't Address the True Causes of the City's Problems," *LAT*, October 22, 1992, sec. Part A; Davis, "Who Killed Los Angeles? Part 2."

66. LCSC, "Reconstructing"; C.A.P.A., "Community Control of Police, 1989 through 1993," folder, *CAPA Report* 94, box 19, CAPA.

67. Clifford et al., "Leaders Lose Feel for L.A. Mayor Bradley and the Council Are Accused of Neglecting L.A.'s Neediest Areas," *LAT*, August 30, 1992, sec. Part A; Thomas Bradley, "Rebuild L.A.: The Blueprint for Our Future," May 2, 1992, folder 31, box 2, RLAC; Rebuild L.A., "RLA Mission Statement," June 20, 1992, folder 2, box 1, RLAC; Rebuild L.A., *Rebuilding LA's Urban Communities: A Final Report from RLA*, 1996, folder 41, box 197, RLAC; Gottlieb et al., *Next Los Angeles*, 178–83; Davis, "Who Killed Los Angeles? A Political."

68. The White House, Office of the Press Secretary, "'Weed and Seed' Program to Aid Needy Los Angeles Communities," May 8, 1992, folder 3, box 5, MTBAP; William P. Barr, "Statement of William P. Barr, Attorney General," May 20, 1992, folder 1, box 4378, MTBAP; U.S. Department of Justice, "The Weed and Seed Strategy," n.d., folder 380, box 23, RLAC; U.S. Department of Justice, "Operation 'Weed and Seed' Reclaiming America's Neighborhoods," 1991, folder 6, box 12, CAPA; Michael J. Rich, "Riot and Reason: Crafting an Urban Policy Response," *Publius* 23, no. 3 (July 1, 1993): 115–34; Ronald J. Ostrow, "Bush Hopes Seed Money Will Sow Roots of Peace in L.A.," *LAT*, May 9, 1992; Miller, *Politics of Community*.

69. Wendy J. Greuel, "Weed and Seed in Los Angeles," 1992, folder 2, box 4378, MTBAP.

70. Ostrow, "Bush Hopes Seed Money."

71. "Weed and Seed in Los Angeles," 1992, folder 2, box 4378, MTBAP; Mayor's Office, "Weed and Seed Update," 1992, folder 14, box 825, MTBAP; U.S. Department of Justice, "City of Los Angeles Weed and Seed," 1992, folder 380, box 23, RLAC; Wendy J. Greuel letter to Tom Bradley, "Weed and Seed Press Conference," August 6, 1992, folder 1, box 4378, MTBAP.

72. Wendy J. Greuel letter to Tom Bradley, Mark Fabiani, and Linda Griego, "Weed and Seed Update," June 8, 1992, folder 15, box 1182, MTBAP; Labor/Community Strategy Center, "Public Hearing," October 1992, folder 15, box 1182; Terree A. Bowers letter to Councilperson, "LAPD Proposal—Los Angeles Weed and Seed Program," November 9, 1992, folder 12, box 825, MTBAP; Mark Ridley-Thomas letter to Terree A. Bowers, "LAPD Proposal—Los Angeles Weed and Seed Program," November 16, 1992, folder 1, box 4378, MTBAP.

73. Mark Ridley-Thomas and Rita Walters, "Motion," 1992, folder 1, box 4378, MTBAP.

74. Urban Strategies Group of the Labor/Community Strategy Center, "Weed and Seed Decried as Objectionable Police Action: Civil Rights and Urban Leaders Call for Rejection of Plan," September 15, 1992, folder 16, box 825, MTBAP.

75. C.A.P.A. "Stop 'Operation Weed and Seed,'" n.d., folder 15, box 12, CAPA; Terree A. Bowers and Edward McGah letter to Thomas J. Rueter, "Urban Strategies Group—'A Call to Reject the Federal Weed and Seed Program in Los Angeles,'" September 30, 1992, folder 12, box 825, MTBAP.

76. Anthony Thigpenn letter to Marcella Howell, "LAPD Weed and Seed," October 20, 1992, folder 6, box 825, MTBAP.

77. LCSC, *Call to Reject.*

78. Henry Weinstein, "Skepticism Greets LAPD's Weed and Seed Proposals," *LAT,* September 18, 1992.

79. Tom Bradley, "Bradley Announces Compromise That Will Enable City to Tap $19 Million in Federal Funds," November 20, 1992, folder 1, box 4378, MTBAP; Presidential Task Force on Los Angeles Recovery, *Presidential Task Force on Los Angeles Recovery Final Report,* January 20, 1993 (Courtesy of Professor Lindsey Lupo).

80. Urban Strategies Group of the Labor/Community Strategy Center letter to Mark Ridley-Thomas, December 14, 1992, folder 16, box 825, MTBAP; Eric Mann, "The Left and the City's Future," *The Nation* 256, no. 17 (May 3, 1993): 586–90; LCSC, *Reconstructing Los Angeles.* On California prison statistics, see Gilmore, *Golden Gulag,* 7, 75–76, 111.

81. "Administrative Order No. 1: Community-Based Policing—Phase I," January 26, 1992, box 30, folder 13, LAWCR; Gottlieb et al., *Next Los Angeles,* 153–57; FBI, UCR Section VI—Law Enforcement Personnel, 2000; Los Angeles Police Department, "LAPD Reaches Milestone Number of Active-Duty Officers," www.lapdonline.org; James Rainey, and Marc Lacy, "Riordan's Budget Spares Only LAPD," *LAT,* September 16, 1993.

82. Richard A. Serrano, "Understanding the Riots-Six Months Later A New Blue Line," *LAT,* November 17, 1992, sec. Special Section.

83. Davis, "Who Killed Los Angeles? Part Two."

84. Human Rights Watch, *Shielded from Justice: Police Brutality and Accountability in the United States,* Human Rights Watch, June 1998.

85. Domanick, *Blue*, 108–24, 149, 164–67, 175–76; Cannon, *Official Negligence*, 527–63.

86. John L. Mitchell, "Bernard Parks' Record as LAPD Chief and City Councilman Is a Mixed Blessing in His Race for L.A. County Supervisor," *LAT*, May 4, 2008; Domanick, *Blue*, 122–25; 159–60, 164–66, 199–201; Rice, *Power Concedes Nothing*, 226–27; Sonenshein, *City at Stake*, 123–29; Human Rights Watch, *Shielded from Justice*.

Epilogue

1. Agee, "Crisis and Redemption."

2. Berger, "Social Movements"; Davis, *Policing the Black Man*; Butler, *Chokehold*; Hayes, *Colony in a Nation*; Gottschalk, *Caught*.

3. Rampart Independent Review Panel, *Report of the Rampart Independent Review Panel*; Blue Ribbon Rampart Review Panel, *Rampart Reconsidered*.

4. Cotton, "Violence"; Katz and Smith, "L.A. Intifada," 24; Katz, *Why Don't American*, 94.

5. Katz and Smith, "L.A. Intifada," 19.

6. Community in Support of the Gang Truce, "No Justice, No Peace!," 1992, folder 42, box 26, CAPA; Vargas, *Catching Hell*, 177; Zinzun, "Gang Truce."

7. "Bloods/Crips Proposal for LA's Face-Lift," n.d., folder Gangs, box 212, SSC.

8. Mike Davis, "In L.A., Burning All Illusions," *Nation* 254, no. 21 (June 1992): 743–46; Michael Zinzun, "We Are All Responsible," 1993, folder 22, box 95, CAPA.

9. Gottlieb et al., *Next Los Angeles*, 126–27; Community In Support of the Gang Truce, "No Set Trippin,'" April 28, 1995, folder 20, box 18, CAPA; Vargas, *Catching Hell*, 194; Hutson et al., "Epidemic"; see also Umemoto, *Truce*.

10. Zinzun, "Gang Truce."

11. Domanick, *Blue*, 133, 153–55, 156; Frontline, "LAPD Blues: The story of Los Angeles' gangsta cops & the corruption scandal that has shaken the once great LAPD," (2001), http://www.pbs.org/wgbh/pages/frontline/shows/lapd/bare.html, accessed January 11, 2017; Randall Sullivan, "The Murder of Notorious B.I.G." *Rolling Stone*, no. 870 (June 7, 2001): 80. For the Pérez transcripts, see Post Conviction Assistance Center, "Pérez Transcripts," http://www.pcaclaw.org/perez.html, accessed January 11, 2017.

12. Frontline, "LAPD Blues: Timeline."

13. Domanick, *Blue*, 156, 170–75; Rice, *Power Concedes Nothing*, 227–28; Charles Rappleye, "Rampart 2," *L.A. Weekly*, January 31, 2001; Charles Rappleye, "Rampart Runneth Over," *L.A. Weekly*, October 11, 2000; Erwin Chemerinsky, "An Independent Analysis of the Los Angeles Police Department's Board of Inquiry Report on the Rampart Scandal," *Loyola of Los Angeles Law Review* 34 (2001): 545–646; Rampart Independent Review Panel, *Report of the Rampart Independent Review Panel: A Report to the Los Angeles Board of Police Commissioners Concerning the Operations, Policies, and Procedures of the Los Angeles Police Department in the Wake of the Rampart Scandal*, November 16, 2000.

14. Bernard Parks, "Rampart Area Corruption Incident," March 1, 2000; Rampart Independent Review Panel, *Report*.

15. Chemerinsky, "Independent Analysis," 550; Rice, *Power Concedes Nothing*, 230–32.

16. Rampart Independent Review Panel, *Report*; Blue Ribbon Rampart Review Panel, "Rampart Reconsidered," 2006, 25; see also Los Angeles County Bar Association

Task Force on the State Criminal Justice System, *Critical Analysis of Lessons Learned: Recommendations for Improving the California Criminal Justice System in the Wake of the Rampart Scandal*, April, 2003.

17. Blue Ribbon Rampart Review Panel, "Rampart Reconsidered," 2006, 1, 18; Gottlieb et al., *Next Los Angeles*, 127; Charles Rappleye, "Rampart 2," *L.A. Weekly*, January 31, 2001.

18. Bill Lann Lee to James K. Hahn, "LAPD Notice of Investigation Letter," May 8, 2000, https://www.justice.gov/crt/lapd-notice-investigation-letter, accessed January 11, 2017; Peter Boyer, "Bad Cops," *New Yorker*, May 21, 2001; H.R.3355—Violent Crime Control and Law Enforcement Act of 1994, 42 U.S.C. § 14141 § (1994); U.S. Department of Justice, "Conduct of Law Enforcement Agencies," June 2, 2016, https://www.justice.gov/crt/conduct-law-enforcement-agencies, accessed January 11, 2017.

19. Bernard Parks, *Rampart Area Corruption Incident*, March 1, 2000; Christopher Stone, Todd Foglesong, and Christine M. Cole, *Policing Los Angeles*, May 2009; Los Angeles Police Department, "Consent Decree Overview," www.LAPDonline.org, accessed January 11, 2017; U.S. v. City of Los Angeles—Consent Decree—Introduction, https://www.justice.gov/crt/us-v-city-los-angeles-consent-decree-introduction, accessed January 11, 2017; U.S. District Court for the Central District of California, *United States of America v. City of Los Angeles, California, Board of Police Commissioners of the City of Los Angeles, and the Los Angeles Police Department: Consent Decree* (September 19, 2000).

20. Rice, *Power Concedes Nothing*, 245–51; Domanick, *Blue*, 234–38; Blue Ribbon Rampart Review Panel, "Rampart Reconsidered." There is some debate over whether CompStat comes from a shortening of "compare statistics" or "computer statistics." See Kohler-Hausmann, *Misdemeanorland*, 38.

21. Rice, *Power Concedes Nothing*, 260–63; Ian Ayres and Jonathan Borowsky, "A Study of Racially Disparate Outcomes in the Los Angeles Police Department"; Blue Ribbon Rampart Review Panel, "Rampart Reconsidered."

22. Blue Ribbon Rampart Review Panel, "Rampart Reconsidered," 2006, 15, 19–20, 25–26. For a discussion of contemporary homicide in Los Angeles, see Leovy, *Ghettoside*.

23. Christopher Stone, Todd Foglesong, and Christine M. Cole, *Policing Los Angeles*, May 2009; Domanick, *Blue*, 279–82, 314–15, 333; Stuart, *Down, Out*; Muñiz, *Police, Power*.

24. Ian Ayres and Jonathan Borowsky, "A Study of Racially Disparate Outcomes in the Los Angeles Police Department," ACLU of Southern California, 2008; Ian Ayres, "Racial Profiling in L.A.: The Numbers Don't Lie," *LAT*, October 23, 2008, sec. Main News; Joel Rubin, "LAPD Rejects Finding of Bias," *LAT*, January 14, 2009, sec. California; sec. Part B; Epp, Maynard-Moody, and Haider-Markel, *Pulled Over*. For the expansion of misdemeanor arrests and racial disparities in New York see Kohler-Hausmann, *Misdemeanorland*.

25. Christopher Stone, Todd Foglesong, and Christine M. Cole, *Policing Los Angeles*, May 2009. For detailed accounts of Bratton and reform in Los Angeles, see Domanick, *Blue*, 223–343; and Rice, *Power Concedes Nothing*, 309–11. On police killings, see the *LAT* "Homicide Report," http://homicide.latimes.com/neighborhood/la-city/officer_involved/true, accessed December 15, 2017.

26. Dennis Romero, "LAPD's Rampart-Era Consent Decree Finally Over," *L.A. Weekly*, May 16, 2013.

27. On the rise of big data, surveillance, and policing see Ferguson, *Rise of Big Data Policing*; Friedman, *Unwarranted*.

28. Dennis Romero, "The Militarization of Police Started in Los Angeles," *L.A. Weekly*, August 15, 2014, http://www.laweekly.com/news/the-militarization-of-police -started-in-los-angeles-5010287, accessed February 11, 2016.

29. David A. Graham, "Can Trump's Justice Department Undo Police Reform?," *Atlantic*, April 4, 2017, https://www.theatlantic.com/politics/archive/2017/04/the -beginning-of-the-end-of-federal-police-reform/521847/, accessed December 22, 2017.

30. President's Task Force on 21st Century Policing, *Final Report of the President's Task Force on 21st Century Policing* (Washington, DC: Office of Community Oriented Policing Services, 2015); Tony Platt, "Obama's Task Force on Policing: Will It Be Different This Time? | Social Justice," Social Justice, February 28, 2015, http:// www.socialjusticejournal.org/obamas-task-force-on-policing-will-it-be-different -this-time/, accessed, March 6, 2017; Ta-Nehisi Coates, "The Myth of Police Reform," *Atlantic*, April 15, 2015, http://www.theatlantic.com/politics/archive/2015 /04/the-myth-of-police-reform/390057/, accessed February 16, 2016; Vitale, *End of Policing*.

31. "L.A. Police Commission Alters Use-of-Deadly-Force Policy; Emphasizes Need to De-Escalate Situations," *KTLA* (blog), March 15, 2016, http://ktla.com/2016/03/15 /los-angeles-police-commission-alters-use-of-deadly-force-policy-emphasizes-need -to-de-escalate-situations/, accessed, March 16, 2016; "Homicide Report," *LAT*, http:// homicide.latimes.com/neighborhood/la-city/officer_involved/true, accessed December 15, 2017; Jason McGahan, "L.A. Police Have Significantly Underreported Officer-Involved Shooting Deaths, Study Says," *L.A. Weekly*, October 13, 2016, http:// www.laweekly.com/news/la-police-have-significantly-underreported-officer-involved -shooting-deaths-study-says-7488797, accessed October 18, 2016; Kate Mather and Cindy Chang, "LAPD Watchdog Takes a Long Look into Allegations of Racial Profiling," *LAT*, November 15, 2016, http://www.latimes.com/local/lanow/la-me-ln-lapd -biased-policing-20161115-story.html, accessed November 18, 2016.

32. Vitale, *End of Policing*; Friedman, *Unwarranted*; Butler, *Chokehold*; Neocleous, *Fabrication*, 99–106.

33. "Still Searching for Justice," *US News & World Report*, https://www.usnews.com /opinion/civil-wars/articles/2017-05-01/25-years-after-los-angeles-riots-police -injustice-continues, accessed May 4, 2017; "Twenty Five Years Later, How Did the Riots Transform L.A.? And Has the City Changed Enough?," *LAT*, April 28, 2017, http:// www.latimes.com/opinion/la-oe-los-angeles-riots-voices-updates-the-chief-s -promise-the-lapd-will-1493352988-htmlstory.html, accessed May 4, 2017; Zusha Elinson, "The 1992 Riots Changed Policing in L.A., but Some Say Not Enough," *Wall Street Journal*, April 29, 2017, sec. US, https://www.wsj.com/articles/the-1992-riots -changed-policing-in-l-a-but-some-say-not-enough-1493467200, accessed May 4, 2017.

34. Simone Weichselbaum, "The Big Problems with Police That Washington Can't Fix," *TIME.Com*, http://time.com/police-shootings-justice-department-civil-rights -investigations/, accessed December 22, 2017.

35. Kate Mather, "African Americans Are Less Trusting of Law Enforcement in Los Angeles County, Poll Finds," *LAT*, May 31, 2016, http://www.latimes.com/local/lanow/la-me-ln-policing-survey-20160531-snap-story.html, accessed June 1, 2016.

36. See the work of Los Angeles area activists involved in the Youth Justice Coalition, http://www.youth4justice.org/, the Los Angeles Community Action Network, http://cangress.org/, Californians United for a Responsible Budget (CURB), http://www.curbprisonspending.org/, the National Day Laborers Organizing Network, https://ndlon.org/, Immigrant Youth Coalition, http://theiyc.org/, and Black Lives Matter, https://blacklivesmatter.com/, among many others. See Hernández, *City of Inmates*, 199–220.

Bibliography

Primary Sources

Manuscript Collections

Amistad Research Center, Tulane University
    John Allen Buggs Papers, 1939–1964
Bancroft Library, University of California, Berkeley, Berkeley, California
    Governor's Commission on the Los Angeles Riots Records
    National Association for the Advancement of Colored People, Region I, Records
Beinecke Rare Book & Manuscript Library, Yale University, New Haven, Connecticut
    The Black Voice
California State Archives, Sacramento, California
    California Council on Criminal Justice Records
    State Office of Economic Opportunity Office Records
California State University, Dominguez Hills, Special Collections, Carson, California
    Glenn M. Anderson Papers
California State University, Los Angeles, Special Collections, Los Angeles, California
    John Holland Papers
    Julian Nava Papers
    Mervyn Dymally Papers
California State University, Northridge, Urban Archives Collections, Northridge,
    California
    Community Relations Committee Records
    Frank Del Olmo Collection
    Julian Nava Collection
    Robert Docter Papers
Hoover Institution Archives, Stanford, California
    Commonwealth Club Records
    Socialist Workers Party Records
The Huntington Library, San Marino, California
    Alexander Pope Papers
    Papers of Edmund D. Edelman
    Collection of Kenneth Hahn
    Loren Miller Papers
    Los Angeles Times Company Records
Library of Congress, Manuscripts Division, Washington, D.C.
    National Association for the Advancement of Colored People Records
Los Angeles City Archives, Los Angeles, California
    Arthur Snyder Papers

City Council Files
City Council Minutes, 1850–1978
Gilbert Lindsey Papers
Human Relations Commission Records
Joel Wachs Papers
Los Angeles Police Department/Bureau of Special Investigations Records
Mark Ridley-Thomas Papers
Pat Russell Papers
Police Department Records PDX/82
Police Department Records, Correspondence and Subject Files PDX/95A
Police Department Records/PDX
Robert Farrell Papers
Los Angeles Public Library, Los Angeles, California
California Collection
Loyola Marymount University, Department of Archives and Special Collections,
William H. Hannon Library, Los Angeles, California
Rebuild L.A. Collection
Moorland-Spingarn Research Library at Howard University
Ralph J. Bunche Oral History Collection
National Archives and Records Administration, Archives II, College Park,
Maryland
Department of Justice Records (RG 60)
FBI Case File 157-LA-2712 (Possible Riot in Watts Area) received through FOIA
Law Enforcement Assistance Association Records (RG 423)
U.S. Civil Rights Commission Records (RG 453)
New York Public Library, Henry W. and Albert A. Berg Collection of English and
American Literature
Berg Collection Un-catalogued Manuscripts
Proquest History Vault (Online Database Access)
Civil Rights during the Johnson Administration, 1963–1969, Part I: The White
House Central Files
Civil Rights during the Johnson Administration, 1963–1969, Part V: Records
of the National Advisory Commission on Civil Disorders Records
(Kerner Commission)
Records of the U.S. Commission on Civil Rights, Special Projects, 1960–1970
Richard Milhous Nixon Presidential Library, Yorba Linda, California and
Washington
Egil ("Bud") Krogh Files
White House Central Files Confidential Files
White House Central Files—HU 3-1
White House Central Files JL—6
White House Central Files LG/Los Angeles
Ronald Reagan Presidential Library, Simi Valley, California
Governor's Papers Governor's Office Files
Governor's Papers Research Unit
WHORM Local Government Files

Schomburg Center for Research in Black Culture, Special Collections, New York, New York

Interreligious Foundation of Community Organizations Records

Southern California Library, Los Angeles, California

20th Century Organization Files

Black Panther Collection

Coalition against Police Abuse Papers

Liberty Hill Foundation Collection

Los Angeles Civil Unrest, 1992 Collection

Meyerson vs. City of Los Angeles Records

Saul Halpert Papers

South Los Angeles 20th Century Documentation Collection

Street Vendors Association Records

Urban Policy Research Institute Records

Watts 1965 Collection

Watts 1965 Oral History Collection

Stanford Green Library, Special Collections, Stanford, California

Bert Corona Papers

Centro de Acción Social Autónomo Papers

Eduardo Quevedo Papers

Ernesto Galarza Papers

Manuel Ruiz Papers

Mexican American Legal Defense and Educational Fund Records

National Council of La Raza Records

State University of New York at Buffalo, University Archives, Buffalo, New York

Elwin H. Powell Papers

UCLA Chicano Studies Research Center, University of California, Los Angeles

The Church of the Epiphany Chicano Civil Rights Archive 1960–1994

Edward R. Roybal Papers 1919–2003

Grace Montañez Davis Papers, 39

Rosalio Muñoz Collection

University of California, Los Angeles Library Special Collections, Charles E. Young Research Library, UCLA, Los Angeles, California.

American Civil Liberties Union of Southern California Records

Augustus F. Hawkins Papers

California Ephemera Collection

Collection of Underground, Alternative and Extremist Literature

Debbie Louis Collection on Civil Rights

Hugh R. Manes Papers

Los Angeles Unified School District Records

Mayor Tom Bradley Administration Papers

Paul Bullock Papers

Rosalio Muñoz Papers

University of California, San Diego, The Library

Herman Baca Papers, 1964–2013 (online access: http://libraries.ucsd.edu/speccoll/testing/html/mss0649a.html)

University of California, Santa Barbara, CEMA 1, Department of Special Collections, University Library, University of California, Santa Barbara, Santa Barbara, California

    Oscar Zeta Acosta Papers

    Samuel L. Williams Papers

University of California, Santa Barbara, Department of Special Collections, Davidson Library, University of California, Santa Barbara

    Lou Cannon—Rodney King Papers

    Stanley K. Sheinbaum Collection

University of Southern California, Regional History Collection, Special Collections, Information Services Division, University of Southern California, Los Angeles, California

    Alphonzo Bell Papers

    Chester Earl Holifield Papers

    Independent Commission on the Los Angeles Police Department Records

    Los Angeles Webster Commission Records

U.S. Citizenship & Immigration Services History Library

    Vertical Files

Newspapers and Periodicals

American County Government	*Los Angeles Times*
Atlantic	*Movement*
Black Enterprise	*Nation*
Chicago Daily Defender	*National Review*
Commentary Magazine	*New York Times*
Economic and Political Weekly	*New York Times Magazine*
FBI Law Enforcement Bulletin	*New Yorker*
Freedomways	*Newsweek*
Frontier	*Police Chief*
Jacobin	*Rolling Stone*
La Opinion	*Time*
L.A. Weekly	*Trans-Action*
Los Angeles Herald-Examiner	*U.S. News & World Report*
Los Angeles Sentinel	*Wall Street Journal*

Government Serials, Publications, and Reports

Attorney General of the United States. "Task Force on Violent Crime." Hearings, Los Angeles, 1981.

Beck, G. N. "SWAT—The Los Angeles Police Special Weapons and Tactics Teams." *FBI Law Enforcement Bulletin*, April 1972.

California Council on Criminal Justice. State Task Force on Gangs and Drugs. *Final Report*. 1989.

California Department of Industrial Relations. *Negroes and Mexican Americans in South and East Los Angeles*. San Francisco: California Department of Industrial Relations, 1966.

California Legislature. Assembly Select Committee on the Administration of
Justice. *Relations between the Police and Mexican-Americans*. Sacramento:
January 28, 1972.

———. *Relations between the Police and Mexican-Americans*. Sacramento: April 21,
1972.

———. *Relations between the Police and Mexican-Americans*. Sacramento: April 28,
1972.

California State Advisory Committee to the U.S. Commission on Civil Rights. *Open
Meeting on: The Immigration and Naturalization Service's Policies and Practices in
the State of California, and the Civil Rights Effects of the Carter Administration's
Proposed Immigration Legislation*. Hearing. Los Angeles, 1978, Robert S. Rankin
Memorial Library, Washington, D.C.

———. *Police-Community Relations in East Los Angeles, California*. San Francisco:
1970.

———. *Report on California: Police-Minority Group Relations*. San Francisco: 1963.

California State Assembly Select Committee on Juvenile Violence. *California State
Assembly Report on the Los Angeles Hearing on Juvenile Violence Held April 26,
1974*. Sacramento: California Legislature, 1974.

California Youth Authority. *AB 3121 Impact Evaluation Final Report*. January 1980.

City of Los Angeles. Community Analysis Bureau. *The State of the City*. Vol. 1. Los
Angeles: Community Analysis Bureau, 1972.

———. *The State of the City*. Vol. 2. Los Angeles: Community Analysis Bureau,
1972.

City of Los Angeles. Office of the Mayor and City Administrative Officer. *Budget,
City of Los Angeles*. Los Angeles: City of Los Angeles, 1977–1978.

———. *Budget, City of Los Angeles*. Los Angeles: City of Los Angeles, 1978–1979.

———. *Budget, City of Los Angeles*. Los Angeles: City of Los Angeles, 1990–1992.

County of Los Angeles. Ad Hoc Subcommittee on Criminal Aliens. *Countywide
Criminal Justice Coordination Committee. Criminal Aliens in the Los Angeles
County Jail Population: Final Report*. Los Angeles: County of Los Angeles,
November 1990.

County of Los Angeles. Commission on Human Relations. *The Urban Reality:
A Comparative Study*. Los Angeles: County of Los Angeles Commission on
Human Relations, 1965.

Davis, Edward M. *LAPD and Computers, 1972–1973*. Los Angeles: LAPD Advance
Planning Division, 1972.

Dunworth, Terence, and Aaron Saiger. *National Assessment of the Byrne
Formula Grant Program*. Washington, D.C.: National Institute of Justice,
December 1996.

Governor's Commission on the Los Angeles Riots. *Violence in the City—An End or a
Beginning?* Los Angeles: Governor's Commission on the Los Angeles Riots,
December 2, 1965.

Guthrie, C. Robert. *Project Sky Knight*. Washington, D.C.: U.S. Dept. of Justice,
Office of Law Enforcement Assistance, 1968.

Hahn, James K. *Civil Gang Abatement: A Community Based Policing Tool of the Los
Angeles City Attorney*. Los Angeles: City of Los Angeles, 1989.

Hamparian, Donna M. "Youth in Adult Courts: Between Two Worlds, West Region, Major Issues in Juvenile Justice and Delinquency Prevention." Washington, D.C.: National Institute for Juvenile Justice and Delinquency Prevention, January 1982.

Independent Commission on the Los Angeles Police Department. *Report of the Independent Commission on the Los Angeles Police Department*. Los Angeles, 1991.

Lasley, James R. *Using Traffic Barriers to 'Design Out' Crime: A Program Evaluation of LAPD's Operation Cul-De-Sac*. Washington, D.C.: National Institute of Justice, November 1996.

Los Angeles Police Department (LAPD). *Annual Report*. Los Angeles: City of Los Angeles Police Department, 1964–1992.

———. "Consent Decree Overview." www.LAPDonline.org, accessed January 11, 2017.

———. *LAPD Mexican-American Community Conference Proceedings and Recommendations*, Los Angeles: City of Los Angeles Police Department, 1967.

———. "LAPD Reaches Milestone Number of Active-Duty Officers." http://www.lapdonline.org/march_2009/news_view/41030, accessed January 11, 2017.

———. *Model Civil Disturbance Control Plan*. Los Angeles: City of Los Angeles Police Department, 1968.

———. *Statistical Digest*, Los Angeles: City of Los Angeles Police Department, 1964–1992.

Los Angeles Regional Criminal Justice Planning Board. *Crime Control in Los Angeles County, 1973–1978*. Department of Justice, 1978.

Parks, Bernard. *Rampart Area Corruption Incident*. Los Angeles: Los Angeles Police Department, March 1, 2000.

President's Task Force on 21st Century Policing. *Final Report of the President's Task Force on 21st Century Policing*. Washington, D.C.: Office of Community Oriented Policing Services, 2015.

Rampart Independent Review Panel. *Report of the Rampart Independent Review Panel: A Report to the Los Angeles Board of Police Commissioners Concerning the Operations, Policies, and Procedures of the Los Angeles Police Department in the Wake of the Rampart Scandal*. November 16, 2000.

Taylor, Zara, and Los Angeles County Commission on Human Relations. *Kids, Crime and Jail: The Color of Juvenile Justice: Report on a Public Hearing Held by the Los Angeles County Commission on Human Relations*. Los Angeles: Los Angeles County Commission on Human Relations, 1988.

U.S. Advisory Commission on Intergovernmental Relations. *Safe Streets Reconsidered: The Block Grant Experience, 1968–1975*. Washington, D.C.: U.S. Advisory Commission on Intergovernmental Relations, 1977.

U.S. Commission on Civil Rights. *Stranger in One's Land*. Washington, D.C.: U.S. Government Printing Office, 1970.

U.S. Commission on Civil Rights, California Advisory Committee. *An Analysis of the McCone Commission Report*. San Francisco, 1966.

———. *Police-Community Relations in East Los Angeles, California*. San Francisco, 1970.

U.S. Congress, House. Committee on Appropriations. Subcommittee on the Department of State, Justice, and Commerce, the Judiciary, and Related Agencies. *Departments of State, Justice, and Commerce, the Judiciary, and Related Agencies Appropriations: Undocumented Aliens.* Hearings. 95th Cong., 2nd Sess., 1978.

U.S. Congress, House. Committee on Education and Labor. Subcommittee on Equal Opportunities. *Juvenile Justice and Delinquency Prevention and Runaway Youth.* Hearings, 93rd Cong., 2nd Sess., 1974.

U.S. Congress, House. Committee on the Judiciary. Subcommittee on Crime. *Police and the Use of Deadly Force.* Hearings, 96th Cong., 2nd Sess., 1980.

U.S. Congress, House. Committee on the Judiciary. Subcommittee on Criminal Justice. *Organized Criminal Activity by Youth Gangs.* Hearings, 100th Cong., 2nd Sess., 1988.

U.S. Congress, House. Committee on Un-American Activities. *Subversive Influence in Riots, Looting, and Burning.* Hearings, Part 1, 90th Cong., 1st Sess., 1967.

———. *Subversive Influence in Riots, Looting, and Burning.* Hearings, Part 3-A (Los Angeles-Watts), 90th Cong., 2nd Sess., 1968.

U.S. Congress, House. Select Committee on Narcotics Abuse and Control. *Federal Law Enforcement Role in Narcotics Control in Southern California.* Hearings, 100th Cong., 2nd Sess., 1988.

———. *Narcotics Trafficking and Abuse in the Los Angeles Area.* Hearings, 99th Cong., 2nd Sess., 1986.

U.S. Congress, Senate. Committee on Governmental Affairs. Permanent Subcommittee on Investigations. *Criminal Aliens in the United States.* Hearings, 103rd Cong., 1st Sess., 1994.

U.S. Congress, Senate. Committee on the Judiciary. *One-Year Drug Strategy Review.* Hearings, 101st Cong., 2nd Sess., 1990.

U.S. Congress, Senate. Committee on the Judiciary. Subcommittee on Juvenile Justice. *Gang Violence and Control.* Hearings, 98th Cong., 1st Sess., 1983.

U.S. Congress, Senate. Committee on the Judiciary. Subcommittee to Investigate Juvenile Delinquency. *School Violence and Vandalism.* Hearings, 84th Cong., 1st Sess., 1975.

U.S. Congress, Senate. Committee on the Judiciary. Subcommittee to Investigate the Administration of the Internal Security Act and Other Internal Security Laws. *Assaults on Law Enforcement Officers.* Hearings, Part 4, 91st Cong., 2nd Sess., 1970.

———. *The Erosion of Law Enforcement Intelligence Gathering Capabilities.* Hearings, 94th Cong., 2nd Sess., 1976.

———. *Extent of Subversion in the 'New Left' Testimony of Robert J. Thoms.* Hearings, Part 1, 91st Cong., 2nd Sess., 1970.

U.S. Department of Commerce, United States Bureau of the Census. *General Social and Economic Characteristics: California.* Washington, D.C.: Government Printing Office, 1960.

———. *General Social and Economic Characteristics: California.* Washington, D.C.: Government Printing Office, 1970.

———. *General Social and Economic Characteristics: California.* Washington, D.C.: Government Printing Office, 1980.

———. *General Social and Economic Characteristics: California*. Washington, D.C.: Government Printing Office, 1990.

U.S. Department of Justice, Law Enforcement Assistance Administration. *Crime Control in Los Angeles County, 1973–1978*. Washington, D.C.: U.S Department of Justice, 1978.

———. *Safe Streets . . . the LEAA Program at Work*. Washington, DC: U.S. Department of Justice, 1971.

U.S. Department of Labor. Immigration and Naturalization Service. *Annual Report of the Immigration and Naturalization Service*. Washington, D.C., 1973.

U.S. District Court for the Central District of California. *United States of America v. City of Los Angeles, California, Board of Police Commissioners of the City of Los Angeles, and the Los Angeles Police Department: Consent Decree*. September 19, 2000.

U.S. General Accounting Office. *Criminal Aliens: INS' Enforcement Activities— Report to the Chairman, Subcommittee on Immigration, Refugees, and International Law, Committee on the Judiciary, House of Representatives*. Washington, D.C.: GAO, November 1987.

Utt, James B. "Poverty Funds to Destroy Police Departments?" *Congressional Record Appendix*, Washington, D.C.: June 12, 1967.

Webster, William H., and Hubert Williams. *The City in Crisis: A Report by the Special Advisor to the Board of Police Commissioners on the Civil Disorder in Los Angeles*. Los Angeles: October 21, 1992.

Other Primary Sources

American Civil Liberties Union (ACLU). "McCone's Modest Measures." *Open Forum*, January 1966.

———. *On The Line: Police Brutality and its Remedies*. Washington, D.C., 1991.

American Civil Liberties Union Southern California Branch. *From the Outside In: Residency Patterns within the Los Angeles Police Department*. Los Angeles: ACLU, 1994.

———. *Law Enforcement: The Matter of Redress*. Los Angeles: Institute of Modern Legal Thought, 1969.

———. *Police Malpractice and the Watts Riot: A Report*. Los Angeles: ACLU, 1966.

Amnesty International. *United States of America: Torture, Ill-Treatment and Excessive Force by Police in Los Angeles, California*. New York: Amnesty International Publications, 1992.

Anonymous. *Implications of California's 1977 Juvenile Justice Reform Law, 1981, Volume 8—The Impact of Changes in the Juvenile Court Process on Juvenile Criminal Offender Handling*. Washington, D.C.: National Institute of Juvenile Justice and Delinquency, 1981. https://www.ncjrs.gov/App/Publications/abstract.aspx?ID=99816, accessed June 29, 2015.

Blue Ribbon Rampart Review Panel. *Rampart Reconsidered: The Search for Real Reform Seven Years Later*. Los Angeles: Blue Ribbon Rampart Review Panel, 2006.

Bradley, Thomas. "A Court System in Which All the People Have a Part." *Judicature* 58 (1974): 270.

———. *The Impossible Dream: Thomas Bradley.* Interview by Bernard Galm. UCLA Oral History Project, 1984.

Bullock, Paul. "Negro and Mexican American Experiences in the Labor Market in Los Angeles: A Comparison, (Statement of Paul Bullock, Assistant Research Economist at Institute of Industrial Relations, UCLA, to Fair Employment Practice Commission March 17, 1966)." Bancroft Pamphlet Folio, pf F869 L8.83. B8, Bancroft Library, Berkeley, CA.

Chandler, Bill, et al. *Tom Bradley Commemorative Booklet.* Los Angeles: City of Los Angeles, 1989.

Cohen, Richard, dir. *Deadly Force.* Documentary. Hound Dog Films, 1980. Distributed by Richard Cohen Films (2009), http://www.imdb.com/title /tt0191942/companycredits?ref_=ttfc_ql_4.

Columbia Broadcasting System. "CBS Reports: Watts: Riot or Revolt? As broadcast over the CBS Television Network." December 7, 1965, F 869 L8.9.N4C62.phot., Bancroft Library.

Hamilton, Cynthia. "Apartheid in an American City: The Case of the Black Community in Los Angeles." Los Angeles: Labor/Community Strategy Center, 1992.

Human Rights Watch. *Shielded from Justice: Police Brutality and Accountability in the United States.* New York: Human Rights Watch, June 1998, https://www.hrw .org/legacy/reports98/police/uspo14.htm, accessed April 20, 2018.

Labor Community Strategy Center (LCSC). *A Call to Reject the Federal Weed and Seed Program in Los Angeles.* Los Angeles: LCSC, 1992.

———. *Reconstructing Los Angeles from the Bottom Up.* Los Angeles: LCSC, 1993.

Los Angeles County Bar Association Task Force on the State Criminal Justice System. *Critical Analysis of Lessons Learned: Recommendations for Improving the California Criminal Justice System in the Wake of the Rampart Scandal.* Los Angeles: Los Angeles County Bar Association, April 2003.

Los Angeles Times Staff. *Understanding the Riots: Los Angeles Before and After the Rodney King Case.* Los Angeles: Los Angeles Times, 1992.

Manes, Hugh R. *A Report on Law Enforcement and the Negro Citizen in Los Angeles.* Hollywood, Calif.: Privately published, 1963.

Post Conviction Assistance Center. "Perez Transcripts." http://www.pcaclaw.org /perez.html, accessed January 11, 2017.

Price, Kendall O., Kent Lloyd, Ellsworth E. Johnson, D. Richard McFerson, and William J. Williams. *A Critique of the* Governor's Commission *on the Los Angeles Riot.* Inglewood, Calif.: Public Executive Development and Research, 1967.

Teilmann Van Dusen, Katherine. *Implications of California's 1977 Juvenile Justice Reform Law, 1981, Volume 6—Transfer to Adult Court: Legislative Change and Its Impact.* Washington, D.C.: National Institute of Juvenile Justice and Delinquency, 1981. https://www.ncjrs.gov/App/Publications/abstract.aspx?ID=99814, accessed June 29, 2015.

Uchida, Craig D., Lawrence W. Sherman, and James F. Fyfe. *Police Shootings and the Prosecutor in Los Angeles County: An Evaluation of Operation Rollout.* Washington, D.C.: Police Foundation, 1981.

Secondary Sources

Abu-Lughod, Janet L. *New York, Chicago, Los Angeles: America's Global Cities.*
Minneapolis: University of Minnesota Press, 1999.
———. *Race, Space, and Riots in Chicago, New York, and Los Angeles.* New York:
Oxford University Press, 2007.
Acuña, Rodolfo. *Anything but Mexican: Chicanos in Contemporary Los Angeles.*
London: Verso, 1996.
Adler, Patricia Rae. "Watts: From Suburb to Black Ghetto." PhD diss., University of
Southern California, 1977.
Agee, Christopher Lowen. "Crisis and Redemption: The History of American Police
Reform since World War II." *Journal of Urban History.* April 28, 2017. http://journals
.sagepub.com/doi/abs/10.1177/0096144217705463.
———. *The Streets of San Francisco: Policing and the Creation of a Cosmopolitan
Liberal Politics, 1950–1972.* Chicago: University of Chicago Press, 2014.
Agyepong, Tera Eva. *The Criminalization of Black Children: Race, Gender, and
Delinquency in Chicago's Juvenile Justice System, 1899–1945.* Chapel Hill: University
of North Carolina Press, 2018.
Alexander, Michelle. *The New Jim Crow.* New York: New Press, 2012.
Alonso, Alex. "Out of the Void: Street Gangs in Los Angeles." In *Black Los Angeles:
American Dreams and Racial Realities*, edited by Darnell M. Hunt and Ana-
Christina Ramón, 140–67. New York: New York Univesity Press, 2010.
Anderson, Elijah. *Code of the Street: Decency, Violence, and the Moral Life of the
Inner City.* New York: W. W. Norton, 2000.
Appier, Janis. *Policing Women: The Sexual Politics of Law Enforcement and the
LAPD.* Philadelphia: Temple University Press, 1998.
Avila, Eric. *Popular Culture in the Age of White Flight: Fear and Fantasy in Suburban
Los Angeles.* Berkeley: University of California Press, 2004.
Bakeer, Donald. *Crips: The Story of the South Central L.A. Street Gang from 1971–
1985.* Los Angeles: Precocious Publishing, 1992.
Baldassare, Mark, ed. *The Los Angeles Riots: Lessons for the Urban Future.* Urban
Policy Challenges. Boulder. Colo.: Westview, 1994.
Balko, Radley. *Rise of the Warrior Cop: The Militarization of America's Police Forces.*
New York, PublicAffairs, 2013.
Balto, Simon. *Occupied Territory: Policing Black Chicago from Red Summer to Black
Power.* Chapel Hill: University of North Carolina Press, forthcoming.
———. "'Occupied Territory': Police Repression and Black Resistance in Postwar
Milwaukee, 1950–1968." *Journal of African American History* 98, no. 2 (April 1,
2013): 229–52.
Barber, Llana. *Latino City: Immigration and Urban Crisis in Lawrence, Massachu-
setts, 1945–2000.* Chapel Hill: University of North Carolina Press, 2017.
Baum, Dan. *Smoke and Mirrors: The War on Drugs and the Politics of Failure.*
Boston: Back Bay Books, 1997.
Bauman, Robert. *Race and the War on Poverty: From Watts to East L.A.* Norman:
University of Oklahoma Press, 2008.

Beckett, Katherine. *Making Crime Pay: Law and Order in Contemporary American Politics*. New York: Oxford University Press, 1997.

Beckett, Katherine, and Steve Herbert. *Banished: The New Social Control In Urban America*. New York: Oxford University Press, 2011.

Beckett, Katherine, and Naomi Murakawa. "Mapping the Shadow Carceral State: Toward an Institutionally Capacious Approach to Punishment." *Theoretical Criminology* 16, no. 2 (May 1, 2012): 221–44.

Behnken, Brian D., ed. *The Struggle in Black and Brown: African American and Mexican American Relations during the Civil Rights Era*. Lincoln: University of Nebraska Press, 2012.

Belew, Kathleen. *Bring the War Home: The White Power Movement and Paramilitary America*. Cambridge, Mass.: Harvard University Press, 2018.

Bell, Jonathan. *California Crucible: The Forging of Modern American Liberalism*. Philadelphia: University of Pennsylvania Press, 2012.

Berger, Dan. *Captive Nation: Black Prison Organizing in the Civil Rights Era*. Chapel Hill: University of North Carolina Press, 2014.

———. "Social Movements and Mass Incarceration: What Is to Be Done?" *Souls* 15, no. 1–2 (2013): 3–18.

Berger, Dan, and Toussaint Losier. *Rethinking the American Prison Movement*. New York: Routledge, 2018.

Bergesen, Albert, and Max Herman. "Immigration, Race, and Riot: The 1992 Los Angeles Uprising." *American Sociological Review* 63, no. 1 (February 1, 1998): 39–54.

Bernstein, Shana. *Bridges of Reform: Interracial Civil Rights Activism in Twentieth-Century Los Angeles*. Oxford: Oxford University Press, 2011.

Bittner, Egon. *The Functions of the Police in Modern Society*. Chevy Chase, Md.: National Institute of Mental Health, 1970.

Bloom, Joshua, and Waldo E. Martin Jr. *Black against Empire: The History and Politics of the Black Panther Party*. Berkeley: University of California Press, 2012.

Blumenson, Eric, and Eva Nilsen. "Policing for Profit: The Drug War's Hidden Economic Agenda." *University of Chicago Law Review* 65, no. 1 (January 1, 1998): 35–114.

Bobo, Lawrence D., Melvin L. Oliver, James H. Johnson Jr., and Abel Valenzuela Jr. *Prismatic Metropolis: Inequality in Los Angeles*. New York: Russell Sage Foundation Publications, 2000.

Boches, Ralph E. "Juvenile Justice in California: A Re-Evaluation." *Hastings Law Journal* 19 (1967): 47.

Bollens, John C., and Grant B. Geyer. *Yorty: Politics of a Constant Candidate*. Pacific Palisades, Calif.: Palisades Publishers, 1973.

Brilliant, Mark. *The Color of America Has Changed: How Racial Diversity Shaped Civil Rights Reform in California, 1941–1978*. Oxford: Oxford University Press, 2010.

Brown, Elaine. *A Taste of Power: A Black Woman's Story*. New York: Anchor, 1993.

Brown, Elizabeth. "Race, Urban Governance, and Crime Control: Creating Model Cities." *Law & Society Review* 44, no. 3–4 (2010): 769–804.

Brown, Michael K. *Whitewashing Race: The Myth of a Color-Blind Society*. Berkeley: University of California Press, 2003.

———. *Working the Street: Police Discretion and the Dilemmas of Reform*. Revised edition. New York: Russell Sage Foundation, 1988.

Brown, Scot. *Fighting for US: Maulana Karenga, the US Organization, and Black Cultural Nationalism*. New York: New York University Press, 2003.

Browne, Simone. *Dark Matters: On the Surveillance of Blackness*. Durham, N.C.: Duke University Press, 2015.

Bullock, Paul. *Aspiration vs. Opportunity: "Careers" in the Inner City*. Ann Arbor: Institute of Labor and Industrial Relations, University of Michigan-Wayne State University, 1973.

———. *Watts: The Aftermath; An Inside View of the Ghetto*. New York: Grove Press, 1969.

Buntin, John. *L.A. Noir: The Struggle for the Soul of America's Most Seductive City*. New York: Three Rivers Press, 2010.

Butler, Paul. *Chokehold: Policing Black Men*. New York: New Press, 2017.

Button, James W. *Black Violence: Political Impact of the 1960s Riots*. Princeton, N.J.: Princeton University Press, 1978.

Cacho, Lisa Marie. *Social Death: Racialized Rightlessness and the Criminalization of the Unprotected*. New York: New York University Press, 2012.

Callinicos, A. T. "Meaning of Los Angeles Riots." *Economic and Political Weekly* 27, no. 30 (July 25, 1992): 1603–6.

Camarillo, Albert M. "Cities of Color: The New Racial Frontier in California's Minority-Majority Cities." *Pacific Historical Review* 76, no. 1 (February 2007): 1–28.

Camp, Jordan T. *Incarcerating the Crisis: Freedom Struggles and the Rise of the Neoliberal State*. Oakland: University of California Press, 2016.

Camp, Jordan T., and Christina Heatherton, eds. *Policing the Planet: Why the Policing Crisis Led to Black Lives Matter*. New York: Verso, 2016.

Cannon, Lou. *Official Negligence: How Rodney King and the Riots Changed Los Angeles and the LAPD*. New York: Times Books, 1997.

Carbado, Devon W. "Racial Naturalization." *American Quarterly* 57, no. 3 (2005): 633–58.

Carby, H. "Figuring the Future in Los(t) Angeles." *Comparative American Studies* 1, no. 1 (2003): 19–34.

Chambliss, William J. "Policing the Ghetto Underclass: The Politics of Law and Law Enforcement." *Social Problems* 41, no. 2 (May 1, 1994): 177–94.

Chaney, Cassandra, and Ray V. Robertson. "Racism and Police Brutality in America." *Journal of African American Studies* 17, no. 4 (December 1, 2013): 480.

Chase, Robert T. "We Are Not Slaves: Rethinking the Rise of Carceral States through the Lens of the Prisoners' Rights Movement." *Journal of American History* 102, no. 1 (June 1, 2015): 73–86.

Chávez, Ernesto. *"Mi Raza Primero!" (My People First!): Nationalism, Identity, and Insurgency in the Chicano Movement in Los Angeles, 1966–1978*. Berkeley: University of California Press, 2002.

Chávez-García, Miroslava. *States of Delinquency: Race and Science in the Making of California's Juvenile Justice System*. Berkeley: University of California Press, 2012.

Chevigny, Paul. *Edge of the Knife: Police Violence in the Americas.* New York: New Press, 1995.

———. *Police Power: Police Abuses in New York City.* New York: Pantheon Books, 1969.

Childs, Dennis. *Slaves of the State: Black Incarceration from the Chain Gang to the Penitentiary.* Minneapolis: University of Minnesota Press, 2015.

Churchill, Ward, and Jim Vander Wall. *Agents of Repression: The FBI's Secret Wars against the Black Panther Party and the American Indian Movement.* Cambridge, Mass.: South End Press, 2002.

Clear, Todd R. *Imprisoning Communities: How Mass Incarceration Makes Disadvantaged Neighborhoods Worse.* New York: Oxford University Press, 2009.

Cleaver, Kathleen, and George Katsiaficas, eds. *Liberation, Imagination, and the Black Panther Party: A New Look at the Panthers and Their Legacy.* New York: Routledge/Taylor & Francis Group, 2001.

Cohen, Jerry, and William S. Murphy. *Burn, Baby, Burn! The Los Angeles Race Riot, August, 1965.* New York: Dutton, 1966.

Cohen, Nathan Edward. *The Los Angeles Riots: A Socio-Psychological Study.* New York: Praeger, 1970.

Cohen, Stanley. *Visions of Social Control: Crime, Punishment and Classification.* New York: Polity, 1991.

Coleman, Sarah. "Iowa, Local Immigration Enforcement and Immigrants' Rights." Paper presented at the Newberry Latino and Borderlands History Seminar. Chicago, Ill., September 22, 2017. In author's possession.

Connor, Micahn. "Creating Cities and Citizens: Municipal Boundaries, Place Entrepreneurs, and the Production of Race in Los Angeles County, 1926–1978." PhD diss., University of Southern California, 2008.

Conot, Robert E. *Rivers of Blood, Years of Darkness.* New York: Bantam Books, 1967.

Cotton, Paul. "Violence Decreases with Gang Truce." *Journal of the American Medical Association* 268, no. 4 (July 22, 1992): 443–44.

Countryman, Matthew. *Up South: Civil Rights and Black Power in Philadelphia.* Philadelphia: University of Pennsylvania Press, 2006.

Cray, Ed. *The Enemy in the Streets: Police Malpractice in America.* New York: Doubleday, 1972.

Crump, Spencer. *Black Riot in Los Angeles.* Los Angeles: Trans-Anglo Books, 1966.

Cuff, Dana. *The Provisional City: Los Angeles Stories of Architecture and Urbanism.* Cambridge, Mass.: MIT Press, 2000.

Cunningham, David. *Klansville, U.S.A.: The Rise and Fall of the Civil Rights–Era Ku Klux Klan.* New York: Oxford University Press, 2012.

———. *There's Something Happening Here: The New Left, the Klan, and FBI Counterintelligence.* Berkeley: University of California Press, 2004.

Currie, Elliott. *Crime and Punishment in America.* New York: Picador, 2013.

Dallek, Matthew. "Up from Liberalism: Pat Brown, Ronald Reagan, and the 1966 Gubernatorial Election." In *Responsible Liberalism: Edmund G. "Pat" Brown and Reform Government in California 1958–1967*, edited by Martin J. Schiesl, 193–216. Los Angeles: Edmund G. "Pat" Brown Institute of Public Affairs, 2003.

Davis, Angela J. *Freedom Is a Constant Struggle: Ferguson, Palestine, and the Foundations of a Movement.* Chicago: Haymarket Books, 2016.

———, ed. *Policing the Black Man: Arrest, Prosecution, and Imprisonment.* New York: Pantheon Books, 2017.

Davis, Edward M. *Staff One: A Perspective on Effective Police Management.* Englewood Cliffs, N.J.: Prentice-Hall, 1978.

Davis, Mike. *City of Quartz: Excavating the Future in Los Angeles.* New York: Vintage Books, 1992.

———. "Who Killed Los Angeles? A Political Autopsy." *New Left Review* 197 (1993): 3–28.

———. "Who Killed Los Angeles? Part Two: The Verdict Is Given." *New Left Review* 199 (1993): 29–54.

De Graaf, Lawrence Brooks, Kevin Mulroy, and Quintard Taylor. *Seeking El Dorado: African Americans in California.* Los Angeles: Autry Museum of Western Heritage, 2001.

Deverell, William. *Whitewashed Adobe: The Rise of Los Angeles and the Remaking of Its Mexican Past.* Berkeley: University of California Press, 2004.

Devine, John. *Maximum Security: The Culture of Violence in Inner-City Schools.* Chicago: University of Chicago Press, 1997.

Domanick, Joe. *Blue: The LAPD and the Battle to Redeem American Policing.* New York: Simon & Schuster, 2015.

———. *To Protect and to Serve: The LAPD's Century of War in the City of Dreams.* Los Angeles: Figueroa Press, 2003.

Donner, Frank. *Protectors of Privilege: Red Squads and Police Repression in Urban America.* Berkeley: University of California Press, 1992.

Dreier, Peter. "America's Urban Crisis a Decade after the Los Angeles Riots." *National Civic Review* 92, no. 1 (Spring 2003): 35–55.

Dreier, Peter, John H. Mollenkopf, and Todd Swanstrom. *Place Matters: Metropolitics for the Twenty-First Century.* Lawrence: University Press of Kansas, 2004.

Dubber, Markus Dirk. *The Police Power: Patriarchy and the Foundations of American Government.* New York: Columbia University Press, 2005.

Duggan, Lisa. *The Twilight of Equality? Neoliberalism, Cultural Politics, and the Attack on Democracy.* Boston: Beacon, 2004.

Dulaney, W. Marvin. *Black Police in America.* Bloomington: Indiana University Press, 1996.

Dunn, Timothy J. *The Militarization of the U.S.-Mexico Border, 1978–1992: Low-Intensity Conflict Doctrine Comes Home.* Austin: CMAS Books, University of Texas at Austin, 1996.

Durán, Robert. "Over-Inclusive Gang Enforcement and Urban Resistance: A Comparison between Two Cities." *Social Justice* 36, no. 1 (115) (January 1, 2009): 82–101.

Edsall, Thomas Byrne, and Mary D Edsall. *Chain Reaction: The Impact of Race, Rights, and Taxes on American Politics.* New York: W. W. Norton, 1991.

Eisinger, Peter K. *Municipal Residency Requirements and the Local Economy.* Madison: Institute for Research on Poverty, University of Wisconsin-Madison, 1980.

Elinson, Zusha. "The 1992 Riots Changed Policing in L.A., but Some Say Not Enough." *Wall Street Journal*, April 29, 2017, sec. US. https://www.wsj.com/articles/the-1992

-riots-changed-policing-in-l-a-but-some-say-not-enough-1493467200, accessed May 4, 2017.

Elkins, Alex. "Battle of the Corner: Urban Policing and Rioting in the United States, 1943–1971." PhD diss., Temple University, 2017.

———. "Stand Our Ground: The Street Justice of Urban American Riots, 1900 to 1968." *Journal of Urban History* 42, no. 2 (2016): 419–37.

———. "The Origins of Stop-and-Frisk." Jacobin, May 9, 2015. http://jacobinmag .com/2015/05/stop-and-frisk-dragnet-ferguson-baltimore, accessed May 15, 2015.

Enns, Peter. *Incarceration Nation: How the United States Became the Most Punitive Democracy in the World*. New York: Cambridge University Press, 2016.

Epp, Charles R. *Making Rights Real: Activists, Bureaucrats, and the Creation of the Legalistic State*. Chicago: University of Chicago Press, 2009.

Epp, Charles R., Steven Maynard-Moody, and Donald P. Haider-Markel. *Pulled Over: How Police Stops Define Race and Citizenship*. Chicago: University of Chicago Press, 2014.

Erie, Steven P. *Globalizing L.A: Trade, Infrastructure, and Regional Development*. Stanford, Calif: Stanford University Press, 2004.

Escobar, Edward J. "Bloody Christmas and the Irony of Police Professionalism: The Los Angeles Police Department, Mexican Americans, and Police Reform in the 1950s." *Pacific Historical Review* 72, no. 2 (May 1, 2003): 171–99.

———. "The Dialectics of Repression: The Los Angeles Police Department and the Chicano Movement, 1968–1971." *Journal of American History* 79, no. 4 (March 1993): 1483–1514.

———. *Race, Police, and the Making of a Political Identity: Mexican Americans and the Los Angeles Police Department, 1900–1945*. Berkeley: University of California Press, 1999.

———. "The Unintended Consequences of the Carceral State: Chicana/o Political Mobilization in Post–World War II America." *Journal of American History* 102, no. 1 (June 1, 2015): 174–84.

Ethington, Philip. "Regional Regimes since 13,000 before Present." In *A Companion to Los Angeles*, edited by William Deverell and Greg Hise, 177–216. Oxford: Wiley, 2010.

———. "Segregated Diversity: Race-Ethnicity, Space, and Political Fragmentation in Los Angeles County, 1940–1994." *Final Report to the John Randolph Haynes Foundation*. Los Angeles: The John Randolph Haynes Foundation, 2000.

Ethington, P. J., W. H. Frey, and D. Myers. "The Racial Resegregation of Los Angeles County, 1940–2000." *Race Contours* (2000): 2001–5.

Evans, Peter B., Dietrich Rueschemeyer, and Theda Skocpol. *Bringing the State Back In*. Cambridge: Cambridge University Press, 1985.

Fagan, Jeffrey. "The Contradictions of Juvenile Crime & Punishment." *Daedalus* 139, no. 3 (Summer 2010): 43–61, 145.

Farber, David. *Taken Hostage: The Iran Hostage Crisis and America's First Encounter with Radical Islam*. Princeton, N.J.: Princeton University Press, 2006.

Fassin, Didier. *Enforcing Order: An Ethnography of Urban Policing*. Cambridge: Polity, 2013.

Feeley, Malcolm, and Austin Sarat. *The Policy Dilemma: Federal Crime Policy and the Law Enforcement Assistance Administration.* Minneapolis: University of Minnesota Press, 1980.

Felber, Garrett. *Those Who Know Don't Say: The Nation of Islam, Black Nationalist Politics, and the Carceral State.* University of North Carolina Press, forthcoming.

Felkenes, George, T. Lasley, Lawrence C. Trostle, and James Lasley. "The Impact of Fanchon Blake v. City of Los Angeles on the Selection, Recruitment, Training, Appointment and Performance of Women and Minorities for the Los Angeles Police Department and the City of Los Angeles." Claremont, Calif.: Center for Politics and Policy, Claremont Graduate School, 1990.

Felker-Kantor, Max. "The Coalition against Police Abuse: CAPA's Resistance Struggle in 1970s Los Angeles." *Journal of Civil and Human Rights* 2, no. 1 (2016): 52–88.

———. "'Kid Thugs Are Spreading Terror Through the Streets': Youth, Crime, and the Expansion of the Juvenile Justice System in Los Angeles, 1973–1980." *Journal of Urban History* 44, no. 3 (2018): 476–500.

———. "Liberal Law-and-Order: The Politics of Police Reform in Los Angeles." *Journal of Urban History.* April 28, 2017. http://journals.sagepub.com/eprint /9SwXk4TBxKVYCbR3hUkA/full.

———. "'A Pledge Is Not Self-Enforcing': Struggles for Equal Employment Opportunity in Multiracial Los Angeles, 1964–1982." *Pacific Historical Review* 82, no. 1 (February 1, 2013): 63–94.

Ferguson, Andrew Guthrie. *The Rise of Big Data Policing: Surveillance, Race, and the Future of Law Enforcement.* New York: NYU Press, 2017.

Fields, Karen E., and Barbara J. Fields. *Racecraft: The Soul of Inequality in American Life.* Reprint edition. London: Verso, 2014.

Fine, Sidney. *Violence in the Model City: The Cavanagh Administration, Race Relations, and the Detroit Riot of 1967.* East Lansing: Michigan State University Press, 2007.

Fischer, Anne Gray. "Arrestable Behavior: Women, Police Power, and the Making of Law-and-Order America, 1930s–1980s." PhD diss., Brown University, 2018.

Flamm, Michael W. *In the Heat of the Summer: The New York Riots of 1964 and the War on Crime.* Philadelphia: University of Pennsylvania Press, 2016.

———. *Law and Order: Street Crime, Civil Unrest, and the Crisis of Liberalism in the 1960s.* New York: Columbia University Press, 2005.

———. "'Law and Order' at Large: The New York Civilian Review Board Referendum of 1966 and the Crisis of Liberalism." *Historian* 64, no. 3–4 (January 1, 2002): 643–65.

Flamming, Douglas. *Bound for Freedom: Black Los Angeles in Jim Crow America.* Berkeley: University of California Press, 2006.

Flusty, Steven. *Building Paranoia: The Proliferation of Interdictory Space and the Erosion of Spatial Justice.* West Hollywood, Calif.: Los Angeles Forum for Architecture and Urban Design, 1994.

Fogelson, Robert M. *Big-City Police.* Cambridge, Mass.: Harvard University Press, 1977.

———. *Violence as Protest: A Study of Riots and Ghettos.* Garden City, N.Y.: Doubleday & Company, 1971.

———. *The Los Angeles Riots, Compiled by Robert M. Fogelson*. New York: Arno, 1969.

Forman, James Jr. "Community Policing and Youth as Assets." *Journal of Criminal Law and Criminology* 95, no. 1 (2004): 1–48.

———. *Locking Up Our Own: Crime and Punishment in Black America*. New York: Farrar, Straus and Giroux, 2017.

———. "Racial Critiques of Mass Incarceration: Beyond the New Jim Crow." *New York University Law Review* 87, no. 1 (April 1, 2012): 21.

Fortner, Michael Javen. *Black Silent Majority: The Rockefeller Drug Laws and the Politics of Punishment*. Cambridge, Mass.: Harvard University Press, 2015.

Foucault, Michel. *Discipline & Punish*. New York: Vintage, 1995.

Frampton, Mary Louise, Ian Haney-López, and Jonathan Simon, eds. *After the War on Crime: Race, Democracy, and a New Reconstruction*. New York: New York University Press, 2008.

Friedman, Barry. *Unwarranted: Policing without Permission*. New York: Farrar, Straus and Giroux, 2017.

Friedman, Lawrence. *Crime and Punishment in American History*. New York: Basic Books, 1993.

Friesema, H. Paul. "Black Control of Central Cities: The Hollow Prize." *Journal of the American Planning Association* 35, no. 2 (1969): 75–79.

Frontline. "LAPD Blues: The Story of Los Angeles' Gangsta Cops & the Corruption Scandal That Has Shaken the Once Great LAPD." 2001. http://www.pbs.org/wgbh/pages/frontline/shows/lapd/bare.html, accessed January 11, 2017.

Frydl, Kathleen. *The Drug Wars in America, 1940–1973*. Cambridge: Cambridge University Press, 2013.

Fulton, William. *The Reluctant Metropolis: The Politics of Urban Growth in Los Angeles*. Baltimore, Md.: Johns Hopkins University Press, 2001.

Gale, Dennis E. *Understanding Urban Unrest: From Reverend King to Rodney King*. Thousand Oaks, Calif.: SAGE, 1996.

García, Mario T. *Memories of Chicano History: The Life and Narrative of Bert Corona*. Berkeley: University of California Press, 1994.

Garland, David. *The Culture of Control: Crime and Social Order in Contemporary Society*. Chicago: University of Chicago Press, 2001.

Gates, Daryl F. *Chief: My Life in the LAPD*. New York: Bantam Books, 1993.

Gilfoyle, Timothy J. "Introduction: New Perspectives on Crime and Punishment in the American City." *Journal of Urban History* 29, no. 5 (July 2003): 519–24.

Gilje, Paul A. *Rioting in America*. Bloomington: Indiana University Press, 1999.

Gillette, Howard. *Camden after the Fall: Decline and Renewal in a Post-Industrial City*. Philadelphia: University of Pennsylvania Press, 2006.

———. "Review Essay: Is This the Neoliberal Moment?" *Journal of Urban History* 36, no. 3 (2010): 393.

Gilmore, Ruth Wilson. *Golden Gulag: Prisons, Surplus, Crisis, and Opposition in Globalizing California*. Berkeley: University of California Press, 2007.

———. "In the Shadow of the Shadow State." *S&F Online*, no. 13.2 (Spring 2016). http://sfonline.barnard.edu/navigating-neoliberalism-in-the-academy-nonprofits-and-beyond/ruth-wilson-gilmore-in-the-shadow-of-the-shadow-state/.

Gilmore, Ruth Wilson, and Craig Gilmore. "Beyond Bratton." In *Policing the Planet: Why the Policing Crisis Led to Black Lives Matter*, edited by Jordan T. Camp and Christina Heatherton, 137–99. New York: Verso, 2016.

Glasgow, Douglas Graham. "The Sons of Watts Improvement Association." PhD diss., University of Southern California, 1968.

Goffman, Alice. *On the Run: Fugitive Life in an American City*. Chicago: University of Chicago Press, 2014.

Goldstein, Alyosha. *Poverty in Common: The Politics of Community Action during the American Century*. Durham, N.C.: Duke University Press, 2012.

Goluboff, Risa. *Vagrant Nation: Police Power, Constitutional Change, and the Making of the 1960s*. New York: Oxford University Press, 2016.

Gómez, David. *Somos Chicanos: Strangers in Our Own Land*. Boston: Beacon Press, 1975.

Gooding-Williams, Robert. *Reading Rodney King/Reading Urban Uprising*. New York: Routledge, 1993.

Goodman, Adam. *The Deportation Machine: Expulsion, Coercion, and Anti-Immigrant Fear Campaigns in US History*. Princeton, N.J.: Princeton University Press, forthcoming.

Gordon, Diana R. *The Justice Juggernaut: Fighting Street Crime, Controlling Citizens*. New Brunswick, N.J.: Rutgers University Press, 1990.

Gottlieb, Robert. *Reinventing Los Angeles: Nature and Community in the Global City*. Cambridge, Mass.: MIT Press, 2007.

Gottlieb, Robert, Regina Freer, Mark Vallianatos, and Peter Freier. *The Next Los Angeles: The Struggle for a Livable City*. Berkeley: University of California Press, 2006.

Gottschalk, Marie. *Caught: The Prison State and the Lockdown of American Politics*. Princeton, N.J.: Princeton University Press, 2014.

———. *The Prison and the Gallows: The Politics of Mass Incarceration in America*. New York: Cambridge University Press, 2006.

Graham, Stephen. *Cities under Siege: The New Military Urbanism*. New York: Verso Books, 2011.

Grogger, Jeffrey. "The Effects of Civil Gang Injunctions on Reported Violent Crime: Evidence from Los Angeles County." *Journal of Law and Economics* 45, no. 1 (April 1, 2002): 69–90.

Hagan, John. *Who Are the Criminals? The Politics of Crime Policy from the Age of Roosevelt to the Age of Reagan*. Princeton, N.J.: Princeton University Press, 2012.

Hagan, John, John D. Hewitt, and Duane F. Alwin. "Ceremonial Justice: Crime and Punishment in a Loosely Coupled System." *Social Forces* 58, no. 2 (1979): 506–27.

Hagedorn, John. *A World of Gangs: Armed Young Men and Gangsta Culture*. Minneapolis: University of Minnesota Press, 2008.

Hagedorn, John, and Perry Macon. *People and Folks: Gangs, Crime, and the Underclass in a Rustbelt City*. Chicago: Lake View Press, 1988.

Hahn, Harlan, David Klingman, and Harry Pachon. "Cleavages, Coalitions, and the Black Candidate: The Los Angeles Mayoralty Elections of 1969 and 1973," *Western Political Quarterly* 29, no. 4 (1976): 507–20.

Hall, Jacquelyn Dowd. "The Long Civil Rights Movement and the Political Uses of the Past." *Journal of American History* 91, no. 4 (March 2005): 1233–63.

Hall, Stuart, Chas Critcher, Tony Jefferson, John Clarke, and Brian Roberts. *Policing the Crisis: Mugging, the State and Law and Order.* 2nd edition. New York: Palgrave Macmillan, 2013.

Halley, Robert M., Alan C. Acock, and Thomas H. Greene. "Ethnicity and Social Class: Voting in the 1973 Los Angeles Municipal Elections." *Western Political Quarterly* 29, no. 4 (1976): 521–30.

Haney-López, Ian. *Racism on Trial: The Chicano Fight for Justice.* Cambridge, Mass.: Belknap Press of Harvard University Press, 2003.

Harcourt, Bernard E. *The Counterrevolution: How Our Government Went to War against Its Own Citizens.* New York: Basic Books, 2018.

———. *Illusion of Free Markets: Punishment and the Myth of Natural Order.* Cambridge, Mass.: Harvard University Press, 2012.

———. *Illusion of Order: The False Promise of Broken Windows Policing.* Cambridge, Mass.: Harvard University Press, 2005.

Harring, Sidney L. *Policing a Class Society: The Experience of American Cities, 1865–1915.* Chicago, Ill.: Haymarket Books, 2017.

Hartnett, Stephen John. *Challenging the Prison-Industrial Complex: Activism, Arts, and Educational Alternatives.* Urbana: University of Illinois Press, 2010.

Harvey, David. *A Brief History of Neoliberalism.* New York: Oxford University Press, 2007.

———. *Rebel Cities: From the Right to the City to the Urban Revolution.* New York: Verso, 2012.

Hayden, Dolores. "'I Have Seen the Future': Selling the Unsustainable City." *Journal of Urban History* 38, no. 1 (January 1, 2012): 3–15.

Hayden, Tom. "Dismantling the Myth of Bill Bratton's LAPD." *Nation,* December 6, 2013.

———. *Street Wars: Gangs and the Future of Violence.* New York: New Press, 2005.

Hayes, Chris. *A Colony in a Nation.* New York: W. W. Norton, 2017.

Hazen, Don, ed. *Inside the L.A. Riots: What Really Happened and Why It Will Happen Again.* New York: Institute for Alternative Journalism, 1992.

Healey, Dorothy Ray, and Maurice Isserman. *California Red: A Life in the American Communist Party.* Urbana: University of Illinois Press, 1993.

Herbert, Steven Kelly. *Citizens, Cops, and Power: Recognizing the Limits of Community.* Chicago: University of Chicago Press, 2006.

———. *Policing Space: Territoriality and the Los Angeles Police Department.* Minneapolis: University of Minnesota Press, 1997.

Hernández, Kelly Lytle. "Amnesty or Abolition? Felons, Illegals, and the Case for a New Abolition Movement." *Boom: A Journal of California* 1, no. 4 (November 1, 2011): 54–68.

———. *City of Inmates: Conquest, Rebellion, and the Rise of Human Caging in Los Angeles, 1771–1965.* Chapel Hill: University of North Carolina Press, 2017.

———. *Migra!: A History of the U.S. Border Patrol.* Berkeley: University of California Press, 2010.

Hester, Torrie. "Deportability and the Carceral State." *Journal of American History* 102, no. 1 (June 1, 2015): 141–51.

Hinton, Elizabeth. *From the War on Poverty to the War on Crime: The Making of Mass Incarceration in America.* Cambridge, Mass.: Harvard University Press, 2016.

Hise, Greg. *Magnetic Los Angeles: Creating the North American Landscape.* Baltimore, Md.: Johns Hopkins University Press, 1999.

Hobson, Emily K. *Lavender and Red: Liberation and Solidarity in the Gay and Lesbian Left.* Oakland: University of California Press, 2016.

———. "Policing Gay LA: Mapping Racial Divides in the Homophile Era, 1950–1967." In *The Rising Tide of Color: Race, State Violence, and Radical Movements across the Pacific,* edited by Moon-Ho Jung, 188–212. Seattle: University of Washington Press, 2014.

Horne, Gerald. *Fire This Time: The Watts Uprising and the 1960s.* 1st Da Capo Press ed. New York: Da Capo, 1997.

HoSang, Daniel. *Racial Propositions: Ballot Initiatives and the Making of Postwar California.* Berkeley: University of California Press, 2010.

HoSang, Daniel, Oneka LaBennett, and Laura Pulido, eds. *Racial Formation in the Twenty-First Century.* Berkeley: University of California Press, 2012.

Hudson, James R. "The Civilian Review Board Issue as Illuminated by the Philadelphia Experience." *Criminology* 6, no. 3 (November 1, 1968): 16–29.

Hunt, Darnell M. *Screening the Los Angeles "Riots."* New York: Cambridge University Press, 1997.

Hunt, Darnell M., and Ana-Christina Ramón, eds. *Black Los Angeles: American Dreams and Racial Realities.* New York: New York University Press, 2010.

Hurewitz, Daniel. *Bohemian Los Angeles and the Making of Modern Politics.* Berkeley: University of California Press, 2007.

Hutson, H. Range, Deirdre Anglin, Demetrios N. Kyriacou, Joel Hart, and Kelvin Spears. "The Epidemic of Gang-Related Homicides in Los Angeles County from 1979 through 1994." *JAMA: The Journal of the American Medical Association* 274, no. 13 (October 4, 1995): 1031–36.

Ingram, James. "The Rules of Ruling: Charter Reform in Los Angeles, 1850–2008." PhD diss., University of California, San Diego, 2008.

Jacobs, Meg. *Panic at the Pump: The Energy Crisis and the Transformation of American Politics in the 1970s.* New York: Hill and Wang, 2016.

Jacobs, Paul. *Prelude to Riot: A View of Urban America from the Bottom.* New York: Vintage, 1968.

Jah, Yusuf, and Shah'Keyah Jah. *Uprising: Crips and Bloods Tell the Story of America's Youth in the Crossfire.* New York: Simon & Schuster, 1997.

James, Joy. *Resisting State Violence: Radicalism, Gender, and Race in U.S. Culture.* Minneapolis: University of Minnesota Press, 1996.

Janssen, Volker. "When the 'Jungle' Met the Forest: Public Work, Civil Defense, and Prison Camps in Postwar California." *Journal of American History* 96, no. 3 (December 2009): 702–26.

Jaynes, Arthur. "Insurgency and Policy Outcomes: The Impact of Protests/riots on Urban Spending." *Journal of Political and Military Sociology* 30, no. 1 (January 1, 2002): 90.

Jeffries, Judson L., and Malcolm Foley. "To Live and Die in L.A." In *Comrades: A Local History of the Black Panther Party*, edited by Judson L. Jeffries, 255–90. Bloomington: Indiana University Press, 2007.

Johnson, Gaye Theresa. *Spaces of Conflict, Sounds of Solidarity: Music, Race, and Spatial Entitlement in Los Angeles*. Berkeley: University of California Press, 2013.

Johnson, James H., Walter C. Farrell, and Melvin L. Oliver. "Seeds of the Los Angeles Rebellion of 1992." *International Journal of Urban and Regional Research* 17, no. 1 (1993): 115–19.

Johnson, James H., Cloyzelle K. Jones, Walter C. Farrell, and Melvin L. Oliver. "The Los Angeles Rebellion: A Retrospective View." *Economic Development Quarterly* 6, no. 4 (November 1, 1992): 356–72.

Johnson, James H. Jr., and Walter C. Farrell Jr. "Fire This Time: The Genesis of the Los Angeles Rebellion of 1992." *North Carolina Law Review* 71 (1993): 1403.

Johnson, Marilynn S. *Street Justice: A History of Police Violence in New York City*. Boston: Beacon Press, 2003.

Johnson, Paula B., David O. Sears, and John B. McConahay. "Black Invisibility, the Press, and the Los Angeles Riot." *American Journal of Sociology* 76, no. 4 (1971): 698–721.

Joseph, Peniel E., ed. *The Black Power Movement: Rethinking the Civil Rights-Black Power Era*. New York: Routledge, 2006.

———. *Waiting 'Til the Midnight Hour: A Narrative History of Black Power in America*. New York: Henry Holt, 2006.

Joyce, Patrick D. *No Fire Next Time: Black-Korean Conflicts and the Future of America's Cities*. Ithaca, N.Y.: Cornell University Press, 2003.

Kafka, Judith. *The History of "Zero Tolerance" in American Public Schooling*. New York: Palgrave Macmillan, 2011.

Katz, Cindi, and Neil Smith. "L.A. Intifada: Interview with Mike Davis." *Social Text* 10, no. 4 (January 1, 1992): 19.

Katz, Michael B. *Why Don't American Cities Burn?* Philadelphia: University of Pennsylvania Press, 2011.

Katznelson, Ira. *City Trenches: Urban Politics and the Patterning of Class in the United States*. New York: Pantheon Books, 1981.

———. *When Affirmative Action Was White: An Untold History of Racial Inequality in Twentieth-Century America*. New York: W.W. Norton, 2005.

Keil, Roger. *Los Angeles: Globalization, Urbanization, and Social Struggles*. New York: J. Wiley, 1998.

Kelley, Robin D. G. *Race Rebels: Culture, Politics, and the Black Working Class*. New York: Free Press, 1994.

———. *Yo' Mama's Disfunktional!: Fighting the Culture Wars in Urban America*. Boston: Beacon Press, 1998.

Kim, Claire Jean. *Bitter Fruit: The Politics of Black-Korean Conflict in New York City*. New Haven, Conn.: Yale University Press, 2000.

King, Martin Luther. *Where Do We Go from Here: Chaos or Community?* Boston: Beacon Press, 2010.

King, Shannon. "'Ready to Shoot and Do Shoot': Black Working-Class Self-Defense and Community Politics in Harlem, New York, during the 1920s." *Journal of Urban History* 37, no. 5 (September 1, 2011): 757–74.

Klein, Malcolm W. *The American Street Gang: Its Nature, Prevalence, and Control.* New York: Oxford University Press, 1995.

———. "Attempting Gang Control by Suppression: The Misuse of Deterrence Principles." *Studies in Crime and Crime Punishment* 2 (1993): 88–111.

———. "'Rock' Sales in South Los Angeles." *Sociology and Social Research* 69, no. 4 (July 1, 1985): 561.

Klein, Malcolm W., and Cheryl L. Maxson. *Gang Involvement in "Rock" Cocaine Trafficking in Los Angeles, 1984–1985.* Ann Arbor, Mich.: Inter-university Consortium for Political and Social Research, 1988.

———. *Gang Structures, Crime Patterns, and Police Responses.* Final report to the National Institute of Justice, April 1996.

Klein, Malcolm W., Cheryl L. Maxson, and Lea C. Cunningham. "'Crack,' Street Gangs, and Violence." *Criminology* 29, no. 4 (November 1991): 623.

Klein, Malcolm W., Cheryl L. Maxson, and Margaret A. Gordon. *Evaluation in an Imported Gang Violence Deterrence Program: Final Report.* Los Angeles: Social Science Research Institute, University of Southern California, 1984.

———. *Police Response to Street Gang Violence: Improving the Investigative Process.* Los Angeles: Center for Research on Crime and Social Control, Social Science Research Institute, University of Southern California, 1987.

Klein, Norman M. *The History of Forgetting: Los Angeles and the Erasure of Memory.* London: Verso, 2008.

Klein, Norman M., and Martin J. Schiesl. *20th Century Los Angeles: Power, Promotion, and Social Conflict.* Claremont, Calif.: Regina Books, 1990.

Knight, Frederick. "Justifiable Homicide, Police Brutality, or Governmental Repression? The 1962 Los Angeles Police Shooting of Seven Members of the Nation of Islam." *Journal of Negro History* 79, no. 2 (April 1, 1994): 182–96.

Kohler-Hausmann, Issa. *Misdemeanorland: Criminal Courts and Social Control in an Age of Broken Windows Policing.* Princeton, N.J.: Princeton University Press, 2018.

———. "Misdemeanor Justice: Control without Conviction." *American Journal of Sociology* 119, no. 2 (September 1, 2013): 351–93.

Kohler-Hausmann, Julilly. "'The Attila the Hun Law': New York's Rockefeller Drug Laws and the Making of a Punitive State." *Journal of Social History* 44, no. 1 (Fall 2010): 71–95.

———. "'The Crime of Survival': Fraud Prosecutions, Community Surveillance, and the Original 'Welfare Queen.'" *Journal of Social History* 41, no. 2 (Winter 2007): 329–54.

———. *Getting Tough: Welfare and Imprisonment in 1970s America.* Princeton, N.J.: Princeton University Press, 2017.

———. "Guns and Butter: The Welfare State, the Carceral State, and the Politics of Exclusion in the Postwar United States." *Journal of American History* 102, no. 1 (June 1, 2015): 87–99.

———. "Militarizing the Police: Officer Jon Burge, Torture, and War in the 'Urban Jungle.'" In *Challenging the Prison-Industrial Complex: Activism, Arts, and*

Educational Alternatives, edited by Stephen John Hartnett, 43–69. Urbana: University of Illinois Press, 2010.

Kramer, Alisa Sarah. "William H. Parker and the Thin Blue Line: Politics, Public Relations and Policing in Postwar Los Angeles." PhD diss., The American University, 2007.

Kramer, Ronald, and Raymond Michalowski. "The Iron Fist and the Velvet Tongue: Crime Control Policies in the Clinton Administration." *Social Justice* 22, no. 2 (60) (July 1, 1995): 87–100.

Kraska, Peter B. *Militarizing the American Criminal Justice System: The Changing Roles of the Armed Forces and the Police.* Boston: Northeastern University Press, 2001.

Krinitsky, Nora. "The Politics of Crime Control: Race, Policing, and Reform in Twentieth-Century Chicago." PhD diss., University of Michigan, 2017.

Kun, Josh, and Laura Pulido. *Black and Brown in Los Angeles: Beyond Conflict and Coalition.* Berkeley: University of California Press, 2013.

Kurashige, Scott. "Between 'White Spot' and 'World City': Racial Integration and the Roots of Multiculturalism." In *A Companion to Los Angeles*, edited by William Deverell and Greg Hise, 56–71. Oxford: Wiley, 2010.

———. *The Shifting Grounds of Race: Black and Japanese Americans in the Making of Multiethnic Los Angeles.* Princeton, N.J.: Princeton University Press, 2008.

Kusmer, Kenneth L., and Joe W. Trotter. *African American Urban History since World War II.* Chicago: University of Chicago Press, 2009.

"L.A. Police Commission Alters Use-of-Deadly-Force Policy; Emphasizes Need to De-Escalate Situations." *KTLA* (blog), March 15, 2016. http://ktla.com/2016/03/15/los-angeles-police-commission-alters-use-of-deadly-force-policy-emphasizes-need-to-de-escalate-situations/, accessed March 16, 2016.

Lang, Clarence. *Grassroots at the Gateway: Class Politics and Black Freedom Struggle in St. Louis, 1936–75.* Ann Arbor: University of Michigan Press, 2009.

Lasley, James R., and Michael K. Hooper. "On Racism and the LAPD: Was the Christopher Commission Wrong?" *Social Science Quarterly* (University of Texas Press) 79, no. 2 (June 1998): 378–89.

Lassiter, Matthew D. "Impossible Criminals: The Suburban Imperatives of America's War on Drugs." *Journal of American History* 102, no. 1 (June 1, 2015): 126–40.

———. "Pushers, Victims, and the Lost Innocence of White Suburbia California's War on Narcotics during the 1950s." *Journal of Urban History* 41, no. 5 (2015): 787–807.

Lebrón, Marisol. *Policing Life and Death: Race, Violence, and Resistance in Puerto Rico.* Berkeley: University of California Press, forthcoming.

Lee, Sonia Song-Ha. *Building a Latino Civil Rights Movement: Puerto Ricans, African Americans, and the Pursuit of Racial Justice in New York City.* Chapel Hill: University of North Carolina Press, 2016.

Leonard, Kevin Allen. *The Battle for Los Angeles: Racial Ideology and World War II.* Albuquerque: University of New Mexico Press, 2006.

Leovy, Jill. *Ghettoside: A True Story of Murder in America.* New York: Spiegel & Grau, 2015.

Lerman, Amy E. *The Modern Prison Paradox: Politics, Punishment, and Social Community*. Cambridge: Cambridge University Press, 2014.

Lerman, Amy E., and Vesla M. Weaver. *Arresting Citizenship: The Democratic Consequences of American Crime Control*. Chicago: University of Chicago Press, 2014.

Light, Jennifer S. *From Warfare to Welfare: Defense Intellectuals and Urban Problems in Cold War America*. Baltimore, Md.: Johns Hopkins University Press, 2003.

Lipsey, Mark W., and Judith E. Johnston. *Impact of Juvenile Diversion in Los Angeles County*. Claremont, Calif.: Claremont Graduate School Center for Applied Social Research, 1979.

Lipsitz, George. *How Racism Takes Place*. Philadelphia: Temple University Press, 2011.

———. "Learning from Los Angeles: Another One Rides the Bus." *American Quarterly* 56, no. 3 (2004): 511–29.

Logan, John R., and Harvey Luskin Molotch. *Urban Fortunes: The Political Economy of Place*. Berkeley: University of California Press, 2007.

Lombardo, Tim. *Blue-Collar Conservatism: Frank Rizzo's Philadelphia and Populist Politics*. Philadelphia: University of Pennsylvania Press, forthcoming.

Loo, Dennis D., and Ruth-Ellen M. Grimes. "Polls, Politics, and Crime: The Law and Order Issue of the 1960s." *Western Criminology Review* 5 (2004): 50.

López, David E., Eric Popkin, and Edward Telles. "Central Americans: At the Bottom, Struggling to Get Ahead." In *Ethnic Los Angeles*, edited by Roger Waldinger and Mehdi Bozorgmehr, 279–81. New York: Russell Sage Foundation, 1996.

Losier, Toussaint. "'The Public Does Not Believe the Police Can Police Themselves': The Mayoral Administration of Harold Washington and the Problem of Police Impunity." *Journal of Urban History*. May 26, 2017. http://journals.sagepub.com /doi/10.1177/0096144217705490.

Lotchin, Roger W. *Fortress California, 1910–1961: From Warfare to Welfare*. New York: Oxford University Press, 1992.

Lupo, Lindsey. *Flak-Catchers: One Hundred Years of Riot Commission Politics in America*. Lanham, Md.: Lexington Books, 2011.

Lynch, Mona Pauline. *Sunbelt Justice: Arizona and the Transformation of American Punishment*. Stanford, Calif.: Stanford Law Books, 2010.

Macías-Rojas, Patrisia. *From Deportation to Prison: The Politics of Immigration Enforcement in Post–Civil Rights America*. New York: New York University Press, 2016.

Malka, Adam. *The Men of Mobtown: Policing Baltimore in the Age of Slavery and Emancipation*. Chapel Hill: University of North Carolina Press, 2018.

Mandel, Jennifer. "Making a 'Black Beverly Hills': The Struggle for Housing Equality in Modern Los Angeles." PhD diss., University of New Hampshire, 2010.

Mann, Eric. *Taking on General Motors: A Case Study of the Campaign to Keep GM Van Nuys Open*. Los Angeles: Institute of Industrial Relations, University of California, Los Angeles, 1987.

Mantler, Gordon Keith. *Power to the Poor: Black-Brown Coalition and the Fight for Economic Justice, 1960–1974*. Chapel Hill: University of North Carolina Press, 2013.

Marable, Manning. *Race, Reform, and Rebellion: The Second Reconstruction and Beyond in Black America, 1945–2006*. 3rd ed. Jackson: University Press of Mississippi, 2007.

Marable, Manning, Ian Steinberg, and Keesha Middlemass. *Racializing Justice, Disenfranchising Lives: The Racism, Criminal Justice, and Law Reader.* N.p.: Palgrave Macmillan, 2007.

Marion, Nancy E. *A History of Federal Crime Control Initiatives, 1960–1993.* Westport, Conn.: Praeger, 1994.

Márquez, John D. *Black-Brown Solidarity: Racial Politics in the New Gulf South.* Austin: University of Texas Press, 2014.

Marx, Gary T. *Undercover: Police Surveillance in America.* Berkeley: University of California Press, 1989.

Massey, Doreen B. *Space, Place, and Gender.* Minneapolis: University of Minnesota Press, 1994.

Mauer, Marc. *Race to Incarcerate.* New York: New Press; distributed by W. W. Norton, 2001.

McClellan, S. "Policing the Red Scare: The Los Angeles Police Department's Red Squad and the Repression of Labor Activism in Los Angeles, 1900–1940." PhD diss., University of California, Irvine, 2011.

McKee, Guian A. *The Problem of Jobs: Liberalism, Race, and Deindustrialization in Philadelphia.* Chicago: University of Chicago Press, 2008.

Meeks, Daryl. "Police Militarization in Urban Areas: The Obscure War against the Underclass." *Black Scholar* 35, no. 4 (January 1, 2006): 33–41.

Meiners, Erica. "Building an Abolition Democracy: Or, the Fight against Public Fear, Private Benefits, and Prison Expansion." In *Challenging the Prison-Industrial Complex: Activism, Arts, and Educational Alternatives,* edited by Stephen John Hartnett. Urbana: University of Illinois Press, 2010.

Melamed, Jodi. *Represent and Destroy: Rationalizing Violence in the New Racial Capitalism.* Minneapolis: University of Minnesota Press, 2011.

Meyer, Marshall W. "Police Shootings at Minorities: The Case of Los Angeles." *Annals of the American Academy of Political and Social Science* 452 (November 1, 1980): 98–110.

Milkman, Ruth. *L.A. Story: Immigrant Workers and the Future of the U.S. Labor Movement.* New York: Russell Sage Foundation, 2006.

Miller, Jerome G. *Search and Destroy: African-American Males in the Criminal Justice System.* Cambridge: Cambridge University Press, 2011.

Miller, Lisa Lynn. *The Myth of Mob Rule: Violent Crime and Democratic Politics.* New York: Oxford University Press, 2016.

———. *The Perils of Federalism: Race, Poverty, and the Politics of Crime Control.* New York: Oxford University Press, 2008.

———. *The Politics of Community Crime Prevention: Implementing Operation Weed and Seed in Seattle.* Burlington, Vt.: Ashgate, 2001.

Model, Paul. "The 1965 Watts Rebellion: The Self-Definition of a Community." *Radical America* 24, no. 2 (1992): 75–88.

Molina, Natalia. *How Race Is Made in America: Immigration, Citizenship, and the Historical Power of Racial Scripts.* Berkeley: University of California Press, 2013.

Monkkonen, Eric. "Toward an Understanding of Urbanization: Drunk Arrests in Los Angeles." *Pacific Historical Review* 50, no. 2 (1981): 234–44.

Moore, Joan W. *Going down to the Barrio: Homeboys and Homegirls in Change.* Philadelphia: Temple University Press, 1991.

———. *Homeboys: Gangs, Drugs, and Prison in the Barrios of Los Angeles.* Philadelphia: Temple University Press, 1978.

Moore, Leonard N. *Black Rage in New Orleans: Police Brutality and African American Activism from World War II to Hurricane Katrina.* Baton Rouge: Louisiana State University Press, 2010.

Morales, Armando. *Ando Sangrando (I Am Bleeding): a Study of Mexican American-Police Conflict.* Fair Lawn, N.J.: R. E. Burdick, 1972.

Muhammad, Khalil Gibran. *The Condemnation of Blackness: Race, Crime, and the Making of Modern Urban America.* Cambridge, Mass.: Harvard University Press, 2010.

Mumford, Kevin J. *Newark: A History of Race, Rights, and Riots in America.* New York: New York University Press, 2007.

Muñiz, Ana. *Police, Power, and the Production of Racial Boundaries.* New Brunswick, N.J.: Rutgers University Press, 2015.

Murakawa, Naomi. *The First Civil Right: How Liberals Built Prison America.* New York: Oxford University Press, 2014.

———. "The Origins of the Carceral Crisis: Racial Order as 'Law and Order' in Postwar American Politics." In *Race and American Political Development*, edited by Joseph Lowndes, Julie Novkov, and Warren Dorian, 234–56. New York: Routledge, 2008.

Murch, Donna. "Crack in Los Angeles: Crisis, Militarization, and Black Response to the Late Twentieth-Century War on Drugs," *Journal of American History* 102, no. 1 (June 1, 2015): 162–73.

———. *Living for the City: Migration, Education, and the Rise of the Black Panther Party in Oakland, California.* Chapel Hill: University of North Carolina Press, 2010.

———. "The Many Meanings of Watts: Black Power, Wattstax, and the Carceral State." *OAH Magazine of History* 26, no. 1 (January 2012): 37–40.

Nelson, Jill. *Police Brutality: An Anthology.* New York: W. W. Norton, 2001.

Neocleous, Mark. *The Fabrication of Social Order: A Critical Theory of Police Power.* London: Pluto, 2000.

———. *War Power, Police Power.* Edinburgh: Edinburgh University Press, 2014.

Neptune, Jessica Helen. "The Making of the Carceral State: Street Crime, the War on Drugs, and Punitive Politics in New York, 1951–1973." PhD diss., University of Chicago, 2012.

Ngai, Mae M. *Impossible Subjects: Illegal Aliens and the Making of Modern America.* Princeton, N.J.: Princeton University Press, 2004.

Nickerson, Michelle, and Darren Dochuk. *Sunbelt Rising: The Politics of Place, Space, and Region.* Philadelphia: University of Pennsylvania Press, 2011.

Nicolaides, Becky M. *My Blue Heaven: Life and Politics in the Working-Class Suburbs of Los Angeles, 1920–1965.* Chicago: University of Chicago Press, 2002.

Nunn, Diane, and Christine Cleary. "From the Mexican California Frontier to Arnold-Kennick: Highlights in the Evolution of the California Juvenile Court, 1850–1961." *Journal of the Center for Families, Children & the Courts* 5 (2004): 3–35.

Oberschall, Anthony. "The Los Angeles Riot of August 1965." *Social Problems* 15, no. 3 (January 1, 1968): 322–41.

Ogletree, Charles J. *Beyond the Rodney King Story: An Investigation of Police Conduct in Minority Communities.* Boston: Northeastern University Press, 1995.

O'Reilly, Kenneth. "The FBI and the Politics of the Riots, 1964–1968." *Journal of American History* 75, no. 1 (June 1, 1988): 91–114.

Orleck, Annelise. *Storming Caesars Palace: How Black Mothers Fought Their Own War on Poverty.* Boston: Beacon Press, 2005.

Oropeza, Lorena. *Raza Sí!, Guerra No!: Chicano Protest and Patriotism during the Viet Nam War Era.* Berkeley: University of California Press, 2005.

O'Toole, James. *Watts and Woodstock.* New York: Holt, Rinehart and Winston, 1973.

Owens, Tom, and Rod Browning. *Lying Eyes: The Truth behind the Corruption and Brutality of the LAPD and the Beating of Rodney King.* New York: Thunder's Mouth Press, 1994.

Pager, Devah. *Marked: Race, Crime, and Finding Work in an Era of Mass Incarceration.* Chicago: University of Chicago Press, 2007.

Parenti, Christian. *Lockdown America: Police and Prisons in the Age of Crisis.* New York: Verso, 1999.

———. *The Soft Cage: Surveillance in America, from Slavery to the War on Terror.* New York: Basic Books, 2007.

Parker, Caitlin. "The Capitalist Games: Privatization, Protest, and the 1984 Los Angeles Olympics," 2014. Paper presented at the Los Angeles History & Metro Studies Group, Huntington Library, San Marino, CA, February 28, 2014. In author's possession.

Parker, William H. *Parker on Police,* edited by O. W. Wilson. Springfield, Ill.: Charles C. Thomas, 1957.

Parrish, Michael. *For the People: Inside the Los Angeles County District Attorney's Office 1850–2000.* Santa Monica, Calif.: Angel City Press, 2001.

Parson, Don. "Injustice for Salcido: The Left Response to Police Brutality in Cold War Los Angeles." *Southern California Quarterly* 86, no. 2 (July 1, 2004): 145–68.

Parson, Donald Craig. *Making a Better World: Public Housing, the Red Scare, and the Direction of Modern Los Angeles.* Minneapolis: University of Minnesota Press, 2005.

Pastor, Manuel, Barbara Cox, and Tomás Rivera Center. *Latinos and the Los Angeles Uprising: The Economic Context.* Los Angeles: The Tomás Rivera Center, 1993.

Payne, James Gregory, and Scott C. Ratzan. *Tom Bradley, the Impossible Dream: A Biography.* Santa Monica, Calif.: Roundtable, 1986.

Peck, Jamie. *Constructions of Neoliberal Reason.* Oxford: Oxford University Press, 2012.

Perlstein, Rick. *The Invisible Bridge: The Fall of Nixon and the Rise of Reagan.* New York: Simon & Schuster, 2015.

———. *Nixonland: The Rise of a President and the Fracturing of America.* New York: Scribner, 2008.

Pettigrew, Thomas F., and Denise A. Alston. *Tom Bradley's Campaigns for Governor: The Dilemma of Race and Political Strategies.* Washington, D.C.: Joint Center for Political Studies, 1988.

Pfaff, John F. *Locked in: The True Causes of Mass Incarceration—and How to Achieve Real Reform.* New York: Basic Books, 2017.

Phillips, Susan A. *Operation Fly Trap: L.A. Gangs, Drugs, and the Law.* Chicago: University of Chicago Press, 2012.

Pihos, Peter C. "Policing, Race, and Politics in Chicago." PhD diss., University of Pennsylvania, 2015.

———. "The Racial Politics of Urban Street Gangs." *Journal of Urban History* 37, no. 3 (May 1, 2011): 466.

Piven, Frances Fox, and Richard A. Cloward. *Poor People's Movements: Why They Succeed, How They Fail.* New York: Vintage Books, 1979.

Platt, Tony. "Obama's Task Force on Policing: Will It Be Different This Time? | Social Justice." *Social Justice*, February 28, 2015, http://www.socialjusticejournal.org /obamas-task-force-on-policing-will-it-be-different-this-time/, accessed March 6, 2017.

Platt, Tony, Jon Frappier, Gerda Ray, Richard Schauffler, Larry Trukillo, Lynn Cooper, Elliott Currie, and Sidney Harring. *The Iron Fist and the Velvet Glove: An Analysis of the U.S. Police.* San Francisco: Crime and Social Justice Associates, 1982.

Pritchett, Wendell E. "Which Urban Crisis?" *Journal of Urban History* 34, no. 2 (January 1, 2008): 266–86.

Provine, Doris M., and Roxanne L. Doty. "The Criminalization of Immigrants as a Racial Project." *Journal of Contemporary Criminal Justice* 27, no. 3 (2011): 261–77.

Pulido, Laura. *Black, Brown, Yellow, and Left: Radical Activism in Los Angeles.* Berkeley: University of California Press, 2006.

Rabig, J. "Broken Deal: Devolution, Development, and Civil Society in Newark, New Jersey, 1960–1990." PhD diss., University of Pennsylvania, 2007.

Rarick, Ethan. *California Rising: The Life and Times of Pat Brown.* Berkeley: University of California Press, 2005.

Rasmussen, Chris. "'A Web of Tension': The 1967 Protests in New Brunswick, New Jersey." *Journal of Urban History* 40, no. 1 (January 1, 2014): 137–57.

Reeves, Jimmie L., and Richard Campbell. *Cracked Coverage: Television News, the Anti-Cocaine Crusade, and the Reagan Legacy.* Durham, N.C.: Duke University Press, 1994.

Reiss, Albert J., Jr. *The Police and the Public.* Revised edition. New Haven, Conn.: Yale University Press, 1973.

Ribeiro, Alyssa. "'A Period of Turmoil': Pittsburgh's April 1968 Riots and Their Aftermath." *Journal of Urban History* 39, no. 2 (2013): 147–71.

Rice, Connie. *Power Concedes Nothing: One Woman's Quest for Social Justice in America from the Courtrooms to the Kill Zones.* New York: Scribner, 2012.

Rich, Michael J. "Riot and Reason: Crafting an Urban Policy Response." *Publius* 23, no. 3 (July 1, 1993): 115–34.

Richter, Kelly. "Uneasy Border State: The Politics and Public Policy of Latino Illegal Immigration in Metropolitan California, 1971–1996." PhD diss., Stanford University, 2014.

Rios, Victor M. *Punished: Policing the Lives of Black and Latino Boys.* New York: New York University Press, 2011.

Robinson, Cedric J. *Black Marxism: The Making of the Black Radical Tradition.* Chapel Hill: University of North Carolina Press, 2000.

———. *The Terms of Order: Political Science and the Myth of Leadership.* Chapel Hill: University of North Carolina Press, 2016.

Roche, Mary Pauline. "Unfinished Business: The Production of Resistance to State Violence in Los Angeles and Derry." PhD diss., University of Southern California, 2004.

Rosenfeld, Seth. *Subversives: The FBI's War on Student Radicals, and Reagan's Rise to Power.* New York: Farrar, Straus and Giroux, 2012.

Ross, Ruth A. *The Impact of Federal Grants on the City of Los Angeles.* Washington, D.C.: Brookings Institution, 1980.

Rothmiller, Mike, and Ivan G. Goldman. *L.A. Secret Police: Inside the LAPD Elite Spy Network.* New York: Pocket Books, 1992.

Rustin, Bayard. "The Watts 'Manifesto' & the McCone Report." *Commentary* 41, no. 3 (March 1966): 29–35.

Saltzstein, Alan L., Raphael Sonenshein, and Irving Ostrow. "Federal Grants and the City of Los Angeles." *Research in Urban Policy* 2 (1986): 55–76.

Sánchez, George J. *Becoming Mexican American: Ethnicity, Culture, and Identity in Chicano Los Angeles, 1900–1945.* New York: Oxford University Press, 1993.

———. "Face the Nation: Race, Immigration, and the Rise of Nativism in Late Twentieth Century America." *International Migration Review* 31, no. 4 (Winter 1997): 1009–30.

———. "Reading Reginald Denny: The Politics of Whiteness in the Late Twentieth Century." *American Quarterly* 47, no. 3 (September 1995): 388–94.

Sassen, Saskia. *The Global City: New York, London, Tokyo.* 2nd ed. Princeton, N.J.: Princeton University Press, 2001.

Sawhney, Deepak Narang. *Unmasking L.A.: Third Worlds and the City.* New York: Palgrave, 2002.

Schept, Judah. *Progressive Punishment: Job Loss, Jail Growth and the Neoliberal Logic of Carceral Expansion.* New York: New York University Press, 2015.

Schoenfeld, Heather. *Building the Prison State: Race and the Politics of Mass Incarceration.* Chicago: University of Chicago Press, 2018.

Schnaubelt, Christopher M. "Lessons in Command and Control from the Los Angeles Riots." *Parameters* 27, no. 2 (Summer 1997): 88–109.

Schneider, Eric C. *Smack: Heroin and the American City.* Philadelphia: University of Pennsylvania Press, 2008.

Schneider, Jack. "Escape from Los Angeles." *Journal of Urban History* 34, no. 6 (2008): 995–1012.

Schrader, Stuart. *Policing Revolution: Cold War Counterinsurgency at Home and Abroad.* Berkeley: University of California Press, forthcoming.

Schrank, Sarah. *Art and the City: Civic Imagination and Cultural Authority in Los Angeles.* Philadelphia: University of Pennsylvania Press, 2011.

Schmidt Jr., Ronald J. *This Is the City: Making Model Citizens in Los Angeles.* Minneapolis: University of Minnesota Press, 2005.

Scott, Allen John. *South-Central Los Angeles: Anatomy of an Urban Crisis.* Los

Angeles: Lewis Center for Regional Policy Studies, Graduate School of
Architecture and Urban Planning, 1993.

Sears, David O., and John B. McConahay. *The Politics of Violence: The New Urban Blacks and the Watts Riot*. Boston: Houghton Mifflin, 1973.

Seigel, Micol. "Violence Work: Policing and Power." *Race & Class* 59, no. 4 (2018): 15–33.

———. "Objects of Police History." *Journal of American History* 102, no. 1 (June 1, 2015): 152–61.

Self, Robert O. *American Babylon: Race and the Struggle for Postwar Oakland*. Princeton, N.J.: Princeton University Press, 2003.

———. "Sex in the City: The Politics of Sexual Liberalism in Los Angeles, 1963–79." *Gender & History* 20, no. 2 (August 1, 2008): 288–311.

Seligman, A. I. "'But Burn—No': The Rest of the Crowd in Three Civil Disorders in 1960s Chicago." *Journal of Urban History* 37 (2011): 230–55.

Shakur, Sanyika. *Monster: The Autobiography of an L.A. Gang Member*. New York: Grove Press, 1993.

Sides, Josh. *L.A. City Limits: African American Los Angeles from the Great Depression to the Present*. Berkeley: University of California Press, 2006.

———, ed. *Post-Ghetto: Reimagining South Los Angeles*. San Marino, Calif.: Published for the Huntington-USC Institute on California and the West by University of California Press, 2012.

———. "Straight into Compton: American Dreams, Urban Nightmares, and the Metamorphosis of a Black Suburb." *American Quarterly* 56, no. 3 (2004): 583–605.

Siegel, Frederick F. *The Future Once Happened Here: New York, D.C., L.A., and the Fate of America's Big Cities*. New York: Free Press, 1997.

Simon, Jonathan. *Governing through Crime: How the War on Crime Transformed American Democracy and Created a Culture of Fear*. Oxford: Oxford University Press, 2007.

———. *Mass Incarceration on Trial: A Remarkable Court Decision and the Future of Prisons in America*. New York: New Press, 2014.

Singh, Nikhil Pal. *Race and America's Long War* (Oakland: University of California Press, 2017).

Skolnick, Jerome H., and James J. Fyfe. *Above the Law: Police and the Excessive Use of Force*. New York: Free Press, 1993.

Skolnick, Jerome H., and Candace McCoy. *Justice without Trial: Law Enforcement in Democratic Society*. New Orleans, La.: Quid Pro, LLC, 2011.

Smith, R. J. *The Great Black Way: L.A. in the 1940s and the Lost African-American Renaissance*. New York: PublicAffairs, 2006.

Soja, Edward W. *Thirdspace: Journeys to Los Angeles and Other Real-and-Imagined Places*. Cambridge, Mass.: Blackwell, 1996.

Sojoyner, Damien M. "Black Radicals Make for Bad Citizens: Undoing the Myth of the School to Prison Pipeline." *Berkeley Review of Education* 4, no. 2 (January 1, 2013).

———. *First Strike: Educational Enclosures in Black Los Angeles*. Minneapolis: University of Minnesota Press, 2016.

Sonenshein, Raphael. *The City at Stake: Secession, Reform, and Battle for Los Angeles*. Princeton, N.J.: Princeton University Press, 2004.

———. *Politics in Black and White: Race and Power in Los Angeles*. Princeton, N.J.: Princeton University Press, 1993.

Sonenshein, Raphael, and League of Women Voters. *Los Angeles: Structure of a City Government*. Los Angeles: League of Women Voters, 2006.

Soss, Joe, Richard C. Fording, and Sanford F. Schram. *Disciplining the Poor: Neoliberal Paternalism and the Persistent Power of Race*. Chicago: University of Chicago Press, 2011.

Southern California Public Radio. "PHOTOS: LA Councilman Art Snyder Remembered as a 'Rascal.'" Southern California Public Radio, https://www.scpr.org/news/2012/11/08/34868/former-la-city-councilman-art-snyder-remembered-ra/, accessed 12/19/2017.

Stein, Judith. *Running Steel, Running America: Race, Economic Policy and the Decline of Liberalism*. Chapel Hill: University of North Carolina Press, 1998.

Steinberg, James, David W. Lyon, and Mary E. Vaiana, eds. *Urban America: Policy Choices for Los Angeles and the Nation*. Santa Monica, Calif.: Rand, 1992.

Stevenson, Brenda. *The Contested Murder of Latasha Harlins: Justice, Gender, and the Origins of the LA Riots*. New York: Oxford University Press, 2013.

Stewart, Gary. "Black Codes and Broken Windows: The Legacy of Racial Hegemony in Anti-Gang Civil Injunctions." *Yale Law Journal* 107, no. 7 (1998): 2249–79.

Stewart-Winter, Timothy. *Queer Clout: Chicago and the Rise of Gay Politics*. Politics and Culture in Modern America. Philadelphia: University of Pennsylvania Press, 2016.

Stone, Christopher, Todd Foglesong, and Christine M. Cole. *Policing Los Angeles Under a Consent Decree: The Dynamics of Change at the LAPD*. Program in Criminal Justice Policy and Management, Harvard Kennedy School, May 2009.

Straus, Emily E. "Unequal Pieces of a Shrinking Pie: The Struggle between African Americans and Latinos over Education, Employment, and Empowerment in Compton, California." *History of Education Quarterly* 49, no. 4 (November 2009): 507–29.

Stuart, Forrest. *Down, Out, and Under Arrest: Policing and Everyday Life in Skid Row*. Chicago: University of Chicago Press, 2016.

Stumpf, Juliet. "The Crimmigration Crisis: Immigrants, Crime, and Sovereign Power." *American University Law Review* 56 (2006): 367–420.

Stuntz, William J. *The Collapse of American Criminal Justice*. Cambridge, Mass.: Belknap Press of Harvard University Press, 2011.

Suddler, Carl. *Presumed Criminal: Youth, Race, and Justice in an American City*. New York: New York University Press, forthcoming.

Sugrue, Thomas J. *The Origins of the Urban Crisis: Race and Inequality in Postwar Detroit*. Princeton, N.J.: Princeton University Press, 1996.

———. *Sweet Land of Liberty: The Forgotten Struggle for Civil Rights in the North*. New York: Random House, 2008.

Sugrue, Thomas J., and Andrew P. Goodman. "Plainfield Burning: Black Rebellion in the Suburban North." *Journal of Urban History* 33, no. 4 (May 1, 2007): 568–601.

Tackwood, Louis E. *The Glass House Tapes*. New York: Avon, 1973.

Taylor, Clarence. "Introduction: African Americans, Police Brutality, and the U.S.

Criminal Justice System." *Journal of African American History* 98, no. 2 (April 1, 2013): 200–204.

Taylor, Keeanga-Yamahtta. *From #BlackLivesMatter to Black Liberation*. Chicago: Haymarket Books, 2016.

Tervalon, Jervey. *Geography of Rage: Remembering the Los Angeles Riots of 1992*. Los Angeles: Really Great Books, 2002.

Theoharis, Jeanne F. "'Alabama on Avalon': Rethinking the Watts Uprising and the Character of Black Protest in Los Angeles." In *The Black Power Movement: Rethinking the Civil Rights-Black Power Era*, edited by Peniel E Joseph, 27–55. New York: Routledge, 2006.

Thompson, Heather Ann. *Blood in the Water: The Attica Prison Uprising of 1971 and Its Legacy*. New York: Pantheon Books, 2016.

———. "Criminalizing Kids: The Overlooked Reason for Failing Schools." *Dissent* 58, no. 4 (2011): 23–27.

———. "Understanding Rioting in Postwar Urban America." *Journal of Urban History* 26, no. 3 (March 1, 2000): 391–402.

———. *Whose Detroit?: Politics, Labor, and Race in a Modern American City*. Ithaca, N.Y.: Cornell University Press, 2001.

———. "Why Mass Incarceration Matters: Rethinking Crisis, Decline, and Transformation in Postwar American History." *Journal of American History* 97, no. 3 (December 1, 2010): 703–34.

Thompson, Heather Ann, and Donna Murch. "Rethinking Urban America through the Lens of the Carceral State." *Journal of Urban History* 4 (July 2015): 751–55.

Tilly, Charles. *The Politics of Collective Violence*. Cambridge: Cambridge University Press, 2003.

———. "State-Incited Violence, 1900–1999." *Political Power and Social Theory* 9 (1995): 161–79.

Tonry, Michael. *Malign Neglect: Race, Crime, and Punishment in America*. New York: Oxford University Press, 1996.

———. *Punishing Race: A Continuing American Dilemma*. New York: Oxford University Press, 2012.

Tullis, Tracy. "A Vietnam at Home: Policing the Ghettos in the Counterinsurgency Era." PhD diss., New York University, 1999.

"Twenty Five Years Later, How Did the Riots Transform L.A.? And Has the City Changed Enough?" *Los Angeles Times*, April 28, 2017. http://www.latimes.com /opinion/la-oe-los-angeles-riots-voices-updates-the-chief-s-promise-the-lapd -will-1493352988-htmlstory.html, accessed May 4, 2017.

Tyler, Bruce Michael. "Black Radicalism in Southern California, 1950–1982." PhD diss., University of California, Los Angeles, 1983.

———. "The Rise and Decline of the Watts Summer Festival, 1965–1985." *American Studies* 31, no. 2 (Fall 1990): 61–81.

Umemoto, Karen. *The Truce: Lessons from an L.A. Gang War*. Ithaca, N.Y.: Cornell University Press, 2006.

Underwood, Katherine. "Pioneering Minority Representation: Edward Roybal and the Los Angeles City Council, 1949–1962." *Pacific Historical Review* 66, no. 3 (1997): 399–425.

Vargas, João Helion Costa. *Catching Hell in the City of Angels: Life and Meanings of Blackness in South Central Los Angeles*. Minneapolis: University of Minnesota Press, 2006.

Vernon, Robert L. *L.A. Justice: Lessons from the Firestorm*. Colorado Springs, Colo.: Focus on the Family Publishers, 1993.

Vigil, Ernesto B. *The Crusade for Justice: Chicano Militancy and the Government's War on Dissent*. Madison: University of Wisconsin Press, 1999.

Vigil, James Diego. "Cholo!: The Migratory Origins of Chicano Gangs in Los Angeles." In *Global Gangs: Street Violence Across the World*, edited by Jennifer M. Hazen and Dennis Rodgers. Minneapolis: University of Minnesota Press, 2014.

———. *Barrio Gangs: Street Life and Identity in Southern California*. Austin: University of Texas Press, 2010.

———. *A Rainbow of Gangs: Street Cultures in the Mega-City*. Austin: University of Texas Press, 2002.

Vitale, Alex S. *City of Disorder: How the Quality of Life Campaign Transformed New York Politics*. New York: New York University Press, 2009.

———. *The End of Policing*. Brooklyn: Verso, 2017.

Wacquant, Loïc. *Punishing the Poor: The Neoliberal Government of Social Insecurity*. Durham, N.C.: Duke University Press, 2009.

Wagner, Bryan. *Disturbing the Peace: Black Culture and the Police Power after Slavery*. Cambridge, Mass.: Harvard University Press, 2009.

Waldinger, Roger. "Not the Promised City: Los Angeles and Its Immigrants." *Pacific Historical Review* 68, no. 2 (1999): 253–72.

Waldinger, Roger David, and Mehdi Bozorgmehr. *Ethnic Los Angeles*. New York: Russell Sage Foundation, 1996.

Walker, Samuel. *Police Accountability: The Role of Citizen Oversight*. Belmont, Calif.: Wadsworth, 2000.

Walker, Samuel. "Employment of Black and Hispanic Police Officers, 1983–1988: A Follow-up Study." *Review of Applied Urban Research* 89-1 (February 1989): 1–8.

Walker, Samuel, and Carol A. Archbold. *The New World of Police Accountability*. New York: SAGE, 2013.

Watson, Dwight. *Race and the Houston Police Department, 1930–1990 a Change Did Come*. College Station: Texas A & M University Press, 2005.

Weaver, Vesla M. "Frontlash: Race and the Development of Punitive Crime Policy." *Studies in American Political Development* 21, no. 2 (2007): 230–65.

Webb, Gary. *Dark Alliance: The CIA, the Contras, and the Crack Cocaine Explosion*. New York: Seven Stories Press, 1998.

Weber, Max. "Politics as Vocation." In *From Max Weber: Essays in Sociology*. Edited by H. H. Gerth and C. Wright Mills. New York: Oxford University Press, 1958.

Weichselbaum, Simone. "The Big Problems with Police That Washington Can't Fix." *TIME.Com*. http://time.com/police-shootings-justice-department-civil-rights-investigations/, accessed December 22, 2017.

Westad, Odd Arne. *The Global Cold War: Third World Interventions and the Making of Our Times.* New York: Cambridge University Press, 2005.

Western, Bruce. *Punishment and Inequality in America.* New York: Russell Sage Foundation, 2006.

Wheeler, Elizabeth A. "More Than the Western Sky: Watts on Television, August 1965." *Journal of Film and Video* 54, no. 2–3 (2002): 11–26.

Widener, Daniel. "Another City Is Possible: Interethnic Organizing in Contemporary Los Angeles." *Race / Ethnicity: Multidisciplinary Global Contexts* 1, no. 2 (April 1, 2008): 189–219.

———. *Black Arts West: Culture and Struggle in Postwar Los Angeles.* Durham, N.C.: Duke University Press, 2010.

Wild, H. Mark. *Street Meeting: Multiethnic Neighborhoods in Early Twentieth-Century Los Angeles.* Berkeley, Calif.: University of California Press, 2005.

Wilson, James Q. *Varieties of Police Behavior: The Management of Law and Order in Eight Communities.* Cambridge, Mass: Harvard University Press, 1968.

Woods, Joseph Gerald. *The Police in Los Angeles: Reform and Professionalization.* New York: Garland, 1993.

Woods, Kristi Joy. "Be Vigorous but Not Brutal: Race, Politics, and Police in Los Angeles, 1937–1945." PhD diss., University of Southern California, 1999.

Yoshino, Erin R. "California's Criminal Gang Enhancements: Lessons from Interviews with Practitioners." *Review of Law and Social Justice* 18, no. 1 (2008): 117–52.

Zimring, Franklin E. *Punishment and Democracy: Three Strikes and You're out in California.* Studies in Crime and Public Policy. Oxford: Oxford University Press, 2001.

———. *When Police Kill.* Cambridge, Mass.: Harvard University Press, 2017.

Zinzun, Michael. "The Gang Truce: A Movement for Social Justice." *Social Justice* 24, no. 4 (December 1, 1997): 258–66.

Index

Page numbers in italics signify graphics.